textbook*plus+*

Equipping Instructors and Students with
FREE RESOURCES for Core Zondervan Textbooks

Available Resources for A Survey of the Old Testament

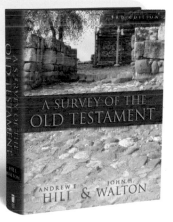

Teaching Resources

- Instructor's manual
- Presentation slides
- Chapter quizzes
- Midterm and final exams
- Sample syllabus
- Image/map library

Study Resources

- Chapter videos
- Quizzes
- Flashcards

*How To Access Resources

- Go to www.ZondervanAcademic.com
- Click "Sign Up" button and complete registration process
- Find books using search field or browse using discipline categories
- Click "Teaching Resources" or "Study Resources" tab once you get to book page to access resources

www.ZondervanAcademic.com

3RD EDITION

A SURVEY OF THE OLD TESTAMENT

ANDREW E. HILL & JOHN H. WALTON

ZONDERVAN®

ZONDERVAN

A Survey of the Old Testament
Copyright © 1991, 2000, 2009 by Andrew E. Hill and John H. Walton

Requests for information should be addressed to:
Zondervan, 3900 *Sparks Dr. SE, Grand Rapids, Michigan 49546*

Library of Congress Cataloging in Publication Data
    Hill, Andrew E.
       A survey of the Old Testament / Andrew E. Hill and John H. Walton.
          p. cm.
       Third ed.
       Includes bibliographical references and index.
       ISBN 978-0-310-28095-8
       1. Bible. O.T. — Introductions. I. Walton, John H., 1952 – II. Title.
    BS1140.2.H54 2000
    221.6'1 — dc21   00 – 020057

Maps by International Mapping
Cover design: Tammy Johnson
Cover photography: Erich Lessing/Art Resource, NY
Interior design: Matthew Van Zomeren

Printed in China

16 17 18 19 20 21 22 23 24 25 26 /GSC/ 25 24 23 22 21 20 19 18 17 16 15 14 13 12 11 10

To the memory of my grandfather

Elmer A. Hill
(1893–1980)
"The wise will inherit honor,
their name will live forever."
(Sirach 37:26)

To my parents

Harvey and Eleanore Walton
for their continuing faith
and encouragement

CONTENTS

Todd Bolen/www.BiblePlaces.com

Part V: The Prophets

Part VI: Epilogue

ABBREVIATIONS

AB	Anchor Bible Commentary Series
ANET	*Ancient Near Eastern Texts*, 3d ed., ed. J. B. Pritchard (Princeton, 1969)
AOTC	Abingdon Old Testament Commentaries
BA	*Biblical Archaeologist*
BAR	*Biblical Archaeological Review*
BASOR	*Bulletin of the American Schools of Oriental Research*
BibSac	*Bibliotheca Sacra*
CAH³	Cambridge Ancient History Series, 3d ed. 12 vols., ed. I. E. Edwards et al. (Cambridge, 1981)
CBC	Cambridge Bible Commentary
CBQ	*Catholic Biblical Quarterly*
DOTP	*Dictionary of Old Testament Pentateuch*
DSB OT	Daily Study Bible Old Testament
EBC	*Expositor's Bible Commentary*, ed. F. E. Gaebelein
ETSMS	Evangelical Theological Society Monograph Series
EvBC	Everyman's Bible Commentary
FOTL	Forms of Old Testament Literature Series
HER	Hermeneia Commentary Series
HSM	Harvard Semitic Monograph Series
HTR	*Harvard Theological Review*
IB	Interpreter's Bible
IBT	Interpreting Biblical Texts Series
ICC	International Critical Commentary
IDB	*Interpreter's Dictionary of the Bible*
ISBE	*International Standard Bible Encyclopedia*, rev. ed., ed. G. W. Bromiley
ITC	International Theological Commentary
JANES	*Journal of the Ancient Near East Society*
JBL	*Journal of Biblical Literature*
JBLMS	Journal of Biblical Literature Monograph Series
JETS	*Journal of the Evangelical Theological Society*
JSOT	*Journal for the Study of the Old Testament*
JSOTSS	Journal for the Study of the Old Testament Supplement Series
MT	Masoretic Text
NAC	New American Commentary
NCBC	New Century Bible Commentary
NIB	*New Interpreter's Bible*
NIBC	New International Biblical Commentary
NICOT	New International Commentary on the Old Testament

NIV	New International Version
NIVAC	NIV Application Commentary
NRSV	New Revised Standard Version
OTG	Old Testament Guides
OTL	Old Testament Library Commentary Series
RB	*Révue Biblique*
RefTR	*Reformed Theological Review*
SBL	Society of Biblical Literature
SBLDS	Society of Biblical Literature Dissertation Series
SBLMS	Society of Biblical Literature Monograph Series
SBT	Studies in Biblical Theology
TB	*Tyndale Bulletin*
TIC	Text and Interpretation Commentary Series
TDOT	*Theological Dictionary of the Old Testament*
TOTC	Tyndale Old Testament Commentary
VT	*Vetus Testamentum*
WBC	Word Biblical Commentary
WCC	Word Communicator's Commentary
WEC	Wycliffe Exegetical Commentary
ZAW	*Zeitschrift für die Alttestamentlishe Wissenschaft*

PREFACE

Why study the Old Testament? This question has echoed down through the centuries of church history, ever since the new covenant of Jesus Christ made the old covenant obsolete (Heb. 8:13). The apostle Paul faced the question, and he responded that the Old Testament was written for the *instruction* and *encouragement* of the Christian church (Rom. 15:4; 1 Cor. 10:11).

We have found the study of the Old Testament a truly exciting enterprise, and we desire to help you enjoy that same exhilaration of discovery and benefit from divine instruction. In Amos 3:8 the prophet proclaims, "The Sovereign LORD has spoken—who can but prophesy?" Exposed to the revelation of God, Amos felt compelled to respond. Although none of us has the privilege Amos had, to function as God's mouthpiece, our response to God's revelation of himself should be no less compelling.

A proper understanding of the nature of the Old Testament helps us gain that fresh excitement and resolve our questions. In approaching the Old Testament as God's self-revelation, we seek to make the Word come alive. To achieve this we could not be content with literary "anatomy"—history of scholarship and summary of content—as important as that is. We have attempted to go beyond that and capture the living spirit that makes these books more than good literature.

Too often survey books fill their pages with summaries of what the Bible says. Unfortunately this leads many to read the survey instead of the Bible itself. This book is intended to be read along with the Bible and not instead of it. We have focused on what the Scriptures intend to communicate. Why does the Old Testament say what it says? Why does it include what it includes? How are genealogies and laws, for example, part of God's self-revelation? As we begin to address these questions, we can become comfortable poring through previously obscure, difficult, or neglected portions of the Old Testament to discover their meaning and value.

Sometimes we may be surprised at what we find. We should also be encouraged when we occasionally meet the unexpected in Scripture—that is, when the Scriptures convince us of the truth of something that changes our minds or leads us down paths once hidden from view. If we acknowledge the authority of Scripture, we must be willing to submit to it by being open-minded about our opinions. God's Word is the final word.

The authority of God's Word is an essential ingredient to our study. We are committed to it and therefore believe that the content of God's Word is true. God has revealed himself in Scripture, and the act of divine inspiration guarantees the authority and integrity of that revelation. These convictions define us as evangelicals. And as evangelicals we are heirs to a long legacy of biblical interpretation by those who were similarly committed to the authority of the Bible. In this we are blessed, and we hold in high esteem those who have preceded us. Nonetheless, we must not become confused about the object of our loyalty. In the end, our commitment is to God's Word, not to the traditional interpretations of it by those who have blazed the trail we follow. We must always be ready to reevaluate our interpretations to ensure that we are attending to the Word rather than being inextricably bound to tradition.

It has been our goal to be objective and to stand by the biblical evidence. At times this has led us to take a more relaxed position on certain issues than our tradition would indicate. In the process of attempting to present some of the directions and insights that have broadened the horizons of interpretation in recent years, we have tried to exercise caution and discretion. A survey cannot offer the documentation or plumb the depths of the evidence that would normally accompany such discussion. Moreover, we have avoided polemical terminology and argumentation. We simply want to help people understand the message and relevance of the Old Testament and, consequently, to experience the excitement of knowing God.

In its structure and format this textbook is intended to complement *A Survey of the New Testament* by Robert H. Gundry, which was published in a revised edition by Zondervan Publishing House in 1994. Following Gundry's lead, we seek to bring together the most significant data from Old Testament historical and literary backgrounds, critical or technical introduction, biblical commentary, and Old Testament theology. The text offers a "synthetic" presentation for all of the Hebrew Bible in the order of the English canon. Each book of the Old Testament is treated according to a basic pattern, as follows:

The Writing of the Book
The Background
Outline of the Book
Purpose and Message
Structure and Organization
Major Themes
Questions for Further Study and Discussion
For Further Reading

Each chapter draws attention to the way in which the literary structure and organization of a given book contribute to the achievement of the biblical writer's message and purpose. An examination of the key theological themes contained in each book brings perspective to its relationship to the Old Testament as a complete collection of books. In addition, because the old covenant finds its fulfillment in the new, pertinent theological relationships between the Old and New Testaments receive attention in regard to subjects such as the covenant, the presence of God, and Messiah.

Further, this survey introduces the reader to a wide range of topics in Old Testament studies including hermeneutics (general and special), history (Israelite and ancient Near Eastern), archaeology, canon, geography, Old Testament theology (biblical and systematic), and basic methodologies of higher criticism.

It is our sincere desire that this textbook will prove to be a readable and useful tool, providing basic but thorough coverage of Old Testament survey and challenging the reader to a serious investigation and personal appropriation of God's truth as revealed in the Old Testament. Above all, we hope this text will bring a new vigor and excitement to the study of the Old Testament as readers learn to discover its story for themselves, understand it, and apply it to their lives, reclaiming it as a substantial part of God's revelation of himself to us. Like the psalmist, may we who study the great works of the Lord in the Old Testament truly learn to delight in them (Ps. 111:2).

IMAGE SOURCES

We are grateful for so many who have provided us photographs and other images, some at reduced prices and others free of charge, to help make this work a visual resource for the ancient world. Credits appear by each photograph, but we would especially recognize the following:

Wikimedia Commons makes photographs available through *http://commons.wikimedia.org* under a variety of licenses. We have benefited greatly from those that have been released into public domain and have sought out appropriate permission for those that have creative commons licensing (cc-by or cc-by-sa). These photographs are not copyright protected in this set but are available for use under the same terms that we used them.

In connection with Wikimedia, we have used a number of photographs from the Yorck Project whose image are indicated as being in the public domain, but with compilation protected under the *GNU Free Documentation License*.

We would like especially to thank Marie-Lan Nguyen, who provided so many photos in public domain on Wikimedia, as well as Rama, who even went and took specific photos that we wanted.

We are grateful to so many who posted their photographs on Flickr and made them available to us when we requested them. Lenka Peacock, Manfred Nader and Peter White were particularly generous and gracious as they allowed us to use many of their photographs.

The Schoyen Collection supplied many photographs at no charge and we are grateful to Elizabeth Sorenssen for her capable help.

Photography Suppliers were very helpful in our endless searches for photographs and we would especially like to acknowledge Todd Bolen (*www.bibleplaces.com*), Zev Radovan (*www.biblelandpictures.com*), Art Resource (*www.artres.com*, with thanks to Ann and Jennifer), and Werner Forman (*www.werner-forman-archive.com*, with thanks to Themis), Jack Hazut (*www.israelimage.net*), and Neil Bierling (*www.phoenixdata systems.com*).

We are also grateful to those who supplied photographs from their personal collections: Frederick J. Mabie, Steven Voth, and John Monson, Michael Greenhalgh, Tim Bulkeley (*http://eBibleTools.com/israel*), Caryn Reeder, Lisa Jean Winbolt, Brian McMorrow, Kim Walton, and the late Maurice Thompson (photographer of the Bible Scene Set), his sons Peter and Andrew, and Geoff Tucker, who scanned the slides for us.

For artwork we are grateful to Susanna Vagt and Alva Steffler.

ACKNOWLEDGMENTS

The publication of the third edition of this textbook affords me yet another opportunity to credit some of those people who have contributed to the success of the project. I remain indebted to those former teachers whose example both nurtured biblical faith and encouraged scholarly achievement, especially Richard D. Patterson and the late Carl B. Hoch.

We have consciously attempted to respond to those many helpful suggestions we have received over the years for making each successive edition of the book an even more useful tool for introducing serious students to the literature, history, and theology of the Old Testament. We thank you for the input, and we trust we have listened well.

I am most grateful to Stanley Gundry and Katya Covrett of the Zondervan Publishing House for making the publication of this third edition possible. Jim Ruark and the Zondervan editorial staff and visual editor Kim Zeilstra also deserve commendation for the many improvements in this edition of the textbook.

To my co-author, colleague, and friend, John Walton, I still extend my apologies for having a surname that precedes "W" in the English alphabet. Seriously, I found our collaboration on the third edition as stimulating as our initial effort in writing the first two editions. I continue to benefit both personally and professionally from my association with John.

Finally, I offer a word of appreciation to my wife, Teri, and the (now-grown) three Js in our lives—Jennifer, Jesse, and Jordan. As always, you remain my primary concern and greatest source of inspiration apart from the Scriptures themselves. May God's good Spirit continue to lead us all on level ground (Ps. 143:10)!

ANDREW E. HILL

There are many people to thank for a project such as this. The staff at Zondervan, particularly Katya Covrett, Kim Zeilstra, and Jim Ruark, have had an immeasurable impact on the shape and quality of the book with their sensitive and discerning editorial work. I am also grateful to my student Jon Kehrer for his careful proofreading of the manuscript.

My family has exercised patience throughout the process. To my wife, Kim, who read most of the manuscript, and to our three Js—Jonathan, Joshua, and Jill—I owe a debt of gratitude. Thanks especially to my father, Harvey Walton, and my son Jon, who both read the first edition meticulously and made many helpful suggestions for making it more readable.

Many of the ideas that make this book unique are the product of the classroom "laboratory." I therefore want to thank the many students who have challenged me, have asked hard questions, have offered their thoughts and ideas, and have motivated me to communicate in more effective ways.

JOHN H. WALTON

The authors and publishers acknowledge with gratitude those who have provided the charts, maps, and photographs. The sources for charts are identified where these items appear. The timelines are provided by Carta, Jerusalem; they were originally published in the *Zondervan NIV Atlas of the Bible* (1989), of which Carl G. Rasmussen is the author, and were adapted by Laura Blost and Rob Monacelli. The composition was performed by Matthew Van Zomeren and Mark Sheeres.

USING THIS BOOK

The authors offer the following suggestions to teachers using this survey.

1. The course need not be structured according to the order of chapters in this book. We have treated the biblical books in canonical order, but other sequences (e.g., chronological) are alternatives. Additionally, there are a number of chapters on various topics interspersed throughout the book. The teacher should evaluate which of those chapters are essential to initiate the course and intersperse the others where they fit best or use them as outside reading or as reading for extra credit.

2. It is an inherent strength in a course when the educational objectives of the teacher correspond to the authors' objectives for the textbook. For teachers who desire to correlate their course objectives to the book's objectives, we recommend the following:

   A. Be able to articulate the purpose and message of each book of the Old Testament.
   B. Be familiar with the major events and people of the Old Testament.
   C. Be able to communicate the "big picture" of the Old Testament and relate the parts to the whole.
   D. Be able to discuss the major theological themes of the Old Testament.
   E. Be able to explain the significance of the Old Testament or any of its parts for a contemporary believer.
   F. Be able to address the foundational significance of the Old Testament for the understanding of the New Testament.

3. We recommend that the Bible be assigned reading alongside this textbook, because the survey does not simply restate the content of the biblical books.

PART I
INTRODUCTION

The path up Mt. Sinai.

APPROACHING THE OLD TESTAMENT

Studying the Old Testament is a monumental task, but proper preparation can help the student to reap a rich harvest. The sovereign God who created the universe, who controls history, and who will accomplish his plan in his time has chosen to speak. That in itself is an act of grace, and we should feel compelled to listen. However, listening may be hindered by many complicating factors. First, God's revelation did not come in the English language or through Western culture. As a result, we may have to work harder to receive the message clearly. The more familiar students can become with ancient Near Eastern culture, particularly that of Israel during the Old Testament period, the more barriers they can eliminate.

A second complicating factor is that even when we are listening, we have a tendency either to be selective about what we hear or to try to make the message conform to what we want to hear. The solution to this is to allow the Bible to speak for itself. We all have assumptions about the Bible. These need to be constantly evaluated and refined lest they distort the teaching of the Bible. The objectives of the biblical authors must not be subordinated to our own objectives, however worthy the latter may be. There are many valuable things to be learned from the Old Testament, but not all are things that the Old Testament is trying to teach. If students desire to reap authoritative teaching from the text, they must learn to discern what the text is teaching rather than superimposing their own ideas on it. When the Bible is allowed to speak from its own vantage point and with its own agenda, the reader can be more open to learn what it is intending to teach.

Self-Revelation

As God's self-revelation, the objective of the Old Testament is that the reader comes to know God better. This process, however, is not intended to be merely cognitive. In addition, knowing God is accomplished by experiencing his attributes. Being able to list God's attributes is but a first step. What must be achieved is that his attributes become the framework of our worldview. By this we mean that our perspective on ourselves, our society, our world, our history, our conduct, our decisions—everything—should be knit together by an informed and integrated view of God. The Old Testament's objective is not transformed lives, though knowing God should transform one's life. The Old Testament's objective is not the adoption of a value system, though a value system would certainly be one outcome of knowing God in a real way. The Old Testament is not a repository of historical role models, dusty hymns, and obscure prophetic sayings, but God's invitation to hear his story.

This story of God begins with creation. The emphasis, however, is not on how the world began, but on how the plan began. Everything was just right for the execution of God's plan. In that sense, creation is simply the introduction to history. God's sovereignty is initially assured by the fact that he created. While this cannot help but deny any claim to sovereignty by other deities, its intention is not to provide polemic against the pagan polytheism of the day. Rather than taking a negative approach that denounces and refutes other deities, the Old Testament takes the positive approach of telling what the one true God is like and what he has done.

As history begins, it will be observed that the Old Testament is concerned with political or social aspects of history only in a secondary way. The primary interest of this history is how God has revealed himself to people in the past. One reflection of this can be found in the names of God that permeate the pages of Scripture. These names portray him as a God who is holy, almighty, most high, and the one who has caused everything to be. Yet he is also a God who hears, sees, and provides. The habitual rebellion and feeblemindedness of humankind shows him by contrast a God of patience and grace.

Just as creation flows into history, so history flows into prophecy. God's plan was initiated in the beginning, was worked out through history, and will continue until all is accomplished. By seeing God's plan worked out in the past (the Pentateuch and the historical books) and projected into the future (prophetic literature), we can begin to appreciate the unfathomable wisdom of God, who is worthy of praise and worship (Psalms and wisdom literature). The Old Testament, then, should be viewed as a presentation of God's attributes in action. We can know who God is and what he is like

"There the angel of the LORD appeared to him in flames of fire from within a bush. Moses saw that though the bush was on fire it did not burn up" (Exod. 3:2). This was a significant step in God's program of revelation. The picture is found in the Golden Hagada, an illustrated Hebrew Bible manuscript from Spain dating to AD 1320.

Z. Radovan/www.BibleLandPictures.com

by hearing what he has done and intends to do. Once we know who he is and what he is like, the appropriate responses are worship, commitment, and service.

The Plan: God with Us

What is this plan that spans the scope of creation, history, and prophecy? We find it communicated throughout the pages of the Bible. God's plan from the beginning was to create a people among whom he could dwell and with whom he could be in relationship. We should not suppose that he needed either a place to live or that he had some psychological need for companionship. His plan emerges naturally as an initiative that expresses his character as a creative, relational, and gracious being.

This plan is reflected in the initial setting of Eden, where God's presence existed in what we might call a cosmic temple, and people were placed in the garden to be near him and to have the opportunity to come to know him. The plan was upset by the disobedience that we call the fall, by which sin entered the picture. Consequently, relationship with God was disrupted and the privilege of being in the presence of God was forfeited as the first couple was driven out of the garden.

The rest of the Bible is the account of God's program to restore his presence to his people and provide means for them to be able to be in relationship with him again. We can offer a brief overview by identifying the seven stages of God's presence.

> **Stages of God's Presence**
> 1. Eden
> 2. Covenant
> 3. Exodus (Bush/Sinai)
> 4. Tabernacle/Temple
> 5. Incarnation (Immanuel)
> 6. Pentecost
> 7. New Creation

In the account of the Tower of Babel (Gen. 11:1–9) we find the people undertaking a project that endeavored to reestablish God's presence on earth. The tower was provided as a means for God to come down and take up his residence in their city and be worshiped. Unfortunately, their concept of God was flawed and when God came down, he was not pleased with the underlying premise of this initiative. His own initiative is introduced in the next chapter of Genesis as he begins to form a covenant with Abram as a means by which he can reveal himself to the world (explained in the next section). He chooses one family with whom he develops a relationship and among whom he will come to dwell. This second stage is the first step of the reclamation project.

God's presence reaches a new level as he appears in the burning bush to Moses and reveals his name (= his character/nature) and the next step of his plan. His presence is made known through the plagues, evident temporarily in the pillar of cloud and fire, and settles on the top of Mt. Sinai, where he reveals how his people can be in relationship with him (the law) and how they can preserve his presence (the rituals and other instructions regarding the tabernacle).

In the next stage God actually initiates a means by which his presence can be established on earth. The Tabernacle is a place of God's dwelling, and by keeping the law and observing rules of purity, the people can enjoy relationship with the God who has come among them. This stage of God's presence is extended eventually into the Temple built by Solomon and lasts through the remainder of the Old Testament. A serious setback is suffered when the rebellion of the Israelites finally causes God's presence to leave the temple allowing it to be destroyed (in Jeremiah and Ezekiel). The covenant benefits are lost as the Israelites are exiled from the promised land and their relationship with God hangs in the balance.

Though they return to the land and the temple is rebuilt, the next stage of God's presence comes in the pages of the New Testament as God sends his Son, Jesus, to be present in human flesh (the incarnation) and take up his residence with us (Immanuel, God with us) as sort of a human tabernacle (John 1:14). It is through Christ that God's presence thus becomes available in a whole new way and also through him that relationship is made available at a whole new level, with the penalty of sin being paid, and a permanent mechanism for relationship being made available.

Though Christ ascended to heaven after the resurrection, he had promised that his presence would not be taken from us, but that a Comforter would be sent. Thus the coming of the Holy Spirit at Pentecost marks the beginning of yet another stage in the availability of God's presence, now *within* his people, and a relationship based on the indwelling of the Holy Spirit. Consequently God's people become the location of God's presence both individually (1 Cor. 6:19) and corporately (1 Cor. 3:16). The veil is torn that restricted access to God's presence (Eph. 2) and relationship is available to all who seek it.

The final stage is yet to come. It is described in Revelation 21:3, "Now the dwelling of God is with men, and he will live with them. They will be his people, and God himself will be with them and be their God."

The Covenant

At the core of this self-revelation, delineating the plan of God, is the covenant. Even the English designation "Old Testament" indicates that the covenant is the core concept of this collection of books (testament = covenant). Through the covenant God both reveals what he is like and obliges himself to a particular course of action. His loyalty (Heb. ḥesed) to the covenant frequently leads him to acts of grace and mercy, but justice is also built into the covenant to ensure accountability by his people.

Z. Radovan/www.BibleLandPictures.com

Since the covenant is the instrument used by God to effect self-revelation, the Old Testament often appears to be the history of the covenant, or of aspects of it, more than a history of Israel. So Genesis 12–50 is a history of the establishment of the Abrahamic covenant. Exodus–Deuteronomy is a history of the establishment of the Mosaic covenant at Sinai. Joshua is a record of God's faithfulness to the covenant, while Judges is a record of Israel's unfaithfulness to the covenant. The books of Samuel and Kings are a history of the covenant of kingship (the Davidic covenant). It is the covenant as God's plan that is more in focus than the people who are involved generation after generation.

Several different approaches to the Old Testament are distinguished from one another by the way each understands the covenant idea and the relationship of the covenants to one another. Are there many different covenants that independently govern periods of history, or are there just one or two governing covenants that have other sub-covenants to offer expansion and explanation? Is there a single unconditional covenant that contains conditional covenants within it, or is the whole a conditional covenant?

These are the questions that, answered different ways by different scholars, define the theological controversies about the Old Testament, its relationship to the New Testament, and its relevance to us today.

"Raise your staff and stretch out your hand over the sea to divide the water so that the Israelites can go through the sea on dry ground" (Exod. 14.16). Israel always looked back on this event as one in which God revealed himself through his actions of deliverance. The crossing of the Red Sea is depicted in this illustration from the Sarajevo Hagada, an illustrated Hebrew Bible manuscript from Spain in the 14th century AD.

The answers given to these questions, however, do not alter the picture of God that the covenant offers. Only the shape of theology is at stake in this issue, not the nature of God as he is revealed in the Old Testament. Even if one is inclined to draw distinct, separating lines between the covenants, the organic unity of the covenants must not be overlooked.

It is this latter characteristic that helps us to see the plan of God as a consistent, unified entity. In this view, the covenant with Abraham established Israel as the "revelatory" people of God—the people through whom he would reveal himself to the world. The law that is given on Sinai is a major part of the revelation that the covenant was established to provide. At the same time, Leviticus, Deuteronomy, and Joshua contain covenant renewals that reinforce the agreement. The Davidic covenant brings to fulfillment some of the initial promises of God to Abraham (e.g., that kings would come from him) and at the same time expands the agreement to include a dynastic line. The prophets speak of future covenants (cf. Isa. 61:8; Jer. 31:31–34; Ezek. 16:60–63; 34:25–30; 37:19–28; Hos. 2:18–20), and these generally relate to the eventual fulfillment of aspects of the previous covenants that had been unrealized because of the failures of the Israelites.

Each covenant will be discussed more fully in the appropriate places in this survey. At this point it is important for us to recognize the centrality and the organic unity of the covenants in the Old Testament as they relate to God's plan and his self-revelation. The covenant is God's initiative for revelation and for relationship. It is the mechanism that he intends to use so that he can again dwell among his people, eventually available in full in the new covenant.

Authority

While it is not improper to study the Bible from a literary perspective and to appreciate it as great literature, we cannot stop there. If the Bible is to be recognized as God's self-revelation, it must be viewed as representing more than the opinion of godly people. In other words, if God is not understood to be the source of the Old Testament, it cannot serve as a *self*-revelation. If God is the source of the Old Testament, it can be understood as possessing authority. We study Scripture because we expect to get an authoritative word from God, not the subjective opinions of people, however valuable or true the latter may be. Authority is what makes the Old Testament more than just fine literature. The New Testament therefore refers to the Old Testament as being God-breathed, or "inspired." Inspiration is that quality that designates the source as God and guarantees that the resulting written product has authority (2 Tim. 3:16).

It stands to reason, then, that if we look to the Bible for authoritative revelation from God, the authority must be vested in what it intends to communicate, not in what the reader wants to hear. This is another way in which the Bible is different from other literature. When we read a novel or a poem, the power of the literature can be measured by its ability to evoke a response from the reader and blend that together with the ideas of the writer to create and recreate new "meanings" each time it is read. In this way a poem could mean one thing to one reader and strike an entirely different chord in another reader. Although this dynamic can be an outcome of the application process in reading the Old Testament (see below), the fact that the written Word has authority while the reader's response does not should warn against intermingling them. The result is that we cannot be content learning our own lessons from Scripture, as valuable as they may be. We must strive to discover what the author intends to communicate, for that is where authority is vested.

What are the implications of the authority the text possesses? The first is that we accept what it says as truth. If God never made a covenant with Abraham or never spoke to Moses on Sinai; if the conquest were just an imaginary polemic for Israel to defend its territorial expansionism; if the Davidic covenant were nothing more than a political ploy by the Davidites to proclaim divine justification for their dynasty, then it is not God's self-revelation but is simple propaganda and has no relevance to us at all. If there is any sense in which this is God's word, it must be taken as truthful.

A second implication is that we need to respond. If the Bible is truly God's authoritative self-revelation, we cannot afford to ignore or neglect him. He expects not only worship, but obedience, justice, loyalty, faithfulness, holiness, righteousness, and love. In short, he wants us to be like him—that is one of the reasons he reveals what he is like.

How to Read the Old Testament

Since the Old Testament is to be understood as God's revelation of himself, we cannot be satisfied to read it for its factual details alone. Those details make up what we can call the "storyline" of the text. The storyline is comprised of the people, places, dates, and events—the raw materials of the history of Israel. The Old Testament is full of such details, often to the extent that the reader can be overwhelmed trying to master them. While the storyline is an essential foundation for understanding the text, it is important to recognize that the mastery of the details of the storyline is secondary to a more central concern. What is more significant than an understanding of the people and events is an understanding of God and his plan. Thus we need to pay attention to

Z. Radovan/www.BibleLandPictures.com

"Then you call on the name of your god, and I will call on the name of the LORD. The god who answers by fire—he is God" (1 Kings 18:24). Here God revealed himself as Israel's God. This important contest on Mount Carmel, where Elijah demonstrates the superiority of Yahweh over Baal and his prophets, is depicted at Dura Europas, one of the earliest preserved synagogues from around AD 245.

what can be called the "plotline" of the Old Testament. The plotline goes beyond the factual content to the message of each book and of the whole. It identifies that which makes the literature not just narrative history, but Scripture. It is concerned with the theology of the text, not just the framework; the substance of the meaning, not just the trivia of the medium. A reader could have absolute mastery of the storyline, and be impacted not at all by the plotline. One could believe that the events took place and the people were historical, but failing to be impacted by the God of the Bible and his story, would miss the point entirely. The compelling reason to read the Bible is not to be found in the sweep of its narrative, but in the reality of the God who is revealed in its pages.

How to Study the Old Testament

If we are to respond to the Old Testament, we must know how to interpret it so we know how to respond. Much of the spiritual truth of the Old Testament is evident even through a superficial reading of the text. In-depth study can yield even greater results but is accompanied by greater difficulties as well. Various principles and methodologies that serve as guides for exegesis and interpretation can only be introduced here but may provide an introduction for the student.

Aspects of Bible Interpretation

One of the main principles of biblical interpretation has already been mentioned: The Bible must be allowed to speak for itself. This is difficult to attain because every interpreter has presuppositions, that is, preformed ideas about what the Bible is, what it says, and how it fits together. These assumptions can shape the interpretation of the text and can slant or distort the interpretation. Presuppositions are often subconscious. When they are not subconscious, they are sometimes considered nonnegotiable. Proper interpretation does not require readers to throw away all presuppositions, but it does insist that readers recognize the presuppositions they hold, constantly reevaluate them for validity, and subordinate them to the text of Scripture.

The object of this principle is to prevent interpreters from manipulating the text to suit their own agendas. If the text is to speak with authority, it must enjoy a certain amount of autonomy from the interpreter.

In literary circles today there continues to be much discussion about the focus of the interpreter's attention. Traditionally the author and his background and intention (either explicit or inferred) had served as the key to interpretation. More recently literary critics have concluded that the impossibility of achieving any confident identification of what the author intended demands that meaning is the result of the impact of the text (an entity isolated from and independent of its author) on the individual reader. As we have said, however, if the Bible is to be considered uniquely authoritative, it cannot always be treated as just another piece of literature. If the biblical text is accepted as authoritative, the intention of the author (human and divine) must remain the focus of the interpreter's attention. One result of this commitment is that the interpreter should not be searching for hidden meanings or mystical symbolism. Another is that the author's message ought not to be ignored or neglected in favor of how the interpreter wants to use the text (a common practice in Bible study groups and sermons).

Procedures of Interpretation

But how do we try to determine the intention of the author? First, the genre of the literature must be determined. In our contemporary literature, biography will be read differently from mystery, and drama differently from limerick. The type of literature affects how that writing will be approached and interpreted. This applies equally to the Old Testament. Prophecy is a different genre from proverbial literature. To begin with, then, the interpreter must identify the genre of what he or she is trying to interpret and discover as much as possible about that genre. This latter endeavor is approached through a wide variety of critical methodologies (see appendix to this book).

Second, it is important to discover all we can about the audience for whom the writing was intended and the circumstances under which it was written. These facts may affect the way certain statements are to be understood.

Third, through an examination of the context, we should try to identify the purpose of the author or editor. This purpose may be addressed explicitly, or it may need to be deduced from observations concerning the author's selection and arrangement of the material that give indications of his rhetorical strategy.

As interpreters, if we can understand the author, the audience, the situation, and the literary genre as well as possible, we are in a good position to put ourselves in the audience and understand the words and, more important, the message of the section that is being interpreted. Interpretation requires us to become, to the best of our abilities, part of the original audience. The message to them is the same as the message to us.

Application of the Old Testament

When presuppositions have been evaluated and selected and methodologies pursued that are consistent with those presuppositions, the goal (to interpret the meaning of the passage) is in sight but not yet achieved. Interpretation is sterile without application. In application we must not simply ask, "What can I learn?" Application cannot be just an aggregate of impressions gained from reading the text. In reading Joshua 1, for example, we might say that we learned to be more courageous. But that is not what we are looking for in application. More specifically, we must ask, "What can I learn from what the text is teaching?" so application can be tied effectively to interpretation. If the interpretation identifies the audience as corporate Israel, the promises made may not be applicable to us as individuals, even though they still teach us about God. If the Old Testament is viewed as God's self-revelation, we will expect in most instances to learn first something about God. From that we will then find out what implications that holds for our view of self, others, or the world around us. In this way the message must seep through to our values, conduct, and worldview and affect our decisions and the attitudes we maintain.

If we feed ourselves only on proof texts, role models, types, and "thoughts for the day," we restrict our ability to know God, for only proper interpretation will bring us the full benefit of God's self-revelation. If God has truly spoken, it is incumbent on us as his creatures to get so absorbed in his Word that it becomes second nature to us. It can convict us, challenge us, and confront us as long as we discharge our responsibility to study the Scriptures conscientiously.

Questions for Further Study and Discussion

1. What are some presuppositions or assumptions commonly held about the Old Testament or about particular books in it?
2. What are some important elements of a "biblical" worldview?
3. What does the Old Testament reveal about God's plan that continues to have relevance today?
4. Compare and contrast the concepts of an inspired Old Testament editor and an inspired Old Testament author.
5. Discuss the various literary genres of the Old Testament in relation to the proposition that the goal of biblical interpretation is the intended meaning of the author as expressed in the text.
6. If focusing on short, isolated passages of the Old Testament can produce a distorted interpretation, what steps are necessary to safeguard a sound exposition of the text?

For Further Reading

Armerding, Carl E. *The Old Testament and Criticism*. Grand Rapids: Eerdmans, 1983.

Barton, John. *Reading the Old Testament*. 2nd ed. Philadelphia: Westminster/John Knox, 1996.

Carson, D. A., and John Woodbridge. *Hermeneutics, Authority and Canon*. Rev. ed. Grand Rapids: Zondervan, 2005.

Conyers, A. J. *How to Read the Bible*. Downers Grove, Ill.: InterVarsity Press, 1986.

Doriani, D. M. *Getting the Message*. Phillipsburg, N.J.: Presbyterian and Reformed, 1996. A practical, nontechnical approach to the essential skills of biblical interpretation.

Fee, Gordon, and Douglas Stuart. *How to Read the Bible for All Its Worth*. 3rd ed. Grand Rapids: Zondervan, 2003. A helpful discussion of how each literary genre in the Bible ought to be read and interpreted.

Goldingay, John. *Approaches to Old Testament Interpretation*. 2nd ed. Downers Grove, Ill.: InterVarsity Press, 2002.

_____. *Theological Diversity and the Authority of the Old Testament*. Grand Rapids: Eerdmans, 1987.

Greidanus, Sidney. *The Modern Preacher and the Ancient Text*. Grand Rapids: Eerdmans, 1988. An excellent treatment of how to incorporate the results of hermeneutically sound exegesis into good sermons.

Hayes, John, and Carl Holladay. *Biblical Exegesis*. Rev. ed. Atlanta: John Knox, 1987.

Longman, Tremper, III. *Literary Approaches to Biblical Interpretation.* Grand Rapids: Zondervan, 1987.

_____. *Making Sense of the Old Testament.* Grand Rapids: Baker, 1998.

_____. *Reading the Bible with Heart and Mind.* Colorado Springs: Navpress, 1997.

McQuilkin, J. Robertson. *Understanding and Applying the Bible.* Chicago: Moody Press, 1983.

Rogerson, John. *Beginning Old Testament Study.* Philadelphia: Westminster, 1982.

Sandy, Brent, and Ronald Giese. *Cracking Old Testament Codes.* Nashville: Broadman & Holman, 1995.

Stuart, Douglas. *Old Testament Exegesis: A Handbook for Students and Pastors.* 3rd ed. Philadelphia: Westminster, 2001.

General Reference

Anchor Bible Dictionary. Ed. by D. N. Freedman. New York: Doubleday, 1992.

Complete Literary Guide to the Bible. Ed. by L. Ryken and T. Longman III. Grand Rapids: Zondervan, 1993.

Dictionary for Theological Interpretation of the Bible. Ed. by K. Vanhoozer et al. Grand Rapids: Baker, 2005.

Dictionary of Biblical Imagery. Ed. by Leland Ryken, James C. Wilhoit, and Tremper Longman III. Downers Grove, Ill.: InterVarsity Press, 1998.

IVP Dictionary of the Old Testament: Historical Books. Ed. by Bill Arnold and H. G. M. Williamson. Downers Grove, Ill: InterVarsity Press, 2005.

IVP Dictionary of the Old Testament: Pentateuch. Ed. by David Baker and T. Desmond Alexander. Downers Grove, Ill: InterVarsity Press, 2003.

IVP Women's Bible Commentary. Ed. by Catherine Clark Kroeger and Mary J. Evans. Downers Grove, Ill: InterVarsity Press, 2002.

This satellite view shows the Middle East, where the events of the Old Testament took place.
NASA/The Visible Earth

GEOGRAPHY OF
THE OLD TESTAMENT

The history of the Israelite nation developed within a specific geographical context. For this reason the Bible takes geography seriously. It records real events taking place in time and space. The Bible is not a portal into an artificial and contrived Narnia-like literary history. The Bible, however, is not simply a collection of ancient annals, nor is it intended to be a gazetteer or topographical manual. Like the science of archaeology, geography expands our knowledge of the setting or background of the biblical narratives and thus enriches our understanding of a given Old Testament text.

The physical world of the Old Testament was the ancient Near East, commonly known today as the Middle East or sometimes Southwest Asia. The Old Testament narratives encompass the region of Mesopotamia in the east, Asia Minor or Anatolia in the north, Syro-Palestine and Egypt in the west, and the Arabian peninsula in the south. The modern states of Iraq and Iran occupy most of ancient Mesopotamia, while Asia Minor is now known as Turkey, and Saudi Arabia controls most of the Arabian peninsula. Nearly four-fifths of Old Testament history takes place in the area of Syro-Palestine on the eastern Mediterranean coast. This territory now includes the states of Syria, Lebanon, Jordan, and Israel.

The Old Testament World

The Fertile Crescent

The world of the Old Testament is usually identified with the "Fertile Crescent." This area included the Nile River valley and delta, the narrow plains along the Mediterranean coast of Syro-Palestine, and the Tigris and Euphrates river valleys. Adequate rainfall and irrigation along these coastal plains and river valleys permitted agriculture and settled life, giving rise to the earliest civilizations of the ancient Near East. The first part of this section describes the major geographical regions adjoining this fertile crescent and the respective peoples and cultures influencing Hebrew history.

Mesopotamia

The name Mesopotamia means "the land between the rivers," namely, the Tigris and Euphrates rivers. The fertile strip of land along the rivers extends some six hundred miles from the mountainous regions on the northern edge of the Fertile Crescent to the expansive **alluvial** plains at the Persian Gulf. Like Egypt, networks of canals irrigated the flood plain, making lower Mesopotamia especially productive agriculturally. Unlike Egypt, Mesopotamia had no natural barriers protecting the region from outside influence and invasion. The city-state cultures of Sumer and Akkad were responsible for spreading early civilization northward along the river basins.

Northern Mesopotamia was the homeland of Israelite origins in that the Hebrew patriarchs lived in the area of Haran in Paddan-Aram between the Tigris and Euphrates. Abraham is identified as an Amorite (Ezek. 16:3), and sometime later Jacob sojourned among Amorite kinfolk in Paddan-Aram (Gen. 28:1–9). We are also told that Abraham migrated from Ur in Mesopotamia (or a "northern Ur" now suggested as an alternative) northward to Haran, and finally to Canaan as he followed the revelation and promise of Yahweh.

Later Israelite history is greatly influenced by the empire nations of Mesopotamia, with the Assyrians, Babylonians, and Persians all controlling the land of Palestine at some point in their rule of the ancient Near Eastern world. Assyria and Babylonia were also responsible for the destruction of the divided kingdoms of the Hebrews and the deportation of thousands of Hebrews into exile in Mesopotamia. Then, under the enlightened rule of Cyrus and the Persians, these Hebrew exiles were permitted to return to their homeland and rebuild the temple of Yahweh.

In ancient times, civilizations often saw their own nation as the center of the world. Ezekiel 5:5 says, "This is what the Sovereign LORD says, 'This is Jerusalem, which I have set in the center of the nations, with countries all around her.'" This Babylonian drawing depicts that kind of worldview. One of the oldest known world maps (6th cent. BC), it depicts Babylon roughly in the center, surrounded by other nations and cities.

Asia Minor/Anatolia

The region of Asia Minor situated northwest of the Fertile Crescent is a rugged, mountainous area. It is a diverse land with rich soil and Mediterranean climate in the west and south, a dry and barren central plateau, and steep mountains in the east toward Armenia. The stores of minerals and metal ores in the central mountain ranges afforded the inhabitants of Anatolia a ready resource for commercial trading with the rest of the ancient Near East for food staples and domestic wares. The peninsula was also the land bridge joining central Asia and southeastern Europe, which meant the area was often subject to invasion and foreign encroachment and influence.

During the second millennium BC the central portion of the region was home to the Hittite Empire, a powerful rival to Egypt for control of Syro-Palestine. The Hittites were a military people, hiring out as mercenaries and exporting military technology throughout the ancient Near East. The Hittite treaty form by which Hittite kings subjugated conquered foes became an important

Caryn Reeder, courtesy of the British Museum

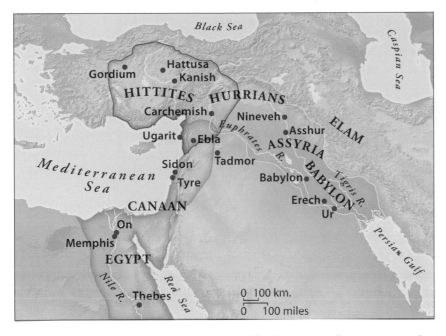

The Near East in the
Late Bronze Age

literary contribution to the ancient world. This treaty form was similar
to that used by the Hebrews for structuring the writing of the covenant
between Yahweh and his people Israel in both Exodus (19–24) and
Deuteronomy. There are also parallels between certain Hittite laws and
the Old Testament, and some biblical scholars even find Hittite influence in the form and practice of history writing in Israel.

During the first millennium BC the people of Urartu dominated east-
ern Asia Minor and warred with the Assyrians for control of northern
Mesopotamia. The Lydians controlled western Asia Minor during the
Neo-Babylonian period (ca. 685–546 BC).

Syro-Palestine

The region of Syro-Palestine, or the **Levant**, constitutes the land bridge
between the continents of Africa and Asia. This four-hundred-mile
strip of fertile land along the Mediterranean coast was bounded on the
west by the Great Sea and in the east by the Arabian desert and the
deep gorge of the Jordan cleft. Syro-Phoenicia, or the northern portion
of this land bridge, essentially encompasses the modern states of Syria
and Lebanon. Palestine, or the southern portion of the land bridge,
essentially includes the modern states of Israel and part of Jordan. Generally Mount Hermon marked the boundary between the northern and
southern portions of the land bridge. (The physical and geographical
features of Syro-Palestine are described later in the section.)

The coast of Syro-Phoenicia had the advantage of natural harbors.
This gave rise to extensive maritime commerce centered in the region,

especially among the Phoenicians and their key ports of Tyre, Sidon, and Byblos. The Phoenicians occupied the northern coast of Palestine from Acco to Ugarit and were merchant traders all along the Mediterranean seaboard for nearly two millennia (cf. Ezek. 27). Both David and Solomon were allied to the Phoenicians, resulting in a Phoenician designed and constructed temple in Jerusalem and a Red Sea port at Elath for Phoenician merchants (1 Kings 7:13–22; 9:26–28). During the period of the divided monarchy, King Ahab of Israel married the Phoenician princess Jezebel. This resulted in the importation of the religion of **Baal** Melqart into the political and religious life of the northern kingdom (1 Kings 16:29–34).

The Arameans occupied the inland regions of Syro-Phoenicia during Old Testament times. They were descendants of the Amorites and Hurrians and settled at the large oasis of Damascus in Aram, or Syria. The Arameans shared a border with Israel and were alternately enemies or allies of the Israelites, depending on the menacing power and presence of Assyria. Two other important centers of civilization were located in Syro-Phoenicia: the city-states of Ebla (ca. 2500 BC) in the northern interior of Syria, and Ugarit (ca. 1500 BC) on the coast of Lebanon.

The region of Palestine, or Canaan, was the land of covenant promise for the Hebrews. However, the presence of the Philistines on the coast and the several Canaanite people groups inland meant Israel would not possess the land of Canaan without conflict. The incomplete conquest

Ancient Egyptian civilization developed around the Nile River. It was a key transportation and trading route and was also valuable because its yearly flood season would revitalize the land for agriculture with water and fresh soil. The result of this annual inundation was that fertile ground lined the Nile on both sides and then abruptly shifted to desert where the flood waters did not reach. Agriculture was therefore limited to a very narrow strip of land.

The Judean Wilderness stretches from the general vicinity of Jerusalem east to the Dead Sea. Its dry desolation forms a protective barrier for the inhabitants of Judah against any would-be adversaries from the east.

Peter White

of Canaan under Joshua left the Hebrews prey to the seductive influence of Canaanite Baalism and its idolatry and immorality (Deut. 7:1–5; Josh. 13:1–7; Judg. 2:11–15). The Philistines controlled the coastal plains and remained a potent enemy of Israel right through the periods of united and divided monarchies, until King Uzziah (767–740 BC) subdued the Philistines (2 Chron. 26:6–15). The Hebrew prophets continued to pronounce judgment on the Philistine cities into the seventh and sixth centuries BC (e.g., Jer. 25:20; Zeph. 2:4–7; Zech. 9:5–7).

Egypt

The land of Egypt lay immediately to the southwest of Palestine and has been known since ancient times as "the gift of the Nile." The Nile River was considered a god by the Egyptians because all life was dependent on the flow of this great watercourse. The final 750 miles of the Nile River bisected the area known as Egypt in antiquity. The river valley was hemmed in by limestone cliffs on the east and desert on the west. The strip of arable land in the river basin measured from 25 miles to nearly 150 miles in width at the delta. The land of Egypt receives up to eight inches of rainfall annually, with large portions experiencing less than one inch. Agricultural activity was based totally on irrigation of the rich alluvial soil deposited along the river basin as a result of the annual flooding.

Ancient Egypt was divided into an Upper Kingdom (along the narrow strip of river valley in the south) and a Lower Kingdom (essentially the delta area in the north). The predictable flood pattern of the Nile and the great natural barriers of mountains and desert on both the eastern and western borders made for a static Egyptian civilization. Historians often refer to the "splendid isolation" of Egypt. This enabled Egyptian civilization to develop a dependable agriculturally based economy, a stable governmental structure, and an ordered society.

The Early Dynastic and Old Kingdom periods of Egyptian history (ca. 3100–2100 BC) witnessed the unification of Upper and Lower Egypt under the pharaoh. This early period was also the time of the building of the great pyramid tombs for the royal family. The Middle Kingdom (2133–1786 BC) and Second Intermediate Period (1786–1570) would have included Abram's sojourn in Egypt (Gen. 12:10–20), the migration of Jacob and his family to Egypt (Gen. 45:16–47:12), and perhaps the oppression of the Hebrews as slaves (Exod. 1:1–14).

The New Kingdom (1570–1085 BC) witnessed the call of Moses as deliverer of the Hebrews and the exodus from Egyptian captivity (Exod. 3–13). By the end of the Late Bronze Age (ca. 1200 BC) Egypt gained control of Palestine under Rameses II, thanks in part to a treaty with the Hittites. Egyptian intervention in Palestine continued with Sheshonk I, who harbored Jeroboam as a political fugitive from Israel (1 Kings 11:40). Later he invaded Judah during the reign of Rehoboam (1 Kings 14:25–26). Thereafter Egypt remained an important and necessary ally of both the Hebrew divided kingdoms against the Mesopotamian imperial powers of Assyria and Babylonia.

Later Hebrew history witnessed considerable direct contact with the Egyptians as well. For example, King Solomon married a daughter of the pharaoh as part of a political alliance (1 Kings 3:1–2), and later

The Shephelah is hilly territory along the western side of Judah, forming a barrier between the cities of Judah and the Philistine Plain. The four valleys through the Shephelah were always inhabited by fortified towns in order to maintain control of the entire region and ensure the security of Jerusalem and the other cities of Judah.

Todd Bolen/www.BiblePlaces.com

The ruins at Tell Balatah are the ancient city of Shechem in the valley between Mount Ebal and Mount Gerizim. Shechem stood along a major juncture of routes running through the Samarian hills.

King Josiah of Judah was killed by Pharaoh Necho in battle at Megiddo (2 Kings 23:28–30).

Egyptian influence can be seen elsewhere in the language and literature of the Old Testament. For example, the Old Testament contains nearly fifty Egyptian "loan words," or vocabulary items directly borrowed from the Egyptian language (like *abrek*, "bow the knee," Gen. 41:43 KJV). There are also the long-acknowledged parallels between Egyptian and Hebrew wisdom literature and love poetry (see chapters 20 and 21, "Hebrew Poetic and Wisdom Literature" and "Job").

Hebrew religion may have been compromised on at least two occasions by the pervasive influence of the **Apis** calf cult of Egypt, namely, the incident of Aaron and the golden calf related in Exodus 32 and Jeroboam's calf worship at Dan and Bethel related in 1 Kings 12. Hebrew statecraft was also influenced by the Egyptians, as the preexilic prophets condemned the Israelites for straying from God and seeking alliances with Egypt (Hos. 7:11). Curiously, Isaiah prophesied that Egypt would one day turn to the Lord and Yahweh would call them his people (Isa. 19:16–25).

The Arabian Peninsula

The Arabian peninsula is a massive, raised plateau. The land is essentially desert, sand dunes, and lava fields surrounded by somewhat fertile coastal fringes. The peninsula is usually divided into three geographical regions: (1) the northwestern area called Arabia of Petra, which includes Petra, Edom, Moab, and the Transjordan; (2) the Arabian desert in the northern and central areas; and (3) the southern coastal strip called Fortunate Arabia. The extensive desert of the Arabian peninsula formed a major physical boundary between the river valley civilizations of Mesopotamia and Egypt. For this reason, travel from east to west in the ancient Near East moved in a north-south direction along the Tigris and Euphrates rivers to Haran and Damascus.

The Transjordan region of Arabia of Petra was home to several nation-states and semi-nomadic tribes that figured prominently in Israelite history. The Moabites and Ammonites were racially homogenous peoples who traced their lineage back to Abraham's nephew Lot and his incestuous relationship with his two daughters (Gen. 19:30–38). They were both monarchical nations, organized and governed by a form of tribal kingship.

It was the nations of Moab and Ammon that denied the Hebrews passage through the southern Transjordan on their way from Egypt to Canaan (Deut. 2:9–37). For this reason no Ammonite or Moabite was permitted to enter the assembly of the Lord (Deut. 23:3). Both nations were enemies to Israel during the days of the Judges right through the Hebrew united and divided kingdoms.

According to 2 Kings 24 and Jeremiah 37, Moab and Ammon aided the Babylonians in the sack of Jerusalem. Even more troublesome for the Hebrews were the gods of Ammon (Milcom or Molech, 1 Kings 11:7; 2 Kings 23:10; Amos 5:23) and Moab (Chemosh, 1 Kings 11:7, 33). Perhaps the Moabite best known to us is the widow Ruth, who pledged allegiance to Yahweh (Ruth 1:16), and eventually found herself in the genealogy of King David (Ruth 4:13–22).

The Edomites lived to the south of Moab from the River Zered to the Gulf of Arabia. Their lineage may be traced to Jacob's older twin, Esau (Gen. 25:19–26). They were a rival nation to the Hebrews from the time of the exodus to the fall of Jerusalem. The prophets Isaiah, Jeremiah, Ezekiel, Joel, Amos, and Obadiah all pronounce **oracles** of doom against Edom, "a people always under the wrath of the Lord" (Mal. 1:2–4). (For more on the place of the Edomites in Old Testament history, see chapter 36, "Obadiah.")

Two other groups of people roaming the northern Arabian peninsula bear mention. The first group, the Amalekites—like the Edomites descendants of Esau (Gen. 36:12, 16)—fought with Israel en route from Egypt to Canaan (Exod. 17:8–16) and were part of a coalition of foreign oppressors of Israel during the period of the Judges (e.g., Judg. 6:3; 7:12). Numbers 24:20 and Deuteronomy 25:17–19 predict the utter annihilation of the Amalekites for their unprovoked assault against Israel during the exodus. The second group, the semi-nomadic Midianites, were descendants of Abraham. They lived in the region of northern Arabia (Gen. 25:1–2, 18). In Habakkuk 3:7 the Cushites and Midianites seem to be equated, so these tribes must overlap in some way. Joseph was

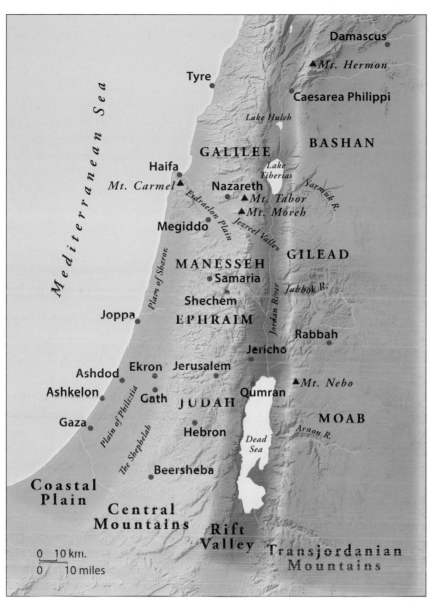

The Holy Land—
Natural Regions

sold to the Egyptians by Midianite traders (Gen. 37:25–36), and Moses married into the Midianite clan of Jethro while exiled in Sinai (Exod. 2:15–22). During the period of the Judges the Midianites were among the foreign peoples oppressing the Hebrew tribes (Judg. 6:2; 7:2).

The Land of Palestine

The land of Palestine took its name from the Philistines (the Pelishtim in Hebrew) who settled along the Mediterranean coast from Joppa to

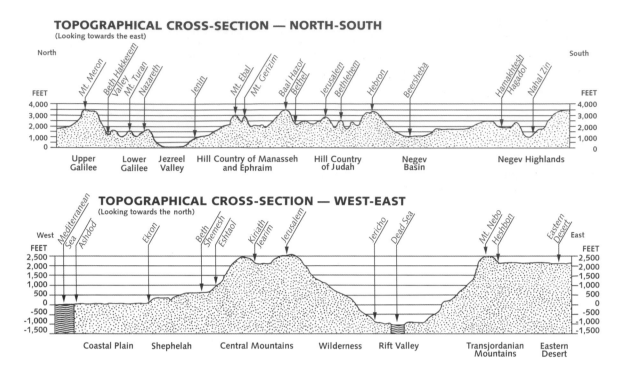

Gaza about 1300–1200 BC. According to the Bible, the Philistine people were connected with Caphtor, usually associated with the island of Crete (Jer. 47:4; Amos 9:7). Prior to the Philistine migrations the region was known as Canaan. This term signified a "land of purple" and was probably derived from the purple dye manufactured by the indigenous peoples from the murex shellfish found in abundance along the Mediterranean coast.

Palestine is often referred to as the geographical and theological center of the ancient world. It was located at the crossroads of the important trade routes of antiquity, the "land between" the continents of Africa, Asia, and Europe. It was also in this general area that Judaism, Christianity, and Islam all had their beginnings. The land area measures approximately 150 miles from Dan to Beersheba (north-south) and 100 miles from the Mediterranean Sea to the Jordan River (east-west), or roughly the size of New Jersey. The climate is typical of the Near East, mild to cold winter depending on the altitude, with some snow at the higher elevations. The rainy season lasts from October to April, with hot, dry, cloudless summer months from May through August.

The land is easily divided into four basic longitudinal, or north-south, geographical regions: the coastal plain, the central hill country, the Jordan rift, and the Transjordan plateau (cf. Deut. 1:6–8). The major latitudinal or east-west geographical divisions of Palestine are connected both with the geographical features of the land and political boundaries of the Israelite divided kingdoms. These divisions included the region of Galilee in the north, Samaria in the north-central area of Palestine, Judah in the south-central portion of Palestine, the Negev (or "dry" **steppe**) in the south, and the Sinai peninsula forming a great natural barrier between Palestine and Egypt.

The Coastal Plain

The coastal plain gradually widens to distances of ten to twelve miles in southern Palestine. This fertile strip of land receives more than 30 inches of rainfall annually off the Mediterranean Sea. Three distinct plains are identified along the coast: Acre (Acco), extending northward from Mount Carmel (twenty-five miles long and five to eight miles wide); Sharon, between Mount Carmel and the port city of Joppa (fifty miles long and ten miles wide); and the plain of the Philistines in the extreme south from Joppa to Gaza. The coastal plain never held primary importance to the Hebrews geographically during Old Testament history. The Phoenicians controlled the northern plain, the Philistines controlled the southern plain, and the plain of Sharon was wasteland, marsh, and dense forest in ancient times.

The Central Hill Country

The region of the central hill country was the most varied geographically and the most important historically in Old Testament times. The majority of Israelite cities were located here, and the territory comprised the bulk of the land area controlled by the Hebrew united and divided monarchies. The mountainous terrain forms the spine, or backbone, of western Palestine and is commonly divided into three major

The Jezreel Valley runs from the northwest to southeast, connecting the coastal plain to the Jordan Rift near Beth-shean. It was a common travel route and therefore became strategically important—and home to numerous conflicts.
Todd Bolen/www.BiblePlaces.com

The Jordan River meanders like a serpent from the area of Mount Hermon in the north through the Sea of Galilee to the Dead Sea in the south of Palestine. If it traveled in a straight line, it would be only seventy miles long, but because of its many curves it actually measures two hundred miles.

geographical sections: Galilee, Samaria (or Ephraim), and Judah. The slopes reach heights of 3,000 to 3,300 feet; the region receives adequate rainfall and was suitable to the Hebrews for agricultural cultivation, including grains, vineyards, and fruit and olive groves.

The principal features of Galilee include Mount Tabor (Judg. 4:6, 12) and the Jezreel Valley. The city of Shechem, flanked by mounts Ebal and Gerizim dominated Samaria (Josh. 8:30–35). Jerusalem was prominently situated at the crossing of the trade routes in Judah (2 Sam. 5:6–12). The strip of land between the coastal plain in the south and the central highlands was known as the Shephelah. This broad and fertile piedmont (or plateau between coast and mountains) was a forested area in Old Testament times and occupied by the Philistines (cf. Judg. 14–15; 1 Sam. 17). During the days of the Judahite monarchy, Beth-Shemesh and Lachish were important fortifications along the southwestern flank of Judah (2 Chron. 25:17–28).

The Jordan Rift

The Jordan River rift, or Jordan cleft, is a great geological depression that begins in Syria in the Lebanon mountains and runs south to the Gulf of Aqabah and the Red Sea. The Jordan River valley that forms the eastern boundary of Palestine is also part of this jagged geological trench.

The Jordan River has its origins on the lower slopes of Mount Hermon and rises from three spring-fed rivulets. The Jordan flows southward from Hermon to the Hula Lake and swamp and then drops quickly some 900 feet and empties into the Sea of Galilee. This inland, freshwater lake is 650 feet below sea level and is surrounded by rounded hillocks. The lake itself is thirteen miles wide and seven miles long. The

Jordan River then flows south from the Sea of Galilee winding its way to the great Salt or Dead Sea, nearly 1,300 feet below sea level — the lowest point on the face of the earth.

During antiquity the region around the Sea of Galilee was heavily populated and intensively cultivated by means of irrigation. Further south, the river valley narrowed and was covered with dense jungle-like vegetation, a habitat for wild animals in Old Testament times (Jer. 49:19; 50:44; Zech. 11:3). The southern end of the river valley was largely unpopulated, except where the Jabbok River entered the Jordan and at the spring-watered oasis of Jericho. Lined with slippery clay-mud hills and thick vegetation, the Jordan Valley still constitutes a natural barrier between Palestine and the Transjordan plateau.

The Dead Sea has no natural outlet, and its mineral-rich waters have a salt content of 30 percent. The limestone cliffs lining the western shore of the Dead Sea are pocked with caves that served as hideaways for bandits, political fugitives, and sectarian religious communities. It was here among the caves of this "badlands"-type landscape that the famous Dead Sea or Qumran community scrolls were found. South of the Dead Sea, the Arabah valley stretches some hundred miles to the Gulf of Aqabah. The inhabitants of this desolate and dry desert fringe mined the iron and copper deposits found in the hills bordering the Arabah, or engaged in the caravan trade that transversed the region.

The Transjordan Plateau

Broadly speaking, the Transjordan plateau is an extensive tableland rising some 2,000 to 6,000 feet above sea level between the Jordan River and the northernmost reaches of the Arabian desert. The region yields some minerals and is suitable for both agricultural and pastoral

Hebron lies about 25 miles south of Jerusalem along the important Ridge Route, which links the cities in the hill country. It was an important commercial and military location and also the city where David began his reign as king (2 Sam. 2:11).

Lepsius Denkmäler

Merchant trade between Canaan and Egypt was common as early 2000 BC. This drawing reproduces a painting from the tomb of Beni Hassan from about the time of Abraham and shows Asiatic (Semitic) merchants bringing their goods to Egypt.

lifestyles. Four major **wadis** or rivers feed the Jordan River from the plateau, including the Yarmuk, Jabbok, Arnon, and the Zered.

The Transjordan tableland may be subdivided into three main plateaus: the Seir mountain plateau in the south (from the Gulf of Elath to the Zered River), the area of Moab and Gilead in the central Transjordan (extending from the Zered to the Yarmuk rivers), and the Bashan plateau in the north (stretching from the Yarmuk to Dan). The King's Highway ran the length of the Transjordan plateau from Bozrah to Damascus.

The Seir plateau is the most rugged of the three, with mountain peaks rising to nearly 6,000 feet. It was here the Edomites and later the Nabateans built their cities amid the rock cliffs. Moab and Gilead contained fertile soil for cultivation and extensive tracts of grazing land for animal herds. Forest remnants can be still be found in Gilead. The largest and most fertile of the plateaus was the region of Bashan. Here the tableland sits some 3,000 to 5,000 feet above sealevel, permitting adequate rainfall for agriculture. The rich volcanic soils of the plain of Bashan made it the best pastureland in the entire Levantine region of the eastern Mediterranean (Ps. 22:12; cf. Amos 4:1).

The Transjordan region was the first area settled by the Hebrews as part of the conquest of Palestine after the exodus from Egypt (Josh. 13:24–31). Throughout Old Testament history the plateau area was often the site of military conflict. The Hebrews, Arameans, Assyrians, Moabites, and Ammonites all vied for control of the trade route centers along the King's Highway and of the fruitful land of Gilead and Bashan, a most valuable commodity in the arid and desert-like environment of most of the Near East.

The Trade Routes

Overland Routes

The prophet Ezekiel's description of Phoenician commerce in the first millennium BC confirms the strategic geographical location of Syro-Palestine (Ezek. 27:12–36). As the land bridge between Africa and Eurasia, Palestine played a prominent role in international trade as early as the third millennium BC.

There were two major international highways linking Mesopotamia and Egypt via Palestine. Both were very ancient routes, their history traceable back to the Early Bronze Age (3000–2100 BC). One was known as "the way of the sea" (or Via Maris in Roman times). The route originated at Qantir (Qantara) in the eastern delta of Lower Egypt, crossed the northern Sinai peninsula, turned north along the coast of the Negev and Judea, and then veered inland through Megiddo to the plain of Beth-Shan. Here the road divided, one artery branching off along the west shoreline of the Sea of Galilee to Dan and Damascus, the other continuing eastward through Bashan to Damascus. At that point the highway turned to the southeast, connecting Babylon and Ur.

The second important trade route was known as "the way of the kings." It too joined Babylon with Egypt, transversing the Sinai desert through Kadesh-Barnea and continuing into the Negev through Edom. The highway then jogged to the north through the Transjordan area of Moab, Ammon, and Gilead to Damascus, and from there into Mesopotamia. King Jehoram identifies the southern portion of this route as "the way of the wilderness of Edom" (2 Kings. 3:8). Secondary roads branching off the King's Highway included a route from Kadesh-Barnea to Elath (perhaps the "way of the Red Sea" in Num. 14:25) and another route to Elath from Bozrah mentioned in the battle that the kings of Sodom and Gomorrah waged against Kedorlaomer (Gen. 14:5–6).

A lesser trade route originated at Elath, extending to Babylon via the Arabian desert with stops at Dumah and Tema. There was also a route northward to Damascus from Dumah. Moreover, some twenty-three regional or local routes crisscrossed Palestine during biblical times (e.g., "the way of the wilderness toward the Red Sea," Exod. 13:18; "the highway from Bethel to Shechem," Judg. 21:19; and "the way of the plain," 2 Sam. 18:23).

The Importance of the Trade Routes

Palestine's location as a corridor for commerce between three continents had great significance for the Israelites. Politically the location made the Hebrews vulnerable to hostile invasion by foreign powers seeking to control the land bridge for military and economic reasons. This forced Israel to engage in international diplomacy, including forging alliances with surrounding pagan powers. On this account Hosea the prophet rebuked the northern kingdom of Israel (Hos. 7:10–11). In their pride and self-sufficiency the Hebrews sought political treaties with Egypt and Assyria, refusing to seek help from the Lord. Of course, this type of political maneuvering was useless. The Egyptians, Assyrians, Babylonians, Persians, and later the Greeks and Romans all

Roads and Routes in
Canaan

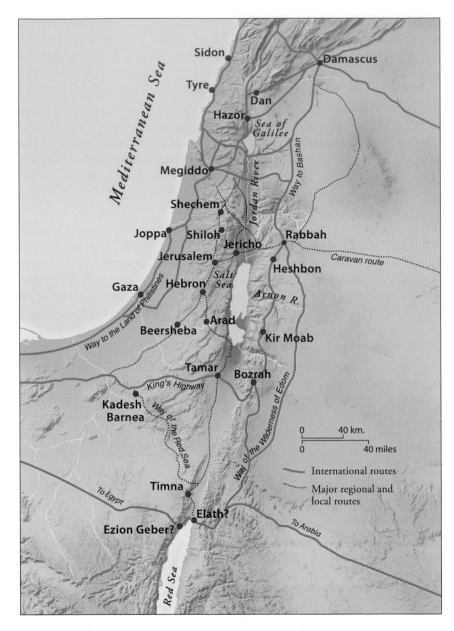

took their turn overrunning Palestine as part of the military expansion
of their empires.

The crucial location of Palestine also had implications for the Israelites socially, economically, and religiously. Trade and commerce fostered the development of a merchant class. Soon the rich were able
to gain control of the institutions of society and oppress the poor,
breaking down covenant community (and equality before God). Economically the prosperity and wealth associated with those engaged in

merchandising encouraged a crass materialism. Naturally, the emphasis on trade and commerce led to Sabbath violations. All this gave rise to pride, arrogance, self-sufficiency, and a false sense of security. Yahweh seemed irrelevant.

The cosmopolitan nature of Syro-Palestine also led to intermarriage between Hebrews and foreign neighbors. This encouraged the **syncretism** of Hebrew religion with the cults of Baal, Chemosh, Milcom, and so on—not separation, uniqueness, and holiness God required of his **elect**. Ultimately it was this "religious pluralism" that led to the overthrow of the Hebrew kingdoms and exile in Assyria and Babylonia (cf. Hos. 4 and Amos 3).

Theological Significance of the Land

Palestine, or the land of Canaan, is also an important theological symbol in the Old Testament. This real estate was a major component in God's initial covenant promise to Abram (Gen. 12:1–3) and is the goal or destination of the Pentateuchal narratives. The exodus from Egypt was divine deliverance for the purpose of bringing the Israelites into "a good and spacious land, . . . flowing with milk and honey" (Exod. 3:8). The land of Canaan was both the goal of covenant obedience before Yahweh and the reward for maintaining his covenant stipulations.

The Hebrew possession of the land of Palestine signaled the displacement of the indigenous Canaanites. The Hebrew conquest under Joshua was "holy war" against the Canaanites. The Old Testament considers the onslaught just punishment meted out by God through theocratic Israel for the gross sin associated with the fertility cult of Baal and Asherah. The Canaanites had defiled the land, and by purging the land of Canaanite presence, the Hebrews themselves were cleansed (Lev. 18:24–30).

Because it was part of God's covenant promise, the land was integrally involved with the Hebrews' covenant relationship with Yahweh. The Ebal ceremony outlined in Deuteronomy 27 and enacted in Joshua 8 formalized the ties between the Hebrews, the Law of Yahweh, and the land of the promise. All three were inextricably bound together under Yahweh's sovereign rule. This meant God's presence and blessing overshadowed Israel as they obeyed the covenant stipulations (Deut. 28:1–14). It also meant that any Israelite trespass of the covenant defiled the land and jeopardized their claim to possess it (Deut. 28:15–68). Practicing the "abominations" of the Canaanites would eventually result in the forfeiture of the land; the land would "vomit" them out as it had the Canaanites (Lev. 18:24–25). Sadly, all this came to pass as a result of the policies and practices instituted by King Manasseh (2 Kings 21:10–15; 24:3). In fact, the length of Israel's exile from the land was directly associated with the concept of sabbatical rest for the covenant land (2 Chron 36:21; see also chapter 6, "Leviticus").

The Old Testament prophets and poets reminded Israel that possession of the land guaranteed neither God's presence nor his blessing (Jer. 7:1–7). The whole earth belongs to the Lord (Ps. 24:1), and he transcends the "land" in that the earth is but his footstool (Isa. 66:1). By the same token, exile from the land of the promise did not necessarily signify God's abandonment, as Ezekiel's chariot vision testifies (Ezek. 1). The throne of Yahweh is movable, and he is capable of seeing and responding to the needs of Israel in any location.

Nehemiah lamented the hollowness of possessing the land of the promise as slaves to foreign powers because of sin and covenant unfaithfulness (Neh. 9:32–37). He understood that right relationship to the land of covenant promise was rooted in right relationship to God in covenant faithfulness.

Finally, even the language and literary images of the Old Testament were influenced by the geography of the land of the promise. Psalm 23 abounds with the imagery of the land, and elsewhere the psalmist likened the righteous to trees planted by flowing waters (Ps. 1:3). The premium on water in the arid climate of the Near East conditioned the language of the prophets as well as the psalmists. The rain and dew are often symbols of God's blessing and vindication (e.g., Joel 2:23; 3:18). Likewise, even the epithets for God such as "Rock, Fortress" and "Refuge" were probably inspired by the rugged and boulder-strewn terrain of the Sinai desert and Judean wilderness (Deut. 32:15). Even the reference to Canaan as a land "flowing with milk and honey" pictured the richness of the land for supporting the lifestyles of pastoralism (i.e., the "milk" of flocks and herds) and agriculture (i.e., the "honey," or nectar of crops and produce).

Questions for Further Study and Discussion

1. Why is a knowledge of geography important to the study of the Old Testament?
2. In what ways did the geography of the ancient Near East influence the history of Israel?
3. What was the theological significance of the land of Canaan for the Hebrews?
4. How was life in Palestine different for the Hebrews from their life as captives in Egypt?

For Further Reading

Aharoni, Yohanan. *The Land of the Bible: A Historical Geography.* 2nd ed. Trans. by A. F. Rainey. Louisville: Westminster John Knox, 1981. Comprehensive and authoritative, an excellent resource.

Aharoni, Yohanan, et al. *Carta Bible Atlas.* 4th ed. (Formerly titled *The Macmillan Bible Atlas.*) New York: Carta, 2002.

Anati, E. *Palestine Before the Hebrews.* New York: Knopf, 1963.

Avi-Yonah, Michael. *The Holy Land: A Historical Geography.* Rev. ed. Grand Rapids: Baker, 1977.

Baly, Denis. *The Geography of the Bible.* Rev. ed. New York: Harper & Row, 1974. A classic, the standard work on the topic.

Bietzel, Barry. *The Moody Atlas of Bible Lands.* Chicago: Moody Press, 1985.

Brisco, T. C. *Holman Bible Atlas.* Nashville: Broadman & Holman, 1999.

Brueggemann, Walter. *The Land: Place as Gift, Promise, and Challenge in Biblical Faith.* 2nd ed. Minneapolis: Augsburg Fortress, 2002. A theological treatment of the "land" as part of Yahweh's covenant promise to Israel and its implications for the Christian church.

Frank, Harry Thomas. *Discovering the Biblical World.* Maplewood, N.J.: Hammond, 1975.

Gordon, R. P. *Holy Land, Holy City: Sacred Geography and the Interpretation of the Bible.* Carlisle: Paternoster Press, 2004.

Hammond Atlas of Bible Lands. 3rd ed. Maplewood, N.J.: Hammond, 2006.

Harper Atlas of the Bible. Ed. by J. B. Pritchard. New York: Harper & Row, 1987.

LaSor, William Sanford. "Palestine." *ISBE.* Rev. ed. Grand Rapids: Eerdmans, 1986. 3:632–49. Technical discussions of Palestine's geology, geography, climate, flora, and fauna.

Lawrence, Paul. *IVP Atlas of Bible History.* Downers Grove, Ill.: InterVarsity Press, 2006.

Monson, J. M. *The Land Between*. Jerusalem: Biblical Backgrounds, 1983. A programmed text designed to be used with the *Student Map Manual* introducing Palestinian history and geography.

_____. *Regions on the Run: Introductory Map Studies in the Land of the Bible*. Biblical Backgrounds, Inc., 1998.

Pritchard, James B., ed. *The Harper Atlas of the Bible*. New York: Harper & Row, 1987. The most comprehensive Bible atlas available.

Rasmussen, Carl G. *The NIV Atlas of the Bible*. Grand Rapids: Zondervan, 1989. Profusely illustrated, useful, and usable for both the specialist and the nonspecialist.

Rogerson, J., and P. Davies. *The Old Testament World*. Englewood Cliffs, N.J.: Prentice-Hall, 1989. Helpful introductory sections on the geography and ecology of ancient Israel.

Sarel, Baruch. *Understanding the Old Testament: An Introductory Atlas to the Hebrew Bible*. Jerusalem: Carta, 1997.

Simmons, J. *The Geographical and Topographical Texts of the Old Testament*. Leiden: Brill, 1959.

Student Map Manual. Jerusalem: Pictorial Archive, 1979.

Van der Woude, A. S., ed. *The World of the Old Testament*. Translated by S. Woudstra. Grand Rapids: Eerdmans, 1986.

Von Soden, Wolfram. *The Ancient Orient: An Introduction to the Study of the Ancient Near East*. Trans. by D. G. Schley. Grand Rapids: Eerdmans, 1994.

Vos, H. F. *Wycliffe Historical Geography of Bible Lands*. Rev. ed. Peabody, Mass.: Hendrickson, 2003.

PART II
THE PENTATEUCH

CHAPTER
3

The importance of the words of the Lord in ancient Israel led to a scribal tradition of careful copying of the Torah. Here the Torah scroll is being copied by hand by a professional scribe using reed pens and feathers, which eventually became the traditional writing tools.

INTRODUCTION TO THE PENTATEUCH

Key Ideas

- Abrahamic covenant as unifying theological theme
- Diversity of literary types and distinctive literary features
- Issues related to the historicity of the narrative texts

The term *Pentateuch* is commonly applied to the first five books of the Old Testament: Genesis, Exodus, Leviticus, Numbers, and Deuteronomy. This Greek expression simply means "five scrolls" and apparently was popularized by the Hellenized Jews of Alexandria in the first century AD. The Hebrew-speaking Jewish community traditionally referred to these five books as the "Torah" (or "instruction" in holiness). Other designations for the Pentateuch include the Book of the Law, emphasizing the covenant stipulations as its defining feature; and the Law of Moses, emphasizing the human mediator as its defining feature.

The Pentateuch was the first divinely prompted literary collection acknowledged as Scripture by the Hebrew community. As such, it is the most important division of the Hebrew **canon**. It always stands first in the threefold division of the Old Testament: Law, Prophets, and Writings. Its supreme rank in the Old Testament canon in respect to authority and holiness is evidenced by its position and separation from the other books in the Septuagint (the Greek translation of the Old Testament). The careful translation of the Hebrew Pentateuch into Greek also confirms the high regard for the collection in the Hebrew community (in contrast to the incomplete and more loosely translated divisions of the Prophets and Writings).

Theme and General Contents

The "five-book" division of the Pentateuch is really a secondary partitioning of what was intended to be a unified, literary whole. The Pentateuch is better understood as a "five-volume" book, a five-part miniseries of sorts. D. J. A. Clines (1979) has convincingly argued that the Pentateuch has two basic divisions, Genesis 1–11 and Genesis 12–Deuteronomy 34. In view of the fall of humankind and the broken fellowship between God and humanity, the first division poses the question, "How can that relationship be repaired or restored?" The second division then provides an answer, or at least a partial answer, to the human dilemma depicted in Genesis 1–11. The solution is rooted in the idea of covenant bonding between God and Abram in Genesis 12:1–3. This passage constitutes the focal point of the second division and actually summarizes the key themes of the Pentateuchal narratives: Yahweh's covenant, Abraham's posterity, divine election and blessing, and the grant of a "promised land."

Part 1 explains the origins of the earth and humankind, explains the nature and purpose of humanity created male and female, records the intrusion of sin into God's good creation, and reveals the character of God, who both judges human sin (as witnessed in the Flood account) and deals mercifully with fallen creation (as seen in the grace extended to Noah and his family).

Part 2 explains how Israel (through Abraham) became the elect covenant people of Yahweh and God's instrument for revealing himself and restoring the broken and corrupted relationship between the Creator and his creation. The Pentateuchal accounts are significant both for Israel, due to their unique covenant relationship with Yahweh, and for the nations of the world, since the destiny of humanity is ultimately tied to Israel's covenant with God.

The unifying theological theme of the Pentateuch is Yahweh's covenant promise to Abram in Genesis 12:3. What humankind was unable to do in all its pride and self-sufficiency (epitomized in the Tower of Babel), God initiated in his covenant promise. The literary plan of the Pentateuch is but an expansion of the three-part covenant promise extended to Abram, as outlined in figure 3.1.

Figure 3.1. The Literary Plan of the Pentateuch

Genesis 1–11: Creation, fall, and judgment

Genesis 12–50: Covenant promise, election of Abraham, and providential preservation of his family

Exodus: Miraculous deliverance of Yahweh's people from bondage in Egypt, covenant relationship expanded to Israel as his people at Sinai, and the law given as a theocratic charter for Israel

Leviticus: Expansion of covenant law for the purpose of holiness among the people of Yahweh, since he will dwell in their midst

Numbers: Testing, purging, and purifying of Yahweh's covenant people in the Sinai wilderness wandering

Deuteronomy: Covenant renewal and the second law-giving as preparation for entry into the land of the promise by the second generation of Yahweh's people

The Literature of the Pentateuch

The Pentateuch, or Book of the Law, is a rich collection of literary genres or types. This diversity of literary types enhances both the artistic nature of the work and the key theological themes unifying the anthology. By the same token, these multiple and complex literary forms have been directly responsible for the ongoing debate over the composition and date of the Pentateuch (see below).

Prose Narrative

Most of the Pentateuchal literature is prose narrative. The narrative is simple but direct and forceful. The text is largely a third-person account of early Israelite history interspersed with prayers, speeches, and other types of direct discourse (e.g., Abraham's intercessory prayer for Sodom in Gen. 18:22–33, Yahweh's speech to Moses in Exod. 3:7–12, and the exchange between Pharaoh and Moses in Exod. 10:1–21).

The narratives artfully blend historical reporting and theological interpretation. This makes the Pentateuch more than a mere register of chronologically ordered events yet something less than pointed religious propaganda serving to explain or justify certain actions, events, institutions, or theological teachings. Perhaps the best example of this blend of historical reporting and theological interpretation is the providential understanding of Joseph's trials as benefiting all of Jacob's family (Gen. 50:15–21).

Figure 3.2. Story Types in Hebrew Narrative

1. Comedic: a story with a happy ending, often characterized by a plot that progresses from problem to solution (e.g., the story of Joseph, Gen. 37–50).

2. Heroic: a story built around the life and exploits of a protagonist or leading character, especially focusing on the struggles and triumphs of the hero or heroine as representative of a whole group (e.g., the story of Abraham and Sarah, Gen. 12–25).

3. Epic: a hero story on a grand scale exhibiting nationalistic interest and often containing supernatural characters and events (e.g., the Hebrew exodus from Egypt, Exod. 12–18).

4. Tragic: a story portraying a change of fortune, usually a movement from prosperity to catastrophe focusing on the outcome of human choice (e.g., the fall of Adam and Eve, Gen. 3).

The language of the Pentateuch is simple and beautiful. It uses anthropomorphic language (i.e., ascribing human qualities to God), and frequent reference to theophany (i.e., a visible and/or audible manifestation of God to a human being). The detailed characterizations and repetitious plots in the stories have led some scholars to use terms like "myth" or "saga," "folklore," and "legend" for portions of the Pentateuchal narratives (especially Genesis). Traditionally, evangelical scholars have balked at employing such labels for the Pentateuchal narratives lest the accounts be thought of as fiction. The inability of modern scholarship to define these genres or literary categories carefully and clearly has also contributed to this reluctance to use these terms. Once again, belief in the historicity of the Old Testament make some scholars reluctant to include Genesis (and the rest of the Pentateuch) in these ill-defined genres. This historical aspect of the Pentateuchal prose narratives is discussed later on.

Figure 3.3. Narrative Structure of the Pentateuch

Genesis 1–11:	Primeval prologue
Genesis 12–50:	Accounts of the patriarchs and matriarchs
Exodus 1:1–12:30:	Israel in Egypt
Exodus 12:31–18:27:	Israelite exodus from Egypt, journey to Mount Sinai
Exodus 19:1–Numbers 10:10:	Israel encamped at Mount Sinai
Numbers 10:11–12:16:	Desert trek from Mount Sinai to Kadesh-Barnea
Numbers 13:1–19:22:	Israel encamped at Kadesh-Barnea
Numbers 20:1–21:35:	Desert trek from Zin to Mount Hor to plains of Moab
Numbers 22–Deuteronomy 34:	Israel encamped on Moab

Ancient Poetry

The Pentateuch contains some of the earliest examples of Hebrew poetry in all the Old Testament. Careful analysis of the way words are spelled, of the meanings words are given, and of the way sentences are put together has demonstrated the antiquity of a number of poetic passages. Among these are Moses' Song of the Sea (Exod. 15), the Balaam Oracles (Num. 23–24), Jacob's Blessing (Gen. 49), and the Song and Blessing of Moses (Deut. 32–33). The dates for the current form of these poetic texts range from the thirteenth to the eleventh centuries BC according to this technical analysis.[1]

Specific poetic forms in the Pentateuch include

- Prayers (e.g., the Aaronic benediction, Num. 6:22–27)
- Songs of praise (e.g., Miriam's song, Exod. 15:21; Israel's song, Num. 21:17–18)

1. Cf. David. N. Freedman, "Divine Names and Titles in Early Hebrew Poetry," in *Magnalia Dei: The Mighty Acts of God*, ed. F. M. Cross et al. (Garden City, N.Y.: Doubleday, 1976), 55–107.

- Victory hymns in epic drama style (e.g., Yahweh's triumph over the Egyptians in Moses' Song of the Sea, Exod. 15)
- Blessings on family members by patriarchs (e.g., the blessing of Rebekah, Gen. 24:60; Jacob's death-bed blessing of his twelve sons, Gen. 49)
- Prophetic utterances (e.g., Yahweh's pronouncement to Rebekah about her twin sons, Gen. 25:23; Balaam's oracles to Israel, Num. 23–24)
- Covenant promises (e.g., Yahweh's promises to Abram, Gen. 12:1–3; 15:1)
- Taunt songs (e.g., Lamech's taunt, Gen. 4:23).

Prophetic Revelation

Prophetic literature in the Old Testament includes both foretelling (or divine revelation) and exposition (or interpretation) of Yahweh's covenant-oriented revelation to Israel. The Pentateuch contains examples of both.

Prophetic revelation in the Law occurs in prose narrative and poetic forms. For example, there is Yahweh's revelation to Abram regarding

The Pentateuch in various places and ways uses the format of ancient treaty for the formulation of the covenant between the Lord and his people. Here is depicted a copy of the treaty carved into the wall of a temple at Karnak (originally inscribed on metal tablets) between the Hittite King Hattushili III and Rameses II of Egypt. It was a bilateral treaty that made peace between the two nations.

Todd Bolen/
www.BiblePlaces.com

the oppression and slavery of his descendants (Gen. 15:12–16) and Moses' prosaic forecast about a prophet who will appear in Israel (Deut. 18:17–20; ultimately fulfilled in Jesus of Nazareth according to John 1:45). Examples of poetic prophecy in the Pentateuch include Jacob's patriarchal blessing, which connects kingship with the tribe of Judah (Gen. 49:8–12), and Moses' lyrical pronouncements over the tribes of Israel (Deut. 33).

The clearest examples of prophetic-like commentary or interpretation of Yahweh's divine revelation are Moses' understanding of Israel's earlier covenant history and God's providential guidance and preservation of his people (in the so-called historical prologue of Deut. 1–4) and Moses' pointed exposition of the stipulations by which Yahweh would enforce covenant keeping in Israel by means of blessings and curses. In each case, instruction to the Israelites is followed by admonitions to covenant obedience (Deut. 4:1–10; 29:9).

Law

The idea of law was not unique to the Hebrews in the ancient Near East. Law collections were published in Mesopotamia as early as 2000 BC, some five centuries (or more) before the time of Moses. The better known of these legal documents are the Sumerian Laws of Ur-Nammu (Ur III Dynasty, 2064–2046, or perhaps his son Shulgi, 2046–1999) and Lipit-Ishtar (king of Isin, 1875–1864), and the Old Babylonian Laws of Eshnunna (nineteenth century BC) and Hammurabi (or Hammurapi, king of Babylon, 1792–1750). The influence of the ancient Near Eastern legal tradition on the form and function of Hebrew law is undeniable and widely documented.[2]

Along with this contemporary cultural influence, the Old Testament affirms the divine origin of Hebrew law through Moses as Yahweh's lawgiver. The Pentateuch is most often associated with Law, as many of the Hebrew titles for the five books attest. The English word *law* translates the Hebrew word *torah*, and Old Testament law includes commandments (Heb. *miṣwāh*), statutes (Heb. *ḥōq*), and ordinances (Heb. *mišpāṭ*). More than six hundred laws are contained in the books of Exodus, Leviticus, Numbers, and Deuteronomy. The purpose of the biblical legislation was to order and regulate the moral, religious or ceremonial, and civil life of Israel in accordance with the holiness necessary for maintaining the covenant relationship with Yahweh.

The purpose of Hebrew law also had implications for the literary form of Old Testament legislation. Old Testament law was covenant law; it was contractual law binding and obligating two separate parties. The covenant law paralleled the so-called suzerainty covenants of the ancient world, especially those of the Hittites. Most exemplary are the Covenant Code (Exod. 20–24) and the book of Deuteronomy.

2. Though outside the scope of this discussion, the parallels between ancient Near Eastern and Old Testament law have been dealt with at length in J. H. Walton, *Ancient Israelite Literature in Its Cultural Context* (Grand Rapids: Zondervan, 1989), 69–94; and H. J. Boecker, *Law and the Administration of Justice in the Old Testament and the Ancient Near East*, trans. J. Moiser (Minneapolis: Augsburg, 1980), 66–176.

The **suzerain** covenants were granted by independent and powerful overlords to dependent and weaker **vassals**, guaranteeing them certain benefits including protection. In return, the vassal was obligated to keep specific stipulations certifying loyalty to the suzerain alone.

In general terms, Old Testament law comprised declarative and prescriptive covenant stipulations for the life of the Hebrew people (quite literally in Deut. 30:15–17). The bulk of the Old Testament legal materials is found in Exodus 20–Deuteronomy 33, and they stem from covenant agreement or renewal ceremonies at Mount Sinai and Mount Nebo. Several important subcategories may be identified:

- Casuistic or case law, usually cast in a conditional "if ... then" formula, making reference to a specific hypothetical legal situation. For example, "If a man is found sleeping with another man's wife; [then] both the man who slept with her and the woman must die. You must purge the evil from Israel" (Deut. 22:22).
- Apodictic law or direct affirmative and negative commands setting the bounds of appropriate behavior in Hebrew society. For example, "You shall have no other gods before me" (Exod. 20:3) or "Honor your father and mother, so that you may live long in the land the LORD your God is giving you" (Exod. 20:12).
- Prohibition or a negative command referring to hypothetical offenses and stating no fixed penalty. For example, "Do not curse the deaf or put a stumbling block in front of the blind, but fear your God. I am the LORD" (Lev. 19:14).
- Death law, a hybrid of the prohibition that makes a distinct legal statement about specific crimes meriting the death penalty. For example, "Anyone who attacks his father or his mother must be put to death" (Exod. 21.15).
- The curse, a development from both the prohibition and the death law addressing crimes committed in secret. The curse was designed to protect the covenant community from uncleanness due to violation of covenant stipulation and to bring divine judgment on the perpetrator of the crime. For example, "Cursed is the man who moves his neighbor's boundary stone" (Deut. 27:17) or "Cursed is the man who kills his neighbor secretly" (Deut. 27:24).

The content of ancient Near Eastern law may be summarized under the traditional headings: civil law, ceremonial law, and cultic law.[3] The subdivisions of civil law included marriage and family, inheritance, property, slaves, debt, taxes, and wages. Common subheadings under ceremonial law were murder, adultery and rape, theft, sexual

3. Despite the limitations of the terms and the ambiguities caused by the obvious overlap in the categories, the traditional rubrics remain helpful categories in discussing the function of Old Testament law. See further, T. Longman, *Making Sense of the Old Testament* (Grand Rapids: Baker, 1998), 110–11; and C. J. H. Wright, *Old Testament Ethics for the People of God* (Downers Grove, Ill.: InterVarsity Press, 2004), 288–301 (who classifies OT legislation under the headings of criminal law, civil law, family law, cultic law, and compassionate law).

deviation, false witness, assault, and liability. Cultic law organized legislation under four major ideas including sacrifices, purification, mode or object of worship, and festival observance.

The Pentateuch as History

Historical Background

The five books of the Law narrate a time span from creation to the death of Moses at Mount Nebo in Moab just prior to the Israelite conquest of Canaan. Obviously, it is impossible to ascertain a date for the origin of our earth and its solar system. While estimates for the date of creation range from tens of thousands to billions of years, it seems best to leave the creation event an "undated mystery."

Roughly speaking, the Pentateuchal narratives from the call of Abram (Gen. 12) to the death of Moses (Deut. 34) may be assigned to the Middle Bronze and Late Bronze ages of ancient Near Eastern history. On a basic chronological continuum this means that the patriarchal period extended from approximately 2000 to 1600 BC, while Moses and the exodus date to about 1500 to 1200 BC (given the early [fifteenth century BC] and late date [twelfth century BC] options for the Israelite exodus from Egypt—see below under "Pentateuchal Chronology").

The patriarchs emerged from Mesopotamian culture founded by the Sumerians but reshaped by the Semitic dynasties of Sargon of Akkad that conquered and absorbed the decaying Sumerian civilization about 2400 BC. The later kingdoms of Sumer and Akkad were in turn influenced by the continuing infiltration of the Amorites from the north and west and the Elamites from the east.

This bronze sculpture is thought to be Sargon, King of Akkad, who founded the first empire known in world history, in southern Mesopotamia about 2350 BC.

Erich Lessing/Art Resource, NY, courtesy of the Iraq Museum, Baghdad, Iraq

Palestine in the Middle Bronze Age was dominated by scattered Canaanite city-states much like Mesopotamia, though not as densely populated or as urban. According to the Egyptian story of Sinuhe, the fame of Palestine's agricultural abundance was widespread. The Canaanites, Amorites, Jebusites, and non-Semitic Hurrians were among the more important people groups occupying Syro-Palestine during this period. Later both the Egyptians and the Hittites influenced Syro-Palestine as they vied for control of this key land bridge (as witnessed by the Amarna tablets and the Boghazköy tablets).

The Egyptians were the most prominent people group shaping the historical background of Pentateuchal history. Abraham's sporadic contact with the land of Egypt eventually gave way to the migration and settlement of Jacob's entire clan in the region of the Nile delta. The Hebrews then resided in Egypt for several centuries, multiplying into a "great nation" while at the same time being thoroughly acculturated into Egyptian civilization. Examples of this acculturation are that not long after the exodus the Hebrews lapsed into worship of what may have been an Egyptian deity (Exod. 32:1–10); during the trek the people clamored to return to Egypt (Num. 11:4–6); and the Pentateuch itself contains some forty-five Egyptian loan words. Ironically, the Exodus narrative pits Moses and Yahweh against the pharaoh and the gods of Egypt, with the central character, Moses, a former Egyptian courtier. (For more on Egyptian history, see "Historical Overview of Old Testament Times," p. 181.

The Egyptian Tale of Sinuhe.

Lenka Peacock, courtesy of the British Museum

Pentateuchal Chronology

Although most of Pentateuchal history may be assigned to the Middle Bronze and Late Bronze ages of ancient Near Eastern history, an exact chronology for the Hebrew patriarchs remains problematic. Some biblical scholars place the characters in a fixed chronological framework, dating Pentateuchal events precisely to the year. For example, Abram's birth is dated to 2166 BC, he began his sojourn in Canaan in 2091, he offered the Mount Moriah sacrifice in 2056, and he died in 1991 BC. Others place the Hebrew patriarchs on a relative chronological continuum, assigning them broadly to the four centuries between 2000 and 1600 BC.

Rudolf Ochmann/Wikimedia Commons, GNU 1.2/CC 2.5

Carved on the wall of Abydos, this is a list of Egyptian pharaohs that offers an early source for chronology.

Figure 3.4. Comparison of Chronological Systems

EARLY EXODUS (LONG SOJOURN)	EARLY EXODUS (SHORT SOJOURN)	LATE EXODUS	RECONSTRUCTIONIST
The Patriarchs 2166 – 1805		2100	
Migration to Egypt 1876		2000	
	The Patriarchs 1952 – 1589	1900	The Patriarchs 1950 – 1650
		1800	
Egyptian Sojourn 1876 – 1446	Migration to Egypt 1660	1700	Migration to Egypt 1650
		1600	
Slavery 1730 or 1580	Egyptian Sojourn 1660 – 1446 Slavery 1580	1500	The Patriarchs 1500 – 1300 Gradual migration
			Egyptian Sojourn 1650 – 1230
		1400	
Wandering 1446 – 1406	Wandering 1446 – 1406	1300	Slavery 1580
			Egyptian Sojourn 1350 – 1230
Conquest and Judges 1406 – 1050	Conquest and Judges 1406 – 1050	1200	
			Conquest and Judges 1230 – 1025
		1100	Conquest and Judges 1230 – 1025
United Kingdom 1050 – 931	United Kingdom 1050 – 931	1000	United Kingdom 1025 – 931
		900	

| Early date for Exodus and 430-year sojourn in Egypt per Masoretic reading of Exodus 12:40 | Early date of Exodus and 215-year sojourn in Egypt per LXX reading of Exodus 12:40 | Late date of Exodus and belief in historicity of patriarchal events | Late date of Exodus and reconstruction of biblical history through use of form criticism |

From John H. Walton, *Chronological and Background Charts of the Old Testament* (Grand Rapids: Zondervan, 1994), 99.

Given the scanty and sometimes ambiguous biblical data relating to Pentateuchal history and chronology, a relative time line for the Hebrew patriarchal period is preferable.

However, even a relative chronological continuum for early Hebrew history is not without problems, as the comparison chart in figure 3.4 demonstrates.

The discussion centers on two principal issues: the interpretation of biblical numerology and the role of archaeology and comparative historical and literary study in understanding biblical history. Scholars committed to a literal reading of the Old Testament **date formulas** affirm the historicity of the Genesis narratives and support an early date for the exodus from Egypt. Those who interpret the Old Testament date formulas figuratively or symbolically usually hold to a late date for the exodus but differ on their understanding of the historicity of the patriarchal narratives. Scholars assuming a skeptical stance toward the Old Testament narratives are regarded as "reconstructionists" because they reject a reading of the text at face value in order to retrieve or establish "real" Old Testament history through the application of historical-critical methodologies to the biblical text.

A second chronological problem arising from the Pentateuchal narratives is the actual date of the Hebrew exodus from bondage in Egypt. The names of the pharaohs of the Hebrew oppression and exodus are not mentioned in the biblical text, and as a result of this ambiguity two distinct positions have emerged from scholarly debate. One position interprets the date formulas of Judges 11:26 and 1 Kings 6:1 literally and assigns the exodus to the fifteenth century BC (Early Date). The alternative view reads the same date formulas symbolically, places a priority on archaeological data and extrabiblical evidence, and dates the exodus to the thirteenth century BC (Late Date). (See further on this in chapter 5.)

Historical Reliability

The source analysis approach that gained prominence during the nineteenth century not only affected the way biblical scholars viewed the Pentateuch as a literary composition, but also had far-reaching implications for the historicity of the patriarchal narratives. Julius Wellhausen, the most influential of the "source critics," asserted that the

Todd Bolen/www.BiblePlaces.com, courtesy of the British Museum

The Amarna Letters are a collection of letters sent from vassal kings in Syria and Canaan to the pharaohs in Egypt. They are important for trying to work out the chronology of the exodus and conquest and for illuminating the political situation in Canaan in the 14th century BC.

Pentateuch conveys no historicity for the patriarchs, but merely reflects patriarchal stories retold in a later age.

It should be noted here that a skeptical stance toward the Old Testament record as history is not peculiar to source analysis. Many present-day scholars espousing the unity of the Pentateuch on the basis of **literary criticism** also deny the essential historicity of the biblical narratives. They speak of "sacred history" and "prose fiction," affirming the theological truth of Scripture but denying that the message reflects historical reality or dismissing the question of historicity as irrelevant.

Three primary reasons have been given for the source critic's skepticism toward historicity: (1) It is assumed that the oral traditions on which the later written documents were based likely suffered from faulty transmission; (2) the historical distance between the actual events of Old Testament history and the documentation of those events seriously undermines the reliability of the written record; and (3) the historical events preserved in these later written documents were no doubt heavily edited by the Hebrew community for theological and political purposes.

Today there are essentially three schools of thought on the historical reliability of the Pentateuchal (and other Old Testament) narratives. One, usually called the orthodox or traditional approach, assumes the supernatural origin of the Old Testament and the complete historical accuracy of the biblical record. The orthodox or conservative biblical scholar appeals to extrabiblical and archaeological resources only to support and elucidate the reliable history of Israel already provided in the Bible.

A second approach, the historical-archaeological, presumes that the Pentateuch (and the Old Testament) is generally reliable. This means that the Old Testament in large measure preserved historical traditions rather than creating them. Archaeological data are employed as objective controls to the accounts of biblical history in lieu of the subjective literary and philosophical hypotheses. Those committed to this view believe that ultimately a proper correlation between archaeological data and biblical tradition will either support the historicity of the Old Testament narratives or permit the proper reconstruction of Israelite history.

The third school of thought is that of the historical reconstructionist. This view takes a skeptical stance toward the biblical narratives on the grounds that they are the work of prescientific ancient and medieval historians. Generally, other ancient extrabiblical sources are considered more reliable than the Old Testament narratives since they are older documents and hence closer to the events they report. The historical-critical scholar uses a variety of methodologies including source, literary, form, and **"tradition history"** criticism to reconstruct the history of Israel in holding that the biblical accounts themselves cannot be taken at face value. Again, it is noteworthy that orthodox or conservative scholars may also use these critical methodologies while presupposing the supernatural origin and the historical reliability of the Old Testament.[4]

So finally, the issue of historical reliability of the Pentateuchal (and other Old Testament) narratives is one of preconvictions about the nature of the biblical text. Proponents of historical reliability are generally committed to the divine inspiration of the biblical narratives assuring an accurate history of Israel. Conversely, proponents of some form of a "reconstructionist" view of Old Testament history generally discount the divine or supernatural origin of the biblical narratives. This preconviction accounts for their critical stance toward the Old Testament as a flawed human and prescientific document and explains the need to reinterpret or recreate Hebrew history in light of extrabiblical literary and archaeological data and contemporary sociopolitical models.

Interpretation of the Pentateuch

The Old Testament and the Christian Church

Ever since the time of the gnostic heretic Marcion (AD second century), the church has been confronted with the problem of determining the rightful place of the Old Testament in the Christian's Bible. Marcion represents one extreme, namely, utter rejection of the Old Testament and its "inferior God." Today the other extreme may be found among those groups who recognize the absolute authoritative nature of the Old Testament writings for the life and doctrine of the church. More recently this application of the authority of the Old Testament, especially the Law, to the life of Christians has witnessed a resurgence in the "theonomics" movement, or Dominion Theology.[5]

The problem of reconciling "law" and "grace" gave rise to multiple methods of interpretation of the Old Testament during the Middle Ages. Since it was believed that revelation was both expressed and hidden in the text of the Bible, several hermeneutical or interpretive approaches were used to understand the proper meaning of the Scriptures. Four basic methods emerged: (1) the literal or plain, taking the Bible at face value; (2) the allegorical or hidden meaning, uncovering "buried" meanings for personal faith; (3) the moral or didactic, directing Christian behavior; and (4) the anagogical, focusing on the consummation of faith and the ultimate hope of the Christian.

Since the Reformation, Protestant churches have attempted to resolve the tension between the "law" of the old covenant and the "grace" of the new covenant by one of two basic approaches. The first heightens the discontinuity of the two covenants, in varying degrees, by means of a "dispensational" interpretation that identifies seven self-contained eras, or dispensations, of divine revelation. This approach

4. See Carl E. Armerding, *The Old Testament and Criticism* (Grand Rapids: Eerdmans, 1983), 1–19.

5. Greg L. Bahnsen, *Theonomy in Christian Ethics* (Nutley, N.J.: Craig Press, 1979). Bahnsen argues that the predominate character of Old Testament Law is moral, hence its content is still binding today. Cf. William S. Barker and W. Robert Godfrey, eds., *Theonomy: A Reformed Critique* (Grand Rapids: Zondervan, 1990).

draws sharp distinctions between Israel and the church and essentially constitutes a messianic suspension of Old Testament law. The second approach, **covenant theology**, emphasizes the continuity of the "covenant of works" and the "covenant of grace" and underscores their interrelationship.[6]

John Goldingay offers a helpful summary of contemporary views regarding continuity and discontinuity between the Old and New Testaments. Ironically, his categories largely parallel those of biblical interpretation during the Middle Ages. The first contemporary view, the Old Testament as a "way of life," equates with the moral interpretive method of the Middle Ages, which views the Old Testament as a handbook on personal ethics. The second, the Old Testament as a "witness to Christ," emphasizes allegorical and typological interpretation much like the "hidden meaning" approach. The third, the Old Testament as "salvation history," calls attention to the God who acts redemptively in human history. Like the anagogical approach, this method points to the Christ event as the fundamental link between the Old and New Testaments. Goldingay's final category, the Old Testament as "Scripture," highlights the development of canon as the authoritative voice for belief and practice in the religious community.[7]

According to John Bright, only the approach that takes seriously the Old Testament as Scripture correctly understands the text and elevates the old covenant to its rightful place in the Christian's Bible. There is a sense in which the other three approaches (the Old Testament as a way of life, as a witness to Christ, and as salvation history) reduce the old covenant to a second rank in comparison with the New Testament. For Bright, this reading of the Old Testament with "New Testament glasses" robs the former of its authority for the Christian church. Since the Old Testament is intrinsically authoritative by virtue of its canonical status in the Christian community, it too is binding on the church in what it teaches explicitly and affirms implicitly. This canonical status also means that the Old Testament is authoritative in its entirety and cannot be appealed to selectively. Only this biblical theological approach preserves the divine authority of the entire Old Testament for the community of the New Testament church. This makes Paul's statement intelligible: "For everything that was written in the past was written to teach us" (Rom. 15:4; 1 Cor. 10: 11).[8]

New Testament Understanding of Old Testament Law

Jesus acknowledged that the law was "legalism" in the sense that it demanded obedience to detailed Old Testament prescriptions and stipulations instituted by Yahweh for Israel (e.g., tithing, Matt. 23:23a). But the true nature of law, according to Jesus, went far beyond the external behavior prescribed by the legal code. Old Testament law comprised

6. Cf. D. P. Fuller, *Gospel and Law: Contrast or Continuum?* (Grand Rapids: Eerdmans, 1980), 1–46.

7. Cf. John Goldingay, *Approaches to Old Testament Interpretation*, 2nd ed. (Toronto: Clements, 2002).

8. Cf. John Bright, *The Authority of the Old Testament* (Reprint, Grand Rapids: Baker, 1975), esp. 151–60, containing examples of the Old Testament's authority in its biblical theology by implicit principle even in those texts superseded by the teachings of the New Testament.

essentially justice, mercy, and faithfulness (Matt. 23:23b). Paul affirmed the law as holy, spiritual, righteous, and good (Rom. 7:12–14).

One of the functions of the Old Testament law was to point out sin in humanity for what it really was—rebellion and disobedience before God. While demonstrating that sin left all persons without excuse before the holy God, the law exposed the human need for divine redemption. It was intended to tutor Israel and thus prepare them (and the world) for the revelation of Jesus of Nazareth as the Christ (Gal. 3:24). Ultimately the sacrificial and ethical demands of Old Testament law **foreshadowed** the New Testament gospel: justification by faith in Jesus Christ.

In one sense, the divinely revealed legal tradition of the Hebrews represents a continuum between the old and new covenants. Jesus fulfilled all the law in his very person and his special ministry as God's **Messiah** (Matt. 5:17). By his teaching, Jesus not only certified the continuing authority of the Old Testament law, but also clarified and illuminated what had been implicit regarding human intent and motives. Biblical law was indeed more than external acts and rituals; it embodied the thoughts of the mind and the intents of the heart (e.g., Jesus' teaching on anger and adultery, Matt. 5:21–32). That Old Testament law was "internal" every bit as much as it was "external" is seen in Jesus' summary of the commandments: "Love the Lord your God with all your heart.... Love your neighbor as yourself " (Matt. 22:37, 39; cf. Deut. 30:1–10). Finally, this love for God that prompts obedience to his commandments marks the true child of God (1 John 5:1–5).

The continuity between the covenants is also demonstrated by the New Testament understanding of Old Testament law. Three specific interpretive approaches may be identified, including (1) the typological (i.e., Old Testament persons, events, and things "foreshadow" the corresponding New Testament entities), (2) the allegorical (i.e., the biblical text is understood figuratively or symbolically), and (3) the didactic (i.e., the instructional value of the Old Testament for today's readers). For example, the book of Hebrews outlines the typological relationship of Old Testament levitical law to the priesthood of Jesus Christ (Heb. 7–9). Paul allegorically interprets Deuteronomy 25:4 in defending apostolic privilege to earn a living by preaching the gospel (1 Cor. 9:8–11). Elsewhere Paul underscores the instructional value of the Old Testament Scriptures for the life of the believer and the Christian church (Rom. 15:4; 1 Cor. 10:11).

Yet we must recognize the contrast or discontinuity between the Old and New Testaments. Their understanding of God, faith, and even law are not identical.[9] Jesus specifically canceled the ceremonial food laws of Leviticus 11 and Deuteronomy 14 in his teaching that all foods are "clean" (Mark 7:14–23; cf. Peter's vision in Acts 10:9–23). Of even

9. For a concise statement on differences between Old Testament and New Testament faith, see Goldingay, *Approaches to Old Testament Interpretation*, 29–37.

greater significance, the levitical legislation related to the office of priest and the institution of animal sacrifice is superseded in the person and work of Jesus Christ as a greater high priest and the "once-for-all" atoning sacrifice for human sin (Heb. 7:15–28; 9:11–14).

However, the undergirding theological principles of Old Testament law remain intact apart from the functional abrogation of aspects of the civil and ceremonial law by New Testament teaching. As "God-breathed" revelation (2 Tim. 3:16), the Old Testament Scriptures are inherently authoritative, whether in explicit teaching or implicit theological idea. So while Jesus Christ is the Passover Lamb, rendering all further animal sacrifices obsolete and unnecessary (1 Cor. 5:7), the New Testament still admonishes all believers in Christ to present themselves as "living sacrifices" unto God (Rom. 12:1–2). Likewise, all believers are obligated to be holy even as God is holy (1 Peter 1:16) because they now constitute a royal priesthood in Christ Jesus (1 Peter 2:9).

Questions for Further Study and Discussion

1. What is the significance of the similarities and differences between the legal literature of the Hebrew Pentateuch and that of the rest of the ancient Near East?
2. Trace the development of the concept of covenant in the Pentateuch.
3. How are the five books of the Pentateuch related literarily and theologically?
4. Define theophany. What is the significance of theophany in the Pentateuchal narratives?
5. How is patriarchal "religion" similar to Mosaic "religion" in the Pentateuch? How is it different?
6. Explain how Moses is an "epic hero" (cf. L. Ryken, *How to Read the Bible as Literature* [Grand Rapids: Zondervan, 1984], 78–81).
7. How are women portrayed in the Pentateuch? Does this compare with the rest of the Old Testament?

For Further Reading

Blenkinsopp, J. *The Pentateuch*. New York: Doubleday, 1992.

Bright, John. *A History of Israel*. 4th ed. Louisville: Westminster John Knox, 2000. Esp. 77–103. Informative section in support of patriarchal historicity.

Carpenter, E. E. "Pentateuch." *ISBE*. Rev. ed. Grand Rapids: Eerdmans, 1986. 3:740–53.

Clines, D. J. A. *The Theme of the Pentateuch*. JSOTSS 10. 2nd ed. Sheffield, England: JSOT Press, 1999. Classic monograph tracing the covenant theme unifying the literature and theology of Pentateuchal narratives.

Dyrness, William A. *Themes in Old Testament Theology*. Downers Grove, Ill.: InterVarsity Press, 1979. Esp. 113–42.

Expositor's Bible Commentary. Vol. 2. "Genesis–Numbers." Ed. by Frank E. Gaebelein. Grand Rapids: Zondervan, 1990. Thoroughly evangelical analysis, including helpful bibliographies.

Fretheim, Terence E. *The Pentateuch*. IBT. Nashville: Abingdon Press, 1996.

Hamilton, Victor. P. *Handbook on the Pentateuch*. 2nd ed. Grand Rapids: Baker, 2005. Practical exposition of Pentateuchal content, excluding discussion of issues related to critical study of Old Testament, but including extensive bibliographies.

Harrison, R. K. *Introduction to the Old Testament*. Grand Rapids: Eerdmans, 1969. Esp. 493–662. Now dated, but still the most comprehensive evangelical review of Old Testament studies, with exhaustive section on the Pentateuch.

Hayes, John H. *An Introduction to Old Testament Study*. Nashville: Abingdon Press, 1979. Esp. 83–198. A useful survey of the historical-critical study of the Old Testament, but giving scant attention to evangelical concerns and responses.

Hayes, John H., and J. Maxwell Miller. *A History of Ancient Israel and Judah*. Louisville: Westminster John Knox, 2006. Esp. 70–212.

Hoerth, Alfred J., Gerald L. Mattingly, and Edwin M. Yamauchi, eds. *Peoples of Old Testament Times*. Grand Rapids: Baker, 1994.

House, P. R. *Old Testament Theology*. Downers Grove, Ill.: InterVarsity Press, 1998.

Kitchen, K. A. *On the Reliability of the Old Testament*. Grand Rapids: Eerdmans, 2003.

Knight, D. A., and G. M. Tucker, eds. *The Hebrew Bible and Its Modern Interpreters*. Philadelphia: Fortress Press, 1985.

Livingston, G. H. *The Pentateuch in Its Cultural Environment*. 2nd ed. Grand Rapids: Baker, 1987. Well-researched introduction to the history and culture of ancient Israel prior to the conquest, with comparative study in ancient nonbiblical religious literature.

Martens, E. A. *God's Design: A Focus on Old Testament Theology*. 3rd ed. Grand Rapids: Baker, 1997.

Millard, Alan R., and Donald J. Wiseman, eds. *Essays on the Patriarchal Narratives*. Winona Lake, Ind.: Eisenbrauns, 1983. Evangelical reexamination of the historical reliability and theological teaching of the Old Testament patriarchal narratives in light of recent research.

Patrick, D. *Old Testament Law*. Atlanta: John Knox, 1985.

Pilch, John. *Introducing the Cultural Context of the Old Testament*. New York: Paulist Press, 1991.

Provan, I., V. P. Long, and T. Longman. *A Biblical History of Israel*. Louisville: Westminster John Knox, 2003. An evangelical and "maximalist" approach to Old Testament history.

Sailhamer, John H. *The Pentateuch as Narrative*. Grand Rapids: Zondervan, 1992.

Sandy, D. Brent, and Ronald L. Giese, eds. *Cracking Old Testament Codes*. Nashville: Broadman & Holman, 1995. A "how-to" guide to interpreting the literature of the Old Testament, including case studies.

Schultz, Samuel J. *The Gospel of Moses*. New York: Harper & Row, 1974.

Scobie, C. H. H. *The Ways of Our God: An Approach to Biblical Theology*. Grand Rapids: Eerdmans, 2003. Comprehensive synthesis of biblical themes discussed in the framework of promise and fulfillment.

Sparks, Kenton L. *Ancient Texts for the Study of the Hebrew Bible.* Peabody, Mass.: Hendrickson, 2005.

Walton, John H. *Ancient Israelite Literature in Its Cultural Context.* Grand Rapids: Zondervan, 1989. A survey of the parallels between the various literary genres common to the Bible and the literature of the ancient Near East.

_____. *Ancient Near Eastern Thought and the Old Testament: Introducing the Conceptual World of the Hebrew Bible.* Grand Rapids: Baker, 2006.

Walton, John H., Victor H. Matthews, and Mark Chavalas, *Bible Background Commentary: Old Testament.* Downers Grove, Ill.: InterVarsity Press, 2000. Social and cultural backgrounds of the Old Testament.

Wenham, G. *Exploring the Old Testament: A Guide to the Pentateuch.* Downers Grove, Ill.: InterVarsity Press, 2003. Helpful sections on the use of the Pentateuch in the New Testament.

Wolf, Herbert M. *An Introduction to the Old Testament Pentateuch.* Chicago: Moody Press, 1991.

Wright, C. J. H. *Old Testament Ethics for the People of God.* Downers Grove, Ill.: InterVarsity Press, 2004.

CHAPTER
4

This mountain, located in modern-day Turkey, is the traditional site where Noah's ark came to rest when the flood waters subsided (Gen 8:4), though the text only mentions the range of mountains.

GENESIS

Key Ideas

- God created, and creation was good.
- Disobedience separated people from God.
- God instituted a program of revelation called the covenant.

Purpose Statement

The purpose of Genesis is to begin the story of the Covenant. Though God created everything just right, sin drew people away from God—so much that they no longer had an accurate idea of what God was like. This was why God decided to make a covenant. The covenant would be with a chosen people, Abraham and his family. The relationship of the covenant was to allow him to use Israel to give people an accurate picture of what he was like. Genesis tells how the covenant was established despite many obstacles.

Major Themes

- Covenant and Election
- Monotheism
- Sin
- Origins

God's Presence

The first three stages of God's presence are presented in Genesis as the cosmos is created as a place for his presence, the privilege of being in his presence is lost, and then God's initiative for restoring his presence is introduced in the Covenant.

Outline

Genesis is the book of beginnings and contains the foundations for much of the theology of the Old Testament. It is the first book of the Pentateuch, also known as the Torah. An understanding of the book's content and message is essential to the study of the rest of the Bible. It is not a book of science, though scientists are right to investigate its claims. It is not a book of biographies, though much can be learned from the lives of men and women portrayed in its pages. It is not a book of history, though history is the path it follows. It is a book of theology, though its task is not accomplished systematically.

"The Lord God said to the serpent, '… You will crawl on your belly'" (Gen. 3:14). Depicted here with two front legs is Bashmu, a serpent chaos creature.
Marie-Lan Nguyen/Wikimedia Commons, courtesy of the Louvre

The Writing of the Book

The book of Genesis does not identify its author in its pages, nor does any other book of the Bible explicitly name the author of Genesis. Traditionally it has been attributed to Moses, and with good reason. The other books of the Torah connect Moses to their writing, and most of the biblical literature treats the Torah as a unit. It is therefore understandable that Moses came to be considered the author of the whole. As has been noted often, who better to put together the book of beginnings?

Logic and tradition aside, however, it is difficult to produce much evidence to connect Moses to the writing of the book. As noted in the appendix on the composition of the Pentateuch, much of the scholarship of the last century has been inclined to divide the book between sources dating largely to the late preexilic and early postexilic periods. Specific challenges to this critical perspective (called "source criticism") on the composition of Genesis have come from computer analysis that contests the criteria by which the various sources are isolated,[1] as well as from alternative critical schools such as redaction criticism (which is interested in how the book was put together).[2] There truly is no end to theories concerning the authorship of this book.

Whoever put Genesis together—whether it was Moses (as we are inclined to think) or someone in the time of David and Solomon or the time of Josiah or the time of Ezra—the book clearly has one outstanding compositional feature: It is organized around eleven sections with each section beginning with "This is the account of . . . ," a device known as a "*toledoth* formula." The first of these formulas comes in 2:4: "This is the account [*toledoth*] of the heavens and earth when they were created." The other ten are connected to individuals (Adam, Noah, Shem, et al.). This suggests that either a compiler used these formulas to indicate the documents that served as his sources, or the author used them to organize his material. Since there is no reason to doubt that some of the material of Genesis was in written form even prior to the time of Moses, we would view someone like Moses as doing mostly the work of a divinely inspired editor rather than the work of an author.

Ashmolean Museum

The Sumerian King List traces kingship, beginning with ten kings who are credited with extraordinarily long reigns—averaging more than 24,000 years each. After the flood, 130 more kingships are recorded with reduced length. This pattern is somewhat reminiscent of the genealogy of Genesis 5 and the reduced life spans after the flood.

The Background

Primeval History (Gen. 1 – 11)

The account of the primeval history in Genesis has been found to have some parallels in the literature of the ancient Near East, particularly that of Mesopotamia. Written about 2000 BC, the Atra-Ḥasis Epic contains an account of creation, growing population, and a destructive flood with similarities to some of the details of Genesis 2–9. The flood story of Atra-Ḥasis, with some modifications, is also found in the eleventh tablet of the famous Babylonian Epic of Gilgamesh. Further information about Mesopotamian concepts of creation have been found in a number of early Sumerian myths as well as in the work entitled Enuma Elish, a hymnic account of the rise of the god Marduk to the head of the Babylonian **pantheon**.

It has been common in some scholarly circles to view Genesis as containing adapted versions of Babylonian mythology. Since Mesopotamia

1. Y. T. Radday and H. Shore, *Genesis: An Authorship Study* (Rome: Biblical Institute Press, 1985).

2. Gary Rendsburg, *The Redaction of Genesis* (Winona Lake, Ind.: Eisenbrauns, 1986).

"They were the heroes of old, men of renown" (Gen. 6:4). This is a picture of the traditional hero figure in early Mesopotamia.

Marie-Lan Nguyen/Wikimedia Commons, courtesy of the Louvre

holds pride of place as the cradle of ancient Near Eastern culture, and since the Babylonian literature is older than the generally accepted dates for the book of Genesis, it has been assumed that the similarities demonstrate biblical dependence on the Babylonian material. This has been affirmed in the minds of these interpreters by the fact that Israel's ethnic roots are traced to Mesopotamia, even by the Bible's own account (Abraham was originally from Mesopotamia).

According to this theory, Israelites borrowed the basic mythological concepts from the Babylonian material but over the centuries adapted them to their distinctive monotheistic outlook. A major difficulty in all this is that it implies that the primeval history is actually only primeval mythology. If Genesis 1–11 is only a revamped mythology, then one does not need to believe that people named Adam, Eve, Cain, Noah, or Shem ever really existed. A mythological perspective usually does not affirm the reality of the Garden of Eden or the ark of Noah, though it depends on how one defines myth. By any definition it is widely acknowledged that the function of Genesis 1–11 in Israel is very similar to the function of myth in the ancient Near East: It embodies the thoughts of how the world originated and operates.

How, then, should we approach comparative studies? Though much is at stake, we cannot afford to ignore the similarities between biblical and ancient Near Eastern literature and hope they will go away. Rather, the ancient Near Eastern material needs to be used to help us gain an appropriate perspective on the Israelite literature preserved for us in the pages of Scripture. The Bible affirms the Mesopotamian roots of the Israelites, and the fact that God chose to use human authors to write the Bible should lead us to expect that there will be some similarities to other literature of the same period. However, we cannot stop there.

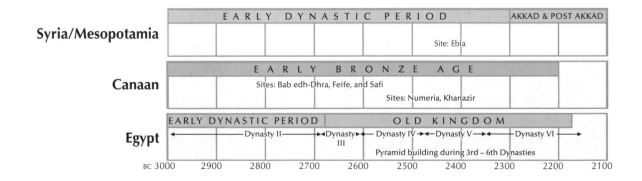

Comparative studies demand that we examine both the similarities and the differences.

When we undertake this type of analysis with the primeval history, we find that differences are considerable and that the similarities can be explained more easily in other ways than by resorting to theories of literary borrowing. As an example, the flood story found in Mesopotamia follows a story line similar to that found in Genesis. A person is warned by deity to build a boat so that he can be spared from an impending flood intended to wipe out the human population. The boat is built; the storm comes; and after the waters subside, the boat comes to rest atop a mountain. Birds are sent out to determine when the inhabitants of the boat may safely disembark. The account ends with the offer of a sacrifice and a blessing bestowed on the survivors.

But the differences must also be considered. Among these are the type of boat, the length of the flood, the people who were saved, the landing place of the boat, the outcome for the hero, and most important, the role of the gods. Many who have done thorough linguistic and literary analysis (e.g., A. Heidel, A. R. Millard, D. Damrosch) conclude that literary dependence cannot be demonstrated. Here, as in most of the parallels in the primeval history, it is considered more likely that Mesopotamian and biblical traditions are based on a common source. Some understand this common source to be a piece of more ancient literature, while others consider it the actual event. In either case, the Mesopotamian literature provides a background for understanding some of the issues of the primeval history of Genesis in contradistinction to the theology of the ancient Near East.

Finally, it should be noted that often when similarities are noted between the Old Testament and the ancient Near East, they can simply be attributed to the fact that the Israelite conceptual world shares the same foundation as surrounding cultures, so we would expect to find them thinking in the same terms, and for that thinking to be reflected in their literature in many ways.[3]

3. For an in-depth study of this phenomenon see J. Walton, *Ancient Near Eastern Thought and the Old Testament. An Introduction to the Conceptual World of the Hebrew Bible* (Grand Rapids: Baker, 2006).

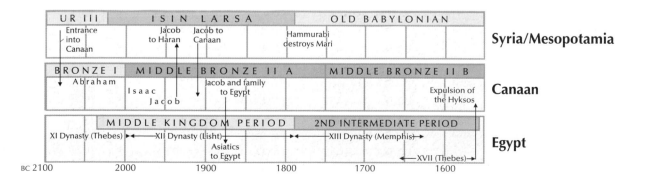

UR III	ISIN LARSA		OLD BABYLONIAN				Syria/Mesopotamia
Entrance into Canaan	Jacob to Haran	Jacob to Canaan	Hammurabi destroys Mari				

BRONZE I	MIDDLE BRONZE II A		MIDDLE BRONZE II B				Canaan
Abraham	Isaac Jacob		Jacob and family to Egypt			Expulsion of the Hyksos	

MIDDLE KINGDOM PERIOD			2ND INTERMEDIATE PERIOD				Egypt
XI Dynasty (Thebes) ►◄──XII Dynasty (Lisht)		Asiatics to Egypt	►◄──XIII Dynasty (Memphis)►		◄──XVII (Thebes)►		

| BC 2100 | 2000 | 1900 | 1800 | 1700 | 1600 |

The Patriarchal Narratives (Gen. 12–50)

In general, the patriarchal narratives ought to be viewed against the background of the archaeological periods designated Middle Bronze I (ca. 2000–1900 BC) and Middle Bronze IIA (ca. 1850–1750 BC). During this time Mesopotamia made the transition from the highly successful Sumerian renaissance of the Ur III period to the Amorite domination of the Old Babylonian period. There is little in this historical background, however, that gives us great insight into the book of Genesis or the lives of the patriarchs. The only passage of Genesis that offers correlation with events in world history is chapter 14, which remains an enigma.

It does seem clear from the archaeological data that through these periods there was a general trend in the social structure of Palestine from a semi-sedentary (sedentary = settled) character to more of an urban character with fortified cities eventually springing up toward the end of Middle Bronze IIA (1900–1700 BC). The Bible's description of the sparsely populated land of Abraham's travels is supported by archaeological analysis. Likewise, the general lifestyle and culture of the patriarchs has been authenticated by archaeological findings.

Though numerous scholars have contested the historicity of the patriarchs, neither the style of the literature nor the nature of the events related in the accounts nor the cultural or geographical setting offers any reason to doubt that what these narratives preserve is realistic and true. Only presuppositions that rule out God's involvement with humankind can sustain the contention that these are merely legends devised to explain Israelite origins. Having said that, it should also be recognized that from a genre perspective, these are identifiable as "Founders Stories" rather than as journalistic history. This label does not undermine the conviction that the events really happened, but it offers a way to understand the criteria by which the author selected and presented his material.

Purpose and Message

The purpose of the book of Genesis is to tell how and why Yahweh came to choose Abraham's family and make a covenant with them. The covenant is the foundation of Israelite theology and identity, and its history is therefore of understandable significance. The book continues the tale of how the covenant was established by detailing the various obstacles to the covenant. Finally, we discover how the Israelites ventured to Egypt, thus setting the scene for the exodus.

The message of the book has several aspects. First of all, it provides an appropriate introduction to the Israelite God, Yahweh. We find that he is the sovereign creator of a world made especially for human habitation. Already in this we can identify an intentional contrast to Mesopotamian theology developing. In the ancient world, something was believed to exist by virtue of having a defined role in an ordered system. Consequently, creation was seen primarily as determining roles and functions for everything in the cosmos. In Mesopotamia this means that creation texts were not as interested, for example, in the material origins of the moon. Instead, the creation of the moon involved its being assigned the role it performed in the cosmos. Since its role was intertwined with the role of the moon god, the origins of both the moon god and the moon itself were linked. Creation referred primarily to this sort of origins. The gods came into being through procreation and as they came into being that to which their role was attached also took its place in the cosmos.

In Israel they shared the belief that creation pertained most importantly to assigning roles (note the description of the roles of the sun, moon and stars in Genesis 1:14). The key difference is that in Israel there was no belief that individual gods were associated with each of the functional aspects of the cosmos. Instead, one God was responsible for establishing all the roles in the cosmos and as a result all of the functionaries of the cosmos become the instruments by which he establishes and maintains order, rather than being viewed as his colleagues or subordinates to whom jurisdiction is delegated.

The earliest known flood story is found in Sumerian literature, and Ziusudra, king of Shuruppak, is the flood hero. This is one of the tablets telling this story.
The Schoyen Collection
MS 3026, Oslo and London

A second aspect of the message of Genesis concerns the role of people in the newly created world, and again a contrast to Mesopotamian thinking is present. A key message of Genesis is that humans were created in the image of God. The world was created for them and with them in mind. The roles of everything in the cosmos are seen in relation to human beings and they are assessed as being "good" when they satisfactorily meet this criterion. When the first human pair are created, they are accorded dignity and entrusted with responsibility (i.e., given their roles). Genesis insists that all this was the design and intention of God. This is a stark contrast to the Mesopotamian mythology that understands humanity as an afterthought of the gods. In Atra-Ḥasis, for instance, people are created to take over the labor that the gods have tired of doing. There is no sense that all creation was undertaken with people in mind, and there was little dignity to offer when slave labor was the only motivation.

Amid this contrast with Mesopotamian theology, it is not the intent of Genesis simply to debate. The point of the Genesis narrative is to establish that Yahweh was sovereignly pursuing a plan of history. People were created with every advantage and were placed lovingly by God in an ideal situation. This is important, for it moves us to the next point of the message of the book. It was this man and woman, not God, who disturbed the equilibrium and brought about the sad state of our present existence.

The Schoyen Collection MS 1989, Oslo and London

The Gilgamesh story is one of the best-known in the ancient world. Here Gilgamesh and Enkidu successfully fight and slay the Bull of Heaven. As a consequence, the gods kill Enkidu, spurring Gilgamesh to go on a quest for immortality that leads him to flood survivor Utnapishtim, who tells him the story of the flood.

It was the continuing failure of humanity as a whole that led Yahweh to send the flood, scatter the people from the plain of Shinar, and eventually work through one man and his family, Abraham. The message of the book is to offer the first eleven chapters as the explanation of why Yahweh has chosen to work through a particular people. It is through them that he plans to reveal himself. Furthermore, it is demonstrated that it was not because of any merit on the part of Abraham that God chose him. Rather, it was an act of God's sovereignty. To Abraham's credit, he responded in obedience and exercised faith that Yahweh would honor his promises.

The message of the patriarchal narratives is that through many difficult situations the patriarchs and, more so, the Lord persevered to result in the establishment of Abraham's family. The text does not hesitate to show the shortcomings of Abraham and his family, but God is faithful and, in his providence, consistently brought good out of intended evil (cf. 50:20).

This is the theological message of the book. There are also other levels on which Genesis has a message. From a geographical standpoint, the book establishes that Abraham and his family were native to Mesopotamia (not Egypt) but spent three generations in Canaan before going down to Egypt. This is significant for their ethnic as well as theological identity.

Finally, Genesis seeks also to explain how Israel came to be organized the way that it was. The message clarifies some of the relationships of the twelve tribes to one another and accounts for the prominence of some and the obscurity of others. The geographical message (travels of the patriarchs), the sociological message (ethnic origins and relationships), and the polemical message (arguing against the ancient Near Eastern worldview) should be understood as subjects the compiler intended to address. But all these should be viewed as subordinate to the theological message, in which the covenant and Yahweh are central.

Structure and Organization

Creation (1:1–2:3)

The creation account is a highly structured literary composition. Using a framework of formulas (e.g., "it was so" and "God saw that it was good"), it presents God as the one who takes what was without purpose, order or function and creates the ordered cosmos. The first three days are occupied with establishing the most basic functions (time, weather and vegetation), while in the next three God fills the cosmos with functionaries and inhabitants. The focus of the composition is that everything is ordered so as to be perfectly suited for people to inhabit. This serves as an apt introduction to who God is and what he has made man and woman to be.

Before the Patriarchs: Primeval History (2:4–11:26)

The primeval history has a universal focus with all humanity as the subject of discussion. In the previous section people were seen in relation to the rest of God's creation. This section begins with people seen in terms of the contrast between their high status and function as originally established on the one hand, and the situation that they brought on themselves by disobedience on the other. The initial disobedience by Adam and Eve brought expulsion from the garden, separation from God, and eventual death. Cain's murder of his brother Abel demonstrated that the new order of things had only become more deeply entrenched.

The passage of time conveyed by the genealogies only made matters worse. Beyond the offenses by Adam, Eve, and Cain, Lamech's attitude showed a boastful glee about his violence. By the time of Noah, violence had become a way of life. The selection of material by the compiler is intended to document in the most graphic terms the moral disintegration that occurred from the fall to the flood.

The flood represented God's punishment on the world, but also his grace. Noah and his family were spared to make a new beginning. Again, some contrast to the Mesopotamian view is evident. There the gods had not planned to spare anyone. Rather, it was an act of betrayal by one of the gods that informed Atra-Ḥasis of the impending disaster. Moreover, while in Genesis it was *humankind* that was saved by sparing Noah and his family, Atra-Ḥasis saved *civilization* by including among his passengers artisans of the various craft guilds. The contrast is that in Genesis God had no intention of saving society; in some ways it was society that needed destroying.

After the flood the blessing was renewed, but degeneration occurred rapidly. The compiler continues to build his case for the insidious effect of humanity's fallen nature, seen even in Noah's own sons. God's eventual response to this occurred when people moved from scheming to make themselves like God to distorting God in their minds so as to make him more like themselves. We believe this to be the threshold that was crossed when the ziggurat (the Tower of Babel) was constructed on the plain of Shinar (11:6). God then placed limitations on people's ability to be united in their misconceptions and waywardness. He did this by causing them to speak different languages that led to geographic scattering. This not only restricted human ability to act in solidarity, but also set the scene for God's change of strategy. God's grace now became evident in his determination to reveal himself to humanity through one man and his family.

The Patriarchs in Palestine: Patriarchal Narratives (11:27–37:1)

While genealogical continuity is established from Noah to Abraham, there is no attempt to establish a faith continuity. Abraham is not introduced as a righteous man, nor is he identified in any way as contrasting with the world around him. Other Scripture makes it clear that Abraham's family did not worship Yahweh (cf. Josh. 24:2). So in a real sense, the Lord came to Abraham "out of the blue." The first contact is described in 12:1–3, where Abraham was instructed to take drastic action to separate himself from his roots so that a new beginning could take place. Yahweh asked Abraham to leave his land, his family, and his inheritance (father's household) and promised him in return his own land, his own family, and his own inheritance (blessing). They did not actually enter into a covenant agreement on this occasion, but the offer was made to do so once the conditions were met.

Chapters 12–22 present the checkered history of the establishment of the covenant between Abraham and the Lord. Once Abraham left his home behind, the next forty or fifty years provided continual suspense concerning how the promises of God would be fulfilled to Abraham. The narrative is artistically executed so as to keep the reader guessing how things might turn out.

The primary approach of the narrator is to introduce various obstacles that place the covenant promises in jeopardy. As each obstacle is surmounted, a successive step is introduced toward the fulfillment of the covenant promises. Obstacles variously take the form of alternate heirs or the form of threatening situations for the primary characters.[4]

The first threat came when Abraham and Sarah went down to Egypt to escape the famine in the land of Canaan. The danger was that the pharaoh might take Sarah into his harem or that a child born to Sarah may not be Abraham's. The threat was eliminated when Abraham and Sarah were escorted out of Egypt.

The first obstacle to overcome regarding an heir was the presence of Abraham's nephew, Lot. Since Abraham and Sarah had no children,

4. L. Helyer, "The Separation of Abram and Lot: Its Significance in the Patriarchal Narratives," *JSOT* 26 (1983): 77–88.

Lot was the apparent heir. His presence with Abraham also could arguably have given him a claim to the land. The obstacle was removed in chapter 13 when Lot chose the plain toward Sodom for his claim, taking him out of the land. This led to the promise to Abraham that all the land would now belong to him and his descendants (13:14–17).

At this point in the text an appendix to the Lot narrative was included recounting how Abraham rescued Lot and many others from an invading army. The reason for including this may be to show that Abraham derived none of his wealth from the Canaanite population (14:21–24), though it is difficult to be certain.

The narrative continues in chapter 15 with the introduction of a second alternate heir, Eliezer, the head of Abraham's household. The Lord indicated, however, that Abraham's heir would be his own child, so another obstacle was removed.

The end of chapter 15 recounts the actual ratification of the covenant between the Lord and Abraham. Again the land was guaranteed to Abraham, but he was also given the information that the land would not actually come into the possession of his family for another four hundred years.

In chapter 16 a third alternate heir came on the scene. In this episode Sarah suggested that since she had been unable to have children, they needed a different plan. Abraham should follow customary procedure whereby a slave in the household serves as a substitute wife in order for the line to be continued. In this manner Ishmael was born, a full and legitimate son of Abraham by the customs of the day.

Thirteen years went by, during which time, we assume, Abraham considered Ishmael his heir. In the midst of receiving instructions for

Susanna Vagt

In ancient Mesopotamia, ziggurats were built to provide a way for the gods to descend to earth and come into their temples. This is probably what the people at Babel had in mind when they declared, "Come, let us build ourselves a city, with a tower that reaches to the heavens" (Gen 11:4).

the sign of circumcision and receiving affirmation from the Lord that he would become a great nation (chap. 17), Abraham was shocked to hear that the promised heir had not yet been born but would be the natural child of Sarah (vv. 15–21). This message was reconfirmed (chap. 18) by the visit of three men to Abraham's tent.

The narrator now keeps us in suspense by relating two significant events that took place prior to the actual arrival of Isaac. The first was the destruction of the cities of the plain, from which Lot and his daughters were delivered. This raised the possibility of Lot's reentering the picture, but the threat was quickly eliminated when he chose to live in the hills.

The second threat was much more serious. Chapter 20 relates an incident in which Sarah was about to be taken into a foreign king's harem, a scene reminiscent of the incident recorded in chapter 12. This time the king was Abimelech of Gerar. This threat was so alarming because Isaac was supposed to be born within the year. If Sarah were taken into Abimelech's harem even briefly, questions would arise as to whether Isaac was actually the son of Abraham. Again the problem was averted when the Lord alerted Abimelech in a dream that Sarah was Abraham's wife and must be restored to him.

Finally, the long-awaited child, Isaac, was born (chap. 21), and the reader is inclined to breathe a sigh of relief that everything has worked out well in the end. But the suspense is not over yet. We find out quickly that Ishmael was not to be so easily dismissed from contention. Nevertheless, even that last obstacle to heirship was removed.

And yet, as we would expect from a skillful narrator, just when it seems that all is well, the largest and most difficult problem imaginable looms over the horizon.

In the account of God's asking Abraham to go and sacrifice his son Isaac (chap. 22), we sense that the narrator has brought us to the climax of the narrative. The Lord had promised Abraham that Isaac was the son through whom the covenant promises would be fulfilled, and so the covenant was again in great jeopardy. All the previous obstacles and threats came from human error or decision. This one came from deity. As the text relates (v. 12), the function of this test was to provide Abraham with the opportunity to demonstrate that he feared God. To be sure, Abraham had been characterized as obedient and full of faith throughout the narrative, but it is much easier to obey when one stands to profit from one's actions. Here Abraham could demonstrate to the Lord that his obedience was motivated by fear of

"Abraham looked up and there in a thicket he saw a ram caught by its horns. He went over and took the ram and sacrificed it as a burnt offering instead of his son" (Gen. 22:13). This sculpture of gold and lapis lazuli was found in a tomb at Ur from a little earlier than the time of Abraham.
Michael Greenhalgh/ArtServe, courtesy of the British Museum

Water is very valuable in the dry climate of the Middle East and could sometimes become a source of contention (Gen. 21:25; 26:19–20). Abraham dug a well at Beersheba and sealed his claim to the water by an oath with Abimelek (Gen. 21:29–31). This well at Beersheba has been used since ancient times.

the Lord, not by what he would gain by obeying. Once the threat was resolved, the promises were repeated to Abraham (vv. 16–18).

The remaining sections of the *toledoth* of Terah continue to offer events pertaining to the establishment of the covenant, though the suspense has been broken. Chapter 23, while recalling the death of Sarah, apparently is included because this relates the only time when Abraham purchased land in Canaan. Since the acquisition of the land was part of the covenant promise, it is important to tell of this first instance.

For Abraham to have a big family, not only must there have been a son, but a son who would marry and have sons of his own. The obstacle to this (chap. 24) was to acquire a wife for Isaac in a way that would neither lead to assimilation with the people of Canaan nor require Isaac to leave the land. This was accomplished by Abraham's having his servant fetch a bride for Isaac from Abraham's extended family.

Finally, the account of Terah's family ends with the identification of Abraham's other children — again, these were potential heirs, so the text shows how they were cared for in the inheritance — and Abraham's death. Amid many obstacles, therefore, the covenant became established.

In keeping with the practice of the narrator, the non-covenant line is traced before the story returns to the main character. So the account of Ishmael precedes that of Isaac, and the account of Esau precedes that of Jacob.

Most of the account of Isaac concerns the conflict between Jacob and Esau and its eventual resolution. The conflict itself was a threat to the covenant because it was serious enough that it could lead to murder and the extinction of Abraham's family (see 27:45). Beyond that, Jacob's leaving the land for some twenty years also threatened to undo the covenant by opening the possibility that the family of Abraham would simply return to Mesopotamia. From a theological standpoint, it is also clear that Jacob was not the man of faith that Abraham became. This leads the reader to wonder whether this might just turn out to be another failed experiment. It is these conflicts that give structure to this section. The covenant is still the main focus.

While most of the account of Isaac is therefore understandable as continuing coverage of the covenant struggle, the narratives that frame the Jacob-Esau conflict prove a bit more difficult to understand. Chapters 26 and 34 appear to be interludes of sorts, since they have little direct relation to the covenant. Like chapters 14 and 23, however, they relate incidents in which agreements were made with people of the land of Canaan. They have covenant significance, for they concern the land and the ethnic distinctiveness of Abraham's family.

The Patriarchs in Egypt: The Joseph Story (37:2–50:26)

The Joseph story is a cohesive narrative with the exception of chapter 38. Like the other interlude chapters, this one concerns an occasion when there was a relationship formed between Abraham's family and the people of the land of Canaan. The episode may also be intended to contribute to the emerging profile of Judah, who had great significance for the later tribal history.

Judah's role in chapter 38 is parallel to Jacob's in chapter 37. Like his father (37:32–33), Judah was deceived and asked to recognize a piece of evidence concerning identity (38:25–26). In this way Judah's actions against Jacob and Joseph were already coming back to haunt him. The end of chapter 38 also shows a younger son forcing his way out just when all seemed lost (vv. 27–30), thus making a "breach" (KJV). This was exactly what Joseph proceeded to do when his story resumes again in chapter 39.[5]

The main intent of the Joseph story appears to be to recount how the family of Abraham ended up in Egypt. In this way it is preparatory for the exodus narratives. Though the covenant is barely mentioned, God's providential care of Joseph and sovereign control of history are evident as the plot develops and is resolved. Perhaps most importantly, it is through Joseph, the representative of Abraham's family, that all the world is blessed (fed in the famine), thus addressing the third clause of the covenant.

Major Themes

The Covenant and Election

The book of Genesis makes it clear that the Lord did not choose Abraham and his family because they were more righteous, more faithful,

5. See especially U. Cassuto, "The Story of Tamar and Judah," *Biblical and Oriental Studies*, vol. 1 (Jerusalem: Magnus, 1973), 29–40 (a reprint of a 1929 article); and Judah Goldin, "The Youngest Son: or, Where Does Genesis 38 Belong?" *JBL* 96 (1977): 27–44.

more pious, or more deserving than any other family. His electing them was an act of grace. Furthermore, while the covenant could not be ratified until Abraham left his family, no clear conditions were placed on the covenant itself. To be sure, the benefits of the covenant could be lost for periods of time, but no mention is made of the possibility of cancellation. The family of Abraham, for good or ill, constituted God's chosen people.

In Christianity, when we speak of the church as God's people, we refer to those who have accepted salvation through faith, specifically faith in Jesus Christ. The church could therefore be identified as the people of God in a soteriological—i.e., salvational—sense. Undoubtedly many Israelites of the Old Testament could be identified as God's people by virtue of their faith in Yahweh. But their divine election and the divine covenant made the Israelites the people of God only in a revelatory sense. By this we mean that God chose them as his instrument of revelation. God revealed himself to the world through Israel—through the law he gave to them; through their history (which demonstrates his benevolence, grace, faithfulness, and sovereignty); through the writing of the Bible; and most of all, through the birth, life, death, and resurrection of Jesus Christ.

Pillars were erected in the ancient world for a number of different purposes. In Genesis 28:18 Jacob sets one up to mark what he has discovered is sacred space. This standing stone has endured from the time and place of ancient Shechem.

The covenant thus became the centerpiece of Israelite theology. It speaks of God's intentions to bless them and honor them as channels of God's revelation. Throughout the Old Testament we learn most about the nature of God by seeing him act in accordance with his covenant promises and by sharing in the benefits of his revelation to and through Israel.

Monotheism

Generally speaking, monotheism is the worship of one God. There are, however, several levels of monotheism, ranging from preference for one deity, to worship of one deity, to believing that only one deity exists. Even the Ten Commandments insist only on a practical monotheism (exclusive worship of one deity) rather than on a philosophical monotheism (only one God exists[6]). This leads us to inquire whether the patriarchs were monotheists. Abraham's relatives apparently practiced the popular polytheistic paganism that was current in Mesopotamia (Josh. 24:2, 14), and the Bible nowhere attributes monotheism to Abraham. Nevertheless, though Abraham is never seen condemning the worship of other gods, there is never a hint that any other god has a place in Abraham's worship. This evidence would lead us to the conclusion that Abraham was at least a practical monotheist. Most people's

6. Though it might be noted that to the extent that the ancient world associated existence with function, it could be maintained that since the first commandment indicates that no other gods function (that is, there are no other gods in Yahweh's presence), it also therefore indicates that other gods do not exist.

Figure 4.1. Theophanies in Genesis

"I am Yahweh"	"I am El Shaddai"
Initiation of agreement	Initiation of fulfillment
Abraham	
Genesis 15:7 – 17	Genesis 17:1 – 8
1. Occasion: Ratification of covenant 2. Emphasis: Giving of land	1. Occasion: Indication of acceptance of covenant (circumcision) 2. Accepts name change; Isaac promised within year 3. Emphasis: Many descendants, nations, kings will come from you
Jacob	
Genesis 28:13 – 15	Genesis 35:10 – 12
1. Occasion: First promise of covenant blessings to Jacob 2. Emphasis: Bringing him back to land and giving it to him	1. Occasion: Indication of acceptance of covenant (destruction of foreign gods, pillar set up) 2. Accepts name change 3. Emphasis: Many descendants, nations, kings will come from you

gods were associated either to a temple in geographical proximity or to the family's ancestral gods. Abraham left all of these behind when he left his land and his father's house.

Also to be considered, however, is the question, "Which God did Abraham worship?" Though the personal name "Yahweh" occurs frequently in Genesis, a problem arises when we read the opening chapters of Exodus. In Exodus 6:2–3 God says to Moses, "I am the Lord [Yahweh]. I appeared to Abraham, to Isaac and to Jacob as God Almighty [El Shaddai], but by my name the Lord [Yahweh] I did not make myself known to them." Though some scholars have suggested that Yahweh and Shaddai were two originally independent deities that became merged, the biblical texts unanimously accept them as alternative names for the same deity.

It seems most likely, from current research, that the patriarchs would have identified their God as "El," with both "Shaddai" and "Yahweh" serving as epithets to describe certain aspects of El's activity. Exodus 6:3 would then be understood as explaining that El Shaddai was the name most appropriately connected with how God interacted with the patriarchs and what he accomplished for them. They did not experience firsthand the significance of the epithet *Yahweh*. It was Moses' generation who would come to know (experience) God as Yahweh.

The book of Genesis helps us see this distinction between Shaddai and Yahweh in the theophanies attributed to each (fig. 4.1). A theophany is a visible and/or audible manifestation of God. Both Abraham and Jacob experienced one "Shaddai theophany" and one "Yahweh theophany." For both, the Yahweh theophany came first and at the initiation of the agreement between God and the patriarch. The emphasis of the Yahweh theophany was on the land that would be given to the patriarch (15:7–17; 28:13–15).

In contrast, the El Shaddai theophanies came when the patriarchs accepted participation in the covenant. In the case of Abraham especially, the actual fulfillment was about to take place. The emphasis was on the element that began to find fulfillment in the patriarchs' lifetimes: descendants. Even in usage apart from the theophanies, the name El Shaddai is most closely connected with descendants (28:3; 43:14; 48:3). Both Shaddai theophanies feature a name change for the patriarch, showing that each considered himself in allegiance with El Shaddai (17:1–8; 35:11–12).

The conclusions to be drawn from this differentiation are that the name Yahweh was connected to the longer-term promises of God to the patriarchs—specifically the land, which even Abraham was told would be a long time coming. The patriarchs could truly be considered then not to have "known" God by his name Yahweh, for the promises that he had been most closely associated with had not yet come to pass. Yet it was now Yahweh who was sending Moses to take the Israelites to the land that had been promised to them in the covenant.

Our conclusion, then, is that Abraham was a practical monotheist worshiping El, who had revealed himself to Abraham through several epithets. Though the patriarchs were aware of the name Yahweh, the name most appropriate to Abraham was El Shaddai. However, it was the name Yahweh that eventually came to be understood as the primary name of Israel's covenant God.

Sin

One of the key themes of Genesis is the introduction of sin into the world and the impact it has had on human history. When Adam and Eve were created, immortality was within their grasp, for the tree of life was in the garden and available for their use. When they gave in to temptation, they were cast from the garden and were denied access to that tree. The desire to be like God that led to their disobedience included a desire for independence, just as children long to gain independence from their parents and make their own decisions.

The punishment was suitable and logical. Independence often brings separation, and so it was with Adam and Eve's relationship to God. Also, as children find out when they become adults, autonomy is not the same as independence. The pronouncement of Genesis 3:16–19 delineates a different sort of dependence. This was the beginning of several cycles of sin and punishment that constitute the primeval history. For Adam and Eve and Cain and Abel the sin was individual in nature. In Lamech's actions (4:23–24) and in the behavior of the "sons of God" (6:1–4), we can identify expansion into the institutions of society (the family and kingship). By the time of Noah, sin completely infiltrated every corner of humanity. The destruction by flood did not eliminate sin, as it progressed again from individual sin (9:20–23) to coordinated acts of rebellion (11:1–9).

The election of Abraham did not put an end to sin. We are particularly struck by Jacob's acts of deception. Again, however, God suited the punishment to the crime. Jacob procured the blessing for himself by disguising himself as Esau (chap. 27). He became the victim of deceit when he married Leah, who was disguised as Rachel. Even more poignant was the deceit of his sons, who produced a bloodied coat to convince Jacob that his son Joseph was dead. In this theme of sin and punishment, we see God's mercy as well as his justice.

Origins

Although, as we have noted, the book of Genesis is not a book of science, it does offer information about origins and therefore has tradi-

Lepsius *Denkmaler*

This troupe of merchants arriving from Canaan in Egypt in the 20th century BC shows the colorful garments worn at that time.

tionally been of some interest to students of science. Those who believe in the trustworthiness of the Bible often find themselves today in the awkward position of trying to reconcile what the Bible says about origins to the scientific consensus about origins. It is important, therefore, to establish precisely what the Bible says about origins.

God created. This is the most basic affirmation of Genesis. Even though Genesis does not recount creation of everything (for example, it does not relate the creation of angels), there is no room given for any other creative power. It is possible, depending on how one translates Genesis 1:1, that the raw material of earth was already in existence when the narrative of the book begins. But one could not infer from this that God was not its creator.

How did God create? The text emphasizes the spoken word of God, but some have felt that this does not rule out the possibility that God could have used an evolutionary sequence or mechanism to do so. Those who reject this possibility contend that God's function as creator must be intended, if nothing else, to emphasize his sovereign control. They see this control threatened by the random, arbitrary, and chance nature of the processes often included in the teaching of evolution. Nevertheless, one could likewise argue that the weather is random, arbitrary, and subject to chance, yet that is not thought of as undermining God's sovereign control of his creation. The fact is, however, that Christian belief affirms that though the weather may have the appearance of being random, God is fully in control. To the extent to which evolution is defined in exclusively naturalistic ways, it is unacceptable to the theology of Genesis, because creation, by the insistence of Scripture, is supernaturalistic.

When did God create? The seven-day structure of Genesis 1 has long created controversy even among conservative interpreters. While some have used it as the basis for a scientific defense of a "young" earth, others have felt that the word "day" was sufficiently flexible to accommodate the long ages proposed by geologists. Still others have contended that the seven-day structure is intended as a literary device

96   A SURVEY OF THE OLD TESTAMENT

GENESIS

rather than as a chronological guide. A more recent theory has suggested that the seven days are to be understood as the seven day dedication of the cosmic temple in the process of which the cosmos becomes operational.[7] All these positions can garner an impressive amount of supporting evidence that can be baffling to the person trying to decide between them.

The difficulty comes in part because we are asking questions that Scripture never intended to address. The point of the text is not to satisfy our curiosity about scientific matters, but to reveal to us the nature of God. Science attempts to explain origins without God; Scripture insists that the most important aspect of origins to understand is that God created. These two philosophies cannot really coexist. Attempts to reconcile the biblical perspective to the scientific perspective are acceptable only as long as they do not compromise what the Bible says.

7. J. Walton, *Genesis* (NIVAC; Grand Rapids: Zondervan, 2001), 146–57.

Questions for Further Study and Discussion

1. How do comparative studies contribute to an understanding of the Old Testament? What dangers do they represent?
2. What would the Israelites have considered the primary impact of the fall?
3. What approach should we take when challenged to reconcile the book of Genesis with modern science?
4. Why would God use multiple names in Genesis and elsewhere in the Old Testament in his revelation of himself?
5. Discuss and contrast the terms "revelatory people of God" and "soteriological people of God" (assisted by the subject index).

For Further Reading

Alter, Robert, *Genesis*. New York: Norton, 1996.

Arnold, Bill T. *Encountering Genesis*. Grand Rapids: Baker, 1998.

Baldwin, Joyce. *The Message of Genesis 12–50*. Downers Grove, Ill.: InterVarsity Press, 1986.

Blocher, Henri. *In the Beginning*. Downers Grove, Ill.: InterVarsity Press, 1984. Evangelical approach to philosophical and exegetical problems encountered in Genesis 1–3.

Brichto, H. C. *The Names of God*. New York: Oxford University Press, 1997. A demonstration of the rationale in the author's use of one name or another and an argument for the unity of the book.

Fields, Weston. *Unformed and Unfilled*. Nutley, N.J.: Presbyterian and Reformed, 1976. A well-written critique of the "Gap theory" that includes discussions of most of the terms of theological significance in Genesis 1–2.

Fokkelman, J. P. *Narrative Art in Genesis*. Amsterdam. Van Gorcum, Assen, 1975.

Garrett, Duane A. *Rethinking Genesis*. Grand Rapids: Baker, 1991.

Hamilton, Victor. *The Book of Genesis*. 2 vols. Grand Rapids: Eerdmans, 1990, 1995.

Hartley, John. *Genesis*. Peabody, Mass.: Hendrickson, 2000.

Hess, Richard S., and D. T. Tsumura. *I Studied Inscriptions from Before the Flood*. Winona Lake, Ind.: Eisenbrauns, 1994.

Kikawada, Isaac, and Arthur Quinn. *Before Abraham Was*. Nashville: Abingdon Press, 1985. A view of the structure of the book of Genesis that rejects the usual division into sources.

Longman, Tremper. *How to Read Genesis*. Downers Grove, Ill.: InterVarsity Press, 2005.

Mathews, Kenneth. *Genesis 1–11:26*. Nashville: Broadman & Holman, 1994.

_____. *Genesis 11:27–50:26*. Nashville: Broadman & Holman, 2005.

Millard, Alan R., and Donald J. Wiseman, *Essays in the Patriarchal Narratives*. Winona Lake, Ind.: Eisenbrauns, 1983.

Ratzsch, Del. *The Battle of Beginnings*. Downers Grove, Ill.: InterVarsity Press, 1995. A very balanced assessment of some of the approaches to the Bible and science.

Ross, Allen. *Creation and Blessing*. Grand Rapids: Baker, 1988. An evangelical treatment using the literary approach to the text.

Sailhamer, John. "Genesis." *EBC*. Vol. 2. Grand Rapids: Zondervan, 1990. 1–284.

Sarna, Nahum. *Genesis*. Jewish Publication Society Commentary. Philadelphia: Jewish Publication Society, 1989.

Waltke, Bruce K. *Genesis*. Grand Rapids: Zondervan, 2001.

Walton, John H. *Ancient Near Eastern Thought and the Old Testament*. Grand Rapids: Baker, 2006. A survey of the conceptual world of the Hebrew Bible.

_____. *The Covenant: God's Purpose, God's Plan*. Grand Rapids: Zondervan, 1994. An analysis of the covenant and its purpose.

_____. *Genesis*. NIVAC. Grand Rapids: Zondervan, 2001.

_____. *Genesis One as Ancient Cosmology*. Winona Lake, Ind.: Eisenbrauns, 2011.

Walton, John H., Victor Matthews, and Mark Chavalas. *The IVP Bible Background Commentary: Old Testament*. Downers Grove, Ill.: InterVarsity Press, 2000.

Wenham, Gordon J. *Genesis 1–15*. WBC. Vol. 1. Waco, Tex.: Word, 1987. A sound presentation of modern evangelical interpretation of Genesis.

_____. *Genesis 16–50*. WBC. Vol. 2. Waco, Tex.: Word, 1994.

_____. *Story as Torah*. Grand Rapids: Baker, 2000.

Westermann, Claus. *Genesis 1–11*. Minneapolis: Augsburg Press, 1984. Translation of German commentary first published in 1974, containing the most thorough presentation of critical scholarship on the book of Genesis.

Youngblood, Ronald. *The Genesis Debate*. Nashville: Thomas Nelson, 1986. Discussion of the issues of Genesis 1–9 reflecting differing evangelical opinions.

The pyramids had been built more than 1,500 years prior to the Israelites' enslavement, but they dominated the landscape then as they continue to do today—monuments to the ambitious building projects of the pharaohs.

Frederick J. Mabie

EXODUS

Key Ideas

- The supremacy of Yahweh over pagan deities
- The exodus as a redemptive event for ancient Israel
- The Mosaic law as a religious and social charter for Israel
- The presence of God symbolized in the tabernacle

Purpose Statement

The purpose of Exodus is to explain how the Israelites became slaves in Egypt and their deliverance from Egyptian oppression. The book also reveals the God whose name is Yahweh and relates how his divine presence came to dwell among his people, Israel.

Major Themes

- Yahweh
- The Ten Plagues
- The Passover
- The Ten Commandments
- The Presence of God

God's Presence

The book of Exodus lays the foundation for the biblical theme of divine presence with God manifest in the call of Moses at the burning bush, the plagues of judgment against Pharaoh and the Egyptians, the awesome Mount Sinai theophany, Yahweh's appearance to Moses, and the instructions for the tabernacle designed to give God an "address" among his people, Israel.

authors-editors of the exilic or postexilic period (ca. 600–400 BC). (See further, Appendix B.)

According to this hypothesis, the oral traditions on which the book of Exodus was based underwent considerable expansion, revision, and rewriting over the course of several centuries (i.e., the ninth to the fifth centuries BC). For this reason critical Old Testament scholarship maintains a stance of suspicion toward the book's literary integrity and skepticism toward its historicity.

An examination of the text of Exodus confirms Mosaic authorship for at least four sections of the book. These four literary units were apparently written in association with the events they record and include the "memorial" of the war with the Amalekites (17:8–16; esp. v. 14), the covenant code (19:1–24:18; cf. 24:4; 34:27), the Song of the Sea (15:1–21), and the additional covenant stipulations (34:1–28; esp. v. 27).

The extensive third-person narratives of the book (including the passage lauding Moses, 11:3), along with the parenthetical insertions intended to bring a later audience up to date (e.g., 16:31–36), suggest that someone other than Moses compiled Exodus in its present form. It seems reasonable to assume that the four passages cited as composed by Moses were collected and arranged by a contemporary, perhaps even his protégé Joshua. The book of Exodus stands substantially as the literary product of Moses. Any later editorial activity is

"So they put slave masters over them to oppress them with forced labor.... They made their lives bitter with hard labor in brick and mortar and with all kinds of work in the fields" (Exod. 1:11, 14). This wall painting from the Tomb of Rekhmire, vizier under Thutmosis III and Amenophis II (18th Dynasty, New Kingdom), depicts slaves making bricks, as the Hebrews were forced to do during their sojourn in Egypt.

Erich Lessing/Art Resource, NY

largely limited to the modernization of archaic or technical terminology and geographical place names (e.g., 15:23). Whether the rest of the narrative and legislation of the book was composed by Moses or dictated to scribes remains unspecified (cf. 25:1; 30:11, 17). Exodus and the rest of the Pentateuch were probably cast in the form of a unified, five-volume book sometime between the days of Joshua and the elders of Israel (Josh. 24:31) and the era of Samuel (1 Sam. 3:19–21).

The Background

Date of the Exodus

The book records events from the birth of Moses to the completion and dedication of the tabernacle at Sinai in the first month of the second year after the exodus from Egypt (cf. 1:1; 2:1–14; 19:1; 40:17). Thus, the actual history of the book covers a span of about eighty-five years.

The main problem for scholars has been determining the century in which the events associated with the departure from Egypt actually took place. Pinpointing the date of the exodus constitutes one of the major chronological problems of Old Testament study, and the complex issue remains a topic of debate. Two basic positions have emerged from the discussions, the so-called Early Date and Late Date views. The chronology of the exodus is further complicated because the migration of Jacob's family to Egypt due to famine in Palestine cannot be precisely calculated either. In an attempt to account for the biblical and extrabiblical chronological and geographical data, four chronological systems have been developed (see fig. 3.4).

Since only two pharaohs of Egypt ruled for more than forty years (the length of Moses' exile in the wilderness during the Hebrew oppression), their reigns have become the focal points of discussion for dating the exodus. The Early Date view identifies Thutmose III (1504–1450) as the pharaoh of the oppression and Amenophis II (1450–1425) as the pharaoh of the exodus. Both reigned during the Eighteenth Dynasty of the period of Egyptian history known as the New Kingdom era and date to the Late Bronze Age of ancient Near Eastern history.

The Late Date position identifies Rameses I (1320–1318) and Seti I (1318–1304) as the pharaohs of the Hebrew oppression and Rameses II (1304–1237) as the pharaoh of the exodus. All were kings of the Nineteenth Dynasty of the Egyptian New Kingdom era and are dated to

"Aaron threw his staff down in front of Pharaoh and his officials, and it became a snake" (Exod. 7:10b). This staff in the form of a coiled serpent was found bearing incantations and prescriptions to secure good health. Serpents were considered magical creatures in ancient Egypt.
Werner Forman Archive/ Fitzwilliam Museum, Cambridge

the century of transition between the Late Bronze and Early Iron ages of ancient Near Eastern history.

The arguments for the two positions are summarized in figures 5.2a and 5.2b.

At issue in the controversy over the date of the exodus is the interpretation of the biblical and extrabiblical data. Proponents of the Early Date position emphasize the literal interpretation of the biblical numbers recorded in Exodus 12:40; Judges 11:26; and 1 Kings 6:1 and selectively appeal to archaeology for support (e.g., both camps cite archaeological evidence from Jericho and Hazor in support of their positions). Those holding to the Late Date view understand the

Figure 5.1a. Early Dating of the Exodus

Suggested early dates:	*Date* BC	*Reigning pharaoh*
	1446	Amenophis II (1450 – 25)
	1440	Amenophis II (1450 – 25)
	1437	Amenophis II (1450 – 25)

Arguments for the Early Date

1. 1 Kings 6:1 indicates the Exodus occurred 480 years prior to the 4th year of Solomon's reign. His 4th year is variously dated at 966/960/957 BC, placing the Exodus at 1446/1440/1437.

2. According to Judges 11:26, Israel had occupied Canaan for 300 years before the judgeship of Jephthah, which is dated between 1100 and 1050. This dates Joshua's conquest between 1400 and 1350. Adding Israel's 40 years in the desert puts the Exodus between 1440 and 1390.

3. Moses lived in exile in Midian 40 years (Acts 7:3; cf. Exodus 2:23) while the pharaoh of the oppression was still alive. The only pharaohs who ruled 40 years or more were Thutmose III (1504 – 1450) and Rameses II (1290 – 1224).

4. The Merneptah Stela (ca. 1220) indicates Israel was already an established nation at this time.

5. The Amarna tablets (ca. 1400) speak of a period of chaos caused by the "Habiru," very likely the Hebrews.

6. The early date allows for the length of time assigned to the period of the judges (at least 250 years). The late date allows only 180 years.

7. The Dream Stela of Thutmose IV indicates he was not the legal heir to the throne (i.e., the legal heir would have died in the tenth plague).

8. Archaeological evidence from Jericho, Hazor, etc., supports a 15th-century date for the Exodus.

9. Exodus 12:40 dates the entrance of Jacob into Egypt during the reign of Sesostris/Senusert III (1878 – 43) rather than during the Hyksos period (1674 – 1567).

Adapted from Andrew E. Hill, *Baker's Handbook of Bible Lists*. Rev. ed. (Grand Rapids: Baker, 2006), 63 – 64. Used by permission.

Figure 5.1b. Late Dating of the Exodus

Suggested late dates:	Date BC	Reigning pharaoh
	1350	Tutankhamen (1361 – 52)
	1290	Rameses II (1304 – 1237)
	1280	Rameses II (1304 – 1237)
	1275	Rameses II (1304 – 1237)
	1225	Rameses II (1304 – 1237)

Arguments for the Late Date

1. The 480 years of 1 Kings 6:1 is a symbolic figure for 12 generations. Because a generation is about 25 years, the actual figure should be 300 years, placing the Exodus around 1266/1260 BC.

2. The 300-year figure cited by Jephthah is merely an exaggerated generalization, since he had no access to historical records.

3. The 40 years Moses spent with the Midianites is not a chronological figure, but a symbolic figure indicating a long period of time.

4. The Merneptah Stela (ca. 1220) indicates Israel was in the land of Palestine by this date. The name "Israel" does not occur in any other historical record or documents before 1220. This would be unlikely had Israel begun occupation of the land 200 years earlier, in 1400.

5. The "Ḥabiru" of the Amarna tablets cannot be identified with the Hebrews. The "Ḥabiru" were a diverse people, native Canaanites. They are attested from the 18th to the 12th centuries BC.

6. With the overlapping of judgeships and the use of symbolic numbers (e.g., 40 years), the period of the judges need not span more than 150 years.

7. That Thutmose IV was not the legal heir to the Egyptian throne in no way proves the legal heir died in the tenth plague.

8. Archaeological evidence from Lachish, Jericho, Bethel, Hazor, Debir, etc., supports a 13th-century date for the Exodus.

9. The 430 years of Exodus 12:40 from the late date for the Exodus places Jacob's entrance into Egypt during the Hyksos period (1730 – 1570). This period of foreign domination in Egypt is a more likely time period for Israel's entrance into Egypt.

10. The civilizations of Edom, Ammon, and Moab were not in existence in the 15th century, thus it would have been impossible for Israel to have had contact with these nations if the Exodus occurred in that century. Since Israel did have such contact, the Exodus must be dated to the 13th century.

11. The Old Testament does not mention the Palestinian invasions of Seti I or Rameses II, very likely because Israel was not yet in the land of Palestine.

12. The Israelites were building Pithom and Raamses (Exod. 1:11), cities of the delta region. Raamses was founded by Seti I (1318 – 1304) and completed by Rameses II (1304 – 1237).

13. Thutmose III was not noted as a great builder.

Adapted from Andrew E. Hill, *Baker's Handbook of Bible Lists*. Rev. ed. (Grand Rapids: Baker, 2006), 64 – 65. Used by permission.

1. E.g., the Late Date view identifies the Arad of Numbers 21:1 with the modern Tell Arad because it is an Iron Age settlement and lacks both Middle Bronze and Late Bronze Age occupation levels. By contrast, the Early Date proponents suggest that Arad should be identified with Tell el-Milh some eight miles southwest of Tell Arad, since it exhibits Middle Bronze Age fortifications.

Rameses II, also known as Rameses the Great, is one of the candidates for the pharaoh in the Exodus narratives. He was the most prominent of the kings of the 19th dynasty and had a reign lasting several decades in the 13th century BC.
Frederick J. Mabie

biblical numbers symbolically and place priority on the extrabiblical historical information and archaeological evidence. The approach adopted in this volume assumes the historical validity of the biblical numbers while recognizing the "slippery" nature of the evidence garnered by both camps from the selective appeal to extrabiblical and archaeological data.[1]

Route of the Exodus

Our understanding of the Hebrew exodus is further complicated by geographical considerations, as the exact route of the Hebrew desert trek and the location of Mount Sinai remain uncertain. Three alternatives have been advanced for the exodus route taken by the Hebrews: the extreme northern Sinai route theory, the central Sinai route theory, and the traditional southern Sinai route theory.

Arguments lending support to the northern route theory include the tentative identification of Baal-Zephon with Ras Kasrun in the northwestern area of the Sinai. Also, the northern route fits Moses' request to Pharaoh for three days to journey to worship Yahweh (Exod. 3:18). The route also marks the shortest distance to Kadesh-Barnea, the immediate objective of the Hebrews. Yet the northern route is the most unlikely option of the three theories, since it keeps the Israelites so close to Egyptian territory. Further, this view discounts the biblical texts indicating that Mount Sinai was an eleven-day journey from Kadesh (Deut. 1:2) and that God

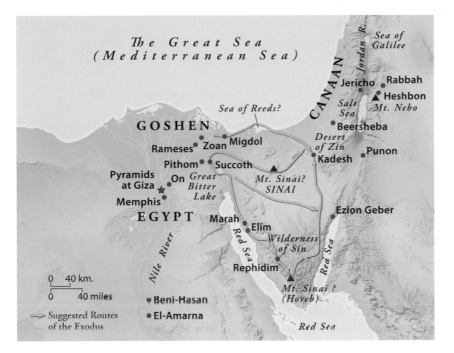

Suggested Routes of the Exodus

deliberately maneuvered the Hebrews away from the occupied areas along the coast (cf. Exod. 13:17).

The central route theory locates Mount Sinai in northwest Arabia, beyond Aqabah, partly on the grounds that the Exodus narrative of the covenant experience describes an active volcano (19:16–25) and partly because the same region is traditionally connected with the homeland of the Midianites (cf. Exod. 3:1; 18:1). Today the central route alternative has largely been discounted by biblical scholars due to the strength of counter-arguments made in separate studies. First, it has been demonstrated that the Sinai theophany is typical of other recorded ancient Near Eastern divine manifestations that do not presuppose an active volcano; there is therefore no need to place Sinai in Arabia, the nearest site for volcanic activity. Second, Moses is identified as being related to the Kenites as well as to the Midianites, and it is believed that the Kenites were a nomadic Midianite clan whose presence in the Sinai region is well attested (cf. Judg. 1:16; 4:11); so there is no need to place Moses in Arabia.

The traditional southern route exodus theory still accommodates all the known biblical and geographical information most convincingly. It seems likely the crossing of "the Sea of Reeds" took place somewhere in the salt marshes and lakes between the Mediterranean Sea and the Gulf of Suez. Lakes Menzaleh, Balah, and Timsah, along with the Great Bitter Lakes have been suggested as possible candidates for the Reed Sea of the Hebrew exodus. The northerly jog in the route is best accounted for by the "wall" of the canal of Shur discovered in the eastern Nile delta.

Certainly the escaped Hebrew slaves would have avoided this Egyptian fortification. Finally, Jebel Musa or Mount Horeb, in the southern Sinai peninsula has been identified as the Mount Sinai of Moses' revelation by Christian tradition dating to the fourth century AD.

Purpose and Message

The message of Exodus is summarized in two passages: the commission of Moses (6:2–9) and the preface to the covenant ceremony at Sinai (19:1–6). The three basic components of the message include (1) the judgment of the oppressor nation Egypt, (2) the deliverance of Israel from slavery in Egypt by the "mighty arm" of Yahweh, and (3) the establishment of Israel as God's special possession among all peoples.

Several themes or emphases unify the Exodus narratives. Judgment and deliverance figure prominently in chapters 1–12, and Yahweh's paternal guidance in the wilderness and the promise of settlement in Canaan follow in 13–18. Theocratic covenant and law combine to form Israel's charter as the people of Yahweh in 19–24, and the book concludes with preparations for worship of the Holy One of Israel (25–40).

The historical purpose of Exodus was the preservation of accounts explaining how the Israelites came to be slaves in Egypt, their deliverance, and their presence in the wilderness of Sinai. The Exodus narrative forms a bridge between the patriarchal stories with the later history of the theocratic nation taking possession of Canaan (cf. 6:4).

The basic theological purpose of the book is divine self-disclosure. God has not only remembered his covenant promises to the Hebrew patriarchs, but also has now revealed himself to Israel as Yahweh (6:2–3). Although this revelation of Yahweh occurs in a variety of manifestations, the end result is that he will take Israel for his people and will be their God (6:7).

Last, the didactic purpose of the book includes instruction on the importance of maintaining covenant relationship with Yahweh and the importance of the law as an instrument for shaping and preserving Israel's identity as Yahweh's people (23:20–23). Only through obedience to the covenant stipulations can Israel be a kingdom of priests to Yahweh and a holy nation, fulfilling her divine destiny among all the nations (19:5–6).

Structure and Organization

The book of Exodus is easily arranged into three large blocks of narrative material based on the sequence of geographical locations for Israel as they journeyed from Egypt to Mount Sinai:

1. Israel in Egypt (1:1–12:36)
2. Israel's wilderness trek (12:37–18:27)
3. Israel at Sinai (19:1–40:38)

Thematically Yahweh's deliverance of the Hebrews from bondage in Egypt as told in Exodus connects the deliverance of Jacob's clan by Joseph (Gen. 46–50) and the deliverance of the Israelite nation by Moses to the threshold of the land of promise (Numbers and Deuteronomy). Exodus as the book of Yahweh's redemption of his covenant people complements Genesis as the book of the inauguration of the covenant and anticipates Leviticus as the book of holiness for the covenant people.

The language and content of Exodus also bear deliberate marks of transitions indicating that the narratives of Genesis, Exodus, and Leviticus are to be read together as a unified document. For example, the repetition in Exodus 1 of the names of Jacob's sons who migrated to Egypt ties the Exodus accounts with the story of Jacob's sojourn in Egypt (Gen. 46–50). Likewise, the concluding passage of Exodus describing the glory of Yahweh's filling the tabernacle (40:34–38) anticipates the departure of Israel from Sinai led by the cloud of guidance (Num. 10:11–35). Last, as in the books of Leviticus and Numbers, the **divine oracle formula** is found repeatedly in Exodus (i.e., "and the LORD said to Moses," 19:21; 25:1; et al.), while the introductory phrase "this is what the LORD has commanded" connects the legislation of Exodus and Leviticus (e.g., Exod. 35:4; Lev. 8:5; 17:2).

Frederick J. Mabie

The symbol of a king or deity with an outstretched arm was a symbol of power and might. "I am the LORD, and I will bring you out from under the yoke of the Egyptians. I will free you from being slaves to them, and I will redeem you with an outstretched arm and with mighty acts of judgment" (Exod. 6:6).

Section 1 tells the story of the judgment of Egypt and the deliverance of Israel from slavery. First, Moses is introduced as God's instrument for securing the release of the Hebrews, and then he is commissioned and equipped to accomplish the task. God's longsuffering and the preeminence of obedience to his commands are underscored in the passage. Yahweh also bestows confirming signs on Moses and appoints Aaron as his spokesman. He affirms the success of the mission by revealing himself as Yahweh—an inexhaustible resource for the task of bringing out the Hebrews. However, before Moses can deliver Israel from Egypt to covenant ratification with Yahweh at Sinai, he must first obey the stipulations of God's earlier covenant terms within his own family (cf. 4:18–26).

God's method for delivering Israel by means of a series of plagues was designed to bring divine judgment upon the Egyptian nation (12:12). The institution of the Passover Feast was a teaching memorial for future generations of Israelites. As a reminder of Yahweh's mighty act in history, it was intended to inspire reverence and prompt worship among the Hebrews (12:14–27).

Section 2 explains how Yahweh turned a mob of former slaves into a "special possession" as his covenant people by means of a covenant agreement at Sinai (19:1–6). It is now widely accepted that the Hebrew covenant with Yahweh parallels the literary form of the Hittite suzerain treaty of the Late Bronze Age. The treaty form was a common way for a ruling lord to exact obedience from vassal states

The traditional site of Mount Sinai in the southern Sinai Peninsula.
Amie Gosselin

in the binding of the servant through carefully prescribed covenant stipulations. Consider some specific elements of the treaty form in the covenant code of Exodus:

Preamble: 20:2a
Historical Prologue: 20:2b
Stipulations: 20:3–17 (= Decalogue); 20:21–23:19
Deposit and Public Reading: 24:7
List of Witnesses: 24:1–11
Blessings and Curses: 23:20–33 (delineated more formally in Leviticus 26)

The final section (chaps. 25–40) gives details of the tabernacle of Yahweh and its furnishings. The very presence of God would be established in the midst of Israel through this Tent of Meeting (25:8). The ordination of Aaron and his sons as priests for the sanctuary helps to explain the inclusion of the genealogy (chap. 6), which legitimized the Aaronic priesthood. The idolatry and rebellion of Egypt judged by Yahweh in the exodus had their parallel in the golden-calf episode when Israel was encamped at Sinai (cf. 32:1–10). The wrath of Yahweh was stayed by the intercessory prayer of Moses for Israel, and the mercy of God made covenant renewal possible (cf. 32:11–34:17). Given Israel's penchant for rebellion and waywardness from God, this pattern characterized much of her history in the Old Testament. Small wonder the new covenant will be one written on the heart, not on tablets of stone (cf. Jer. 31:31–34).

Major Themes

Yahweh

The revelation of the name Yahweh (or Jehovah) to Moses as the divinely appointed deliverer of Israel marked a new stage in God's progressive self-disclosure to the Hebrew people. The name is usually translated "I AM" and connotes the personal, eternal, and all-sufficient aspects of God's nature and character.

At issue is the occurrence of the name "Yahweh" in the Genesis records. Some biblical scholars have assumed that the Hebrew patriarchs did not know the name Yahweh for God. They argue that the name Yahweh was written into the text of Genesis anachronistically (i.e., after the fact) or else the book is a compilation of later writings that included the divine name. In contrast, those biblical scholars committed to the antiquity and integrity of the Pentateuch have asserted that it is more reasonable to assume that the patriarchs knew the name Yahweh but were unfamiliar with the radical new dimension of theological meaning for the name that stemmed from Israel's exodus experience.

The unveiling of the divine name Yahweh was not the only way in which God revealed himself to Israel during the exodus experience (see p. 92). Several other types of theophanies are reported in the Pentateuchal narratives. For example, Yahweh revealed his nature and person as well as his will and divine purposes for Israel by a variety of means, including

- The angel of the Lord (Exod. 3:2; 14:19)
- Other angelic agents (Exod. 23:20; 33:2)
- Miraculous event (Exod. 8:16–19)
- A flame in a bush (Exod. 3:2)
- Fire, smoke, thunder, and lightning at Sinai (Exod. 19:18–20)
- Vision and dream (cf. Num. 12:6–8)
- Voice and direct communication (Exod. 24:1)
- The cloud of glory (Exod. 16:10)
- The cloud of guidance and pillar of fire (Exod. 40:34–38)
- "Face to face" with Moses (Exod. 33:11; cf. vv. 20–23)

More important than the variety of divine manifestations to the Hebrews was the content they disclosed to Israel about this covenant God, Yahweh. He was a God

- Who remembered his previous covenant obligations (2:24)
- Of judgment and deliverance (12:27)
- Transcendent, yet immanent (19:10–15; 25:1–9)
- Who rules the nations for the providential benefit of his elect, Israel (15:4–6, 13–18)
- Unique and holy, far above and more powerful than the gods of the nations (15:11; 18:10–12)
- Gracious and merciful, who relents of anger and responds favorably to intercessory prayer and repentance (32:11–14)

The Ten Plagues

The text of Exodus declares that the confrontation between Moses and Pharaoh is actually a cosmic struggle between the true God, Yahweh, and the false gods of the Egyptian religion (cf. Exod. 12:12; 15:11; 18:11). Yahweh elevated Moses to a position "as God" so that Moses could oppose Pharaoh as an equal, since the office of the pharaoh was the physical expression of the sun god Aten, or Ra (cf. Exod 7:1).

Although many biblical scholars attempt to identify a particular deity as the object of each of the ten plagues (see fig. 5.2), it seems better to understand the plagues collectively as judgment against the whole pantheon of Egyptian gods. However, the final two plagues do appear to be aimed at the primary Egyptian deity and his earthly representative, the pharaoh. By blotting out the sun in Egypt and permitting daylight in Goshen, and by interrupting the pharaonic cycle of deity in the death plague, Yahweh showed himself Lord to the Egyptians.

The "miraculous" nature of the signs and wonders brought by Yahweh against Egypt continues to generate discussion among biblical scholars, given the prominence of antisupernaturalist assumptions in our post-**Enlightenment** era. The terms "signs" and "wonders" (Exod. 7:3) express the idea of a **miracle** demonstrating one's power. The word

Figure 5.2. The Plagues and the Gods of Egypt

Plague	Reference	Possible Egyptian Deity Directed Against
Nile Turned to Blood	Exodus 7:14 – 25	Khnum: guardian of the Nile Hapi: spirit of the Nile Osiris: Nile was bloodstream
Frogs	Exodus 8:1 – 15	Heqt: form of frog; god of resurrection
Gnats (Mosquitoes)	Exodus 8:16 – 19	
Flies	Exodus 8:20 – 32	
Plague on Cattle	Exodus 9:1 – 7	Hathor: mother-goddess; form of cow Apis: bull of god Ptah; symbol of fertility Mnevis: sacred bull of Heliopolis
Boils	Exodus 9:8 – 12	*Imhotep: god of medicine
Hail	Exodus 9:13 – 35	Isis: goddess of life Seth: protector of crops
Locusts	Exodus 10:1 – 20	Isis: goddess of life Seth: protector of crops
Darkness	Exodus 10:21 – 29	Re, Aten, Atum, Horus: all sun gods of sorts
Death of Firstborn	Exodus 11:1 – 12:36	The deity of Pharaoh: Osiris, the giver of life

These are only some of the gods whom the plagues may have been directed against. This listing is not necessarily conclusive.
*Perhaps too early for this deity to have been involved.

From John Walton, *Chronological and Background Charts of the Old Testament*, (Grand Rapids: Zondervan, 1994), 85.

miracle may be understood as either the intensification of natural law or phenomena or the superseding of natural law or phenomena.

Today the ten plagues are often interpreted as a sequence of natural cause-effect phenomena associated with the regular flood cycle of the Nile River. This is the case not only among scholars committed to antisupernatural presupposition, but also among certain traditions predisposed toward a "literary" understanding of the Exodus narrative.[2] Here the miraculous is seen in the providential timing of the events, the severity of the natural disasters, and the fact that Moses had foreknowledge of each plague in its sequence. Moreover, the phenomenological character of the plague narrative is attributed to the "prescientific" worldview of the Hebrew writer. According to this view, the ancient Hebrews did not understand the natural world as a closed system governed by the laws of physics, but as a completely and constantly open system in which Yahweh was free to intervene according to his divine purposes. In general, scholars holding to a naturalistic interpretation today view the plague narration as embellished literary and liturgical tradition.

By contrast, biblical scholars committed to the plague narrative literally and historically as Yahweh's supernatural intervention into the created order are quick to note the instantaneous aspects of the plague sequence rendered at the command of Moses and Aaron (e.g., Exod. 8:16–17). Also, the response of the magicians (Exod. 7:22; 8:18–19) is difficult to understand if the plagues are merely "intensification" of a natural sequence of events to which the Egyptians were accustomed. Finally, the isolation of the Hebrews in Goshen from the nine plagues and the death of the firstborn are inexplicable apart from the supernatural activity and purpose.

How did the Egyptian magicians perform counter-miracles against Aaron (7:8–13) and duplicate the effects of the first two plagues (7:14–8:15)? These diviners of Pharaoh's were a powerful and revered priestly class in Egyptian society. They were devotees of the moon god, Thoth, who was also the god of magic and divination. According to the teaching of both the Old and New Testaments, these kinds of idolatrous religious systems are energized by demonic powers (cf. Deut. 32:16–17; Ps. 106:36–37; Acts 16:16–18; 1 Cor. 10:20; 2 Thess. 2:8–12).

How do we explain the "hardening of Pharaoh's heart"? First, God was already aware of Pharaoh's stubbornness (Exod. 3:19–20). The series of signs and wonders (i.e., the plagues) were used by God to confirm Pharaoh in his sinful rebellion against Yahweh in oppressing the Israelites and refusing to release them to worship God (7:3–4). Pharaoh continued to harden his heart through the two miracles of Moses and Aaron and the first five plagues (7:8–8:32). Even his own magicians admitted the limitations of their power before Yahweh

2. E.g., J. K. West, *Introduction to the Old Testament*, 2nd ed. (New York: Macmillan, 1981), 161–64; and William Sanford LaSor, David A. Hubbard, and Frederick W. Bush, *Old Testament Survey*, 2nd ed. (Grand Rapids: Eerdmans, 1996), 69–70.

(8:19), yet Pharaoh steeled his resistance to the truth that Yahweh is Lord (cf. 7:5).

After the sixth plague, we are told, the Lord himself hardened Pharaoh's heart (Exod. 9:8–12). It would seem that Pharaoh no longer has an option to relent and obey the command of Yahweh. God's course of judgment for Egypt became irrevocable. God had given Pharaoh over to the sinfulness of his own heart, confirming him in his rebellion through the signs and wonders (cf. Rom. 1:24, 26, 28). Henceforth, he and the Egyptians were without excuse before God and deserved the death penalty (or death plague; cf. Rom. 1:20, 32).

It is possible that the pharaoh's hardening his heart against God is akin to the sin of blasphemy of the Holy Spirit condemned by Jesus in the New Testament (cf. Mark 3:28–30). Even as Jesus' enemies attributed the miraculous works of God to Satan, so Pharaoh in his rejection of God's signs and wonders had willfully denied God's activity in human history. Implicitly he attributed the divine works to the demonic by not acknowledging Yahweh (Exod. 5:2), by calling for counterfeit signs from his magicians (7:11), and by ignoring their discernment of the "finger of God" intervening in Egyptian history (8:19).

The Schøyen Collection MS 2064, Oslo and London

The Passover

The historical context of the original Passover event (Exod. 12) was the last plague against Pharaoh, the Egyptians, and the Egyptian gods. This death plague forced the Hebrew flight from oppression and bondage (vv. 21–27). Future generations are commanded to observe the Passover as a feast commemorating the Hebrew deliverance accomplished by the mighty arm of Yahweh (contra the "mighty arm of Pharaoh," cf. 13:14).

The Feast of Unleavened Bread accompanied the Passover memorial as a reminder of the great haste in which the Israelites departed from Egypt (12:11). Later on, the ordinance for the dedication of the firstborn to the Lord with statutory offerings was designed as a perpetual reminder of the mercy of Yahweh in sparing all those firstborn from the "destroyer" in the Israelite homes that had been sprinkled with the Passover blood (Exod. 12:23; 13:2; 22:29–30; Num. 3:13, 40–51).

As a memorial feast, the Passover ceremony had important educational implications for the Hebrew family. The actual instruction took the form of question and response. The meaning of the Passover for the Hebrews was summarized in the formal answer of the father to his

The Laws of Ur Nammu or Shulgi are a collection of Sumerian laws that includes a prologue followed by a list of casuistic law—that is, if … then statements. "If a fire breaks out and spreads into thornbushes so that it burns shocks of grain or standing grain or the whole field, [then] the one who started the fire must make restitution" (Exod. 22:6). Dating to just before 2000 BC, this is the oldest collection of laws yet found.

son's question, "What does this service mean?" The father responded, "It is the sacrifice of the Lord's Passover, for he passed over the houses of the people of Israel in Egypt when he slew the Egyptians but spared our houses" (cf. 12:24–27).

In Egypt, the Apis bull was revered as a god, particularly in Memphis. One live bull succeeded another as representatives of the Apis, and figurines were common. After the bull was sacrificed, it was transformed into the god Osiris.

Loïc Evanno/Wikimedia Commons courtesy of the Louvre, GNU 1.2/CC 2.5

The New Testament writers understood the Old Testament Passover typologically as a precursor of Jesus' dying sacrificially as the Lamb of God who takes away the sin of the world (cf. John 1:29; 1 Cor. 5:7). The parallels between the Passover and the death of Christ are significant in number and kind (e.g., cf. Exod. 12:46 and Num. 9:12 with John 19:36).

The institution of the Lord's Supper, or Eucharist, is rooted in the Passover rite, both from the standpoint of a memorial feast (cf. Luke 22:7–30) and in the atoning deliverance of the Paschal Lamb of God (cf. Rev. 5:6–14).

The Ten Commandments

Also known as the Decalogue or "Ten Words," the Ten Commandments are recorded in Exodus 20:1–17 and repeated in Deuteronomy 5:6–21. In contrast to the rest of the divinely revealed legislation of the Pentateuch, Moses is not cited as the mediator of these injunctions. Instead, God himself writes the commandments on tablets and speaks directly to all the Hebrews (20:1; 32:16). Interestingly, Yahweh indicates he has spoken to the people from heaven, not from Mount Sinai, after delivering the Ten Commandments to the Israelites (20:22; cf. Lev. 25:1)—perhaps denoting the perfect and eternal character of the Decalogue.

Only two of the statutes are cast in the form of positive imperatives: the fourth, "Remember the Sabbath day . . . ," and the fifth, "Honor your father and mother . . ." (Exod. 20:8–12). Eight of the ten laws are prohibitions (i.e., they take the form "You shall not . . ."). The particular grammatical construction employed shows that these commands were to have binding authority for the current and all future generations of Hebrew people. The harsh tone of the Decalogue created by the repetition of the most severe negation possible in the Hebrew language served to underscore the absolute nature and permanent character of this divine law.

The Ten Commandments are patterned after the literary format of the Hittite suzerain-vassal treaty with a preamble, historical prologue,

This relief from the Hittite capital of Hattusha shows a priest before an altar and a bull.

M. Willis Monroe

and a list of basic stipulations (see "Structure and Organization"). The first four statutes circumscribe the relationship of the vassal (Israel) to the suzerain (Yahweh), while the last six commandments order human relationships within the vassal (Israelite) community. Ultimately the Decalogue was an extension of Yahweh's grace to Israel already demonstrated in the exodus from Egypt. The Ten Commandments brought a sense of righteousness to Israel's religion and social life. Israel's covenant obedience was but a response of gratitude to the grace of God, not a burdensome duty by which they earned or merited God's favor and redemption.

(The variations in the Deuteronomy 5 rendering of the Decalogue are accounted for by the covenant renewal procedure, in which the basic covenant stipulations were modified or adapted to accommodate changing historical and sociological circumstances.)

According to G. E. Mendenhall, the purpose of covenant is to create new relationships, whereas the purpose of law is to regulate existing relationships by ordering the means or fixing the conditions required for maintaining an association. The explicit purpose of the Decalogue is stated in Exodus 22:20: "... that the fear of God will be with you to keep you from sinning." The Ten Commandments express the eternally perfect moral character of Yahweh, and as such they constituted the basic principles governing (or "ordering the means of") the life of faith for the Hebrews.[3]

As law, the Decalogue is connected with covenant in that these regulations summarize the covenant stipulations requisite for maintaining the agreement between Yahweh and Israel. The Decalogue probably also

3. Cf. G. E. Mendenhall, *The Tenth Generation* (Baltimore: Johns Hopkins University Press, 1973), 198–214, esp. 200.

functioned as a general statement of criminal law for Israelite society, delineating "serious crime" in relation to covenant with Yahweh. This was essential to the well-being of the nation, because an offense against Yahweh's covenant jeopardized the entire covenant community.

In the New Testament, Jesus summarized the theological and social dimensions of the covenant stipulations in the Decalogue in two commandments (Matt. 22:36–39; cf. Deut. 6:5); and emphasized that the essence of the Old Testament law is justice, mercy, and faith (cf. Matt. 23:23).

The Presence of God

One important outcome of the covenant agreement between Yahweh and Israel was the very presence of God accompanying the Hebrews on their journey from Egypt to the plains of Moab via Mount Sinai. Although this mysterious presence of God was made manifest to Israel in alternative forms—a cloud and a pillar of fire—the essential thrust of the Pentateuchal narrative is the "Lord dwelling in the midst of his people" (Exod. 25:8).

The tabernacle structure described in Exodus 25–40 was designed to symbolize the active presence of the Lord among the Hebrews. The tabernacle was also called the Tent of Meeting, because there God convened his assemblies with Israel, with the holy priesthood ordained to represent the Hebrew people before Yahweh (cf. Lev. 1:1). In part, the presence of God associated with the tabernacle restored the intimate fellowship enjoyed by God and man and woman in the garden experience before the fall (Gen. 3:8).

The New Testament renews this theme of God's presence among humankind with the announcement found in John's gospel that "the Word became flesh and lived [or 'tabernacled'] among us" (1:14; cf. Isa. 7:14). Perhaps this return of the "divine presence" to Israel fulfilled Haggai's prophecy about the latter glory of the temple being far greater than the glory of the former (i.e., Solomon's) temple (Hag. 2:9; cf. Luke 2).

Questions for Further Study and Discussion

1. What is the significance of the name Yahweh for our understanding of the book of Exodus?
2. How do we explain Yahweh's hardening of Pharaoh's heart? What does this disclose about God's dealings with nations?
3. How is God portrayed in the Song of Moses and Miriam in Exodus 15? How does this compare with the way he is depicted elsewhere in the book?
4. What is the relationship between covenant and law?
5. Is one's understanding of the message of the book affected by one's position regarding the route and date of the exodus from Egypt? Explain.
6. What was the nature and purpose of the tabernacle for Hebrew religious and social life?
7. Characterize Moses on the basis of how he is portrayed in the Exodus accounts.

For Further Reading

Beegle, D. M. *Moses, The Servant of Yahweh*. Ann Arbor, Mich.: Pryor Pettengill, 1979.

Bimson, J. J. *Redating the Exodus and Conquest*. JSOTSS 5. Sheffield, England: Almond Press, 1981.

Brisco, T. V. "Exodus, Route of the." *ISBE*. Rev. ed. Grand Rapids: Eerdmans, 1982. 2:238–41.

Cassuto, U. *A Commentary on the Book of Exodus*. Trans. by I. Abrahams. Jerusalem: Magnes Press, 1967. Classic Jewish commentary, sensitive to the book as literature and rejecting the conclusions of source criticism. Excellent discussion of the book's message.

Childs, B. S. *The Book of Exodus*. OTL. Philadelphia: Westminster, 1974. Detailed and technical study of Exodus's place in the Old Testament canon, with thought-provoking theological discussion.

Clements, R. E. *Exodus*. CBC. Cambridge: Cambridge University Press, 1972.

Cole, R. A. *Exodus: An Introduction and Commentary*. TOTC. London: Tyndale, 1973. Brief but well-researched and readable. Thoroughly evangelical in perspective. Helpful introductory sections on the historical background and theology of Exodus.

Davis, J. J. *Moses and the Gods of Egypt*. 2nd ed. Grand Rapids: Baker, 1998.

Durham, J. I. *Exodus*. WBC. Vol. 3. Waco, Tex.: Word, 1987. Extensive bibliography but a disappointing assessment of the historicity of the Exodus narratives. Blindly committed to source analysis.

Ellison, H. L. *Exodus*. DSB-OT. Philadelphia: Westminster, 1982. Insightful contemporary application of the book's message to Christians corporately and individually.

Enns, Peter. *Exodus*. NIVAC. Grand Rapids: Zondervan, 2000. Balanced Christological interpretation of the exodus event, with timely contemporary application of the book's message.

Fretheim, Terence E. *Exodus*. Interpretation. Louisville: John Knox, 1991.

Gowan, Donald E. *Theology in Exodus: Biblical Theology in the Form of a Commentary*. Louisville: Westminster John Knox, 1994.

Hyatt, J. P. *Exodus*. NCBC. London: Marshall, Morgan, & Scott, 1971.

Hoffmeier, James K. *Israel in Egypt: The Evidence for the Authenticity of the Exodus Tradition*. 2nd ed. New York: Oxford University Press, 1999. Analysis of the historical and archaeological evidence in support of the biblical record concerning Israel in Egypt.

_____. "Moses." *ISBE*. Rev. ed. Grand Rapids: Eerdmans, 1983. 3:415–25.

Kaiser, Walter C. "Exodus." *EBC*. Vol. 2. Grand Rapids: Zondervan, 1990. 287–497.

_____. *Toward Old Testament Ethics*. Grand Rapids: Zondervan, 1983. Esp. 81–111. Lucid exposition of the legislation of the Decalogue and covenant code.

Longman, Tremper, and Daniel G. Reid. *God Is a Warrior*. Grand Rapids: Zondervan, 1995. A tracing of the development of the "divine warrior" motif through the Old and New Testaments.

Miller, P. D. *The Divine Warrior in Early Israel*. Cambridge: Harvard University Press, 1973.

Motyer, J. Alec. *The Message of Exodus*. Downers Grove, Ill.: InterVarsity Press, 2005. Insightful theological reflection upon the character of God.

Sarna, Nahum M. *Exodus*. JPS Torah Commentary. Philadelphia: Jewish Publication Society, 1991.

Schoville, Keith N. *Exodus and Leviticus*. BBC. Vol. 2. Nashville: Abingdon Press, 1994.

Shea, W. H. "Exodus, Date of the." *ISBE*. Rev. ed. Grand Rapids: Eerdmans, 1982. 2:230–38.

Stuart, Douglas. *Exodus*. Nashville: Broadman & Holman, 2006.

Walton, J. H. "Exodus, Date of." *DOTP*. Downers Grove, Ill.: InterVarsity Press, 2003. 258–72.

Wright, C. J. H. *God's People in God's Land*. Grand Rapids: Eerdmans, 1990. Exegesis and interpretation of Old Testament law as it applies to family, land, and property, with insightful application to Christian social ethics.

_____. "Ten Commandments." *ISBE*. Rev. ed. Grand Rapids: Eerdmans, 1988. 4:786–90.

_____. *Old Testament Ethics for the People of God*. Downers Grove, Ill.: InterVarsity Press, 2004.

Leviticus provides regulations for governing the sacred space in and around the tabernacle. This is a full-sized reconstruction of the tabernacle that is set up in the Negev (Timna). Todd Bolen/www.BiblePlaces.com

LEVITICUS

Key Ideas

- The holiness of God
- The purity of the covenant community
- The principle of substitution in the sacrificial ritual
- The principle of mediation in the service of the priests
- The redeeming of time by means of the liturgical calendar

Purpose Statement

The purpose of Leviticus is to provide a manual or handbook on holiness designed to instruct the Hebrew community in holy worship and holy living so that they might imitate God's holiness and enjoy the presence and blessing of God.

Major Themes

- Holiness
- Sacrifice
- Sabbath Rest and Sabbatical Year

God's Presence

Leviticus affirms God's presence with his people in the requirements of the sacrificial system (especially the fellowship offerings), the various purity laws intended to establish a standard of holiness for Israel appropriate to their covenant relationship with God, and the legislation ensuring reverence for his sanctuary in their midst. All this was necessary in order that God might maintain his dwelling place among the people and walk among them as their God (26:11–12).

An Outline of Leviticus

I. Approaching a Holy God
- A. Laws about Sacrifice (1–7)
  1. Burnt offering (1:1–17)
  2. Grain offering (2)
  3. Peace offering (3)
  4. Sin offering (4:1–5:13)
  5. Guilt offering (5:14–6:7)
  6. Instructions for priests 6:8–7:38
- B. Laws about the Consecration of Priests (8–10)
  1. Anointing of Aaron and his sons (8)
  2. Aaron's sacrifice (9)
  3. Death of Nadab and Abihu (10)

II. Living in the Presence of a Holy God
- A. Laws about "Clean" and "Unclean" Things (11–15)
  1. Food (11)
  2. Childbirth (12)
  3. Leprosy and skin diseases (13–14)
  4. Discharges and secretions (15)
- B. Laws about Holiness (16–25)
  1. The Day of **Atonement** (16)
  2. Taboo on eating and drinking blood (17)
  3. Laws about sexuality (18)
  4. Civil and ceremonial laws (19)
  5. Various laws and punishments (20)
  6. Laws for priests (21–22)
  7. Feasts and calendar (23–25)

III. Covenant Blessings and Curses (26)

IV. Appendix: Laws about Vows and Gifts (27)

L eviticus, the third book of the Pentateuch, is a manual of priestly regulations and duties and a handbook of instructions prescribing practical "holy living" for the Israelite covenant community. The Hebrew title of the book, "And he called," is taken from the opening verse of the text, "And the LORD called unto Moses" (KJV). The English name "Leviticus" derives from the Greek title *Leuitikon*, given in the Septuagint and meaning "pertaining to the Levites."

The Writing of the Book

The human author of Leviticus is not mentioned in the book. Yet the phrase "the LORD said to Moses" occurs more than twenty-five times

Leviticus 1: Altars were the center of ritual in the ancient world. Many of those found by archaeologists had horns on the four corners, such as this limestone altar from Beersheba. While the symbolism of the horns is not clear, fugitives of most crimes (but not intentional murder—see, for example, 1 Kings 2:28–32) could find asylum by grasping the horns of the altar in an appeal to God's mercy. Cutting off the horns made an altar useless for religious purposes (Amos 3:14).

Dr. Tim Bulkeley, www.eBibleTools.com

in the text (at least once in every chapter except 2, 3, 9, 10, and 26), Orthodox Jewish and Christian scholars have traditionally attributed the book to Moses, the lawgiver of Israel. Although no divine commandment is given for the recording of this legislation delivered to Moses, it is simply assumed by analogy to the book of Exodus that Moses wrote down the words spoken to him by the Lord (cf. Exod. 17:14; 24:4; 34:27).

Scholars holding to the traditional Mosaic or single-author view set forth two options for the date of writing of Leviticus: (1) those committed to an early date for the Israelite exodus from Egypt assign the work to the first half of the Late Bronze Age (ca. 1400 BC), while (2) those inclined toward a late date for the Hebrew exodus place the writing of the book in the early Iron Age (ca. 1200 BC).

Biblical scholars who hold to some form of the multiple authorship or Documentary Hypothesis for the composition of the Pentateuch assign the whole of Leviticus to the Priestly (P) source. This Pentateuchal literary strand is distinguished by the unmistakable priestly and liturgical interests of the levitical order such as rituals, purity laws, and genealogies. According to this theory, the P document was composed by one or more unknown levitical priests between 550 and 450 BC. When the Priestly contributions were then added to the other documents or strands of written tradition (J, E, and D) about 400 BC, the result was the complete Pentateuch as we know it today. (See further, Appendix B.)

A third position on the authorship of Leviticus mediates between the traditional Mosaic view and the Documentary approach. This view maintains that the P source is preexilic in date but not Mosaic in origin. Arguments supporting this alternative are grounded in the

Leviticus 2: Food offerings were common in sacrifices made in the ancient world. This Egyptian relief shows the food stacked high.

Frederick J. Mabie

similarities between the teachings of Leviticus and the books of Judges and Samuel on topics like personal holiness, war, and blood sacrifice (e.g., Lev. 17:10–16 and 1 Sam. 14:33–34) and the quotations of Leviticus in Old Testament books that are clearly preexilic or exilic in origin (e.g., Deut. 26:14; Ezek. 18:13; 20:9).

When all the available evidence is taken into account, there are no compelling reasons for denying the antiquity and authenticity of the book of Leviticus. Moses is explicitly and repeatedly cited as the recipient of Yahweh's commandments, and everywhere the book assumes a desert context. The numerous Mesopotamian legal parallels to Leviticus support an early date for the book (at least to the time of the united monarchy). Ezekiel's extensive appeal to the legislation of Leviticus shows the work at least predates the Babylonian exile. On a more practical note, careful examination of Leviticus reveals that much of the legislation is ill-suited for the civil and ceremonial context of the postexilic Hebrew community. Finally, linguistic analysis of the so-called P source exhibits considerable discontinuity with other biblical Hebrew texts from identifiable, later chronological time periods.[1]

Whether Moses compiled the materials of Leviticus himself or dictated the revelation to scribes remains unclear. However, it seems likely that the content and arrangement of the legal materials were standardized very early in the Hebrew covenant experience. This was necessary since they constituted a handbook for priestly procedure and function.

1. E.g., R. Polzin, *Late Biblical Hebrew: Toward an Historical Typology of Biblical Hebrew Prose*, HSM 12 (Missoula, Mont.: Scholars Press, 1976). Cf. Y. T. Radday et al., "Genesis, Wellhausen and the Computer," *Zeitschrift für die alttestamentlische Wissenschaft* 94 (1982): 467–81. This study notes considerable similarities between the so-called J and P sources in sections of Genesis and suggests that stylistic differences in biblical texts are determined more by the distinctiveness of literary genres than by assuming multiple authorship and the evolutionary development of the written sources.

The Background

Chronology

The book of Leviticus originates in the revelation of Yahweh given to Moses from the "tent of meeting" (1:1) and at Mount Sinai (25:1) during Israel's eleven-month sojourn at Sinai after the exodus from Egypt (cf. Exod. 19:1; 40:17; Num. 10:11).

(For the historical background of Leviticus, see the previous chapter.)

Given an early date for the Hebrew exodus (i.e., the fifteenth century BC), Moses or his scribe recorded the legislation of Leviticus during the first half of the period known as the Late Bronze Age (1550–1200 BC). In ancient Near Eastern chronology, this corresponds to the Eighteenth Dynasty of the New Kingdom in Egypt, with Thutmose III (1504–1450) the pharaoh of the Hebrew oppression and Amenophis II (1450–1425) the likely pharaoh of the exodus.

Given a late date for the Hebrew exodus (i.e., the thirteenth century BC), Moses transcribed or dictated the legislation of Leviticus during the transition from the Late Bronze Age to the Early Iron Age (1200–900). This corresponds with the Nineteenth Dynasty of the New Kingdom in Egypt, with Rameses II (1304–1237) the likely pharaoh of the exodus.

Cultural Background

The Hebrews were not alone in the ancient Near East in their practice of ritual purification and animal sacrifice. Highly structured priestly classes in charge of sanctuaries or temples are known in virtually all of the religious traditions concurrent with Hebrew faith as recounted in the Old Testament. Ceremonial washing and anointing or purification rites before worship or service before the gods were common to both Mesopotamian and Egyptian religion. Sacrifice, both animal and human, was commonplace in ancient Near Eastern religion as well.

Canaanite religions included "peace offerings" and "whole" or "burnt offerings" similar to those of Hebrew practices.

Despite these similarities in priestly office and form of ritual, the Hebrew religion remained distinct from other ancient Near Eastern religions in several ways. The differences include:

- The idea of direct divine revelation and theophany
- The concept of strict monotheism
- The understanding of the origin and impact of human sin

Kim Walton, courtesy of the Oriental Institute Museum

An offering stand from Megiddo. "The priest shall take a handful of fine flour and oil, together with all the incense, and burn this as a memorial portion" (Lev. 2:2).

- The highly ethical and moral nature of Hebrew religion in contrast to the Canaanite fertility cult
- The holy and righteous character of Yahweh in contrast to the capricious behavior of the pagan deities
- The prohibition of human sacrifice[2]

Purpose and Message

The central teaching of the book is summarized in the command to "consecrate yourselves and be holy, because I am holy ..." (Lev. 11:44–45). The first part of Leviticus outlines the requisite procedures for worshiping Yahweh (chaps. 1–10), and the second section prescribes how the covenant people of God are to translate the idea of holiness into daily living (chaps. 11–27).

Leviticus is basically a manual or handbook on holiness designed to instruct the Hebrew community in holy worship and holy living so that they might enjoy the presence and blessing of God (cf. Lev. 26:1–13). The laws and instructions were to transform the former Hebrew slaves into a "kingdom of priests and a holy nation" (cf. Exod. 19:6).

Structure and Organization

Leviticus is a natural extension of the narrative found in Exodus 25–40. The Exodus account concludes with the assembly and dedication of the tabernacle, and Leviticus begins with God addressing Moses from "the tent of meeting" about the prescriptions for the worship and service to take place there. The use of the simple conjunction "and" in Leviticus 1:1 (omitted in the NIV) indicates that the two books are to be read as one continuous record. Finally, the distribution of the divine oracle introductory formula "the LORD said to Moses" (e.g., Exod. 31:1; 33:1; 34:1; 39:1; 40:1; Lev. 1:1; 4:1; 6:1) and the concluding formula "Moses did as the LORD commanded" supports the interrelatedness of Exodus and Leviticus (e.g., Exod. 40:16; Lev. 8:13; 16:34).

The laws of Leviticus have affinity with the larger block of Pentateuchal legal material. First, like Exodus and Deuteronomy, the legislation of Leviticus is cast within the framework of historical narrative (e.g., chaps. 8–10; 24). Second, the divine oracle formula is repeated consistently throughout Leviticus (in which the phrase begins twenty of the twenty-seven chapters) and the Pentateuch as a whole. Third, the repetition of key words and the opening and closing formulae are used to mark literary units or related units of legislation. (For example, the phrase "this is the law" or "this is the thing" identifies chapters 6–17 as a literary unit [6:8; 7:1; 11:1; 17:2], and the recurring "I am the LORD your God" is a standard refrain in chapters 18–26.) The formu-

2. For discussions of similarities and differences between Israelite and ancient Near Eastern religion and religious literature, see J. Bottéro, *Religion in Ancient Mesopotamia* (Chicago: Univ. of Chicago Press, 2001); J. Assmann, *In Search for God in Ancient Egypt* (Ithaca: Cornell Univ. Press, 2001); R. S. Hess, *Israelite Religions* (Grand Rapids: Baker, 2007); J. Walton, *Ancient Near Eastern Thought and the Old Testament* (Grand Rapids: Baker, 2006).

lation of legislation to meet specific needs of the Hebrew community remains a constant in Leviticus (e.g., 24:10–23; cf. Exod. 18:13–27; Num. 15:16).

The presentation of the legislation in Leviticus is logically ordered in connection with the construction and dedication of the tabernacle in Exodus 40:1–33. A "tent of meeting" for Yahweh presumes religious activity of some sort and authorized personnel to conduct such activity. Leviticus documents the nature and purpose of Hebrew liturgy for the tabernacle, including the various sacrifices (chaps. 1–7) and the requirements for the priesthood in charge of the worship.

The remainder of the book contains laws regulating the life of the Hebrew people so they might reflect God's holiness as his people in the routine of daily living (cf. Exod. 19:6). Chapters 11–16 address various impurities inhibiting proper worship and community relationships, while chapters 17–25 constitute practical guidelines for holy living so that Israel's religious and "secular" life might not be mutually exclusive.

The last two chapters of the book (26–27) reinforce the covenantal context of the levitical legislation. The basic purpose of the book is outlined in chapter 26, including the recitation of the covenant blessings and curses. This chapter also connects the legislation with the covenant-making process at Sinai so that Israel might be his people and Yahweh might be their God (26:15–46). The concluding chapter appears to be an appendix, attached because covenant relationship is

An Egyptian relief showing a fellowship offering being prepared. "You are to give the right thigh of your fellowship offerings to the priest as a contribution" (Lev. 7:32).

really "oath taking" before Yahweh (cf. the similarity in the concluding formulas in 26:46 and 27:34). The laws involving vows and gifts further instruct the people on the solemn and sacred nature of their vows before God.

Major Themes

Holiness

The central teaching of Leviticus is summarized in the command "consecrate yourselves and be holy, for I am holy" (Lev. 11:44–45). The first part of the book gives the procedures for approaching the Holy One of Israel in worship (chaps. 1–10). The second prescribes how those joined covenantally to God translate the idea of Yahweh's holiness to the sphere of daily living (chaps. 11–27). The basic purpose of Leviticus, then, was to provide instruction for the Hebrew community in "holy worship" and "holy living," so that as the covenant people they might enjoy the blessing of Yahweh's presence (cf. 26:1–13).

The Old Testament word *holiness* essentially conveys the notion of "separation" from the mundane for service and/or worship to Yahweh, who himself is wholly separate from his creation. The legislative holiness of Leviticus could prove effective only as Israel practically implemented the ideal of "the holy" into the everyday human experience. At issue was discernment between the holy and the common and between the clean and the unclean (10:10–11).

Applying the concepts of the holy, common, clean, and unclean to the physical, moral, and spiritual realms of life was basic to the ancient Hebrew worldview. The distinctions allowed the people to order their relationship to the natural world in such a way that they might indeed "be holy" as the Creator is holy.

On the basis of levitical law, everything in life was either holy or common for the Hebrews. Those things determined common were subdivided into categories of clean and unclean. Clean things might become holy through sanctification or unclean through pollution. Holy things could be profaned and become common or even unclean. Unclean things could be cleansed and then consecrated or sanctified to be made holy. The relationship of these concepts is illustrated in figure 6.1.[3]

Common (i.e., clean) things or persons devoted to God become holy through the mutual efforts of human activity in sanctifying (or consecrating) and of the Lord as the sanctifier (cf. Lev. 21:8). Uncleanness may be caused by disease, contamination, infection, or sin; it could be cleansed only by ritual washing and sacrifice. Hence the importance of the instructions regarding sacrifices in the book of Leviticus. The presence of the holy God resided in the Israelite camp within the tab-

3. Cf. Gordon J. Wenham, *The Book of Leviticus*, NICOT (Grand Rapids: Eerdmans, 1979), 18–29.

Figure 6.1. The Cycle of Sanctification

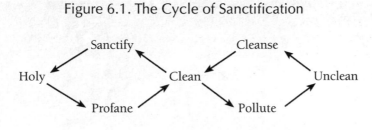

ernacle, and therefore it was imperative to prevent the unclean from coming into contact with the holy (7:20–21; 22:3; cf. Num. 5:2–3). Failure to prevent contamination resulted in death (Num. 19:13, 20; cf. Num. 15:32–36; Josh. 7).

The apostle Paul understood the atonement in the age of the new covenant in a similar way. All human beings are unclean because of inherited sin due to the fall of Adam (Rom. 5:6–14). The redemptive work of Jesus Christ washes (elevates to cleanness) and sanctifies (makes holy) the repentant sinner (1 Cor. 6:9–11). The exhortation to practical holiness (e.g., Matt. 5:48; 1 Peter 1:16) can be realized only as the believer in Christ yields to the Spirit of God in obedience to the teachings of righteousness found in Scripture (Rom. 6:15–23; 8:12–17).

Sacrifice

The ritual sacrifice was but one way the Hebrew people might gain access to their God Yahweh, the Holy One of Israel (in addition to prayer, Jer. 29:12; repentance and contrition, Isa. 66:2; et al.). The idea of sacrifice was not unique to the Hebrews in the ancient world, as animal, grain, and drink offerings to deities were common to the religious cults of Mesopotamia and Syro-Palestine. While the parallels between Israelite and ancient Near Eastern sacrificial practices attest the universal need for humanity to placate the gods, the Hebrew sacrificial system was distinctive in that it was divinely revealed and was directed toward the goal of personal and community holiness (fig. 6.2).

Five basic types of sacrifices, or offerings, were instituted as part of formal, corporate worship and personal celebration in Hebrew religious expression: (1) cereal or grain offering, (2) fellowship or peace offering, (3) whole burnt offering, (4) sin offering, and (5) guilt or trespass offering (see fig. 6.2). These sacrifices, described in Leviticus, fell into two categories: (1) those offered spontaneously to God in praise and thanksgiving for blessings received or favors granted (e.g., the cereal or grain offering and the three types of peace offerings, Lev. 2:1–16; 3:1–17), (2) those demanded by Yahweh on the occasion of sin in the Hebrew community (e.g., the burnt, sin, and trespass or guilt offerings, Lev. 1:3–17; 4:1–5:13; 5:14–6:7). The former were grateful responses

"When anyone brings from the herd or the flock a fellowship offering to the LORD, ... it must be without defect or blemish to be acceptable" (Lev. 22:21). The Standard of Ur from the third millennium BC shows animal gifts being brought.

Michael Greenhalgh/ArtServe, courtesy of the British Museum

to the goodness of God, while the latter were necessary to purify the holy place from the desecration brought on by sin. These purifying sacrifices led to reconciliation with Yahweh and restored the penitent sinner to fellowship with other persons and God.

According to Leviticus 17:11, the principle of life is represented in the blood. Thus, blood upon the altar was necessary for the symbolic cleansing of God's presence (cf. Heb. 9:21–22). The word "atonement" used here represents the word group related to the Hebrew root *kpr*. In its verbal forms it refers to the purging of holy objects from the effects of sin. So the altar would be purged on behalf of the offerer whose sin or impurity had ritually tarnished it. The purpose was to maintain the sanctity of God's presence in their midst. The ritual, like a disinfectant, is normally remedial but can be preventative. This decontamination of the sanctuary renders the offerer clean and paves the way for his reconciliation with God. The same term is applied to the great Day of Atonement ritual of Leviticus 16, known today as Yom Kippur.

The teaching in both the Old Testament and the New Testament clearly indicates that animal sacrifices were not intended to save people from their sins or to get them to heaven. Instead, they preserved the holiness of God's presence and a healthy relationship between the people and God. The believer under the old covenant was counted as righteous on the basis of faith in Yahweh and faithfulness to the covenant and its stipulations (e.g., Gen. 15:6; Hab. 2:4). The external act of

Figure 6.2. The Sacrificial System

Name	Portion Burnt	Other Portions	Animals	Occasion or Reason	Reference
Burnt offering	All	None	Male without blemish; animal according to wealth	Propitiation for general sin, demonstrating dedication	Lev. 1
Meal offering or tribute offering	Token portion	Eaten by priest	Unleavened cakes or grains, must be salted	General thankfulness for firstfruits	Lev. 2
Peace offering a. Thank offering b. Vow offering c. Freewill offering	Fat portions	Shared in fellowship meal by priest and offerer	Male or female without blemish according to wealth; freewill; slight blemish allowed	Fellowship a. For an unexpected blessing b. For deliverance when a vow was made on that condition c. For general thankfulness	Lev. 3 Lev. 22:18–30
Sin offering	Fat portions	Eaten by priest	Priest or congregation: bull; king: he-goat; individual: she-goat	Applies basically to situation in which purification is needed	Lev. 4
Guilt offering	Fat portions	Eaten by priest	Ram without blemish	Applies to situation in which there has been desecration or desacrilization of something holy or there has been objective guilt	Lev. 5:1–67

From John H. Walton, *Chronological and Background Charts of the Old Testament* (Grand Rapids: Zondervan, 1994), 22.

"A man or woman who is a medium or spiritist among you must be put to death. You are to stone them; their blood will be on their own heads" (Lev. 20:27). Israel was not the only ancient nation to use capital punishment. This Syrian "Hadad Inscription" presented by Panamuwa condemns any member of the royal household who plots destruction to be stoned by a same-sex relative.

Emily Katrencik, courtesy of the Pergamon Museum, Berlin

ritual sacrifice was symbolic and representative of the internal attitude and disposition of the heart. Psalmist, sage, and prophet reiterated the truth that God does not desire sacrifice, but repentance leading to obedience (cf. 1 Sam. 15:22–23; Ps. 51:16–17; Prov. 21:3; Isa. 1:12–17; Jer. 7:21–23; Hos. 6:6; Amos 5:21–24; Mic. 6:6–8).

In his lovingkindness God granted forgiveness to anyone manifesting "the broken and contrite heart" of sincere repentance (e.g., 2 Sam. 12:13; Ps. 51:1, 16–17). The effectual removal of guilt and forgiveness of sin were accomplished through confession and the petition and intercession of prayer to the gracious and merciful Lord (e.g., Exod. 32:11–13, 30–35; Isa. 6:5–7). Ultimately the purpose of Hebrew sacrifice was to worship God and to preserve God's presence in their midst. The rituals served to instruct the Israelites in the principles of God's holiness, human sinfulness, substitutionary death as a response to human transgression, and the need for repentance. They provided cleansing and renewed fellowship within the community and with Yahweh.

These rituals furnished illustrations and a basis for understanding the redemptive work of Jesus of Nazareth as Messiah. John the Baptist recognized and proclaimed Jesus as the Lamb of God who takes away the sin of the world (John 1:29–34). Jesus himself understood his role as the good shepherd who lays down his life for his sheep (John 10:1–21). Elsewhere New Testament writers interpreted the crucifixion of Jesus Christ as the "once for all" sacrifice for the sins of humanity (e.g., Rom. 5:6–11; Heb. 10:10, 12). The writer to the Hebrews in fact connected the Day of Atonement ceremony with the death of Jesus Christ, which became an atoning sacrifice through the offering of his body (Heb. 9–10; cf. Lev. 16).

Finally, the New Testament writers found the new covenant equivalent of ritual sacrifice in "spiritual sacrifices" offered by Christians to God through Christ Jesus (1 Peter 2:5). These spiritual sacrifices include

- Generous and cheerful giving (Phil. 4:18)
- Worship, especially praise and thanskgiving (Heb. 13:15–16; cf. Ps. 50:13–14)
- Prayer (Rev. 5:8; 8:3–4)
- Evangelism (Rom. 15:16–17; cf. Isa. 66:20)
- Selfless service to Christ—even to death (Rom. 12:1–2; Phil. 2:17; 2 Tim. 4:6; Rev. 6:9)

Interestingly, all the levitical expiatory or atoning sacrifices were for "unwitting" covenant violations. There was no specific sacrifice for premeditated and malicious covenant transgression or rebellion.

Figure 6.3. Jewish Special Days

Special Days	Hebrew Name	Day	Reference	Reading (Megilloth)	Commemoration
Passover (Feast of Unleaven Bread)	Pesach	14 Nisan	Exod. 12 (Lev. 23:4–8)	Song of Solomon	Deliverance from Egypt
Pentecost	Shavuoth	6 Sivan	Deut. 16:9–12 (Lev. 23:9–14)	Ruth	Celebration of the harvest
9th of Ab	Tish'ah be'ab	9 Ab	No direct reference	Lamentations	Destruction of temple 586 BC and AD 70
Day of Atonement	Yom Kippur	10 Tishri	Lev. 16 (23:26–32)		Sacrifices for sins of the nation
Feast of Tabernacles	Succoth	15–21 Tishri	Neh. 8 (Lev. 23:33–36)	Ecclesiastes	Wanderings in the wilderness
Dedication	Chanukah	25 Kislev	John 10:22		Restoration of the temple in 164 BC.
Lots	Purim	13–14 Adar	Esther 9	Esther	Failure of plot against Jews by Haman

From John H. Walton, *Chronological and Background Charts of the Old Testament* (Grand Rapids: Zondervan, 1994), 22.

Sabbath Rest and Sabbatical Year

The levitical prescriptions for holiness in Hebrew life extended even to the calendar. The great religious festivals were ordered according to the agricultural calendar of Palestine so that the Israelites might acknowledge Yahweh as their provider and sustainer (Lev. 23:4–44). The command to observe one day in seven as a Sabbath rest to God prefaces this religious calendar (Lev. 23:1–3).

The Sabbath ordinance reminded Israel that Yahweh was the Creator (cf. Exod. 20:8–11). It also brought a sense of "timelessness" to the worship of Yahweh and a sense of "holiness" to the human idea of time. Keeping one day holy to God meant rest and refreshment for humankind and animals, but more important, it sanctified the human endeavor so that in the other six days of the week one might truly "eat, drink, and find enjoyment in one's labor" as a gift from God (cf. Eccl. 2:24–26; 5:18–20).

The Sabbath was a covenant sign between Yahweh and Israel denoting Israel's special relationship with God and testifying that Israel's holiness was rooted in the Holy One, not in law and ritual (Exod. 31:12–17; cf. Lev. 26:2). By the time of Jesus, the practical and humanitarian benefits of the Sabbath had been obscured if not forfeited by the legalism of Judaism (cf. Matt. 12:1–4; Mark 7:1–13).

The Hebrew religious calendar provided for a "sabbath" of rest for the land of the promise as well. After six years of sowing, cultivating, and harvesting, the land was to lie fallow in the seventh year (Lev. 25:1–7). Practically speaking, the poor and socially disadvantaged were the beneficiaries of the sabbatical year, as they could glean the produce of the fallow land (Exod. 23:11). The laws of Deuteronomy expanded the sabbatical program to include the cancellation of debts, generous relief for the poor, and the release of Hebrew slaves (Deut. 15:2–18). The sabbatical cycle culminated in the Jubilee, or year of emancipation (Lev. 25:8–24). After seven sabbatical-year cycles, the land was "sanctified" in the fiftieth year. Along with the sabbatical year sanctions, property reverted to the families of its original owners.

The Sabbath and sabbatical-year ordinances were designed to foster social and economic equality and to inculcate important covenant community principles in Hebrew society, including (1) thanksgiving for past provision and faith in God's continued sustenance during the fallow year, (2) forgiveness in the remission of debts, (3) respect of persons created in the image of God in the manumission or release of slaves, and (4) the practice of generosity and the idea of stewardship in the redistribution of the covenant land.[4]

According to the prophet Jeremiah, neglect of the sabbatical laws and the consequent rejection of the covenant instruction inherent

---

4. Cf. John H. Yoder, *The Politics of Jesus* (Grand Rapids: Eerdmans, 1972), 64–77

in the commands were responsible for the fall of Jerusalem and the
Hebrew exile in Babylon (cf. Jer. 25:8–14; 2 Chron. 36:17–21). Once
the sabbatical cycle was interrupted, the community naturally rejected
the legal instruction undergirding the sabbath principles. God had no
choice but to exile his people "until the land enjoyed its sabbath rests"
(2 Chron. 36:21; cf. Lev. 18:28).

Questions for Further Study and Discussion

1. What does the legislation of Leviticus reveal about Yahweh?
2. How were the Hebrew sacrifices different from the pagan offerings made to pagan deities? How were they the same? Is the concept of sacrifice "bargaining" with God? Explain your answer.
3. Does the legal code of Leviticus motivate covenant obedience by works of the law or divine grace? Explain.
4. How do the levitical laws compare in severity with other legal codes of the ancient Near East? What purpose did the stringent penalties for violation of levitical law serve for the Israelite community?
5. Why did God seek to order Hebrew life with a ceremonial, or liturgical, calendar? Discuss the value of a liturgical calendar for the church today.

For Further Reading

Beckwith, Roger, and Martin Selman, eds. *Sacrifice in the Bible*. Grand Rapids: Baker, 1995.

Budd, Philip J. *Leviticus*. NCBC. Grand Rapids: Eerdmans, 1996.

Carpenter, E. E. "Sacrifices and Offerings in the Old Testament." *ISBE*. Rev. ed. Grand Rapids: Eerdmans, 1988. 4:260–73.

Dawn, Marva J. *Keeping the Sabbath Wholly*. Grand Rapids: Eerdmans, 1989. Sabbath principles for the church.

_____. *The Sense of Call: A Sabbath Way of Life for Those Who Serve God, the Church, and the World*. Grand Rapids: Eerdmans, 2006.

de Vaux, Roland. *Ancient Israel: Its Life and Institutions*. Vol. 2. Trans. by J. McHugh. New York: McGraw-Hill, 1961.

Gammie, John. *Holiness in Israel*. Minneapolis: Augsburg Fortress Press, 1989.

Gane, Roy. *Leviticus–Numbers*. NIVAC. Grand Rapids: Zondervan, 2004.

Hamilton, Victor P. *Handbook on the Pentateuch*. Grand Rapids: Baker, 1982. 245–311.

Harris, R. Laird. "Leviticus." *EBC*. Vol. 2. Grand Rapids: Zondervan, 1990. 501–654.

Harrison, R. K. *Leviticus: An Introduction and Commentary*. TOTC. Downers Grove, Ill.: InterVarsity Press, 1980. Somewhat brief, but a most readable commentary with useful introductory sections. Thoroughly evangelical in its stance, with concern for contemporary application.

Hartley, John E. *Leviticus*. WBC. Vol. 4. Waco, Tex.: Word, 1992. Helpful Hebrew word studies.

Hill, Andrew E. *Enter His Courts with Praise!* Grand Rapids: Baker, 1996. Old Testament worship for the New Testament church.

Kaiser, Walter C. "Leviticus." *IB*. Rev. ed. Vol. 1. Nashville: Abingdon Press, 1994.

Levine, Baruch A. *Leviticus*. JPS Torah Commentary. Philadelphia: Jewish Publication Society, 1989.

Milgrom, Jacob. *Leviticus 1–16; Leviticus 17–22; Leviticus 23–27*. AB Vols. 3, 3A, 3B. New York: Doubleday, 1991, 2000, 2001. Extensive treatment of Jewish sources on levitical law.

Noth, M. *Leviticus: A Commentary*. OTL. Trans. by J. E. Anderson. Philadelphia: Westminster, 1965.

Porter, J. R. *Leviticus*. CBC. Cambridge: Cambridge University Press, 1976.

Ringgren, H. *Religions of the Ancient Near East*. Trans. by J. Sturdy. Philadelphia: Westminster, 1973.

Rooker, Mark. *Leviticus*. NAC 3A. Nashville: Broadman & Holman, 2000.

Ross, Allen. *Holiness to the Lord: A Guide to the Exposition of the Book of Leviticus*. Grand Rapids: Baker, 2002.

Schoville, Keith N. *Exodus and Leviticus*. Nashville: Abingdon Press, 1994.

Snaith, N. H., ed. *Leviticus and Numbers*. NCBC. London: Nelson, 1967.

Walton, John H. "Equilibrium and the Sacred Compass: The Structure of Leviticus." *Bulletin for Biblical Research* 11.2 (2001): 293–304.

Wenham, Gordon J. *The Book of Leviticus*. NICOT. Grand Rapids: Eerdmans, 1979. Best commentary in English on the topic. Clear exposition with appreciation for ancient Near Eastern backgrounds to Old Testament sacrifice and ritual. Complete discussion of Old Testament relationships to the New Testament and the theological significance of the book.

The report of the scouts concerning the fortified cities of Canaan discouraged the Israelites from entering the land and resulted in forty more years in the wilderness. "The people who live there are powerful, and the cities are fortified and very large" (Num. 13:28). This fortress at Arad from the later Iron Age illustrates the idea of fortified cities. Todd Bolen/www.BiblePlaces.com

NUMBERS

Key Ideas

- God's faithfulness to his covenant promises
- Divine testing of human motives
- God communicating his truth through the medium of culture
- God's sovereign rule of the nations

Purpose Statement

The purpose of Numbers is to contrast the faithfulness of God with the faithlessness and rebellion of the Israelites. The former is seen in God's keeping of his covenant promise to make Israel a numerous people (as shown by the census). The latter is attested by the record of Israel's grumbling about their living conditions, rebellion against God's leadership, and refusal to enter the land. Thus, the people tested God at every level even while God was providing their every need.

Major Themes

- The Census Numbers
- The Testing by Yahweh
- The Revelation of God in Human Culture
- The Balaam Oracles

God's Presence

God's presence is confirmed in the cloud that covered the tabernacle and led the people in their journey through the Sinai wilderness, in the distribution of the power of the Spirit to the seventy elders of Israel, and in the daily provision of food and water (cf. 1 Cor. 10:3–4).

Outline

I. Preparations for Departure from Sinai
   A. Numbering and Organization of the Tribes (1–4)
   B. Special Legislation (5–6)
   C. Tribal Offerings for the Tabernacle (7)
   D. Purification of the Levites (8)
   E. Passover (9:1–14)
   F. The Cloud of Guidance and the Silver Trumpets (9:15–10:10)

II. From Sinai to Kadesh
   A. Arrangement of the Tribes Marching (10:11–36)
   B. Grumbling and Unrest (11:1–15)
   C. God's Provision of Food (11:16–35)
   D. Insubordination of Aaron and Miriam (12)
   E. The Twelve Spies (13–14)
   F. Supplemental Laws (15)
   G. Rebellion of Korah and Others (16–17)
   H. Duties of Priests and Levites (18)
   I. Purification Ritual for the Unclean (19)
   J. Miriam's Death and Moses' Sin (20:1–21)

III. From Kadesh to the Plains of Moab
   A. Aaron's Death (20:22–29)
   B. Defeat of Arad, Sihon, and Og (21)
   C. Balak and Balaam (22–24)
   D. Israel's Idolatry and Immorality at Baal-Peor (25)
   E. Second Numbering of Israel (26)
   F. Inheritance Case of Zelophehad's Daughters, Part 1 (27:1–11)
   G. Selection of Joshua as Moses's Successor (27:12–23)
   H. Additional Legislation on Offerings and Vows (28–30)
   I. War Against Midian (31)
   J. The Transjordan Tribes (32)
   K. Itinerary of Israel's Journey from Egypt to Canaan (33:1–49)
   L. Allotment of Transjordan Lands (33:50–34:29)
   M. Levitical Cities and Cities of Refuge (35)
   N. Inheritance Case of Zelophehad's Daughters, Part 2 (36)

The book of Numbers is the fourth book of the Pentateuch, and it continues the story of the Israelite exodus from Egypt, the covenant ceremony at Mount Sinai, and the journey to Canaan. The book highlights the wilderness testing and rebellion of the covenant people during the formative period of the Hebrew nation's relationship with Yahweh.

The Hebrew title of the book, "in the wilderness," is taken from the opening verse. The name is appropriate, because Numbers records the significant events associated with the period of "desert wandering" prior to the death of Moses and the Hebrew occupation of Canaan. The English title "Numbers" is a translation of the Greek Old Testament name for the book, "Arithmoi," reflecting the two census takings of the Hebrews related in chapters 1 and 26.

The Writing of the Book

Traditionally, Jewish and Christian scholars have credited the writing of Numbers to Moses, the Hebrew lawgiver. Yet the book itself contains only one reference to Moses as an author of the material, and that is specifically limited to the itinerary of the Israelites in their desert trek from Egypt to Moab (Num. 33:2). Elsewhere the text implies that the priests were also recording and preserving the divine instructions and regulations, especially those pertinent to their duties associated with the tabernacle (cf. 5:23).

Biblical scholars holding to some form of the Documentary Hypothesis for the composition of the Pentateuch regard the book as a patchwork of four (or more) literary sources (see further Appendix B). Essentially Numbers 1–10 is assigned to the block of Priestly (P) materials extending from Exodus 35 through Numbers 10. Chapters 11–36 of Numbers are considered a composite of the Yahwist (J) and Elohist (E) sources, and two different P traditions (with portions of 11–14, 16, and 20–25 assigned to J and E and portions of 13–17, 20, and all of 25–36 assigned to P). According to this source analysis, Numbers underwent expansion, revision, and rewriting until the book took its final form at the hands of Priestly editors in the fifth century BC.

Mounting evidence against the late date for the Priestly source has spurred growing appreciation for the antiquity of many of the traditions preserved in Numbers. Gordon Wenham has argued that the great familiarity of Deuteronomy with Numbers suggests that all of Numbers predates Deuteronomy. This leads Wenham to conclude that if J, E, and P are legitimate Pentateuchal sources, they can no longer be regarded as originating in widely different periods of history.[1]

As with Leviticus, the introductory formula "and the LORD said to Moses" appears in every chapter of the book. Until more solid evidence surfaces to the contrary, it may be assumed by analogy to the book of Exodus that the bulk of the text in Numbers is the literary product of Moses, stemming from the fifteenth or thirteenth century BC (depending on the date of the Hebrew exodus).

Z. Radovan/www.BibleLandPictures.com

"The LORD bless you and keep you; the LORD make his face shine upon you and be gracious to you; the LORD turn his face toward you and give you peace" (Num. 6:24–26). This priestly benediction was inscribed in Hebrew on this silver amulet, dating to the beginning of the 6th century BC. It is the earliest object with the divine name yet found.

1. G. J. Wenham, *Numbers: An Introduction and Commentary*, TOTC (Downers Grove, Ill.: InterVarsity Press, 1981), 23.

However, the references to Moses in the third person in the narrative (e.g., Num. 12:3; 15:22–23) and the sporadic editorial insertions designed to update a later audience (e.g., 13:11, 22; 27:14; 31:53) suggest that the book took its final form sometime after Moses' death. It seems correct to assume that the substantial portions of the history and legislation of Numbers originated with Moses during the thirty-eight years of desert wandering that the book recounts (cf. Num. 33:38; Deut. 1:3). Whether he transcribed the words of Yahweh himself or dictated them to a scribe is unclear. But Numbers and the rest of the Pentateuch

Wilderness Wanderings

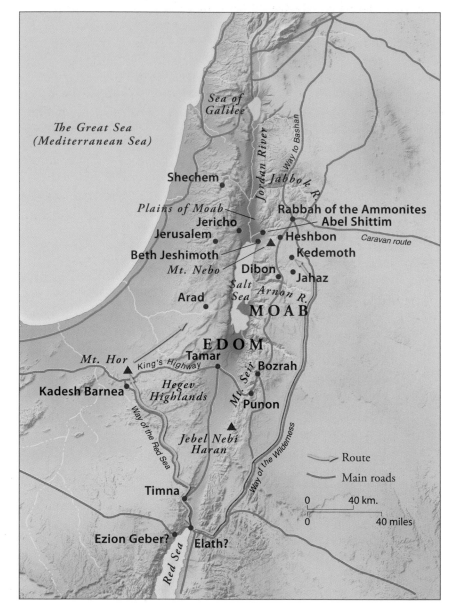

were cast in the form of a unified, five-volume book sometime between the days of Joshua and the elders of Israel (Josh. 24:31) and the era of Samuel (cf. 1 Sam. 3:19–21).

The Background

According to the date formulas given in the Pentateuch, the book of Numbers covers a span of some thirty-eight years and nine months. This period of early Hebrew history is commonly known as the wilderness or desert wanderings. The events associated with the desert trek of the first generation of Hebrews after the exodus from Egypt are narrated in three distinct stages: (1) a twenty-day period at Mount Sinai from the completion of the tabernacle to the taking up of the cloud of guidance (1:1–10:11), (2) the thirty-eight-year "sentence" of wilderness wandering from Sinai to Kadesh for the first generation of Hebrews who came out of Egypt, due to their unbelief and rebellion (10:11–20:13; cf. 33:38), and (3) a six-month duration at the end of thirty-eight years when the second generation after the exodus journeyed from Kadesh to the plains of Moab (20:14–36:13; cf. 33:38 and Deut. 1:3).

The complete log of key date formulas found in the Pentateuch for marking the development of Hebrew history after the exodus is shown in figure 7.1.

Figure 7.1. Timetable after the Exodus

Exodus from Egypt	15th day of first month	Exod. 12:2, 5; Num. 33:3
Arrival at Mount Sinai	1st day of 3rd month	Exod. 19:1
Yahweh reveals himself at Sinai	3rd day of 3rd month	Exod. 19:16
Completion of tabernacle	1st day of 1st month of 2nd year	Exod. 40:1, 16
Command to number Israel	1st day of 2nd month of 2nd year	Num. 1:1
Departure from Sinai	20th day of 2nd month of 2nd year	Num. 10:11
Arrival at Kadesh	1st month of 40th year?	Num. 20:1
Death of Miriam	1st month of 40th year?	Num. 20:1
Death of Aaron and thirty days of mourning	1st day of 5th month of 40th year	Num. 20:29
Departure for Moab	1st day of 6th month of 40th year?	Num. 20:22; 21:4
Moses addresses Israel in Moab	1st day of 11th month of 40th year	Deut. 1:2–3
Death of Moses and thirty days of mourning	?	Deut. 34:8
Joshua and Israel enter Canaan	10th day of 1st month of 41st year	Josh. 1:19

The precise dating of these "years" after the exodus from Egypt is unknown. The relative dating of the events is entirely dependent upon one's view of the date of the exodus. An early date for the exodus places the events of Numbers around 1400 BC, while the late date pushes the narrative nearer 1200 BC (see chap. 3, esp. fig. 3.4).

The narrative of Numbers contains numerous references to ancient regions and cities on the periphery of Palestine. The biblical record also indicates that organized kingdoms were firmly established in these border regions. For example, early opposition to the Hebrews during their wilderness wanderings came from Canaanites and Edomites in the Negeb and from the Moabites, Ammonites, and Midianites in the Transjordan (cf. Num. 21 and 31).

Critical scholars have challenged the historicity of these narratives relating Hebrew encounters with foreign nations and peoples for lack of supporting archaeological evidence. The archaeological picture of the Transjordan is incomplete, and disagreement over site identification and selective appeal to available archaeological data further confuse the issue. Yet experience has shown that calling into question the historicity of the biblical text is unwarranted, because subsequent archaeological discoveries tend to confirm Scripture (as in the case of the Nabonidus Chronicle and the book of Daniel).[2]

Purpose and Message

The book of Numbers in literary terms is a diary of Israel's early days of covenant relationship with Yahweh (cf. Deut. 8:1–10). Israel experienced firsthand the tragic consequences of disobedience to the covenant stipulations (e.g., Num. 16:25–50; 25:1–18). The book's message is twofold: first, one of God's patience and faithfulness in the face of Israel's continual grumbling and rebellion, and second, one of further disclosure of the nature and character of Israel's covenant God, Yahweh.

The austere holiness of Yahweh remains constant throughout, but other facets of God's person are revealed during this developmental stage of Israel's covenant relationship with the Lord. The desert experience gave Israel glimpses of Yahweh as a patient and faithful provider, a sovereign and providential intervener, a compassionate responder to intercessory prayer, and a jealous and just God (cf. Exod. 34:6–7).

The book of Numbers serves an important historical purpose in its cataloging of early Hebrew experiences outside of Egypt. The record of Israel's journey from Sinai to the plains of Moab continues the narratives of Exodus and Leviticus and helps explain the Hebrew presence in the land of Canaan. Numbers everywhere anticipates the occupation of the land of the covenant promise, thus bridging the legislation of Sinai and the conquest of Palestine. (For example, the section 33:50–36:13 is

2. Cf. Wenham's discussion of recent archaeological investigation related to sites associated with Numbers 21, 31, and 32 in *Numbers*, 154–63, 209–16.

devoted to the possession, distribution, holiness, and inheritance rights of the land of Canaan—cf. 26:52–56; 33:51–53; 35:31–34; 36:9.)

Theologically, the purpose of Numbers was to preserve the accounts of the initial phases of the practical outworking of God's recently established covenant with Israel. The book emphasizes

- The holiness of God
- The sinfulness of humanity
- The necessity of obedience to Yahweh
- The tragedy of disobedience to Yahweh's commands
- The utter faithfulness of God to his covenant agreement with Israel

Pragmatically, part of the purpose of Numbers was to order and organize the former Hebrew slaves into a unified community of God prepared to fulfill their covenant obligations. The intent of Numbers was to transform an oppressed people into a kingdom of priests and a holy nation through civil and ceremonial legislation, religious instructions, administrative census takings, tribal marching and camping arrangements, priestly ordinances, the cloud of guidance, and laws related to the allotment and inheritance of the land.

Finally, the tragic examples of covenant disobedience preserved in Numbers were a stern warning to future generations of the Hebrew nation. Moses understood the didactic value of these historical object

"In the first month the whole Israelite community arrived at the desert of Zin, and they stayed at Kadesh" (Num. 20:1). Kadesh Barnea is an oasis in the Eastern Sinai desert along the southern border of Canaan where the Israelites spent much of their time prior to entering the Promised Land.
Z. Radovan/www.BibleLandPictures.com

lessons for covenant obedience, hence his departing reminder to Israel to "take heed" to the works of the Lord accomplished during the desert wandering (Deut. 4:9; cf. Pss. 78:40–55; 95:9–11). The New Testament echoes this truth, acknowledging that the record of the Old Testament was inscripturated for a warning to the Hebrews and for the instruction of the church of Jesus Christ (cf. Rom. 15:4; 1 Cor. 10:11).

Structure and Organization

The book of Numbers almost defies dissection into logical literary units, making it perhaps the most difficult Old Testament book in which to identify order and structure. Rather than despairing, several Old Testament commentators have suggested that the complexity of the book's literary structure only affirms the integrity of the biblical accounts and the honesty of the Hebrew scribes responsible for preserving the record. Instead of forcing the material into an artificial structure for the sake of the reader, these scribes faithfully reproduced the written tradition they had received.

Some general observations may be made in respect to the overall structure of the book, however. Roughly speaking, the book is ordered in chronological sequence according to the date formulas contained in the text. This may help account for the seemingly disjointed nature of the composition, as portions were simply recorded and added to the growing history as the events occurred. Also, Numbers 1–10 is part of the larger block of material originating with Israel's sojourn at Sinai. Key themes unifying that extensive literary unit (Exod. 19–Num. 10) include founding of the tabernacle, the formation of the covenant community, and the anticipation of possessing Canaan as the land of the promise.

Numbers conveniently divides into three chronological periods of events and revelation bridged by narrative accounts of the intervening journeys of the Israelites. This schema may be outlined as follows:

1:1 – 10:10	Israel encamped at Sinai
10:11 – 13:25	Journey from Sinai to Kadesh (first postexodus generation of Hebrews)
13:26 – 20:21	Israel encamped at Kadesh
20:22 – 21:35	Journey from Kadesh to Moab (second generation)
22:1 – 36:13	Israel encamped on the plains of Moab

All five sections reinforce the basic message of Numbers — the faithfulness of Yahweh in the face of Israel's rebellion and the dire con-

"So Moses made a bronze snake and put it up on a pole. Then when anyone was bitten by a snake and looked at the bronze snake, he lived" (Num. 21:9). Moses made this bronze snake shortly after the Israelites came out of Egypt, where charms of a foe were often used to ward off that foe. Specifically, snakes were sometimes included on amulets to ward off snakes. This bronze snake was found at a shrine in Timna, an ancient site in the Negev.

Z. Radovan/www. BibleLandPictures.com

sequences attached to covenant disobedience. The numberings of the tribes and additional covenant legislation serve to affirm God's providential keeping of Israel while she was captive in Egypt and his fulfillment of promises made to Abraham about "a great nation" (Gen. 12:2; 17:5–6). The trek from Sinai to Kadesh and the events associated with that destination also underscore Yahweh's faithfulness (e.g., the provision of manna and quail, Num. 11:4–15) and the folly of rebelling against God (e.g., Korah's story, Num. 16).

In a touch of irony the meek and faithful character of Moses becomes a **foil** for the pride, selfishness, disobedience, and rebellion of Aaron, Miriam, and others. Yet even Moses fails God miserably at Meribah and becomes a foil for the unchanging faithfulness of Yahweh.[3]

The last sections of Numbers tangibly demonstrate Yahweh's covenant faithfulness and his good intentions to bring them into the land of the promise with the defeat of enemies along the way and the appointment of Joshua as Moses' successor. Even the Aaronic benediction of 6:24–26 returns to Israel full-circle in chapters 22–24, when Yahweh overturns the curses of the pagan **seer** Balaam so that he pronounces blessings upon the people of God.

Finally, the book represents a collection of diverse literary sources and features, including the four poems of Balaam (chaps. 22–24), and the ballad of Heshbon (21:27–30) — both non-Hebrew compositions originally; the quotation of poetry from the Book of the Wars of the Lord (21:14–18) — perhaps a Hebrew military document of some sort; the two formulaic census lists from which the book takes its name (chaps. 1 and 26); the travel log composed by Moses (chap. 33); extensive historical narrative interspersed with direct discourse; and the interweaving of narrative and legal materials (including both apodictic and case law).

Major Themes

The Census Numbers

The enumeration or enrollment of peoples (whether local or national) was an administrative procedure common to the ancient Near East. The census had three primary functions: (1) ascertaining and recruiting manpower for war (cf. Num. 1:3), (2) allotment of work assignments in the corvée — forced labor gangs — and the religious cult (e.g., Num. 3:4), and (3) establishing a basis for taxation (cf. Moses' census for a sanctuary tax in Exod. 30:11–16). Along with the instructions for ordering the Hebrew tribes in marching and camping formations (chap. 2), the census takings had the practical effect of contributing to the organization of former slaves into a unified people of God (fig. 7.2).

3. It must be remembered that Moses' sin went beyond simple disobedience to God's command to speak instead of striking the rock. Moses' anger and self-promoting statements are tantamount to insubordination as he and Aaron usurp Yahweh's preeminent place before the people of Israel (Num. 20:2–13; esp. v. 10). The severity of Moses' punishment (i.e., denial of entry into Canaan) seems justified, given the nature of responsibility associated with those exercising leadership gifts in the Old Testament and given Yahweh's consistently harsh judgment of rebellion elsewhere in Numbers.

Figure 7.2. Arrangement of the Twelve Tribes around the Tabernacle

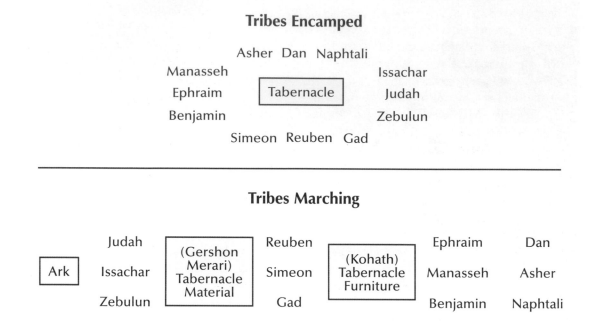

Tribes Encamped

Asher Dan Naphtali

Manasseh   Issachar

Ephraim   Tabernacle   Judah

Benjamin   Zebulun

Simeon Reuben Gad

Tribes Marching

Judah	(Gershon Merari) Tabernacle Material	Reuben	(Kohath) Tabernacle Furniture	Ephraim	Dan
Ark Issachar		Simeon		Manasseh	Asher
Zebulun		Gad		Benjamin	Naphtali

Figure 7.3. Census Figures in Numbers 1 and 26

Tribe	Reference	Figures	Reference	Figures
Reuben	1:20 – 21	46,500	26:5 – 11	43,730
Simeon	1:22 – 23	59,300	26:12 – 14	22,200
Gad	1:24 – 25	45,650	26:15 – 18	40,500
Judah	1:26 – 27	74,600	26:19 – 22	76,500
Issachar	1:28 – 29	54,400	26:23 – 25	64,300
Zebulun	1:30 – 31	57,400	26:26 – 27	60,500
Ephraim	1:32 – 33	40,500	26:35 – 37	32,500
Manasseh	1:34 – 35	32,200	26:28 – 34	52,700
Benjamin	1:36 – 37	35,400	26:38 – 41	45,600
Dan	1:38 – 39	62,700	26:42 – 43	64,400
Asher	1:40 – 41	41,500	26:44 – 47	53,400
Naphtali	1:42 – 43	53,400	26:48 – 50	45,400
Totals		603,550		601,730
Greatest decrease: Simeon (37,100)				

Adapted from William Sanford LaSor, David A. Hubbard, and Frederick W. Bush, *Old Testament Survey* (Grand Rapids: Eerdmans, 1982), 167. Used by permission.

The command for the first enlistment of Israel was given in the second month of the second year after the exodus (Num. 1:1). This census numbered the first generation of postexodus Israelites, all males twenty years of age and older. The command for a second enlistment of all Israelite males of fighting age came in the fortieth year after the exodus, and it numbered the second generation of postexodus Israelites (cf. 20:1, 22–29; 33:38). The census figures are compared in figure 7.3.

If these numbers are understood literally and the men of military age comprise approximately one-fourth of the population, then the projections for the total number of Israelites ranges anywhere from two to three million people. Supporters of a literal interpretation of the census figures note that this view corresponds well with Pharaoh's fear of the rapidly multiplying Hebrews overrunning Egypt and with the promises made to Abraham about becoming a great nation (cf. Exod. 1:7–12; Gen. 12:2; 17:5–6).

Yet critics contend that, given the inability of the Sinai wilderness to sustain such large numbers of people and animals and given Israel's failure to subdue and displace the Canaanites, such rapid population growth is unlikely and therefore the numbers cannot be understood literally. These difficulties associated with a literal reading of the census figures in Numbers have prompted alternative approaches to interpreting these and other numbers in the Pentateuch.

It has been suggested, though not widely accepted, that the census totals in Numbers are "misplaced" census lists from the era of David's monarchy. Other biblical scholars view the numbers as part of the writer's "epic prose" style, intended to emphasize the cumulative wholeness of Israel and the magnitude of Yahweh's miraculous deliverance. Still others discount the numbers as either artificial literary fiction or pious exaggerations hopelessly corrupted by the centuries of rewriting and revising the Pentateuchal sources.

The most widely accepted alternative approach contends that the Hebrew word for "thousand" has been mistranslated due to confusion arising from the lack of vowel markings in earlier Hebrew manuscripts. This means that the same cluster of consonants could be read as "clan," "tribe," or "unit" (e.g., Judg. 6:15; Zech. 9:7) or even "chieftain" or "armed warrior" (e.g., Gen. 36:15). Hence, the census lists of Numbers record either military "units" of an unspecified number of warriors or individual (armed) fighting men. Such accounting lowers the Israelite army to a figure somewhere between 18,000 and 100,000 men, with the total Hebrew population numbering between 72,000 and 400,000 people.

It is argued that these drastically reduced figures are more consistent with available historical and archaeological data regarding population patterns during the period of the Hebrew exodus. This approach

As the Israelites enter Canaan, Moabite King Balak hires a prophet, Balaam, to curse the Israelites (Num. 22–24). This prophet is referred to in this inscription from Deir Alla from the mid-first millennium BC.

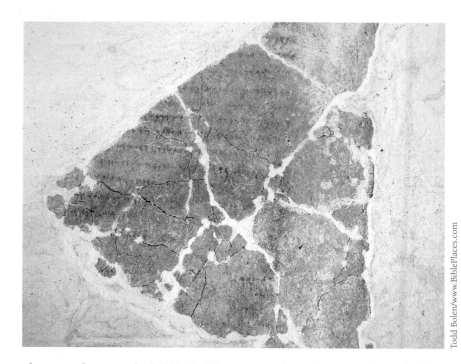

Todd Bolen/www.BiblePlaces.com

also corroborates the biblical affirmations about the size of Israel when compared with surrounding nations (cf. Exod. 23:29; Deut. 7:1–7). Yet it must be emphasized that none of the interpretive options for the Numbers census figures is without problems or inconsistencies. Generally speaking, one's view of Scripture determines one's stance on the biblical numbers, with one end of the spectrum inclined toward literalness, the other end skeptical about their historicity and reliability, and between them a moderate view of openness toward alternative readings.

The Testing by Yahweh

Probationary experience or testing is a repeated theme in the Pentateuch, and it becomes a major theme in the book of Numbers. The Genesis narrative records early humankind's probationary experience in the garden of God (2:15–17). Moreover, the presence of a "tempter" in the garden coupled with the New Testament expression "elect angels" suggests that even the angelic hosts were subjected to some kind of testing or probationary experience (cf. 1 Tim. 5:21). Elsewhere God tested Abraham's faith in calling for the sacrifice of Isaac (Gen. 22:1–14), and Joseph was divinely motivated to test the loyalty of his brothers (Gen. 44:1–17).

Moses described Israel's forty-year sojourn in the wilderness as a "test" of faith in Yahweh and covenant loyalty (Deut. 8:1–2). The purpose of Yahweh's testing was to humble the Israelites so that they might learn total dependence on him, teach obedience to his commandments, and show them the true condition of their "hearts." The New Testament commentary on this episode of Israelite history is found in Stephen's speech before the Sanhedrin (Acts 7:39; cf. Heb. 3:16–4:4); he indicated that the Hebrews failed because they never came out of Egypt in their hearts.

The Old Testament accounts of the lives of Abraham (Gen. 22), David (Pss. 17:3; 26:2), Job (23:10), and many others suggest that testing by Yahweh is common to the experience of God's elect. The **chronicler** and the prophet Jeremiah both understand Yahweh as a God who tests the heart and mind (1 Chron. 29:17; Jer. 11:20). In fact, David invited the testing of God because he knew it was beneficial in keeping the faithful of God on the way everlasting (Ps. 139:23). Ultimately, the testing of God diagnoses the root of human motive and attitude, thus preventing the holy name of Yahweh from being profaned (Isa. 48:10–11). This testing exposes and condemns unbelief and rebellion, leaving human beings without excuse before God.

By the same token, human beings are not to put God to the test (Deut. 6:16). The prophet Malachi helps illuminate this prohibition in his careful instructions to postexilic Israel. On the one hand he commends putting God to the test from the standpoint of obedience and faith (3:10). On the other, he discourages putting God to the test from the standpoint of disobedience and unbelief (3:15). The word found in Malachi 3:15 also appears in the Old Testament texts describing Israel's testing of God during the desert sojourn (Exod. 17:2; Pss. 66:10; 78:18, 41; 95:9). Those who "tested" God out of unbelief and disobedience erred in their hearts, had no regard for the ways of God, and were punished accordingly (cf.

A panorama of the land of Moab, where the Israelites were opposed by the Amorite kings Sihon and Og (Num. 21).

Bible Scene Multimedia/Maurice Thompson

Ps. 95:9–11). By contrast, the word for testing in Malachi 3:10 is the same one found in Job 23:10; Pss. 17:3; 26:2; 139:23. There it connotes the purification and strengthening of faith for those who put God to the test from a position of trust and obedience to his commandments.

The New Testament agrees with the Old Testament understanding of God's testing humankind. Even Jesus was tested in every respect as we are so that he might be our sympathetic High Priest (Matt. 4:1–11; Heb. 4:14–16). The use of two different words for testing in the book of James conforms to the Old Testament language pattern and substantiates Old Testament teaching. God tests human beings with a view toward approving faith and developing godly character traits (James 1:2–4), but he does not tempt individuals with the purpose of inciting evil or disapproving faith (1:12–15). That is the work of Satan as the enemy of the righteous. Finally, like King David before him, the apostle Paul recognized the "redemptive" benefits of divine testing (Rom. 5:1–11).

The Revelation of God in Human Culture

The book of Numbers illustrates the different ways Yahweh reveals himself to Israel in the context of ancient Near Eastern culture. For example, the freedom of God to work outside the cultural norms of that time is demonstrated in the Mosaic legislation establishing "cities of refuge" for those guilty of the crimes of involuntary or accidental manslaughter (Num. 35:9–28; cf. Deut. 4:41–43; 19:1–13; Josh. 20–21). The concept of a haven for the protection of the "manslayer" was designed to short-circuit the ancient Near Eastern custom of blood vengeance, in which the near kinsman of the victim was obligated to avenge the death of his deceased relative by killing the manslayer. The

While the Israelites were wandering in the wilderness on their way to Canaan, they encamped in the desert of Zin. There they grumbled against the Lord because of their thirst (see Num. 20:1–2).

Jack Hazut

Sidebar 7.4. Society and Culture in the Old Testament

Students of the Old Testament frequently raise two related questions as a result of encountering the cultural conventions associated with the world of the Bible. First, how did Israel's unique covenant faith relate to and interact with the social and cultural practices of the ancient Mediterranean world? Second, what was God's relationship to the sociocultural patterns of those ancient societies?

Christopher Wright has offered a biblically based assessment of the range of ancient Israel's responses to contemporary culture. The approach respects the dignity of human beings made in God's image, recognizes the reality (and consequences) of the fall, and gives place to the importance of human responsibility for the social impact of cultural norms. His broad classifications may be arranged under three headings:

1. Practices abhorrent to God and rejected as socially prohibited to Israel, including the idolatrous, the perverted (e.g., deviant sexual behavior, occultic activities), those things destructive of persons (e.g., human sacrifice), and callousness to the poor.
2. Toleration of certain social customs without explicit divine command or sanction, often addressed by a developing theological critique indicating that such customs fell short of God's highest standards, and usually regulated by legal safeguards intended to soften or eliminate their worst effects (e.g., polygamy, divorce, slavery).
3. Divine acceptance and affirmation of shared sociocultural patterns, especially the importance of family and kinship, customs related to hospitality, the idea of social justice, appreciation for the arts, and the value of a strong work ethic.

institution of the cities of refuge was unique in the ancient world and elevated Hebrew social and moral life to a higher plane than the surrounding nations.

The landmark decision of Moses in the inheritance case of Zelophehad's daughters constitutes another example of Yahweh overturning ancient Near Eastern legal custom in his dealings with the Hebrews as his special people (Num. 27:1–11; 36:1–13). In Mesopotamian law, daughters did not normally inherit shares in the family estate. This was apparently standard practice among the Hebrews as well (cf. Deut. 21:15–17). But the legislation in Numbers elevates the status of women in Hebrew society in contrast to the neighboring peoples and also indicates Yahweh's intention to fulfill his promises regarding the covenant land (Num. 33:50–36:1; cf. Gen. 12:1; 17:8).

Yet God also chose to accommodate aspects of his revelation to the cultural conventions of the ancient Near East. Examples here include the utilization of human language and human agents to convey divine

"Whenever the ark set out, Moses said, 'Rise up O Lord! May your enemies be scattered; may your foes flee before you'" (Num. 10:35). Relief from the temple of Ramses III at Medinet Habu with the enthroned pharaoh being carried in procession using poles, just as the ark was. Note the griffin flanking the throne (as the cherubim flanked the ark) and the protective wings of the goddess standing behind the throne.

Manfred Näder, Gabana Studios Germany

truth (e.g., Num. 33:2), the command for the census taking (Num. 1:2), and the legislation regarding Nazirite vows (Num. 6:1–21)—all reflecting practices common to ancient Near Eastern civilizations. An interesting illustration of this cultural conformity in divine revelation entails the laws protecting against a husband's jealousy for a woman suspected of adultery (Num. 5:11–31). In Mesopotamian law, the accused party took an oath before the gods (e.g., the river god, Id) and then plunged (or was thrown) into the river. The gods would see that justice prevailed, determined by whether the defendant was spared (denoting innocence) or was caused to drown (denoting guilt). Although the procedure for the Hebrew "adultery test" was more enlightened than the Mesopotamian river ordeal, it was still a male-dominant legal tradition in that the test was given only to a female.

Of course, the intent of Yahweh was to establish holiness among the people of Israel and prevent criminal violation of the covenant stipulations, whether his revelation took conventional social and legal forms or totally superseded them. Looking at Yahweh's revelation in the context of human culture yields two important principles: (1) God demonstrates his respect and appreciation for human culture by working through it rather than above or outside it, and (2) the higher goals of covenant obedience and personal and corporate holiness may necessitate **supracultural** approaches to relational ministry carried out in the name of Yahweh.

The Balaam Oracles

The antiquity of Balaam's poetic utterances as preserved in Numbers 22–24 has long been recognized. They constitute an important contribution to the early Israelite poetry comprising the so-called Primary History of the Hebrew Bible.[4]

Undoubtedly the poetry is more widely known for the humorous misadventures of a pagan prophet hired by the Moabite Balak to curse Israel and thus assist Moab in defeating them in battle (Num. 22:1–6). At first the Lord commands Balaam not to go with Balak; then he relents and lets the seer follow Balak to the Israelite camp. A verbal exchange with the angel of the Lord and his own donkey ensues, apparently due to divine detection of Balaam's impure motives (cf. 22:32). Ironically, Balaam pronounces only blessings upon the people of Israel and curses upon the nations of Moab, Edom, and Amalek (24:15–24).

The inclusion of the Balaam oracles in the Numbers narrative enhances the basic message of Yahweh's covenant faithfulness to Israel by reminding them they are a "blessed" people (22:12), nurtured and protected by Yahweh's very presence (23:21–22). The poetry also serves to encourage Israel as they journey toward the land of the promise by demonstrating Yahweh's sovereign control over the nations in the region. Moreover, it extends the promise of future messianic kingship in the prophecy of the star and scepter (24:17; cf. Gen. 49:10).

Later Balaam joined with the Midianites and indirectly succeeded in cursing Israel by inciting them to participate in the idolatry and immorality of the Baal cult of Peor (Num. 25:1–3; cf. 31:8–16). In the New Testament, Balaam is cited as an example of a false prophet corrupted by greed and the desire for personal gain (Jude 11).

A fragmentary inscription written in Aramaic on a plastered wall at Deir 'Allah in Jordan recounts another story of a seer named Balaam conveying the message of the gods to a disobedient nation. If this is indeed the Balaam of Numbers 22–24, the text gives evidence of the prophet's lasting and widespread renown as a "diviner."[5]

4. Cf. William F. Albright, "The Oracles of Balaam," *JBL* 63 (1944): 207–53; and David N. Freedman, *Pottery, Poetry, and Prophecy: Studies in Early Hebrew Poetry* (Winona Lake, Ind.: Eisenbrauns, 1980), 77–178. Freedman's corpus of early Hebrew poetry constituting the "Primary History" includes The Testament of Jacob (Gen. 49), The Song of the Sea (Exod. 15), The Oracles of Balaam (Num. 23–24), The Testament of Moses (Deut. 33), The Song of Deborah (Judg. 5), and several poetic fragments (Exod. 17:16, Num. 6:24–26; 10:35–36; 12:6–8, 21:17–18, 27:30; Deut. 34:7; and Josh. 10:12–13).

5. A translation and discussion of the text, along with its implications for Old Testament study is published in J. Hoftijzer and G. van der Kooij, *Aramaic Texts from Deir 'Allah* (Leiden: Brill, 1976).

Questions for Further Study and Discussion

1. How does the book of Numbers portray Moses? How does it portray Yahweh?
2. Why does the writer of Numbers give such a prominent place to the complaints, unbelief, rebellion, and punishment of the Hebrew people?
3. What does Numbers teach about Yahweh and his revelation in relationship to human culture?
4. How does the purpose of the cities of refuge described in Numbers 35:6–34 relate to Yahweh's covenant with Israel?
5. What do the portraits of women in the book of Numbers suggest about the role of women in ancient Hebrew society?
6. How are we to understand Yahweh's command to Israel to "take vengeance" on the Midianites (31:1–2)?
7. What does Yahweh's interaction with a pagan prophet like Balaam tell us about his intervention in history?

For Further Reading

Allen, Ronald B. "Numbers." *EBC*. Vol. 2. Grand Rapids: Zondervan, 1990. 657–1008.

Ashley, Timothy R. *Numbers*. NICOT. Grand Rapids: Eerdmans, 1993. Develops the theological relevance of the book.

Brown, Raymond. *The Message of Numbers*. BST. Downers Grove, Ill.: InterVarsity Press, 2002.

Budd, P. J. *Numbers*. WBC. Vol. 5. Waco, Tex.: Word, 1984. Helpful bibliographies.

Cole, R. Dennis. *Numbers*. NAC 3B. Nashville: Broadman & Holman, 2000.

Davies, E. W. *Numbers*. NCBC. Grand Rapids: Eerdmans, 1995.

Gane, Roy. *Leviticus–Numbers*. NIVAC. Grand Rapids: Zondervan, 2004.

Harrison, R. K. *Numbers*. WEC. Chicago: Moody Press, 1990.

Levine, Baruch. *Numbers*. AB. Vol. 4A. New York: Doubleday, 1993.

Maarsingh, B. *Numbers: A Practical Commentary*. TIC. Trans. by J. Vriend. Grand Rapids: Eerdmans, 1987.

Milgrom, J. *Numbers*. JPS Torah Commentary. Philadelphia: Jewish Publication Society, 1990.

Noth, Martin. *Numbers*. OTL. Trans. by J. D. Martin. Philadelphia: Westminster, 1968.

Olson, Dennis T. *Numbers*. Interpretation. Louisville: John Knox, 1996.

Pilch, John J. *Introducing the Cultural Context of the Old Testament.*
    New York: Paulist Press, 1991.

Riggans, W. *Numbers.* DSB-OT. Philadelphia: Westminster, 1983.
    Useful parallels between the teaching of Numbers and the
    ministry of Jesus Christ.

Sturdy, J. *Numbers.* CBC. Cambridge: Cambridge University Press,
    1976.

Wenham, G. J. *Numbers: An Introduction and Commentary.* TOTC.
    Downers Grove, Ill.: InterVarsity Press, 1981. Easily the best
    commentary on the topic. Readable, thoroughly researched,
    solidly evangelical, insightful exposition, and thoughtful
    contemporary application.

_____. *Numbers.* OTG. New York: Continuum, 1997.

The ruins of a high place at Hazor. "Destroy completely all the places on the high mountains and on the hills and under every spreading tree where the nations you are dispossessing worship their gods. Break down their altars, smash their sacred stones and burn their Asherah poles in the fire; cut down the idols of their gods and wipe their names from those places" (Deut. 12:2–3).

Steven Voth

DEUTERONOMY

Key Ideas

- The importance of a central worship place
- The emphasis on the name of God
- The organization of laws with reference to the Ten Commandments
- The centrality of loving and obeying the covenant God

Purpose Statement

The purpose of Deuteronomy is to summarize and renew the covenant in preparation for entering into the land. In the process it organizes laws in a way that the spirit behind the Ten Commandments will be understood. It is the charter document of Israel that emphasizes that there is one God, one people of God, one sanctuary, and one law.

Major Themes

- Law
- Central Sanctuary
- History as Theology
- Retribution Principle

God's Presence

Deuteronomy reviews God's presence with his people in the events of the Exodus, at Sinai, and during the wilderness wandering. In the presentation of the law it reiterates the essential elements by which the people will experience God's presence and be in relationship with him.

Outline

I. First Speech of Moses
   A. Preamble (1:1–5)
   B. Historical Prologue (1:6–3:29)
   C. Introduction to Stipulations: Exhortation to Obey the Law (4:1–43)

II. Second Speech of Moses
   A. Introduction to Speech (4:44–5:5)
   B. Stipulations (5:6–26:19)
     1. The Decalogue (5:6–21)
     2. Response of the people (5:22–33)
     3. Elaboration of the Decalogue (6:1–26:15)
       a. Commandment 1 (6–11)
       b. Commandment 2 (12)
       c. Commandment 3 (13:1–14:21)
       d. Commandment 4 (14:22–16:17)
       e. Commandment 5 (16:18–18:22)
       f. Commandment 6 (19–21)
       g. Commandment 7 (22:1–23:14)
       h. Commandment 8 (23:15–24:7)
       i. Commandment 9 (24:8–16)
       j. Commandment 10 (24:17–26:15)
     4. Concluding exhortation (26:16–19)
   C. Document Clause (27:1–10)
   D. Curses and Blessings (27:11–28:68)

III. Third Speech of Moses: Final Charge (29–30)

IV. Last Words of Moses
   A. Miscellaneous Matters (31)
   B. Song of Moses (32)
   C. Blessing of Moses (33)
   D. Death of Moses, Transition to Joshua (34)

The book of Deuteronomy does not give a "second law" as the name suggests, but rather provides an important summary of the history of the wilderness period and organization of the legal material. Framed in the words of Moses shortly before his death, the book tries to give the Israelites a broad perspective on the events of the previous generation as it affords the opportunity for the renewal of the covenant.

The Writing of the Book

The dating of Deuteronomy has served as the basis for two popular critical theories of modern times: the Documentary Hypothesis of the

Pentateuch (see pp. 764–69) and the theory of the Deuteron-omistic History (see pp. 205–8). Both models have traditionally dated Deuteronomy to the latter part of the seventh century BC, contrary to the claims of the book itself, and viewed it as the foundation document for the reforms of King Josiah in 622 (2 Kings 23:1–3). While its function in Josiah's reform is unquestioned, there is a growing opinion that Deuter-onomy contains much material that must be viewed as considerably earlier than the seventh century. As a result, studies on the nature, content, and origin of the earliest form of Deuteronomy abound.

One reason scholars have for not retaining Moses' association with the book is that Deuteronomy teaches that worship should be centralized at one sanctuary (Deut. 12). It is maintained that such centralization could not have been an issue before the temple was built in Jerusalem. Furthermore, there is no historical evidence for true concern about centralization until the time of Josiah, or perhaps a bit earlier, in the reign of Hezekiah. Also, these scholars contend that the warn-ing about kingship (chap. 17) must have originated after the founding of the monarchy.

These objections beg the question to the extent that they deny Moses logically anticipating the issues that would need to be addressed. We see no reason to deny that the book is indeed an accurate record of the words of Moses.[1] It is not necessary that Moses personally committed them to writing, but the nature of the book and its unity suggest that it was written down quite close to the time when the speeches were given. Moses can be affirmed as the dominant, principal, and determinative voice in the book, and he is credited with at least some of the writing. A few sections, such as chapter 34, might be better understood as having been appended at a later time.

The unity of the book is evidenced by the fact that it takes the structure of an ancient Near Eastern vassal treaty. More than fifty such treaties have been discovered in the ancient Near East ranging in time from the mid-third millennium to the mid-first millennium BC. Almost half of them are from the archives of the Hittite Empire in the mid-second millennium.

Studies have shown that each general time period tends to have its own characteristic outlines for setting forth the terms of the treaty. It has been argued that Deuteronomy follows the form of the mid-second millennium treaties as compared with those of other time periods, therefore demonstrating that the book can be dated with confidence to

"Do not move your neighbor's boundary stone set up by your predecessors in the inheritance you receive in the land" (Deut. 19:14). Marked stones were often used to separate one field from another and to indicate what land belonged to whom. This is a royal boundary marker (*kudurru*) from the Kassite period (second half of the second millennium BC).
Marie-Lan Nguyen/Wikimedia Commons, courtesy of Bibliotheque Nationale de France

1. D. Block, "Recovering the Voice of Moses: The Genesis of Deuteronomy," *JETS* 44 (2001): 385–408.

"Go up into the Abarim Range to Mount Nebo in Moab, across from Jericho, and view Canaan, the land I am giving the Israelites as their own possession. There on the mountain that you have climbed you will die and be gathered to your people" (Deut. 39:49–50). From Mount Nebo on the eastern side of the Dead Sea Moses would have been able to see much of the land of Israel before his death.

Todd Bolen/www.BiblePlaces.com

all this there are two statements of God's authority (6:4; 10:17) and numerous warnings against worshiping other gods. The overall message of these chapters is that God should be the Israelites' first priority and final authority. That is what the first commandment is all about.

Commandment 2: Divine Dignity (Deut. 12)

"You shall not make for yourself an idol."

This section concerns how God is to be treated. The significance of the central sanctuary in this context is that it is intended to prevent the Israelites from simply taking over Canaanite sanctuaries and converting them to sanctuaries for Yahweh. Such conversions would make Israel too vulnerable to the influences of pagan religion, while the use of one central sanctuary would preserve uniformity in religious teaching and practice.

The main concern lies in how the ritual aspect of worship takes place. The Lord is not to be treated the way the Canaanites treated their gods, nor worshiped that way (12:4, 30–31). Canaanite ritual was often manipulative and self-serving. In contrast, Israelite ritual was expected to acknowledge the true and unique nature of the Lord as sovereign and autonomous. Anything less jeopardizes his dignity. Ritual must never accommodate pagan standards, and it must not be an end in itself. True worship must give God his proper place and cannot be manipulative or self-serving. Thus, the second commandment is seen to go far beyond a prohibition against the use of idols, though the key distinction it offers is that the presence of Israel's God cannot be mediated by an image.

Commandment 3: Commitment to Deity (Deut. 13:1 – 14:21)

"You shall not misuse the name of the LORD your God."

Commitment to God ought to be reflected in one's conduct. Chapter 13 introduces a hypothetical example of the most basic and blatant offense—enticement to worship other gods. Whether the offense is committed by a highly respected religious authority, a good friend, or a large group of people, the wickedness must be purged. God does not hold guiltless those who do not take him seriously, and neither should the Israelites hold such people guiltless. While seriousness about God requires severe action in blatant cases, it requires a response that is above reproach in the more subtle areas of conduct. So chapter 14 uses the dietary laws as an example. The truly committed person would demonstrate that devotion in diet.

Jack Hazut

Phylacteries of one of the modern Jewish sects. "These commandments that I give you today are to be upon your hearts.... Tie them as symbols on your hands and bind them on your foreheads" (Deut. 6:6, 8).

The Central Sanctuary

The idea of one sanctuary in Israel was symbolically related to the concept of one God. In the ancient Near East different cities had different patron deities with temples constructed in their honor. Therefore, it was proper for Israel, who had just one God, to have just one legitimate temple. However, one could find numerous temples to the same deity in the ancient Near East. But the theology of God's continual special presence in the temple in Jerusalem made it impossible for more than one shrine to be maintained. God's presence could not be represented by idols as it was in other religions, and the rituals had to be performed in God's presence. Centralization was therefore important for reasons of theology as well as for safeguarding orthodox religious practice. It was the failure to accomplish centralization that created many of the religious problems occurring before the exile.

History as Theology

In Israel, history was not viewed as the simple sequence of events evaluated in terms of cause and effect, but it was God in action. History is the evidence of Israel's election—the working out of the details represented in the statement, "I will be your God and you will be my people." History does not flow at random. It was not coincidence or human endeavor that brought Israel out of Egypt after four hundred years and led them to the land promised to Abraham. History is revelation and requires response; that is why it was crucial to the covenant.

The fact that God had acted in history on their behalf served as the clarion call for the Israelites to accept the Lord's benevolent rule. It was insisted (Deut. 4) that the Israelites should learn the lessons of history; this exhortation was repeated in the New Testament concerning the revelation in history of who God is (Rom. 15:4; 1 Cor. 10:1–13). While God's hand may be seen in all of history and lessons can be learned from any segment of world history, the history of Israel is unique as a specially designed vehicle of God's self-revelation.

The Retribution Principle

Conforming to God's expectations is rewarded, and violating God's commands brings punishment. That is how God operates with nations. This also came to be understood as the way God deals with individuals, a concept disclosed in the context of poetry and the wisdom literature. God's expectations of Israel were delineated in the law and recorded as stipulations of the covenant. The blessings of the covenant would be forfeited if its conditions were not met, though this does not mean that the covenant would become entirely null and void. The curses attached to the covenant figured prominently later on in the indictment brought by the classical, preexilic prophets.

Questions for Further Study and Discussion

1. What significance can be attached to Deuteronomy's having a standard treaty format? What does that add to our understanding of the book?
2. How is our understanding of the theological concept of law enhanced by interpreting Deuteronomy as an exposition of the Decalogue?
3. What are the strengths and weaknesses of the theory that Deuteronomy 6–26 expounds the spirit of the Ten Commandments?
4. Is history still revelation? Suggest a contemporary theology of history.
5. Some consider Deuteronomy to contain the most significant theology of the Old Testament. In what ways can this view be supported?

For Further Reading

Brown, Raymond. *The Message of Deuteronomy*. Downers Grove, Ill.. InterVarsity Press, 1993.

Craigie, Peter C. *The Book of Deuteronomy*. Grand Rapids: Eerdmans, 1976.

_____. *The Problem of War in the Old Testament*. Grand Rapids: Eerdmans, 1978. Helpful chapter on the topic of Israel's "holy war" against the Canaanites.

Kaufman, Stephen A. "The Structure of the Deuteronomic Law." *Maarav* 1, 2 (1978–79): 105–58.

Kline, Meredith G. *The Treaty of the Great King*. Grand Rapids: Eerdmans, 1963. Evangelical exposition of the treaty format of Deuteronomy and its implications.

McCarthy, Dennis J. *Treaty and Covenant*. Rome: Biblical Institute Press, 1978. The most thorough study of the formal aspects of treaties of the ancient Near East and the biblical covenant.

McConville, J. G. *Deuteronomy*. Downers Grove, Ill: InterVarsity Press, 2002.

Mendenhall, George E. *Law and Covenant in Israel and the Ancient Near East*. Pittsburgh: Biblical Colloquium, 1955. The first major presentation in English of the comparison between treaty and covenant.

Merrill, Eugene. *Deuteronomy*. Nashville: Broadman & Holman, 1994.

Nicholson, E. W. *Deuteronomy and Tradition*. Philadelphia: Fortress Press, 1967.

Thompson, John A. *Deuteronomy*. Downers Grove, Ill.: InterVarsity Press, 1974. Brief but solid evangelical commentary.

Tigay, Jeffrey. *Deuteronomy*. Philadelphia: Jewish Publication Society, 1996.

Walton, John H. "Deuteronomy: An Exposition of the Spirit of the Law." *Grace Theological Journal* 8 (1987): 213–25.

Weinfeld, Moshe. *Deuteronomy and the Deuteronomic School*. New York: Oxford University Press, 1972.

_____. *Deuteronomy 1–11*. Garden City, N.Y.: Doubleday/Anchor Books, 1991.

Wright, Christopher. *Deuteronomy*. Peabody, Mass.: Hendrickson, 1996.

CHAPTER
9

Numbers 33 contains the itinerary of the Israelites as they traveled from Egypt through the desert until they reached the land of Canaan. Egyptian pharaohs sometimes carved the itineraries of their military campaigns, listing all the places along the way. This is an itinerary of Thutmose III (15th century BC) carved into the walls at Karnak. Frederick J. Mabie

HISTORICAL OVERVIEW OF OLD TESTAMENT TIMES

Chronology

A few words about chronology are necessary to an overview of the history of the Old Testament period. Readers may well wonder how dates can be assigned to all the events and personages of this ancient period of history when records give, at best, a phrase such as "In the third year of King X." There are many sources from Israel and the ancient Near East that give relative chronology (the third year of one king is the first year of another), and from those data a substantial grid of people and events can be constructed. To establish an absolute chronology (the king began his reign in 465 BC), some fixed point must be determined to which the grid of the relative chronology may be attached.

For the ancient Near East, this fixed point is supplied by the Eponym lists of Assyria. The Eponym lists record for each year a designated official who is honored by having the year named after him. In the list his name is given along with one or two of the most significant events of "his" year, usually military campaigns. Fortuitously, in the year of Ishdi-Sagale, governor of Guzana, the list reports that a solar eclipse occurred. Astronomers can calculate when solar eclipses took place, and therefore the year of Ishdi-Sagale can be identified positively as 763 BC. This is the primary anchor for the absolute chronology of the ancient Near East, and it is not contested. As a result, it can be determined that the Eponym lists cover the years 893–666 BC. Since each king of Assyria during this period is (predictably) among those honored, the dates of Assyria can be established for that span of more than two centuries. This is the period of the Neo-Assyrian Empire, so synchronisms of most of the nations of the ancient Near East are made with Assyria for that time. In this way Assyria has become the foundation for the chronology of the ancient Near East.

We should not assume, however, that all chronological problems are thereby solved. Often there are conflicting data with the relative chronology scheme that introduce uncertainties for absolute dating. On other occasions events or people are not related in the textual material to the grid of relative chronology—for instance, the failure of the account of the exodus to name the pharaoh who

Age Palestine as a backdrop and therefore offers general information. Lists of cities in Palestine are also given in the Egyptian execration texts. Most are otherwise unknown, though Jerusalem and Shechem are mentioned. As the period progresses there is more and more contact with Egypt and extensive caravan travel between Egypt and Palestine.

Egypt to the Exodus

Roughly concurrent to the Early Dynastic Period in Mesopotamia was the formative Old Kingdom in Egypt that permanently shaped Egypt both politically and culturally. This was the age of the great pyramids. In the Sixth Dynasty, contemporary with the dynasty of Akkad in Mesopotamia, disintegration became evident. From the mid-twenty-second century until about 2000 BC, Egypt was plunged into a dark period known as the First Intermediate Period, which was characterized by disunity and, at times, practical anarchy. Order was finally restored when Mentuhotep reunited Egypt, and Amenemhet I founded

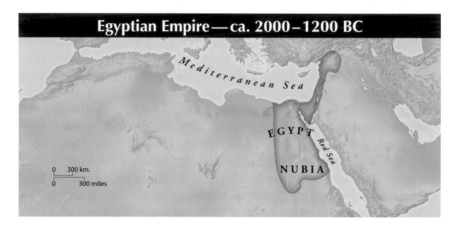

the Twelfth Dynasty, beginning a period of more than two centuries of prosperous growth and development.

The Twelfth Dynasty developed extensive trade relations with Syro-Palestine and is the most likely period for initial contacts between Egypt and the Hebrew patriarchs. By the most conservative estimates, Sesostris III would have been the pharaoh who elevated Joseph to his high administrative post. Others would be more inclined to place the emigration of the Israelites to Egypt during the time of the Hyksos. The Hyksos were Semitic peoples who had begun moving into Egypt (particularly the delta region) as early as the First Intermediate Period. As the Thirteenth Dynasty ushered in a gradual decline, the reins of power eventually fell to the Hyksos (whether by conquest, coup, or consent is still indeterminable), who then controlled Egypt from about the middle of the eighteenth century to the middle of the sixteenth century. It was during this time that the Israelites began to prosper and multiply in the delta region, waiting for the covenant promises to be fulfilled.

After nearly two centuries of foreign domination at the hands of the Hyksos, the Egyptians finally set about restoring their nation to their

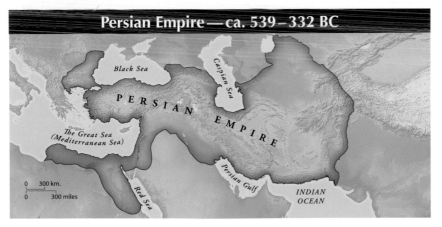

own control. In an explosion of nationalistic fervor, the Hyksos were driven from the land and the Eighteenth Dynasty was established under the Egyptian pharaoh Ahmose. It was perhaps in a reaction against foreigners that the Israelites were reduced to slavery by the newly established regime. It should be noticed that the Egyptians did not fear the military might of the Israelites but rather were afraid that the Israelites would join forces with the enemy and be driven out (Exod. 1:10). The Egyptians did not want the Israelites to leave, perhaps having become economically dependent on them in some way (see Gen. 47:6).

In the Eighteenth and Nineteenth dynasties Egypt reached the height of its political power, though there were periods of decline. Thutmose III, in the first half of the fifteenth century, extended Egypt's territorial control through Palestine and north as far as Qadesh on the Orontes in Syria. In the south, Egypt pushed up the Nile to include both upper and lower Nubia among its conquests. Thutmose III's son and successor, Amenhotep II, is identified as the pharaoh of the exodus by those favoring a fifteenth-century date for this event (see chapter 5 for a discussion of the dating of the exodus).

By the close of the fifteenth century, Egypt had reached the limits of its expansion and had begun a decline fostered by military stagnation and an increased standard of living that reduced concern for maintaining foreign interests. The results of this decline are amply documented in the Amarna archives from the fourteenth century BC. The central figure of this period and the one blamed for many of Egypt's troubles was the controversial pharaoh Akhenaten. In an attempt to break the power of the priesthood of Amon-Re, Akhenaten deserted the capital at Thebes, where the cult of Amon-Re was centered, and constructed a new capital city about two hundred miles north at modern el-Amarna (Akhetaten), dedicated to the god Aten (the god of the sun disk). This political strategy was only part of a much larger attempt to establish an almost monotheistic worship of Aten that engulfed art, literature, and nearly every other aspect of Egyptian culture for almost half a century.

The correspondence from the Amarna archives portrays an Egypt that has lost its international respect and is no longer capable of maintaining order among the petty city-states of Palestine, let alone defending its interests in Syria against the Hittites or honoring its treaty with the Mitannian Empire in its death throes in western Mesopotamia. Some holding to a fifteenth-century date for the exodus contend that the Israelites were making a successful incursion into Canaan at this time, taking advantage of Egyptian neglect of the area. But it is unlikely that the "Ḥabiru" people mentioned as troubling the kings of Palestine should be equated with the "Hebrews." This does not rule out the possibility that the Israelites were among those peoples designated as Habiru who motivated the kings of Canaan to plead with the pharaoh to send auxiliary troops, but usage of the term *Ḫabiru* (or *Ḫapiru*) shows it cannot be restricted to an identification of the Israelites.

As the thirteenth century began, Egyptian reputation was restored by the Nineteenth Dynasty, primarily by Ramesses II (the Great). Most who maintain that the exodus occurred in the thirteenth century would view this pharaoh as the one who witnessed the mighty hand of God in delivering the Israelites from Egypt.

The Late Bronze Age (1500–1200 BC)

While Egypt was experiencing the decline of the Eighteenth Dynasty and the Amarna Age, the Late Bronze Age began in Syro-Palestine. During this period the Syro-Palestine corridor had a significant role to play. Because this was an age of international trade, control of the trade routes became a great economic advantage. The overland trade routes from Egypt to Anatolia (Asia Minor) and Mesopotamia all passed through Syro-Palestine, and the growing sea trade on the Mediterranean was dependent on the hospitable ports of the Syrian coast (Byblos, Tyre, Sidon, and Ugarit in particular). As a result, each of the military powers desired to expand their control into Syro-Palestine, and many of the great battles of this era took place in Syro-Palestine. According to the earlier chronology, this was the period of the judges of Israel, and the constant burden of foreign oppression described in the book of Judges would fit the profile of this period, though the great political powers are not listed among the oppressors of Israel.

This small portion of a large relief depicts Rameses III's great battle against the Sea Peoples (some of whom were the Philistines). The relief is from the temple of Rameses III at Medinet Habu, across the Nile from Thebes, and dates from the early 12th century BC.

Vying with Egypt for control of Syria at the beginning of this period was the Hurrian kingdom of Mitanni, located along the upper Tigris and Euphrates in northern Mesopotamia, the area the Bible refers to as Aram-Naharaim (Judg. 3:8–10). It was the influence of the Mitannian king Shaustatar that prevented Egypt's Thutmose III from extending his control north of Qadesh. Mitanni was soon overshadowed, however, by the emergence of the Hittites in Anatolia, who were to become the dominant political force in the Near East for the next two and a half centuries. As both Egypt and Mitanni reached periods of decline in the latter part of the fifteenth century, they set aside their differences and made an alliance to protect their mutual interests in Syria from the upstart Hittites, but to no avail.

The fourteenth century brought expansion of Hittite influence into Syria under the guidance of Shuppiluliuma I, at the expense of the dormant Egyptians and the floundering Hurrians. With the reestablishment of a strong Assyrian state in 1362, Mitanni came under pressure from both east and west, finally breaking apart about 1350. It is possible that the first oppressors of Israel in the judges period were peoples who had been displaced from Mitanni (Judg. 3:7–11).[3] The Assyrians did not, however, attempt to expand to the west, preferring to exert their influence on Urartu to the north and Babylon to the south. Meanwhile, the cities of Syria had gradually come under the control of the Hittites.

The thirteenth century brought the resurgence of Egypt as the Nineteenth Dynasty began to reverse the devastating policies that had characterized the Amarna period. The capital was moved to the delta region in the north, and control over Palestine was exerted more forcefully. In the mid-thirteenth century Ramesses the Great began to challenge the Hittite control of Syria. Both Egyptian and Hittite records preserve accounts of the famous battle of Qadesh, in which Ramesses, though surprised by the Hittite forces, managed to avoid humiliation. The resulting occupation of territory suggests that the Hittites retained control of Amurru and Qadesh and perhaps even made gains to the south. Eventually a treaty was made between Hattushili III (Hittites) and Ramesses II, probably motivated by renewed interest in Syria on the part of the Assyrian king Shalmaneser I.

The resulting picture of the Late Bronze Age is an ever-shifting stalemate between major political powers, with Syria and, to a lesser extent, Canaan caught in the middle. If the Israelites were in Canaan during this time, they would have been largely unaffected by the international events. Canaan was too far south and too insignificant (compared with Syria) for the northern powers to be interested. The troop movements of the Egyptians during the thirteenth century would have had little effect, for the Israelites were largely settled in the hill country away

3. Cushan-Rishathaim could represent a Hebrew attempt at rendering a Hurrian name such as Kuzzarishti. Although this name is not found among known Hurrian names, it is made up of elements frequently attested in Hurrian names.

from the major routes of travel. But the balance of power was about to undergo a dramatic change.

Iron Age I (1200–1000 BC)

The beginning of the Iron Age brought the fall of the Hittite Empire, the destruction of many of the major port cities of Syria including Ugarit, Tyre, and Sidon as well as fortified cities such as Megiddo and Ashkelon, a lull in Assyrian power, and substantial decline in Egyptian influence. Much of this political upheaval is blamed on the invasion by a coalition of tribes called the Sea Peoples who appear to have come from the Aegean region by ship as part of a massive population movement. It is difficult to ascertain what role they had in the destruction of fortified cities and the fall of the Hittite Empire, but records show they were repelled by the Egyptians after massive sea battles exacted heavy casualties. One of the Sea People tribes, the Philistines, settled on the southwest coast of Canaan. It is from them that the name Palestine is derived.

This period brought the technological development of iron tools and weapons, knowledge of which helped establish Philistine supremacy over Israel (see 1 Sam. 13:19–23).

The resulting situation in the Near East was that international politics was virtually eliminated. With no major powers left to exert control, relatively minor skirmishes in localized areas replaced the massive military campaigns of empires. The resulting power vacuum allowed for the development of empire building on a smaller scale such as that most evident in tenth-century Israel.

The Empire of David and Solomon (1000–900 BC)

Iron Age II extends from 1000 to 586 BC, but it is preferable to cover this period of history in shorter segments. Toward the end of the Judges period the Philistines had been contained by the activities of Samson, though they were in control of Judah (Judg. 15:11). During the time of Samuel, they overran the hill country and destroyed Shiloh (1 Sam. 4) but were later driven back (1 Sam. 7). Saul was successful in maintaining the equilibrium throughout most of his reign, but after the battle of Mount Gilboa (in which Saul was killed), the Philistines occupied most of the midsection of Canaan.

When David came to the throne, one of his first tasks was to regain control of Israelite territory. This was accomplished from his newly conquered, fortified base in Jerusalem. After the Philistines were subdued, David's military success continued with the eventual subjugation of most of Syro-Palestine. Some countries were annexed, with military

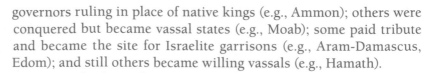

governors ruling in place of native kings (e.g., Ammon); others were conquered but became vassal states (e.g., Moab); some paid tribute and became the site for Israelite garrisons (e.g., Aram-Damascus, Edom); and still others became willing vassals (e.g., Hamath).

As a result of David's successes, Solomon inherited an empire that stretched from the elbow of the Euphrates in the north to the borders of Egypt in the south. Even Egypt entered into a marriage alliance with him (the pharaoh's daughter joined Solomon's harem) as he built a navy and extended his trade to the far reaches of the Mediterranean and south along the full length of the Red Sea. Although his economic success was great, Solomon's military capability did not match his father's. Though he fortified strategic cities such as Megiddo, Hazor, and Gezer and built up his cavalry and chariotry, very little military success is recorded for Solomon in the Old Testament (2 Chron. 8:3–6). Though his wisdom was widely recognized and the prosperity of his realm unparalleled, the empire declined under his guardianship and was on the verge of collapse when his son Rehoboam took the throne. Military neglect and a heavy tax burden on the people appear to have been Solomon's most obvious political faults, and the authors of Kings and Chronicles likewise point out his spiritual failures.

Internal unrest and unquenched rebellion among the vassals left Rehoboam with little more than the capital city and the wilderness that lay to the south. The kingdom deteriorated even more a few years later when Shishak (known as Sheshonq I in Egyptian records), the pharaoh of Egypt, raided Judah, sacking many of the fortified cities and receiving heavy tribute in return for bypassing Jerusalem.

The Rise of the Aramaeans (950–800 BC)

Even as one of Solomon's officials, Jeroboam, gained control over the northern kingdom of Israel, the reins of political power in the region fell into the hands of the Aramaean states in the region of Syria. The Aramaeans as a people are first mentioned as living along the upper Euphrates toward the end of the Late Bronze Age. In the wake of the incursion of the Sea Peoples, they began to move into Syria. After gaining independence from Israel in the later years of Solomon, Damascus became the center of a new Aramaean state that had achieved unification by the mid-ninth century. For much of the ninth century Aram was the major political power in the west. It led the western states in coalitions against the developing Assyrian threat and served as a buffer between the Assyrians and Israel for much of the time. There were also

The Syrian king Hazael attacked Israel during the reigns of Joram, Jehu, and Jehoahaz (2 Kings 8:28; 10:32; 13:22) and received tribute from Jehoash, king of Judah, in order to prevent attack (2 Kings 12:17–18). This ivory plaque depicts King Hazael framed by lotus flowers (8th century BC).

numerous battles between the Aramaeans and the northern kingdom of Israel, with Aram maintaining a decisive edge. As the century drew to a close, Hazael, the king of Aram, had successfully overrun and occupied most of Israel.

The First Assyrian Threat and the Resurgence of Israel (850–750 BC)

Nearly concurrent with the rise of the Aramaeans came the resurgence of Assyrian imperialism. This began in the reign of Ashurnasirpal II, who undertook a number of annual campaigns along the upper Euphrates, terrorizing the inhabitants through a policy of ruthless intimidation. This was expanded into a more logical military strategy by his successor, Shalmaneser III, who concentrated on gaining control of the upper Euphrates. Then in 853 Shalmaneser turned his attention to western expansion and launched a campaign into Aram. He was met at Qarqar on the Orontes by a coalition of western states joined by Ben-Hadad of Aram and Ahab, king of Israel. Though Shalmaneser claimed victory, evidence suggests that the coalition had successfully blocked his entry into the west.

During the two centuries of their existence as separate states (ca. 930–720), Israel and Judah had sporadic skirmishes as well as periods of alliance. In the northern kingdom, Israel, Jeroboam was occupied with an enormous task of reorganization to achieve complete autonomy

Pharaoh Shishak (Sheshonq) invaded Israel soon after the division of the kingdom (about 925 BC). On this wall engraving at Karnak, he lists many of the cities that he claims to have conquered.

from Jerusalem. He attempted to portray himself as a reformer rather than as an innovator, but in so doing enraged those loyal to the temple in Jerusalem and brought a condemnation on his kingdom that is traced methodically through the books of Kings. Jeroboam's son succeeded him but was assassinated after only two years. Thus began the pattern of frequent change in dynasties in the northern kingdom.

The next dynasty in the north was established by Baasha, who had wiped out Jeroboam's line. It was at this time that the escalation of tensions between Israel and Judah brought the Aramaeans into Israel. His line likewise did not last, but was replaced by the politically successful house of Omri. During the Omride ascendancy the capital of the northern kingdom was moved to Samaria. It was a period of peaceful relations and even included intermarriage with the Davidic line from Jerusalem. Omri's son Ahab was married in political alliance to the Tyrian princess Jezebel. Though this was a beneficial political arrangement, it proved disastrous for Israel, because Jezebel was intent on imposing the worship of her native deity Baal Melqart on the Israelite population. This blatant violation of the covenant was vigorously opposed by the prophet Elijah and led eventually to a public outcry and conservative backlash that brought down the Omride line.

The house of Jehu undertook a bloody purge and also reversed foreign policy. Jehu paid tribute to Shalmaneser III and became a cooperative Assyrian vassal. As Assyrian influence in the west declined toward the end of the century, Jehu's dynasty again became embroiled in skirmishes with the Aramaeans, becoming an occupied Aramaean state by the end of the century.

Judah enjoyed a bit more stability if only because the same dynasty remained in power from the tenth to the sixth century. The line of David, however, failed to maintain an exemplary spiritual posture and remained isolated from international politics. In the first half of the ninth century Asa and his son, Jehoshaphat, attempted some spiritual reform, but much of that was undone by Jehoshaphat's alliance with the house of Ahab, whereby he imported Baalism under Jezebel's influence. Subsequently, when Jehu obliterated the house of Omri in the north, Judah lost a king as well (Jehoshaphat's grandson, Ahaziah), and the Davidic line came within an heir of being wiped out. The infant Joash was rescued and returned to the throne six years later.

Judah was not involved in the conflicts with either the Aramaeans or the Assyrians. The trade routes skirted their country, which was therefore of little value to foreign powers.

The early eighth century witnessed the decline of both Assyria and Aram. Assyria was occupied with internal difficulties and pressure from Urartu. Jeroboam II, the most successful king of Jehu's dynasty, recovered Israelite territory from the Aramaeans and made vassals of

Hamath and Damascus. Meanwhile, in the south, Azariah (Uzziah) collected tribute from the Ammonites and was successful against the Philistines and Arabians. Between Jeroboam II and Azariah, the territorial control nearly equaled that of David. This was a prosperous time for Israel and Judah, but military success led to decadence and social and spiritual decay. It was this decline that set the stage for the development of classical prophecy, for although Israel and Judah were autonomous and trouble-free, a major crisis lay just over the horizon.

The Neo-Assyrian Empire (745–630 BC)

After a lapse of half a century, the Assyrian Empire returned much stronger than before under the capable leadership of Tiglath-Pileser III in 745. This was to become the first "world class" empire known to history and the first of a line of empires that culminated in the Roman Empire. First on the Assyrian king's agenda was to consolidate dominion of Syria, which had come under the influence of Urartu, and to regain control of the trade routes. Over his first eight to ten years the king accomplished this goal and established a strong military presence in Syria. As part of this process he collected tribute from Menahem, the king of Israel.

Tiglath-Pileser III became the first king of the Neo-Assyrian Empire in about 745 BC.

Marie-Lan Nguyen/Wikimedia Commons, courtesy of the Louvre

While Tiglath-Pileser was pursuing this agenda, however, Rezin, king in Damascus, had his own plan. He had sponsored an upstart, Pekah, from Israel and helped him secure the throne, and together they planned to do the same sort of thing in Judah. Ahaz, the Judaean king, though encouraged by the prophet Isaiah to trust the Lord for deliverance from this threat, chose to summon Tiglath-Pileser to deal with the co-conspirators. The result was the second western campaign in the years 734–732. Pekah was replaced on the throne of Israel by Hoshea, and all but the environs of Samaria were annexed as part of the Assyrian state. Rezin was killed and Damascus destroyed. In the process Ahaz became an Assyrian vassal.

Tiglath-Pileser was succeeded to the throne by Shalmaneser V, who reigned for only about five years. Very little is known of him, but most significantly, it was during his reign that Hoshea of Israel rebelled against Assyria. Shalmaneser's campaign to the west began a three-year siege of Samaria. Upon its fall, the survivors were deported, the city destroyed, and the northern kingdom of Israel annexed entirely to the Assyrian Empire in 722.

When Sargon II came to the throne, the Assyrian Empire was well established. Most of Sargon's attention was focused on Urartu and Elam, although there were three major western campaigns. Though Hezekiah of Judah was anti-Assyrian, there was little direct action against Judah in these campaigns. That was to change, however, when Sargon's son, Sennacherib, came to the throne in 704.

During the reign of Sargon, Babylon had declared its independence under the leadership of Merodach-baladan. For twelve years Sargon had been unable to deal with this rebel; Merodach-baladan was finally driven from the throne but escaped. The wily Babylonian had not been idle in the meantime, and when Sennacherib came to power, Merodach-baladan ascended the throne in Babylon and enjoyed the support of concurrent rebellions against Assyria throughout the empire, including one by Hezekiah of Judah. Sennacherib, however, had learned a lesson from his father and went immediately to the source of the trouble. Merodach-baladan became the target of a strategic campaign that quickly subdued Babylon.

Having quenched the uprising in the south, Sennacherib undertook a campaign against the western coalition in 701. He came south along the Phoenician coast and collected tribute from Sidon to Acco. After seizing some cities on the coastal plain, he proceeded down into Philistine territory to Ekron. Having cut off the other allies, he was then ready to move against Judah, which was cut off from any potential help. Hezekiah paid tribute at this point, but to no avail. Then, when all seemed lost, Hezekiah trusted the Lord for deliverance and the Assyrian army was mysteriously slaughtered during the night. Sennacherib's account does not report the outcome of the siege.

Hezekiah was succeeded by his son, Manasseh, who adopted a pro-Assyrian position. His long reign spanning the first half of the seventh century came at the height of Assyrian strength and territorial control. Sennacherib's son, Esarhaddon, extended the empire to Egypt and successfully subjugated the north, but it was left to Esarhaddon's son, Ashurbanipal, to capture Thebes in 663. This was the pinnacle of the Assyrian Empire's power, but the cracks of deterioration were already becoming evident.

Empires in Transition (650 – 600 BC)

Ashurbanipal had inherited an empire at its peak, but decline began in the 650s as Psammetichus gradually cleared the Assyrians out of Egypt. About this time, also, there was civil war in Babylon, led by Ashurbanipal's brother with the support of the Elamites and the Chaldeans. Though this attempt was unsuccessful, the Assyrian king continued to be worn down by revolts. The last several years of his reign are very confused, and it appears that his son assumed kingship before Ashurbanipal died. Shortly after the death of Ashurbanipal in 627, the Babylonians successfully achieved their independence, and the days of Assyrian strength were gone.

In Judah, the decline of Assyria was good news to Josiah, who had ascended the throne at the age of eight, just two years after the death of his grandfather, Manasseh. The reform that Josiah undertook in 628 and furthered in 622 took full advantage of the lack of Assyrian presence. At the same time, however, Egypt was strengthening its position in Palestine. Egypt attempted simultaneously to maintain friendly relations with Assyria and to benefit from Assyria's inability to maintain control of the west. As a result, by the 630s the major trade route was controlled by Egypt, and Egypt had a greater presence in Palestine than did Assyria.

The Neo-Babylonian Empire (600–550 BC)

When the Babylonians declared independence from the Assyrians in 626, it was the Chaldean Nabopolassar who claimed the throne. For the next decade he successfully maintained control of Babylon but was unable to extend his rule any farther into Assyrian territory. It was clear that Assyria was losing its grasp on the empire, however, and Nabopolassar was not the only one scrambling to take over Assyrian interests. To the east, Cyaxares the Mede was also moving against major Assyrian strongholds. In 614 one of those, the city of Assur, fell to the Medes, and outside the ruins of the city the late-arriving Nabopolassar and the victorious Cyaxares made a pact to join their forces against the floundering Assyrians. Their joint armies were able to bring down the mighty capital of Nineveh just two years later, in 612 BC. The beleaguered Assyrian government retreated west and regrouped with its headquarters in Haran.

Sinsharishkun had died in the fall of Nineveh, so Ashuruballit assumed the throne, destined to become Assyria's last king. In 610 Haran capitulated, and the Assyrians were forced to retreat another fifty miles west to Carchemish on the west bank of the upper reaches of the Euphrates, just inside modern-day Turkey. Here, though reinforced by the Egyptians under Pharaoh Necho, the Assyrian Empire ended when Nebuchadrezzar,[4] crown prince of Babylon and commander-in-chief of the armies, stormed Carchemish and scattered what was left of the Assyrians, pursuing them as far south as Hamath and claiming Syria for the Babylonian realm. That very year Nabopolassar died, and Nebuchadrezzar rushed back to Babylon, where he assumed the throne of what had now become the Neo-Babylonian Empire.

Nebuchadrezzar was one of the most successful kings known to history. He ruled from 605 to 562 and distinguished himself in both

4. The forms "Nebuchadrezzar" and "Nebuchadnezzar" both appear in the Hebrew Scriptures, but on the basis of the Akkadian language the authors prefer the form with r.

military matters and domestic undertakings, foremost of which was the beautification of the city of Babylon. The Assyrian Empire had been divided between the Babylonians and their allies, the Medes. The Babylonians received the Tigris and Euphrates basins from a line just east of the Tigris (approximating the boundary between the modern states of Iraq and Iran) and all of the western states extending as far north as the southeast section of Asia Minor. The Medes ruled the eastern regions (modern-day Iran), Urartu (between the Black and Caspian seas), and the eastern section of Asia Minor. Eventually Nebuchadrezzar was able to extend his domain to include Egypt (568).

The establishment of the Neo-Babylonian Empire had far-reaching effects on Judah. Apparently hoping to contribute to the downfall of Assyria, Josiah attempted to stop the advance of the Egyptian armies hurrying to provide assistance to Ashuruballit at Carchemish. This proved to be a fatal decision, because Josiah, who had accomplished more reform than any of his Davidic predecessors, was killed in the losing effort. He was succeeded to the throne in turn by three sons and a grandson. Jehoahaz, the first son, was taken into exile in Egypt after serving only three months; this occurred upon Necho's return from Syria in 609. Jehoiakim, a second son, was placed on the throne instead. Once Nebuchadrezzar had defeated the Assyrian-Egyptian coalition and claimed control of Syro-Palestine, Jehoiakim became a Babylonian vassal; this lasted until he rebelled in 598. By the time Nebuchadrezzar came west, Jehoiakim had died and his son, Jehoiachin, was on the throne. The city of Jerusalem was set under siege and surrendered on March 16, 597. Jehoiachin was taken to exile in Babylon along with many of the people, including the prophet Ezekiel. Nebuchadrezzar set Zedekiah, Josiah's third son, on the throne.

Almost from the start, Zedekiah became involved in seditious schemes against the Babylonians, and finally, with the promise of Egyptian support, he rebelled in 589. The Babylonian army arrived in 588 and blockaded Jerusalem to prevent its stockpiling supplies while other fortified cities were defeated. That summer the siege was lifted briefly, as the Babylonians were diverted to meet an Egyptian force, and then was reinstated. By the following summer, July 587, the walls were breached and Jerusalem was sacked, the temple burned, and the people deported to Babylon.

The Neo-Babylonian Empire did not long survive the death of Nebuchadrezzar. He was succeeded by four relatively obscure and apparently incompetent kings, and one could say the handwriting was on the wall long before that fateful feast of Belshazzar on the eve of the fall of Babylon the Great. In fact, Cyrus had begun moving to consolidate his power within five years of the death of Nebuchadrezzar.

The Medo-Persian Empire (550–450 BC)

When the Babylonian king Nabonidus negated his treaty with the Medes and realigned himself with Cyrus and the Persians in 556, it gave Cyrus the opportunity he had been waiting for to move against the Medes. He defeated them in 550 and became the ruler of the new Medo-Persian Empire. Over the next decade he was able to defeat the Lydians, a major political force in western Anatolia, and extend his control in the east as far as the Indus valley. He was now poised to move against Babylon. Since numerous segments of the population had good reason to be disgruntled with the policies and prospects of Nabonidus, Cyrus was reportedly welcomed into Babylon (October 16, 539 BC) as deliverer rather than having to resort to a long siege.

Cyrus was anxious to be recognized as a benevolent liberator rather than as a conquering tyrant, and he set policies toward that end. These policies included granting permits for many of the peoples deported by the Babylonians to return to their homelands and rebuild their temples. The Israelites were among them. Nevertheless, such permission assumed loyalty to the Medo-Persian crown and acceptance of its sovereignty; so although Israel was restored to the land, she was still without a king.

Cambyses, the son of Cyrus, was able to add Egypt to the empire in 526, but he died in an unfortunate accident on the return journey. (According to Herodotus, Cambyses was wounded by his own sword as he attempted to mount his horse and died of the resulting infection.) After some struggle, the throne was secured by Darius the Great, who, because of the difficulties surrounding the succession, was now faced with revolts in every quarter of the empire. By 519, however, he was able to put down the revolts and secure his rule.

By the beginning of the fifth century, the Persians were coming into contact with the Athenians because of some rebellions against Darius in the western cities of Anatolia. This led Darius eventually to attempt an invasion of Greece, which failed miserably when his army was driven into the sea at the Battle of Marathon (490). When Darius died in 486, it was left to his son, Xerxes, to renew the attempt. Disaster followed disaster, however, as the Persians were defeated at Thermopylae and Salamis in Greece and continued to suffer losses as they retreated through Anatolia.

Xerxes was assassinated, and he was succeeded by his son, Artaxerxes I, who officially sponsored the rebuilding of the walls of Jerusalem at the request of his Jewish cupbearer, Nehemiah. War with the Greeks dragged on, yet the Persian Empire remained in power for another century until the lightning conquest by the young warrior Alexander the Great in 331.

Questions for Further Study and Discussion

1. Why is chronology important to the study of the Old Testament?
2. What impact did the Late Bronze Age have on the social, cultural, and religious history of the Hebrews?
3. What did technological development during the Iron Age mean for Hebrew history?
4. How do we account for the rise of the Israelite monarchy to empire status under David and Solomon?
5. What is the relationship between the Hebrew prophetic movement and the rise of empire nations in Mesopotamia in the first millennium BC?
6. How was Persian military and political policy different from that of Assyria and Babylonia? What did this mean for the Hebrews?
7. How does Old Testament history contribute to the "fullness of time" (Gal. 4:4 NRSV) as understood by the apostle Paul?
8. What did Old Testament history contribute to the understanding of Messiah during the intertestamental period?

For Further Reading

The Cambridge Ancient History Series. 3rd ed. Vols. 1–3. The standard, exhaustive reference work on the history of the ancient Near East.

The Cambridge History of Iran. 4 vols. Cambridge: Cambridge University Press, 1983, 1985. Vols. 2–3.

The Cambridge History of Judaism. D. W. Davies and Louis Finkelstein, eds. Cambridge: Cambridge University Press, 1984. Vol. 1. Introduction: The Persian Period.

Coogan, Michael D. *Oxford History of the Biblical World.* New York: Oxford, 1998.

Hayes, John, and J. Maxwell Miller. *Israelite and Judaean History.* Philadelphia: Westminster, 1977. An exploration by a number of contributors of the current state of scholarship on the various periods of Israelite history.

Hoerth, Alfred J., Gerald Mattingly, and Edwin Yamauchi, eds. *Peoples of the Old Testament World.* Grand Rapids: Baker, 1994.

Kuhrt, Amélie. *The Ancient Near East.* 2 vols. London: Routledge, 1995.

Merrill, Eugene. *Kingdom of Priests.* Grand Rapids: Baker, 1987.

Miller, J. Maxwell, and John Hayes. *A History of Ancient Israel and Judah.* Philadelphia: Westminster, 1986. Probably the most thorough presentation of Israelite history against the background of the ancient Near East, though evangelicals will find it overly reconstructive.

Nemet-Nejat, Karen Rhea. *Daily Life in Ancient Mesopotamia.* Westport, Conn.: Greenwood, 1998.

Oates, Joan. *Babylon.* London: Thames & Hudson, 1979.

Pitard, Wayne. *Ancient Damascus.* Winona Lake, Ind.: Eisenbrauns, 1987.

Provan, Iain, V. Philips Long, and Tremper Longman. *Biblical History of Israel.* Louisville: Westminster John Knox, 2003.

Saggs, H. W. F. *The Greatness That Was Babylon.* New York: Mentor, 1962.

_____. *The Might That Was Assyria.* London: Sidgwick & Jackson, 1984. Like the preceding title, an excellent introduction to its subject.

Sasson, Jack. *Civilizations of the Ancient Near East.* New York: Simon and Schuster, 1995.

Snell, Daniel C. *Life in the Ancient Near East.* New Haven: Yale University Press, 1997.

Thiele, Edwin R. *The Mysterious Numbers of the Hebrew Kings.* Rev. ed. Grand Rapids: Zondervan, 1983.

Van de Mieroop, Marc. *A History of the Ancient Near East, ca. 3000–323 BC.* London: Blackwell, 2004.

Van Der Woude, A. S. *The World of the Bible.* Grand Rapids: Eerdmans, 1986. An excellent introduction to geography, history, archaeology, and manuscripts.

Wiseman, Donald J. *Peoples of Old Testament Times.* Oxford: Clarendon, 1973.

Yamauchi, Edwin M. *Persia and the Bible.* Grand Rapids: Baker, 1989.

PART III
THE HISTORICAL BOOKS

CHAPTER 10

Shalmaneser III ruled Assyria in the middle part of the 9th century BC. and fought a western coalition of nations, including Israel. This stele records his victories and farther down shows Jehu, king of Israel, submitting to the Assyrian monarch and paying tribute.

INTRODUCTION TO THE HISTORICAL BOOKS

The English arrangement of the historical books of the Old Testament includes Joshua, Judges, Ruth, 1 and 2 Samuel, 1 and 2 Kings, 1 and 2 Chronicles, Ezra, Nehemiah, and Esther. In the Hebrew arrangement, Joshua, Judges, and the books of Samuel and Kings constitute a group referred to as "the Former Prophets." Labeling them as prophetic suggests that these books are primarily theological in nature rather than annalistic. The prophets play a prominent role in most of these books; but more important, the books share a prophetic view of history in which cause and effect are tied to the blessings and curses of the covenant.

The remainder of the books—Ruth, Chronicles, Ezra, Nehemiah, and Esther—form part of the section of the Hebrew canon called "the Writings."

The Deuteronomistic History

Theory

In the first half of the twentieth century it was common for source critics to subject the books of Joshua–Kings to the same kind of analysis used on the Pentateuch, identifying identical sources (i.e., Jahwist, Elohist, Deuteronomist, Priestly; see Appendix B). At the same time, a growing number of scholars were denying the presence of the Pentateuchal sources in the early historical books, suggesting instead that they were made up of small, originally independent literary units woven together by an editor or series of editors. The latter view was adopted and defended in detail in 1943 by Martin Noth, who was a longtime professor of Old Testament at the University of Bonn.

The theory presented by Noth maintained that Deuteronomy–2 Kings was a unified work written substantially during the exilic period. Noth called this "the Deuteronomistic History" because he believed it was designed to show how the theology of Deuteronomy was reflected in the history of Israel. This theory still provides the framework for most of the current research on the historical books.

The earliest history of the world is found in lists such as this one of kings who ruled in southern Mesopotamia before the flood. These lists are distinguished by the great lengths of reign attributed to the kings (as high as 43,200 years).

The Schoyen Collection
MS 2855, Oslo and London

Composition

Despite the wide acceptance of the concept of a Deuteronomistic History comprising Deuteronomy – 2 Kings, a number of different theories have arisen as to when and how the work came together. The most common view today is that the initial editing of the work took place as early as the time of Hezekiah at the end of the eighth century, but that the first edition was largely the product of the time of Josiah's reform toward the end of the seventh century. A subsequent edition was considered to have been compiled with certain sections added during the exile, with the work being virtually complete by about 550 BC. Variations in theories of composition focus largely on the questions of date and the number of editions.

Characteristics

This so-called Deuteronomistic History shares with the book of Deuteronomy a common perspective on history and theology. Israel's history is viewed in terms of their loyalty to the covenant. Obedience to the law and faith in the Lord bring the blessings and prosperity of the covenant (Deut. 28), while disobedience and apostasy bring the curses listed there. Dependence on formulaic phrases (e.g., "the Israelites did evil in the eyes of the LORD" in Judges; "walked in the ways of Jeroboam" as the common indictment of the northern kings in the books of Kings) and the rhetorical use of speeches to recapitulate at important junctures (cf. Deut. 4; Josh. 23; Judg. 2:11 – 23; 1 Sam. 12; 2 Sam. 7; 1 Kings 8; 2 Kings 17:7 – 23) are among the stylistic similarities.

Message

The message of the Deuteronomist is brought out by repetition. Recurring formulas identify the author's primary concerns. For example, failure to depart from the sins of Jeroboam is the condemnation of each of the kings of the northern kingdom — even Zimri, who reigned for only seven turbulent days and would have found it difficult to initiate a programmatic reform during that time had he been so inclined. For the kings of the Davidic dynasty in Judah, the primary standard of evaluation was how they measured up to David for faithfulness and how successful they were in carrying out reform toward centralized worship in Jerusalem and extermination of apostasy. These are typically considered the themes of the preexilic edition of the book assigned to the time of Josiah.

The so-called exilic edition (that is, produced during the Babylonian exile) is thought to be more concerned to develop the theme of sin and punishment. In pursuit of the answer to the exiles' question "Where did things go wrong?" the suggestion is made that things went wrong right from the start and that the pattern continued virtually unabated throughout the long history of the monarchy. The constant presence of the prophetic word to kings during this period confirmed that the Lord gave plenty of warning and ample opportunity to respond. God's patience and faithfulness to the covenant were totally vindicated. It can be seen, then, that the message of these books was tied closely to the covenant.

Though it is common to hear sermons built on the role models (good or bad) offered by the various people who cross these pages, it should be evident that God is the main character. This is not revelation of Joshua, Samson, David, Elijah, or Josiah. It is revelation of God.

Critique

While many commendable insights have resulted from this Deuteronomistic approach over the years, some aspects warrant reconsideration. There should be no objection to the fact that Joshua – 2 Kings shares the perspective of Deuteronomy as its foundation. However, the many scholars who view Deuteronomy as compiled to promote the reform of Josiah are thereby forced to date the Deuteronomistic History no earlier than that.

Scholars with more conservative presuppositions, by contrast, have not on the whole been convinced of this late date of Deuteronomy. They are inclined to accept the book as largely the work of Moses, in accordance with the book's own claim. The result is that there are far fewer restrictions concerning the compilation date of the historical material. The text of Scripture does not designate a single author for these historical books, so we are not compelled to support a single-authorship model. The books of Kings mention sources used in the writing process, so it seems likely that editorial activity was involved. This does not require abandoning a conservative view of inspiration, for editors can be inspired as well as authors.

Another important observation is that while the books included in the Deuteronomistic History share a common perspective, it must also be recognized that each book has a distinctive literary style. The cycles of Judges differ considerably from the programmatic overview of Kings, though they both emphasize God's patience despite the unfaithfulness of Israel. Joshua concerns the fulfillment of the covenant promise

The Neo-Assyrian Empire dominated Israel for over a century. Much of our knowledge of this period comes from the historical records preserved in the royal inscriptions. This inscription recounts the conquests of Sargon II, who completed the deportation of the northern kingdom. The text mentions success against the "House of Omri"—a reference to Israel.
The Schøyen Collection MS 2368, Oslo and London

of the land, while Samuel addresses the establishment of the covenant of kingship. The former features an annalistic style using reports and lists, and the latter is more anecdotal. As a result, each of the books must be recognized as autonomous from a literary standpoint, though there are editorial techniques that draw them together also.

If one is inclined, as we are, to assign Deuteronomy to an earlier date, it would not be unreasonable to view Joshua and Judges as independent products of the united monarchy period, with Samuel written during the divided monarchy (though possibly as early as Solomon) and Kings completed and combined with the others by means of light editing during the exilic period. There would be no objection to referring to this final product as a Deuteronomistic History.

Concept of History in Israel and the Ancient Near East

When historians study the records of a civilization, they are interested in identifying what model of history is assumed by those documents. As an example, it is said that present Western civilization has adopted a linear model. In this, history is seen as a straight line moving from point A, the beginning, to point Z, the end along the continuum of time. Cause and effect are viewed in strictly naturalistic terms as opposed to supernatural.

By contrast, cause and effect in the world of the ancient Near East is viewed almost entirely in supernatural terms. Even when natural cause and effect was evident or obvious, it was judged insignificant compared with the supernatural aspect. Time appears to be of much less importance, evidenced by the lack of any system of absolute chronology (instead, the dates were identified only by the year of the king's reign). It has been suggested that rather than a linear view of history, there was a cyclic view that was built on the pattern of the regular cycle of the seasons. In this view there is a fixed sequence of several stages through which history passes, returning eventually to an original point.

The cyclic view can be subsumed under a more comprehensive model called "recurrence." This takes into account both biblical and Near Eastern approaches to history and places the greater emphasis on recurring patterns of history rather than on the mythical focus of the cycles. Some of this perspective is retained in the modern adage that those who do not learn from the errors of history are doomed to repeat them.

In the ancient Near East, the key to the patterns of historical recurrence was sought out by use of omens. It was believed that the action of deity had innumerable related effects throughout the natural world in addition to influencing history. As a result, if one could record unusual occurrences in nature that happened around the time of a particular event, it would be possible to use those data to know when a similar event would recur. For example, observations of the alignment or motion of heavenly bodies, the activity of animals, the flight of birds, or the configurations of the entrails of sacrificed animals would regularly be compared with past observations of the same phenomena in order to discover whether they indicated good or ill fortune. If the omens suggested that catastrophic events were about to recur, attempts would be made to dodge destiny through recitation of the appropriate incantations. History and theology merged because belief in supernatural cause and effect in history prompted ritual activity.

The fact that deity was believed to play such a central role in the historical events of the ancient Near East, combined with the arbitrary and capricious nature of deity, made the omen system necessary. In contrast, the monotheism of the Israelites greatly simplified the matter. They did not have to concern themselves with dozens of deities who might influence history with no discernible rhyme or reason. Furthermore, divination, omens, and incantations were prohibited to Israelites by the law; therefore, given the recurrence worldview, they saw the need to conform to the covenant and keep the law (rather than relying on certain rituals) in order to exert some control over history. Yahweh was defined by his attributes, which were constant, and he had committed himself to specific obligations through the covenant.

As a result, theology and history merged in Israel, not through ritual, but through the covenant. The actions of deity could not be predicted, altered, or in any way manipulated by ritual. Rather, whenever Israel was unfaithful to the covenant, the Lord could be expected to punish in accordance with the covenant. Human activity and decisions fall into particular patterns, and to the same extent, God's cause-and-effect activity in history follows corresponding patterns. Both the cycles of the book of Judges and the reports of endless apostasy in the books of

Tiglath-Pileser III (744–727 BC) was a great king who ushered in Assyria's golden age. His annals include records of his victories and is of interest especially because it mentions "Menahem of Samaria" (2 Kings 15:14–23).

Todd Bolen/
www.BiblePlaces.com,
courtesy of the British Museum

The Assyrians were fond of huge, carved stone reliefs that would display their great victories. This is part of the relief of Sennacherib's victory over the fortified city of Lachish in Judah in 701 BC. It is of interest that he portrays this battle, because his armies were decimated by the Lord as they camped outside Jerusalem (2 Kings 18:35–36), and therefore that was one battle for which he was not able to boast of victory.

Caryn Reeder, courtesy of the British Museum

Kings bear witness to the principle of recurrence. It is the foundation of Deuteronomic theology. The ancient concept of history can therefore be described as theological in contrast to the Western view, which is entirely secular.

Purpose of History Writing in Israel and the Ancient Near East

As would be expected, one's concept of history is reflected in the purpose for recording history. In Western societies there are numerous reasons why history might be written. In a textbook, history is written for purposes of teaching about events or perhaps so that lessons might be learned from the experience of others. Journalists record history for information's sake but often attempt to identify and analyze elements of cause and effect. These genres of **historiography** are largely driven by a desire to record what actually happened. The print media may also have other agendas such as defending certain principles or promoting certain opinions. Different historical media or genres may have different purposes, and it is important for the readers of that history to know what the purposes were.

In the ancient Near East there were various genres of history writing as well. Studies have suggested that the historiography of the ancient Near East was rarely intended to present an objective view of what actually happened. More often, propaganda was clothed in historical attire with the purpose of benefiting those in power. Royal inscriptions were often self-serving documents whereby a king could boast of his accomplishments, embellishing the positive, ignoring the negative, and at times taking credit for the achievements of his predecessor. When the purpose is self-aggrandizement and the rewards are power and prestige, accuracy becomes of little concern. As a result, historiographical documents of the ancient Near East have to be interpreted very carefully if an accurate account of the events is to be reconstructed. The purpose of this historiography was to support the king, not to offer an objective account of what "really happened."

Some interpreters of the past have contended that Israel's historiography likewise reflected an agenda of royal, dynastic legitimation. So, for instance, the fact that the Davidic dynasty received divine endorsement through the covenant recorded in 2 Samuel 7 has fostered suspicion concerning its authenticity. Yet it must be admitted that there is actually very little that the Deuteronomist has to say about the Davidic dynasty that is positive. Even David himself is portrayed in such a way that his faults are as evident as his achievements. The book of 2 Samuel would make very ineffective propaganda.

While the historiography of the ancient Near East focuses generally on the king and his military and domestic achievements, it is clear that Israel's historical narratives are motivated by theological concerns. The purpose of the historical literature of the Bible is to show the ways in which the Lord has acted in history to fulfill his covenant promises and to carry out his agenda. One could call it didactic (giving instruction) in the sense that it is revelation of who God is by recording what he has done. To the extent that the covenant affirms special status for Israel, this emphasis could be viewed as having propagandistic value; but such a purpose for the literature is negated by the continual emphasis on the failures and unfaithfulness of Israel. Both didactic literature and propagandistic literature will be selective about the events and details recorded. The selection of the didactic author will be motivated by a desire to focus on the lesson in view.

Deity is seen as the central cause of the events of history in the ancient Near East as a whole, but nothing in the historiographical literature functions specifically to reveal God. There is likewise no

Tips for Reading Old Testament Historical Literature

- Think of the books as theological rather than historical.
- Remember that the main focus of the literature is God and his covenant, not people or events.
- Remember that historical cause and effect is seen largely in terms of the role of God rather than the actions of people.

historiographical work that treats the kind of large time span covered by the Deuteronomistic History. Israel's God is revealed as One who has a plan for history and who intervenes to ensure that the plan is executed. While Israel's neighbors believed that their gods at times intervened in history, the intervention was generally done to maintain a status quo. The God of Israel, however, intervened at times to work toward a goal that had never yet been achieved. He also intervened to punish his own people when necessary. All God's intervention is focused toward a single goal: the execution of his plan.

Understanding Historical Literature

The Old Testament historical literature needs to be understood within the frame of reference that it is a strategic part of God's self-revelation. As we noted earlier, a modern tendency is to regard the message of the historical literature as being the role models offered by the persons who cross its pages. In contrast, as God's self-revelation, its intention is to convey instruction about and knowledge of God. This message is conveyed not so much by individual narratives, but by the patterns and cycles of history portrayed generation after generation.

Some readers are inclined to look for new insights and lessons in each account. But rather than our seeking out "lessons from the life of Asa" or "lessons from the life of Saul," the text continually points us to patterns, themes, and motifs that we ought to see as weaving the historical tapestry into a picture of the sovereign God of the covenant. The significance of each thread is the contribution it makes to the tapestry; by itself the thread has little to offer. The quality of its color has no inherent value, but its function in the tapestry helps to create dimension and hue. So the narratives must be approached through their context, and God must be seen as the focus. This tapestry will be unveiled as each biblical book is studied in its turn.

Questions for Further Study and Discussion

1. How can we accommodate both the supernaturalistic view of Old Testament story and the current trend toward analyzing human-natural cause and effect behind historical events?
2. Why was divination forbidden to Israel?
3. Why is history an important part of God's self-revelation?
4. If an account of history is selective, is truth compromised? Explain. What are the implications of selectivity for biblical inerrancy?

For Further Reading

Albrektson, Bertil. *History and the Gods*. Uppsala: Lund, 1967. A stimulating study comparing the Israelite and ancient Near Eastern views of history.

Alter, Robert. *The Art of Biblical Narrative*. New York: Basic Books, 1981.

Cate, Robert L. *An Introduction to the Historical Books of the Old Testament*. Nashville: Broadman & Holman, 1994.

Chisholm, Robert B. *Interpreting the Historical Books: An Exegetical Handbook*. Grand Rapids: Kregel, 2006.

Fretheim, Terence. *Deuteronomic History*. IBT. Nashville: Abingdon Press, 1983.

Gese, Hartmut. "The Idea of History in the Ancient Near East and the Old Testament." *Journal for Theology and the Church* (1965): 49–64.

Halpern, Baruch. *The First Historians*. San Francisco: Harper and Row, 1988.

Hamilton, Victor. *Handbook on the Historical Books*. Grand Rapids: Baker, 2001.

Howard, David M. *An Introduction to the Old Testament Historical Books*. Chicago: Moody Press, 1993.

Knoppers, Gary N. and J. Gordon McConville. *Reconsidering Israel and Judah*. Winona Lake, Ind.: Eisenbrauns, 2000.

Long, Burke O. *First Kings: With an Introduction to Historical Literature*. Grand Rapids: Eerdmans, 1984.

Long, V. Philips. *The Art of Biblical History*. Grand Rapids: Zondervan, 1994. Reprinted in Moisés Silva, gen. ed., *Foundations of Contemporary Interpretation*. Grand Rapids: Zondervan, 1996. 281–429.

_____. *Israel's Past in Present Research*. Winona Lake, Ind.: Eisenbrauns, 2000.

Polzin, Robert. *Moses and the Deuteronomist.* San Francisco: Harper & Row, 1980.

_____. *Samuel and the Deuteronomist.* San Francisco: Harper & Row, 1989.

Tadmor, Hayim, and Moshe Weinfeld. *History, Historiography and Interpretation.* Jerusalem: Magnes, 1984.

Van Seters, John. *In Search of History.* New Haven: Yale University Press, 1983.

Walton, John H. *Ancient Near Eastern Thought and the Old Testament.* Grand Rapids: Baker, 2006.

Weinfeld, Moshe. *Deuteronomy and the Deuteronomic School.* New York: Oxford University Press, 1972.

"Then Joshua built on Mount Ebal an altar to the LORD, the God of Israel" (Josh. 8:30). These remains of a stone structure on Mount Ebal are suggested by some archaeologists to be the altar built by Joshua. The mountain in the background is Gerizim. Z. Radovan/www.BibleLandPictures.com

JOSHUA

Key Ideas

- The faithfulness of God in fulfilling covenant promises
- The conquest and apportionment of the land
- The importance of obedience

Purpose Statement

The purpose of the book of Joshua is summarized nicely in Joshua 21:43–45: "So the LORD gave Israel all the land, . . . and they took possession of it and settled there. The LORD gave them rest on every side. . . . The LORD handed all their enemies over to them. Not one of all the LORD's good promises to the house of Israel failed; every one was fulfilled." The book shows how God kept his covenant promise to give the land to Israel.

Major Themes

- Covenant and Land
- Ban
- Divine Warrior
- Sovereign Involvement
- Corporate Solidarity

God's Presence

God's presence with the Israelites is confirmed by his deliverance of the land to them and their recommitment to relationship is indicated in the covenant ceremony in Joshua 8.

Outline

I. Entrance into the Land
   A. Preparation for Entering the Land (1–2)
   B. Crossing the Jordan (3–4)
   C. Circumcision (5:1–12)

II. Conquest Narratives
   A. The Commander of the Lord's Army (5:13–15)
   B. Jericho (6)
   C. Ai (7–8)
      1. Defeat at Ai (7:1–5)
      2. Achan's offense (7:6–26)
      3. Victory at Ai (8:1–29)
      4. Reading of the Law at Ebal and Gerizim (8:30–35)
   D. Southern Coalition (9–10)
      1. Treaty with Gibeon (9)
      2. Battle at Gibeon (10)
   E. Northern Coalition (11)
   F. List of Conquests (12)

III. Description of Allotment of Land
   A. Settlement of Prior Claims (13–17)
      1. Reuben, Gad, and Half-Manasseh in Transjordan (13)
      2. Caleb (14)
      3. Judah (15)
      4. Manasseh and Ephraim (16–17)
   B. Remainder of Tribes (18–19)
   C. Cities of Refuge Established (20)
   D. Levitical Cities Allocated (21)

IV. Covenant Matters
   A. Potential Violation in Altar Building (22)
   B. Covenant Exhortations to Tribal Leaders (23)
   C. Covenant Renewal at Shechem (24)

Joshua was one of the outstanding persons of the Old Testament: assistant to Moses (Exod. 24:13; 32:17; 33:11), one of the twelve spies (Num. 14), successful general (Exod. 17). Courageous and godly, he served as God's instrument for bringing the people of Israel into the Promised Land. The book rightly bears his name, but in the end it must be realized that the book is not about Joshua—it is about God.

The Writing of the Book

Scholarly study of the book of Joshua has focused on two separate yet related issues: composition and historicity.

Composition

Early in the twentieth century it was not unusual to see references to the "hexateuch," a group that contained six books—the Pentateuch plus the book of Joshua. Though some still maintain that approach, it is much more common today to find Joshua included in the work referred to as the Deuteronomistic History.

The view that Joshua was part of a "hexateuch" was based on the assumption that the Pentateuchal sources (see chap. 3) are traceable into Joshua. This has been largely rejected in favor of the theory that a **Deuteronomistic school** was responsible for the composition of the historical group of books from Joshua through 2 Kings. Nevertheless it is still valid to understand the close connection that the narrative of Joshua has to the Pentateuch since the destination of God's people since the beginning of the covenant was the land promised to Abraham. To this theme the book of Joshua provides a fitting climax.

If Joshua is included in the work of the Deuteronomistic historian, the date set for the writing of the book will be dictated by one's theory regarding the Deuteronomistic school. Scholars who attribute the foundation of the school to a book of Deuteronomy first compiled in the late seventh century and accepted by Josiah as the basis of his reform must of necessity date most of the history writing to Josiah's time or later. Scholars who are open to an earlier date for Deuteronomy, however, are at liberty to consider a much wider range for the composition of the historical books.

A number of elements in the book of Joshua suggest an early date for its composition. Among the most convincing, Joshua 16:10 mentions that the Canaanites were not driven out of Gezer and lived there "to this day." First Kings 9:16 reports that Pharaoh conquered Gezer and killed all the Canaanites living there. This suggests that at least this part of Joshua was written before the time of Solomon. Other examples include Joshua 15:63, which records that the Jebusites still inhabited

Pharaoh Merneptah's stela (13th century BC) commemorates his victory over all his enemies. Israel is included in the list of conquered peoples, making this the earliest extrabiblical reference to the nation.

Todd Bolen/
www.BiblePlaces.com,
courtesy of the Cairo Museum

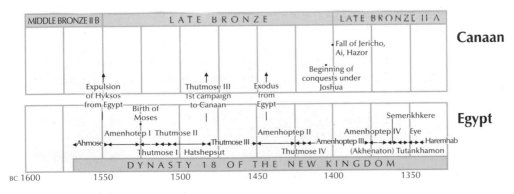

MIDDLE BRONZE II B	LATE BRONZE			LATE BRONZE II A		Canaan
			Fall of Jericho, Ai, Hazor			
			Beginning of conquests under Joshua			
Expulsion of Hyksos from Egypt	Thutmose III 1st campaign to Canaan	Exodus from Egypt				
	Birth of Moses				Semenkhkere	Egypt
	Amenhotep I Thutmose II		Amenhoptep II	Amenhoptep IV Eye		
Ahmose	Thutmose I Hatshepsut	Thutmose III	Thutmose IV	Amenhoptep III (Akhenaton) Tutankhamon	Haremhab	
	DYNASTY 18 OF THE NEW KINGDOM					
BC 1600	1550	1500	1450	1400	1350	

"At that time the LORD said to Joshua, 'Make flint knives and circumcise the Israelites again'" (Josh. 5:2). Circumcision in Israel was a mark of God's covenant, but was a practice elsewhere in the ancient world for other reasons. This relief in the Egyptian tomb of Ankhmahor depicts a priest performing circumcision.

Werner Forman Archive

Jerusalem, and 13:6, which emphasizes the Sidonians rather than the city of Tyre, which had become dominant by the time of David.

For those who accept the Mosaic authorship of Deuteronomy, there are no restrictions as to how soon after Joshua's lifetime the book could have been written. On the one hand, Joshua 8:32 gives an indication that there was scribal activity among the Israelites during that lifetime, so there is no reason to rule out the possibility that this is a contemporary record. On the other hand, there is no reason to demand that it was given its final form by Joshua himself. Joshua is not identified as the author of the book. The time of Samuel is one possibility. The frequent reference to phenomena observable "to this day" may well suggest that some time had passed between the events related and the composition of the book.

Historicity

Some scholars are inclined to see the book of Joshua as an unrealistic portrayal of the conquest. In place of the large-scale invasion recorded in Joshua that subdued the native peoples within a relatively short period, they hold that a localized, gradual, piecemeal conquest (supposedly described in Judg. 1) is more likely. Their consensus on Joshua is that it is composed of etiological legends (fictional stories contrived to give some explanation for an observed phenomenon or situation), a theory they support by pointing to the recurring comment "until this day" (4:9; 5:9; 7:26; 8:28–29; 9:27; 10:27; 13:13; 14:14; 15:63; 16:10).

Others have found no persuasive reasons to reject the biblical account as presented. First, they see no contradiction entailed between the accounts of the conquest in Joshua and Judges 1. While some verses in Joshua seem to suggest that the entire land was conquered (e.g., 11:23; 21:43–45), these must be balanced against other statements in the book that clearly indicate there was still much to be done (e.g., 13:1–6; 17:12–13; 18:2–3; 23:4–5, 13). It is the latter situation that is in view in Judges 1. The former condition is not contradictory to this, but represents a theological assertion to the effect that God had fulfilled his promises in putting the entire land under the Israelites' control. The major powers of the area had been defeated by Joshua, so by default the territory that they had controlled now belonged to Israel. Israel's control, however, was neither accepted nor enforced. This accounts for the apparent discrepancy.

Second, there is still much discussion concerning the nature of so-called etiological legend. Depending on one's definition, it is possible to consider some of the elements in Joshua etiological in nature (e.g., the naming of the Valley of Achor in 7:26). The more important issue is whether the explanation given for the event or situation can be considered historical or not. If one insists that the label *etiological* implies that the explanation is fictional or legendary, then such a label must be discarded. Brevard Childs, however, has demonstrated that such a narrow view of the category is not sustainable.[1] As a result, even if these narratives should be considered etiological, there is no reason to deny a factual basis to the account.

Beyond this, however, it must be seriously questioned whether these narratives can be assigned to the category of etiology. The purpose of etiological narrative is to give explanation of and assign cause to situations or phenomena. Is that the purpose of the biblical author in introducing these accounts to the reader? While it may be admitted that etiological information is given, it is a different matter to see that as the author's purpose. An etiological purpose would not account for the theological cohesiveness that is evident in the selection and arrangement of the material.

Another challenge to the historical authenticity of the book of Joshua comes, not from literary analysis, but from the archaeological record. One would expect that archaeology had great potential for confirming the destruction of Canaanite cities and the repopulation of the land by the Israelites. These are events that excavation should be able to detect and provide details for. Yet the nature of the data leaves the picture controversial and unclear.

Theoretically, what is needed is to find a period of time when each of the cities mentioned in Joshua 1–12 shows evidence of being occupied and when three of them—Jericho, Ai, and Hazor—show signs of being destroyed.[2] When clear-cut answers are not forthcoming, some

1. Brevard S. Childs, "A Study of the Formula 'Until This Day,'" *JBL* 82 (1963): 279–92; and "The Etiological Tale Re-examined," *VT* 24 (1974): 387–97.

2. Jericho was destroyed at the end of Middle Bronze Age II, traditionally about 1550 BC, and not occupied again until about 1400. There was subsequent destruction in the fourteenth century. The site traditionally identified as Ai was unoccupied between 2400 and 1200 BC. Hazor also shows a destruction level at the end of Middle Bronze Age II and another in the thirteenth century, which is thought to coincide with the incident reported in Judges 4–5.

reject the biblical record, others reject the archaeological results, and still others seek to harmonize the two by making adjustments to one or the other or both.

The date of the conquest most naturally suggested by the text of Scripture, about 1400 BC, has frequently been rejected by archaeologists because destruction and occupation levels of the relevant cities did not correlate to this time period. Those who used the archaeological record to identify a more suitable date concluded that the end of the thirteenth century provided the closest correlations to the biblical account. As more and more difficulties arose with this date, many rejected the biblical picture of a conquest altogether in favor of the view that Israel gained control of Canaan over a long period of time by means of peaceful infiltration by independent nomadic groups that eventually banded together and became "Israel." Because this model depends on increasingly suspect sociological concepts (especially with regard to nomadism and tribal organizations), it gave way to a model portraying the "conquest" as a peasant revolt instigated by a group from Egypt but carried out primarily by disenchanted internal factions. This model suffers from a total lack of biblical support and represents something of a modern Marxism superimposed on ancient cultures with little sociological evidence.

John Bimson has put forth a theory that seeks to deal with the problem in a totally different way. Many of the cities listed in the conquest narratives of Joshua show evidence of their city walls having been destroyed at the end of the period that archaeologists have designated Middle Bronze II. This era has traditionally been considered to have ended about 1550 BC, and the destruction of cities in Canaan was attributed to the Hyksos or to the Egyptians who were chasing the Hyksos out of Egypt.

Bimson has gathered evidence to suggest that the end of Middle Bronze II should be revised to about 1420 BC and that the destructions should be seen as having been wrought by the Israelites under Joshua. Jericho and Hazor both saw substantial city walls destroyed at the end of Middle Bronze II. Ai is more of a problem, for there is some dispute about whether the site has been identified properly. Scholars are exploring various alternatives to the traditional identification with Khirbet et-Tell, which was not occupied between 2400 and 1200 BC and thus did not make a very good candidate.[3] Bimson's view has the disadvantage that most archaeologists believe that the dates of the archaeological periods cannot be manipulated so radically.

The Background

As we have seen, the dates of the exodus and the conquest are matters of ongoing dispute that will not be resolved here. However, whether

3. For a summary of Bimson's position, see "Redating the Exodus," *BAR* 14 (1987): 40–52; for a full treatment, see his book *Redating the Exodus and the Conquest*, 3rd ed. (Sheffield, England: n.p., 1988). Though Bimson's position is controversial and may still undergo some adjustment, it may be commended for attempting to interpret the archaeological data with integrity while respecting the authority of the biblical text. For more information about the archaeology related to the conquest, see J. Walton, "Exodus, Date of" in *Dictionary of the Old Testament: Pentateuch*, ed. D. Baker and T. D. Alexander (Downers Grove, Ill.: InterVarsity Press, 2003), 258–72.

the events of Joshua took place at the end of the fifteenth century or sometime in the thirteenth, they occur after the expulsion of the Hyksos from Egypt in the mid-sixteenth century and before the invasion of the Sea Peoples about 1200 BC.

The expulsion of the Hyksos brought the powerful Eighteenth Dynasty to the throne of Egypt. By the mid-fifteenth century the dynasty was firmly established and at the peak of its strength. At this same time (about 1460) the New Kingdom of the Hittite Empire also took shape, and over the next two centuries the Egyptians and the Hittites competed for control of the trade routes and the ports of Syro-Palestine. During most of this period, a third power center was located in northern Mesopotamia. Until about 1350 this was the Hurrian Empire of Mitanni along the upper Euphrates. When the Hittites overthrew the Hurrian capital, the power void was filled by the Assyrians, who dominated the east for most of the thirteenth century. The result of this triad of competing political powers was a stalemate, with continual adjustments and shifts of advantage based on the skillfulness of the respective kings and armies and the effectiveness of their diplomatic strategies.

At stake in this international game of intrigue was control of the busy seaports of the Syrian coast—Byblos, Ugarit, and Sidon being among the most prosperous—and the overland trade routes, particularly the Coastal Highway that guided caravans and troops from Egypt

Jericho is the city well known because Joshua and the Israelites witnessed the collapse of its walls without a sword or battering ram. "Then the LORD said to Joshua, 'See, I have delivered Jericho into your hands, along with its king and its fighting men'" (Josh. 6:2). Jericho was a ten-acre site guarding the fords of the Jordan against those entering the land from the east as the Israelites did.

Joshua and the Israelites suffered their first defeat in battle between Ai and Bethel (Josh. 7:1-5), because of the sin of one Israelite. Later they returned and successfully took the towns (Josh. 8:9–23). The site of Bethel is still disputed by some, but this place, called Beitin, is the consensus choice.

through major cities in Palestine, through Damascus, Hamath, and Aleppo, and finally east to the Euphrates and down through the heartland of Mesopotamia to the Kassites, who controlled Babylonia.

Palestine and Syria at this time were checkered with independent or loosely confederated city-states, each anxious to benefit from the economic opportunities its location provided. Letters found at the ancient Egyptian capital Tell el-Amarna, written from petty kings of Canaanite city-states to the Egyptian court in the fourteenth century, provide reliable information about this situation. The fourteenth century saw a decline in the power of Egypt through the Eighteenth Dynasty before the final glory days of the Nineteenth. The city-state kings who wrote the letters sought military assistance from the dormant Egyptians. It is clear from the correspondence that Egyptian control of Palestine had diminished and the Canaanite kings were shuffling for political power. The lack of Egyptian control had caused two problems: (1) some city-states were taking advantage of Egyptian absence to enlarge their territories, and (2) groups of displaced peoples posed a threat in attempting to carve out a new home by driving out the current inhabitants. The Amarna letters refer to these people as "the Ḥabiru."

Some scholars have wondered whether the Ḥabiru might refer to the Hebrews, for given an early date of the exodus, the timing would be about right. Further study, however, has shown that while the Israelites could have been included, the term Ḥabiru refers to a much broader range of peoples.

As the Nineteenth Dynasty came to power in Egypt and began its ascent, the tension between the Egyptians and the Hittites increased. The first half of the thirteenth century saw a major confrontation between their two armies at Qadesh on the Orontes River in Syria. Fighting to a stalemate, Rameses II of Egypt was unable to wrest control of Amurru and Qadesh from the Hittites. By mid-century, peace was established between the two powers, with Egypt retaining control of Palestine and the port cities of Syria as far north as Ugarit. The Hittites would rule the Orontes and inland territory in Syria.

The resulting picture in Palestine during the conquest (at whichever date) is that Egypt had at least nominal control of the area, but locally a network of city-states governed. Egypt's primary interest was securing the trade routes and maintaining their garrisons. Even in the times of greatest strength, Egypt probably would have intervened in Palestine only when their own interests were threatened. During periods of Egyptian weakness, the people of Palestine were on their own.

Purpose and Message

There are two popular misconceptions about the book of Joshua. One is that it is just the story of a courageous and godly person; the other, it is a military record of the conquest. Both must be passed over in identifying the reason why the book was written. Regarding the first, the lack of biographical details and a dearth of expressions of approval or disapproval of Joshua's actions suggest that Joshua is not really the

In a service of thanksgiving after the defeat of Ai, Joshua sacrificed to the Lord on Mount Ebal (Josh. 8:30–35). The law was read for the Israelites who were in the valley between Mount Ebal (background) and Mount Gerizim (foreground).
Bible Scene Multmedia/ Maurice Thompson

focus of the material, though he certainly plays a central role in the events of the book. As to the second, a close examination reveals that there is actually very little given of the details of military strategy and achievement—only the barest sketch of an outline. Furthermore, neither biography nor military history explains the land allotment segment in chapters 13–19. Any identification of the purpose of the author must include all sections of the book.

These misconceptions dispelled, we see that when military strategies are described in the text, they are God's strategies, not Joshua's. In each battle narrative, only enough information is given to convey that (1) God was the one who engineered the victory, and (2) God's instructions were carried out in placing the defeated cities under the ban.

The orientation of the texts toward the role of God is evident in several places. The incidents identified in figure 11.1 show that this is not simply military history. Rather, a theological point is being made even though military records are used to get the point across.

Figure 11.1. Theological Purpose in the Book of Joshua

God instructs the Israelites to enter the land	1:1 – 9
God has gone before them to terrify the occupants of the land	2:9 – 11
God brings them across the Jordan	3 – 4
Circumcision required for rededication	5:1 – 12
The commander of the Lord's army	5:13 – 15
God-given strategies	6:2 – 5; 8:2
God-given victories	6:16; 8:7; 10:42
Defeat when God's instructions had been violated	7:5 – 12

Based on this orientation toward the role of God, on including every segment of the writing, and on the comments made by the narrator, it is evident that the purpose of the book is to convey how God kept his covenant promise to bring the Israelites into the land he had showed to Abraham. The faithfulness of God in carrying out his end of the covenant is important to affirm. It explains why there is frequent reference to the Lord's giving the land to the people and why his role gets so much attention.

The message is that God keeps his promises, no matter how impossible they may seem. God's covenant with Abraham is something that he took very seriously and intended to fulfill. God was determined to carry it out and is capable of carrying it out.

Structure and Organization

The first section of the book (1–5) gives some details concerning the Israelites' entering the land. From the start, the text focuses on the covenant, expressing God's intention to bring them into the land that he promised to Abraham (1:2–6) and exhorting them to keep the law (1:7–8). It is clear from the text that God gave the instructions to enter the land. The story of the spies in Jericho is told at length, not because of the military strategy it discloses, but because of the information gained by the spies. The inhabitants of the land were all fearful *because they had heard what the Lord had done for Israel*. The conclusion in 2:24 is theological and covenant focused: "the LORD has surely given the whole land into our hands."

The crossing of the Jordan was accomplished with the help of a sign from God, and a memorial was built to acknowledge that fact. The narrative includes a consecration to the Lord (3:5) and prominently features the ark of the covenant (e.g., 3:8). Again, the conclusion emphasizes the work of God (4:23–24). The renewal of the rite of circumcision (chap. 5) also serves as a rededication to the covenant in preparation for God's fulfillment of his promises.

The second section of the book is the most familiar to Christians in general. In the important introduction (5:13–15) Joshua is confronted by one who identifies himself as the commander of the Lord's army. This event has some parallels to the episode of the burning bush in the life of Moses, but its greatest significance is that it again demonstrates that the Lord is the one who will do the fighting and will enable the Israelites to possess the land. It is the Lord's army who will conquer.

Gibeon: In Joshua 9 the Gibeonites use a ruse to make a treaty with Israel, and in Joshua 10 the city is besieged by a Canaanite coalition, "because Gibeon was an important city, like one of the royal cities" (Josh. 10:2).
Bible Scene Multimedia/ Maurice Thompson

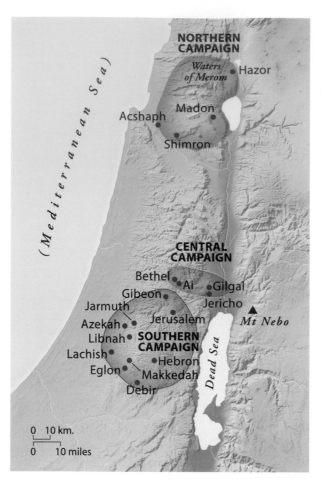

NORTHERN
CAMPAIGN

*Waters
of Merom* •Hazor

Acshaph• Madon•

Shimron•

(Mediterranean Sea)

CENTRAL
CAMPAIGN

Bethel• •Ai •Gilgal

Gibeon•
Jarmuth•   •Jericho

Azekah• •Jerusalem   ▲
Libnah• SOUTHERN   *Mt Nebo*
Lachish• CAMPAIGN *Dead Sea*
Eglon• •Hebron
    Makkedah•
  Debir•

0   10 km.
0   10 miles

The Conquest

The actual conquest narratives begin with the famous battle of Jericho. The emphasis on carrying out the ban (6:17–21) and the fact that the instructions they received resemble a ritual more than a battle plan set the tone for the narratives as conveying the covenantal aspects rather than the military aspects of the conquest, though military records would have been used as sources.

Chapter 7 provides one of the most detailed accounts of the conquest narratives, and it concerns not a military encounter, but a covenant issue: the violation of the ban. The defeat at Ai (7:2–5) showed again that the Lord was the one granting victory or defeat. The discovery of the violator, Achan, and the appropriate punishment of the crime cleared the way for subsequent victory (chap. 8). This event was followed by the building of an altar and the reading of the law on mounts Ebal and Gerizim to give recognition to the Lord for giving the people this first foothold in the land.

Chapter 9 functions, first, to give background for the conflict related in chapter 10 and, second, to explain why an action that was ostensibly a covenant violation (making a treaty with inhabitants of the land) was tolerated by the Lord. The reason is that the Gibeonites' deception of Joshua exonerated the Israelites from punishment.

The account of the battle of Gibeon in chapter 10 also serves to point out the Lord's part in bringing the victory. God's involvement was evident both in honoring Joshua's request about the sun and moon (10:12–15) and in sending hail to batter the enemy (10:10–11). (The ancient book of Jashar, which has not been preserved, is referred to as confirming these events.) The mopping-up operation (10:16–43) showed Joshua's faithfulness in following God's instructions regarding "the ban" (see below).

The northern coalition was the next army to confront the Israelites. But since there is no mention of a specific, miraculous divine intervention, the narrative has nothing to report about the battle. It tells only who was involved and reports that the Lord delivered the enemy into the Israelites' hands (11:8). Chapter 12 concludes this section by listing the kings who were defeated.

Section three gives detailed descriptions of the boundaries of the territory allotted to each tribe and in so doing helps us to identify the purpose of the book of Joshua. Since God was enabling Israel to possess the land, he also supervised their disposition of it. This constituted the fulfillment of God's promise. The narrative makes this point explicit in the conclusion of this section: "So the LORD gave Israel all the land, ... and they took possession of it and settled there. The LORD gave them rest on every side.... The LORD handed all their enemies over to them. Not one of all the LORD's good promises to the house of Israel failed; every one was fulfilled" (21:43–45). That is what the book of Joshua is all about.

Chapters 22–24 concern Israel's response to the occupation and focus on the covenant. Especially important is the covenant renewal at

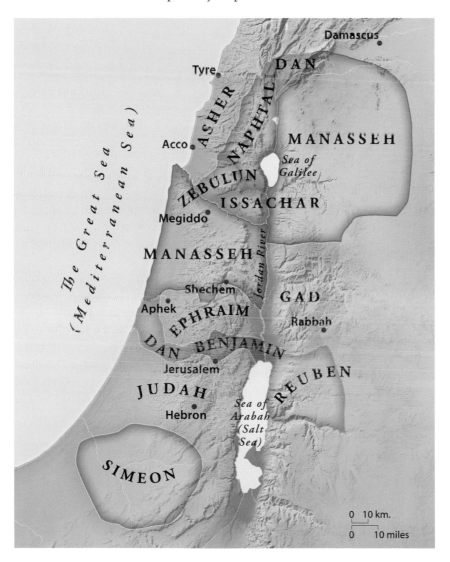

Tribal Territories

Shechem containing a restatement of what God had done and what the Israelites agreed to do.

Major Themes

Covenant and Land

In Israel's perception of herself as the covenant people of God, nothing is more central than the land. God had promised Abraham a land, though it was not to belong to his family for some four centuries (Gen. 15:13–21). The delivery of that land into the hands of Israel is the focus of the book of Joshua. Forever after, the land is viewed in the history and literature of Israel as evidence of God's having chosen them as his covenant people and bestowing his favor on them. When Israel's offenses against the Lord required judgment, the worst sentence that the prophets could deliver was the threat of banishment from the land. In the same manner, the hope of restoration and a future kingdom were both rooted in the promise that the Lord would regather Israel to the land.

The book of Joshua, then, has great theological significance, for its narratives demonstrate, more than anything else could, that the Lord was keeping the covenant promises he had made to Abraham. Just as Israel did not come out of Egypt by its own power, so the land was not taken by Israel's military might or by Joshua's strategies.

The Ban

A prominent theme of Joshua is found in the instructions regarding how the conquered cities of Palestine were to be treated. Legislation on the ban—"destroy them totally; ... show them no mercy"—is found in Deuteronomy 7:1–11 and 20:10–18, and it is instituted in Joshua 6:17–19. The term *ban* is inadequate to convey the meaning of the concept, but it is widely used for lack of suitable alternatives. The verb has lately been defined as follows: "Consecrate something or someone as a permanent and definitive offering for the sanctuary; in war, consecrate a city and its inhabitants to destruction; carry out this destruction; totally annihilate a population in war; kill."[4] The concept is not unique to Israel, for it occurs also in the ninth-century inscription of Mesha, king of Moab.

Yet the question often arises, Why the ban? Why did God command the complete annihilation of the occupants of the land? Ethicists and philosophers over the centuries have debated this, and various explanations have been offered. Scripture suggests that the Canaanites brought this destruction on themselves by their own wickedness (Deut. 9:5). This is indicated not only in their abhorrent practices (e.g., fertility rites

---

4. *TDOT*, 5:188.

In Joshua 11 a northern coalition was formed, led by the principal city of Hazor, to oppose the Israelites' settlement in the land. This is the excavation of the palace at Hazor.

Z. Radovan/www.BibleLandPictures.com

and child sacrifice), but also in their resistance to the action of the Lord (cf. Josh. 9:1–4; 10:1–5; 11:1–5).[5]

The Divine Warrior

The Lord is frequently described, from the time of Samuel, as "YHWH of armies." But he is seen earlier, in the book of Joshua (10:14), as engaging in combat on behalf of the Israelites as a divine warrior. In the Old Testament this motif is related to Yahweh as Creator (Isa. 45:12–13) and describes his role in the exodus (Exod. 15; Deut. 33:2–3) and in the return from the exile as related in the prophetic literature (e.g., Isa. 51:9–11; 52:7–12). When the Israelites set out from Sinai with the ark in the lead, the formula recited by Moses addressed Yahweh as one going forth in battle (Num. 10:35).

The significance of this theology is laid out clearly in Proverbs 21:31: "The horse is made ready for the day of battle, but victory rests with the LORD."

Sovereign Involvement

It seems clear that the element of direct divine involvement cannot be removed from the book of Joshua without severely damaging its theological intent. The book is insistent that the Lord sovereignly acts in history in order to execute his plan and carry out his promise. This is not portrayed as haphazard involvement like that evidenced in the polytheistic theology of the ancient Near East. Rather, it is part of the ongoing, consistent plan of God that is delineated by the historical literature, projected further by the prophetic literature, and brought to a

5. This observation comes from Lawson Stone.

climax in the birth, life, and death of Jesus the Christ. Technically, we should not refer to this as intervention, because that implies that God's actions are imposed from the outside on something that is operating on its own. Alternatively, history is seen as the outworking of God's plan. What we sometimes call miracles, the text refers to as signs.

The exodus and the conquest represent the first great demonstration of the sovereignty of God in the history of Israel. What he had promised to an undistinguished emigrant from Mesopotamia who traveled to Canaan and raised a small family, which left the land two generations later, came true. Though more than four hundred years had gone by, the land of Canaan again belonged to the family of Abraham.

Corporate Solidarity

In Joshua 7 the consequences of Achan's sin first fell on all Israel as they lost a battle against Ai (with thirty-six Israelite casualties), and then the punishment fell on Achan's family, who were all stoned to death. In the individualistic orientation of our culture, it seems grossly unfair that so many should suffer for one person's offense. It even seems contrary to the dictates of the law (Deut. 24:16), though other passages warn us against reading that law too simplistically (Exod. 20:5–6).

The sense of national or ethnic identity was much stronger for Israel than it is in today's Western societies, though corporate identity still survives in areas where teamwork is necessary and "team spirit" is valued (e.g., small companies, the military, or organized sports). This solidarity was reflected positively in the laws of levirate marriage (Deut. 25:5–10) and land redemption (Lev. 25), which provided that family members come to the aid of a disadvantaged member of the clan. Negatively, all could suffer for the sake of one.

Besides the account of Achan, we see evidence of this practice in the destruction of the families of Korah, Dathan, and Abiram (Num. 16:27–33). In these cases, innocent parties shared in the punishment of an individual, not because they shared his guilt, but because they had a share in his identity. Achan's violation of the ban resulted in his being included in the ban. By bringing himself under the ban, he doomed his family to being treated as Canaanites, and the function of the ban was to obliterate all lines of continuity.

Questions for Further Study and Discussion

1. If the book of Joshua is intended to be read as theology rather than biography or military history, how should we approach the book in Bible study and exposition?
2. How is corporate identity a factor in our understanding of God's action in history?
3. Compare Joshua and Moses religiously, militarily, and politically.
4. How does the story of Rahab function in the book of Joshua?

For Further Reading

Bartlett, John. *Jericho*. Grand Rapids: Eerdmans, 1983.

Boling, Robert. *Joshua*. Garden City, N.Y.: Doubleday, 1982. A good historical and archaeological treatment with helpful, though not evangelical, exegetical notes.

Craigie, Peter C. *The Problem of War in the Old Testament*. Grand Rapids: Eerdmans, 1978. A thorough study of the concept of war from both textual and ethical perspectives.

Hess, Richard. *Joshua*. Downers Grove, Ill.: InterVarsity Press, 1996.

Howard, David. *Joshua*. Nashville. Broadman, 1999.

Kitchen, Kenneth A. *Ramesses II: Pharaoh Triumphant*. London: Aris and Phillips, 1982. A superb historical account drawing heavily on the inscriptional material yet very readable.

Longman, Tremper, III, and Dan Reid. *God Is a Warrior*. Grand Rapids: Zondervan, 1995.

Miller, J. Maxwell. "Archaeology and the Israelite Conquest of Canaan: Some Methodological Considerations." *Palestine Exploration Quarterly* 109 (1977): 87–93.

Walton, John H. "Joshua 10:12–15 and Mesopotamian Celestial Omen Texts." In *Faith, Tradition, and History*. Ed. by A. R. Millard, J. K. Hoffmeier, and D. W. Baker. Winona Lake, Ind.: Eisenbrauns, 1994. 181–90.

Wiseman, Donald J. *Peoples of Old Testament Times*. Oxford: Oxford University Press, 1973. Summary of the history of many of Israel's neighbors during the Old Testament period.

Woudstra, Marten. *The Book of Joshua*. Grand Rapids: Eerdmans, 1981. A good commentary from an evangelical perspective emphasizing the book's theology.

Younger, Lawson. *Ancient Conquest Accounts*. JSOTS 98. Sheffield, England: JSOT Press, 1990.

CHAPTER
12

This is the archaeological dig at the site of Hazor, the most prominent Canaanite city of the period. During the cycles of the Judges, God sold the Israelites "into the hands of Jabin, a king of Canaan, who reigned in Hazor" (Judg. 4:2).   Copyright 1995–2009 Phoenix Data Systems

JUDGES

Key Ideas

- The cycles of the Judges period
- God's justice and grace
- God's sovereign provision of deliverers
- Covenant failure by the people, the priests, and the tribal leadership
- The role of the Spirit of the Lord

Purpose Statement

The purpose of Judges is to show the failure of the Israelites to keep their part of the covenant. The cycles show how God demonstrated his power and mercy by delivering them time after time after his justice had demanded that he bring punishment. The book shows that neither the leadership of the Judges nor the tribal leadership succeeded in helping the people remain faithful. Instead, the leaders were as bad as the people.

Major Themes

- The Nature of Charismatic Leadership
- Spirit of the Lord
- Israel's Apostasy

God's Presence

God's Presence is jeopardized as the covenant is repeatedly violated and the role of the ark and tabernacle are obscured.

Outline

    I. Background: Failure to Drive Out the Canaanites (1:1–2:5)

   II. Introduction: Cycle of Apostasy (2:6–3:6)

  III. Cycles: "The Israelites Did Evil in the Eyes of the Lord"
       A. Othniel (3:7–11)
       B. Ehud (3:12–31)
       C. Deborah (4–5)
       D. Gideon (6–8)
          1. Abimelech (9)
          2. Tola and Jair (10:1–5)
       E. Jephthah (10:6–12:7)
          1. Ibzan (12:8–10)
          2. Elon (12:11–12)
          3. Abdon (12:13–15)
       F. Samson (13–16)

  IV. Tribal Depravity: "Everyone Did as He Saw Fit"
       A. Danites (17–18)
       B. Benjaminites (19–21)

When Joshua renewed the covenant with the people at Shechem, the Israelites insisted they would never forsake the Lord for other gods after all he had done for them. Joshua responded that they were incapable of serving the Lord, would be unfaithful, and would bring disaster on themselves (Josh. 24:16–20). For several centuries, as Joshua's apprehensions proved well founded, the Lord periodically provided leaders to come to the aid of Israel just when they seemed to be on the brink of extinction. These leaders were called "deliverers," or "ones bringing justice"—the "judges" for whom the book is named.

The Writing of the Book

There is no indication anywhere in Scripture as to the identity of the author or the compiler of the book. Jewish tradition identifies Samuel as the author, though no evidence is available to support such a claim. Recent scholarship has generally included the book within the Deuteronomistic History, as discussed earlier (see p. 205).

    The consensus today is that the book comprises narratives that may have been composed nearly contemporary with the events and put in a theological-literary setting by a compiler at a later date. So, for instance, the Song of Deborah (Judg. 5) is frequently dated to the premonarchical period, while the narrator's refrain, "In those days Israel had no king" (e.g., 17:6; 18:1), gives clear evidence that at the time he was writing the nation had a king. From such indications we understand that the book's composition involved a process that may have consumed several centuries. This does not pose a threat to those holding a traditional view of inspiration, for other books of the Bible were clearly compiled over centuries by numerous hands (e.g., Psalms).

The Background

Chronology

The dating of the period of the judges depends, of course, on one's view of the date of the exodus and the conquest. Given a thirteenth-century date for the exodus, the judges period would cover most of the twelfth and eleventh centuries BC, which corresponds roughly to what archaeologists have called Iron Age I. The earlier, fifteenth-century date of the exodus would yield a judges period twice as long, extending from the fourteenth century through the eleventh and including both Iron Age I and the period referred to as the Late Bronze Age II.

Some internal evidence for the dating of the book exists, but it is not conclusive. Adding up the years of each oppression and the years of rest noted at the end of each cycle yields a total of 410 years, but this is too many to fit even the longer period. Some discrepancy has been accounted for by assuming that numbers are rounded off, but it is likewise probable that at least some of the oppressions and judges are more local rather than national and coincide (cf. Judg. 10:7). As a result, we cannot date the judges period precisely with confidence. It

This stone relief from the palace of Ashurbanipal shows Assyrian troops on horseback pursuing Arabs on camels. Camels were a valuable commodity in the ancient world because of their speed and their ability to survive in the desert. An army with camels was also a commodity. "There was no number to [the Midianites] and their camels; and they came to the land of Israel, and laid it waste" (Judg. 6:5).

Werner Forman Archive/The British Museum

The Israelites often adopted the worship of Baal, the Canaanite storm god, during the Judges period. In Judges 2:11–12 this is cited as the main reason for their continuing struggles: "Then the Israelites did evil in the eyes of the LORD and served the Baals. They forsook the LORD, the God of their fathers, who had brought them out of Egypt."
Marie-Lan Nguyen/Wikimedia Commons, courtesy of the Louvre

does appear, however, that the period cannot be limited to Iron Age I, for Judges 11:26 affirms without dispute that at the time of Jephthah, Israel had already been in the land for three hundred years. The longer period also seems to correlate more easily with the information given in 1 Kings 6:1, where 480 years are said to have transpired between the exodus and the dedication of the temple by Solomon.

The Historical Background

Late Bronze Age II witnessed empires struggling in a virtual stalemate with the advantage constantly shifting from one power to another. As the Egyptians and Hittites vied for control of the lucrative trade routes and seaports of Syro-Palestine, the Mitannian Empire and later the Assyrians provided a third political center whose allegiance could shift the balance of power from one side to the other. Though some of the most powerful and distinguished kings in history reigned during this time (e.g., Rameses the Great), the book of Judges offers no acknowledgment of them. Since the territory occupied by the Israelites was primarily confined to the hill country and away from the major trade routes, the struggles of the empires may have had little impact on them. More important, however, the narrator of Judges seems more interested in the theological implications of history, allowing him to ignore important international events as being superfluous to his purpose.

All of this changed dramatically in a series of events traditionally attributed to the Sea Peoples' incursion into the ancient Near East from the Mediterranean at the end of the thirteenth century BC. The stalemate ended as the Hittite Empire fell, the Egyptians relapsed into internal struggles, and the trade that the empires had sought to control by their military expansion was devastated in the destruction of a number of the prosperous seaports. The result was a political vacuum in which there were no international powers threatening the peoples of Palestine. This opened the way for the growing influence of the Philistines (one of the groups of the Sea Peoples who settled on the southern coast of Palestine) and the infiltration of the Aramaean tribes from the

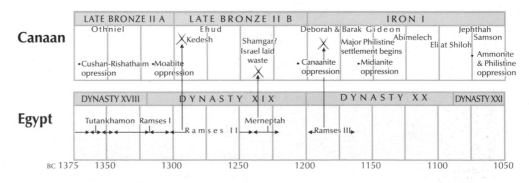

	LATE BRONZE II A	LATE BRONZE II B		IRON I		
Canaan	Othniel	Ehud Kedesh	Shamgar? Israel laid waste	Deborah & Barak	Gideon Major Philistine settlement begins Abimelech Eli at Shiloh	Jephthah Samson
	•Cushan-Rishathaim	•Moabite opression		•Canaanite oppression	•Midianite oppression	•Ammonite & Philistine oppression
	DYNASTY XVIII	DYNASTY XIX		DYNASTY XX		DYNASTY XXI
Egypt	Tutankhamon Ramses I	Ramses II	Merneptah	Ramses III		
BC 1375	1350	1300	1250	1200	1150	1100 1050

northeast, who were to become a dominant political force during the time of the Israelite monarchy.

Cultural Background

When the Israelites came into Canaan, they found, not a unified country, but numerous city-states with separate governments. At times these city-states were loosely confederated as allies, and more frequently they were aligned with major powers, especially Egypt, that often dominated the region. The correspondence from some of these cities found in the Amarna letters shows that they did not always receive the help from Egypt that they expected or needed, and also that they were not above implicating one another in conspiracies against the pharaohs. Yet the narratives of the book of Joshua show that they could work together against a common enemy when the need arose. In contrast, Israel was organized politically by a tribal structure. Each clan descended from Jacob's sons had its own leaders.

Purpose and Message

The purpose of the book of Judges is to explore what happened theologically during the years between Joshua and David. The Lord had given the Israelites the land, and they had formalized their commitment to

A mountain is an obvious place to gather an army. Deborah instructed Barak to gather an army on Mount Tabor in order to incite Sisera, the commander of Jabin''s army, to battle. It worked, and the Israelites triumphed (Judg. 4:1–24).
Todd Bolen/
www.BiblePlaces.com

Abimelech "went to his father's home in Ophrah and on one stone murdered his seventy brothers" (Judg. 9:5). Standing stones, like these from Gezer, were used in ancient Israel for a variety of purposes; they were often designated sacred space and thus became the site for rituals.

Dr. Tim Bulkeley,
www.eBibleTools.com

remain faithful to him by covenant at Shechem (Josh. 24). But there ensued centuries of failure, finally brought to an end by the Lord's formal installation of kingship by covenant (2 Sam. 7). How was God working between these covenants, and why were the Israelites not enjoying the blessings of the covenant?

The message of the book is that the problem was not the Lord's fault, but was created and sustained by Israel's continued disobedience. The judges period was characterized by acts of depravity, not just individually, but on the tribal level. This is conveyed by the two sets of refrains that recur in their respective sections of the book. Each cycle in chapters 3–16 is introduced by the observation that "the Israelites did evil in the eyes of the Lord" (2:11; 3:7, 12; 4:1; 6:1; 10:6; 13:1), indicating the tendency toward theological apostasy. The second refrain serves as an "inclusio" by appearing at the beginning and end of chapters 17–21 (17:6; 21:25): "In those days there was no king in Israel; everyone did as he saw fit." The first half of the phrase is used in two other places as well to sustain the narrative in between (18:1; 19:1).

This second section (chaps. 17–21) is not so distinctly covenant oriented as the first section (chaps. 2–16), though covenant violations abound. It rather shows that injustice was the natural by-product of the Israelites' apostasy. Since the refrain appears to blame the conditions on the lack of kingship, some have seen this section as an apologetic for monarchy. Though this seems to us doubtful, the refrain shows that tribal leadership was ineffective in maintaining conformity to God's covenant and rule.

In these refrains can be seen an obvious contrast to David, who "had done what was right in the eyes of the Lord" (1 Kings 15:5), but the books of Kings show that the monarchy was also unsuccessful in keeping people faithful to the covenant. Yet in all these times, though apostasy and injustice brought punishment, the mercy of the Lord was also evident. In the books of Kings, God's mercy is evident in his raising up of prophets to warn the people; in Judges it is evident in his raising up judges to deliver the people. The message emphasized Yahweh's longsuffering grace in the face of continual and rampant apostasy and injustice among his people. Covenant failures of the people were met by covenant faithfulness from the Lord.

Structure and Organization

The first section of the book establishes the failure of Israel to carry out the directions of the Lord to purge the land of the Canaanites. The result was that, although the land had been formally given into the control of the Israelites by virtue of the conquest, it was neither possessed nor controlled by them. This failure to rid the land of Canaanites led in turn to the apostasy of Israel that characterized the judges period. The book of Joshua has made it clear that there was no possibility of blaming the Lord for doing only a partial job. Judges 1 likewise discounts this possibility. The Lord's refusal to drive out the inhabitants of the land was a direct result of the people's disobedience—a point made in the speech of "the angel of the Lord" at the end of the first section (2:1–5).

The next part (2:6–3:6) introduces the cycles that constitute the theological framework of the period. Formulas are used through most of the cycles to demonstrate that the pattern is typical. First, the people did evil in the eyes of the Lord—usually described in broad terms indicating the practice of worshiping Canaanite deities. The typical response was for the Lord to punish them, doing so by sending foreign oppressors. It is noteworthy that on only one occasion were the Canaanites the oppressors (chap. 4).

As might be expected, the people would eventually cry out to the Lord to deliver them. Yet neither in the introduction to this section (chap. 2) nor in the actual cycles (chaps. 3–16) do we read that the people offered repentance. They cried for help, but with the exception of 10:10–16 there is no indication that repentance or reform accompanied that cry. Nevertheless, the Lord would raise up a deliverer as an act of compassion, and this deliverer would bring liberation during his lifetime, only to have the cycle begin all over again once he died.

This is the cycle of apostasy introduced in chapter 2 and then followed through six full repetitions in chapters 3–16. The major intrusion into this is chapter 9, which recounts an occasion when Abimelech, one of the sons of Gideon, tried to make himself king. This aborted attempt served as an early warning to the Israelites that monarchies are only as successful as the king who sits on the throne.

Chapters 17–21 show that the Israelites, despite this cycle of human apostasy and divine deliverance, failed to establish a just and righteous social order. There was no consistent basis for ethics and morality. The book thus ends in a scene of gloom and depression. Kingship was a logical and moral option to pursue. But the reason why a king was needed, as inferred from Judges, was to help the people do what was right in the eyes of the Lord, so that oppression would not come. Merely to have someone in charge who would go out and fight their battles for them (1 Sam. 8:20) missed the point of the Judges narrator entirely.

This Babylonian seal depicts the hero Gilgamesh kneeling with an outstretched lion above his head. Lions were dangerous foes, and one who defeated a lion was considered great. The Israelite judge Samson killed a lion with his bare hands (Judg. 14:6).

Werner Forman Archive

Major Themes

The Nature of Charismatic Leadership

The office of judge in this period of Israelite history is not easy to define. The judges were not elected, nor did they inherit their office. They were not appointed in any official way, nor were they anointed. They are referred to as charismatic leaders because they spontaneously took leadership roles when the need arose. Thus, it can be affirmed that God raised them up to deliver Israel.

Though a similar term to that rendered "judge" is used to describe tribal leaders in the Mari texts and magistrates in Phoenician and Punic literature, the function of the judge in Israel can best be determined by developing a profile from the book of Judges. The most prominent tasks undertaken by the judges were military in nature. In this sense the judge was establishing justice for the Israelites who were oppressed by other peoples. There is very little civil function mentioned for the judges, though it is generally assumed that disputes would have been brought to these persons for resolution.

There is even less information given for any sort of spiritual function. The situation of Deborah does not clarify the matter, for she is identified as a prophetess. The judges had no relation to the tabernacle or to the ark of the covenant, and they did not call the people back to Yahweh. Though the Lord is identified by the narrator as the one who raised up the judges, there is little evidence to conclude that they were chosen on the basis of their spirituality. Gideon, Jephthah, and Samson all acknowledged the Lord in their speech and acted in his name, but—typical of the times—had major blemishes on the record:

Gideon was blamed for improper worship involving the ephod he made (8:27), Jephthah performed child sacrifice (11:30–40), and Samson habitually cavorted with Philistine women, thereby undermining his ability to accomplish his task (chaps. 14–16).

We must conclude, therefore, that the judges were not intended to be spiritual role models, nor was their spirituality necessarily a criterion for God's raising them up. Indeed, the text never implies that it was. This is not to suggest that the judges did not act in faith; rather, it warns us not to place them on too high a pedestal. There were unquestionably some unethical things done by certain judges (e.g., 3:20; 15:4–5). The Bible does not express approval even though it acknowledges that deliverance was still possible nevertheless.

The task of the judge was to be a deliverer—in fact, the Lord's instrument for providing deliverance. In 2 Kings 13:5 the same term, "deliverer," is used and probably refers to a foreign king. It could thus be concluded that the person might at times be unaware that he was functioning as a deliverer and did not necessarily intend to be so. The fact that deliverance was accomplished does not imply approval of the means used. Of Samson it is noted that the Lord was using even his bad choices to accomplish his purposes (14:4). Acting as deliverer was part of the larger role of being responsible for procuring justice for the people. This was the basic job description of the kings of the ancient world, and it would seem that functionally the office of judge was not greatly different from king. They differed primarily in the way one came to the office and in the fact that there was no political machinery to support the office of judge.

It is very possible that many of the judges exercised only local jurisdiction, but this is a difficult point to prove. A distinction is often made today between "major" and "minor" judges, though this reflects their treatment in the book more than their historical importance or the extent of their influence or jurisdiction. The designation "major" is used for those judges who are directly connected to the cycles of the book (Othniel, Ehud, Deborah/Barak, Gideon, Jephthah, and Samson). These are also the ones apparently raised up by God for a specific task. These judges had experiences with prophets (Deborah, herself a prophetess, was used by the Lord to raise up Barak); angels (Gideon, Samson's parents), and the Spirit of the Lord (Othniel, Gideon, Jephthah, Samson). These experiences were the evidence of the Lord's role in directing and empowering the charismatic leaders of Israel.

The Spirit of the Lord

The Spirit of the Lord plays a prominent role in the book of Judges. It was under his power that several of the judges accomplished their tasks, and this therefore demonstrated that the Lord was at work and

with and manifested through the forces of nature. They were capricious and unpredictable and not particularly prone to moral behavior. Their demands were largely ritual in nature, and it was thought that the temple and sacrifice satisfied their needs. And since they had needs that they were dependent on humans to provide, the gods could be manipulated.

These two views of deity—Israelite monotheism and Canaanite polytheism—were mutually exclusive. The monotheistic view that was accepted in theory at Sinai involved sophisticated philosophical adjustments that most of the people simply never made. Once the Israelites had arrived in the land and had scattered to their respective territories, the ever-present Canaanite religion influenced the way they thought about God. Not only did they worship the Canaanite gods, but as even the prophets indicated at a much later date, they treated the Lord as if he were one of the pagan deities.

If the first few generations failed to remain theologically distinct, it is no surprise that the problem lasted a long time, for the system had been set up so that the law would be transmitted within the family (Deut. 6:4–9). Though it is clear that Israel remembered their history during the judges period (6:13; 11:14–27), there is little to suggest that the details of the law had penetrated their worldview. The priesthood was most to blame for this lapse (for example, see Judg. 17–21; 1 Sam. 2–4), and their failure may have hastened the decline of priestly influence.

Questions for Further Study and Discussion

1. How does the book of Judges illustrate the need to distinguish between the plan of God and the will of God? How can God's plan be carried out by people who are not self-consciously seeking to do God's will? (Consider the book of Habakkuk and Genesis 50:20 in your answer.)
2. What validity was there in Gideon's oracle of the fleece and in Jephthah's vow? Would these be legitimate methods to use today, and if so, under what conditions or restrictions?
3. Can someone who is empowered by the Spirit of the Lord do things contrary to God's will? Explain your answer.
4. What theological conclusions can be drawn from the continuity and discontinuity observable between the Old Testament and New Testament roles of the Spirit?

For Further Reading

Block, Daniel. *Judges, Ruth*. Nashville: Broadman & Holman, 1999. The most helpful of all commentaries on the book.

Boling, Robert. *Judges*. Garden City, N.Y.: Doubleday, 1975. Helpful archaeological and historical information. Exegetically good, though not evangelical.

Cundall, Arthur, and Leon Morris. *Judges and Ruth*. TOTC. Downers Grove, Ill.: InterVarsity Press, 1968.

de Vaux, Roland. *The Early History of Israel*. Philadelphia: Westminster, 1978. A comprehensive treatment of scholarly reconstructions of the literature and history of this era.

Gray, John. *Joshua, Judges, Ruth*. NCBC. Grand Rapids: Eerdmans, 1986.

Kitchen, Kenneth A. *Pharaoh Triumphant: The Life and Times of Ramesses II*. London: Aris and Phillips, 1982. A very thorough and delightful reconstruction of the life and accomplishments of Rameses the Great, drawing heavily on the inscriptional data.

Soggin, J. A. *Judges*. Philadelphia: Westminster, 1981. Heavy on literary and reconstructive analysis, light on exegetical.

Wilcock, Michael. *The Message of Judges*. Downers Grove, Ill.: InterVarsity Press, 1992.

Yadin, Yigael. *The Art of Warfare in Biblical Lands*. London: Weidenfeld and Nicolson, 1963. A compendium of information about weapons, armaments, defenses, fortifications, and strategies used in the various periods of Old Testament history.

Younger, K. Lawson. *Judges, Ruth*. NIVAC. Grand Rapids: Zondervan, 2002.

On the threshing floor, good grain was separated from the heads by pulling a heavy sledge with bits of sharp rock over the grain. Then the threshed grain was tossed in the air to separate the kernels from the chaff. The winnowing process is portrayed in this Egyptian painting from the Tomb of Menna. It was to the threshing floor that Ruth went to propose marriage to Boaz (Ruth 3:1–6).

Manfred Näder gabana Studios Germany

RUTH

Key Ideas

- God's faithfulness and loyalty stimulated by people's faithfulness and loyalty to one another
- David's faith shown to be the legacy of his ancestors
- The light of loyalty dispersed during the apostasy of the Judges period
- The concept of kinsman-redeemer introduced

Purpose Statement

The purpose of Ruth is to show that when people are faithful, God is faithful. It provides a contrast to the book of Judges showing that faithfulness survived in Israel among some of the common folk. God preserved such families of faithfulness, and that is the very background from which David came.

Major Themes

- Kinsman Redeemer
- Hesed

God's Presence

The book begins with the apparent absence of God's presence indicated by the famine and resulting in Israelites leaving the land. It is not hard to understand God's absence in light of the setting in the Judges period. Nevertheless the book shows that God is still present with his people as his care is demonstrated to Naomi and Ruth.

Outline

The touching story of Ruth introduces the reader of the Old Testament to one of the lynchpins of the covenant. As a record of an incident that occurred during the judges period, it offers a stark contrast to the negative perspective of Israelite faith offered there. Rather than Israelites abandoning their loyalty and deserting the worship of Yahweh for other gods, the story portrays Ruth acting out of loyalty and embracing Yahweh, denouncing other gods, even as that which becomes the Davidic line hovers on the brink of extinction.

The Writing of the Book

No author is named for the book, so it remains anonymous. Though it is placed after Judges in the English Bible, following the lead of the Septuagint and Vulgate, the Jewish ordering counts it among the third division of the canon, the Writings. As a result, the book is not considered to be part of the Deuteronomistic History.

The opening verse implies that the judges period is past, and the closing genealogy suggests that the audience would have been familiar with David. If the genealogy is not a later addition, the book is a product of the monarchy period at the earliest. Other factors such as the language and customs (e.g., levirate marriage) have been used by some to support a preexilic date, by others to defend a postexilic date. There is no consensus on the matter, although a preexilic date is gaining support and seems to us to be favored by the evidence.

The Background

Historical Background

Little can be offered to place this story with any confidence in a particular part of the judges period. The Moabites oppressed Israel early in the period and were driven out by Ehud (Judg. 3), so we would not expect that the story occurred then. If the genealogy at the end of the book is complete, the events would most logically be placed toward the end of the twelfth century BC, roughly contemporary with Jephthah.

Not much is known about Ruth's people, the Moabites, during the judges period aside from the brief oppression at the time of Ehud. The Moabites were a kindred people to the Israelites, descended from Abraham's nephew Lot (Gen. 19:37). They occupied the territory across the Dead Sea from Judah. They had shown hostility toward the Israelites at the time of Moses (Num. 21–25) but were sympathetic to David's cause when he was a fugitive from Saul (1 Sam. 22:3–4). Later they were subdued by David (2 Sam. 8:2).

Literary Background

Rich in dialogue, the book of Ruth has all the literary trappings of a dramatic play in four scenes. This has contributed to a growing number of scholars treating the book as folklore. Its literary qualities have long been appreciated, from its succinct prose to its skillful character development. Its pastoral setting, portrayal of common people, and lack of a villain qualify it as an **idyll**, though idylls are usually fictional. Robert Hubbard has built a case for the classification "short story," which would not preclude historical accuracy.[1]

Purpose and Message

Because the book ends with David, many have seen in it a message concerning the king. The question is, what point is the book making about him? Is it an attempt to explain and excuse his foreign ancestry? Does it intend to show divine providence at work in preserving the line to which he was heir? Others, seeing the book's connection to David as secondary, think the purpose is either to promote conversion of foreign peoples or to discourage Israelite intermarriage with them. Both ideas are difficult to support because of the turn of events traced in the book and because of its gentle tone.

Although David should not be ignored in determining the intent of the author, the actual purpose of the narrative may supersede a narrow focus on David alone. The judges period that provided the setting was notorious for its apostasy and covenantal ignorance and offense; faith was at a premium. How did the faith of Israel survive? We suggest that it survived in the families of common folk such as Elimelech and Naomi. The overall picture was grim, but there were faithful individuals. This issue is not without significance for the reader's understanding of David. As the historical narratives move from the judges period to the monarchy, the reader may find a faith like David's difficult to reconcile. How could faith like this still exist after four hundred years of conditions such as those described in the book of Judges? The story of Ruth, drawn from David's ancestry, offers an explanation of the survival of faith.

1. Robert L. Hubbard, *The Book of Ruth* (Grand Rapids: Eerdmans, 1988), 47–48. As is common with short stories, the book of Ruth can entertain as well as instruct.

Questions for Further Study and Discussion

1. What are the various ways in which *ḥesed* is expressed in the book?
2. What significance would the Israelites attach to the fact that Ruth was from Moab?
3. What did the principle of levirate marriage imply regarding the family culture of ancient Israel?
4. Why did the book of Ruth become associated with the Feast of Pentecost in later Judaism?

For Further Reading

Atkinson, David. *The Wings of Refuge.* Downers Grove, Ill.: InterVarsity Press, 1983.

Block, Daniel. *Judges, Ruth.* Nashville: Broadman & Holman, 1999.

Bush, Frederic. *Ruth/Esther.* Dallas: Word, 1996.

Campbell, Edward F. *Ruth.* Garden City, N.Y.: Doubleday, 1975. Straightforward and helpful, though not evangelical.

Cundall, Arthur, and Leon Morris. *Judges and Ruth.* TOTC. Downers Grove, Ill.: InterVarsity Press, 1968.

Gray, John. *Joshua, Judges, Ruth.* NCBC. Grand Rapids: Eerdmans, 1986.

Hubbard, Robert L. *The Book of Ruth.* Grand Rapids: Eerdmans, 1988. The best of the commentaries on Ruth: evangelical, thorough, insightful, and readable.

Luter, A. Boyd, and Barry C. Davis. *God Behind the Seen.* Grand Rapids: Baker, 1995.

Sasson, Jack M. *Ruth.* Baltimore: Johns Hopkins University Press, 1979. A sociological approach that offers many stimulating and some radical suggestions.

After Saul was anointed king by Samuel (1 Sam. 10:1) and proclaimed king by the people (10:24), he made his home at Gibeah (10:26). This is a view of the excavated palace at Gibeah, not far from Jerusalem.

David Bivin/www.BiblePlaces.com

1–2 SAMUEL

Key Ideas

- The institution of kingship
- The process toward establishing a covenant with David's line
- The importance of divine kingship

Purpose Statement

The purpose of the books of Samuel is to tell the story of the establishment of the kingship covenant with David. God's plan was to have an earthly king who would give a good example of what God's kingship was like. David is shown to be the legitimate choice of God, but also is shown to have been at times an obstacle rather than an instrument of God's rule.

Major Themes

- Ark of the Covenant
- Kingship
- Davidic Covenant
- Assessment of Saul
- Assessment of David

God's Presence

God's presence with David as he battled Goliath is expanded into his presence with David and his line as appointed kings. His presence is restored to a central position as the ark is brought into Jerusalem.

Outline

    I. The Shiloh Traditions (1 Sam. 1:1–4:1a)

   II. The Ark Narrative (1 Sam. 4:1b–7:1)

  III. The Institution of the Monarchy (1 Sam. 7:2–12:25)

  IV. The Reign of Saul (1 Sam. 13–15)

   V. David's Rise to Power (1 Sam. 16:1–2 Sam. 5:10)

 VI. David's Successes (2 Sam. 5:11–9:13)

VII. David's Failures (2 Sam. 10–24)
    A. Men Acting Against Him: The Succession Narrative (2 Sam. 10–20)
    B. God Acting Against Him: Appendix (2 Sam. 21–24)

The books of 1 and 2 Samuel fall together naturally as a unit and originally constituted a single book. Together they cover the period of the transition from the judges through the establishment of the monarchy, including the reigns of Saul and David. Although the Septuagint combines the books of Samuel with the books of Kings under the title "Kingdoms," the Hebrew text traditionally has referred to these books as the books of Samuel in recognition of the significant role of Samuel in the establishment of the monarchy.

The Writing of the Book

The events of the book took place in the last half of the eleventh century and the early part of the tenth century BC, but it is difficult to determine when the events were recorded. There are no particularly persuasive reasons to date the sources used by the compiler later than the events themselves, and good reason to believe that contemporary records were kept (cf. 2 Sam. 20:24–25). If the books are part of a larger "Deuteronomistic" work, the compiler would have worked late in the period of the divided monarchy.

The Background

Sources for this period of history are scarce. Neither Egypt nor Mesopotamia was in any position to look beyond its borders, so smaller nations of Syro-Palestine were left to squabble among themselves. Threats to Israel posed especially by the Philistines necessitated a greater amount of cooperation among the tribes than was the case previously, and these are directly responsible for the decision to switch to a monarchic

This ivory plaque from Megiddo, dating from the 12th–13th centuries BC, depicts a ruler, perhaps the king of Megiddo, sitting on his throne, surrounded by attendants who are inspecting prisoners. Of interest is the portrayal of cherubs flanking the throne, the same way that the Lord is understood as being enthroned upon the cherubim.

Z. Radovan/
www.BibleLandPictures.com

form of government. Saul had occasional victories over the Philistines, but he died in the battle at Mount Gilboa and the Philistines overran at least the central portion of Palestine. It was left to David, therefore, to drive out the Philistines. David was also successful in extending Israelite control over most of Syro-Palestine through a series of conquests and treaties.

Purpose and Message

As we noted in the introduction to historical literature, these books do not have a strictly historical purpose. That is, this is not history for history's sake. Neither are these books biographical in intent, though certainly some biographical data are included. The major purpose is theological. As Genesis gives us the history of the establishment of the Abrahamic covenant, so Samuel gives us the history of the establishment of the Davidic covenant (2 Sam. 7). The emphasis in these books and ultimately in the covenant itself is the development of the proper concept of divine authority.[1]

The message has several aspects to it. The primary message is that the Davidic covenant was established by God. People may choose kings, as they did Saul, but God chooses dynasties. Even though the people chose the first king and God did not approve of either their motivation for or their concept of kingship, the institution of a monarchy was in God's plan for Israel (Deut. 17:14–20).

Surely another concern of the narrator was to demonstrate to the reader that David was not a usurper of the throne, but painstakingly avoided taking any action against the house of Saul. This concern is pursued to make it clear that God placed David on the throne, lest anyone think of David as a renegade who plotted to seize the throne, assassinated the king and his rightful heirs, and then attempted to excuse his atrocities by claiming divine approval and guidance. This is not, however, a whitewash of David. The narrative portrays David in all his humanity and refuses to obscure in any way his weaknesses or the punishments he received at the hand of God. The second half of 2 Samuel then turns to problems within David's family and kingdom with the message that David's own failures were magnified in his children

---

1. W. J. Dumbrell, "The Content and Significance of the Books of Samuel: Their Place and Purpose Within the Former Prophets," *JETS* 33 (1990): 50.

to the extent that the covenant was put in jeopardy, with the story to be continued into the books of Kings.

Structure and Organization

The Shiloh traditions (1 Sam 1:1–4:12) introduce us to Samuel and give us the information that even from birth there was something unique about him. This is appropriate, for he was the one who was going to serve the important transitionary function between the period of the judges and the monarchy. After relating the circumstances surrounding his birth and arrival at the temple, the narrative draws a contrast between Samuel and Eli, and Eli's rebellious sons. The prophetic word of the demise of the house of Eli came to Samuel and established his reputation as a man of God. He also wore the linen ephod of the priest. The wretched condition of the priesthood is exemplified in Eli's house and demonstrates the extent of the apostasy of the judges period.

The judges period ended in exile of a sort—a self-imposed exile of the Lord represented in the ark of the covenant's being captured by the Philistines and taken out of the land of Israel. Usually the victory of one army over another was thought to signal the victory of the gods of that nation over the gods of the defeated nation. The fact that the ark had been captured would have naturally led to the conclusion that the Philistine god, Dagon, was more powerful than the Israelite God, Yahweh. The events in chapters 5–6 are reported to dispel any such idea. With Yahweh's demonstration of his power over the idol of Dagon and also his plague on the Philistine people, it became clear that the Lord had not been overpowered, but had rejected and therefore abandoned the Israelites. The theme of divine abandonment is well-known in the ancient Near East.

This self-imposed exile marked a distinct break between the period of the judges and the monarchy. The account of the return of the ark from exile uses language that is reminiscent of the exodus.[2] It is of theological interest that the ark's temporary housing continued through

2. A. F. Campbell, *The Ark Narrative* (Missoula, Mont.: Scholars Press, 1975), 203ff.

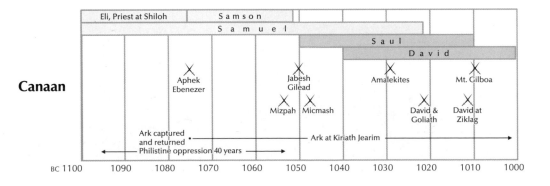

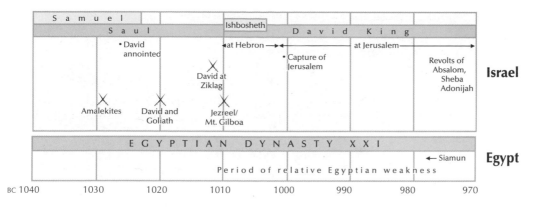

S a m u e l							
S a u l			Ishbosheth	D a v i d K i n g			

Israel

EGYPTIAN DYNASTY XXI

Egypt

Period of relative Egyptian weakness

← Siamun

BC 1040   1030   1020   1010   1000   990   980   970

all of Saul's reign and that the ark was not officially brought back into prominence until David brought it to Jerusalem (2 Sam. 6). This suggests that both Samuel and Saul were transitional figures.

The Institution of the Monarchy

A section on the institution of the monarchy begins at 1 Samuel 7. At the outset, Samuel is functioning not only as prophet and priest, but also as judge. Despite all the political power vested in Samuel, he was still not a king. That condition led to the request by the people that Samuel preside over a change in the form of government, from judges to kings. This was not supposed to be as big a change as the people imagined it would be. Both systems ought to have been theocratic in nature. Even when there was a human king, he was supposed to be only the representative of the divine King. The fact that the people had

Steve Nicholls

"The LORD said, 'Rise and anoint him [David]; he is the one.' So Samuel took the horn of oil and anointed him.... And from that day the Spirit of the LORD came upon David in power" (1 Sam. 16:12–13). Deity was understood to be the one who anointed kings. In this picture of the temple at Kom Ombo, Egypt (from the Ptolemaic era, third to first centuries BC), the anointing oil is portrayed by ankh signs, the Egyptian symbol of life.

not understood this is reflected in the Lord's analysis that the people had rejected him, not Samuel. If the Lord was not king, a human king would not meet their expectations.

Mention of Samuel's disappointment may suggest that he considered himself the most appropriate candidate for the position. This is supported by the references to Samuel's age and his sons' waywardness (8:4–5). In fact, the NIV confirms this in the translation, "It is not you they have rejected, but they have rejected me as their king" (8:7).

Chapter 9 introduces both Saul and a literary device into the text. The format of the text regarding the united monarchy (Saul, David, and Solomon) is to relate the appointment of a king, describe his potential and successes, and finally recount his failures and the results of those failures (fig. 14.1). Saul's installation included several steps showing Samuel, the Lord, and the people all having distinctive roles to play in his appointment. It is notable that the terminology used by the Lord in describing Saul's appointed function (9:16–17) and the incident at Jabesh Gilead (chap. 11) both seem to portray Saul more as a judge than a king. Also, as with many of the judges, Saul seemed well-intentioned but lacking in spiritual depth and a sound knowledge of the Lord. This is not unexpected, since he came on the scene after four hundred years of general apostasy that characterized the judges period. A judge was expected to be a deliverer, and that is what the people expected of a king as well. At the beginning, Saul succeeded in doing this, fulfilling his potential. But God expected more of a king, and Saul was unable to meet the requirements.

The conclusion of this section (chap. 12) indicates that the people's insistence on having a king was really a willful rejection of the Lord's rule over them. Their primary error was that they assumed they were being oppressed because they had no king to lead them into battle; in reality they were being oppressed for their sin. Kingship would not cure this problem; it would make it worse. Therefore, chapter 12 also

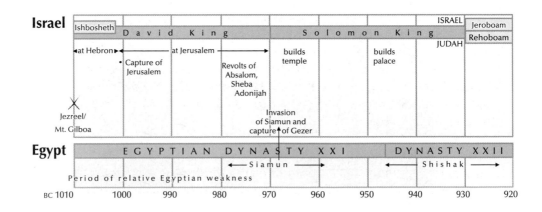

Figure 14.1. Narrative Emphasis in the History of the United Monarchy

	Saul	David	Solomon
Appointment	1. By Samuel 2. Public process 3. Activated by the Spirit	1. By Samuel 2. Long process 3. By people	1. By David 2. By Zadok and Nathan
Successes and potential	Victory over Ammonites	1. Taking of Jerusalem 2. Defeat of Philistines 3. Bringing ark back 4. Covenant 5. Expansion of empire	1. Dream and request for wisdom 2. Wisdom and adminis-tration of empire 3. Building of temple
Failures	1. Impatient offering 2. Placing people under improper oath 3. Disobeying instruc-tions in Amalekite war	1. Adultery with Bath-sheba and murder of Uriah 2. Wrongful taking of census	1. Foreign wives' religious practices accommo-dated 2. Labor and tax on people
Results of failures	Bad judgment, incompe-tence, and jealousy	1. Bloodshed within fam-ily (Amnon, Absalom, Adonijah) 2. Rebellion in kingdom (Absalom, Sheba)	1. Military problems 2. Division of kingdom

established the continuing importance of the prophetic office to pro-vide God's guidance to the king.

One might ask, why did God appoint Saul if he knew the king would fail? But that is the wrong question. God used Saul to bring temporary deliverance for Israel—in the same way he had used Gideon, Samson, and other judges. They all had their failures, yet God accomplished his plan despite them. Saul had the potential to succeed, but he did not develop into a man who knew God. His lack of spiritual insight and sound judgment becomes clear as the text recounts his failures.

The Vindication of David

Chapters 13–15 concern the failures of Saul. It is significant that although chapters 19–28 appear to have enough damaging information about Saul to convince readers that he was unsuitable for the throne, there is some concern to show the failures of Saul independently from and prior to his relationship with David. The point is that David did not cause Saul's failure; rather, Saul had disqualified himself before David ever came on the scene.

It is difficult to dissect Saul's offense of offering the sacrifice for the consecration of the soldiers prior to battle (chap. 13). Saul was in an awkward position. Samuel had not come to offer the sacrifice in preparation for battle, and Saul dared not go into battle without it—yet the opportunity for attack was passing quickly and the army was beginning to desert. What would be the most appropriate course of action? Saul acted in his best judgment and reluctantly offered the sacrifice. In doing so, he followed a Canaanite model of kingship, in which the king had certain priestly prerogatives. When Samuel arrived and learned what Saul had done, he was absolutely livid. This is an example of Saul's inability to make wise decisions. The wisdom that was the natural endowment of a true king had escaped Saul; he neither possessed it nor requested it. One could not succeed as king on good intentions.

Chapters 14 and 15 continue to show how Saul's lack of wisdom surfaced in consistently bad decisions. His leadership ability gradually eroded to the point that he gave in easily to the people's demands on him (14:45; 15:15, 24). This was the legacy of Saul, and it led the Lord to direct Samuel to anoint Saul's successor.

Although the history of David's rise continues to reveal the shortcomings of Saul, the narrative is arranged around David and tells his story. From his anointing in 1 Samuel 16 to his enthronement in 2 Samuel 5, the text is oriented toward David. As previously mentioned, the concern of the narrator here was to demonstrate that even though David was destined by the Lord to rule Israel, he did not usurp the throne of Saul.

There are three major points supporting the narrator's contention. The first is Saul's animosity. There is a firm case built in these narratives that Saul was consistently the initiator of the antagonism that grew up between him and David. It was Saul who threw spears at David, who sent men to arrest David during the night, and who pursued David around the wilderness of Judah. This point is also made by the narrator's clear statements of Saul's motivation in various situations when David was sent against the Philistines (1 Sam. 18:17–25).

In the Valley of Elah, the Philistines gathered against the Israelites for battle and put Goliath of Gath as their champion. David confronted the giant and defeated him there (1 Sam. 17).

Bible Scene Multimedia/
Maurice Thompson

The second and most extensive proof is David's nonaggression. This is demonstrated in his friendship and covenant with Jonathan, Saul's son and heir to the throne (18:1–4; 19:1–7; 20:1–42). Similarly, David's marriage to Michal, Saul's daughter, even though he considered himself unworthy to marry into Saul's family, shows David's benevolent attitude toward them (18:17–29). The major evidence, however, in the narrator's case is the two occasions on which David could have killed Saul—and was urged to do so, but refused (1 Sam. 24 and 26).

Furthermore, a number of narratives strive to demonstrate that David was not involved in actions taken against Saul and his house.[3] He was not in the battle in which Saul was killed, so he could not be blamed for assassination under the cover of battle (1 Sam. 28–29). The text goes to great lengths to describe David's activities with the Philistines and how he was dismissed from taking part in the battle—all to vindicate David on this point.

After Saul's death, the kingdom fell to his son, Ish-Bosheth, but Abner, who had been Saul's commander-in-chief, seems to have been in charge. When he and Ish-Bosheth had a falling out, Abner determined to deliver the kingdom to David. Unfortunately, while he was on his mission to David, Abner was assassinated. The narrator was careful to establish that there were hard feelings between Abner and Joab (2 Sam. 2) so that the reader can understand that when Joab killed Abner, he did so for personal reasons rather than at David's command (2 Sam. 3:28–39). Likewise, the narrator wanted to establish that David neither killed nor ordered the killing of Ish-Bosheth (2 Sam. 4).

Another sign of the text's vindicating David of action against Saul's house lies in the treatment of David's wife Michal. Through most of his reign she was out of favor, but this had nothing to do with her being Saul's daughter. The narrator told the story of Michal's ridicule of David that led to her fall from favor (2 Sam. 6:16–23). Then there was the case of Shimei—a descendant of Saul who was put to death by Solomon on David's instruction. As the text relates, however, this execution was not without good reason (2 Sam. 16:5–13; 19:16–23; 1 Kings 2:36–46) and was not motivated by Shimei's relationship to Saul.

A final case is presented in the appendix of Samuel, and this was perhaps the most suspicious to observers of the royal house. Seven members of the house of Saul were executed because of their lineage (2 Sam. 21). Again, however, it is explained that David did not instigate

"Then he took his staff in his hand, chose five smooth stones from the stream, put them in the pouch of his shepherd's bag and, with his sling in his hand, approached the Philistine" (1 Sam. 17:40). The sling stones typically used in the ancient world were not small pebbles, but stones the size of a fist, such as these that were found in the city of Lachish. Armies had divisions of slingers because the sling was considered a formidable weapon.

Todd Bolen/
www.BiblePlaces.com,
courtesy of the British Museum

3. For further discussion, see P. Kyle McCarter, "The Apology of David," *JBL* 99 (1980): 489–504.

this action, and the circumstances are used to suggest that it was done at the Lord's bidding (vv. 1, 14).

Part of the stated evidence of David's innocence in these acts of aggression is the severe action that he took against those who were responsible. He executed the Amalekite who claimed to have killed Saul (2 Sam. 1:1–16) as well as those who killed Ish-Bosheth (2 Sam. 4). He even censured and eventually doomed Joab for the assassination of Abner (2 Sam. 3:28–39; 1 Kings 2:28–34). Also to be noticed are the **lament** taken up for Saul (2 Sam. 1:17–27) and the preservation of Jonathan's son Mephibosheth in keeping with David's covenant with Jonathan (2 Sam. 9). All this was used by the narrator to demonstrate David's nonaggression toward the house of Saul.

The third point supporting the contention of the narrator is his interest in presenting statements affirming David's innocence or destiny. Such statements were made by Samuel when David was anointed (1 Sam. 16:12–13) and by Samuel's spirit (1 Sam. 28:16–18). The story of Nabal and Abigail may have been related for the very purpose of recording Abigail's testimony that David represented the voice of the people (1 Sam. 25:30). Most significant are the statements by Jonathan (1 Sam. 19:4–5; 20:14–15; 22:16–18) and by Saul himself (1 Sam. 20:31; 24:16–22; 26:21–25).

Some allege that all this represents no more than a propaganda campaign aimed at legitimizing David's claim to the throne. There can be no doubt that the narrator was presenting evidence by which he intended to legitimize David's claim to the throne. Furthermore, there can be no doubt that this material had propagandistic value. The most serious question, however, is whether propagandistic misinformation was given to hide the facts. On the one hand, our high view of Scripture prohibits such a view of the text. On the other hand, we find it difficult to substantiate that misinformation was involved here, because David is not treated very well by the text overall. Incidents of deception, poor judgment, and even murder of civilians permeate the narratives from 1 Samuel 21–2 Samuel 3. There is therefore no reason to suspect that the narrator construed the text to favor David. Rather, the narrator was demonstrating that David was legitimately appointed to the throne by the Lord, leading inexorably to the establishment of the Davidic covenant.

This massive structure, referred to as the stepped stone structure, supported the platform on which the Israelite royal palace was built (2 Sam. 5:9) and is sometimes referred to by its Hebrew term, Millo.

Steven Voth

David's successes as king are presented in 2 Samuel 5–9. They include his conquests and his establishment of Jerusalem as the new capital city. This was crowned by bringing the ark of the covenant out of exile and placing it back in operation. It should not be thought coincidental that this was followed immediately by the formation of the Davidic covenant, which stood as the charter for the new era. Thus, in chapter 6 David reestablished the throne of Yahweh (i.e., the ark), while in chapter 7 Yahweh established the throne of David.

The Davidic covenant was the centerpiece of the narrator's agenda. Everything in the narrative up to this point had been moving in this direction. From here on in the narrative, everything is to be understood in light of this covenant.

The Succession Narrative (2 Sam. 10–20) has as its main focus the family of David. The foundation of this section is David's adultery with Bathsheba and his subsequent arrangement for the death of her husband, Uriah. (Some would contend that the Succession Narrative begins with chapter 9, and that is possible. In our opinion, however, the story of David's kindness to Mephibosheth is better suited to the section on David's rise and successes, for it brought to conclusion his obligation to the house of Saul through his covenant with Jonathan.) Chapter 10 relates how the Israelites got into war with the Ammonites. Chapter 11 gives the details of the actual crimes, and chapter 12 recounts how David was confronted with his sin by Nathan the prophet and records the announcement of the punishment. The case that Nathan presented to David was designed to have David pass judgment on himself. Though the legal situation was different (adultery and murder vs. theft), the common ground was that both David and the rich man of the parable acted treacherously with no compassion or pity (12:6). The judgment passed on David's house became the litany of his family history (12:10–12).

It may not be coincidental that David decreed a fourfold restitution (12:6) and that the ensuing narratives eventually record the loss of four heirs to the throne of David (the child by Bathsheba, 2 Sam. 12; Amnon, 2 Sam. 13; Absalom, 2 Sam. 18; and Adonijah, 1 Kings 2),[4] but we can be certain of the legacy of sexual misconduct and violence that overshadowed David's family. In either case, the purpose of the narrator was to trace the effects of David's conduct (as epitomized in the Bathsheba affair) in the conduct of his children. This does not reflect a didactic concern for showing how sons tend to walk in their father's footsteps. Rather, there was a theological agenda designed to document how human sin and bad judgment jeopardized the Davidic covenant as far back as David himself. We have already

When an army was defeated, the survivors became slaves for the victors. The Philistines who survived the battle with the Israelites would have become slaves such as these pictured in Egyptian reliefs from Medinet Habu (1 Sam 17:51–53).

Kim Walton, courtesy of the Oriental Institute Museum

---

4. This observation comes from H. C. Brichto.

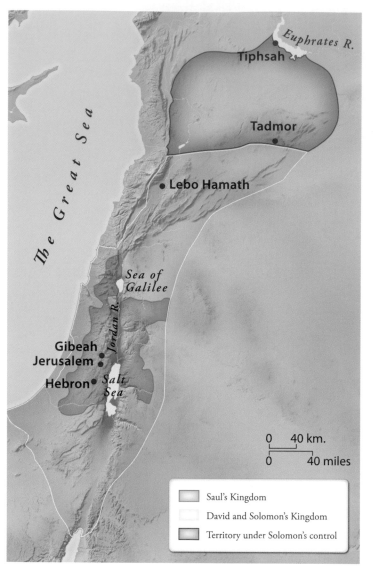

The Kingdoms of Saul, David, and Solomon

Euphrates R.
Tiphsah

Tadmor

Lebo Hamath

The Great Sea

Sea of Galilee

Jordan R.

Gibeah
Jerusalem
Hebron   Salt Sea

0   40 km.
0   40 miles

Saul's Kingdom
David and Solomon's Kingdom
Territory under Solomon's control

seen how covenant jeopardy was a theme in the patriarchal narratives of Genesis. Here, as there, the covenant jeopardy brought into sharp focus the sovereignty and grace of God.

So the narratives of 2 Samuel 13–20 tell of how Amnon's incest led to his murder by Absalom and how Absalom successfully dethroned his father David, but was killed in the ensuing battle against David's forces. In both cases sexual misconduct and murder are reminiscent of David's crimes. Though chapter 20 does not involve a son of David, it has significance here because it shows that tension was already building that threatened to rend the kingdom. The point is made: the result of the unrest in David's house was that the unity of the kingdom and, therefore, the covenant was in jeopardy. The text is careful to note, however, that though there was failure and jeopardy, the Lord still supported David and was faithful to him, despite these acts of others against him. This is most evident in the fact that the rebellions of Absalom and Sheba were unsuccessful.

Though the Succession Narrative picks up again in 1 Kings, the book of 2 Samuel comes to a close with an appendix that reflects on events in David's life that could be inferred to be failures because of apparent action of God against him. Chapters 13–20 had focused on human action against David. Chapters 21 and 24, which frame this section, both relate cases of God's taking action against David—namely, through famine and plague. This circumstance is balanced by the central sections, which report some successful exploits of David, but above all insist that the Lord supported him in giving him victory over his enemies (chap. 22) and making the covenant with him (23:1–7).

Major Themes

The Ark of the Covenant

The ark of the covenant was the most important religious artifact in Israel. Built at Sinai under the supervision of Moses, it represented Yahweh's presence in their midst. Occupying the place in the temple that was given over to the idol of the deity in most of the religions of the ancient Near East, the ark was nevertheless considered only the footstool of Yahweh's throne.

One reason why idols were prohibited in Israelite religious practice is that they were commonly used in pagan rituals to obligate or force the deity to act in the way desired by the worshipers. Unfortunately the ark was at times subject to this same abuse. The foremost example of this, recorded in 1 Samuel 4, occurred when the sons of Eli decided to take the ark into battle in an attempt to assure their victory over the Philistines. The theory was that a deity would not allow himself to be captured. But the Lord was not going to respond to such manipulation. It was the Lord himself who directed the comings and goings of the ark. The ark was not really taken captive, but instead departed from Israel (1 Sam. 4:21).

Likewise, when the time came, the ark returned to Israel on a cart without a driver (1 Sam. 6:10–16). There was even an abortive reinstallation attempt when the ark was not handled properly (2 Sam. 6:1–11), leaving David to wonder how the ark could come to him (v. 9). All of this demonstrated the autonomy of the ark; it operated only at the initiative of the Lord.

From the havoc wreaked in Philistia by the presence of the ark (1 Sam. 5), to the destruction in Israelite Beth Shemesh for profaning the ark when it returned from Philistia (1 Sam. 6:19–20), to the punishment of Uzzah when David was trying to bring the ark to Jerusalem (2 Sam. 6), the ark is seen to be much more than a relic. There was no other physical object that had the endowment of Yahweh's presence as the ark did. We can therefore see that the successful installation of the ark in Jerusalem at the beginning of David's reign was not simply a ritual, but designated the Lord's approval of the new era and his favor on David. This theology of the ark is supported in Psalm 78:54–72.[5]

Kingship

From a biblical standpoint, kingship over Israel was the prerogative of Yahweh (Judg. 8:23; 1 Sam. 8:7; 12:12). The function of the king was to maintain justice, both in a domestic sense in society and in an international sense by means of an effective military force. In the judges period the Lord raised up and empowered individuals to accomplish this purpose. The people of Samuel's day viewed kingship as a

5. This section draws heavily on Campbell, *The Ark Narrative*, 199–210.

more permanent office that would eliminate the need to wait for the Lord to raise up a deliverer.

It was this perspective on kingship that caused the Lord to be angry. There was nothing wrong with having a monarchic form of government. We should remember that even as early as the Abrahamic covenant it was promised that kings would come from Abraham's family (Gen. 17:6). Likewise, the appointment of a king was anticipated in the book of Deuteronomy (17:14–20). The crime of the people, then, was not their request for a king, but their expectation that a human king could succeed where they believed the Lord had failed.

Saul was chosen as the one who would "go out before us and fight our battles" (1 Sam. 8:20). That this view was ultimately flawed is shown in 1 Samuel 17. There we learn that Saul was unwilling to fight the Israelites' battles for them, so he offered a reward to anyone who would go out and fight Goliath.[6] In contrast, the true king—David—fully realized that it was the Lord who fought their battles for them (1 Sam. 17:37, 46). A proper monarchy still had to function as a theocracy rather than replace it. The king was to be viewed as the earthly head of God's theocratic kingdom.

The Davidic Covenant

As the central focus of the books of Samuel and a significant aspect of Old Testament theology in general, the covenant made with David merits some close examination. At least three points require discussion: (1) What did the Lord promise David? (2) Was the covenant conditional or unconditional? (3) What impact did the covenant have on the rest of Israelite history?

1. *What did the Lord promise David?* First, the Lord promised to make David's name great (2 Sam. 7:9). This was similar to the promise made to Abraham (Gen. 12:2), so immediately a parallel is seen between these two great covenants. Second, the Lord promised a place in which he would plant Israel (2 Sam. 7:10), and again a parallel can be seen in the promise of land to Abraham. The further promise to make the land a place of security (2 Sam. 7:10–11) is reminiscent of the Lord's promise that he would curse those who cursed Abraham (Gen. 12:3). We conclude, therefore, that the first part of the Davidic covenant merely positions David in the line of Abraham and shows the subordination of that covenant to the Abrahamic covenant.

The departure from the Abrahamic covenant begins in 2 Samuel 7:12. There it is promised that David's descendant would be established on the throne after him. Though this was similar to the Abrahamic covenant in that it dealt with descendants, it was clearly a new development. David's successor would construct the temple that David had so much wanted to build (2 Sam. 7:1–7). The Lord would have a parental

---

6. This observation comes from Matt Condron.

relationship with him that evokes discipline rather than rejection (2 Sam. 7:14). Furthermore, this successor would also have the opportunity to extend the terms of the covenant to his successor and so on.

The terminology used indicates that this covenant would better be described as open-ended rather than eternal. The word translated "forever" (Heb. ʿolam) in verses 13 and 16 is the same word used with regard to the covenant with Eli and his house in 1 Samuel 2:30. (For other important occurrences of this word, see 1 Samuel 1:22; Deuteronomy 15:17; and Jeremiah 17:4.) Yet it is clear that that covenant could be cut off by the Lord in the case of insubordination. In fact, the Lord had done exactly that.

With this understood as an open-ended covenant, what was guaranteed to David was that his son would succeed him and would not be rejected (as Saul had been). The potential existed for continuance beyond that point, but there were no guarantees. That David understood the terms is indicated in 2 Samuel 7:29, when he prayed that the Lord might be pleased to extend the blessings continuously to his line.

2. *Was the covenant conditional or unconditional?* It has often been noted that there are no conditions set on the covenant in 2 Samuel 7. This only means that the promises made to David were unconditional. However, as we have seen, the covenant was subject to periodic renewal, so we would expect that there must have been criteria by which it was decided whether or not the covenant would be renewed to the next generation. Indeed, such conditions became clearly evident when the covenant was discussed with Solomon. In 1 Kings 2:4, David instructed Solomon about the covenant; in 1 Kings 6:12 and 9:4–5, the Lord spoke to Solomon about it; and in 1 Kings 8:25, Solomon reported his understanding of the covenant in his prayer of dedication for the temple.

Conditions are clearly stated in each of these passages: "If you walk before me in integrity of heart and uprightness, as your father David did, and do all I command and observe my decrees and laws, I will establish your royal throne over Israel forever [i.e., indefinitely], as I promised David your father when I said, "'You shall never fail to have

This early Aramaic inscription from Tell Dan (9th cent. BC) mentions the battle of Ben-hadad, king of Aram, against the "House of David," which is recorded in 1 Kings 15:20. It is the earliest archaelogical reference to David.

Z. Radovan/
www.BibleLandPictures.com

a man on the throne of Israel'" (1 Kings 9:4–5). The Bible states clearly, then, that David was promised unconditionally that his son would succeed him and serve a full term, but the terms beyond that were conditional on the conduct of his son. The potential existed for unlimited continuity. We suggest that there were no conditions placed on David because he had already met the conditions.

3. *What impact did the covenant have on the rest of Israelite history?* When Solomon failed to meet the conditions of the covenant, did it become null and void? This issue is addressed in 1 Kings 11:32–39. Verses 34–35 imply that allowing Solomon to remain on the throne for all his days fulfilled the promise made to David. The Lord was free to take the kingdom from him and give it to someone else (see also 11:12–13). However, as an act of grace, not of obligation, the Lord promised to leave one tribe under the control of David's line (11:36). This was not required by the covenant arrangements in 2 Samuel 7, but was done for the sake of David. Although a new arrangement, somewhat similar to the one made with David, was made with Jeroboam (11:38), the promise of a continued "lamp" and the understanding that reduced control was only temporary (11:39) sustained the hope of the Davidic line through the ensuing centuries (2 Chron. 21:7; cf. Ps. 89).

The hope that someday a Davidic king would come who would meet the conditions and bring the restoration of the full Davidic covenant was the foundation for the messianic theology as we see it in the prophets. Jeremiah 33:14–22 may be the clearest statement of this, presenting a renewal of the Davidic covenant through an ideal Davidic king. Rather than a new David, this individual could be construed as a new Solomon, a shoot growing out of a cut-off stump (Isa. 11:1).

This view of the Davidic covenant helps us to understand the long history from the fall of Jerusalem even to the present, during which time there has been no Davidic king on the throne. The New Testament came to recognize Jesus as the one who would bring the renewal of the Davidic covenant. By meeting the conditions, the way was cleared for a truly eternal kingdom.

Assessment of Saul

Saul has often been viewed as a man tormented by jealousy and paranoia, and one can easily see how such an impression could be formed by reading the narratives of 1 Samuel 18–30. But Saul certainly had not always been so. In the earlier section of Samuel, Saul is portrayed as a shy, sincere, and likable sort. He is presented as just the kind of individual whom people would naturally choose as king. What brought the change? Why did Saul fail?

One factor identified by the narrative was the Spirit of the Lord. The Spirit came upon Saul (1 Sam. 10:10), empowering him for the task of kingship. Then this Spirit was replaced by an evil spirit from the Lord (1 Sam. 16:14). From that point on, Saul lost the empowering from God that was essential to be a successful king. Saul did not make good decisions, nor did he maintain justice.

But even before this time there were indications that all was not well. Saul's failure seemed to be fueled by his lack of spiritual sensibility. He was sincere but superficial. This was evident early on when Saul appeared totally unaware of Samuel's identity or function (1 Sam. 9:10–15), even though Samuel's home was barely five miles from Saul's. Further evidence is found in Saul's inability to recognize that a serious offense had been committed when he offered the sacrifice before battle (13:8–12) and when he failed to execute Agag (15:13–35). Even Jonathan, his son, condemned Saul's lack of good sense (14:29).

Although the Syrians would later give both Israel and Judah trouble, they were among the peoples that David is recorded as subduing in 2 Samuel 8. This basalt relief from the Syrian palace depicts two Aramaean palace officials (Late Hittite era, 9th century BC).

Erich Lessing/Art Resource, NY, courtesy of the Museum of Oriental Antiquities, Istanbul, Turkey

An episode near the end of Saul's life—when he decided to use divination to gain information (1 Sam. 28)—suggests that he never quite understood some of the basic tenets of orthodox Israelite theology. It is true and to his credit that he did not worship other gods, but it is likely he failed to see how Yahweh was different from them. Since he was an Israelite of the eleventh century BC, Saul's shortcoming is understandable and puts him in no different category from most of the populace or even the judges who had served Israel over the previous centuries. But that is exactly the point. A king had to be in a different category. Saul neither had nor acquired the theological sophistication to see and perform his role in proper perspective or to function in it successfully.

Assessment of David
Just as Saul has tended to be despised by ancient and modern readers of the Bible, so David has frequently been put high on the pedestal of a spiritual giant. Yet again we must be careful to offer a textually

informed appraisal. In contrast to Saul, there can be no doubt of David's heart for God, spiritual sensitivity, and theological sophistication.

Yet David committed a number of serious errors. These came, not from ignorance of what is right, but from being impulsively driven by the need of the moment without reflecting on the consequences. His lies cost people their lives (1 Sam. 21); his temper jeopardized his royal destiny (1 Sam. 25); his duplicity led him to execute civilians (1 Sam. 27); his lust entangled him in a murderous plot (2 Sam. 11); his unwillingness to take firm disciplinary action contributed to the bloodshed within his family (2 Sam. 13–14); and his pride brought a pestilence that devastated the land (2 Sam. 24). Yet God chose David and affirmed that he walked in accordance to his law. David was loyal to the Lord and recognized when he had committed sin. A balanced view of David recognizes his godliness, but realizes that, like any of us, he was not immune to lapses in judgment. A balanced view will focus not on David himself, but on how he was used by God. At times David's character made him an instrument of God's plan. Unfortunately, his flaws sometimes positioned him as an obstacle.

Questions for Further Study and Discussion

1. What is the theological significance of viewing Samuel and Saul as transitional figures?
2. If Saul was not God's choice, how ought we to understand 1 Samuel 9–10?
3. How can a monarchic government function also as a theocracy? What might the resulting theology of kingship look like?
4. What are the significant points of continuity and discontinuity between the Abrahamic and Davidic covenants?
5. What is the contribution of Psalm 89 to our understanding of the Davidic covenant?

For Further Reading

Alter, Robert. *The David Story: A Translation with Commentary of 1 and 2 Samuel*. Scranton, Pa.: Norton, 1999.

Anderson, Arnold. *2 Samuel*. WBC. Vol. 11. Waco, Tex.: Word, 1989.

Arnold, Bill T. *1 and 2 Samuel*. NIVAC. Grand Rapids: Zondervan, 2003.

Baldwin, Joyce G. *1 and 2 Samuel*. TOTC. Downers Grove, Ill.: InterVarsity Press, 1988. Brief but insightful evangelical treatment.

Bergen, Robert. *1 and 2 Samuel*. Nashville: Broadman & Holman, 1996. The best of the evangelical commentaries.

Birch, B. *The Rise of the Israelite Monarchy*. Missoula, Mont.: Scholars Press, 1976.

Carlson, R. A. *David: The Chosen King*. Uppsala: Almqvist & Wiksell, 1964.

Dothan, Trude. *The Philistines and Their Material Culture*. New Haven: Yale University Press, 1982.

Dumbrell, W. J. "The Content and Significance of the Books of Samuel: Their Place and Purpose within the Former Prophets." *JETS* 33 (1990): 49–62. An excellent treatment of the purpose and themes of the books.

Evans, Mary J. *1 and 2 Samuel*. Peabody, Mass.: Hendrickson, 2000.

Fokkelman, J. P. *Narrative Art and Poetry in the Books of Samuel*. Assen, the Netherlands: Van Gorcum, 1986. Extremely detailed analysis of the narrative from a literary perspective.

Gordon, Robert P. *I and II Samuel: A Commentary*. Grand Rapids: Zondervan, 1986. Highly recommended evangelical treatment.

Gunn, David. *The Fate of King Saul*. Sheffield, England: JSOT Press, 1980.

_____. *The Story of David*. Sheffield, England: JSOT Press, 1982.

Hertzberg, H. W. *1 and 2 Samuel*. Philadelphia: Westminster, 1964.

Ishida, T. *Studies in the Period of David and Solomon.* Winona Lake, Ind.: Eisenbrauns, 1983.

Klein, Ralph W. *1 Samuel.* WBC. Vol. 10. Waco, Tex.: Word, 1983.

Long, V. Phillips. *The Reign and Rejection of King Saul.* Atlanta: SBLDS 118 (1989).

McCarter, P. Kyle. *1 Samuel.* Garden City, N.Y.: Doubleday, 1980.

_____. *2 Samuel.* Garden City, N.Y.: Doubleday, 1984. The best and most up-to-date commentaries on these books.

_____. "The Apology of David." *JBL* 99 (1980): 489–504.

Miller, Patrick, and J. J. M. Roberts. *The Hand of the Lord.* Baltimore: Johns Hopkins University Press, 1977.

Polzin, Robert. *Samuel and the Deuteronomist.* Indiana Studies in Biblical Literature. Bloomington: Indiana University Press, 1993.

Tsumura, David. *First Samuel.* NICOT. Grand Rapids: Eerdmans, 2006.

Whybray, R. N. *The Succession Narrative.* London: n.p., 1968.

The Ain Dara temple in Syria evidences a tripartite plan very similar to Solomon's Temple. This view looks straight into the Holy of Holies. Notice the footprints moving in, indicating the deity entering his temple.

John Monson

1–2 KINGS

Key Ideas

- Kingship—good and evil
- The prophetic voice as the royal conscience
- Worship—Yahwism vs. Baalism
- Covenant blessings (repentance and restoration) and curses (judgment and exile)

Purpose Statement

The books of Kings continue the story of kingship begun in Samuel, and their primary purpose is to record the "covenant failure" of the Hebrew united and divided monarchies. The biblical narrative implicitly balances the notion of God's sovereignty and the reality of human freedom and declares that God was justified in exiling his people for the failure of the kings of Israel and Judah to uphold the ideals of the Davidic covenant.

Major Themes

- Assessment of King Solomon
- Preclassical and Classical Prophecy
- Dynastic Succession and Charismatic Leadership
- The Golden Calf Cult

God's Presence

The books of Kings report God's presence manifest in the form of a cloud of glory filling Solomon's temple at its dedication (1 Kings. 8:10–11). The reality of the divine presence associated with the Jerusalem sanctuary is accented in the foil of divine abandonment of the temple and the fall of the Hebrew monarchies and the exile of God's people (cf. Ezek. 10:18–19).

Outline of 1 and 2 Kings

I. King Solomon (1 Kings)
   A. His Succession (1–2)
   B. His Wisdom (3)
   C. His Reign (4–11)

II. King Rehoboam (12:1–22)

III. Kingdoms of *Israel* and Judah from 931 to 853 BC
   A. *Jeroboam I* (12:22–14:20)
   B. Rehoboam (14:21–33)
   C. Abijah (15:1–8)
   D. Asa (15:9–24)
   E. *Nadab* (15:25–32)
   F. *Baasha* (15:33–16:7)
   G. *Elah* (16:8–14)
   H. *Zimri* (16:15–20)
   I. *Omri* (16:21–28)
   J. *Ahab* (16:29–34)

IV. Prophetic Ministries of Elijah and Elisha
   A. Elijah and *King Ahab* (1 Kings 17:1–22:40)
   B. King Jehoshaphat (1 Kings 22:41–50)
   C. *King Ahaziah* (1 Kings 22:51–2 Kings 1:18)
   D. Elisha and *King Jehoram* (2 Kings 2:19–8:15)

V. Kingdoms of *Israel* and Judah from 852 to 722 BC
   A. Jehoram (8:16–24)
   B. Ahaziah (8:25–29)
   C. *Jehu* (9–10)
   D. Athaliah and Joash (11–12)
   E. *Jehoahaz* (13:1–9)
   F. *Jehoash* (13:10–25)
   G. Amaziah (14:1–22)
   H. *Jeroboam II* (14:23–29)
   I. Azariah (15:1–7)
   J. *Zechariah* (15:8–12)
   K. *Shallum* (15:13–16)
   L. *Menahem* (15:17–22)
   M. *Pekahiah* (15:23–26)
   N. *Pekah*/Assyrian Campaign Against Israel (15:27–31)
   O. Jotham (15:32–38)
   P. Ahaz (16)
   Q. *Hoshea* (17:1–6)
   R. Fall of Samaria to Assyria (17:4–41)

VI. Kingdom of Judah from 729 to 587/586 BC
   A. Hezekiah/Assyrian Campaign Against Judah (18–20)
   B. Manasseh (21:1–18)
   C. Amon (21:19–26)
   D. Josiah (22:1–23:30)
   E. Jehoahaz (23:31–35)
   F. Jehoiakim/First Babylonian Invasion (23:36–24:7)
   G. Jehoiachin/Second Babylonian Invasion (24:8–17)
   H. Zedekiah (24:18–20)

VII. Fall of Jerusalem to Babylonia (25:1–21)

VIII. Historical Appendix A: Governor Gedaliah (25:22–26)

IX. Historical Appendix B: Jehoiachin in Exile (25:27–30)

This silver-coated bronze figurine of a calf was found inside the miniature clay shrine in the sanctuary at Ashkelon (Middle Bronze Age, 2000–1750 BC). The bull was associated with the storm god Baal in Canaanite religion, whom both Israel and Judah turned to worshiping instead of Yahweh (1 Kings 16:31; 2 Kings 21:3).
Z. Radovan/ www.BibleLandPictures.com

The books of Kings conclude the history of Israel from its origins in the clan of Abraham, as recorded in Genesis, to the fall of Jerusalem that ended Hebrew national independence. The two books are in the section of the Hebrew Bible designated the "Former Prophets" (Joshua, Judges, Samuel, and Kings), which is comprised of Israelite annals presenting a theological interpretation of Hebrew history emphasizing covenant relationship with Yahweh and the attendant national blessings and curses conditioned by obedience to his covenant stipulations. The two books of Kings document the covenant history of Israel from King David's death and Solomon's succession to the throne through the demise of the divided kingdoms of Israel and Judah.

The separation of Kings from Samuel is somewhat artificial. Early Greek manuscripts of the Old Testament classify Samuel and Kings as *Basileiai* ("reigns, kingdoms") in four volumes: Samuel = First and Second Books of "Kingdoms," Kings = Third and Fourth Books of "Kingdoms." The division of Kings from one book in the Hebrew Old Testament into two books in the Greek Old Testament was simply a matter of convenience due to the length of the record. English Bibles have adopted the fourfold division of the history books in the manner of the Septuagint (Greek Old Testament), but retained the Hebrew titles of Samuel and Kings.

The Writing of the Book

Like most of the Old Testament historical books, the authors of the Kings annals remain unknown. The Jewish tradition preserved in the Babylonian Talmud (*Baba Bathra* 15a) attributes the books of Kings to Jeremiah the prophet. This association may have been based on the similarities between Jeremiah 52 and 2 Kings 24–25. It has also been noted that the history recorded in Kings gives a prominent place to the lives of the Old Testament prophets and the accuracy of the prophetic word in relationship to the Israelite and Judean monarchies. However, there is little concrete evidence for identifying the writer on the basis of context, theological theme, and purpose of writing.

Two distinct theories of the authorship and unity of the Kings history prevail among biblical scholars. The traditional view accepts Jewish lore and identifies the prophet Jeremiah as the compiler of the books. Those who discount this tradition nonetheless argue that the books of Kings bear the mark of a single author or compiler who was an eyewitness of the fall of Jerusalem. It is suggested that this writer skillfully spliced many historical sources into a unified script to portray the two kingdoms' "covenant failure" and the divine rationale for foreign exile. Most supporters of this view of authorship admit that the two historical abstracts appended to 2 Kings (25:22–26, 27–30) are later additions to the book.

The alternative view generally understands 1–2 Kings to be the product of the so-called Deuteronomistic school that supposedly began sometime in the late eighth or early seventh century BC and was closely aligned with the southern monarchy. The literary activity of these "Deuteronomistic editors" was motivated by specific theological interests, namely, the purity of temple worship and the centrality of the temple cult in Jerusalem, the fulfillment of previous prophetic revelation related to Hebrew kingship, and the reality of the blessings-and-curses formulas of the book of Deuteronomy for the history of the Israelite monarchies.

"When the queen of Sheba heard about the fame of Solomon and his relation to the name of the LORD, she came to test him with hard questions" (1 Kings 10:1). This stone relief found in South Arabia and dating to the first millennium BC depicts the "Lady from Saba (Sheba)." The writing on her forehead is her name written in Sabean script.
Z. Radovan/
www.BibleLandPictures.com

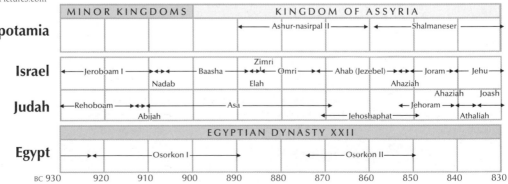

	MINOR KINGDOMS		KINGDOM OF ASSYRIA				
Syria/Mesopotamia			←——— Ashur-nasirpal II ———→	←——— Shalmaneser ———→			
Israel	←——— Jeroboam I ———→ Nadab	←→←→ Baasha ←—→	Zimri Elah Omri →←→	←——— Ahab (Jezebel) →←→ Ahaziah	←— Joram →←→	Jehu →—	
Judah	←——— Rehoboam →←→ Abijah	←——————— Asa	———————→	←——— Jehoshaphat ———→	←— Jehoram →←→ Athaliah	Ahaziah Joash	
	EGYPTIAN DYNASTY XXII						
Egypt	←—→←→	←——— Osorkon I ———→		←——— Osorkon II ———→			
	BC 930 920 910 900 890 880 870 860 850 840 830						

According to this theory, Kings was composed in two redactions, or editorial stages: the first, labeled the preexilic stage of writing, was associated with the reforms of King Josiah in Judah around 600 BC; the second, the exilic stage, was prompted by the release of King Jehoiachin from prison in Babylonian captivity and dated near 550 BC. The first stage presumably explains the clear pro-Judahite bias in the Kings history.

Opponents of this view are quick to point out that actual evidence for the Deuteronomistic History hypothesis is scant. No consensus exists among its advocates as to the origin and extent of the History. The basic theological concerns identified with the Deuteronomistic school are in fact tenets of covenant teaching central to Hebrew theology from the time of Moses. Notable variances between Deuteronomy and Kings on points of thematic emphasis and style abound (e.g., Deuteronomy is hortatory or sermonic narrative and prescriptive whereas Kings is formulaic historical narrative and evaluative). Even more problematic is the widely acknowledged similarity between Deuteronomy's structure and the Hittite suzerain treaty of the second millennium BC All this puts the idea of a Deuteronomistic school in the time of Josiah in considerable doubt.[1]

The unknown compiler of Kings makes reference to three specific sources utilized in assembling the "covenant history" of Israel's monarchies. The "Book of the Acts of Solomon" (1 Kings 11:41), the "Book of the Chronicles of the Kings of Israel" (mentioned seventeen times, e.g., 1 Kings 14:19), and the "Book of the Chronicles of the Kings of Judah" (mentioned fifteen times, e.g., 1 Kings 15:23) are all named as resources the reader might consult for verification or further information. These documents were probably official court histories kept by royal scribes (cf. 2 Sam. 8:16; 20:24–25) and very likely paralleled the royal annals of Mesopotamian civilizations of Assyria and Babylonia.

Biblical scholars have proposed that there are some other sources for Kings, though none are cited in the text:

1. For a nontechnical discussion of the standard Deuteronomistic History and the "Deuteronomic Reformation," see B. W. Anderson, *Understanding the Old Testament*, 4th ed. (Englewood Cliffs, N.J.: Prentice-Hall, 1986). Recent studies on the antiquity and unity of Deuteronomy include R. Polzin, *Moses and the Deuteronomist* (New York: Harper & Row, 1980); *Samuel and the Deuteronomist* (New York: Harper & Row, 1989); and Gordon Wenham, "The Date of Deuteronomy: Linch-Pin of Old Testament Criticism," *Themelios* 10, no. 3 (1985): 15–20; and 11, no. 1 (1986): 15–18.

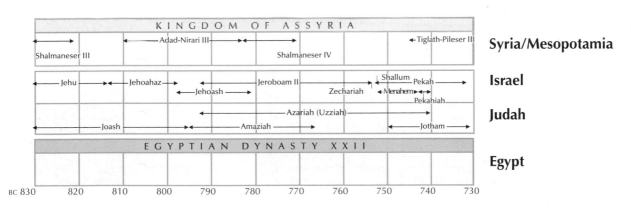

KINGDOM OF ASSYRIA										Syria/Mesopotamia
Shalmaneser III	←— Adad-Nirari III —→			Shalmaneser IV				←— Tiglath-Pileser III		
←— Jehu —→	←— Jehoahaz —→ ←— Jehoash —→		Jeroboam II		Zechariah	Shallum Menahem Pekahiah	Pekah			Israel
			Azariah (Uzziah)							Judah
←— Joash —→		←— Amaziah —→					←— Jotham —→			
EGYPTIAN DYNASTY XXII										Egypt
BC 830	820	810	800	790	780	770	760	750	740	730

1. The "Succession Narrative" or "Court History of David" (a united monarchy narrative comprised of 2 Samuel 9–20, with 1 Kings 1–2 usually associated with the present books of Samuel)
2. A conjectured "Dynasty of Ahab" record (perhaps contained within 1 Kings 16–2 Kings 12)
3. The Elijah-Elisha prophetic cycle (contained within 1 Kings 17–19, 21; 2 Kings 1–13)
4. An Isaiah source (since Isa. 36:1–39:8 is almost identical with 2 Kings 18:13–20:19)
5. An independent prophetic source that contained biographies of Old Testament prophets associated with the Israelite monarchies (e.g., Ahijah, 1 Kings 11:29–33 and 14:1–16; Micaiah, 1 Kings 21:13–28; and certain unnamed prophets, 1 Kings 12–13 and 20:35–43)

"Now Mesha king of Moab raised sheep, and he had to supply the king of Israel with a hundred thousand lambs and with the wool of a hundred thousand rams. But after Ahab died, the king of Moab rebelled against the king of Israel" (2 Kings 3:4–5). The military exploits of the Moabite king are recorded on the Mesha Stele (840–820 BC) and include his interactions with Israel.

Z. Radovan/
www.BibleLandPictures.com

Although hypothetical, these proposed contributions do fit the context of the Kings history, and they have gained widespread acceptance among biblical scholars as probable sources underlying the composition of Kings.

Given the available evidence, we do best to assign the books of Kings to an anonymous compiler-author of the sixth century BC. Whether he was a prophet or not is uncertain, but he understood the covenantal nature of Israel's relationship to Yahweh and its implications for Hebrew history. The book was probably composed in Palestine sometime between the fall of Jerusalem (587/586 BC) and the decree of King Cyrus of Persia that permitted the Hebrews to return to their homeland (539 BC). It is possible that the book may have been composed in two stages. Most of the history of Hebrew kingship could have been completed between the fall of Jerusalem and the Babylonian reprisal for the assassination of the governor Gedaliah (a third deportation in 582 or 581 BC, which was described in the first historical appendix, 2 Kings 25:22–26 and Jer. 52:30). The final edition of the work may have been published sometime after the release of King Jehoiachin from prison in Babylon by Nebuchadrezzar's successor, Evil-Merodach (ca. 562/561 BC, reported in the second historical appendix, 2 Kings 25:27–30). A date of 550 BC appears reasonable for the completed Kings record.

The Background

The books of Kings represent a selective history of Israel from the closing days of King David's reign until the Babylonian conquest of Jerusalem. By way of chronology,

1–2 Kings documents the political history of Israel during the united monarchy, beginning about 970 BC, through the Assyrian exile of the northern kingdom of Israel (722 BC) and the Babylonian exile of the southern kingdom of Judah (587/586 BC).

Two historical footnotes are attached to the end of 2 Kings. The first (25:22–26) recounts King Nebuchadrezzar's appointment of Gedaliah as governor of Judah and Gedaliah's assassination by a group of Jewish conspirators led by one Ishmael sometime between 586 and 582 BC. The second (25:27–30) records the release of King Jehoiachin from prison in Babylon after the death of King Nebuchadrezzar (March 562 or 561 BC).

The Kings history surveys the Israelite "golden age" of united empire under King Solomon, the split of the monarchy during the reign of Rehoboam, and the ebb and flow of the political and religious fortunes of the divided kingdoms of Israel and Judah until their collapse. Israelite interaction with the surrounding foreign powers is also integrated into the Kings account (see fig 15.1).

Archaeology has made significant contributions to the illumination and substantiation of the biblical record in 1–2 Kings. Specific discoveries include the unearthing of sites associated with the periods of both

Figure 15.1. Foreign Powers Mentioned in the Books of Kings

Egyptians	An unnamed pharaoh	1 Kings 3:1
	Shishak (945 – 924)	1 Kings 11:40
	So or Osorkon (726 – 715)	2 Kings 17:4
	Necho (609 – 594)	2 Kings 23:29 – 35
Aramaeans	Rezon (940 – 915)	1 Kings 11:23 – 25; 15:18
	Tabrimmon (915 – 900)	1 Kings 15:18
	Ben-Hadad I (900 – 860)	1 Kings 15:18, 20
	Ben-Hadad II (860 – 841)	1 Kings 20
	Hazael (841 – 806)	2 Kings 8:15
	Ben-Hadad III (806 – 770)	2 Kings 13:3
	Rezin (750 – 732)	2 Kings 15:37
Phoenicians	Ethbaal (874 – 853)	1 Kings 16:31
Edomites	Hadad (?)	1 Kings 11:14 – 22
Moabites	Mesha (853 – 841)	2 Kings 3:4ff.
Assyrians	Tiglath-Pileser III (745 – 727)	2 Kings 15:19 – 22
	Shalmaneser V (727 – 722)	2 Kings 17:3 – 6
	Sargon II (721 – 705)	Isaiah 20:1; 2 Kings 18:17
	Sennacherib (704 – 681)	2 Kings 18 – 19
Babylonians	Merodach-Baladan II (703)	2 Kings 20:12 – 13
	Nebuchadrezzar (604 – 562)	2 Kings 24 – 25
	Evil-Merodach (562 – 560)	2 Kings 25:27 – 30

The temple of Arad is the only known Iron Age temple of Yahweh that has been excavated. Although there was only supposed to be one temple (Solomon's in Jerusalem), the biblical text makes it clear that prohibitions against competing worship sites were often not obeyed.

Peter White

the united and the divided Hebrew monarchies (e.g., Megiddo, Hazor, Gezer, Samaria, Beersheba, Arad, Lachish, and Dan). Extrabiblical inscriptional evidence from Assyria, Babylonia, and Syro-Palestine has greatly supplemented our understanding of the classical Hebrew language, both Hebrew and ancient Near Eastern chronology, and Hebrew political history, religious experience, social customs, and daily life. All this is disclosed in the context of ancient Near Eastern culture—e.g., the Moabite or Mesha Stone, the Black Obelisk of Shalmaneser III, the Sennacherib Prism, the Assyrian Annals, the Babylonian Chronicle, and the Lachish letters.

Two of the most outstanding archaeological finds related to the Kings account are the famous Siloam Inscription commemorating the completion of Hezekiah's water tunnel (cf. 2 Kings 20:20; 2 Chron. 32:2–4) and the Babylonian "prison-ration" tablets dated to 595 and 570 BC, which mention daily foodstuff allotments for exiled King Jehoiachin of Judah and his entourage (cf. 2 Kings 25:27).

Chronology of the Books

The United Monarchy
The Dynasty of Saul
    Saul (?–1011 BC)
    Ish-bosheth (1011–1009 BC)
The Dynasty of David
    David (1011–971 BC)
    Solomon (971–931 BC)

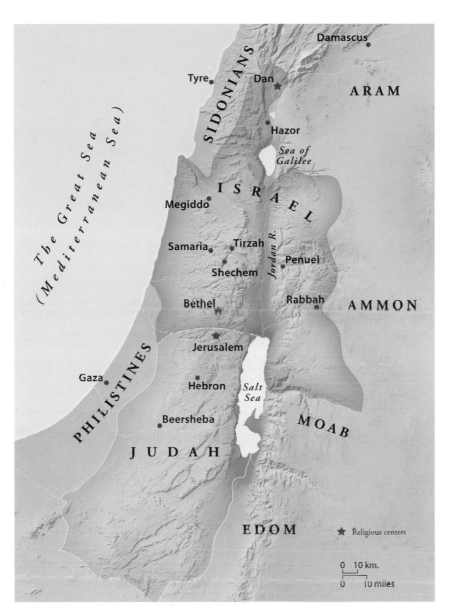

The Two Kingdoms
930–722 BC.

Fixing a date for the beginning of kingship in Israel is complicated by the loss of a phrase during the process of manuscript transmission in 1 Samuel 13:1, which capsulizes the reign of Saul. The figures for both Saul's age at his ascension to the throne and the length of his reign have dropped out of the Hebrew text. The Septuagint inserts the number "thirty" and gives thirty-two years as the length of Saul's reign. Other Bible versions understand the length of Saul's reign as forty-two years, based on the apostle Paul's speech in Pisidian Antioch (cf. Acts 13:21).

Ish-bosheth, or Esh-baal, Saul's fourth son, attempted to continue the Saulide dynasty and waged civil war with David for two years as king of Israel (2 Sam. 2:1–11; 4:1–12; 1 Chron. 8:33; 9:39).

David's forty-year tenure as king of Israel may be divided into two phases. The first, his rival kingship over Judah, was centered in Hebron and lasted for seven years and six months (2 Sam. 2:11). The second began sometime after the assassination of Ish-bosheth when David was installed as king of all Israel and reigned in Jerusalem for thirty-three years (2 Sam. 5:1–5).

Solomon's forty-year reign is usually touted as Israel's "golden age." After his death the monarchy split into the divided kingdom of Israel and Judah (figs. 15.2a and 15.2b).

Figure 15.2a. The Kings of Israel (Northern Kingdom)

	Hayes and Hooker	Thiele	Bright	Cogan and Tadmor
Jeroboam	927 – 906	931 – 910	922 – 901	928 – 907
Nadab	905 – 904	910 – 909	901 – 900	907 – 906
Baasha	903 – 882 (880)	909 – 886	900 – 877	906 – 883
Elah	881 – 880	886 – 885	877 – 876	883 – 882
Zimri	7 days	885	876	882
Omri	879 – 869	885 – 874	876 – 869	882 – 871
Ahab	868 – 854	874 – 853	869 – 850	873 – 852
Ahaziah	853 – 852	853 – 852	850 – 849	852 – 851
Jehoram (Joram)	851 – 840	852 – 841	849 – 843/2	851 – 842
Jehu	839 – 822	841 – 814	843/2 – 815	842 – 814
Jehoahaz	821 – 805	814 – 798	815 – 802	817 – 800
Jehoash (Joash)	804 – 789	798 – 782	802 – 786	800 – 784
Jeroboam II	788 – 748	793 – 753	786 – 746	789 – 748
Zechariah	6 months	753 – 752	746 – 745	748 – 747
Shallum	1 month	752	745	747
Menahem	746 – 737	752 – 742	745 – 737	747 – 737
Pekahiah	736 – 735	742 – 740	737 – 736	737 – 735
Pekah	734 – 731	752? – 732	736 – 732	735 – 732
Hoshea	730 – 722	732 – 722	732 – 724	732 – 724

Chronologies for the Hebrew monarchies (see also Figure 15.2b) will vary between one and ten years depending on the source consulted. The sources cited are J. H. Hayes and P. K. Hooker, *A New Chronology for the Kings of Israel and Judah* (Atlanta: John Knox, 1988); E. R. Thiele, *The Mysterious Numbers of the Hebrew Kings*, rev. ed. (Grand Rapids: Zondervan, 1983); J. Bright, *A History of Israel*,

The Divided Kingdom

The Israelite (northern) kingdom was less stable politically than the Juda-hite (southern). Both its shorter duration as an independent nation (some 209 years) and the violence associated with succession to the throne attest this fact. The Kings historian characterized all nineteen—or twenty, if one includes Omri's rival Tibni (1 Kings 16:21)—rulers of Israel as "evil" because they perpetuated the "golden calf" cult of Jero-boam. An average reign for an Israelite monarch was but ten years, with nine different ruling families laying claim to the throne. Charisma was as useful as ancestry for ascending the throne, but it was no guarantee of preservation; seven kings were assassinated, one committed suicide, one was stricken by God, and one was deposed to Assyria. (See fig. 15.3.)

Figure 15.2b. The Kings of Judah (Southern Kingdom)

	Hayes and Hooker	Thiele	Bright	Cogan and Tadmor
Rehoboam	926 – 910	931 – 913	922 – 915	928 – 911
Abijah	909 – 907	913 – 911	915 – 913	911 – 908
Asa	906 – 878 (866)	911 – 870	913 – 873	908 – 867
Jehoshaphat	877 – 853	872 – 848	873 – 849	870 – 846
Jehoram	852 – 841	853 – 841	849 – 843	851 – 843
Ahaziah	840	841	843/2	843 – 842
Athaliah	839 – 833	841 – 835	842 – 837	842 – 836
Joash (Jehoash)	832 – 803 (793)	835 – 796	837 – 800	836 – 798
Amaziah	802 – 786 (774)	796 – 767	800 – 783	798 – 769
Azariah (Uzziah)	785 – 760 (734)	792 – 740	783 – 742	785 – 733
Jotham	759 – 744	750 – 732	750 – 735	758 – 743
Ahaz	743 – 728	735 – 716	735 – 715	743 – 727
Hezekiah	727 – 699	716 – 687	715 – 687/6	727 – 698
Manasseh	698 – 644	697 – 643	687/6 – 642	698 – 642
Amon	643 – 642	643 – 641	642 – 640	641 – 640
Josiah	641 – 610	641 – 609	640 – 609	639 – 609
Jehoahaz	3 months	609	609	609
Jehoiakim	608 – 598	609 – 598	609 – 598	608 – 598
Jehoiachin	3 months	598 – 597	598/7	597
Zedekiah	596 – 586	597 – 586	597 – 587	596 – 586

3d ed. (Philadelphia: Westminster, 1981); and M. Cogan and H. Tadmor, *Second Kings*, in AB, vol. 11 (Garden City, N.Y.: Doubleday, 1988). In addition, see J. Finegan, *Handbook of Biblical Chronology* (Princeton: Princeton Univ. Press, 1964); and W. R. Wifall, "The Chronology of the Divided Monarchy of Israel," *Zeitschrift für die Alttestamentliche Wissenschaft* 80 (1968): 319 – 37.

Figure 15.3. Divided Kingship "Scorecard"

Israel . . .	Judah . . .
20 kings	19 kings, 1 queen
9 ruling dynasties (or families)	2 ruling dynasties (or families)
7 assassinations	5 assassinations
1 suicide	2 "stricken by God"
1 "stricken by God"	3 exiled to foreign lands
All judged "evil" by the Kings historian	8 judged "good" by the Kings historian

The southern kingdom persisted about a century and a half longer (totaling some 345 years). In contrast to Israel, the reigns of Judah's nineteen kings and one queen averaged more than seventeen years per monarch. The dynasty of David was sole claimant to the southern throne, enhancing political stability. Queen Athaliah's reign of terror was the only interruption to Davidic succession. Yet Judah had its share of political intrigue, as five kings were assassinated, two were stricken by God, and three were exiled to foreign lands. The Kings historian reported that eight of Judah's rulers were "good" because they followed the example of David and obeyed Yahweh (i.e., Asa, Jehoshaphat, Joash [Jehoash], Amaziah, Azariah [Uzziah], Jotham, Hezekiah, and Josiah). (See fig. 15.3.)

The prophets and prophetesses of Yahweh served as the "conscience" of the king during the monarchical era. The prophetic voices influencing the throne as recorded in the books of Kings are arranged chronologically in figure 15.4.

Purpose and Message

The books of Kings relate the history of the Hebrew united and divided monarchies in their "covenant failure." The narrative focuses on the figures primarily responsible for covenant keeping in Israel—the kings and the prophets. The prophetic voice has a prominent place in the story of kingship because those divinely appointed messengers functioned as the conscience of the monarchies.

The history of the Hebrew nation is told through the lives of the Israelite and Judean kings as representatives of the nation, because the fortunes of the king and the plight of the people were entwined. Rebellion and disobedience in the form of idolatry and social injustice on the part of the king brought divine retribution on the nation in several forms, including oppression by surrounding hostile powers, overthrow of the royal dynasties, and ultimately exile into foreign lands. Conversely, the blessing of Yahweh's favor in the form of peace, security, prosperity, and deliverance from foes rested upon the people of God when the king was obedient to the law of Moses (or instituted religious and social reforms after repentance and revival).

The accounts of the rival Hebrew monarchies in Kings also convey the story of alternative modes of kingship competing in Israel and Judah. Indeed, part of the purpose of the Kings history is the legitimization of the Davidic dynasty through the agency of the prophetic office. This was because the kingship covenant previously announced by Nathan sanctioned the tribe of Judah and the family of David as rightful heirs to the Hebrew throne (cf. 2 Sam. 7:1–17).

The most obvious purpose of the Kings narrative is to complete the written history of Hebrew kingship as a sequel to the books of Samuel. The record of Hebrew monarchies implicitly balances the notion of God's sovereign hand in Israel's covenant history and the reality of human freedom and accountability for those joined to him in covenant relationship. This prophetic view of Israelite history served both to admonish the king and people for past breaches in covenant keeping and to warn them of the grave consequences attached to continued disobedience to Yahweh's covenant stipulations. By the same token, 1–2 Kings contained a word of exhortation and offered a word of hope to Israel and Judah. God still ruled human history and remained faithful to his agreement with the Hebrews as his "elect" (cf. Ps. 115:5–6).

Figure 15.4. Prophets and Prophetesses in the Monarchical Era

Prophets	Kings	Reference
Nathan	David, Solomon	1 Kings 1
Ahijah	Solomon, Jeroboam, Abijah	1 Kings 11:26–40; 14:1–16
"Man of God"	Jeroboam	1 Kings 13:1–10, 20–32
"Lying Prophet"	Jeroboam	1 Kings 13:11–19
Jehu	Baasha, Elah	1 Kings 16:1–4, 12–13
Elijah	Ahab, Ahaziah, Jehoram	1 Kings 16:29–19:21; 2 Kings 1:1–2:12
Elisha	Ahaziah, Jehoram, Jehu, Jehoahaz, Jehoash	2 Kings 2:13–8:15; 13:14–21
Zedekiah and other "lying prophets"	Jehoshaphat, Ahab	1 Kings 22:5–12
Micaiah	Jehoshaphat, Ahab	1 Kings 22:13–28
Jonah	Jeroboam II	2 Kings 14:25
Isaiah	Hezekiah	2 Kings 19–20
Huldah	Josiah	2 Kings 22:14–20

The repeated references to fulfilled prophecy and the two historical appendices especially called to mind the Davidic covenant and God's promise to establish kingship forever in Israel (2 Sam. 7:1–17).

Structure and Organization

The historical record of Hebrew kingship in 1–2 Kings is ordered chronologically from the accession of Solomon to the fall of Jerusalem, with some exceptions, given the writer's thematic interests. Examples of thematically arranged materials include

- The summary account of Solomon's administration (1 Kings 4) appended to the narrative describing his great wisdom (1 Kings 3)
- The overview of Solomon's architectural achievements (1 Kings 5:1–7:12) prior to the dedication of the temple (1 Kings 8:62–66)
- Certain events related to the reigns of Jeroboam I and Hezekiah (cf. 1 Kings 13; 14:1–20; 2 Kings 18:7–19:37; 20)
- The condensed version of the prophetic ministries of Elijah and Elisha

The histories of the divided monarchies are recounted simultaneously through the interweaving of concurrent kingships in the northern and southern kingdoms. Variations from this basic pattern include the cycle of Elijah and Elisha narratives that interrupts the chronicle of the Omri/Ahab and Jehoram dynasties (see the outline above).

The accounts of the ministries of Elijah and Elisha are important not only as representative biographies of the nonliterary prophetic

Figure 15.5. Baal (of the Canaanites) vs. Elijah and Elisha (of Yahweh)

Baal, as storm-god, controls the rains.	Elijah commands drought (1 Kings 17:1).
Baal ensures agricultural fertility and bountiful harvests.	Israel experiences famine and drought, yet Elijah and Elisha provide grain and oil miraculously (2 Kings 4:1–7, 42–44).
Baal controls lightning and fire.	Elijah commands fire from heaven in the name of Yahweh (1 Kings 18:38; 2 Kings 1:10–12; 2:11).
Baal controls life and death.	Elijah and Elisha heal and raise the dead in the name of Yahweh (1 Kings 17:7–24; 2 Kings 4:8–37; 5:1–20).

Parallels according to L. Bronner, *The Stories of Elijah and Elisha* (Leiden: Brill, 1968), 50–85.

Todd Belen/www.BiblePlaces.com

This high place at Dan could have been constructed when Jeroboam became the first king of the northern kingdom of Israel. At that time he built two golden calves and placed them at Dan and Bethel to keep his people from returning to Jerusalem to worship (1 Kings 12:26–30). This sin persisted and was the basis for the indictment of the northern kingdom.

movement, but also as tracts of faith commemorating key figures in a religious drama with cosmic implications. After his marriage to the Phoenician princess Jezebel, King Ahab installed Baalism as the official religion of the northern kingdom (1 Kings 21:25–26). In contrast, the biographies of Elijah and Elisha stand as monuments to uncompromised faith in Yahweh as the God of the Israelites (cf. 1 Kings 18:16–18). They served as living testimonies of God's covenant faithfulness to Israel and his supremacy over the Canaanite storm god, Baal. Figure 15.5 shows how the ministries of Elijah and Elisha refuted popular understanding of Baal's basic character and power.

The Kings history is similar to other ancient annals in that it is a brief and formulaic reporting of the key political and military events of a given king's reign. The characteristic formula framing Judahite kingship includes (1) the introduction of the king by name, the name of his father, and his accession (usually synchronized with the reign of his Israelite counterpart); (2) among the biographical details recited, the king's age at accession, the length of his reign, the name of the queen mother, Jerusalem as the capital city of the king, and an evaluation of the king's moral character and spiritual leadership; and (3) identification of additional sources documenting facts about the king's reign, a death and burial statement, and an announcement of his successor. The biographical sketch for the Israelite kings typically contained the same information, except for the name of the royal city (usually Samaria) and the name of the queen mother (usually omitted).

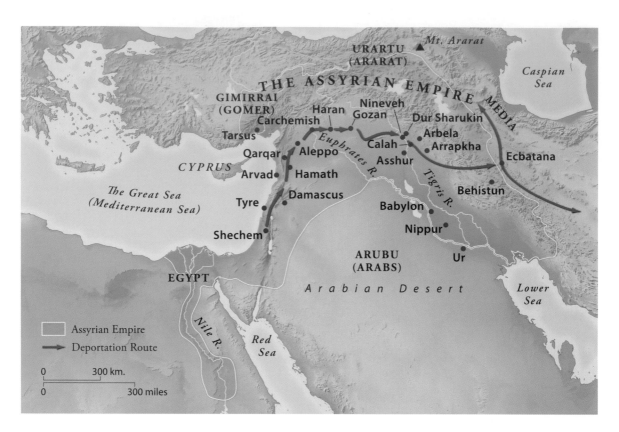

Assyrian Empire

Sandwiched into this selective rehearsal of the king's reign were prophetic speeches (e.g., 1 Kings 18:20–29), direct discourse (e.g., 2 Kings 18:19–27), wisdom sayings (e.g., 1 Kings 20:11; 2 Kings 14:9), and poetic materials (e.g., 1 Kings 22:17; 2 Kings 19:21–28).

Major Themes

Assessment of King Solomon

The reign of Solomon ushered in the "golden age" of Hebrew history. As king, he was "loved by Yahweh" (the meaning of the name Jedidiah, cf. 2 Sam. 12:24–25); was divinely bestowed with the gift of wisdom (1 Kings 3); brought unprecedented peace, wealth and prosperity, glory and splendor to Israel during his tenure on the throne (1 Kings 10:14–29); achieved international fame as a master builder (1 Kings 6:1–7:12) and sage (1 Kings 10:23); and was an ardent student of the "arts and sciences" (1 Kings 4:29–34).

Yet the latter years of Solomon's rule were marked by steady political decline and religious and moral decay. Ironically King Solomon fell prey to the seductions of the foreign women within the royal harem (1 Kings 11:1–3). Consumed by sensuality and materialism, he was unable to avoid the "snare" about which he had repeatedly warned others (e.g., Prov. 5:1–14; 7:6–27).

The Kings historian rightly attributes the division of Israel's united monarchy to Solomon's sin of idolatry (cf. 1 Kings 11:33, perhaps foreshadowed in 3:3). However, the collapse of the empire was merely the regrettable by-product of years of gross mismanagement of the affairs of state by Solomon.

The policies and programs instituted by Solomon contributing to the eventual split of the kingdom included

1. Political alliance to foreign nations by marriage (e.g., 1 Kings 3:1–2)
2. Tendencies toward religious syncretism in an effort to appease both the Canaanite and Hebrew populations in Palestine (i.e., participation in both the Hebrew religion associated with Yahweh and the Canaanite cults of Baal and other deities, 1 Kings 11:1–8)
3. The geographical realignment of Israel into twelve administrative districts in an attempt to erase old tribal boundaries and loyalties (a practice similar to "gerrymandering" in modern politics, cf. 1 Kings 4:7–19)
4. The proliferation of state bureaucracy (1 Kings 4:22–28)
5. Lavish building projects that required slave labor among both the non-Hebrew and Hebrew residents of Israel (1 Kings 9:15–22; cf. 5:13–18 and 12:9–11)

Dr. Tim Bulkeley, www.eBibleTools.com

This stone altar in Megiddo shows one of the forms that "high places" would take, though this one is much earlier than the Israelite monarchial period.

6. The influx of pagan political and religious ideology in Jerusalem as a result of international trade and commerce (cf. 1 Kings 9:26–28; 10:22–29)
7. The revolt of satellite states as Solomon's military power waned (with the ensuing loss of foreign tribute as revenue compensated for by increased taxation of the Israelites, 1 Kings 11:9–25)

It is small wonder that when the split of the kingdom came at Rehoboam's accession, the rallying cry of the seceding ten northern tribes became, "Now look after your own house, David" (1 Kings 12:16). The old tribal loyalties had resurfaced and Israel was now a house divided.

Preclassical and Classical Prophecy

The development of Hebrew kingship prompted the emergence of parallel nonwriting (or preclassical) and writing (or classical) prophetic movements in Israel. In the Elijah-Elisha cycle the Kings historian freely weaves a representative biography of the personality and ministry of the nonwriting prophets to the Hebrew kingship.

Although somewhat artificial, certain general distinctions have been made between the preclassical and classical prophets. The former slightly predate the latter. The records of the non-writing prophets tend to be preserved in story form, including accounts of their miraculous signs confirming divine authority in their message. The ministry of the nonwriting prophet was essentially to the royal family, and their message was one of judgment and national destruction for covenant violation.

By contrast, the message of the classical (or writing) prophets (e.g., Hosea, Amos, Isaiah) was generally preserved in oracle form and was often underscored with symbolic behavior rather than miraculous event. The prophets took their message to the political and religious leaders of the monarchies as well as to the populace. In some cases their prophetic ministry was even expanded to the surrounding nations (see chap. 32).

Dynastic Succession and Charismatic Leadership

The type of kingship associated with Judah is usually called the "**dynastic succession**" model of royal rule. In this, one family claimed (or in David's case, is divinely granted, cf. 2 Sam. 7) royal authority in perpetuity. At a monarch's death the throne passed to the eldest son, thus establishing a sequence of kings from the same ruling family in dynastic succession for generations. Often the aging king appointed his successor or arranged a tenure of coregency for his successor in order to guarantee the smooth transition of power.

In preparation for building the temple, Solomon sought out the best materials he could find, which included cedar wood from the cedars of Lebanon (1 Kings 5:6).

Ryan McBride

By contrast, the northern kingdom of Israel combined the dynastic succession model of kingship with the charismatic leadership model typical of the era of the Hebrew judges. In this case, God raised up a gifted and able male or female leader for Israel to respond to political and religious crises (e.g., Gideon in Judg. 6–7). This leader was empowered by the Holy Spirit—an anointing often manifested by extraordinary physical strength, courage, and spiritual zeal. Charismatic leadership was not handed down from one generation to the next. Rather, God commissioned deliverers from different Hebrew tribes and families on the basis of inherent abilities, covenant faith, and historical circumstances. This random and sporadic investiture of charismatic leaders was no doubt designed to instill faith in Yahweh as the ultimate sovereign in Israel.

Unlike Judah, dynastic succession in Israel was conditional. The ruling family's claim to the throne was contingent on the king's obedience to the statutes of God, according to Ahijah's prophecy to Jeroboam (1 Kings 11:37–38). Failure to obey the commands of Yahweh brought a pronouncement of disaster on the royal household from the prophet of God (1 Kings 14:10–11). Often this prophetic curse included the charge to the succeeding king to systematically execute the family of his predecessor (sometimes resulting in little more than a "bloody coup" in later Israelite history, cf. 1 Kings 16:3–4, 11–12). God then appointed a new king "up from the dust" to lead the people of Israel through the word of his messenger (1 Kings 16:2).

The Golden Calf Cult

The Hebrew term for "calf" is a flexible word connoting any male or female animal of the bovine family. The New English Bible translates "bull-calf," and this is probably the best approximation of the identity of the molten gold symbols of a young bull worshiped by Israel during the wilderness wanderings (Exod. 32) and later in the northern kingdom of Israel under Jeroboam I (1 Kings 12).

All evidence seems to indicate that the Hebrews borrowed the bull-god symbol from the Egyptians, probably the Apis-bull cult of Memphis. Apis was the sacred bull later known as the incarnation of the son of **Osiris**. This sacred bull was a fertility deity who gave life, health, and strength to the king and agricultural and reproductive fertility to the kingdom. It seems very likely that Jeroboam brought the bull-god symbol back to Israel from Egypt as a result of his exile there until the death of Solomon (1 Kings 11:40).

Upon returning to Israel, Jeroboam possibly also combined elements of the Canaanite bull-god worship once he assumed the throne. This would explain the presence of both Canaanite and Egyptian motifs characteristic of the Israelite "calf cult."

The bull gods that Jeroboam erected at the shrines of Dan and Bethel were not originally intended to represent idols of a foreign religious cult. Jeroboam's religious reforms were designed to win the allegiance of the Yahwists in the northern kingdom and thus prevent them from making the three annual pilgrimages to the temple in Jerusalem that was controlled by the southern kingdom. It is conjectured that these bull-calves of Jeroboam were intended to be symbols representing Yahweh in some way, perhaps as pedestals for his throne or platforms for his very presence. Thus, the bulls, like the fortification of Shechem and the border cities near Judah, were a political strategem used by Jeroboam to consolidate his power and authority in Israel.

Whatever the initial intentions of Jeroboam, it is clear that the golden bull gods soon became identified with religious ideology and practice much different from Yahwism. Ahijah acknowledged the images as "other gods" (1 Kings 14:9), and by the time of Hosea the bull gods were repudiated by the prophet as "idols, not God" (Hos. 8:4–5). By that time the golden bull became associated with the Canaanite fertility cult deities. The worship of the calf god was thoroughly entwined with the rituals of Baalism (Hos. 10:5; 11:1–2; 13:1–2). The progression from false idols to fertility cult, astral worship, and human sacrifice in Israel is outlined in 2 Kings 17:15–17.

This breach of covenant not only brought an end to the dynasty of Jeroboam, but ultimately led to the dissolution of the nation of Israel by Yahweh in his anger (2 Kings 17:18).

Figure 15.6. Military Conflicts of Israel

Approx. Date (Thiele)	King of Israel	Opposing Country	Opposing King	Aggressor	Victor
925	Jeroboam	Syria	Rezon	Syria	Syria
925	Jeroboam	Philistia		Philistia	Philistia
925	Jeroboam	Moab		Moab	Moab
912	Jeroboam	Judah	Abijam	Judah	Judah
909	Nadab	Philistia		Israel	Philistia
895	Baasha	Judah	Asa	Israel	Judah
890	Baasha	Syria	Ben-hadad I	Syria	Syria
885	Zimri	Civil War	Omri	Omri	Omri
881	Omri	Civil War	Tibni	Omri	Omri
877	Omri	Moab		Israel	Israel
853	Ahab	Syria	Ben-hadad I	Syria	Israel
853	Ahab	Syria	Ben-hadad I	Israel	Israel
853	Ahab	Assyria	Shalmaneser III	Assyria	Israel
853	Ahab	Syria	Ben-hadad I	Israel	Syria
850	Jehoram	Moab	Mesha	Moab	Moab
845	Jehoram	Syria	Ben-hadad I	Syria	Israel
845	Jehoram	Syria	Ben-hadad I	Syria	Israel
841	Jehoram	Syria	Hazael	Israel	Syria
820	Jehu	Syria	Hazael	Syria	Syria
810	Jehoahaz	Syria	Hazael	Syria	Syria
798	Jehoash	Syria	Ben-hadad II	Israel	Israel
795	Jehoash	Syria	Ben-hadad II	Israel	Israel
793	Jehoash	Syria	Ben-hadad II	Israel	Israel
790	Jehoash	Judah	Amaziah	Judah	Israel
780	Jeroboam II	Syria	Ben-hadad II	Israel	Israel
735	Pekah	Judah	Ahaz	Israel	Judah
733	Pekah	Assyria	Tiglath-pileser III	Assyria	Assyria
722	Hoshea	Assyria	Shalmaneser V	Assyria	Assyria

Figure 15.6. Military Conflicts of Israel (cont.)

Place of Battle	Territory Gained	Reason for Agression	Scripture
	Syria	Revolution for freedom	None
Mt. Zemaraim	Philistia	Revolution for freedom	None
Gibbethon	Moab	Revolution for freedom	None
	Various cities	To regain territory	2 Chron. 13:2–20
	None	To gain back lost territory	1 Kings 15:27
	Ramah	To gain control of route north	1 Kings 15:16–17
Ramah	Naphtali	In response to Asa's call	1 Kings 15:20; 2 Chron. 16:4–5
Various cities	Israel	Take throne	1 Kings 16:17–18
Tirzah	Israel	To totally control throne	1 Kings 16:22
	Moab	Conquest of Moab	
Samaria	None	Conquest of Israel	1 Kings 20:1–21
Aphek	None	To chase from country	1 Kings 20:22–30
Qarqar	None	Conquest of Israel	
Ramoth-gilead	None	To take back subjugated city	1 Kings 22:29–37; 2 Chron. 13:28–31
	Moab	Revolution for freedom	2 Kings 3:4–27
Various cities	None	To gain control of territory	2 Kings 6:8
Samaria	None	Conquest of Israel	2 Kings 6:24–7:8
Ramoth-gilead	None	To take back subjugated city	2 Kings 8:28–29
Various cities	Transjordan	To gain control of territory	2 Kings 10:32–33
Various cities	Various cities	To gain control of territory	2 Kings 13:3–7, 22
Various cities	Various cities	Recovery of cities	2 Kings 13:25
Various cities	Various cities	Recovery of cities	2 Kings 13:25
Various cities	Various cities	Recovery of cities	2 Kings 13:25
Beth-shemesh	None	Show of strength, revenge	2 Kings 13:12; 14:11–13
Various cities	Control of Syria	Conquest of northern territory	2 Kings 14:25–28
Jerusalem	None	To persuade to join alliance against Assyria	2 Kings 15:37; 16:5–6
Various cities	Naphtali	Subjugation, responding to Ahaz's request	2 Kings 15:29
Samaria	Israel	Conquest of Israel	2 Kings 17:4–6

Figure 15.7. Military Conflicts of Judah

Approx. Date (Thiele)	King of Israel	Opposing Country	Opposing King	Aggressor	Victor
925	Rehoboam	Egypt	Sheshonq I	Egypt	Egypt
912	Abijam	Israel	Jeroboam	Judah	Judah
900	Asa	Ethiopia (Egypt)	Zerah	Egypt	Judah
895	Asa	Israel	Baasha	Israel	Judah
853	Jehoshaphat	Syria	Ben-hadad I	Judah	Syria
853	Jehoshaphat	Edom, Moab, Ammon		Edom, Moab, Ammon	Judah
850	Jehoshaphat	Moab		Moab	Moab
845	Joram	Edom		Edom	Edom
845	Joram	Libnah		Libnah	Libnah
842	Joram	Philistia, Arabia		Philistia, Arabia	Philistia, Arabia
841	Ahaziah	Syria	Hazael	Judah	Syria
796	Joash	Syria	Hazael	Syria	Syria
794	Amaziah	Edom		Judah	Judah
790	Amaziah	Israel	Jehoash	Judah	Israel
785	Uzziah	Philistia, Arabia		Judah	Judah
743	Uzziah	Assyria	Tiglath-pileser III	Assyria	Assyria
738	Jotham	Ammon		Judah	Judah
735	Ahaz	Israel, Syria	Pekah, Rezin	Israel, Syria	Judah
735	Ahaz	Edom		Edom	Edom
735	Ahaz	Philistia		Philistia	Philistia
733	Ahaz	Assyria	Tiglath-pileser III	Assyria	Assyria
715	Hezekiah	Philistia		Judah	Judah
701	Hezekiah	Assyria	Sennacherib	Assyria	Judah
650	Manasseh	Assyria	Ashurbanipal	Assyria	Assyria
609	Josiah	Egypt	Necho	Judah	Egypt
607	Jehoiakim	Moab, Syria		Moab, Syria	
605	Jehoiakim	Babylon	Nebuchadnezzar	Babylon	Babylon
597	Jehoiachin	Babylon	Nebuchadnezzar	Babylon	Babylon
586	Zedekiah	Babylon	Nebuchadnezzar	Babylon	Babylon

Figure 15.7. Military Conflicts of Judah (cont.)

Place of Battle	Territory Gained	Reason for Agression	Scripture
Various cities	Various cities	Conquest of Judah	1 Kings 14:25–28; 2 Chron. 12:2–12
Mt. Zemaraim	Various cities	To regain territory	2 Chron. 13:2–20
Mareshah	None	Conquest of Judah	2 Chron. 14:9–15
Ramah	Ramah	To gain control of route north	1 Kings 15:16–17
Ramoth-gilead	None	To take back subjugated city	1 Kings 22:29–37; 2 Chron. 18:28–34
En-gedi	None	Conquest of Judah	2 Chron. 20:1
	Moab	Revolution for freedom from Israel	2 Kings 3:4–27
	Edom	Revolution for freedom from Judah	2 Kings 8:22; 2 Chron. 21:8–10
	Libnah	Revolution for freedom from Judah	2 Kings 8:22; 2 Chron. 21:10
Jerusalem	None	Plundering	2 Chron. 21:16–17
Ramoth-gilead	None	To take back subjugated city	2 Kings 8:28–29; 2 Chron. 22:5–6
Various cities	Various cities	To subjugate cities of Judah	2 Kings 12:18; 2 Chron. 24:23–24
Valley of Salt	Edom	Conquest of Edom	2 Kings 14:7; 2 Chron. 25:11–13
Beth-shemesh	None	Show of strength, revenge to Israel mercenaries	2 Kings 13:12; 14:11–13; 2 Chron. 25:17–24
Various cities	Various cities	Subjugation of cities	2 Chron. 26:6–7
	None in Judah	Conquest of northern territory	(Not in Scripture)
		Subjugation of Ammon	2 Chron. 27:5
Jerusalem	None	To persuade to join alliance against Syria	2 Kings 15:37; 16:5–6; 2 Chron. 28:5–6
	Edom	Plundering	2 Chron. 28:17
Various cities	Various cities	Plundering	2 Chron. 28:18
	None	Subjugation of territory	2 Chron. 28:20
Various cities	Various cities	Subjugation of Philistia	2 Kings 18:8
Jerusalem	None	Conquest of Judah	2 Kings 18:13–19:27; 2 Chron. 32:1-23
	None	Subjugation of Judah	2 Chron. 33:11
Megiddo	Control of Judah	To stop Egypt from aiding Assyria	2 Kings 23:29; 2 Chron. 35:20–24
Various cities	Various cities	Plundering on command from Babylon	2 Kings 24:2
Jerusalem	None	Subjugation and captives	2 Chron. 36:6
Jerusalem	Judah	Subjugation and captives	2 Kings 24:10–12; 2 Chron. 36:10
		Conquest of Judah	2 Kings 25; 2 Chron. 36:13–21

Questions for Further Study and Discussion

1. What is the relationship between prophecy and kingship in 1–2 Kings?
2. What was the political and religious significance of the "bloody coups" for the northern kingdom of Israel?
3. What purpose do the accounts of Elijah and Elisha serve in the Kings history?
4. How is Solomon's request for wisdom an example of "dramatic irony" on the part of the Kings historian?
5. In light of G. E. Mendenhall's article "The Monarchy," discuss the problem of mixing politics and religion in the Hebrew monarchy.
6. Examine 1–2 Kings for instances when the Old Testament historian recorded Yahweh's intervention in human history. How does this compare with the nature and frequency of divine interventions in Joshua, Judges, and Samuel?
7. Discuss whether the Solomon narrative (1 Kings 1–11) is the Hebrew equivalent of the literary form known as "epic drama" (cf. Leland Ryken, *How to Read the Bible as Literature* [Grand Rapids: Zondervan, 1984], 78–81).

For Further Reading

Albright, William F. *The Biblical Period from Abraham to Ezra*. New York: Harper & Row, 1963.

Bright, J. *A History of Israel*. 3rd ed. Philadelphia: Westminster, 1981. The definitive sourcebook for the history of Israel from the patriarchal to the Maccabean periods.

Brueggemann, Walter. *1 and 2 Kings*. London: Smyth and Helwys, 2000.

Cogan, Mordechai. *1 Kings*. AB 10. New York: Doubleday, 2001.

Cogan, Mordechai, and Hayim Tadmor. *Second Kings*. AB. Vol. 11. Garden City, N.Y.: Doubleday, 1988.

Coogan, Michael. *Imperialism and Religion: Assyria, Judah and Israel in the Eighth and Seventh Centuries BCE*. Missoula, Mont.: Scholars Press, 1974.

Coogan, Michael, ed. *The Oxford History of the Biblical World*. New York: Oxford University Press, 1998.

de Vaux, R. *Ancient Israel*. New York: McGraw-Hill, 1961. Valuable discussions on the civil institutions of ancient Israel (e.g., the Israelite concept of the state, kingship, royal officials, administration of the kingdom).

De Vries, S. J. *First Kings*. WBC. Vol. 12. Waco, Tex.: Word, 1985. Extensive bibliographies. View of 1 Kings as the product of the Deuteronomistic school.

Gray, J. *First and Second Kings*. 2nd ed. OTL. Philadelphia:
    Westminster, 1970. An indispensable commentary for its
    treatment of the Hebrew text, historical background, and
    annalistic sources of Kings, though his reconstructionist Hebrew
    history is not always agreeable to evangelicals.

Hayes, J. H., and J. Maxwell Miller. *Israelite and Judean History*.
    Philadelphia: Westminster, 1977.

Hobbs, T. R. *Second Kings*. WBC. Vol. 13. Waco, Tex.: Word, 1985.
    Extensive bibliographies. View of 2 Kings as "tragic drama" from a
    single author interpreting Israelite and Judean covenant failure.

House, Paul R. *First and Second Kings*. NAC. Vol. 8. Nashville:
    Broadman & Holman, 1995. Insightful literary reading of the
    biblical narrative.

Howard, David M. *An Introduction to the Old Testament Historical
    Books*. Chicago: Moody Press, 1993. Extensive bibliographies with
    excellent discussions of the message and theological themes of
    Kings.

Jones, G. H. *First and Second Kings*. NCBC. Grand Rapids: Eerdmans,
    1984.

Long, Burke O. *1 Kings*. FOTL. Vol. 9. Grand Rapids: Eerdmans, 1984.
    A form-critical analysis of the book, especially helpful with genre
    identification.

_____. *2 Kings*. FOTL. Vol. 10. Grand Rapids: Eerdmans, 1991. See
    above.

Malamat, M. "The Last Kings of Judah and the Fall of Jerusalem."
    Israel Exploration Journal 18 (1968): 137–56.

_____. "Origins of Statecraft in the Israelite Monarchy." *BA* 28 (1965):
    34–65.

Matthews, Victor H., and Don C. Benjamin. *Old Testament Parallels:
    Laws and Stories from the Ancient Near East*. 2nd ed. New York:
    Paulist Press, 1997. Esp. 155–90.

Mendenhall, G. E. "The Monarchy." *Interpretation* 29 (1975): 155–70.
    A provocative socioeconomic analysis of Hebrew kingship during
    the united monarchy, addressing the problems of political and
    religious syncretism in Israelite society.

Merrill, E. H. *Kingdom of Priests: A History of Old Testament Israel*.
    Grand Rapids: Baker, 1987.

Newsome, J. D., ed. *A Synoptic Harmony of Samuel, Kings, and
    Chronicles*. Grand Rapids: Baker, 1986.

Patterson, R. D., and H. J. Austel. "First and Second Kings."
    EBC. Vol. 4. Grand Rapids: Zondervan, 1988. 3–300. Largely
    descriptive commentary with theological emphasis, containing
    useful historical information in the "Notes" sections.

Payne, David F. *Kingdoms of the Lord*. Grand Rapids: Eerdmans, 1981.

Porten, B. "The Structure and Theme of the Solomon Narrative." *Hebrew Union College Annual* (1967): 93–128.

Provan, Iain W. *First and Second Kings*. NIBC. Peabody, Mass.: Hendrickson, 1995.

Rice, Gene. *Nations under God: A Commentary on First Kings*. ITC. Grand Rapids: Eerdmans, 1990.

Satterthwaite, Philip E., and J. Gordon McConville. *Exploring the Old Testament: A Guide to the Historical Books*. Vol. 2. Downers Grove, Ill.: InterVarsity Press, 2007.

Wiseman, Donald J. *Chronicles of the Chaldean Kings*. London: British Museum, 1956.

_____. *First and Second Kings*. TOTC. Downers Grove, Ill.: InterVarsity Press, 1993.

Wiseman, Donald J., ed. *Peoples of Old Testament Times*. Oxford: Clarendon, 1973.

Wood, L. J. *Israel's United Monarchy*. Grand Rapids: Baker, 1979. Detailed study of the Hebrew united monarchy, including in-depth discussions of the reigns and personalities of Saul, David, and Solomon.

Yamauchi, Edwin M. *Foes from the Northern Frontier*. Grand Rapids: Baker, 1982.

CHAPTER 16

Arad was near the southern border of Israel. Excavators uncovered a large altar and this Holy of Holies from the period of the Israelite monarchy. Although there were to be no temples to compete with the one Solomon built in Jerusalem, the Arad temple confirms the biblical statements that some were.

Peter White

1–2 CHRONICLES

Key Ideas

- The retelling of the past to inspire hope in the present
- The reigns of David and Solomon idealized
- The centrality of temple worship
- The validation of the priests and Levites as community leaders

Purpose Statement

The books of Chronicles retell the story of the God of history, more specifically the biography of the God of Israel's history—especially Davidic kingship. The sermon-like narrative is a theology of hope for the post-exilic Hebrew community, affirming that God is faithful and he will restore Davidic kingship and fulfill his promises to raise up a shepherd-king like David to rule over Israel (cf. Jer. 33:15–16; Ezek. 34:23–24).

Major Themes

- Worship in the Old Testament
- The Chronicler's Vocabulary
- Typology

God's Presence

The books of Chronicles teach that God's presence is more important than a king's presence, and obedience to God is more important than political power and national status. The centrality of the temple, the proper worship of Yahweh, and the authoritative role of the priests and Levites underscored the divine presence associated with Solomon's temple as a house of prayer (cf. 2 Chron. 5:14; 6:40).

Outline

I. Genealogical Prologue
   A. Patriarchs (1 Chron. 1)
   B. Israel's Sons (2–3)
   C. Families of Judah (4:1–23)
   D. Simeon (4:24–43)
   E. Reuben, Gad, Manasseh (5)
   F. Levi (6)
   G. Issachar, Benjamin, Naphtali, Ephraim, Asher (7)
   H. Saul (8)
   I. Returning Exiles (9)

II. United Monarchy
   A. David's Reign (1 Chron. 10–29)
     1. Saul's death (10)
     2. David's ascension (11–12)
     3. Return of the ark of the covenant (13–17)
     4. David's conquests (18–20)
     5. Organization of David's kingdom (21–27)
     6. David's preparations for the temple (28:1–29:9)
     7. David's farewell and death (29:10–30)
   B. Solomon's Reign (2 Chron. 1–9)
     1. Solomon's kingship (1)
     2. Construction of the temple (2:1–5:1)
     3. Dedication of the temple (5:2–7:22)
     4. Solomon's activities (8–9)

III. History of Judah
   A. Rehoboam (10–12)
   B. Abijah (13:1–14:1)
   C. Asa (14:2–16:14)
   D. Jehoshaphat (17:1–21:1)
   E. Jehoram (21)
   F. Ahaziah (22:1–9)
   G. Athaliah and Joash (22:10–24:27)
   H. Amaziah (25)
   I. Uzziah (26)
   J. Jotham (27)
   K. Ahaz (28)
   L. Hezekiah (29–32)
   M. Manasseh (33:1–20)
   N. Amon (33:21–25)
   O. Josiah (34:1–36:1)
   P. Jehoahaz (36:2–4)

      Q. Jehoiakim (36:5–8)
      R. Jehoiachin (36:9–10)
      S. Zedekiah (36:11–16)

IV. The Exile (36:17–23)

Like Samuel and Kings, 1 and 2 Chronicles were originally one book. The text was divided into two books when the original Hebrew was translated into Greek. Chronicles follows Ezra–Nehemiah in the Hebrew Bible, suggesting it was accepted into the Old Testament canon at a later date or was viewed as an appendix to the Writings since it supplemented the histories found in Samuel and Kings. The English version follows the Greek Old Testament in placing Chronicles after Kings and prior to Ezra–Nehemiah.

The Hebrew title of the book is literally "the words of the days," or "the events" of the monarchies. While the Hebrew title is characteristically taken from the first verse, here the title phrase is actually found in 1 Chronicles 27:24. The books are called "The Things Omitted" in the Greek Septuagint, that is, things passed over by the histories of Samuel and Kings. The English title "Chronicles" is a shortened form of Jerome's suggestion that the history be called "a chronicle of the whole divine history."

As literary history, the books of Chronicles supplement the records of Samuel and Kings, rehearsing the history of Israel from the patriarchs (by way of genealogy) through the fall of the southern kingdom of Judah to Babylon. As theological history, the Chronicles concentrate on the legitimization of priestly and levitical authority and the contributions of the Hebrew united and Judahite monarchies to the religious life of Israel.

The Writing of the Book

The Chronicles are an anonymous composition. The stylistic and linguistic similarities with Ezra–Nehemiah have led many biblical

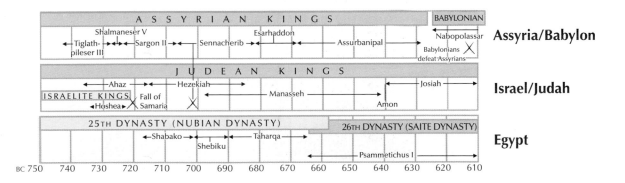

scholars to conclude that a single "chronicler" was responsible for all four books. Based on Jewish tradition assigning the Chronicles to Ezra the scribe (Babylonian Talmud: *Baba Bathra* 15a), W. F. Albright championed the view that Ezra and the chronicler were the same person.[1] At one time there was an overwhelming consensus that Ezra and Chronicles were the product of a single author. More recently, the identification of the chronicler with Ezra the scribe has been contested and is no longer as widely accepted.

Furthermore, during the last two decades biblical researchers have questioned the literary ties between Chronicles and Ezra–Nehemiah. Today most Old Testament scholars recognize the unity of the two books of Chronicles but separate it from the books of Ezra and Nehemiah, citing thematic differences such as the lack of Davidic messianism, "second exodus" overtones, and the "pan-Israelite" emphasis in the latter. At present it seems best to recognize the books of Chronicles as a unified composition written by an unknown "chronicler." Given the writer's pointed interests in the temple and its priestly and levitical personnel, it is likely that he was a priest or Levite employed in the service of the temple. The exact relationship of the chronicler's writings to the books of Ezra–Nehemiah remains an open question.

The Chronicles are, with Ezra–Nehemiah, probably the latest books of the Old Testament in respect to the date of composition. The date of their writing has been placed anywhere from the reforms of the prophets Haggai and Zechariah (ca. 515 BC) to well into the Greek period (with dates ranging from 300 to 160 BC). The last dated event in Chronicles is the record of Cyrus's decree permitting the Hebrews to return to Palestine from exile in Babylonia (ca. 538 BC; cf. 2 Chron. 36:22–23). However, if Zerubbabel's genealogy in 1 Chronicles 3:17–21 is ordered in chronological sequence, this internal evidence moves the date of Chronicles nearer 400 BC than 500 BC. The widely acknowledged associations between Chronicles and Ezra–Nehemiah (whether or not Ezra is identified as the chronicler) also suggest a date near 400 BC (see chap. 17).

Considerable attention has been given to the numerous sources used by the chronicler in compiling his history of Israel. In addition to extensive appeal to canonical sources such as the Pentateuch and Samuel–Kings, the chronicler explicitly cites noncanonical records and official documents as well. The array of sources employed by the chronicler's sources may be divided into the following categories:

1. Genealogical records (1 Chron. 4:33; 5:17; 7:9, 40; 9:1, 22; 2 Chron. 12:15)
2. Letters and official documents (1 Chron. 28:11–12; 2 Chron. 32:17–20; 36:22–23)

---

1. Cf. William F. Albright, "The Date and Personality of the Chronicler," *JBL* 40 (1921): 104–24.

3. Poems, prayers, speeches, and songs (e.g., 1 Chron. 16:8–36; 1 Chron. 29:10–22; 2 Chron. 29:30; 35:25)
4. Other histories, including the Book of the Kings of Israel and Judah (2 Chron. 27:7; 36:8), the Book of the Kings of Judah and Israel (2 Chron. 16:11; 25:26; 28:26; 32:32), the Chronicles of David (1 Chron. 27:24), the Commentary on the Book of Kings (2 Chron. 24:27), the Directions of David, King of Israel, and the Directions of Solomon His Son (2 Chron. 35:4)
5. Prophetic writings, including the Chronicles of Samuel, Nathan, and Gad (1 Chron. 29:29), the Prophecy of Ahijah and the Visions of Iddo the Seer (2 Chron. 9:29), and the Records of Shemaiah, Jehu and Isaiah (2 Chron. 12:15; 20:34; 32:32)

The Background

Historical Background

The genealogies of 1 Chronicles trace the heritage of covenant faith from Adam to David, with particular attention given to the Hebrew patriarchs and the twelve sons of Jacob. The actual history addressed in Chronicles spans the Hebrew united monarchy from the close of Saul's reign to the Babylonian captivity of Judah (ca. 1020–586 BC). The accounts of David's and Solomon's kingships are focused on events and figures associated with the ark of the covenant and the construction and dedication of Yahweh's temple. The chronicler's history of the

The Temple Mount, as it is called today, is where Solomon's temple stood in ancient times. "Then Solomon began to build the temple of the LORD in Jerusalem on Mount Moriah" (2 Chron. 3:1).
Todd Bolen/
www.BiblePlaces.com

divided kingdoms virtually ignores the northern side. The books of Chronicles conclude with this same emphasis on Yahweh's temple, as expressed in the edict of Cyrus, King of Persia, permitting the return of the Hebrew exiles to Palestine to rebuild the edifice (ca. 538 BC; cf. 2 Chron 36:22–23).

The backdrop for the writing of Chronicles was the postexilic period of Hebrew history. Whether the books are assigned to 500, 400, or 300 BC, the conditions in postexilic Jerusalem were essentially the same. Judah remained an insignificant and struggling backwater province throughout the entire Persian period and into the Greek period. Hebrew national and political life was overshadowed by the pagan "super empires" of Persia and Greece, and Hebrew religion was challenged by the rival temple and worship of the Samaritans, the great Persian cult of **Ahura Mazda**, and the Greek mystery religions.

The despair over the apparent failure of Zerubbabel and others to inaugurate the messianic kingdom in Judah as predicted by Haggai and Zechariah, coupled with the disappointment of the seemingly shallow and short-lived religious reforms carried out by Ezra and Nehemiah, prompted the chronicler's "theology of hope," couched in the annals of Israelite history. The present distress would one day give way to the restoration of Israel, according to the theocratic ideal expressed in Chronicles. The second exodus envisioned by Zechariah was delayed but not canceled. The kingdom of God would eventually break into human history, and Jerusalem would indeed be established as the political and religious focal point of the nations (cf. Zech. 8:1–8; 14:9–21).

This Sumerian text from about 2000 BC is one of the most complete records known of temple construction and dedication. As such, it is a valuable source for understanding Solomon's building and dedication of the temple of the Lord.
Rama/Wikimedia Commons, courtesy of the Louvre

Historical Reliability

The chronicler exercised considerable freedom in selecting, arranging, and modifying the extensive source material from which he composed his history. This condition has led many biblical scholars to disparage the integrity and historical reliability of the chronicler's record. In fact, the accuracy of the book of Chronicles has been called into question more than any other book of the Old Testament except Genesis.

Specific accusations leveled against the validity of the chronicler's history include the bias shown in omitting material from Kings related to the northern kingdom; the neglect of the sins of David and the apostasy of Solomon and the overemphasis on the favorable character traits and deeds of the Hebrew kings; the tendency to modify material from Samuel and Kings in moralizing and theologizing terms (e.g., 2 Sam. 24:1 compared with 1 Chron. 21:1); the addition (or fabrication?) of historical material not found in Samuel–Kings

"They destroyed the high places and the altars throughout Judah and Benjamin and in Ephraim and Manasseh" (2 Chron. 31:1). This is one such high place excavated in the northern town of Dan.
Kim Walton

(e.g., 2 Chron. 33:18–20); and the inclination to enlarge (or exaggerate?) the numbers reported in the parallel accounts of Samuel–Kings (e.g., 2 Sam. 23:8 compared with 1 Chron. 11:11).

Scholars who are committed to the trustworthiness of the books of Chronicles as a historical document have responded to these charges with a variety of arguments. For example, the chronicler's omission of materials from Samuel–Kings should not be understood as intentional deception. Rather, the writer assumed the reader's working knowledge of the earlier Hebrew histories. This allowed the compiler carefully and deliberately to select only those excerpts that had direct bearing on the religious life of the Israelite community or promoted the theology of hope the Chronicles were intended to convey.

Likewise, the skeptical stance toward the historical accuracy of the chronicler's "additions" to the history of the Hebrew kings is unwarranted, given his wide appeal to sources outside the Samuel–Kings narrative. Many of these sources are identified by name and may actually represent older traditions than those underlying the Samuel–Kings narratives. More important, archaeological data and extrabiblical historical materials have corroborated the chronicler's record in those instances where the different sources converge or overlap.[2]

Several explanations have been offered for the chronicler's "embellishment" of the numbers and statistics taken from the parallel Samuel–Kings narrative (fig. 16.1). Clearly, some of the numerical discrepancies can be attributed to scribal error (e.g., 2 Kings 24:8; 2 Chron.

2. Cf. J. M. Myers, *First Chronicles*, in AB, vol. 12 (Garden City, N.Y.: Doubleday, 1965), 240; and S. Japhet, "The Historical Reliability of Chronicles," *JSOT* 33 (1985): 83–107.

36:9). Others reflect a rounding off of totals rather than exact readings. It is even suggested that the chronicler may have introduced the ancient equivalent of allowing for inflation in his numerology (since he was writing some five hundred years after the time of David). Last, it is possible that portions of the books of Chronicles may have been based on older (and perhaps more reliable?) Hebrew texts and manuscripts than the Samuel–Kings accounts.

The chronicler's modification of the historical narratives of Samuel–Kings proves more difficult to assess. Here the concept of Yahweh's continuing and progressive revelation in Hebrew history and the consequent development of Hebrew theology aids our understanding of the chronicler's use of the ancient sources. For instance, 2 Samuel 24:1 states that the Lord incited David to take a census, whereas the parallel account in 1 Chronicles 21:1 attributes the instigation to Satan. This seems an unmistakable example of later development of Hebrew theology regarding the "agency of Satan" in Yahweh's sovereign design to test motive and punish sin among humanity (cf. Job 1–2 and Daniel's expansion of Hebrew understanding of resurrection from the dead in 12:2, based on Isa. 26:19).

Another category of conflicting reports in the Samuel–Kings and Chronicles parallels finds its solution by analogy to the New Testament quotation of Old Testament passages. Even as the New Testament writers both quoted and interpreted Old Testament texts for specific theological purposes, so also the Old Testament writers, in a similar vein, under the inspiration of the Holy Spirit, made appeal to earlier documents at their disposal. This kind of interpretive quotation has sometimes been labeled "inspired exposition." Apparently God is free to interpret his own record![3]

Purpose and Message

The chronicler's message centers on the Israelite united monarchy and the crucial roles played by David and Solomon in establishing and maintaining the temple of Yahweh in Jerusalem. The chronicler highlighted David's kingship to communicate the centrality of the temple, while Solomon's success was directly tied to the proper worship of Yahweh. The new exodus and restoration of the Hebrew community predicted by the prophets could only be realized as postexilic Jerusalem imitated the model of past faithfulness and obedience in worship and service to the Lord of Hosts.

For postexilic Jerusalem, the chronicler's message concerned Yahweh's election of Israel (which was implicit in the extensive genealogical catalogs at the beginning of the work; 1 Chron. 1–9) and the providential activity of Yahweh in Israel's history (as seen in the accounts

3. Cf. S. Lewis Johnson, *The Old Testament in the New* (Grand Rapids: Zondervan, 1980), 39–51. For a discussion of variant readings in the Samuel-Kings and Chronicles parallels, see J. Barton Payne, "Validity of Numbers in Chronicles," *Near East Archaeological Society Bulletin* 11 (1978): 5–58, and the pertinent sections of his commentary "1, 2 Chronicles" in *EBC* (Grand Rapids: Zondervan, 1988), 4:302–562. For a more strained approach harmonizing these variant readings see G. L. Archer, *Encyclopedia of Bible Difficulties* (Grand Rapids: Zondervan, 1982).

Figure 16.1. Numbers in Chronicles that Disagree with Old Testament Parallels

Higher	Lower		Parallel Passage	Evaluation of Chronicles
(a)	1 Chron. 11:11	300 slain by Jashobeam, not 800	2 Sam. 23:8	Scribal error
(b) 18:4		Hadadezer's 1000 chariots and 7000 horsemen, not 1000 chariots and 700 horsemen	8:4	Correct
(c) 19:18a		7000 Syrian charioteers slain, not 700	10:18a	Correct
(d)	19:18b	and 40,000 foot soldiers, not horsemen	10:18b	Correct
(e) 21:5a		Israel's 1,100,000 troops, not 800,000	24:9a	Different objects
(f)	21:5b	Judah's 470,000 troops, not 500,000	24:9b	More precise
(g)	21:12	Three years of famine, not seven	24:13	Correct
(h) 21:25		Ornan paid 600 gold shekels, not 50 silver	24:24	Different objects
(i, j) 2 Chron 2:2, 18		3,600 to supervise temple construction, not 3,300	1 Kings 5:16	Different method of reckoning
(k) 2:10		20,000 baths of oil to Hiram's woodmen, not 20 kors (= 200 baths)	5:11	Different objects
(l) 3:15		Temple pillars 35 cubits, not 18	7:15	Scribal error
(m) 4:5		Sea holding 3000 baths, not 2000	7:26	Scribal error
(n)	8:10	250 chief officers for building temple, not 550	9:23	Different method of reckoning
(o) 8:18		450 gold talents from Ophir, not 420	9:28	Correct or scribal error
(p)	9:16 (Chron. is same)	300 gold bekas per shield, not 3 minas	10:17	Different method of reckoning
(q)	9:25	4000 stalls for horses, not 40,000	4:26	Correct
(r) 22:2		Ahaziah king at age 42 years, not 22	2 Kings 8:26	Scribal error
(s)	36:9	Jehoiachin king at age 8, not 18	2 Kings 24:8	Scribal error

Compared with its parallels, Chronicles is the same once, higher 10 times, and lower 7 times. Total disagreements: 19 (j repeats i) out of 213 parallel numbers.

From J. Barton Payne, "1, 2 Chronicles," *EBC*, vol. 4 (Grand Rapids: Zondervan, 1988), 361.

of David's and Solomon's reigns, e.g., 1 Chron. 18–20). The rehearsal of Israel's past became a guarantee of God's continued intervention to accomplish his covenant purposes for the Hebrews as his special possession (e.g., 1 Chron. 17:16–27).

The historical review of Judah (the southern kingdom) underscored another key message for postexilic Jerusalem, namely, the divine retribution (in the form of judgment and exile) associated with the blessings and curses conditioning Yahweh's covenant with Israel. Respect for divinely appointed authority figures and obedience to the covenant stipulations were absolutely essential for the success of the postexilic community.

The chronicler conveyed several important purposes in his reassessment of Israelite history. First, his emphasis on Davidic and Solomonic kingship was intended to demonstrate the continuity between preexilic and postexilic Hebrew history. More important, the kingdom of Judah was set forth as the rightful heir of the covenant promises made by Yahweh to the "true Israel." The incorporation of the genealogies of Jacob's descendants reminded Israel of their former tribal unity and called the whole people once again to band together in covenant unity before Yahweh. Only by faithful adherence to Yahweh's covenant stipulations could Israel recapture the glory days of the past described by the chronicler.

The chronicler's fixation with the Davidic and Solomonic kingdoms was more than a plea for the return of the "good old days" of Israel's history. Those kingships served as models of an "ideal" Israel under theocratic rule for the present community. The centrality of the temple, the proper worship of Yahweh, and the authoritative role of the priests and Levites in the temple service demonstrated the supremacy of the Hebrew God and the superiority of Hebrew religion in the face of encroaching paganism.

Finally, the chronicler's history offered hope in postexilic Jerusalem by assuring the present community that of the sovereign Lord of Hosts, having been active during the reigns of David and Solomon, would continue providentially to intervene in Hebrew history to accomplish the prophetic vision of Zion as the political and religious center of the nations (cf. Zech. 14:12–21).

Structure and Organization

The chronicler was a theologian and religious teacher as well as a historian. His interpretive and apologetic history of Israel was designed to awaken covenant faith and evoke hope in the midst of the beleaguered postexilic Hebrew community. The macrostructure of Chronicles highlights this hopefulness in that the first book opens with the building of the first temple (with Gentile help) and the second book closes with the edict of a Gentile king commanding the building of the second temple (cf. 2 Chron. 36:22–23). An expanded version of this so-called Cyrus **colophon** in 2 Chronicles appears in Ezra 1:1–3, thus bridging the history of the chronicler and the books of Ezra–Nehemiah. The connection of the Ezra–Nehemiah reforms with Israel's "temple history" reinforces the chronicler's theocratic ideal and the expectation of a "new exodus."

It is assumed that the historical materials of Chronicles were spliced in at least two distinct stages. The original work comprising 1 Chronicles 10–2 Chronicles 34 was probably compiled in conjunction with the prophetic ministries of Haggai and Zechariah about 500 BC. The second stage of the history saw the addition of 1 Chronicles 1–9 and 2 Chronicles 35–36 in association with the reforms of Ezra and Nehemiah (ca. 450–400 BC).

"Now Hiram king of Tyre sent messengers to David, along with cedar logs, stonemasons and carpenters to build a palace for him" (1 Chron. 14:1). Due to the weight of the cedar logs, these materials were probably shipped by boat along the Mediterranean coast, as portrayed in this Assyrian relief from Dur-Sharrukin.
Marie-Lan Nguyen/Wikimedia Commons, courtesy of the Louvre

The genealogies of 1 Chronicles 1–9 preface the review of the Davidic and Solomonic monarchies (1 Chron. 10–2 Chron. 9). Unfortunately, the chronicler's catalog of obscure (and unpronounceable!) Hebrew names is better known as an antidote for insomnia than for its literary merit. Yet the section does make important contributions to the overall plan and purpose of the book. The genealogies call attention to the unity of "all Israel" (a necessary theme after the fall of the divided monarchies). The chronicler's spotlight shines upon Judah and Levi—the tribes of kingship and priesthood in Israel. Carefully tracing the lines of Aaron and David to Abraham calls to mind the covenant Yahweh made with the patriarch. The recitation of these lineages both legitimized the religious and political leadership of Israel and testified to God's faithfulness in making a great nation of Abraham's descendants (Gen. 12:2; cf. 17:2).

The section outlining the reigns of Saul and David presents a study of contrasts. Saul's disobedience, failures, and neglect of the ark of the covenant serve as a literary foil for David's faithfulness, triumphs, and careful attention to the ark of God (1 Chron. 10–29). In keeping with the chronicler's interest in the "theocratic ideal," David's return of the ark to Jerusalem, his preparations for the building of the temple, and his arrangements for the temple service take center stage in the narrative (chaps. 13–17, 21–29).

The history of Judah, the southern kingdom and successor to the Davidic covenant, concludes the chronicler's narrative (2 Chron. 10–36). Special attention is given to the "good" kings of Judah, exalting those whose reforms directly affected Yahweh's temple and Hebrew worship. In fact, even as David is cast as a "second Moses" and Solomon a "second Joshua," so kings Hezekiah and Josiah are idealized as Davidic and Solomonic type figures because of their cleansing of the temple and restoration of proper worship in Jerusalem. This concluding section also emphasizes the importance of the prophetic word for maintaining covenant relationship with Yahweh and the reality of divine retribution in light of the blessings and curses appended to the covenant code (cf. 2 Chron. 36:17–21).

Rebellion before God and disobedience to his covenant jeopardized not only Hebrew kingship, but also the temple of Yahweh. King Nebuchadrezzar of Babylon taught Judah this dreadful and costly lesson when he terminated Davidic kingship, deported the Hebrews to Babylonia from the land of covenant promise, and laid waste the temple of the Lord of Hosts—the very symbol of Yahweh's theocratic presence and rule among the Israelites. And yet, just as the word of the Lord was fulfilled in Judah's defeat and exile, so it was fulfilled in the promise of return and restoration under King Cyrus (cf. 2 Chron. 36:21–22).

Babylonian Deportation

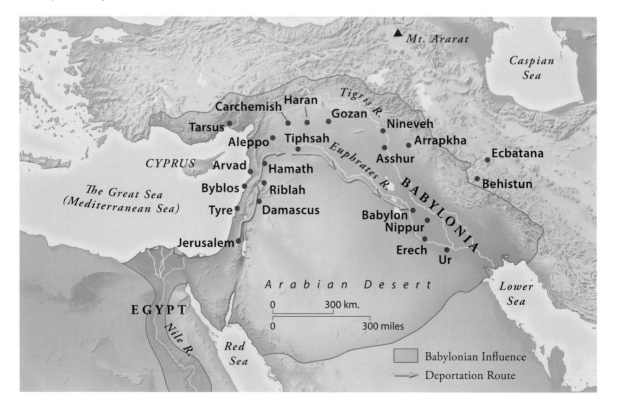

During the reign of Saul, Bethshean was a Philistine city. Saul and Jonathan's bodies were taken there after their defeat (1 Sam. 31:10–12). During David's conquest of the Philistines he must have taken the city, because it is listed as part of Solomon's kingdom (1 Kings 4:12; 1 Chron. 7:29).

Major Themes

Worship in the Old Testament

The worship of Yahweh was an integral part of the chronicler's theocratic ideal for postexilic Jerusalem. The records of Hebrew worship in the Chronicles are representative of the wide range of Israelite religious experiences and are useful as a summary statement of Old Testament worship in general.

Although the chronicler emphasized the former, he clearly understood the importance of both corporate and individual worship (1 Chron. 15:29; 2 Chron. 31:20–21). The chronicler also offered examples of ordered and priestly led worship in keeping with the liturgical calendar (2 Chron. 35:1–19) and the spontaneous response to Yahweh's steadfast lovingkindness (1 Chron. 16:28–34; cf. Hezekiah's celebration of two Passover's in one year!—2 Chron. 30:13–22). The private aspect of worship is more implicit in Chronicles (e.g., 1 Chron. 16:23–27), but gatherings for public worship abound in the two books (1 Chron. 16:36; 29:9; 2 Chron. 5:2–14; 6:3–11). More important, the chronicler recognized that the true worship of Yahweh was motivated both by the fear of the Lord (2 Chron. 6:31, 33), and love for God with a whole heart (1 Chron. 28:9; 2 Chron. 19:9).

That the chronicler valued worship as an attitude, a condition of human heart and mind, is demonstrated in the discussion that follows (cf. 1 Chron. 16:10–11; 28:9; 2 Chron. 15:12, 15). In addition, worship for the Hebrews was an active experience before God, not passive. Acknowledging the worth of God and giving him the reverence and adoration due his name included the following gestures, acts, and movements: drink offerings and **libations**, the presentation of sacrifices and burnt offerings, bowing down, burning incense, giving thank offerings and votive gifts, prayer in various postures, fasting, ritual washing and cleansing, dancing, tearing of the clothes (in repentance), feasting, and observing the great religious festivals (cf. 2 Chron. 29:12–19, 31–36; 32:13–27; 34:12; 34:22–28).

Of special importance to the chronicler was the significance of worship as word. There was the word of oath taking, of praise and thanksgiving, of prayer, joyful song, confession, and liturgical responses by the Hebrew congregation (cf. 1 Chron. 15:29; 16:4, 9, 23, 36, 40; 17:16–27; 2 Chron. 15:15). Preeminent in the chronicler's theocratic ideal was worship as a place, namely, the temple of Yahweh (cf. 2 Chron. 5:2–7:10). Yet he also acknowledged that true worship of the Lord God of Israel is not limited by the bounds of time or the confines of a "sacred place" (cf. 2 Chron. 6:12–23).

Finally, some mention of the personnel directing Hebrew worship is pertinent, because the chronicler devotes large sections of his record to the role of the priests and Levites in the religious life of the nation. The priests and Levites were the Old Testament equivalent of professional clergy, since they were supported by the offerings and votive gifts of

Megiddo guarded an important passage through the Carmel range into the Jezreel Valley that provided an international travel route for merchants and armies. It was logical for Solomon to fortify the site, and many battles took place in that valley guarded by the city. In one battle, the godly king Josiah was killed by the armies of Pharaoh Necho when he attempted to keep the Egyptians from passing through his land (2 Chron. 35:20–24).

the people. They were consecrated solely to the service of God through the institution of Yahweh's sanctuary.

Basically the priests were the descendants of Aaron, Israel's first high priest, and they were responsible for guiding and representing the Hebrews in the sacrificial and festival worship. The rest of the Levites (i.e., the other male members of the tribe of Levi) were assigned to specific tasks related to the maintenance and services of the Lord's sanctuary.

The chronicler gives special attention to the role of the priests and Levites for several reasons. The building of the temple and a permanent home for the ark of the covenant meant that the Levites no longer had to serve as porters for the sanctuary (cf. Num. 4:1–49). In the Chronicles the Levites were assigned, by royal decree, to service guilds such as singer, musician, gatekeeper, and teacher of the law and judge (cf. 1 Chron. 24–26; 2 Chron. 17:7–9; 19:11).

This centralization of responsibility for official religion in the office of the Hebrew king sanctioned priestly and levitical authority, and when kingship ceased in Israel they became the heirs of divine administration. The chronicler assumed that the priests and Levites would bring in the new order and reestablish theocracy in Israel. However, Malachi and others censured the priesthood and the Levites for their failure to keep their sacred trust before God (e.g., Mal. 1:6–2:9). According to the New Testament and a Christian perspective of Hebrew history, this only served to heighten the priesthood of Jesus, the surety of a better covenant (Heb. 7:20–22).

The Chronicler's Vocabulary

The chronicler's repeated use of standard expressions related to the attitude and intent of the heart of individual and corporate Israel indicate that he understood divine retribution as more than the mere mechanical cause-and-effect concept of "sowing and reaping."[4]

First, the emphasis on "repentance" in Chronicles reveals that the compiler knew the mercy of Yahweh and his gracious capacity for turning from wrath in the face of genuine repentance by his people (e.g., 2 Chron. 12:6–12; cf. Exod. 32:11–14). Illustrations of past repentance are recited as concrete examples assuring God's continued response of merciful forgiveness to those who return to him (2 Chron. 15:4; 32:26). The enduring lovingkindness of Yahweh is exhibited in his willingness to receive those from the apostate northern kingdom who turn to him (2 Chron. 30:6–9), and even the wicked Manasseh experienced Yahweh's mercy (2 Chron. 33:12–14).

Other stock phrases giving evidence of the chronicler's awareness of the need to balance the "internal" and "external" factors of true religion include his attention to "rejoicing and serving God with a pure

4. Often the chronicler used the repetition of key vocabulary items to logically connect a variety of literary sources. Cf. Andrew E. Hill, "Patchwork Poetry or Reasoned Verse: Connective Structure in 1 Chronicles xvi," *VT* 33 (1983): 97–101.

Peter White

"It was Hezekiah who blocked the upper outlet of the Gihon spring and channeled the water down to the west side of the City of David. He succeeded in everything he undertook" (2 Chron. 32:30). Hezekiah did this by digging what is now known as "Hezekiah's tunnel." This is the entry by the spring that still runs through the tunnel today.

heart" (e.g., 1 Chron. 28:9; 29:9, 19; 2 Chron. 16:9), "generous giving and faithfulness" (e.g., 1 Chron. 29:1–9, 14, 17; 2 Chron. 19:9), and "thankful and joyful celebration and worship" (e.g., 1 Chron. 16:4, 7; 23:30; 29:13).

Typology

Formal **typology** is one aspect of biblical hermeneutics or interpretation. Typology is a method of exegesis that establishes historical correspondence between Old Testament events, persons, or objects and ideas and similar New Testament events, persons, or objects and ideas by way of foreshadowing or prototype. Usually the Old Testament correspondent is identified as the "type"; the New Testament correspondent expressing the Old Testament truth in a greater way is regarded the "antetype." For example, the writer of the epistle to the Hebrews understands the priesthood of Melchizedek in the Old Testament (Gen. 14:17–24; Ps. 110:4) as the prototype of the superior priesthood of Jesus Christ (Heb. 7:1–22). In the same manner, the tabernacle (and later the temple) were symbols or types of the new covenant, foreshadowing Christ's eternal sacrifice (Heb. 9:6–14).

In describing the preparations for and construction of the temple of Yahweh, the chronicler portrayed David as a "second" Moses and Solomon as a "second" Joshua.[5] Specifically, David was prohibited from completing the temple even as Moses was denied the privilege of leading the Hebrews into the land of covenant promise (cf. Num. 20:2–11; 1 Chron. 22:8).

Likewise, Solomon exemplified Joshua in that both were chosen as successors privately and given public acclaim, both received popular support without political or military resistance, both were exalted by God, and both led the Hebrew people into an era of "rest" and "blessing." Finally, both Joshua and Solomon were given the same charge in assuming their leadership roles, a charge "to be strong and courageous" (Deut. 31:6; cf. 1 Chron. 22:13) because "the LORD goes before you" (Deut. 31:6, 8, 23; Josh. 1:5, 9; cf. 1 Chron. 22:11, 16), and "he will never leave you nor forsake you" (Deut. 31:6, 8; Josh. 1:5, 9; cf. 1 Chron. 28:20).

---

5. Cf. R. B. Dillard, "The Chronicler's Solomon," *Westminster Theological Journal* 43 (1981): 207–18; and H. G. M. Williamson, "The Accession of Solomon in the Book of Chronicles," *VT 26* (1976): 351–61.

Questions for Further Study and Discussion

1. Why is King David the "ideal" king for the chronicler?
2. How does the chronicler's recitation of the history of Israel demonstrate the goodness of God?
3. What are the strengths and weaknesses of typology as a method of biblical interpretation?
4. How are we to explain the **variant** readings between the parallel passages of Samuel–Kings and Chronicles? What does this mean for the doctrine of biblical inspiration?
5. Why does the chronicler make the temple of God the focal point of his history?
6. What is the relationship between reflection on the past and the worship of Yahweh?
7. What significance does the chronicler's rehearsal of Israelite history have for individual and corporate Christianity today?
8. What do we learn about worship from the Chronicles that is relevant for Christian worship today?

For Further Reading

Ackroyd, P. R. *Israel Under Babylonia and Persia*. Oxford: Clarendon Press, 1970.

_____. "The Chronicler as Exegete." *JSOT* 2 (1977): 2–32.

_____. "History and Theology in the Writings of the Chronicler." *Concordia Theological Monthly* 38 (1967): 501–15.

Allen, Leslie C. *1, 2 Chronicles*. Communicator's Commentary 10. Waco, Tex.: Word, 1987. Insightful application of the chronicler's message to the contemporary setting.

Braun, R. *1 Chronicles*. WBC. Vol. 14. Waco, Tex.: Word, 1986. Useful discussion of theological themes, with extensive bibliographies.

_____. "Chronicles, Ezra and Nehemiah: Theology and Literary History." In *Studies in the Historical Books of the Old Testament*, J. A. Emerton, ed. VT Supplement 30. Leiden: Brill, 1979. 52–64.

Bright, John. *A History of Israel*. 4th ed. Louisville: Westminster John Knox, 2006.

Coggins, R. J. *The First and Second Books of Chronicles*. CBC. Cambridge: Cambridge University Press, 1976.

DeVries, S. J. *1–2 Chronicles*. FOTL. Vol. 11. Grand Rapids: Eerdmans, 1989. Helpful analysis of each literary unit in Chronicles by structure, genre, setting, and intention according to form criticism but undermines the historical integrity of the books.

Dillard, R. B. *2 Chronicles*. WBC. Vol. 15. Waco, Tex.: Word, 1987. Extensive bibliographies.

Dumbrell, W. J. "The Purpose of the Books of Chronicles." *JSOT* 27 (1984): 257–66. Concise statement of theological and historical purposes in Chronicles.

Fishbane, M. *Biblical Interpretation in Ancient Israel*. Oxford: Clarendon, 1985. 385–407. Penetrating discussion of historical exegesis in the chronicler.

Freedman, David N. "The Chronicler's Purpose." *CBQ* 23 (1961): 436–42.

Goldingay, John. "The Chronicler as Theologian." *Biblical Theology Bulletin* 5 (1975): 99–121.

Hill, Andrew E. *1 and 2 Chronicles*. NIVAC. Grand Rapids: Zondervan, 2003.

Japhet, S. *I and II Chronicles*. OTL. Louisville: Westminster/John Knox, 1993. Comprehensive literary and historical analysis of the books. Must reading for the serious student.

_____. "The Historical Reliability of Chronicles." *JSOT* 33 (1985): 83–107.

McConville, J. G. *I and II Chronicles*. DSB–OT. Philadelphia: Westminster, 1984. Insightful contemporary application of the chronicler's message.

McKenzie, Steven L. *1–2 Chronicles*. AOTC. Nashville: Abingdon Press, 2004.

Myers, J. *First Chronicles*. AB. Vol. 12. 2nd ed. Garden City, N.Y.: Doubleday, 1986.

_____. *Second Chronicles*. AB. Vol. 13. 2nd ed. Garden City, N.Y.: Doubleday, 1986.

Newsome, J. D. *A Synoptic Harmony of Samuel, Kings, and Chronicles*. Grand Rapids: Baker, 1987.

_____. "Toward a New Understanding of the Chronicler and His Purposes." *JBL* 94 (1975): 204–17.

Payne, J. Barton. "1, 2 Chronicles." *EBC*. Vol. 4. Grand Rapids: Zondervan, 1988. 303–562. Helpful discussions of the variant readings between the parallels of Samuel–Kings and Chronicles.

Selman, Martin J. *1, 2 Chronicles*. TOTC. Vols. 10a, 10b. Downers Grove, Ill.: InterVarsity Press, 1994. Informative introductory sections on the chronicler as an interpreter and the chronicler's message.

Thompson, J. A. *1, 2 Chronicles*. NAC. Vol. 9. Nashville: Broadman & Holman, 1994.

Tuell, Steven. *First and Second Chronicles*. IBC. Louisville: John Knox, 2001.

Wilcock, M. *The Message of Chronicles*. Downers Grove, Ill.: InterVarsity Press, 1987.

Williamson, H. G. M. *I and II Chronicles*. NCB. Grand Rapids: Eerdmans, 1982. Informative introductory section on the chronicler and his sources.

_____. *Israel and the Book of Chronicles*. Cambridge: Cambridge University Press, 1977.

Wilson, R. R. *Genealogy and History in the Biblical World*. New Haven: Yale University Press, 1977.

_____. "Between 'Azel' and 'Azel': Interpreting the Biblical Genealogies." *BA* 42 (1979): 11–22.

After an attempt to stop the temple construction, King Darius I of Persia decreed that the Jews were allowed to resume construction (Ezra 6:1-12). This relief shows Darius seated, with Xerxes I, his son and successor (the Ahasueras in the book of Esther), standing behind him.

Werner Forman Archive/Archaeological Museum, Teheran

EZRA–NEHEMIAH

Key Ideas
- The physical restoration of the city of Jerusalem
- Yahweh as a covenant-keeping God
- Religious and social reform as the aftermath of repentance

Purpose Statement

The purpose of the books of Ezra and Nehemiah is to show the numerous ways that God was faithfully at work in restoring the people of Israel to their land after the Babylonian exile. God providentially brought favor with the Persian rulers and helped the Israelites overcome the obstacles presented by their enemies as they rebuilt the temple and walls of Jerusalem and established the Law of Moses as the foundation of society.

Major Themes
- Yahweh as Covenant Keeper
- Restoration Period Reforms and the Seeds of Pharisaism

God's Presence

God's presence in Ezra and Nehemiah is implicit in the rebuilding and dedication of the second temple—(Ezra 3 and 6). The Israelite understanding of the divine presence is also implicit in the community confession and covenant renewal ceremony (Ezra 10), and in the reforms of priesthood, Sabbath keeping and the reorganization of post-exilic Judah around the Torah of Moses (suggesting the need for the holiness of the people is still a requirement in view of God's covenant relationship with his people).

Outline

I. Sheshbazzar and Zerubbabel Narrative (Ezra)
   A. Decree of Cyrus (1:1–4)
   B. Return under Sheshbazzar (1:5–11)
   C. Return under Zerubbabel (2)
   D. Rebuilding the Altar and Temple (3–6)

II. Ezra's Memoirs: Part 1 (Ezra)
   A. Ezra's Arrival (7–8)
   B. Ezra's Religious and Social Reforms (9–10)

III. Nehemiah's Memoirs: Part 1 (Nehemiah)
   A. Nehemiah's Arrival (1–2)
   B. Rebuilding the Wall of Jerusalem Despite Opposition (3–4)
   C. Nehemiah's Economic and Social Reforms (5:1–7:73a)

IV. Ezra's Memoirs: Part 2 (Nehemiah)
   A. Reading of the Law (7:73b–8:12)
   B. Worship and Confession (8:13–9:37)
   C. Covenant Renewal (9:38–10:39)

V. Nehemiah's Memoirs: Part 2 (Nehemiah)
   A. Repopulation of Jerusalem (11:1–12:26)
   B. Dedication of the Wall of Jerusalem (12:27–13:3)
   C. Further Social and Religious Reforms of Nehemiah
      (13:4–31)

Ezra and Nehemiah were contemporaneous reformers of the postexilic period. Like their predecessors, Haggai and Zechariah, they had complementary ministries in Jerusalem of both a physical and spiritual nature. Ezra, a priest and scribe who was skilled in the law of Moses, is best remembered for his reading of the Torah to the postexilic community and the consequent religious revival it inspired (cf. Neh. 8:1–12). Nehemiah is well known for the administrative skill he demonstrated in organizing the restoration community to repair and rebuild a large section of the wall of Jerusalem destroyed by the Babylonians in 587 BC.

Both men came to Jerusalem from Susa in Persia during the reign of Artaxerxes I (464–424 BC), and both were members of some standing in Persian royal circles. By virtue of his levitical pedigree, it is suggested that Ezra held a position akin to secretary or counsel for Jewish affairs in the royal cabinet (cf. Ezra 7:1–6), while Nehemiah was a cupbearer to King Artaxerxes (Neh. 1:11; 2:1–2). Prayerful zeal for the plight of the restoration community in Jerusalem motivated both men to journey to Palestine from Persia. Their efforts to reform the religious,

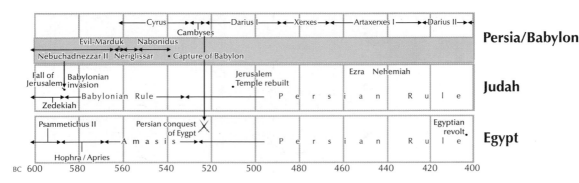

social, and economic life of the Hebrew city were rooted in a nationalistic sense of pride for the tradition of the Hebrew forefathers (e.g., Neh. 2:3) and a genuine concern for the reputation of the name of Yahweh in the midst of pagan opposition (cf. Ezra 9:1–15; Neh. 1:4–11).

Ezra and Nehemiah form a single book in the Hebrew Old Testament. Along with other historical books like Samuel, Kings, and Chronicles, it was divided into two books in the Septuagint. Ezra and Nehemiah actually comprise the second volume of a two-part work by the chronicler that presents a theological interpretation of Hebrew history. The two parts of Chronicles constitute the first volume of that history. The books of Ezra and Nehemiah are placed after 1–2 Chronicles in the Greek, Latin, and English Bibles. The reverse order in the Hebrew Old Testament may indicate the order of acceptance of the books into the canon.

Two books in the Old Testament **Apocrypha** are entitled "Esdras," the Greek equivalent of the name Ezra. The apocryphal 2 Esdras is an apocalyptic work of the late first century AD and has no connection with the historical Ezra. The apocryphal 1 Esdras dates to the second century BC and includes material from 2 Chronicles 35:1 through the end of the Old Testament book of Ezra, with Nehemiah 7:73–8:12 forming an appendix to the text. Though the book of 1 Esdras has some value for comparative analysis with the biblical texts of Chronicles, Ezra, and Nehemiah, the book is generally considered inferior both historically and theologically to the Old Testament book of Ezra (e.g., 1 Esd. 5:70–73).

The Writing of the Book

The majority view among biblical scholars today, regardless of theological persuasion, attributes the combined books of Ezra–Nehemiah to the postexilic chronicler. It is assumed that this compiler of the books of Chronicles also edited the book of Ezra–Nehemiah because 2 Chronicles 36:22–23 constitutes a colophon, or closing inscription, presupposing the introductory verses of Ezra 1:1–2. Jewish tradition

The Cyrus Cylinder describes Persian King Cyrus II's victory over Babylon (538–530 BC) and gives an example of his releasing captive peoples to return to their homelands. How this decree of Cyrus affected the Jewish people is recorded in Ezra 1.
Caryn Reeder, courtesy of the British Museum

identified Ezra the scribe as the chronicler of the postexilic history narrated in 1–2 Chronicles and Ezra–Nehemiah (so Babylonian Talmud: *Baba Bathra* 15a). Although this idea remains a possibility, most interpreters regard the chronicler as an anonymous compiler of Hebrew historical sources.

The actual composition of the books of Ezra–Nehemiah occurred in stages and was probably completed around 400 BC The sequence of writing and compiling may be outlined as follows: (1) Ezra and Nehemiah draft individual memoirs (ca. 440–420 BC); (2) the chronicler combines the Ezra and Nehemiah memoir sources, deliberately interweaving the materials; (3) the chronicler adds the Sheshbazzar/Zerubbabel narrative to the memoirs to form a prologue, or introduction, to the Ezra and Nehemiah autobiographies.

The intentional interweaving of memoir materials from Ezra and Nehemiah has raised some suspicion among certain biblical scholars as to the integrity of the compiler and the historical accuracy of the narratives. Far from being confused or dishonest, the compiler artfully documented a very pragmatic history of the Hebrew restoration period, emphasizing particular religious themes (including covenant keeping, purity of religion, separation from foreigners, etc.). This practice of conveying a religious message in the context of the historical narrative is a common tendency in Old Testament history writing (see chap. 10). The phenomenon is typical of ancient Near Eastern historical texts as well.[1]

This approach to the composition of Ezra–Nehemiah need not compromise the biblical teaching of the writing of Old Testament Scripture by the inspiration of the Holy Spirit (2 Tim. 3:16). The chronicler was no doubt inspired in a manner similar to Luke as he compiled early Christian historical sources about the life and teaching of Jesus Christ into his gospel account (cf. Luke 1:1–4).

Ezra is one of two Old Testament books containing substantial sections of text written in the Aramaic language and not the Hebrew

---

1. Cf. E. Speiser, "Ancient Mesopotamia," in *The Idea of History in the Ancient Near East*, ed. R. C. Denton (New Haven: Yale University Press, 1955), 37–76. S. Mowinckel, "Israelite Historiography," *Annual of the Swedish Theological Institute in Jerusalem* 2 (1963): 4–26; J. J. Finkelstein, "Mesopotamian Historiography," *Proceedings of the American Philosophical Society* 107 (1963): 461–72; and P. Michalowski, "History as Charter," JAOS 103/1 (1983): 237–48.

language (Ezra 4:8–6:18; 7:12–26; cf. Dan. 2:4–7:28). By the Persian period, Aramaic was the language of international trade, making it difficult to determine the place of writing for the memoir sources of Ezra and Nehemiah. Whether he completed his work in Persia or Palestine, it is certain the chronicler had access to the Persian state archives, since the Aramaic passages of Ezra appear to be verbatim quotations of official letters and related governmental documents.

It is possible, therefore, that Ezra or Nehemiah wrote the Sheshbazzar/Zerubbabel narrative or that they aided the chronicler's effort in some way by virtue of their good standing with the Persian king Artaxerxes (cf. Ezra 7:1–10; Neh. 1:1–11). The Hebrew adaptation of the Cyrus edict (Ezra 1:2–4) and the Artaxerxes letter (Ezra 7:12–26) suggest that the final compilation of the books of Ezra–Nehemiah occurred in Palestine.

It is widely recognized that the chronicler's compilation of Ezra and Nehemiah was motivated by keen theological interests. The more important themes identified as shaping the careful construction of the literature include covenant renewal in the restoration community (e.g., Nehemiah 8–10), the rebuilding and dedication of the wall of Jerusalem as a physical demonstration of God's fulfillment of earlier promises to restore the remnant of Israel (cf. Zeph. 3:19–20; Hag. 2:1–9), the historical and theological continuity between preexilic and postexilic

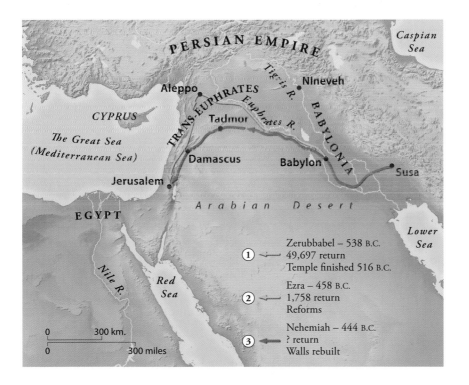

The Three Returns

Sebastià Giralt

Israel (e.g., the institution of the temple, installation of officers like the priests and temple servants, and the importance of the Torah of Moses as the guide for Hebrew religious and social life), and the legitimacy of the restoration community's religious, political, economic, and social agenda as God's elect (cf. Neh. 9:32–37).

The Background

The Jerusalem of Ezra and Nehemiah was little different from the Jerusalem to which Haggai and Zechariah had prophesied some sixty years earlier (ca. 520–518 BC; cf. Ezra 5:1–2). The reconstructed second temple was a mere shadow of the magnificent edifice erected by Solomon (cf. Ezra 3:12). Rather than inspiring the hope of covenant restoration in the community, the building served only as a monument to remind the people of messianic expectations dashed by the reality of Medo-Persian domination. Indeed, the promise of Yahweh to make Jerusalem an ensign among the nations was all but forgotten as postexilic Judah subsisted on the remote fringes of a pagan empire that was at that time controlling most of the known world (cf. Hag. 2:20–23).

In fact, the very existence of the Hebrew postexilic community appeared threatened by the opposition of hostile enemies surrounding

Jerusalem during the governorship of Zerubbabel (ca. 520 BC; cf. Ezra 4:1–5; 5:1–7). This situation had not really changed by the time Ezra and Nehemiah arrived on the scene in the mid-fifth century BC. Nehemiah's initiative to repair the walls of Jerusalem was undertaken against considerable resistance offered by a coalition of local alien enemies, including Sanballat (the Samaritan governor in control of the province of Judah), Tobiah (called "the Ammonite" and an influential member of the Jerusalem aristocracy by marriage), Geshem (an Arab official), and the Arabs, Ammonites, and citizens of Ashdod (Neh. 4:1–9).

The earlier call to religious and social reform by the prophets Haggai and Zechariah had seemingly little impact. Only a generation later, the prophet Malachi (ca. 500–475 BC) rebuked the people for breaking faith with Yahweh and called them to repentance and covenant renewal. Now, two generations after Malachi's preaching, Ezra and Nehemiah encountered similar religious apathy and social decay. In fact, the reforms instituted by Ezra and Nehemiah were directed against many of the very same covenant violations decried by the postexilic prophets. These included spiritual apathy and improper worship, social injustice, divorce, intermarriage with foreign women, neglect of the tithe, moral laxity, and abuse of authority on the part of the priests.

The exact date of Ezra's arrival in Jerusalem remains a disputed issue among biblical scholars. Three options for the chronology of Ezra's ministry in Jerusalem have emerged from the discussion. According to the traditional view, Ezra arrived in Jerusalem during the seventh year of King Artaxerxes I, or 458 BC (cf. Ezra 7:8).

Michael Greenhalgh/ArtServe, courtesy of the British Museum

"In the month of Nisan in the twentieth year of King Artaxerxes, when wine was brought for him, I took the wine and gave it to the king" (Neh. 2:1). For protection from assassination by poisoning, the king had a cupbearer. This was a high adminstrative position that Nehemiah held for King Artaxerxes of Persia.

The second view is established on the assumption that the text of Ezra 7:8 has been corrupted through the course of manuscript transmission and should read the "thirty-seventh" year of Artaxerxes I, instead of the "seventh." This would place Ezra in Jerusalem in 428 BC during Nehemiah's second term as governor of the community. This view is the weakest of the three because the hypothesis of a textual error in Ezra 7:8 has virtually no supporting textual-critical evidence.

The third view argues that Ezra ministered in Jerusalem during the seventh year of the reign of King Artaxerxes II, or 398 BC. This chronology for Ezra's arrival presumes that the priest Johanan mentioned in Nehemiah 12:22 and the high priest Johanan named in the late fifth-century Elephantine papyri are to be identified as the same person.

Despite the problems encountered in reconciling the relationship of Ezra and Nehemiah as coreformers in Jerusalem, the traditional view continues to provide the most satisfactory explanation of all the evidence. A date of 458 BC for Ezra's arrival in Jerusalem is preferred. The date for Nehemiah's arrival in the postexilic community is firmly fixed during the twentieth year of the reign of King Artaxerxes I, or 445 BC.

The following chronology of the later postexilic period of Hebrew history supplements the time line on page 331.

> Xerxes, king of Persia (485–465 BC)
> Esther, Xerxes queen (1:1), ?
> Artaxerxes I, king of Persia (464–424 BC)
> Return of Ezra (Ezra 7:7–8), (458 BC)
> Return of Nehemiah (Neh. 2:1–2), (445 BC)
> Nehemiah, governor of Judah for twelve years (Neh. 13:6), (445–433 BC)
> Nehemiah's second governorship (Neh. 13:7), (after 433 BC to ?)[2]
> Darius II, king of Persia (423–405 BC)
> Artaxerxes II Mnemon, king of Persia (404–359 BC)
> Chronicler compiles 1–2 Chronicles and Ezra–Nehemiah, (ca. 400–380 BC)

Purpose and Message

Historical

The books of Ezra and Nehemiah report a significant portion of the history of Israel during the postexilic, or Persian, period. The highly stylized account documents key events roughly from the edict of Cyrus in 538 BC to Nehemiah's second governorship in Jerusalem (sometime after 433 BC). This record of restoration history is contained in three distinct literary sources, as explained earlier. The essential content of the three sources may be summarized as follows: (1) the Hebrew return

2. Nehemiah's second governorship must have ended by 407 BC, since the Egyptian Elephantine papyri of the fifth century BC mention a certain Bagoas as governor of Judah.

to Jerusalem from Babylonian exile, including the rebuilding of the altar and temple; (2) the arrival and ministry of Ezra, including the religious reform of the community based on the law of Moses; and (3) the arrival and ministry of Nehemiah, including the repair of the Jerusalem wall and continued social and economic reform in the restoration community.

The purpose of the books is historiographic, given the need to preserve the record of the return to Jerusalem from Babylonia by the former Hebrew exiles. As such, the accounts highlighted Yahweh's faithfulness and thereby instilled hope in postexilic Israel by demonstrating God's providential working among human kings and governments. Theologically, the narrative recounting the ministries of Ezra and Nehemiah in restoring Jerusalem physically and spiritually affirmed Yahweh's promises to renew the remnant of Israel. Pragmatically speaking, the history probably stems from the obligation placed on Ezra and Nehemiah to chronicle their experiences for the sake of reporting to the king of Persia. The covenant renewal ideas discussed below reinforce this understanding of the basic purpose of the two books.

Theological

The dominant theological idea of the memoir material of both Ezra and Nehemiah is covenant renewal in the postexilic community. The call to

"Ezra the priest brought the Law before the assembly.... He read it aloud from daybreak till noon as he faced the square before the Water Gate in the presence of the men, women and others who could understand. And all the people listened attentively to the Book of the Law" (Neh. 8:2–3). That scene is depicted in this wall painting from the Dura Europos, one of the earliest surviving synagogues (AD 245).

spiritual renewal and social justice by the two reformers was aimed at correcting abuses and gross misconduct among the returned remnant and instilling hope and boosting the morale of the people. It was important for the community despairing over God's apparent neglect to recognize that obedience to covenant stipulations was a mandatory prerequisite for Yahweh's blessing and restoration of Israel as his special possession. While Ezra and Nehemiah no doubt recorded their memoirs simply to preserve a small piece of history for posterity, the more profound message of God's providential rule of human activity for the ultimate benefit of his "elect" was most welcome news (e.g., note how "the hand of God" was upon Ezra [7:9] and Nehemiah [2:8], and the repetition of epitaphs like "the God of heaven" [Ezra 7:11–28; Neh. 2:1–8]).

The theme of covenant renewal is also part of the chronicler's theological agenda in the arrangement of the historical sources of Ezra and Nehemiah. For the chronicler, the return from exile in Babylon was a new exodus for Israel. He understood the covenant relationship between Yahweh and the Hebrew people as an important link bridging historical and religious continuity from the preexilic to the postexilic periods of Israelite history.

Although subservience to the Persian overlord prohibited the reestablishment of Israel as a nation-state ruled by a "Davidic" king, the covenant renewal event served to legitimize the postexilic community as the "heir" of that tradition and the people of the restoration as the "covenant people" of God. The particular emphasis on religious purity and social exclusiveness in the community now helped maintain Hebrew identity as a "separate people," since the vibrant nationalism associated with the political independence of the preexilic period was but a memory.

Finally, the chronicler reaffirmed and expanded the notion of God's sovereign rule of human history. The inclusion of the Sheshbazzar/Zerubbabel narrative as a prologue to the Ezra and Nehemiah memoirs underscored God's involvement in the restoration of Israel by revealing Yahweh's role in prompting Persian kings to permit Israel to return to her land and rebuild the temple. Two additional theological truths of great importance for the restoration community are implicit in the careful splicing of the historical and memoir sources: (1) the people may have hope in the present because the work of God on behalf of Israel in the past stands as the model for Yahweh's participation in the future of the community, and (2) the ministry of Ezra and Nehemiah in restoring Jerusalem attested God's ability to continue to raise up his servants to accomplish his purposes and fulfill his promises to Israel.

Structure and Organization

The book of Ezra opens with a recitation of Cyrus's proclamation for the restoration of Jerusalem (Ezra 1:1–4), and the book of Nehemiah concludes with the reforms of Nehemiah implemented during his second stint as Persian-appointed governor of Jerusalem (Neh. 13:6–30). Generally speaking, the books recount postexilic history from about 538 BC to sometime after 433 BC—a span of some hundred years.

These overlapping accounts of the ministries of Ezra and Nehemiah in postexilic Jerusalem give evidence of careful literary construction. The author-editor used a variety of written sources of several different literary types, or genres. Three large units of material may be readily distinguished: (1) the Sheshbazzar/Zerubbabel narrative (Ezra 1–6),

(2) the Ezra autobiography (Ezra 7 – 10; Neh. 7:73 – 10:39), (3) the Nehemiah autobiography (Neh. 1:1 – 7:73; 11:1 – 31:31).

The outline of the complete composition reveals the deliberate weaving or interleaving of the literary units by the compiler:

Sheshbazzar/Zerubbabel Narrative (Ezra 1 – 6)
Ezra's Memoirs: Part 1 (Ezra 7 – 10)
Nehemiah's Memoirs: Part 1 (Neh. 1:11 – 7:73a)
Ezra's Memoirs: Part 2 (Neh. 7:73b – 10:39)
Nehemiah's Memoirs: Part 2 (Neh. 11 – 13)

These sections of the two books are logically arranged according to the compiler's theological purposes, related to Yahweh's reaffirmation of covenant relationship with Israel. The literary units work together to describe the sequence of Hebrew migrations back to Palestine and the physical rebuilding and spiritual renewal of Jerusalem.

The variety of literary types within these larger units includes

- First-person memoir material from the autobiographies of Ezra and Nehemiah and third-person narrative materials (e.g., Ezra 8:35 – 36)
- Historical documents and official correspondence (e.g., the Cyrus edict in Aramaic, Ezra 6:3 – 5; and the communication between Tattenai and Darius, Ezra 5:7 – 17)

Second Chronicles 32:5 describes Hezekiah extending the walls of Jerusalem, and this extension is what is generally thought to be referred to in Nehemiah 3:8: "They restored Jerusalem as far as the broad wall." Excavations have revealed portions of this wall.
Peter White

- Speeches and prayers (e.g., Neh. 9:5–37)
- Songs (e.g., Ezra 3:11)
- Numerous catalogs and census records of individuals and families who participated in the return to Jerusalem from exile (e.g., Ezra 2:2–70)
- An inventory list of temple vessels returned to Jerusalem (Ezra 1:9–11)

The historical reliability of Ezra and Nehemiah has been confirmed by continuing archaeological discoveries. Extrabiblical evidence garnered from inscriptions on papyri, official seals, and commemorative vessels substantiates the biblical account at several points, including the names of significant characters in the biblical narrative (e.g., Sanballat, Neh. 2:10, and Judahite priests like Jehoiada and Johana, Neh. 12:2; 13:28), the Hebrew understanding of postexilic chronology (e.g., the placement of Geshem the Arab in the first half of the fifth century BC (Neh. 6:1–6), and the illumination of particular events in postexilic Hebrew history (e.g., Nehemiah's expulsion of Jehoiada's son, Neh. 13:28).[3]

The exact nature of the relationship between the ministries and reforms of Ezra and Nehemiah proves more difficult to assess. Neither Ezra nor Nehemiah mentions the other in his memoirs, and apart from one reference in Nehemiah 8:9, they do not appear together as coworkers in the text. Yet this is hardly sufficient reason for doubting the contemporaneous aspects of their ministries. Neither Haggai nor Zechariah mentions the other, and they prophesied in Jerusalem during the same two-year period. It may well be that the compiler juxtaposed the memoirs of Ezra and Nehemiah to emphasize the complementary ministry of the two, based on the earlier pattern of Haggai and Zechariah.

Major Themes

Yahweh as Covenant Keeper

The labors of Ezra and Nehemiah to rebuild and reform postexilic Jerusalem were largely inspired by the theological truth of Yahweh as covenant keeper (cf. Neh. 9:32). God's faithfulness to his word as a keeper of covenant oath meant "there is still hope for Israel" (Ezra 10:2). It was the certainty of this teaching that energized the postexilic prophets to announce messages of hope and encouragement to the restoration community as well (cf. Zech. 1:3; Mal. 1:2). Perhaps more important was the faith of these postexilic servants who trusted God for the accomplishment of feats that served as concrete manifestations of his covenant-keeping ability (e.g., the reconstruction of the second temple and repair of the Jerusalem city wall).

3. Cf. Edwin M. Yamauchi, "The Archaeological Background of Ezra" and "The Archaeological Background of Nehemiah," *Bibliotheca Sacra* 137 (1980): 195–211, 291–309.

Yahweh's willingness to return to those who returned to him assured the postexilic community of his desire to bless and restore the covenant people (Hag. 2:4–9; Zech. 1:16–17; Mal. 3:6–7). As a covenant-keeping God, Yahweh heard and responded to the petitions of Israel and declared them "his people" (Ezra 7:9–10, 27–28). Indeed, the very presence of a remnant of Israel in the land of Palestine was a gracious token of God's covenant-keeping nature (cf. Ps. 111:4–5, 9).

Restoration Period Reforms and the Seeds of Pharisaism

The reordering of Hebrew society under Ezra and Nehemiah had both immediate and far-reaching implications. Two primary concerns shaped the reform of the restoration community. The first was the prevention of another Hebrew exile, since the loss of the land of covenant promise was unthinkable. The second was the preservation of the ethnic identity of the Israelites while they languished beneath the Persian yoke in a fringe province surrounded by hostile people groups.

Excursus: Old Testament Scribes

The development of writing systems in the ancient Near East led to the rise of a professional class of scribes, and this held true for Hebrew society in Old Testament times. In preexilic Israel these official secretaries were key figures in both religious and civil administration (cf. 2 Sam. 8:16–17; 20:23–26).

During the period of the Hebrew monarchies the scribes functioned as "diplomats" in a way, since their expertise in the languages and literature of the day facilitated international correspondence (cf. 2 Kings 18:18–26). The scribes also wrote personal letters and public documents (e.g., Isa. 50:1; Jer. 36:18) and recorded legal, military, and financial data for the monarchy (cf. 1 Kings 4:3; 2 Kings 22:3–4; 2 Chron. 24:11; 2 Chron. 26:11). The Levites also served as scribes and recorders for the temple (2 Chron. 34:13, 15).

After the fall of the Hebrew monarchies, the scribal class in postexilic Israel was tied solely to the temple and more narrowly focused as to function. These temple scribes were essentially a class of scholars who devoted themselves to copying, preserving, publishing, and interpreting the Law of Moses for the Hebrew people. Ezra is often identified as the precursor of this scribal class (Ezra 7:1–10). By New Testament times, the scribes formed a powerful religious and political class in Judaism. They became major opponents of the ministry of Jesus, accusing him of violating Jewish law (cf. Matt. 23:2).

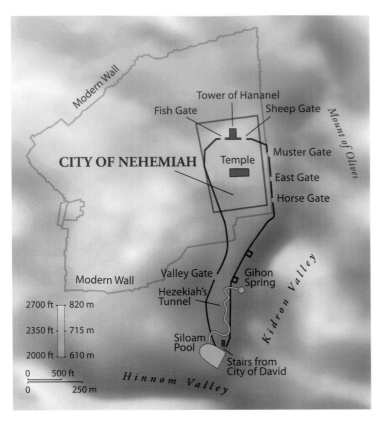

Nehemiah's Jerusalem

Specific measures taken by Ezra and Nehemiah to ensure Hebrew possession of the land of the promise included the covenant renewal ceremony (cf. Neh. 9:38–10:27), the rehabilitation of the priesthood (e.g., Ezra 10:18–44), the reinstitution of temple ritual and Sabbath observance (Neh. 8:13–18; 13:15–22), and the introduction of the law of Moses as the rule of community life (Neh. 8:1–12). Attempts to maintain the ethnic purity of the Israelite community included social and economic reforms based on covenant principles (e.g., Neh. 11:1–2), renewed emphasis on the ceremonial purity of the entire populace of Jerusalem (cf. Neh. 10:28–39), and the divorce and expulsion of foreigners from the assembly of God (Ezra 10:1–8; Neh. 9:1–5; 13:1–3).

The immediate consequences of these reforms had a considerable impact on the nature and structure of postexilic Hebrew society. Israel's identity as the people of God took on a new dimension as temple and priest replaced state and king as the stabilizing institutions of the Hebrew community. The law of Moses became the charter or constitution by which society was reorganized into a priestly "temple-state." Religious, social, and economic policy was now determined by the Torah, bringing a new emphasis on Hebrew "exclusiveness" and "separation" from the Gentiles and their polluted world order.

Perhaps more significant was the metamorphosis that took place in the offices of priest and scribe. In the preexilic period a scribe was a high-ranking cabinet member of the state bureaucracy (e.g., 2 Sam. 20:24–25; 2 Kings 18:18) who never functioned as a priest. The role of the scribe was redefined with the arrival of Ezra. As a priest-scribe he became the model for a later class of religious professionals whose sole task was the study and exposition of Scripture (cf. Ezra 7:10).

The long-term ramifications of this restructuring of Hebrew society emerged in the attitudes and teachings of later Judaism. Unfortunately, the consequences for Hebrew religion were mostly negative. Yet the historical and theological developments traced from the postex-ilic period through the intertestamental period contribute greatly to the understanding of New Testament backgrounds, especially Jesus' encounters with the religious elite of Palestine in the first century AD.

For example, the zealous but misguided appeal to Mosaic law for community rule eventually led to a pharisaical legalism that tithed "pepper seeds" with ruthless calculation but ignored the very essence of Torah—faith, justice, and mercy (Matt. 23:23). To ensure commu-nity obedience to covenant stipulations related to personal purity, the Mosaic code was "fenced in" or supplemented by a legal hedge called the oral law, or "tradition of the elders" (cf. Matt. 15:1–9). Gradually the supplemental code displaced the primary code of Moses, prompting Jesus to decry a religion that neglected the law of God to cling to the traditions of men (cf Mark 7:1–9).

The idea of Hebrew exclusiveness fostered by Ezra slowly degener-ated into an unhealthy preoccupation with the separation from the "unclean" lifestyle of the Gentiles. As a result, the majority of the Jews were blinded to their divine commission as a light to the nations (Isa. 42:6; Luke 2:32) and desensitized to their own spiritual bankruptcy (Luke 5:27–31, 10.25–37).

Finally, the study and teaching of the law of Moses continued to be divorced from the priesthood. For their part, the priests were more concerned about political and economic issues due to the influence of **Hellenism** on the ruling aristocracy of Jerusalem. By New Testament times, however, a professional class of scribes or "lawyers" had usurped the priestly role as spiritual leaders of the people. Jesus condemned them as little more than "blind guides" and "whitewashed tombs" (Matt. 23:16, 27). Small wonder the multitudes were astounded at the teaching of Jesus as one who spoke with authority (cf. Mark 1:22)!

Questions for Further Study and Discussion

1. How were Ezra and Nehemiah complementary reformers?
2. What is the significance of the reading of the law of Moses by Ezra (Neh. 8) for postexilic Israelite history?
3. How were the migrations of the Hebrew exiles from Babylonia to Palestine a "new exodus"?
4. How does the response of Ezra and Nehemiah to the sins of the Hebrews align with rest of the teaching of the Bible on the attitude of the righteous to sin?
5. How is Nehemiah a good example of doing the work of God from an administrative perspective?
6. How are we to understand the Hebrew separation from "all foreigners" in Nehemiah 9? Is this a form of racism?
7. How are we to understand the marriage reforms recorded in Ezra 9–10 and Nehemiah 13? What are the ethical implications of this mass divorce legislated by Ezra and Nehemiah? How do these accounts of mandatory divorce compare with other teachings of Scripture on divorce?

For Further Reading

Ackroyd, P. R. *Exile and Restoration*. Philadelphia: Westminster, 1968.
_____. *Israel Under Babylon and Persia*. London: Oxford University Press, 1970. A standard work on the historical background of the postexilic period by the acknowledged expert on the topic.
Berquist, Jon L. *Judaism in Persia's Shadow*. Minneapolis: Fortress Press, 1995.
Bickerman, E. *From Ezra to the Last of the Maccabees*. New York: Schocken, 1962.
Blenkinsopp, Joseph. *Ezra–Nehemiah—A Commentary*. OTL. Philadelphia: Westminster, 1988.
Breneman, Mervin. *Ezra, Nehemiah, Esther*. NAC. Nashville: Broadman & Holman, 1993. Insightful application of the books' message to the contemporary situation.
Bright, John. *A History of Israel*. 4th ed. Louisville: Westminster John Knox, 2006. The standard history of Israel in English.
Brown, Raymond. *The Message of Nehemiah*. Downers Grove, Ill.: InterVarsity Press, 1998. Insightful commentary on the contemporary relevance of Nehemiah's message.
Clines, D. A. *Ezra, Nehemiah, Esther*. NCBC. Grand Rapids: Eerdmans, 1984.
Cross, Frank M. "A Reconstruction of the Judean Restoration." *JBL* 94 (1975): 4–18. A careful study of the problems of postexilic

chronology, supporting the traditional view of Ezra arriving in Jerusalem in 458 BC.

Davies, P. R., ed. *Second Temple Studies*. Vol. 1. JSOTSS 117. Sheffield, England: Sheffield Academic Press, 1991.

Davies, P. R. and J. M. Halligan, eds. *Second Temple Studies*. Vol. 3. JSOTSS 340. Sheffield, England: Sheffield Academic Press, 2002.

Eskenazi, T. C. "The Structure of Ezra–Nehemiah and the Integrity of the Book." *JBL* 107 (1988): 641–56.

Eskenazi, T. C., ed. *Second Temple Studies*. Vol. 2. JSOTSS 175. Sheffield, England: Sheffield Academic Press, 1994.

Fensham, F. C. *The Books of Ezra and Nehemiah*. NICOT. Grand Rapids: Eerdmans, 1982. Thorough, conservative, well researched and well organized. Most readable, with useful application of the books' message to the contemporary situation. Probably the best evangelical commentary currently available.

Holmgren, F. C. *Ezra and Nehemiah: Israel Alive Again*. ITC. Grand Rapids: Eerdmans, 1987.

Kidner, Derek. *Ezra and Nehemiah*. TOTC. Downers Grove, Ill.: InterVarsity Press, 1979.

Klein, Ralph. *Ezra and Nehemiah*. NIB 3. Abingdon Press, 1999. 663–851.

Myers, J. M. *Ezra–Nehemiah*. AB. Vol. 14. New York: Doubleday, 1965.
_____. *I and II Esdras*. AB. Vol. 42. New York: Doubleday, 1974.
_____. *The World of the Restoration*. Englewood Cliffs, N.J.: Prentice-Hall, 1968.

Packer. J. I. *A Passion for Faithfulness: Wisdom from the Book of Nehemiah*. 2nd ed. Wheaton, Ill.: Crossway Books, 2000.

Throntveit, Mark. *Ezra-Nehemiah*. IBC. Atlanta: John Knox, 1992.

Williamson, H. G. M. *Ezra, Nehemiah*. WBC. Vol. 16. Waco, Tex.: Word, 1985. Detailed historical and linguistic analysis, careful exegesis, insightful exposition and application. Less useful than it might be due to awkward format.

Yamauchi, Edwin M. "Ezra and Nehemiah." *EBC*. Vol. 4.Grand Rapids: Zondervan, 1988. 546–771. Informative discussion on the contributions of Persian history, language, and biblical archaeology to the understanding of the life, times, and message of Ezra and Nehemiah.
_____. *Persia and the Bible*. Grand Rapids: Baker, 1990.

Although most of the events of the book of Esther take place in the old Elamite capital of Susa, Darius I chose Persepolis, some 300 miles to the southeast, as the site for a royal seat for the Persian Empire. Building continued during the reign of Xerxes (Ahasueras).

ESTHER

Key Ideas

- God is at work even when he is behind the scenes.
- The schemes of the wicked are doomed.
- God's plan for his people cannot be thwarted.

Purpose Statement

The purpose of the book of Esther is to show that God can accomplish his purposes just as easily through "coincidences" as he can through grand miracles of deliverance. Though he works behind the curtain, he is just as much in control. Events that others see as chance or fate, can be seen by believers as signs of God's sovereignty.

Major Themes

- Purim
- People of God

God's Presence

This book demonstrates that God is present with his people in many different ways, some more subtle than others. His presence can be felt even in foreign lands and works on behalf of his people even in the face of mighty opponents.

Outline

    I. Esther's Rise to Power (1–2)

    II. Mordecai's Refusal to Bow
       A. Haman's Anger: Mordecai's Jeopardy (3:1–6)
       B. Xerxes' Decree: Israel's Jeopardy (3:7–15)

    III. Plan for Deliverance: Esther's Jeopardy (4–5)

    IV. Esther's First Banquet
       A. Xerxes' Insomnia: Mordecai Remembered (6:1–5)
       B. Haman's Humiliation: Mordecai Honored (6:6–13)

    V. Esther's Second Banquet
       A. Xerxes' Anger: Haman Exposed and Doomed (7)
       B. Xerxes' Decree: Israel Given Right to Defend Itself (8)

    VI. Israel's Enemies Destroyed (9:1–19)

    VII. Purim Observed (9:20–32)

    VIII. Resulting Stature of Mordecai (10:1–3)

It would be difficult to find a more riveting, dramatic, and suspense-filled plot in the pre-Hellenistic world than the book of Esther. Although the book is in the center of a number of swirling controversies, they all fade into the background as we are introduced to the colorful cast: pompous and impressionable Xerxes/Ahasueras, who is thwarted by his unruly and defiant Queen Vashti and repeatedly manipulated by all; the diabolical archvillain, Haman; and above all, the beautiful, wise, and courageous Esther at center stage.

The Writing of the Book

There is no indication that the story was intended to be performed as a stage play, but it could be easily adapted to such a medium. Despite the fine literary characteristics, the vindictive nature of some of the action in the book and, more particularly, the absence of any mention of God have occasionally brought objections regarding its inclusion in Scripture. Furthermore, though actual events can appear more contrived than fictitious ones, modern interpreters have often considered the plot too artificial to stake a claim to historical accuracy. This has prompted the search for a consensus concerning the genre of the book.

    The book gives no indication as to its author, and though some have speculated that Mordecai may be a candidate, there is little evidence available to promote any theories. So we must consider the author anonymous. Whoever it was, he or she shows great skill as a narrator and had access to court records (cf. 10:2). The author demonstrates a breadth of knowledge about the operation of the Persian court and appears to possess information that would have been known only to Mordecai and Esther.

The setting of the book is the Persian Empire of the early to mid-fifth century BC, so obviously it must have been written after that time. Though there are no Hebrew manuscripts of the book that date earlier than the eleventh century AD, analysis of the Hebrew language used in the book indicates that it is older than the second century BC. It is most likely that the book was written down in the fourth or even the late fifth century BC.

In the Greek translation, the book has over a hundred additional verses. This longer version was available as early as Jerome in the fourth century AD and already had a long tradition by then. In this expanded form the story included such passages as a dream of Mordecai that reveals to him the plot against the king, letters from Mordecai and Xerxes, and prayers of Mordecai and Esther. These additions served the function of inserting God more obviously into the plot, but they have no claim to authenticity.

The Background

By the early part of the fifth century, the Achaemenid rulers of Persia were secure enough in the East to attempt expansion across the Mediterranean at the expense of the Greeks. Though this expansion was decidedly unsuccessful, the Persian Empire controlled the Near East longer than the Neo-Assyrian and Neo-Babylonian empires combined, and it ruled much more territory than any of its predecessors.

Xerxes I is identified with Ahasueras (KJV) and reigned from 486 to 465 BC. He was the son of the eminently successful Darius the Great, who had annexed parts of India and Eastern Europe into his expanding empire. Darius's confrontations with the Greeks, however, did not have so favorable an outcome, as the rout at Marathon (490 BC) attested. Though Xerxes was able to crush rebellions in Egypt and Babylon, the humiliation of the Persians at

This text from the time of Xerxes was found at Persepolis. It preserves a list of peoples under the rule of the Achaemenid kings.

the hand of the Greeks continued in the defeats suffered at Salamis and Mycale and in the embarrassing loss of the entire Persian fleet at Eurymedon. The primary source for this period is the earliest of the Greek historians, Herodotus, a contemporary of Xerxes and his son, Artaxerxes.

Though the details offered in Esther give it a ring of authenticity and suggest a realistic historical setting for the book, many have drawn the conclusion that this book is not intended as an accurate chronicling of events. This opens up the question of literary genre: Is this history? Is it a historical novel? Is it parable or allegory? Belief in the authority of Scripture does not eliminate this question, for there is nothing wrong with a story being a parable if that is what its author intended it to be. As interpreters we would be remiss to treat something as factual if it were not intended by the author to be so.

What are the claims of the book? The most forthright statement occurs in 10:2, where the reader is referred to the court records of the Persian Empire to verify at least the stature of Mordecai. This falls short of suggesting that all the events of the book could be verified from the court records. But it does give an indication that the author was concerned about verification, thus implying an intention to be historically rooted. Though this would be further supported by the authenticating details woven through the fabric of the plot, historical fiction often thrives on authenticating details.

The most serious objection to the authenticity of the book is the inability of contemporary sources to identify most of the principle players, notably Vashti, Esther, Mordecai, and Haman. Herodotus includes somewhat lengthy discussion of the exploits of Xerxes' queen Amestris, but various attempts to identify her as either Vashti or Esther have not gained widespread support. While this is problematic and potentially threatening to the credibility of the narrative, it is not sufficient to outweigh the book's own insistence on its accuracy.

Defending the accuracy of the book, however, does not obligate the interpreter to insist that the book's primary intention is to record his-

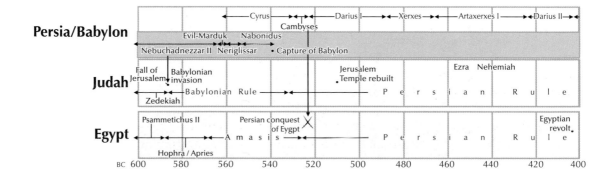

tory. The literary style and features of the book do not favor classifying the book as one that is intended only to chronicle history. On the contrary, it possesses many of the characteristics of the modern short story, with fast-paced action, narrative tension, irony, and reversal. The blend of these literary features with a historical setting and a theological purpose, however, suggest that the book of Esther is in a class by itself. There is nothing like it in ancient literature, and in the Bible only the story of Joseph comes close.

An Egyptian die reminiscent of the purim (lots) that figure prominently in the book of Esther.
Kim Walton, courtesy of the Oriental Institute Museum

Purpose and Message

The book of Esther has very particular points to make about the saving acts of the Lord. Israel's history was replete with accounts of the signs and wonders of the Lord on behalf of his covenant people. The mighty plagues, the deliverance from Egypt, the parting of the sea, and the crumbling of the walls of Jericho were classic examples of Yahweh's highly visible deliverance of Israel. More recently, the return of the exiles from their Babylonian captivity was evidence of God's continuing ability to accomplish the impossible.

But God is not so visible in the book of Esther. Yet, where others may see coincidences, Israel saw the Lord at work. A king's insomnia could just as easily bring deliverance as receding waters. In the course of this book it therefore becomes evident that the well-known themes of prophecy and wisdom could still fuel the hopes of Israelites even though they were scattered among the nations. The prophetic theme of God's protection of Israel and the judgment of her enemies (e.g., Zech. 1:21) was operating as the plot unfolded. Even more evident is the wisdom theme that God would prosper the righteous and bring to naught the schemes of the wicked (cf. Ps. 37:12–15).

The message comes through clearly: God's methods may vary, but his purposes do not. His workings may be obscured to skeptics by the disguise of coincidence, but the people of God recognize his sovereign hand in the ebb and flow of history. His name is not mentioned, but his influence is unmistakable.

Structure and Organization

There is a growing consensus among those analyzing Esther that the plot is built and the message is conveyed through the technique of reversal. This occurs when the current state of affairs is turned around or when the plot develops in a way that is opposite or contrary to what one would expect. Among the most notable examples of this phenomenon are the elevation of Mordecai, the downfall of Haman, and the Jews' destroying their enemies rather than being destroyed by them.

"If it pleases the king, . . . let the king, together with Haman, come today to a banquet I have prepared for him" (Esth. 5:4). A similar banquet with the king and the queen is portrayed in this Assyrian relief.

The effect of reversal is heightened by the use of irony throughout the narrative. Irony occurs when the reader has information that the characters do not. Perhaps the most striking example of this occurs when Haman comes into the court to ask permission to execute Mordecai, and before he can ask, the king requests Haman's opinion concerning how to bestow a great honor. The irony is heightened when Haman assumes that the king means to honor him and reaches a climax when Haman is then forced to personally bestow the honor on Mordecai whom he sought to kill. The reader has knowledge that neither of the characters have.

Haman is the main target for the irony of the text. He thinks he is being honored by being invited to Esther's banquets when in actuality he is being set up. He seeks to destroy the Jews and then is reduced to begging for his life from a Jewess. Not least of all, he is hung on his own gallows. All these turns make him almost a comic figure whom the narrative cannot resist humiliating time and again.

The significance of the irony is that it demonstrates that there is always more going on than meets the eye and more possibilities available than any single person understands or is aware of. God's control cannot be calculated, God's solution cannot be anticipated, and God's plan cannot be thwarted, because no one has all the necessary information. It is the effective use of irony and reversal that serve throughout the plot to make the message plain. The narrative tension created by the crisis into which Mordecai and the Jews are thrown headlong is resolved through an apparently circumstantial chain of events that could not have been guided by anyone but a sovereign God.

The basic flow of the plot is evident as one reads through the narrative. As can be seen from the outline, the first five chapters set up the situation, moving Esther into the palace and establishing the feud between Mordecai and Haman that escalates into an attempt by Haman to exterminate the Jews. The major turn takes place in chapter 6, between the two banquets, just before Esther exposes Haman. From that point the prediction of Haman's wife becomes nearly self-fulfilling as Haman is executed and his genocidal plot is reversed. Mordecai and Esther gain high positions and the favor of the king, and the Jews are saved from their enemies.

Major Themes

Purim

The book of Esther is read annually at the Jewish celebration of the Feast of Purim ("lots"). The festival, observed in late February/early March, commemorates the deliverance reported in the book and, likewise, the book establishes the celebration of the festival. A number of interpreters have concluded that the book itself was written to provide an explanation for the celebration of the feast. Others have seen chapter 9 as a later addition to the narrative that seeks to legitimize a non-Israelite festival. Neither explanation is necessary or persuasive. If the events recorded in the book actually took place (as we would affirm), it is logical and understandable that a feast would be established to commemorate the occasion. The name "Purim" is entirely appropriate, for God's deliverance does not come by the angel of the Lord slaying the enemy in the night, but by means that others would view as chance. The theology of Purim affirms that God is no less at work in the latter than in the former (cf. Prov. 16:33).

The People of God

We recall from the chapter on Genesis that God chose Abraham and his family to become the people of God in the sense that his revelation would come through them. They were to be the "revelatory" people of God. Upon reaching the book of Esther, the reader has been brought through a 1,500-year story of God's self-disclosure through his people Israel despite themselves. Now Esther perhaps implies that a shift took place in the postexilic period. The deliverance of Israel recorded in this book was not done in such a way that it bore witness to the world of God's power. Rather it was accomplished so as to confirm believers in their faith in a sovereign God, while skeptics might easily dismiss it as coincidence.

Certainly it was always God's desire that the people through whom he was revealing himself would be in a proper relationship with him (i.e., the revelatory people of God would also respond with faith). But in the postexilic period, the spiritual condition of the people moved to the top of the agenda, and the revelatory function seems at best to have been put on hold until the righteous remnant would emerge (cf. Dan. 9:24). The book of Esther illustrates this shift. The comment of Haman's wife demonstrates that, to a large extent, the revelatory purpose of God was achieved: "Since Mordecai, before whom your downfall has started, is of Jewish origin, you cannot stand against him—you will surely come to ruin" (6:13). This was the same woman who earlier had urged Haman to build the gallows on which to hang Mordecai (5:14). But in this change of heart she recognized that the Jews were a people specially blessed and protected, and she thus attested indirectly to the sovereignty of their God.

Questions for Further Study and Discussion

1. If God has shifted to using more subtle methods of deliverance, is it still appropriate to speak of the existence of a "revelatory" people of God?
2. Of what importance for the message and purpose of the book of Esther is the question of its historicity?
3. How does the book of Esther in the Old Testament compare with the Additions to Esther in the Old Testament Apocrypha?
4. What does the character of Esther contribute to our understanding of the role of women in the Old Testament?
5. How does the literary device of "reversal" help to unify the book of Esther?

For Further Reading

Baldwin, Joyce G. *Esther.* TOTC. Downers Grove, Ill.: InterVarsity Press, 1984. Excellent, though brief, evangelical treatment.

Berg, Sandra Beth. *The Book of Esther.* Missoula, Mont.: Scholars Press, 1979. A dissertation, but very readable and informative.

Bush, Frederick. *Ruth and Esther.* Waco, Tex.: Word, 1996.

Clines, David J. A. *Ezra, Nehemiah, Esther.* Grand Rapids: Eerdmans, 1984. A well-done, though brief, commentary.

Fox, Michael. *Character and Ideology in the Book of Esther.* 2nd ed. Grand Rapids: Eerdmans, 2001.

Gordis, R. "Religion, Wisdom and History in the Book of Esther: A New Solution to an Ancient Crux." *JBL* 100 (1981): 359–88.

Jobes, Karen. *Esther.* NIVAC. Grand Rapids: Zondervan, 1999.

Luter, A. Boyd, and Barry C. Davis. *God Behind the Seen.* Grand Rapids: Baker, 1995.

Moore, Carey. *Esther.* New York: Doubleday, 1971.

_____. *Studies in the Book of Esther.* New York: Ktav, 1982. A collection of several dozen of the most significant articles on the book of Esther, with about a hundred pages of introduction by Moore.

Talmon, S. "Wisdom in the Book of Esther." *VT* 13 (1963): 419–55.

Wright, J. Stafford. "The Historicity of the Book of Esther." In *New Perspectives on the Old Testament.* Ed. by J. Barton Payne. Waco, Tex.: Word, 1970. 37–47.

CHAPTER
19

The Dead Sea Scrolls were found in the caves at Qumran in the late 1940s. These scrolls are important discoveries because they provide manuscripts of many Old Testament books originating a thousand years earlier than the manuscripts previously available. Steven Voth

ARCHAEOLOGY AND THE OLD TESTAMENT

The purpose of archaeology is to recover the material culture of the peoples of antiquity and, so doing, attempt to reconstruct their history and lifestyles. To achieve this goal requires the cooperation of a large number of technical specialists, first to retrieve information and objects from below the surface of a chosen site and then to evaluate and interpret their significance. Many sites of ancient cities preserve a layer of remains for each of the successive occupations of the settlement through their history. Each layer covers over the remains of the previous habitation. Excavation of these layers is painstakingly tedious, and methods have been designed to uncover one layer at a time to reveal the remains of each successive settlement.

The most common objects found in Near Eastern archaeology are pieces of pottery. These can be classified by their characteristics and are helpful in developing a chronology of the site. Works of art such as statues or reliefs are found much less frequently. Tools and weapons reveal the technologies and skills of the people. Architecture also gets much attention. From the various types of common houses to the most magnificent palaces, architecture can provide archaeologists and historians with an important key to understanding how people lived.

Perhaps the greatest contributions to an archaeologist's task are finds that contain some written record. This would include every form of writing from graffiti on pottery shards to large royal archives. Seals, coins, funerary inscriptions, letters, building inscriptions, jar handles—all sorts of writing help archaeologists fulfill their task.

Near Eastern archaeology has much to contribute to biblical study, for the history and culture that it seeks to reconstruct overlap considerably with the background of the Bible. As a result, scholars and interpreters have often looked to archaeology to provide information that will help them understand the Bible better. Though historically the field of Near Eastern archaeology was developed largely by those who were interested in advancing biblical understanding, that is not a universal goal among scholars today. It must always be remembered that Near Eastern archaeology and biblical studies are independent disciplines, even though they are certainly not unrelated.

What Archaeology Can Do for the Bible

The primary contribution of archaeology to biblical studies is the illumination it provides about life in Bible times. This enlightenment includes (1) the construction of a historical framework that makes use of information given in the Bible and supplements it with the finds of archaeology; (2) the reconstruction of political situations that might supply cause-and-effect explanations for some of the events recounted in the Bible; and (3) the recovery of customs and practices that suggest reasons why people of antiquity acted the way they did. The last category is especially helpful when it sheds light on religious beliefs and practices in the ancient Near East.

A secondary aspect of archaeology's role is authentication. Archaeology occasionally helps those who seek to confirm that names, places, and events of the Bible are authentic and reliably reported. It must be recognized, however, that more often than not, archaeology is unable to provide such confirmation and at such times can make the apologist's task more difficult. Archaeology is capable of providing facts (e.g., Sennacherib was indeed king at the same time as Hezekiah and did conduct a campaign against Jerusalem), but frequently the significance of archaeological data is dependent on one's interpretation of the data, and, as experience has demonstrated, interpretations can change or be incorrect. Sometimes this works to the apologist's advantage, sometimes not; but this factor has to be taken into account when archaeology is used for apologetical purposes.

The Babylonian story of creation is called Enuma Elish. This cuneiform tablet (7–8th century BC) describes the god Marduk battling for a position of supremacy over the other gods. Such theomachy, or war between the gods, is unknown in Israel's religious system, where Yahweh is the sovereign unique God. The tablet contains an account of creation, but its overall intent is to proclaim the fifty names of Marduk as he ascends to the head of the divine council.

Z. Radovan/
www.BibleLandPictures.com

A third area in which archaeology has made a considerable contribution to biblical studies is linguistics. Through archaeology, the field of comparative Semitics (the study of the group of related languages classified as Semitic) has grown and enriched our understanding of Hebrew, thereby offering exegetical insights that would have been otherwise impossible. Furthermore, understanding the languages of the ancient Near East is one of the best ways to become acquainted with the cultural background of the Old Testament.

What Archaeology Cannot Do for the Bible

The inherent limitations of archaeology are assessed most clearly in Edwin Yamauchi's compilation of the information "fractions" an archaeologist must live with.

1. Only a fraction of the evidence survives in the ground.
2. Only a fraction of possible sites has been detected.
3. Only a fraction of detected sites has been excavated.
4. Only a fraction of any site is excavated.
5. Only a fraction of what has been excavated has been thoroughly examined and published.
6. Only a fraction of what has been examined and published makes a contribution to biblical studies.[1]

With such restrictions, we must understand that there is much information archaeology could potentially provide that it never actually will. This silence of archaeology often proves to make the interpreter's task more difficult than does the information archaeology discloses.

Another important limitation is that the main point of the biblical writings is beyond archaeology's ability to confirm: the sovereign role of God. The authors of Scripture were not so much interested in how the walls of Jericho fell down as in the fact that the Lord caused them to fall down. Archaeologists could theoretically find the walls and maybe even speculate on the scientific cause of their collapse, but they cannot address, either to confirm or deny, the role of God in the event. Archaeologists might theoretically find traces of Abraham, but they cannot prove that the Lord made a covenant with him and brought it to pass. Archaeology has information to offer on the fall of Jerusalem and the return from the Babylonian exile, but none of the data could possibly prove that the Lord was controlling those events.

For the authors of Scripture, history is a theological tool by which God reveals himself. Archaeology can authenticate history, but it cannot authenticate theology, and from the biblical perspective, history devoid of theology is meaningless.

Ancient kings kept palace records of important events. Such records of Israel are alluded to in Scripture but did not survive (1 Kings 11:41; 14:19, 29). Similar records survived in other nations, however. This tablet is one of 15,000 tablets from the Royal Archives of a palace in Ebla, Syria, the oldest royal archive surviving (mid-third millennium BC).

Erich Lessing/Art Resource, NY, courtesy of the National Museum, Aleppo, Syria

What Archaeology Has Done for the Bible

One could page through the Bible enumerating all the archaeological findings pertaining to a particular account or event, but instead this

1. Edwin M. Yamauchi, *The Stones and the Scriptures* (Philadelphia: Lippincott, 1972), 146–62.

section offers a brief survey of the types of finds that contribute to biblical studies and mentions some key examples of each type. The bibliography at the end of this section lists more complete sources.

Archives

The Epic of Atrahasis is an early Babylonian text (early 2nd millenium BC) that presents the creation of humanity and its near-extinction at the flood. It is an important text to understand ancient thought about human origins: humans were created to serve the gods.

Todd Bolen/
www.BiblePlaces.com

More than a dozen major archives (including royal libraries) have been discovered in the ancient Near East in addition to a number of smaller archives, especially from cities of Assyria and Babylonia. Most of these finds have been royal archives, but some personal archives such as those found at Nuzi have proved very helpful. No Israelite archives have been unearthed, though a few collections of ostraca (pieces of broken pottery that were sometimes written on) have been found, notably at Samaria and Lachish.

A large proportion of many of the archives is made up of economic texts, comprising mostly the documentation of various business transactions (e.g., receipts). While these at times contribute to biblical studies, much more significance is attached to other classes of literature. Mythological texts, treaties, wisdom literature, epics, historiographical documents (e.g., royal correspondence), and even occasional references to prophecy have all come to light. Religious texts such as omens, incantations, hymns, and prayers are often included among the tablets and provide a background against which the faith of Israel can be examined. Since the archives provide written records and literature, they have more to offer students of the Bible than any other kind of archaeological find.

Ebla. The Italian archaeological team digging at Tel-Mardikh in northern Syria in the mid–1970s determined that they had found the site of the prominent third-millennium city of Ebla. When the royal palace was located and excavated, archaeologists were stunned to discover the archives as well, consisting of thousands of clay tablets. In the years since, many unsubstantiated and now disregarded claims were made about the contents of those tablets, and to this day some of the basic scholarly evaluation is still in process.

The primary significance of the Ebla archive as it has been analyzed thus far is historical. The history of third-millennium Syria was largely unknown prior to the find, and it is now being penciled in as a result of the translation and interpretation of the tablets. The implications of the findings at Ebla for Old Testament studies remain ambiguous and contested.

Mari. The city of Mari was located on the upper Euphrates some three hundred miles northwest of Babylon, just ten miles from today's Iraqi border in modern Syria. Mari was a prominent city in the latter part of the third millennium and in the first third of the second millennium. The archives were housed in the palace of Zimri-Lim, one of the most splendid such buildings of ancient times. Covering some eight acres, the palace had more than 260 rooms and courtyards that housed schools, bakeries, wine cellars, and even bathrooms with indoor plumbing.

A major contribution is the data Mari provides for understanding the political situation in the eighteenth century BC, when Hammurabi of the First Dynasty of Babylon was enlarging his empire. Before the Mari discovery, little more than Hammurabi's own inscriptions attested to the political situation; now a much more balanced view is available. Also of great interest is the largest collection of prophecies extant in the literature of the ancient Near East. This provides comparative material for studying the Israelite institution of the prophets, for in these texts we can discover what prophets of other countries were like and what kinds of prophecies they uttered.

Nuzi. The Nuzi archive is the most important personal library uncovered in the ancient Near East. It dates from the time of the Hurrian empire of Mitanni from 1500 to 1350 BC. As a personal archive it features a large number of family documents, such as marriage contracts, adoption agreements, and land transfers. Consequently the scholars who studied the archive saw the potential for shedding light on the family affairs scattered about the patriarchal narratives of Genesis (even though the patriarchs may have been as much as half a millennium earlier). Though many of the initially suggested parallels have been modified or rejected over time, the archive still offers substantial insight into the family lifestyle of the mid-second millennium BC. So, for instance, when Abraham and Sarah decide that Sarah's handmaid, Hagar, should be used to produce an heir (Gen. 16:1–4), they are simply following a common custom that is attested in the marriage contracts of the Nuzi archives.

Amarna. The Amarna archive preserves almost four hundred documents of correspondence that passed between the pharaohs of Egypt and the nations of the Near East in the fourteenth century BC. These letters document the political complexity of that time, including the loosening of Egypt's iron grip on Syro-Palestine and the corresponding rise of the New Kingdom of the Hittite Empire. Especially poignant are the letters from the petty kings of Canaanite city-states that express pleading, cajoling, backbiting, and protesting—at one moment groveling before the mighty pharaoh, at the next admonishing him as one would an incompetent child.

When providing these kinds of data, archaeology is in its glory.

Hattushash. Hattushash (the modern Boghazköy in upper Asia Minor) was the capital of the mighty Hittite Empire that was the dominant force in the ancient Near East throughout most of the Late Bronze Period (1500–1200 BC). Until the discovery of Hattushash and its archives at the turn of the twentieth century, the Hittites were virtually unknown as a people and their political influence was unrecognized. Rarely does archaeology equal the impact of revealing a previously "lost" people of such significance as the Hittites. Besides making the Hittite language and culture accessible to scholars for the first time, the archives provided excellent examples of numerous types of literature. Perhaps the find's greatest impact on biblical studies came from almost three dozen treaties all using a format that has also been recognized in the structure of the book of Deuteronomy and in several of the covenants between the Lord and Israel.

Emar. The Late Bronze Age town of Emar, subject to the Hittite kings, was located at the bend on the upper Euphrates until its destruction at the beginning of the twelfth century. Among the most important of the 800 texts found there were ritual texts from the Temple library that help us to understand worship at Emar and the festivals and rituals that they observed. There are also many legal texts that continue to shed light on daily life.

Ugarit. Ugarit was a bustling seaport and city-state in northern Syria in the Late Bronze Age. Until it fell prey to the widespread destruction that came with the incursion of the Sea Peoples at the end of the thirteenth century, this city thrived on the lively sea trade, transporting goods from Mediterranean ships across land to the Euphrates and from there down into Babylonia. Besides political and diplomatic developments of this period, the archives disclosed a new language, Ugaritic, which is very closely related to Canaanite and is among the closest relatives of Hebrew. The mythological texts of Ugarit greatly expanded our knowledge of Canaanite religion in general and the god known as Baal in particular. Most important was a set of six tablets that contain stories of Baal's defeat of the god Yamm (representing chaos), the building of a palace for Baal, and the struggle between Baal and Mot (death) that explains mythologically the cycle of the seasons. The portrayal of Baal and the recounting of his escapades and how he is treated all offer further insight into the Canaanite worship of Baal.

Ashurbanipal's Library at Nineveh. The first of the large archival discoveries, Ashurbanipal's library at Nineveh is still arguably the richest literary trove in the history of archaeology. It was this archive that first introduced the modern world to ancient classics such as the Gilgamesh Epic, with its startling parallel to the biblical flood account, and Enuma Elish, which discloses some of the Babylonian theology of creation. Other well-known finds include the Epic of Adapa, the Hymn to Shamash, and two wisdom compositions that grapple with issues similar to those found in the book of Job ("Ludlul bel Nemeqi" and "The Babylonian Theodicy"). This literature has provided the materials necessary to undertake extensive comparative studies between Israelite and Mesopotamian literature that greatly enhance our understanding of the Bible, particularly by elucidating the differences between Israelite and Mesopotamian theology.

The Gilgamesh Epic (with copies dating from throughout the biblical period) records the tales of the great king-tyrant Gilgamesh. It is well-known for including a story of a great flood, which has been seen to contain parallels to the biblical account of Noah in Genesis 6–9.

The Dead Sea Scrolls

Though the initial discovery of biblical manuscripts in the caves of the Dead Sea region was not made by archaeologists, the Dead Sea Scrolls have pride of place among the most significant contributions of archaeology to biblical studies. The Jewish community that lived in the self-supporting village of Qumran on and off from early in the second century BC until the second revolt against Rome in the second century AD produced scrolls of many of the Old Testament books as well as other literature.

When these scrolls were found in the late 1940s, they provided manuscripts of the Old Testament that were a thousand years older than any previously available. They not only increased the credibility of the Masoretic manuscripts that had been the basis of all current English translations, but also provided important information for understanding the transmission of the text of the Old Testament. While the Dead Sea Scrolls remain the oldest manuscript evidence available for much of the Old Testament, an important discovery in 1979 produced the earliest extant fragment of biblical text. In a Jerusalem family tomb from the time of Jeremiah, two small silver scrolls were found that were inscribed with the benediction from Numbers 6:24–26.

Monuments and Inscriptions

Some of the monuments and inscriptions unearthed by archaeologists name kings of Israel or Judah. Others refer to events that are known from the pages of the Old Testament. The examples cited in this section are among the most significant artifacts of this kind.

The Mesha Inscription. When King Mesha of Moab came to the end of his reign, he had a monument inscribed recounting all his accomplishments. Called the Moabite Stone, the inscription includes a report of how Moab had come under the domination of Israel during the reign of Omri, but had regained its independence and recaptured some territory from Israel during the reign of Ahab or Ahaziah. Thus, the stone contains some history on which the Bible is silent. It also provides the only extrabiblical reference to the concept of placing things under the ban as Joshua did at Jericho (see Josh. 6:17–19). It is clear, therefore, that this practice was not unique to Israel.

The Stele of Shalmaneser III. The first Assyrian king to have contact with the Israelites was Shalmaneser III. Inscriptions speak of his western campaigns against coalitions that include kings Ahab (at the Battle of Qarqar in 853 BC) and Jehu. The black obelisk that preserves the accounts of Shalmaneser's campaigns from his eighteenth to thirty-first years pictures Jehu—or perhaps his representative—bowing before him with the tribute signifying submission to Assyrian suzerainty. This occurred in 841 BC, Jehu's first year on the throne, after the obliteration of the line of Ahab.

This collection of pottery is dated to the Iron Age (1200–1000 BC) and was found in the City of David. Various characteristics of pottery allow it to be used by archaeologists for dating the layers of a site.

Z. Radovan/
www.BibleLandPictures.com

The left column is partially cut off, showing only fragments:

Third, a
the Old Test
from Scriptu
of the Israel
only brief tr
findings ind
influential k
by contrast,
focus on his
the spineless
vert Israel to
details that
and theologi
the internatio

Finally, l
reconstruct t
groups ment
already been
Phoenicians,
Perhaps most
as three of the
have undergo

Places. Ar
lical places in
people — that
this informati
Nineveh that fi
as Ur and Haze
important cent

Events. Son
by without the
human author
they rarely dig
earlier, is the b
neser III gives
a large coalitio
the Assyrian ki
the Israelites to

Still other e
Testament are
fall of Samaria
provide comple
thing of only pa
Lachish to Senn

Sennacherib's Prism. A notable event during the divided monarchy was the siege of Jerusalem by Sennacherib in the days of Isaiah and Hezekiah, and the subsequent deliverance of the Israelites by the Lord. Theologically the deliverance demonstrated the Lord's power over the mightiest and most feared empire on the face of the earth, and that in response to the trust of King Hezekiah. Politically it marked Judah's success in avoiding the fate of the northern kingdom of Israel; Judah was not destroyed and annexed by Assyria. The Bible reports the details of this classic confrontation in three places—2 Kings 18–19; 2 Chronicles 32; Isaiah 36–37; Sennacherib's account of these campaigns became known with the discovery of an inscribed hexagonal clay cylinder, or prism (see photo, p. 367). Sennacherib details his success against forty-six cities of Judah and his deportation of more than 200,000 Israelites. He also boasts of imprisoning Hezekiah in Jerusalem by subjecting the city to siege.

The prism gives no hint of Sennacherib's suffering a defeat and does not record the outcome of the siege on Jerusalem, but it notes how he received increased tribute from Hezekiah. Thus, the inscription confirms the military details as presented in the Bible but fails to provide any substantiation of the role ascribed to the Lord or the victory claimed in Scripture. Likewise, it says nothing to contradict the version of the events recorded in Scripture.

The Cyrus Cylinder. The deportation programs practiced by Assyria and Babylon were designed to eliminate ethnic identities of conquered peoples and to assimilate them into a common mixed stock that would foster loyalty to the empire and diminish ethnic and political distinctions. This posed a great threat to the Lord's covenant with Israel as an ethnic and political entity. When the Medo-Persian Empire took over from the Babylonians, Cyrus instituted a new approach to foreign policy. This policy was built on the philosophy that offering increased autonomy to subject peoples would increase loyalty to the empire, not undermine it. That is, if oppression were decreased, the likelihood of revolt would be reduced. As a result, many of the subjugated people were allowed to return to their homelands and rebuild their communities and sanctuaries.

The Cyrus Cylinder, a clay cylinder containing the royal decree granting various peoples permission to return, does not mention Judah specifically, but Scripture reports that Judah enjoyed such a benevolence (see photo, p. 332).

Court Chronicles

The official annals and chronicles of the court report on military campaigns and the internal affairs of a kingdom. They provide not only information on events, but also their chronology. The chronicles most

event on the walls of Sennacherib's palace in Nineveh. The fall of the city to Nebuchadrezzar's forces more than a century later is the background for the Lachish letters, some military correspondence depicting the critical situation on the eve of the collapse of Judah. Both of these destructions are further supported by data gleaned from ongoing excavations at the site.

What Archaeology Has Not Done for the Bible

Despite all the help that archaeology has provided for biblical studies, much remains to be done. There are many pieces of information that archaeology seems capable of supplying but has not yet delivered. We have already mentioned that there is very little textual evidence for the Old Testament that dates from those times. It is quite possible that an Israelite archive would contain such data, but as yet no such archive has been found.

Another gap in our archaeological information is that no individual Israelite is referred to by name in contemporary literature prior to passing references to Omri and David in ninth century BC inscriptions. Certainly we would hope that someday archaeologists will find inscription references to the kings of the united monarchy. There are likewise personages from later history who have yet to appear in contemporary extrabiblical materials, including Daniel, Esther, and Nehemiah—all of whom held important posts in foreign administrations. From a much earlier period, we could cite Joseph. The most notable foreigner who still remains a mystery to modern historians is Darius the Mede, mentioned in the book of Daniel.

There are some events recorded in the Bible for which archaeological data have served to increase confusion rather than understanding. Notable among these are the exodus from Egypt and the conquest of the land of Canaan. The excavations at the various cities mentioned in the book of Joshua have produced a number of different reconstructions of the actual course of events. In some cases the archaeological data are interpreted primarily to discredit scriptural accounts. In others the biblical text is accepted as accurate, and therefore the archaeological data are viewed and interpreted with considerable skepticism. Between these two poles are numerous theories attempting to reconcile the Bible to archaeology or archaeology to the Bible. Though archaeology has not been able to settle the disputes concerning these events, continuing excavation keeps the windows of hope open.

Finally, there are probable material remains that archaeologists have not succeeded in uncovering. For instance, no trace of the palace or the temple of Solomon has been unearthed. One reason, of course, is that it is difficult to conduct excavations in places still inhabited today.

In conclusion, in reflecting on what archaeology has and has not been able to accomplish, we are reminded that while archaeology is capable of providing much useful information to the study of the Bible, it is also capable of creating confusion. Sound scholarship cannot be so subjective as to rely heavily on archaeology when it supports the favored position but to reject it outright when it offers contradictory data. A proper use of archaeology requires a consistent approach to its findings and an understanding of its methods and techniques.

Questions for Further Study and Discussion

1. What stance should we take when archaeological data appear to conflict with the biblical record?
2. If an Israelite royal archive were to be discovered, what sorts of documents would we expect to find in it? What areas of biblical study would be potentially influenced, and how?
3. What cautions ought we to exercise in developing parallels between the Old Testament and the ancient Near East?

For Further Reading

Dever, William G. *What Did the Biblical Writers Know and When Did They Know It?* Grand Rapids: Eerdmans, 2001.

_____. *Who Were the Early Israelites and Where Did They Come From?* Grand Rapids: Eerdmans, 2003.

Hoerth, Alfred J. *Archaeology of the Old Testament.* Grand Rapids: Baker, 1997.

Hoffmeier, James, and Alan Millard. *The Future of Biblical Archaeology.* Grand Rapids: Eerdmans, 2004.

King, Philip J. *Amos, Hosea, Micah: An Archaeological Commentary.* Philadelphia: Westminster, 1988.

King, Philip J. and Lawrence Stager. *Life in Biblical Israel.* Louisville: Westminster John Knox, 2002.

Kitchen, Kenneth A. *On The Reliability of the Old Testament.* Grand Rapids: Eerdmans, 2003.

McRay, John. *Archaeology and the New Testament.* Grand Rapids: Baker, 1991.

Matthews, Victor H. *Manners and Customs in the Bible.* Peabody, Mass.: Hendrickson, 1988. Probably the most helpful of the books on manners and customs.

Mazar, Amihai. *The Archaeology of the Land of the Bible.* Garden City, N.Y.: Doubleday, 1990.

Meyers, Eric. *The Oxford Encyclopedia of Archaeology in the Near East.* 5 volumes. New York: Oxford University Press, 1996.

Millard, Alan. *Nelson's Illustrated Wonders and Discoveries of the Bible.* Nashville: Thomas Nelson, 1997. Beautifully illustrated with very balanced, readable text.

Nakhai, Beth Alpert. *Archaeology and the Religions of Canaan and Israel.* Boston: ASOR, 2001.

Paul, Shalom, and William Dever. *Biblical Archaeology.* Jerusalem: Keter, 1973.

Rainey, Anson and R. Steven Notley. *The Sacred Bridge.* Jerusalem: Carta, 2006.

Richard, Suzanne. *Near Eastern Archaeology: A Reader.* Winona Lake, Ind.: Eisenbrauns, 2003.

Sasson, Jack. *Civilizations of the Ancient Near East.* New York: Scribners, 1995.

Schoville, Keith N. *Biblical Archaeology in Focus.* Grand Rapids: Baker, 1978. A fine textbook from a well-established evangelical archaeologist.

Shanks, Hershel, ed. *Recent Archaeology in the Land of Israel.* Washington, D.C.: Biblical Archaeology Society, 1984.

Stern, Ephraim. *The New Encyclopedia of Archaeological Excavations in the Holy Land.* New York: Simon and Schuster, 1993, 4 vols. The most important reference resource, giving summary site reports for most of the major excavations in Israel.

Stern, Ephraim. *Archaeology of the Land of the Bible, Vol. 2.* New York: Doubleday, 2001.

Walton, John H., Victor Matthews, and Mark Chavalas. *The IVP Bible Background Commentary: Old Testament.* Downers Grove, Ill.: InterVarsity Press, 2000.

Yamauchi, Edwin M. *The Stones and the Scriptures.* Philadelphia: Lippincott, 1972.

CHAPTER
20

"Wisdom is too high for a fool; in the assembly at the gate he has nothing to say" (Prov. 24:7). The important men of the city would often sit at the gate and discuss important issues. This gate at Beersheba has benches that would allow such conversations.   Todd Bolen/www.BiblePlaces.com

HEBREW POETIC AND WISDOM LITERATURE

Key Ideas
- Fear of the Lord
- Theodicy
- Retribution Principle
- Instruction
- Personification of Wisdom

Introduction

The boundaries of poetic literature in the Old Testament are not easy to delimit, since little is known about the exact nature of biblical Hebrew poetry. Unlike its classical and modern counterparts, ancient Hebrew poetry has no distinctive scheme of accentuation, meter, or rhythm to differentiate it from prose. Only within the past two centuries has this fact been fully appreciated in biblical scholarship.

The most significant early contribution to the study of Hebrew poetry was made by Bishop Robert Lowth in the mid-eighteenth century. He noted parallelism, or the counterbalancing of ideas in phrases, as a fundamental feature distinguishing Hebrew poetry from prose. His delineation of the various types of parallelism remains basic to the understanding of Old Testament poetic structure.

J. Hoftijzer in 1965 published an analytical method for identifying Hebrew poetry based on the distribution of the marker for the direct object in Old Testament texts. F. I. Andersen and David N. Freedman refined this approach for separating Hebrew poetry from prose through a "prose particle" counting method that takes into account additional markers of narrative style in the Hebrew Bible.

Old Testament texts exhibiting prose-particle densities of 15 percent or more are considered prose in nature, while those demonstrating prose-particle densities of 5 percent or less are regarded as poetic. Old Testament prophetic literature yielding densities between 5 and 15 percent is labeled "**oracular prose**," connoting its poetic tendencies.

"Listen to your father, who gave you life, and do not despise your mother when she is old" (Prov. 23:22). The family unit was very important in the ancient world. This Egyptian statue depicts a family of four.

Werner Forman Archive/ Egyptian Museum, Cairo

The most recent development in the study of Old Testament poetry is the application of modern linguistic terminology and methodology to the Hebrew text.[1] Here the assumption is that biblical Hebrew is not unique as a language and consequently can best be analyzed by the same procedures contemporary linguists use on other languages. This has led to a greater appreciation of Old Testament poetry as literature and has in some instances enhanced our understanding of the meaning of biblical texts. No doubt the traditional descriptions and analytical methods applied to Hebrew poetry will continue to undergo change as modern linguistic and literary research influences biblical studies.

Today biblical scholars acknowledge that poetry comprises about one-third of the Hebrew Old Testament. This poetry ranges from brief extracts (Gen. 4:23–24; Num. 21:18; 1 Sam. 18:7) to complete compositions like songs, hymns, and oracles (Gen. 49:2–27; Exod. 15:1–18; 1 Sam. 2:1–10) in the Pentateuch and historical books, to the long and ornate poetic works of Job and the Psalms, to the bold and vivid oracular prose of Isaiah 40–66, Nahum, and Habakkuk.

Psalms, Proverbs, Song of Songs, and Lamentations are entirely poetic in form. Most of Job and portions of Ecclesiastes are poetic, while the prose narratives in the books of Genesis, Exodus, Numbers, Deuteronomy, Judges, and 1–2 Samuel contain substantial poetic sections. The prophetic books of Obadiah, Micah, Nahum, Habbakuk, and Zephaniah are composed completely in oracular prose (with the exception of the **superscriptions** or title verses). This is also true for major portions of Isaiah, Jeremiah, Ezekiel, Daniel, Hosea, Joel, and Amos. In the Old Testament only Leviticus, Ruth, Ezra, Nehemiah, Esther, Haggai, and Malachi contain little or no poetic material.

Although the Old Testament wisdom books are usually poetic in form, they are classified as wisdom literature for other reasons. To the Hebrews, "wisdom" constituted "skill in living" that combined the powers of observation, the capacities of human intellect, and the application of knowledge and experience to daily life. Wisdom literature may be didactic or instructional in nature, or argumentative in a reflective or speculative sense. Wisdom sought to teach practical moral principles for behavior or prompted the reader rationally to investigate

---

1. E.g., Michael O'Connor, *Hebrew Verse Structure* (Winona Lake, Ind.: Eisenbrauns, 1980).

the many problems associated with human existence—all from a viewpoint firmly rooted in "the fear of the Lord."

The wisdom literature of the Old Testament includes the instructional books of Proverbs and Song of Songs and the speculative books of Job and Ecclesiastes, along with select wisdom psalms (e.g., 1, 37, 49, 112) and portions of the prophetic books employing wisdom terminology or themes (e.g., Isa. 40:12–17, 21–26; Amos 3:10; 5:4, 6, 14).

Poetry and Wisdom in the Ancient Near East

Poetry in the Ancient Near East

Israel was the beneficiary of a long and well-developed literary tradition in the ancient Near East. While the earliest Hebrew poetry extant dates to the thirteenth or twelfth centuries BC, the rudiments of Egyptian poetry can be traced to a triumph hymn for the pharaoh dated near 3200 BC. Poetic couplets occur in the famous Pyramid Texts of the Fifth Dynasty (ca. 2350 BC), and matching couplets appear as early as 2300 BC in the victory hymn for Pepi I:

> This army returned in safety,
> After it had hacked up the land of the [Sand] Dwellers.
> This army returned in safety,
> After it had crushed the land of the Sand Dwellers.[2]

Scholars have long recognized the similarities between Psalm 104 and the sun hymn of Akhenaten. For example, compare the excerpt from the Aten Hymn with Psalm 104:25–26 (fig. 20.1a). The same holds true for the Egyptian Love Songs of the New Kingdom (ca. 1570–1085 BC) and the biblical Song of Songs. Note the affinities between Song 31 from Egypt and the Song of Songs 4:1–7 (fig. 20.1b).

These same kinds of poetic traditions developed concurrently in ancient Mesopotamia. Parallel couplets occur already in the building inscription of Gudea, prince of Lagash (ca. 1900–1800 BC). Old Babylonian kingdoms (ca. 1900–1600 BC) canonized earlier Sumerian literature, including poetic hymns and prayers like the "Prayer to Any God":

> In ignorance I have eaten that forbidden of my god,
> In ignorance I have set foot on that protected by my goddess.

This period also saw the composition of Neo-Sumerian prayers and hymns such as the long "Hymn to Shamash":

> At thy rising the gods of the land assemble;
> By thy frightful brilliance the land is overwhelmed.
> Of all countries (even) those different in languages,
> Thou knowest their plans; thou art observant of their course.

2. ANET, 3rd ed. (Princeton: Princeton University Press, 1969), 228.

Figure 20.1a — Similarities in Poetry: 1

Aten Hymn

The ships are sailing north and south as well,
For every way is open at thy appearance.
Thus fish in the river dart before thy face,
Thy rays are in the midst of the great
  green sea.*

*From *ANET*, 3d ed. (Princeton: Princeton Univ. Press, 1969), 370.

Psalm 104:25 – 26

There is the sea, vast and spacious,
  teeming with creatures beyond number —
  living things both large and small.
There the ships go to and fro,
  and the leviathan, which you formed
    to frolic there.

All mankind rejoices in thee;
O Shamash, all the world longs for thy light.[3]

Probably the most notable Old Babylonian poetic literary works are the Gilgamesh Epic (containing the Babylonian flood story) and the Enuma Elish (the Babylonian creation epic). An excerpt from the Enuma Elish follows:

When on high the heaven had not been named,
Firm ground below had not been called by name,
Naught but primordial Apsu, their begetter,
(And) Mummu-Tiamat, she who bore them all,
Their waters commingling as a single body;
No reed hut had been matted, no marsh land had appeared,
When no gods whatever had been brought into being,
Uncalled by name, their destinies undetermined —
Then it was that the gods were formed within them.[4]

Though Egyptian and Mesopotamian culture influenced Syro-Palestine, equally important are the ancient Near Eastern parallels to biblical poetry found in the Canaanite literature discovered at Ras Shamra, or Ugarit. The written poetry of Ugarit dates to approximately 1400–1200 BC, but these were probably preceded by at least two centuries of oral recitations.

Ugaritic poetry is similar to its Hebrew counterpart in vocabulary and style. For example, the identification of hundreds of parallel (or A/B) word pairs that also occur in Hebrew poetry indicate that the Old Testament poets used a common parallelistic poetic tradition. The Ugaritic epics of Baal, Ahqat, and Keret also contain poetic features like chiasmus, numerical climax, and synonymous and synthetic parallelism. Note the parallelism and chiasmus in this sample text from the Baal Epic:

I tell thee, O Prince Baal,
I declare, O Rider of the Clouds.
Now thine enemy, O Baal,

---

3. Ibid., 388.
4. Ibid., 60–61.

Now thine enemy wilt thou smite,
Now wilt thou cut off thine adversary.
Thou'lt take thine eternal kingdom,
Thine everlasting dominion.[5]

Like the Hebrew psalter, some Ugaritic texts include superscriptions, subheadings, colophons, and on occasion even musical notations. These striking similarities between Ugaritic and Hebrew poetry point to a common West Semitic linguistic and literary heritage.

Wisdom in the Ancient Near East

Biblical wisdom literature, like Hebrew poetry, must be understood in an international context. The Bible touts the sapiential tradition of the Egyptians (e.g., Exod. 7:22; 1 Kings 4:30), of the Edomites and Arabians (e.g., Jer. 49:7; Obad. 8), and the Babylonians (e.g., Isa. 47:10; Dan. 1:4).

5. Ibid., 130–31.

Figure 20.1b — Similarities in Poetry: 2

Egyptian Love Song 31

One, the lady love without a duplicate,
more perfect than the world,
see, she is like the star rising
at the start of an auspicious year.
She whose excellence shines, whose body
    glistens,
glorious her eyes when she stares,
sweet her lips when she converses,
she says not a word too much.
High her neck and glistening her nipples,
of true lapis her hair,
her arms finer than gold,
Her buttocks droop when her waist is girt,
her legs reveal her perfection;
her steps are pleasing when she walks
    the earth,
she takes my heart in her embrace.
When she comes forth, anyone can see
that there is none like that One.†

†From W. K. Simpson, ed., *The Literature of Ancient
Egypt*, rev. ed. (New Haven: Yale Univ. Press,
1973), 315–16.

Songs of Songs 4:1–7

How beautiful you are, my darling!
    Oh, how beautiful!
    Your eyes behind your veil are doves.
Your hair is like a flock of goats
    descending from Mount Gilead.
Your teeth are like a flock of sheep just shorn,
    coming up from the washing.
Each has its twin;
    not one of them is alone.
Your lips are like a scarlet ribbon;
    your mouth is lovely.
Your temples behind your veil
    are like the halves of a pomegranate.
Your neck is like the tower of David,
    built with elegance;
on it hang a thousand shields,
    all of them shields of warriors.
Your breasts are like two fawns,
    like twin fawns of a gazelle
    that browse among the lilies.
Until the day breaks
    and the shadows flee,
I will go to the mountain of myrrh
    and to the hill of incense.
All beautiful you are, my darling;
    there is no flaw in you.

"For these commands are a lamp, this teaching is a light, and the corrections of discipline are the way to life" (Prov. 6:23). Good teaching was highly valued in the ancient world. Much teaching was done in the home, but some children attended scribal schools, where they learned reading and writing. This Egyptian relief from the tomb of Princess Sesh-seshet Idut shows scribes at work.

Werner Forman Archive

Surviving Egyptian wisdom literature consists of two basic types, or genres: instructions and discussions. The instructions, or teachings, are largely the product of the pharonic court as the king prepared his son to assume the administration of the monarchy. The examples of speculative wisdom include political satire and skeptical treatises on the ironies of life. The essence or governing principle of Egyptian wisdom was the concept of *maat*, the embodiment of truth, justice, and order.

Both types of Egyptian wisdom literature contain striking parallels to the Hebrew wisdom of the Old Testament. For example, portions of the "Teachings of Amenemope," an Egyptian sage writing near 1200 BC, exhibit remarkable similarities in language and theme with the "Sayings of the Wise" in Proverbs (22:17–24:23). Note the associations between Amenemope,

> Guard yourself from robbing the poor, from being violent to the weak. Do not associate with the rash man nor approach him in conversation.[6]

and Proverbs 22:22–23,

> Do not exploit the poor because they are poor
>   and do not crush the needy in court,...
> Do not make friends with a hot-tempered man,
>   do not associate with one easily angered.

The discussion literature of Egyptian wisdom includes works like "The Dispute Over Suicide," "The Tale of the Eloquent Peasant," and

---

6. John H. Walton, *Ancient Israelite Literature in Its Cultural Context* (Grand Rapids: Zondervan, 1989), 192; quoting from translation by John Ruffle, "The Teaching of Amenemope and Its Connection with the Book of Proverbs," *TB* 28 (1977).

"The Song of the Harper." These writings are contemplative, analytical, even pessimistic in tone and mood and are reminiscent of the wisdom assembled by the Preacher (or Qoheleth) in Ecclesiastes. The discussions address topics such as finding meaning and joy in life, social injustice, the problem of evil, and the reality of pain and death in a fashion akin to the biblical books of Job and Ecclesiastes. Note, for example, the similarities on the topic of enjoyment in life between the Harper Song,

This Sumerian tablet was one often copied by students in Sumerian schools. After each line citing underachievement or misbehavior it says, "caned me."

Kim Walton, courtesy of the Oriental Institute Museum

> Let not thy heart flag.
> Follow thy desire and thy good.
> Fulfill thy needs upon earth, after the command
>   of thy heart.
> Until there come for thee that day of mourning.[7]

and Ecclesiastes 8:15,

> So I commend the enjoyment of life, because nothing is better for a man under the sun than to eat and drink and be glad. Then joy will accompany him in his work all the days of the life God has given him under the sun.

Although the Bible reports a significant wisdom tradition among the Edomites, little written evidence remains that might indicate the extent or content of Edom's wisdom. The book of Job probably preserves remnants of the influence of Edomite wisdom tradition on the Hebrew sages, in that the name Job is a shortened form of Jobab (an Edomite king mentioned in Genesis 36:34, not to be identified with Job). One of Job's friends is from an Edomite clan (Eliphaz the Temanite, Job 2.11), and the land of Uz was apparently located in or near Edom (cf. Lam. 4:21).

If "Massa" is a proper name in Proverbs 30:1 and 31:1 (so RSV; elsewhere translated "oracle"), then the words of Agur son of Jakeh (30:1–33) and King Lemuel (31:1–9) may reflect the influence of Arabian wisdom on the developing Hebrew wisdom tradition. Massa has been identified with the tribes settled in northwestern Arabia near Teman (cf. Gen. 25:14; 1 Chron. 1:30).

Mesopotamian wisdom literature also contains instructions in the form of proverbs and fables along with discussions related to **theodicy** (i.e., the vindication of divine attributes like holiness and justice in respect to the existence of evil). One text, "A Man and His God," is known as the Sumerian Job. Note the similarity between the lament in that writing,

> Never has a sinless child been born to its mother,...
> a sinless workman has not existed from of old.[8]

7. ANET, 467.

8. Ibid., 590.

The Admonitions of Ipuwer (probably 2000 BC) is an Egyptian wisdom composition which consists of six poems of a court sage who levies social criticisms against Pharaoh's administration and hopes for an ideal king who will set things right. This is similar to the hope in the Psalms of a future Davidic ideal king. It is one of a number of wisdom compositions known from ancient Egypt.

and Job 15:14–16,

> "What is man, that he could be pure,
>   or one born of woman, that he could be righteous?
> If God places no trust in his holy ones,
>   if even the heavens are not pure in his eyes,
> how much less man, who is vile and corrupt,
>   who drinks up evil like water!"

Yet another Mesopotamian text, "The Babylonian Theodicy," has friends making speeches to a tormented man whose gods have forsaken him. Still another, "The Dialogue of Pessimism," reflects on the emptiness and irony of human existence from the perspectives of indulgence and abstinence in a similar vein to the Preacher's contrasts of excess and asceticism (Eccl. 7:14).

While the many similarities between ancient Near Eastern wisdom literature and the Hebrew wisdom of the Old Testament are certainly not just coincidental, the resemblances are as much the product of the universal nature of attempts to cope with the problems associated with human existence as they are a result of any cultural or literary borrowing. The search for meaning and purpose in life, the mystery of life and death, the reality of suffering, pain, injustice, and the relationship of the divine to the problem of evil are questions common to the human experience—whether Egyptian, Babylonian, or Hebrew.

Moreover, despite the special thematic and literary relationships that may be demonstrated between ancient Near Eastern and Hebrew wisdom, one fundamental difference remains. Unlike the other ancients who paid homage to assorted pantheons of deities, the Israelite wisdom of the Old Testament acknowledged only one God, Yahweh (Prov. 22:17–19). Thus, the Hebrews denied materialism (since matter was created by God), pantheism (because Yahweh as creator was above all creation), and dualism (since creation was originally made "good" by God). Ideologically this meant that the Hebrews owed allegiance to Yahweh alone and had neither room nor time for these false deities and competing religious systems. Practically speaking, however, the facts of Hebrew history indicate that this was not always the case.

Literary Character of Hebrew Poetry

The two distinctive features of Hebrew poetry (including the poetic wisdom books) are rhythm of sound and rhythm of thought. Rhythm of sound is the regular pattern of stressed or unstressed syllables in lines (or stichs) of Hebrew poetry; it may also be the repetition of sounds through devices like alliteration or assonance. Rhythm of thought or sense is the balancing of ideas in a structured or systematic form. The primary vehicle for conveying rhythm of thought in biblical poetry is a feature described as "parallelism of members." A pervasive mode of thought in ancient Near Eastern literary circles, this parallelism was elevated with exceptional artistry by the Hebrew poets. Although Hebrew parallelism is beyond absolute and rigid categorization, it can be understood by biblical example from the Psalms.

Rhythm of Thought

1. *Semantic Parallelism (based on word usage)*

Using Synonyms
24:2   for he founded it upon the seas
       and established it upon the waters.

Using Similar Terms
1:5   Therefore the wicked will not stand in the judgment,
       nor sinners in the assembly of the righteous.

Using Matched Pairs
9:8   He will judge the world in righteousness;
       he will govern the peoples with justice.

Using Opposites
37:16   Better the little that the righteous have
       than the wealth of many wicked.

2. Progressive Parallelism (based on logical sequence)

Using Cause and Effect

37:4   Delight yourself in the LORD
         and he will give you the desires of your heart.

Using Sequence

37:29   the righteous will inherit the land
         and dwell in it forever.

Using Deduction

16:8   I have set the LORD always before me.
         Because he is at my right hand, I will not be shaken.

Using Metaphors

18:31   For who is God besides the LORD?
         And who is the Rock except our God?

Using Explanation

5:10b   Banish them for their many sins,
         for they have rebelled against you.

3. Grammatical Parallelism (based on choice of grammatical forms)

Using parallel parts of speech

19:7–8   The law of the LORD is perfect, reviving the soul.
         The statutes of the LORD are trustworthy, making wise
            the simple.
         The precepts of the LORD are right, giving joy to
            the heart.
         The commands of the LORD are radiant, giving light
            to the eyes.

Using Word Order

1:2   But his delight is in the law of the LORD,
         and on his law he meditates day and night.

Using Ellipsis

18:41   They cried for help, but there was no one to save them—
         to the LORD, but he did not answer.

Rhythm of Sound

The second distinctive feature of Hebrew poetry, rhythm of sound, is demonstrated through a variety of techniques used by the ancient poet.

1. *Acrostic poem.* An acrostic is verse in which the initial letters of consecutive lines of a stanza form an alphabet, word, or phrase. The Old Testament in Hebrew contains thirteen complete alphabetic acrostic poems (Pss. 9 and 10, 25, 34, 37, 111, 112, 119, 145; Prov. 31:10–31; Lam. 1, 2, 3, 4) and perhaps one incomplete alphabetic acrostic (Nah. 1:2–10). More than a matter of personal style, the acrostic poem was

Alva Steffler

a mnemonic tool, or memory device, in the ancient scribal schools. Although it was somewhat artificial, as a literary feature it conveyed ideas of order, progression, and completeness within the poetic message. Unfortunately this aspect of Hebrew poetry cannot be appreciated fully in translation (though the acrostics are often identified in the margins or in footnotes in many English versions).

A sample of the Hebrew alphabetic acrostic is offered in English translation (fig. 20.2). Psalm 112 contains twenty-two lines, one for each letter of the Hebrew alphabet. The first six lines of the psalm have been translated to form an acrostic. Note that the English rendering is somewhat strained.

2. *Alliteration.* A common feature in Old Testament poetry is alliteration, the consonance of sounds at the beginning of words or syllables. Again, the English translation is inadequate to represent the resonant cadence of the Hebrew *š* (sh) and *l* (l) in Psalm 122:6:

Transliteration: *ša^{a}lû š^{e}lôm y^{e}rûšalaim*
Translation: "Pray for the peace of Jerusalem."

3. *Assonance.* Assonance is the rhythm of sound using the correspondence of vowel sounds, often at the end of words. Like alliteration, assonance may serve as a literary ploy to emphasize an idea or theme or to set

The ancients believed that the world was surrounded by waters above and below (Job 26:5–13) and that both the earth and the sky were held up by pillars. "The pillars of the heavens quake" (Job 26:11). This ordered cosmos was at the root of much wisdom literature, which itself was founded on the value of order.

a certain tone for the poem. An example of this feature appears in Psalm 119:29, with the *e* class vowels Seghol and Sere and the *i* class Hiriq.

Transliteration: *derek-šeqer hāsēr mimmenî / weṯôrāṯeka ḥannēnî*
Translation: Keep me from deceitful ways, / be gracious to me through your law.

4. *Paronomasia.* The Hebrew poets and especially the prophets often incorporated paronomasia, or word play, into their poems and oracles. This word play consisted of the repetition of words similar in sound, but not necessarily in meaning, to heighten the intended impact of the message. The prophet Amos saw a basket of summer fruit (Heb. *qayis*) and announced the end (Heb. *qēs*) of the nation of Israel (Amos 8:2). On his deathbed Jacob predicted Judah (Heb. *yehûdâ*) would be praised (Heb. *yôḏûkā*) by his brothers (Gen. 49:8). And the prophet Isaiah ended his Song of the Vineyard with this masterful stroke (5:7b):

And he looked for justice [*mišpāṭ*]
    but saw bloodshed [*miśpāḥ*];
for righteousness [*ṣedāqâ*],
    but heard cries of distress [*ṣeʿāqâ*]!

5. *Onomatopoeia.* The use of words that sound like what they describe was another feature conditioned by the orality of Hebrew poetry. The Israelite poets enhanced the vividness of their description of the reality around them by dipping into the rich cache of onomatopoeic words in the Hebrew vocabulary. Samples of onomatopoeia in the Old Testament include the simple interjection "woe" (Heb. *ʾôy*) as in Isaiah 24:16, the "thunder" (Heb. *raʿam*) in Psalm 81:7, even the quaking of the earth (Heb. *rāʿaš*) in Psalm 68:8, and the hoofbeats of horses (Heb. *dahªrôṯ dahªrôṯ*) in Judges 5:22.

6. *Ellipsis.* The omission of a word or words that would complete a given parallel construction is common in Hebrew poetry and has been marked as one of the criteria for distinguishing poetry from prose. An example is found in Psalm 115, where "their idols" in verse 4 is understood in verses 5–7.

Figure 20.2. Acrostic Structure

aleph	(a)	Ah, the happiness of the one who fears the Lord,
beth	(b)	because of his commandments he delights exceedingly!
gimel	(g)	Great on the earth will be his "seed";
daleth	(d)	descendants of the upright will be blessed.
heh	(h)	Honor and riches are in his house;
waw	(w)	without end his righteousness endures.

7. *Inclusio.* The inclusio is a special form of the repetition common to Hebrew poetry. The device is sometimes called an envelope figure, since by repeating keywords and phrases the poet returns to the point from which he began. For example, Psalm 118 begins (v. 1) and ends (v. 29) with the lines:

Give thanks to the LORD, for he is good; / his love endures forever.

Rhythm of Form

1. *Meter.* Meter has been assumed in Hebrew poetry on the basis of analogy with other kinds of poetry. Recent studies have challenged this assumption (e.g., James Kugel and Michael O'Connor). The exact nature of meter remains a topic of discussion because the formal characteristics constituting Hebrew poetry are still ill-defined.

The two common methods of gauging Hebrew meter are counting the stressed or accented syllables in line pairs (or distichs) of poetry and counting the total number of syllables in the two lines of poetry. For example, the normal pattern is a three-stress first line followed by a two-stress second line (3 + 2, the so-called *qinah*, or **dirge** meter, of Lamentations). Other common patterns include three-stress couplets (3 + 3) and two- and four-stress lines (2 + 2 and 4 + 4). These approaches do not describe meter so much as they provide a guide to its structure. The concept of syllable counting as a reflection of Hebrew poetic meter continues to be a topic of debate among biblical scholars. Recent research that connects syntactical and statistical analysis with modern linguistic methodology and comparative poetics offers the most promise for unraveling the complexities related to understanding meter in Hebrew poetry.

2. *Strophe.* Strophic patterns, the grouping of lines into larger units, are not readily discernible in most Hebrew poetry. While certain acrostic poems exhibit an alphabetic strophic structure (e.g., Ps. 119; Lam. 1, 2, and 4), most attempts to isolate these larger units of biblical poetry remain unconvincing.

On occasion, Old Testament poems contain refrains or repeated lines of text that may indicate strophic structure (e.g., Pss. 42:5, 11; 43:5; 107:8, 15, 21, 31; or 136), but more often there are no formal markers of stanzas in the poem. Thus, while greater structures of symmetry are assumed to exist in Hebrew poetry, there is at present no methodology that will demonstrate these strophic patterns with consistency and certainty.

Life Situation and Genre

Like all other poetry, that in the Bible is an expression of human creative energy filtering and responding to all facets of reality comprising the experiences of life in a language of images (e.g., birth, Gen. 25:23; life, Eccl. 3:1–9; death, 2 Sam. 1:17–27; blood revenge, Gen. 4:23–24; war, Josh. 10:12–13; and marriage, Gen. 24:60). Israel's poetry was shaped further by an intense faith in the God Yahweh, because he had acted in history on behalf of his people (cf. Exod. 15:1–18, 21; Judg. 5:1–31), and by an inherent desire to celebrate the worth and meaning of human existence (cf. Pss. 92, 112, 127, 128; Eccl. 5:18–20). It is for these reasons that Old Testament poetry transcends the historical setting of ancient Israel and informs the very fabric of modern culture (perhaps explaining why the Psalms remain the most popular literature in all the Bible).

The poetry of the Old Testament was also musical in nature. It was usually intended to be sung or chanted to the accompaniment of musical instruments (e.g., Deut. 31:30–32:44; Pss. 5, 6). The musicality of Hebrew poetry aggrandized the artistry of the literary form, added an important liturgical dimension, and aided the oral transmission of the poetry. Although the "orchestral scores" for Old Testament poetry are now lost, vestiges of its musicality remain, particularly in the Psalms. This Israelite hymnbook retains superscriptions denoting the specific accompanying instruments (e.g., Pss. 54, 55, 67, 150), the composer or recipient (Pss. 70, 72, 73, 77, 81), the occasion prompting the composition (Pss. 45, 70, 92, 100), and the musical tune or arrangement to which the poem was (played and) sung (Pss. 12, 22, 39, 57, 58, 80).

A general thesis regarding the types of Hebrew poetry has emerged by scholarly consensus. Early poetry was brief and limited to one

"My tongue is the pen of a skillful writer" (Ps. 41:1). Scribes were important because of their ability to read and write, which was not a skill everyone in the ancient world had the time and opportunity to acquire.

Rama/Wikimedia Commons, courtesy of the Louvre, CeCILL/CC 2.0

situation or event; mixing types and greater length began during the era of the Conquest, accelerated under the united monarchy, and reached its zenith during the exile and shortly thereafter.

Several basic poetic types, or genres, have been identified: the no longer extant historical anthologies (e.g., Num. 21:14; Josh. 10:13), victory songs (Exod. 15:1–18; Judg. 5:1–31), curses (Num. 21:27–30), taunt songs (Isa. 14:1–27; 47:1–15), funeral dirges and eulogies (2 Sam. 1:17–27; Jer. 9:17–22), wisdom songs (Pss. 1, 37), royal songs (Pss. 20, 21, 45), hymns (Pss. 8, 29), songs of trust (Pss. 11, 62), thanksgiving poems (Pss. 18, 30, 65), laments (Pss. 27, 28) and penitential poems (Pss. 32, 38), songs of litigation (Isa. 45:20–21; Mic. 1:1–7), love poems (Song 4:1–7), wedding songs (Ps. 45), and predictive poetry (Gen. 49:1–27; Num. 23:8–10, 19–24).

The Idea of Wisdom

Terms and Definitions

The idea of wisdom stems from the need for people to cope with the reality of human existence for sheer survival. This desire to gain mastery over life through the powers of reason marks one of the universal phenomena of ancient and modern societies.

Another pervasive aspect of the human wisdom tradition is the belief that the accumulated knowledge of experience and observation can be taught to the succeeding generation. For this reason, much of the literature published by the sages or keepers of the wisdom traditions takes the form of instructions designed to "steer" one safely and successfully through the course of life.

The concept of "the fear of the Lord" distinguished Hebrew wisdom from its ancient Near Eastern counterparts. For Israel, wisdom and the knowledge of God were inseparable because God was the source and dispenser of insight and understanding (cf. Job 12:13; Prov. 2:5–6; Isa. 31:1–2). This "Yahweh orientation" of Hebrew wisdom meant that the knowledge of God had implications for Israel's emotional and spiritual life (as expressed in Old Testament poetry) and for their physical and experiential life (as reflected in Old Testament wisdom).

The word for "wisdom" originally denoted some kind of technical skill, aptitude, or ability like that necessary for crafting wood and metal, artistic design and architecture, sea navigation, and even politics. The most common word for wisdom, *hokmâ*, reflected this practical aspect of the term in several different Old Testament contexts. For example, Bezalel and Oholiab were given special "wisdom" in artistic design and craftsmanship for their work in the construction of articles and utensils for the tabernacle (Exod. 31:1–11). In another time and place, Solomon's architectural genius demonstrated in the planning and building of the temple in Jerusalem was attributed to this same expertise, or "wisdom" (1 Kings 5:9–18). Elsewhere, the word was applied to the handiwork of artisans (cf. 1 Kings 7:14; Isa. 44:9–17).

Equally important are the philosophical and intellectual connotations of this term. The word also means "superior mental ability." So the translation "intelligence" is appropriate in Job 38:36 and 39:17. The same expression is applied to the intellectual brilliance and vast knowledge of Solomon as the writer of songs and proverbs (1 Kings 4:29–34). The term itself is morally neutral, so "wisdom" may also include the devious conniving of Jonadab and Absalom (2 Sam. 13) and the clever scheming of Joab and the wise women of Abel and Tekoa amid difficult circumstances (2 Sam. 14; 20:16–22).

In respect to wisdom proper, this same Hebrew word has acquired a derived meaning equivalent to "experience" or even "good common sense" (cf. Job 32:7; Prov. 1:7). Essentially the wisdom mentioned in these texts connotes the judicious or skilled application of the powers of human reason to the issues of life. Other Old Testament wisdom terminology includes a series of related words usually translated in the following manner: "understanding, knowledge" or even "discernment" (Prov. 1:5; 3:5; 4:1), "insight, sensibility, intelligent, clever, have success" (Prov. 12:8; 16:20; 19:14; 21:11), "aptitude" or "skill" (Prov. 10:23; 11:12), and "prudence, success, good results" (Prov. 3:21; Isa. 28:29).

In the Old Testament, then, wisdom is basically the very practical art of being prudent, sensible, and skillfully insightful so that one might prosper and have good success in life. It is the ability to discern and achieve order. When one can perceive order in the world, order in international and national relations, order in human behavior, and order in one's own heart, wisdom is achieved. Wisdom therefore results in disciplined and proper behavior, learning how to do what is right and just and fair (Prov. 3:1–5). Wisdom taps the life experience of accumulated years and harnesses that knowledge and understanding for the purpose of safety, long life, right behavior, sound moral character, happiness, material prosperity, and integrity (cf. Prov. 1:33; 2:8–9; 3:1–2). Ultimately wisdom results in the ability to steer through life in a way that wins favor and a good name in the sight of both humanity and God (Prov. 3:4).

The Form of Wisdom

The sage, or wise person, was an important figure in Israelite society from the earliest days of the monarchy. The sage is cited, along with the priest and the prophet, as one of the three sources of authoritative guidance for the community of God (cf. Jer. 18:18; Ezek. 7:26). It appears that royal counselors were part of the corps of professional officers comprising the cabinet in the courts of David and Solomon (2 Sam. 8:16–18; 20:23–26; 1 Kings 4:1–6).

Hence the setting of wisdom as a professional circle of wise men played a significant role in the royal court of the united monarchy and King Solomon (1 Kings 4:32–33; Prov. 25:1). In fact, biblical scholars suggest that the wisdom of Proverbs was in effect a school textbook for the royal family and the elite of society. They were trained in the ways of wisdom so that in the future they might be wise and productive leaders of the next generation of Israelites (cf. the "my son" formula in Prov. 1:8; 2:1; 3:1; 4:1; et al.).

There are essentially two genres of wisdom literature in the Old Testament. The first and most prevalent type is didactic or practical wisdom. The book of Proverbs is the most representative example of this practical instruction. Didactic wisdom consists of wise sayings or popular proverbs that advocate all sorts of prudential habits, skills, and virtues (e.g., Prov. 21:23; 22:3; 23:22). These utilitarian lessons were aimed at developing moral character, personal success and happiness, safety, and well-being. In one sense, didactic wisdom was a practical exposition of and ethical commentary on the law of Moses.

The second type of Old Testament wisdom is that found in Ecclesiastes, or Qoheleth, and to some extent Job. The genre is usually categorized as philosophical, speculative, or even pessimistic wisdom. This strand of wisdom tradition is critical, reflective, and questioning as it delves into the deeper and more vexing issues confronting humankind. The skepticism characteristic of this speculative and philosophical literature portrays most vividly the emptiness and folly of the search for insight and understanding apart from God (Eccl. 1:1–18; 12:12–14).

Figure 20.3. Proverbial Speech Forms

1. The proverb: "Before his downfall a man's heart is proud, / but humility comes before honor" (Prov. 18:12).
2. The folk saying: "The laborer's appetite works for him; / his hunger drives him on" (Prov. 16:26).
3. The paradoxical: "He who is full loathes honey, / but to the hungry even what is bitter tastes sweet" (Prov. 27:7).
4. The analogous: "Like cold water to a weary soul / is good news from a distant land" (Prov. 25:25).
5. The absurd: "Of what use is money in the hand of a fool, / since he has no desire to get wisdom" (Prov. 17:16).
6. The classification: "If a man is lazy, the rafters sag; / if his hands are idle, the house leaks" (Eccl. 10:18).
7. The proportional or relative value: "Better a meal of vegetables where there is love than a fattened calf with hatred" (Prov. 15:17).
8. The cause and effect or consequential: "Wealth is worthless in the day of wrath, / but righteousness delivers from death" (Prov. 11:4).

Hebrew wisdom is like a mountain full of precious gemstones that must be carefully mined out of sediment and rock formations one by one. The basic unit of Hebrew wisdom is the proverb. The proverb is merely an analogy attempting to uncover basic truth about life by means of comparison. Characteristically the *proverb* is a popular saying expressing in pithy terms certain observed regularities in the external world of nature or in human behavior. There are several other types or patterns of the proverbial speech form, as shown in figure 20.3.

Hebrew wisdom literature is a composite of several wisdom speech forms.

1. In Proverbs the *parable* is usually understood as a "warning speech" (e.g., the warning against adultery in 6:20–35).
2. The *precept* is an authoritative instruction or regulation for behavior based on the rules and values and religious tenets of society. The ethical aspects of this literary form connect Hebrew wisdom with the moral codes of Hebrew law (e.g., "Do not withhold good from those who deserve it, / when it is in your power to act," Prov. 3:27).
3. The *riddle* is a puzzling question stated as a problem calling for mental acumen to solve it (e.g., Samson's riddle, "Out of the eater, something to eat; / out of the strong, something sweet," Judg. 14:14).
4. The *fable* is a brief tale embracing a moral truth using people, animals, or inanimate objects as characters (cf. Jotham's fable about the trees choosing a king, Judg. 9:7–20).

Other literary categories and devices used by biblical wisdom writers include the *wise saying* (a generalization about the way of wisdom based on the insight of experience or a folk expression of plain common sense — Prov. 18:18; 20:19), the *numerical proverb* (which takes the form of culminating numerical progression — Prov. 6:16–19; 30:18–31), the *rhetorical question* (Prov. 5:16; 8:1), *allegory* (the personification of wisdom in Proverbs 8–9 and the "old age" poem in Ecclesiastes 12:1–8), and *satire* and *irony* (Prov. 11:22; Eccl. 5:13–17).

The Practice of Wisdom

The Bible knows only two "paths" of life. Either one follows the way of the righteous, or one walks in the way of the wicked (Ps. 1). In the New Testament, Jesus affirmed this basic description of the course of life as a choice between "the narrow way" and "the broad way" (Matt. 7:13; 12:30). In Proverbs those who walk the narrow path of righteousness are called "wise" (10:8, 14), "upright" (11:3, 6), and "righteous" (10:16, 20); those who carelessly speed down the broad road are labeled "fools" (10:1, 8, 14), "wicked" (10:3, 6, 7), and "unfaithful ones" (11:3).

Werner Forman Arch ve/Egyptian Museum, Cairo

"The Almighty is beyond our reach and exalted in power; in his justice and great righteousness, he does not oppress" (Job 37:23). Justice in the ancient world was the responsibility of the gods. In Egypt, it was the gods' responsibility to establish *maat*, order in the world. This painting shows the god Horus with the goddess Maat.

Of singular importance here is the notion that "the way of wisdom" is not so much knowledge and intellect as it is behavior and character. More than pithy sayings and clever maxims, true wisdom is a lifestyle. Biblical wisdom is a code of ethics rooted in the legal tradition of the law of Moses. Its purpose is to school one's attitude, character, and behavior in the fear of the Lord so he or she might walk in the way of goodness and keep to the paths of righteousness (Prov. 2:20).

The antithesis of the wise man in wisdom literature is the fool. Various terms are used to caricature the fool in the Old Testament wisdom, including the naive youth who is untutored and easily deceived (Heb. *petî*, Prov. 14:15), the person who is stupid in practical affairs and shameless in religious affairs (Heb. *kesîl*, Prov. 1:1), the one whose obstinance leads into folly (Heb. *'ĕwîl*, Prov. 1:7), those who are crude and dull like beasts (Heb. *ba'ar*, Prov. 12:1), the brutal and the godless (Heb. *nābāl*, Prov. 17:7), the babbler and scoffer (Heb. *lēṣ*, Prov. 1:22), and the deluded, mad, and irrational (Heb. *hōlēl*, Prov. 28:4). All these foolish ones are characterized by disdain for wisdom and instruction, the rejection of discipline and correction, and insolence and irreverence before the Lord God.

The New Testament confirms this understanding of the way of wisdom as divine instruction that prompts the practical outworking of godliness in human behavior. According to the book of James, those who are truly wise demonstrate their insight by a "good life" and works done in "meekness of wisdom." Unlike earthly wisdom, godly wisdom is pure, peaceable, loving, gentle, open to reason, submissive, full of mercy and good works, impartial, and sincere (3:13–18).

The Person of Wisdom

The ancient Hebrews recognized that wisdom was more than mere teachings of the sage or the accumulation of experience over the years of life. The basic goal of Hebrew wisdom was a proper relationship to Yahweh, the very God of Wisdom (Job 12:13; Isa. 31:1–2). This "Lord who is wise" has revealed his knowledge and understanding in creation, and he continues to display his wisdom in his providential rule of the nations (e.g., Ps. 104:24; Prov. 3:19; Isa. 10:13). As the God of wisdom he also grants this gift to humanity, to those searching for it like hidden treasure (Prov. 2:4; 1 Kings 3:28; Dan. 2:21).

The Old Testament expression "the fear of the Lord" best conveys this relational dimension of Hebrew wisdom (Ps. 111:10; Prov. 1:7). The fear of the Lord was the source of Hebrew wisdom and actually connoted a complex of interrelated attitudes and actions:

1. The desire to get understanding that arises from a choice grounded in the human will (Prov. 1:29; 2:5).
2. Awe and reverence for the God of creation and redemption that elicits genuine worship and willing obedience to his commands (Prov. 24:21).
3. Dread at God's holiness and trepidation of his divine judgment (Eccl. 12:13–14).
4. Faith and trust in God's plan for human life, and a rejection of self-reliance (Ps. 115:11; Prov. 3:5–6).
5. Hating and avoiding evil, and refusing to envy sinners (Prov. 3:7; 9:13; 16:6; 23:17).
6. Generally the reward of prosperity and long life to the prudent (Prov. 10:27; 14:27; 19:23).
7. Disciplined instruction that instills wisdom, humility, and honor (Prov. 15:33; 22:4).

The personification of wisdom in the book of Proverbs also illustrates the personal aspects of the fear of the Lord. Wisdom is portrayed both as an itinerant female pedagogue seeking students at the city gates (Prov. 8:1–12) and as a preexistent master architect participating in God's creative works (Prov. 8:22–31). In each case, emphasis is placed on the experience of a relationship with the "person of wisdom."

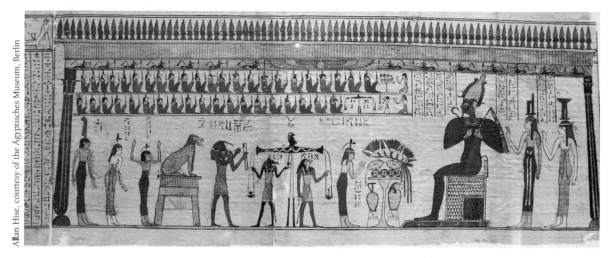

The New Testament further develops this concept of the person of wisdom by identifying Jesus Christ as "the master architect" of creation (Col. 1:15–17). Elsewhere the apostle Paul indicates that the Christian's walk in the way of wisdom begins when he or she acknowledges that God is the source of life in Jesus Christ and that God made this Jesus our wisdom, righteousness, holiness, and redemption (1 Cor. 1:30).

The Content of Wisdom

Theodicy

The topics addressed in Old Testament wisdom literature are as numerous and varied as the human experience, yet there are recurring themes in the speculative and instructional wisdom writings.

The philosophical discussions of Job and Ecclesiastes focus on questions related to the notion of theodicy (i.e., the reality of pain, suffering, and death in the world in relationship to God's holiness and justice). Specific issues addressed in the discussions of speculative Old Testament wisdom include human suffering, poverty, and social injustice (e.g., Job 21:7–26), the "crookedness" of life (especially the prosperity of the wicked—Eccl. 8:14–15; 9:11–12), the fact of evil and death (Eccl. 9:1–6), the afterlife (Eccl. 3:16–22), and purpose and meaning in this life (Eccl. 4:1–3).

The Retribution Principle

The idea of divine retribution based on the merits (or demerits) of human behavior is a common theme in the poetic and wisdom literature of the Old Testament. The retribution principle is rooted in the

"My heart does not reproach me for any of my days" (Job 27:6). The heart was the source of evil and good actions and as such could be checked to determine the goodness of a person's life, a common theme in the wisdom literature. This picture from the Book of the Dead shows a person's heart being weighed in the judgment of the dead, while a monster waits to devour the soul if found unworthy.

blessings and curses of the Mosaic covenant (Deut. 28). The rewards or punishments appended to the legislation of Yahweh's pact with Israel stipulate that obedience to the commands of God will bring divine blessing, whereas disobedience to the Lord's statutes will send the curses of Yahweh upon the Hebrews. This fundamental teaching of Old Testament theology is examined from four complementary perspectives in the following chapters (Job, Psalms, Proverbs, and Ecclesiastes).

Instruction

Didactic wisdom literature is essentially practical social commentary based on the ethical demands of Hebrew law. Hence the instructions and warnings of the sayings in the book of Proverbs aimed at regulating daily life cover a diversity of topics, including familial relationships (23:22–25), retribution and discipline (3:12; 28:10), friendship (17:17), control of the tongue (26:18–28), marriage and adultery (5:1–23), the poor and the needy (14:21, 31), the wise contrasted with the foolish (18:1–16), the industrious contrasted with the sluggardly (26:13–16), drunkenness (23:29–35), life and death (13:14), anger (29:22), kingship (20:28), etiquette (25:2–7), indebtedness (11:15), wisdom (1:7), and the fear of the Lord (2:5–6).

Questions for Further Study and Discussion

1. How do we account for the similarities between the poetry and wisdom literature of the Hebrews and that of the rest of the ancient Near East?
2. What is the relationship between Old Testament wisdom literature and the so-called prosperity gospel espoused in some sectors of the Christian church today?
3. How do the apocryphal wisdom of Sirach (Ecclesiasticus) and the Wisdom of Solomon compare with the canonical Old Testament wisdom in style and theme?
4. What is the relationship of wisdom literature to the ethical teachings of the Prophets?
5. Select a psalm and try to identify examples of the various types of parallelism that characterize Hebrew poetry.
6. What role should wisdom literature have in the teaching of the contemporary Christian church? Is there a place for the "sage" in today's church?
7. How does our understanding of the life situation of the Hebrew poet aid in the interpretation of biblical poetry?

For Further Reading

Alter, Robert. *The Art of Biblical Poetry*. New York: Basic Books, 1985.

Anderson, B. W. *Out of the Depths: The Psalms Speak for Us Today*. 3rd ed. Philadelphia: Westminster Press, 2000. Informative discussion of the structure and content of the various psalm types.

Andersen, F. I., and David N. Freedman. *Hosea*. AB. Vol. 24. Garden City, N.Y.: Doubleday, 1980.

Brueggemann, W. *Israel's Praise: Doxology against Idolatry and Ideology*. Philadelphia: Fortress Press, 1988.

Bullock, C. Hassell. *An Introduction to the Old Testament Poetic Books*. Rev. ed. Chicago: Moody Press, 1988.

Carson, D. A. *How Long O Lord? Reflections on Suffering and Evil*. 2nd ed. Grand Rapids: Baker, 2006.

Crenshaw, J. L. *Old Testament Wisdom: An Introduction*. Rev. ed. Louisville: Westminster John Knox, 1998. A comprehensive introduction to the idea of wisdom and wisdom literature in the Bible and the ancient Near East.

Crenshaw, J. L., ed. *Studies in Ancient Israelite Wisdom*. New York: Ktav, 1976.

Estes, D. J. *Handbook on the Wisdom Books and Psalms*. Grand Rapids: Baker, 2005.

Freedman, David N. *Pottery, Poetry and Prophecy*. Winona Lake, Ind.: Eisenbrauns, 1982.

Gammie, John, and Leo G. Perdue, *The Sage in Israel and the Ancient Near East*. Winona Lake, Ind.: Eisenbrauns, 1990.

Gordis, R. *Poets, Prophets, and Sages*. Bloomington: Indiana University Press, 1971.

Gray, G. B. *The Forms of Hebrew Poetry*. Reprint. New York: Ktav, 1972.

Hoftijzer, J. "Remarks Concerning the Use of the Particle *ʾt* in Classical Hebrew." *Oudtestamentische Studien* 14 (1967): 1–99.

Holladay, W. L. *The Psalms through Three Thousand Years*. Minneapolis: Fortress Press, 1993.

Kidner, Derek. *The Wisdom of Proverbs, Job and Ecclesiastes: An Introduction to Wisdom Literature*. Downers Grove, Ill.: InterVarsity Press, 1985.

Knight, D. A., and G. A. Tucker, eds. *The Hebrew Bible and Its Modern Interpreters*. Chico, Calif.: Scholars Press, 1985.

Kugel, James. *The Idea of Biblical Poetry: Parallelism and Its History*. Reprint. Baltimore: Johns Hopkins University Press, 2004. A case against the ideas of parallelism and meter in Hebrew poetry and for Hebrew poetry as essentially a synthetic composition (i.e., the second half of a poetic line sharpens or emphasizes the first).

Longman, Tremper, III. *How to Read the Psalms*. Downers Grove, Ill.: InterVarsity Press, 1988.

Lowth, Robert. *Lectures on the Sacred Poetry of the Hebrews*. Boston: Crocker & Brewster, 1829. Reprint.

Matthews, V. H., and D. C. Benjamin. *Old Testament Parallels*. 3rd ed. New York: Paulist, 2006. Contemporary English translations of ancient Near Eastern documents, including poetry and wisdom.

Murphy, R. E. *The Tree of Life*. 3rd ed. Grand Rapids: Eerdmans, 2002.

_____. *Wisdom Literature*. FOTL 13. Grand Rapids: Eerdmans, 1982. Classification and analysis of individual units of biblical wisdom literature according to genre.

_____. *Wisdom Literature and Psalms*. Nashville: Abingdon Press, 1983.

Noth, Martin, and D. W. Thomas, eds. *Wisdom in Israel and in the Ancient Near East*. VT Supplement 3 (1955). Rowley Festschrift.

O'Connor, Michael. *Hebrew Verse Structure*. Winona Lake, Ind.: Eisenbrauns, 1980. An attempt to move the study of Hebrew poetry away from the emphasis on parallelism and meter by shifting the focus to Hebrew syntax through the application of modern linguistic techniques.

Peterson, E. H. *Answering God: The Psalms as Tools for Prayer*. San Francisco: Harper, 1989.

Pritchard, J. B., ed. *ANET*. 3rd ed. Princeton: Princeton University Press, 1969.

von Rad, Gerhard. *Wisdom in Israel*. Trans. by J. D. Martin. Nashville: Abingdon Press, 1972.

Ryken, Leland. *How to Read the Bible as Literature*. Grand Rapids: Zondervan, 1984.

_____. *Words of Delight*. 2nd ed. Grand Rapids: Baker, 2005. Especially "Biblical Poetry," 159–289.

Scott, R. B. Y. *The Way of Wisdom*. New York: Macmillan, 1971. A popular introduction to canonical and extracanonical wisdom literature, including historical background, literary forms, and contemporary significance.

Simpson, W. K., ed. *The Literature of Ancient Egypt*. Rev. ed. New Haven: Yale University Press, 1973.

Sparks, Kenton L. *Ancient Texts for the Study of the Hebrew Bible*. Peabody, Mass.: Hendrickson, 2005.

Walton, John H. *Ancient Israelite Literature in Its Cultural Context*. Grand Rapids: Zondervan, 1989. Useful survey and discussion of the parallels between Old Testament and ancient Near Eastern literature according to genre. Extensive bibliographies.

_____. *Ancient Near Eastern Thought and the Old Testament: Introducing the Conceptual World of the Hebrew Bible*. Grand Rapids: Baker, 2006.

In Job 28, mining is used as an illustration to compare how deep and unattainable wisdom is. This copper mining installation is at Timna in the Negev. Bible Scene Multimedia/Maurice Thompson

JOB

Key Ideas

- It is not true that only the wicked suffer.
- God's justice cannot be reduced to a simple formula like the retribution principle.
- God's infinite wisdom is the key to acknowledging his justice.

Purpose Statement

The purpose of the book of Job is to test God's policies concerning justice. The conclusion is God's justice cannot be assessed because we can never have enough information to do so. Instead his justice must be inferred from his wisdom.

Major Themes

- Retribution Principle
- Wisdom, Justice, and Sovereignty of God
- Mediator

God's Presence

The developing theme of God's presence is not advanced in the book, though he makes his presence manifest for the final discourses of the book used to drive home the point.

Outline

I. Prologue (1–2)

II. Dialogues
  A. Job's Opening Lament (3)
  B. Cycle 1: Consolation
    1. Eliphaz (4–5)
    2. Job (6–7)
    3. Bildad (8)
    4. Job (9–10)
    5. Zophar (11)
    6. Job (12–14)
  C. Cycle 2: The Fate of the Wicked
    1. Eliphaz (15)
    2. Job (16–17)
    3. Bildad (18)
    4. Job (19)
    5. Zophar (20)
    6. Job (21)
  D. Cycle 3: Specific Accusations
    1. Eliphaz (22)
    2. Job (23–24)
    3. Bildad (25)
    4. Job (26–27)

III. Interlude: Hymn to Wisdom (28)

IV. Discourses
  A. Discourse 1: Job
    1. Reminiscence (29)
    2. Affliction (30)
    3. Oath (31)
  B. Discourse 2: Elihu
    1. Introduction and theory (32–33)
    2. Verdict on Job (34)
    3. Offense of Job (35)
    4. Closing statement of summary (36–37)
  C. Discourse 3: God
    1. Speech 1 (38–39)
    2. Speech 2 (40–41)
  D. Job's closing statements (40:3–5; 42:1–6)

V. Epilogue (42:7–17)

The book of Job leads us to consider one of the basic philosophical questions of human existence. It has been found to be a very practical book because the questions have not changed much over the last five thousand years of history. We still seek reasons for personal and corporate suffering and wonder what logic can be used to understand our life experiences. The book of Job offers a biblical perspective on suffering (to be distinguished from offering an explanation of suffering).

The Writing of the Book

There can be little doubt that the form of Job we now possess has the unified structure of a literary composition. Much speculation, however, has been given as to what process may have been involved in the production of the work. Literary critics have been quick to identify particular sections as later additions. Prominent among these would be the Elihu speeches (chaps. 32–37), the Hymn to Wisdom (chap. 28), the second speech of Yahweh (40:6–41:34), and the prose prologue and epilogue, which are often presented as adopted from an ancient Epic of Job.

The most contested section is that containing the speeches of Elihu. Some scholars note that Elihu is not mentioned among the friends in either the prologue or the epilogue, and they contend that he does not really add anything new to the debate. The latter objection will be addressed in the discussion on the structure of the book. As to the former, there is good reason for Elihu to be omitted in the narrative portions of the book. In the prologue he would not be mentioned because of his lack of status. His introduction of himself in chapter 32 makes it plain that he was not one of the recognized wise men; he was rather like a graduate student daring to reprimand his professors for their lack of insight. That Elihu is not mentioned in the epilogue can be explained in that he had not committed offense in his response to Job. The other friends advised Job in effect to confess to unknown or unreal sins to appease an angry deity. Elihu did not so misconstrue God and was not called to account. There is therefore no reason to consider Elihu's speeches as secondary additions.

Once it is recognized that Job is wisdom literature, it is possible to accept, as most scholars do, that the dialogue presented is not offered as a reporter's transcript quoting the precise words of each person

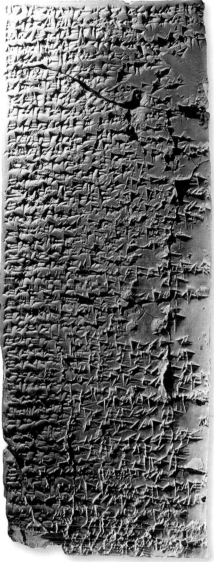

The Schøyen Collection MS 3025, Oslo and London

"... Amid disquieting dreams in the night ... fear and trembling seized me" (Job 4:12–14). Gilgamesh, the ancient hero, was also troubled by dreams and sought their interpretation, since they were considered to be communication from the gods. This tablet records the dream of Gilgamesh.

involved. A high view of biblical inspiration requires one to take into consideration the literary genre of a book in order to understand how it ought to be interpreted.

The result of this is that the composition of the book of Job may not have occurred until centuries after the experiences of the man. While this would allow more room for the possibility of sections being added to the core of the work, the evidence that such a process actually took place is vague, and we see no need for such a theory of composition. The unified structure argues for the integrity of each section, and we believe that each section makes a unique contribution to the purpose of the whole. To put it another way, the book would fall short of accomplishing its purpose if any of the sections were deleted.

The individual named Job shows no indication of being an Israelite. The place names rather suggest that he was Edomite. Consequently there is no mention of the covenant or the law, and God is rarely identified as Yahweh (El Shaddai is more frequent). Since the book is a work of Wisdom, there is little information of a historical nature in its content to help us to date either its events or its composition. Traditionally the events of the book have been dated roughly to the patriarchal era because the lifestyle and longevity of Job are most similar to those found in Genesis. It is further pointed out that the existence of roving bands of Sabaeans and Chaldeans (Job 1:15, 17) suits best the early second millennium BC. There are no real problems with this view, though it must be recognized that the evidence is scant.

In contrast, it is not considered likely that the book was composed that early. While some have attempted to make connections to the Persian period, the orthography of the book appears to be preexilic, and many scholars now hold to a date during the divided monarchy. Evidence is extremely difficult to establish, and in any case, the timeless nature of the message makes the dating of the book a moot point.

The Background

While ascertaining historical background is neither possible nor pertinent, it is necessary to discuss the literary background of a book such as Job. The book contains a variety of literary genres, including dialogue (chaps. 4–27), soliloquy (e.g., chap. 3), discourse (e.g., chaps. 29–41), narrative (chaps. 1–2), and hymn (chap. 28). These literary genres are common to wisdom literature but are rarely mixed in so sophisticated and skillful a manner as found in Job.

Wisdom literature of the ancient Near East features a few compositions that address the same general philosophical questions. A Sumerian work entitled "Man and His God" (Ur III period, about 2000 BC) is a monologue by a person who does not understand why he is suffering. At the end he is shown what his sin was and therefore concludes that there is no such thing as undeserved suffering.

In an Akkadian monologue, "Ludlul bel Nemeqi" (I will praise the lord of wisdom), dating to the latter half of the second millennium BC, a man who considers himself in favor with Marduk, the chief god of the Babylonians, wonders why he is suffering. In the end his sins are forgiven, so again the solution is that there is no such thing as a righteous sufferer (fig. 21.1).

A third piece, "The Babylonian Theodicy" (about 1000 BC), takes the form of a dialogue between a sufferer and his friend. The friend offers the standard lines of advice and explanation only to find each refuted by the sufferer. The conclusion finally reached is that the behavior of the gods cannot be analyzed or understood—whatever evil men do is done because the gods made them that way (fig. 21.2).

Although the literature from Mesopotamia shows some general similarities in form and content to the book of Job, the latter has a much higher level of sophistication both in literary form and in philosophical depth and integrity.

If the genre of Job is to be identified based on a correlation with these Mesopotamian pieces, an argument could be made against those who view the book as a stage play, though certainly it could be adapted to that use. Likewise, because wisdom literature by definition makes frequent use of hypothetical situations and dialogue, there is no reason to overemphasize the historicity of the conversation. Equally, there is no reason to doubt that the narrative is based on the experiences of real people.

Job 40:4, "I am unworthy—how can I reply to you? I put my hand over my mouth" (Job 40:4). In the ancient world, putting your hand over your mouth was a sign of submission, as with this dignitary appearing before the throne of King Darius of Persia.
Z. Radovan/
www.BibleLandPictures.com

Figure 21.1. Excerpt from Mesopotamian Wisdom: 1

My lofty head is bowed down to the ground,
Dread had enfeebled my robust heart.
A novice has turned back my broad chest.
My arms, though once strong, are both paralyzed.
I, who strode along as a noble, have learned to slip by unnoticed.
Though a dignitary, I have become a slave.
To my many relations I am like a recluse.
My family treats me as an alien.
The pit awaits anyone who speaks well of me,
While he who utters defamation of me is promoted.
My slanderer slanders with god's help;
I have no one to go by my side, nor have I found a helper.
What strange conditions everywhere!
When I look behind, there is persecution, trouble.
Like one who has not made libations to his god,
Nor invoked his goddess at table,
For myself, I gave attention to supplication and prayer:
To me prayer was discretion, sacrifice my rule.
The day for reverencing the god was a joy to my heart;
The day of the goddess's procession was profit and gain to me.
The king's prayer — that was my joy,
And the accompanying music became a delight for me.
I instructed my hand to keep the god's rites,
And provoked the people to value the goddess's name.
I made praise for the king like a god's,
And taught the populace reverence for the palace.
I wish I knew that these things were pleasing to one's god!
What is proper to oneself is an offence to one's god.
Who knows the will of the gods in heaven?
Who understands the plans of the underworld god?
He who was alive yesterday is dead today.
For a minute he was dejected, suddenly he is exuberant.
One moment the people are singing in exaltation,
Another they groan like professional mourners.
My god has not come to the rescue in taking me by the hand,
Nor has my goddess shown pity on me by going at my side.
Then the Lord took hold of me,
The Lord set me on my feet,
The Lord gave me life,
The Babylonians saw how Marduk restores to life,
And all quarters extolled his greatness:
Who thought that he would see his Sun?
Who imagined that he would walk along his street?
Who but Marduk restores his dead to life?
Apart from Sarpanitum which goddess grants life?

From "Ludlul bel Nemeqi," in *Babylonian Wisdom Literature*, trans. W. G. Lambert (New York: Oxford Univ. Press, 1960): I:73 – 79, 92 – 95, 98; II:10 – 13, 23 – 42, 112 – 20; IV:2 – 4, 29 – 36.1.

Figure 21.2. Excerpt from Mesopotamian Wisdom: 2

Sufferer III

23 My friend, your mind is a river whose spring never fails,
24 The accumulated mass of the sea, which knows no decrease.
25 I will ask you a question; listen to what I say.
26 Pay attention for a moment; hear my words.
27 My body is a wreck, emaciation darkens [me],
28 My success has vanished, my stability has gone.
29 My strength is enfeebled, my prosperity has ended,
30 Moaning and grief have blackened my features.
31 The corn of my fields is far from satisfying [me],
32 My wine, the life of mankind, is too little for satiety.
33 Can a life of bliss be assured? I wish I knew how!

Friend VI

56 O palm, tree of wealth, my precious brother,
57 Endowed with all wisdom, jewel of [gold],
58 You are as stable as the earth, but the plan of the gods is remote.
59 Look at the superb wild ass on the [plain];
60 The arrow will follow the gorer who trampled down the fields.
61 Come, consider the lion you mentioned, the enemy of cattle.
62 For the crime which the lion committed the pit awaits him.
63 The opulent nouveau riche who heaps up goods
64 Will be burnt at the stake by the king before his time.
65 Do you wish to go the way these have gone?
66 Rather seek the lasting reward of (your) god!

Sufferer VII

67 Your mind is a north wind, a pleasant breeze for the peoples.
68 Choice friend, your advice is fine.
69 Just one word would I put before you.
70 Those who neglect the god go the way of prosperity,
71 While those who pray to the goddess are impoverished and dispossessed.
72 In my youth I sought the will of my god;
73 With prostration and prayer I followed my goddess
74 But I was bearing a profitless corvée as a yoke.
75 My god decreed instead of wealth destitution.
76 A cripple is my superior, a lunatic outstrips me.
77 The rogue has been promoted, but I have been brought low.

Friend XXIV

254 O wise one, O savant, who masters knowledge,
255 In your anguish you blaspheme the god.
256 The divine mind, like the centre of the heavens, is remote;
257 Knowledge of it is difficult; the masses do not know it.
258 Among all the creatures whom Aruru formed
259 The prime offspring is altogether ...

(Continued on following page.)

260 In the case of a cow, the first calf is lowly,
261 The later offspring is twice as big.
262 A first child is born a weakling.
263 But the second is called an heroic warrior.
264 Though a man may observe what the will of the god is, the masses do
     not know it.

Sufferer XXVII
287 You are kind, my friend; behold my grief.
288 Help me; look on my distress; know it.
289 I, though humble, wise, and a suppliant,
290 Have not seen help and succour for one moment.
291 I have trodden the square of my city unobtrusively,
292 My voice was not raised, my speech was kept low.
293 I did not raise my head, but looked at the ground,
294 I did not worship even as a slave in the company of my associates.
295 May the god who has thrown me off give help,
296 May the goddess who has [abandoned me] show mercy,
297 For the shepherd Šamaš guides the peoples like a god.

Excerpts from "The Babylonian Theodicy," in *Babylonian Wisdom Literature*, trans. W. G. Lambert (New York: Oxford Univ. Press, 1960).

Purpose and Message

The purpose of the book of Job is to explore God's policies concerning justice, especially as it regards the suffering of the righteous. This investigation takes two major directions. First, the satan[1] implies in 1:9–11 that God's policy of blessing the righteous is counterproductive to the development of true righteousness. Blessing induces people to be righteous for what they stand to gain from it. He suggests that his claim can be demonstrated by cutting off Job's blessings. The satan's contention is that righteousness purely for righteousness' sake does not exist and, indeed, cannot exist in the system that God operates. God's policies are placed on trial here, not Job. Second, Job wonders how God can possibly allow the righteous person to suffer. Again, it is God's policies that are on trial.

In carrying out this purpose, the book refuses to take any shortcuts. The narrator goes to great pains to establish Job's impeccable reputation. The easy solutions of the ancient Near East are thereby discounted from the start as well as rejected in the shallow philosophy of Job's friends. In the end, it is not important to the purpose of the book that God vindicated Job. The audience knew of Job's innocence from the start. What is essential to the development of the book's purpose is that Job vindicates God's policy of blessing righteous people by maintaining his integrity even when he is not being blessed for it.

---

1. "The satan" is used throughout rather than "Satan" to reflect that the Hebrew text also uses the definite article indicating that this is a title (= adversary) rather than a proper name.

The message of the book in regard to the satan's concern is that God's practice of blessing the righteous is not a hindrance to the development of true righteousness. In regard to Job's situation, the message is that God is not always under obligation to make sure that the righteous receive blessing and *only* blessing. The world is more complex than that. In both cases God's justice is inferred from his wisdom. Though we cannot get enough information to vindicate God's justice, we do have enough information to be convinced of his benevolent wisdom. God's self-defense, if it can be called that, is conducted by establishing that his wisdom exceeds all human wisdom.

While this purpose and message offer an understanding of the book on the level of its plot, some have wondered what might have given the Israelites an interest in this piece of literature that seems to have originated outside their society. A common answer has been that the book of Job may have become of interest to the Israelites who were experiencing the Babylonian exile and trying to reconcile that event with their view of God.

Although the book unquestionably contains discussion and information that would be invaluable to the exiles (especially the idea that God's wisdom is the basis on which his justice may be vindicated), the scenario in Job seems too unlike Israel of the sixth century to invite too close a correlation. Most obviously, the book is insistent on Job's absolute innocence and vindicates him in the end. Such could hardly be said of Israel. Undoubtedly, however, the minority who were righteous in Israel may well have taken solace and found comfort in the teachings of the book of Job.

Kim Walton, courtesy of the Oriental Institute Museum

"One day the angels [sons of God] came to present themselves before the Lord" (Job 1:6). These were members of the heavenly assembly. In the ancient world this was a divine council made up of the major gods. This cylinder seal impression shows a procession of gods with their mythological animals.

In this situation we see the broader categories of God's attributes. Omniscience is only one small and relatively insignificant part of God's infinite wisdom. Omnipotence is likewise only one aspect of God's sovereignty. Similarly, mercy is sometimes a more personalized reflection of God's justice. The broader categories help us focus more on who God is instead of on what he can do for a particular person.

Mediator

The question of whether Job could or would be aided by a mediator (referred to by a variety of Hebrew terms) arises several times in the book (5:1; 9:33; 16:18–22; 19:25–27; 33:23). Job pleads for the intercession of a mediator and appears convinced that such a one will arise (19:25–27), though the exact nature of his expectation is a matter of continuing controversy. Some see in Job's affirmations a belief in the resurrection of the body, while others translate and interpret the text to convey only his confidence that he will be vindicated and restored before his death.

Regardless of Job's position on the timing of his vindication, the role of the mediator is clear. He is an individual (most would agree that it is God himself whom Job expects) who would serve as defense attorney in court to afford Job a fair hearing and a just verdict. Additionally, some of the terminology used to describe the mediator portrays him as a near relative (kinsman-redeemer; see chapter 13, "Ruth") who would appear at the height of the crisis to bring relief by providing a dignified resolution.

It is important that though the mediator issue dominates the dialogue section, it fades into the background as the book reaches its conclusions. In the end, no mediator is necessary and none appears. Job's claim of having been treated unjustly dissipates in the face of God's challenges, and his need for a kinsman-redeemer is eliminated by his restoration.

Questions for Further Study and Discussion

1. How can the information gleaned from the book of Job be used to comfort someone who is suffering?
2. What does the book offer as an appropriate response to suffering?
3. Does God operate by means of the retribution principle today? Explain your answer.
4. Is there any observable connection between the retribution principle and the Pharisees' view of the law? Explain.

For Further Reading

Andersen, Francis I. *Job*. TOTC. Downers Grove, Ill.: InterVarsity Press, 1976. Excellent treatment by a renowned evangelical linguist.

Atkinson, David. *The Message of Job*. Downers Grove, Ill.: InterVarsity Press, 1991. Pastoral approach to suffering based on the experience of Job.

Clines, D. J. A. *Job 1–20*. WBC. Vol. 17. Waco, Tex.: Word, 1989.

Gordis, Robert. *The Book of God and Man*. Chicago: University of Chicago Press, 1965. Thematic treatment from a Jewish background.

Hartley, John. *The Book of Job*. Grand Rapids, Eerdmans: 1988. Conversant with scholarship, evangelical (though not always in a traditional sense), thought-provoking, thorough, and arguably the best.

Pope, Marvin. *Job*. New York: Anchor: 1965. Good treatment from an ancient Near Eastern backdrop in particular.

Tsevat, Matitiahu. "The Meaning of the Book of Job." In *The Meaning of the Book of Job and Other Biblical Studies*. New York: Ktav, 1980. A seminal article, originally published in 1966, on the book of Job and the retribution principle.

Westermann, Claus. *The Structure of the Book of Job*. Philadelphia: Fortress Press, 1981. A helpful form-critical study.

Zuck, Roy B., ed. *Sitting with Job*. Grand Rapids: Baker, 1992. A collection of some of the more important articles on Job.

The Psalms often used the imagery of a shepherd for God and the sheep for his people. "Know that the LORD is God. It is he who made us, and we are his; we are his people, the sheep of his pasture" (Ps. 100:3).

PSALMS

Key Ideas

- Recognition of the kingship and sovereignty of God
- Conduct and destiny of the righteous and the wicked
- God's comfort and defense in times of crisis
- Importance of praise in all of its variations
- Role of nature and creation

Purpose Statement

The purpose of the book of Psalms is to use the familiar hymns of Israel to provide a cantata-like presentation of God's kingship through his anointed representatives, the kings of David's line. In the process it shows God as one who delights in rewarding the righteous and who will bring punishment to the wicked. The themes and message of the book are embedded in Psalms 1, 2, and 145.

Major Themes

- Retribution Principle
- Kingship
- Nature and Creation

God's Presence

The psalms speak often of a desire to be in God's presence in the temple and of the delight to be found in the law that provides a guideline for being in relationship with God. The book also testifies to God's presence with individuals in crisis and with his people in troubled times. God is praised for his presence with his people.

Outline

> (Based on the view that an editor's agenda is behind the arrangement of the psalms, it must be remembered that this approach is still speculative. The table in figure 22.2 helps to explain the outline.)

  I. Introduction (1–2)

 II. David's Conflict with Saul (3–41)

III. David's Kingship (42–72)

IV. The Assyrian Crisis (73–89)

 V. Introspection about the Destruction of the Temple and the Exile (90–106)

VI. Praise and Reflection on the Return and the New Era (107–145)

VII. Concluding Praise (146–150)

The book of Psalms is one of the best-loved and most-used books of the Old Testament, yet at the same time it is one of the most problematic in the canon. Questions surrounding authorship, composition, theology, interpretation, application, and function all contribute to the book's complexity. The fact that many believers through the ages have found comfort from its pages in time of need, never once considering any of those questions, stands as testimony to the power of God to minister through the books of Scripture.

The Writing of the Book

Two aspects of the writing need to be considered: the authorship of individual psalms and the composition of the psalter as a whole. Since some of the psalms purport to have been written in the mid-second millennium BC, while others are clearly postexilic (i.e., after 539 BC), we know that (1) the final composition of the whole did not take place until sometime after the exile, and (2) thus, the editor (the person or persons responsible for collecting and organizing the psalms) is to be differentiated from the author (the composer of individual psalms). We will use the terms *author* and *editor* to distinguish these functions (realizing that there are multiple authors and undoubtedly multiple editors).

Authorship

The main source of information for the authorship of the psalms comes from the psalm titles. Of the 150 psalms, all but 34 have titles of some sort. Of the 116 titles, 100 indicate an author (and often other information as well, such as musical style or directions for performance), and of those 100, 73 are attributed to David. Other authors identified are Moses (90), Solomon (72, 127), Asaph (50, 73–83), Heman (88), Ethan (89), and the group called the Sons of Korah (42, 44–49, 84–85, 87). There has been some question as to whether the persons named in the titles are being designated as authors or as dedicatees. For instance, Psalm 72 seems to be a blessing on Solomon (by David) rather than a psalm that Solomon would have written.

Others have wondered about the reliability of the titles. Would we consider them inspired? Even the oldest manuscripts of the Old Testament contain the titles, though they are not part of the composition proper. If they are later additions by an editor, they are still very ancient and therefore have a claim to authenticity. It is difficult to prove that they are inspired, but most conservative interpreters treat them as accurate.

Composition

The book of Psalms is divided into five books as follows:

Book I: 1–41
Book II: 42–72
Book III: 73–89
Book IV: 90–106
Book V: 107–50

This division is older than our oldest manuscripts, but until recently, interpreters had few clues as to its significance. Some headway has been made in the recognition that smaller collections exist within the larger whole. Among collections that have been identified:

Davidic Group I: 3–41
Sons of Korah Group I: 42–49
Davidic Group II: 51–65
Asaph Group: 73–83
Sons of Korah Group II: 84–88 (exc. 86)
Congregational Praise Group I: 95–100
Halleluyah Group: 111–117
Songs of Ascent to Jerusalem: 120–134
Davidic Group III: 138–145
Congregational Praise Group II: 146–50

Marie-Lan Nguyen/Wikimedia Commons, courtesy of the Louvre

This Neo-Sumerian royal hymn to Inanna celebrates the marriage of Iddin-dagan in the sacred marriage festival. The Old Testament has no such fertility ritual, but Psalm 45 is a royal wedding hymn.

"Singers and dancers alike say, 'All my springs are in you'" (Ps. 87:7). It was common to have singers and dancers present at important events in the ancient world. This tomb painting shows Egyptian musicians and dancers.

The Yorck Project/Wikimedia Commons, GNU

The editor has woven these smaller collections together into the five-book structure to produce the larger composition that we call the book of Psalms. What purpose guided the editor as individual psalms and collections of psalms were set in their places?

One helpful suggestion is that the editor's purpose is discernible by the "seam" psalms. These are the psalms that come at the end of each of the first four books (i.e., 41, 72, 89, and 106). The theory speculates that these have been used by the editor to mark transitions from one book to the next, so that by examining them carefully we may be able to distinguish the primary topic of each book. These data would be supplemented by other evidences of editorial activity such as the comment in Psalm 72:20, which notes the end of the prayers of David even though many Davidic psalms appear later in the psalter.

The most significant evidence of the editor's work and purpose is thought to be represented in Psalms 1 and 2, which many consider an introduction to the whole book.

The point to note here is that these observations combine to suggest there is a definitive, purposeful arrangement of the psalms that offers a message that transcends what any individual psalm has to offer. In the same way that the writers of the historical literature took narratives from various sources and edited them into a unified composition with a particular theological agenda in mind, so it may be with the editor of Psalms. Just as some historical literature (especially Kings) was compiled in stages, so, it is likely, was the book of Psalms.

Evidence that the five books of Psalms were not initially compiled all at one time comes from the psalm manuscripts found among the Dead Sea Scrolls. These manuscripts date to the last century and a half BC. Among the thirty-odd Psalms manuscripts available, the psalms of books I–III are almost always in the same order as they are in the Bible. The order of the psalms in books IV and V, however, frequently varies from that found in the Old Testament. This seems to suggest that books I–III had already attained final form by the second century BC, whereas books IV–V may still have been under development. It is possible, then, that the editorial arrangement was not fixed until just before the time of Christ.

Thus, the book of Psalms is made up of individual poetic compositions written during a thousand-year period by several persons. These compositions were at various times gathered into small collections, which in turn were arranged in stages into a larger work edited with a particular theological agenda in mind.

The Background

It is more appropriate to speak of the literary background of the book of Psalms than of a historical background. Study of the Mesopotamian and Egyptian hymns and prayers has provided much information by which we can better understand the psalms. In a comparative study like this, it is necessary to consider both similarities and differences to gain a balanced picture. Aspects of both form and content can contribute to the analysis (fig. 22.1).

Form

The psalms of the Bible can be classified into three general categories—praise, lament, and wisdom—with a number of subcategories as well. For the most part, each psalm falls into only one of the classifications—one exception being Psalm 22, in which verses 1–21 are a lament psalm and verses 22–31 are a praise psalm. Both the praise and lament psalms have typical characteristics that make them easily identifiable. For instance, the lament psalms generally contain a vocative in the first line (e.g., "O Lord"; cf. Pss. 3–7), and congregational praise psalms almost always start with an imperative call to praise (e.g., "Sing to the Lord"; cf. Pss. 96, 98).

Additionally, each psalm type follows a fairly consistent format. Lament psalms regularly include elements such as complaint, petition, confession of trust, and vow of praise.

The psalms of Mesopotamia do not contain distinctly lament compositions. Instead, lament and praise are characteristically combined into single entities. In this we can see both similarity and difference with the Psalms. The difference lies in the Babylonians' combining praise and lament; the commonality is that Israelites and Babylonians use generally the same forms of lament when they are complaining about deity and similar forms of praise when they are praising deity.

Figure 22.1. Excerpt from a Mesopotamian Psalm
Prayer to the Moon-God

O Sin, O Nannar, glorified one ...,
Sin, unique one, who makes bright ...,
Who furnishes light for the people ...,
To guide the dark-headed people aright ...,
Bright is thy light in heaven ...
Brilliant is thy torch like fire ...
Thy brightness has filled the broad land.
The people are radiant; they take courage at seeing thee.
O Anu of heaven whose designs no one can conceive,
Surpassing is thy light like Shamash thy first-born.
Bowed down in thy presence are the great gods; the decisions of the
    land are laid before thee;
When the great gods inquire of thee thou dost give counsel.
They sit (in) their assembly (and) debate under thee;
O Sin, shining one of Ekur, when they ask thee thou dost give the
    oracle of the gods.
On account of the evil of an eclipse of the moon which took place
    in such and such a month, on such and such a day,
On account of the evil of bad and unfavorable portents and signs
    which have happened in my palace and my country,
In the dark of the moon, the time of thy oracle, the mystery of the
    great gods,
On the thirtieth day, thy festival, the day of delight of thy divinity,
O Namrasit, unequaled in power, whose designs no one can
    conceive,
I have spread out for thee a pure incense-offering of the night; I
    have poured out for thee the best sweet drink.
I am kneeling; I tarry (thus); I seek after thee.
Bring upon me wishes for well-being and justice.
Make my god and my goddess, who for many days have been angry
    with me,
In truth and justice be favorable to me; may my road be propitious;
    may my path be straight.
After he has sent Zaqar, the god of dreams,
During the night may I hear the undoing of my sins; let my guilt be
    poured out;
(And) forever let me devotedly serve thee.

From "Sumero-Akkadian Hymns and Prayers," in *ANET*, 3d ed. (Princeton: Princeton Univ. Press, 1969), 386.

One type of praise, however, is common in the Bible but does not occur in Mesopotamian literature. Israelite psalms manifest both "descriptive praise" and "declarative praise," but only the former appears in Mesopotamia. Descriptive praise extols God for who he is; it focuses on the attributes of God. Declarative praise is usually the praise of a person thanking God for answering his prayer about a specific instance in the past.

Content

In reading the psalms and prayers of the Babylonians, someone who was familiar with the Bible would surely recognize a general similarity in the matters of praise and in the situations that brought complaints to God. Petitions are also similar. Yet many differences would also be immediately apparent. Descriptive praise is of a different nature in the Babylonian materials, where there is a tendency simply to list attributes and epithets (titles) of deities. There is very little of the Israelite imperative approach to praise, in which the hymn requests the worshiper to join in praise to God.

Several differences are also observable in lament psalms. Most obvious is the fact that most of the laments of Mesopotamia are used in conjunction with magical rituals and incantations intended to coerce the deity to comply with the petition. In these rites the Mesopotamian worshiper accepts the idea that the deity considers him or her guilty of offense, though the person has no idea what the offense might be. He or she does not assume that the god is consistent or just; the worshiper merely seeks to appease him by performing the appropriate ritual.

The case in Israel is far different. In the laments in the book of Psalms, the worshiper most frequently considers himself innocent and therefore seeks vindication. There is no hint of magic, incantation, appeasement, or manipulation. When the Israelite author does consider himself guilty (e.g., Ps. 51), the offense is typically of an ethical or moral sort, whereas the offense in the Mesopotamian laments would more likely be cultic (e.g., the failure to offer appropriate sacrifice).

In conclusion, many of the similarities have to do with general content or literary style. The differences are more substantial and most frequently are related directly or indirectly to the contrasting views of God and how he is worshiped. This shows us that from a literary standpoint, the psalms do not represent too great a departure from

Hymns to gods are known throughout the ancient world. This is an Egyptian hymn to Osiris, the god of the netherworld.
Kim Walton, courtesy of the Oriental Institute Museum

what can be found throughout the ancient Near East. The uniqueness of the psalms is found in the way they reflect the theological distinctiveness of Israel.

Purpose and Message

Since we have identified two levels of composer—author and editor—we must also address two levels of purpose.

Author

Very little can be said about purpose at the level of the author. Each author would have had a specific purpose for each composition. Older commentaries have offered suggestions for the historical situation that lay behind each psalm, but this practice was highly speculative and did not produce satisfying results. By contrast, it is probable that many of the compositions were written to meet liturgical needs. More recently some scholars have been inclined to identify festivals or rituals behind each psalm. Unfortunately, our only knowledge of specific rituals comes from other ancient Near Eastern literature. In order to substantiate this theory these scholars must assume that Babylonian festivals (such as the enthronement festival), otherwise unknown in Israel, were adopted, regularly observed, and had a well-developed liturgy. Evidence for this remains very tentative.

"Sit at my right hand until I make your enemies a footstool for your feet" (Ps. 110:1). Here the bound, captive enemies of Egypt are engraved "under the feet" of the giant statue of Pharaoh.
Eric Baker

In the end we must be willing to consider the whole range of possible situations. Some of the psalms would have been motivated by a particular historical occurrence. (For instance, thirteen of them cite historical instances in their titles: 3, 7, 18, 34, 51, 52, 54, 56, 57, 59, 60, 63, 142. All are Davidic, and all but one are in books I or II.) Others would have been written for various liturgical occasions. Still others may have been private devotional thoughts. The point is that there is no unified purpose or message to be identified at the authors' level.

Editor

We have already suggested that Psalms 1 and 2 serve as an introduction to the book as a whole and that the "seam" psalms are instrumental in helping us to discern the editor's agenda. What conclusions can be drawn from these about the editor's purpose and message?

Psalm 1 draws a brief but sharp distinction between the conduct of the righteous person and that of the wicked person. It also addresses their respective destinies. We find that this accurately introduces one of the major themes of Psalms: concern for the vindication of the righteous and the punishment of the wicked.

Psalm 2 presents the idea that God has chosen the Israelite king and will defend him against the conspiracies of the nations. This provides a national aspect to parallel the individual aspect of Psalm 1.

Figure 22.2. A Cantata about the Davidic Covenant

Introduction Psalms 1 – 2		Ps. 1. Ultimate vindication of the righteous Ps. 2. God's choice and defense of Israelite king	
Book	Seam	Theme	Content
Book 1	41	David's conflict with Saul	Many individual laments; most psalms mention enemies
Book 2	72	David's kingship	Key psalms: 45, 18, 51; 54 – 64; mostly laments and "enemy" psalms
Book 3	89	Eighth-century Assyrian crisis	Asaph and Sons of Korah collections; key psalm: 78
Book 4	106	Introspection about destruction of temple and exile	Praise collection: 95 – 100; key psalms: 90, 103 – 105
Book 5	145	Praise/reflection on return from exile and beginning of new era	Halleluyah collection: 111 – 117; Songs of Ascent: 120 – 134; Davidic reprise: 138 – 145; key psalms: 107, 110, 119
Conclusion 146 – 150		Climactic praise to God	

These two levels of message (individual and national) come together in David. He stands as the righteous person who is in need of vindication from God. He is also the king of Israel par excellence who represents not only the nation of Israel, but also all the successive kings of his line. God chose him as king and made a covenant of kingship with him.

The seam psalms, then, help us to see how these two aspects of the editor's message are going to be addressed. In Psalm 72, the seam between books II and III, we see a transition from David to Solomon. This psalm includes elements of both covenanted kingship and righteous rule. Reverting to the seam between books I and II, we can discern a transition from the monarchy of Saul, when David was hunted and persecuted, to David's vindication in coming to the throne after the death of Saul. Psalm 89, the seam between books III and IV, shows a covenant in disarray and a people confused and under siege. This would bring to mind the preexilic monarchy perhaps from Solomon to the fall of Jerusalem as the focus of book III, though it may have more specific reference to the eighth-century Assyrian crisis. The last seam, Psalm 106, is a litany of the failures of Israel and a plea to regather the people from exile, clearly suggesting an exilic context for book IV.

This analysis of Psalms 1 and 2 and the seam psalms has led to the conclusion that the five books of the psalter are intended to trace the history of Israel, particularly with regard to the Davidic covenant, which is the covenant of kingship. Intertwined with this is consideration of the righteous man and his response. The "righteous man" potentially refers to any righteous person in Israel who seeks to understand the national dilemma and cope with the national failures. How does the godly person view the demands on conduct when the nation is going astray and God's actions are not always comprehensible? These are presented as poetic reflections intended to convey the consistency of God's justice and faithfulness to the covenant and the righteous.

David is a prime example of the righteous man vindicated. He was vindicated in his conflict with Saul, in his conflict with Absalom, and ultimately on a national and eschatological scale in the development of the Davidic covenant. This shows us a "wisdom" aspect to the editor's message (the righteous will be vindicated) as it addresses the individual and an "eschatological" aspect (God's commitment to Davidic kingship) addressing the nation.

Structure and Organization

Just as Kings and Chronicles contain theological reflection about God through a recitation of history, so Psalms may use the arrangement of liturgical compositions to reflect on the nature of God and the response of the individual. In many ways, therefore, the psalms would resemble

"Praise him with trumpet sound. Praise him with lute and harp" (Ps. 150:3). Instruments were part of many occasions in the ancient world. This wall painting in the Egyptian tomb of Rekhmire shows musicians playing harp and lute.

a cantata. The arrangement is not based on the circumstances or dates when the psalms were composed, but on other factors. For instance, Psalms 138–145 are in the so-designated postexilic section, yet they are Davidic psalms. Why would the author place them there? This is the kind of question we need to address.

We have seen that the seam psalms and introductory psalms appear to indicate a general agenda, but the question has been raised whether individual psalms or even collections of psalms were set in an order to suit that agenda. Some psalms certainly seem to be placed specifically with the intention of fulfilling the editor's agenda as we have identified it. Among the most persuasive are these:

45　Coronation Hymn for David
48　Correlation to the conquest of Jerusalem by David
51　Repentance concerning sin with Bathsheba
78　Reflection on the fall of Samaria and the northern kingdom
90　Moses' anticipation of exile beginning the exilic section
103　Critical discussion of God's forgiving the sins of the nation
110　The return of victorious kingship with theocratic and eschatological focus
119　Correlation to the establishment of the law as the focus of the postexilic community.

These psalms are all placed exactly where one would expect them to be in a presentation of the sort we have been discussing. There are many

"Great is the LORD and most worthy of praise, in the city of our God, his holy mountain" (Ps. 48:1). Jerusalem during the reign of David was quite different from modern Jerusalem. The walls would have started about where the southern wall is today. The southern spur that was the City of David occupies most of this picture, circumscribed roughly by the road as it stretches to the south of the modern city.

more individual psalms for which a rationale of placement can be identified, suggesting that the editor's work did involve such arranging.

There are also cases in which entire collections seem to have been set in place. We would not expect that all the Asaph psalms were placed together where they are by mere coincidence. It is more logical to assume that the editor used the tone of the Asaph collection or something that stood out in the collection to decide where it would best fit in his cantata.

The best examples of this kind of thematic placement appear in book V. The Halleluyah collection (111–117) appropriately follows

Psalm 110 with its recurring themes of God's faithfulness, deliverance, and theocracy. The "Songs of Ascent" (120–134) were originally composed for the pilgrimage feasts for which thousands of Israelites journeyed to Jerusalem. In this new context they would reflect on *the* return to Jerusalem after decades of exile. The themes of deliverance and trust in God are also quite fitting. Finally, the last Davidic collection (138–145) functions to give David the "last word" before the grand finale. The closing psalm in the group, 145, is particularly well-suited to this purpose.

Much has yet to be done in identifying the rationale of each psalm or collection, but enough is evident to conclude that an editorial intention did exist and that the editorial purpose can be identified, at least in its broad strokes.

Book I contains mostly laments, and many of the psalms make some mention of the psalmist's enemies. As the writer cries out to God for vindication and deliverance, we can easily see the correlation of this book to the time David spent in the wilderness fleeing from Saul. Psalms 3–13 would parallel 1 Samuel 19–23, the beginning of David's troubles with Saul. Psalm 18 reports deliverance from enemies and could correlate to 1 Samuel 24, where David spares Saul's life and Saul stops the chase. Psalms 23–24 appear strikingly appropriate to 1 Samuel 25, when God provides for David's needs through the wisdom of Abigail. Parallels to David's second sparing of Saul's life can be seen in Psalms 27–30. In general the tone of the psalms in the first book fits well with this period in David's life.

We have already mentioned some of the individual psalms in book II (45, 48, 51). As a whole the psalms can be correlated with the events of David's reign as recorded in 2 Samuel. Another major section of laments in Psalms 54–64 would parallel the crisis represented in Absalom's rebellion, with David being driven from the throne by his own son (note esp. 55:12–14, 21).

Book III is more difficult to assess than the other books. This is because it is composed of two collections that, we assume, have been placed according to chronology. Psalm 78 appears to offer the most insight to its orientation, with a possible correlation to the fall of the northern kingdom. Because the seam psalm (89) offers a crisis and, apparently, a resolution of the crisis, the book may be limited to the Assyrian crisis in the latter half of the eighth century BC, though it could refer to the entire period from Solomon to the fall of Jerusalem.

Book IV begins with a psalm of Moses and ends with a recapitulation of a history of rebellion, leading to a hope and a plea for restoration. Along the way it includes a small collection of praise psalms (95–100) that appropriately presents the affirmations of hope and faith sustained in the exile. Themes in this small collection include the Lord as King, a new song, deliverance, idol worshipers put to shame, Yahweh above all gods, judgment on the nations, and the continuing faithfulness of the Lord. Psalm 102 is a fitting plea for the Lord to have compassion on Zion. The book concludes with a series (104–106) surveying the mighty and gracious deeds of the Lord, from creation and sovereignty, to election and covenant, to the rebellion and failures of the people.

Finally, book V begins with Psalm 107, the Israelites' thankfulness to God for regathering them. The roles of Psalm 110, of Psalm 119, and of the three collections in this book have already been discussed. Psalm 145 provides a conclusion to book V, while Psalms 146–150 serve as the finale to the entire cantata.

Major Themes

Two of the major themes in the book of Psalms are those introduced in Psalms 1 and 2: the retribution principle and kingship.

The Retribution Principle: Part 2

The retribution principle can be summed up in two two-part affirmations: (1) The righteous will prosper and the wicked will suffer, and (2) those who prosper are righteous, while those who suffer are wicked. The first of these affirmations is generally supported in Psalms and throughout Scripture (cf. Ps. 1). It was acknowledged, however, that exceptions existed (compare the English proverb "crime doesn't pay").

Some of the biblical psalms were written to be accompanied by stringed instruments (Pss. 4, 6, 54, 55, 61, 67, 76). This wall painting in the tomb of the Egyptian scribe Jeserkareseneb (15th century BC) shows a man and woman playing stringed instruments.

Werner Forman Archive

The second affirmation, although it is not given the support of Scripture, was clearly believed by many Israelites. This is obvious from the actions and concerns of Job's friends, as related in the book of Job, and also from the statements in many of the psalms (e.g., Ps. 37).

For the Israelites, this principle was a theological issue: If God is a just God, how can the righteous suffer or the wicked prosper? Though this question still perplexes even at times today, the situation was much worse for the ancient Israelites. The reason is that today we find consolation in the belief that even if the righteous person does not prosper here on earth, he or she has the expectation of heaven. Likewise, we are assured that the wicked will face the judgment of God for eternity rather than escape unscathed. Because of these assurances, the justice of God is not so seriously questioned, although we continue to struggle with theology as we try to cope with our circumstances.

The ancient Israelites did not have the advantage of these assurances. God had not yet revealed to them the fact that judgment of the righteous and wicked would take place after death with each group receiving just rewards. All that the Israelites knew of God's justice was its execution in this life (cf. Pss. 27.13, 91:5-8). This made the retribution principle a much more serious matter for them than for us.

The lament psalms reflect this concern the most. The psalmist complains to the Lord because enemies have gained the upper hand even though the psalmist is the righteous one. He pleads for God to intervene and put his enemies to shame and in so doing vindicate him. The psalmist does not consider himself absolutely righteous, but he is more righteous than his enemy, and he feels he certainly does not deserve the degree of persecution that has come his way.

The degree of persecution or suffering is important, because if God is just, the wicked person should suffer in proportion to his wickedness and the righteous person should prosper in proportion to his righteousness. It is not just for a very wicked person to be punished in a very small way.

This observation can help us understand what is often considered one of the most difficult problems in the book of Psalms. Several of the lament psalms include a curse or imprecation on the writer's enemies—sometimes of a general sort (28:4), sometimes more specific (137:9). Some whole psalms are devoted to this type of expression (58, 109). Once we understand the need for the retribution principle to be carried out proportionately, we can see that these pleas for God's judgment are simply an outgrowth of beliefs about who God is and how he will act. Desperately wicked people had to be punished by God in drastic ways if his justice were to be upheld. The specific call for drastic punishment was the psalmist's way of asserting how wicked his enemy was, emphasizing the need for God to exercise his justice by righteous judgment.

Psalms as a book confirms that it is legitimate for righteous people to expect God to prosper them for their righteousness and for God to bring the destruction of the wicked. It is never promised, however, that there will be no exceptions to that general rule. David is held up as an example of a righteous man who was vindicated, and it is in the nature of God to work in that way. But life is not always that simple,

Excursus: Devotional Use of the Psalms

The book of Psalms uses the praise, complaint, and exhortation of God's people to reveal the character of God. As readers to whom the authority of God's Word is important, our task is to submit ourselves to the God who is here revealed. Praise psalms extol the attributes and actions of God and compel us to kneel before him. Wisdom psalms explore theological principles for means to comprehend God's ways. Lament psalms help us to see God through the emotional struggles of a believer in crisis who is thrown to dependence on him.

The historical books help us learn more about God by telling us his stories. The psalms give us a different perspective by helping us come into contact with God through our daily experiences and the questions that arise from them. When journalists want to find out about a person, they don't just read the biography, they also interview the people who knew him or her best. When someone applies for a job, the employer doesn't stop with reading the applicant's resume, but also checks the references. These analogies show the difference in how the historical literature and the psalms reveal God to us. Unquestionably, an interview or references are more likely to be subjective than a biography or resume. But the subjective aspect can be just as important a guide to knowing the individual.

When we relate to God day by day, it is usually this subjective aspect that poses the hard questions. We often grapple with affirming God's attributes, not because we have philosophical reservations, but because our experience leads us to question his attributes. The true affirmation of his attributes comes through acknowledging them even when our life experiences do not seem to support them. That is the long-term effect that Psalms should have on us. Affirmation of God's attributes is the goal of our devotional reading. This process prepares us for or sustains us through trial and loss. It likewise keeps God in focus and everything in perspective when life goes smoothly.

Even in our devotional use of psalms, however, we must be careful to interpret properly. We cannot allow our picture of God or our expectations of him to be distorted by twisting or manipulating the information given about him to our own advantage. The fact that God prospered or delivered someone in a particular situation is testimony to what God can do, not a promise that he will always do so for us. Each psalm and the book of Psalms as a whole contribute to our understanding of God. Though this composite picture of God may serve to satisfy our emotional ups and downs, it still must be developed from the text. We cannot afford a distorted picture of God derived from an uninformed handling of the text, for especially in times of crisis we must avoid misleading ourselves with false hopes dependent on misconstrued promises.

and Scripture does not offer a firm rule that will hold in every case. The book of Job has already shown us that answers to the hard situations in life are not always forthcoming. Psalms also teaches us that trust in the sovereign will of God is proper, whatever one's circumstances.

Kingship

There are nine psalms scattered through the psalter that specifically concern the king: 2, 18, 21, 45, 72, 89, 110, 132, 144. Of these, four are attributed to David (18, 21, 110, 144), and three have important editorial functions (2, 72, 89). They are at times considered messianic psalms, and in terms of the continuum that exists from David through his dynasty to the eventual ideal Davidic king (Messiah), that is accurate. Nevertheless, in most cases it is inappropriate to see these psalms as dealing specifically and exclusively with the ideal Davidic king. More often than not, they are more generic and could be applied to any Davidic monarch.

Psalm 2 sets the tone with the affirmation of the Lord's choice and protection of the king. Psalm 18 praises God for delivering the king from his enemies (vv. 37–50). Many of the psalms in this set either ask for deliverance, victory, or blessing for the king or discuss the covenant that established kingship. It is affirmed that God promised victorious kingship to the kings who trust in him and that he is fully able to carry out that promise. This is best viewed as relating to the future ideal king, for there was not an abundance of kings in David's line who trusted the Lord. In contrast, the coming, ideal king would exercise perfect trust and would therefore enjoy all the blessings of God on his reign.

Nature and Creation

Several praise psalms focus on God's relationship to nature. This was an important matter to address for several reasons. Israel was an agricultural community, which means that the people were dependent on the climate for their livelihood and even their survival. God's favor or disfavor was most easily inferred from the bounty of the harvest. The blessings and curses connected to the covenant were tied to the produce of the land.

Another reason for this emphasis is that much popular theology of the day concerned the world around them. The gods the Canaanites most highly esteemed were fertility gods, and most of the foreign gods were intertwined with the forces of nature. It was important, then, for the God of the Israelites to be distinguished from these other gods; he is not bound by nature or identified with the forces of nature in the same way.

In the psalms addressing God and his creation (8, 19, 29, 65, 104) several important points are established. God is the Creator and maintains and orders all of creation (104). Creation and nature reveal the glory of God (19). Humankind has been placed at the head of creation (8). The forces of nature are instruments of his power and blessing (29, 65). God is thereby elevated above nature in a way that was not possible in the polytheistic systems of the ancient Near East.

Questions for Further Study and Discussion

1. How can the reader of Psalms find a balance between the message of each psalm as an individual composition and the message of each psalm as a part of the larger whole? Is either aspect more important than the other?
2. What is the significance of the psalm types for interpreting the book of Psalms?
3. How does the retribution principle apply today?
4. How and when might lament psalms be used in corporate worship?
5. How do we strike a balance between the contextual view of the royal psalms and the messianic view? How does a passage such as Luke 20:41–44 affect our view?
6. How should our understanding of the form, content, purpose, and message of the book affect our devotional use of psalms?

For Further Reading

Allen, Leslie. *Psalms 101–150*. WBC. Waco, Tex.: Word, 1983.

Anderson, A. A. *Psalms*. NCB. 2 vols. Grand Rapids: Eerdmans, 1972.

Anderson, B. W. *Out of the Depths*. Philadelphia: Westminster, 1983.

Bullock, C. Hassell. *Encountering the Book of Psalms*. Grand Rapids: Baker, 2001.

Craigie, Peter. *Psalms 1–50*. WBC. Waco, Tex.: Word, 1983. The best evangelical commentary on Psalms.

Goldingay, John. *Psalms*. Vol. 1: *Psalms 1–41*. Grand Rapids: Baker, 2006.

Hayes, John H. *Understanding the Psalms*. Valley Forge, Pa.: Judson, 1976.

Firth, David, and Philip Johnston. *Interpreting the Psalms: Issues and Approaches*. Downers Grove, Ill.: InterVarsity Press, 2006.

Johnston, Philip S. *Shades of Sheol*. Downers Grove, Ill.: InterVarsity Press, 2002.

Kidner, Derek. *Psalms 1–72* and *Psalms 73–150*. TOTC 14a, b. Downers Grove, Ill.: InterVarsity Press, 1973, 1975.

Kraus, Hans-J. *Psalms 1–59*. Minneapolis: Augsburg Press, 1988. Most helpful commentary from a nonevangelical perspective.

_____. *Psalms 60–150*. Minneapolis: Augsburg Press, 1989.

_____. *Theology of the Psalms*. Trans. by Keith Crim. Minneapolis: Augsburg Press, 1986.

Lewis, C. S. *Reflections on the Psalms*. New York: Harcourt, 1958.

Longman, Tremper, III. *How to Read the Psalms*. Downers Grove, Ill.: InterVarsity Press, 1988. An excellent introduction to the book.

McCann, J. Clinton. *A Theological Introduction to the Book of Psalms*. Nashville: Abingdon Press, 1993.

Miller, Patrick. *Interpreting the Psalms*. Philadelphia: Fortress Press, 1986.

Van Gemeren, Wilhelm. "Psalms." *EBC*. Vol. 5. Grand Rapids: Zondervan, 1991. 3–860.

Walton, John H. "The Psalms: A Cantata about the Davidic Covenant." *JETS* 34 (1991): 21–31.

Westermann, Claus. *Praise and Lament in the Psalms*. 1965. Reprint, Atlanta: John Knox, 1981. The forerunner for treatment of the psalm types.

Wilson, Gerald. "Evidence of Editorial Divisions in the Hebrew Psalter." *VT* 34 (1984): 337–52.

_____. "The Function of Untitled Psalms in the Hebrew Psalter." *Zeitschrift für die alttestamentliche Wissenschaft* 97 (1985).

_____. "The Qumran Psalms Manuscripts and the Consecutive Arrangement of Psalms in the Hebrew Psalter." *CBQ* 45 (1983): 377–88.

_____. "The Use of Royal Psalms at the 'Seams' of the Hebrew Psalter." *JSOT* 35 (1986): 85–94.

_____. *Psalms*. Vol. 1. NIVAC. Grand Rapids: Zondervan, 2002.

"Wisdom has built her house; she has hewn out its seven pillars" (Prov. 9:1). This is a massive structure at Luxor, Egypt, with seven sets of pillars.
Frederick J. Mabie

PROVERBS

Key Ideas
- The fear of the Lord is the beginning of wisdom.
- The way of wisdom leads to life.
- A proverb illustrates a general principle, not a promise.
- Wisdom leads to an understanding of the retribution principle.

Purpose Statement

The purpose of the book of Proverbs is to collect the wisdom of ancient Israel and offer both instruction and example in godly living. The wisdom compiled in the book functioned to shape character and promote virtue in keeping with the commandments of Moses. More specifically, the purpose of the book is stated in the prologue to the wisdom collections and may be summarized as a lifestyle of knowing wisdom and instruction and learning the fear of the Lord (1:2–7).

Major Themes
- The Fear of the Lord
- The Retribution Principle: Part 3
- Human Speech
- Human Sexuality

God's Presence

God's presence is manifest in the book of Proverbs in the personification of wisdom (chaps. 8, 9), since God is the source and giver of wisdom, and in the theological principle of the fear of the Lord rooted in Israel's covenant relationship with Yahweh.

The Retribution Principle: Part 3

The retribution principle expressed in the blessings and curses of the Pentateuchal covenant formulas resurfaces in the wisdom literature of the Old Testament. The expectation of reward for the nation's conformity to the law of God is logically applied to the individual Hebrew "God-fearer" in the proverbial wisdom.

The tangible benefits of walking in the way of wisdom are conditioned by two important assumptions of the sages. First, proverbial wisdom presumes that the "vertical" dimension of covenant relationship with Yahweh has been a firmly established pattern of life. The practice of covenant loyalty and faithfulness is presupposed as part of a godly lifestyle. Second, the "blessings" of the path of wisdom are contingent on the premise that the "horizontal" dimensions of covenant relationship with Yahweh have been demonstrated practically in doing what is "right and just and fair" (Prov 2:9).

More important, the "ideal" paradigm of obedience—an adherence to the way of wisdom that naturally yields the "profits" of prosperity, peace, health, and long life—is qualified by the reality of human sin and the "crookedness" of a fallen world. So the Preacher reminds us that the race is not always won by the swift, nor the battle by the strong, but "time and chance happen to them all" (Eccl. 9:11–12).

The truisms of Proverbs are not absolute promises, but general principles based on careful observation of the human experience. The psalmist recognized the inherent flaw of mechanically ascribing the corporate blessings and curses of covenant law to the individual situation (e.g., Ps. 73). Here the writer questions his life of integrity in the face of the apparent ease and success of the wicked. Not until he

The Instruction of Amenemope is an Egyptian wisdom composition that contains numerous parallels to Proverbs 22–23. It exalts a life of contemplation and endurance rather than a fast-paced and "successful" life.

entered the Lord's sanctuary did he gain perspective on the incongruities of life. Even Job's rebuttal to the "counsel" of his friends mocked a rigid interpretation of the retribution principle, as he satirically noted "the tents of marauders are undisturbed" (Job 12:1–6).

Finally, equal attention must be given to character development as part of the benefits of walking in the way of wisdom. More than material prosperity, the better fruits of understanding are the qualities of personal character such as discretion, prudence, wise dealing, righteous behavior, justice, and integrity. In fact, the words translated "prosperity" in Proverbs 13:21 and 21:21 (NIV) are better rendered "well-being" and "righteousness" respectively. Ultimately the way of wisdom is keeping to the path of righteousness, because only men and women of integrity will remain in the land (2:20–21).

Human Speech

The book of Proverbs has much to say about the use and abuse of the "tongue." In fact, three of the abominations in the warning against the seven sins God hates are directly related to human speech. Wisdom teaching on human speech in Proverbs can be summarized as follows.[2]

First, words have great power, for even death and life are in the power of the tongue (18:21). They may be used to wound or heal one's spirit (12:18; 15:4), shape attitudes and perceptions (18:8; 29:5), and form beliefs and convictions (10:21; 11:9). But the mouths of the wicked spread discord and strife like a "scorching fire" (16:27–28), in contrast to the mouth of the righteous, which is like a fountain or tree of life dispensing truth and knowledge (10:11; 15:2, 4, 7).

Second, words are sometimes futile as well. Human speech cannot serve as a substitute for concerted action (14:23), nor can it change the facts or conceal hidden motives or disguise one's inner character (24:12; 26:23–28).

Finally, Proverbs gives instructions on human speech at its best. The words of the wise spring from righteous character and reflective deliberation (12:17; 14:5). The words of the wise are marked by the qualities of honesty (16:13), brevity (10:14), serenity (15:1), and aptness (15:23).

Human Sexuality

The wisdom of Proverbs extols the virtue of (monogamous) marriage and warns against the folly of sexual license. The insights of the Hebrew sages on the intricacies of the male-female relationship remain a valid resource for addressing the problems associated with human sexuality in the modern era. The biblical affirmations, admonitions, and guidelines for this aspect of human life include

2. This is a summary of Derek Kidner's excellent essay on the theme "Words." See *The Proverbs: An Introduction and Commentary*, TOTC (London: Tyndale, 1964), 46–49.

- The value of wisdom instruction as an antidote for sexual sin (2:16)
- The sanctity of marriage and the appropriateness of erotic (heterosexual) love within marital bonds (5:15–23; 18:22)
- The need to guard and discipline the "eyes" and "mouth," as these are the primary gates for the temptations that lead to unchastity (5:1–6; 7:21–23; cf. Job 31:1)
- Being aware of the destructiveness of jealousy stemming from adultery (6:20–35)
- Being aware of the dangers spawned by "idleness" (7:6–9)
- The importance of the family unit in teaching and enforcing sexual mores (7:1–5, 24–27)
- Being aware of the subtlety of sexual sins (23:26–28)
- The easy manner in which sexual sins are rationalized, thus hardening the heart to godly moral principles (7:14–20; 30:20)
- The need to evaluate and choose a marriage partner based on internal standards related to character, not external standards related to physical attraction and "sex appeal" (31:10–31; cf. 1 Peter 3:1–6)
- The necessity for mates to avoid quarreling and maintain open channels of communication (19:13; 27:15)

In many respects, the instructions of Proverbs on human sexuality and marriage constitute a practical commentary on the Genesis account of the creation of man and woman and their union as one flesh (Gen. 2:18–25).

Questions for Further Study and Discussion

1. What is "the fear of the Lord"? How does this idea relate to the teachings of the law of Moses?
2. What does Proverbs 31:10–31 suggest about the role of some women in ancient Israel?
3. How is the content of the New Testament book of James similar to the wisdom of Proverbs?

For Further Reading

Atkinson, David. *The Message of Proverbs*. Downers Grove, Ill.: InterVarsity Press, 1996.

Garrett, Duane, A. *Proverbs, Ecclesiastes, Song of Songs*. NAC. Vol. 14. Nashville: Broadman, 1993. 347–432. Includes a useful summary of the various interpretive approaches to the book.

Kidner, Derek. *The Proverbs: An Introduction and Commentary*. TOTC. London: Tyndale, 1964. Useful introductory section on the themes of Proverbs.

Koptak, Paul E. *Proverbs*. NIVAC. Grand Rapids: Zondervan, 2003.

Longman, Tremper, III. *How to Read Proverbs*. Downers Grove, Ill.: InterVarsity Press, 2002. Practical guide to interpreting and applying biblical wisdom to everyday life.

_____. *Proverbs*. Grand Rapids: Baker, 2006.

McKane, W. *Proverbs: A New Approach*. OTL. Philadelphia: Westminster, 1970. Highly specialized and technical study, somewhat ponderous; demanding but rewarding reading.

Mouser, W. E. *Walking in Wisdom: Studying the Proverbs of Solomon*. Downers Grove, Ill.: InterVarsity Press, 1983. A most readable introductory guide to the literary forms of Proverbs, with emphasis on interpreting biblical wisdom and its contemporary application.

Murphy, Roland E. *Proverbs*. WBC 22. Nashville: Word, 1998.

Ross, Allen P. "Proverbs." *EBC*. Vol. 5. Grand Rapids: Zondervan, 1991. 883–1134.

Scott, R. B. Y. *Proverbs, Ecclesiastes*. AB. Vol. 18. Garden City, N.Y.: Doubleday, 1965. A good introduction to wisdom literature in general.

Thompson, J. M. *The Form and Function of Proverbs in Israel*. The Hague: Mouton, 1974.

van Leeuwen, Raymond. "Proverbs." *NIB* 5:19–264. Nashville: Abingdon Press, 1997. Solid exegetical analysis and theological reflection from a progressive evangelical perspective.

"What does man gain from all his labor at which he toils under the sun?" (Eccl. 1:3).
Labor under the hot sun of the Middle East would be very difficult and would not be
worth the effort unless good compensation were involved. This stone relief from the
palace of Sennacherib shows prisoners being forced by guards to work in a stone quarry.

Werner Forman Archive/The British Museum

ECCLESIASTES

Key Ideas
- Life should not be expected to be self-fulfilling.
- Frustrations in life are unavoidable.
- The seasons of life must be accepted.
- Enjoyment of life comes only through a God-centered worldview.

Purpose Statement
The purpose of the book of Ecclesiastes is to demonstrate that there is nothing in life that is able to bring self-fulfillment or give meaning to life. Frustration and troubles are unavoidable, and we should not expect answers to why things happen. Rather than pursuing self-fulfillment, we should enjoy the good things of life as a gift from God. We should recognize that troubles help to shape us as people. A God-centered approach to life accepts both success and adversity as coming from the hand of God.

Major Themes
- The Retribution Principle: Part 4
- Experience vs. Revelation
- Epicureanism vs. Piety

God's Presence
Because it is interested in exploring life "under the sun" it offers very little reflection on the presence of God and does not advance this theme.

one's case. Qoheleth built his case without any presupposition about revelation. He made no reference to the Law or the Prophets, and nothing was said about Israel's place in God's plan or the covenant. His approach was philosophical and based on experience and wisdom. The absence of the standard Israelite elements of theology does not suggest ignorance or rejection of them by Qoheleth, but may reflect an attempt to address a wider audience.

Epicureanism vs. Piety

Some have worried about Qoheleth's "enjoy life" philosophy. It has seemed perhaps too close to the Epicurean dictum "Eat, drink, and be merry, for tomorrow we die." Moreover, he said little about a life of piety, faith, or even good works. What of discipline, virtue, and morality? Where is repentance or a sense of sinfulness? We must recognize that the book of Ecclesiastes is not intended to be a systematic theology. Qoheleth's primary purpose was to establish that life "under the sun" cannot offer fulfillment and to offer an alternate worldview. The philosophy expressed is not simply "enjoy life," but "enjoy life and fear God." This is not abandonment of all for a life of pleasure; it is a responsible, optimistic integration of life and faith. The result is that few books of the Bible offer as clear a challenge to our contemporary Western worldview. Enjoyment of life comes not in the quest for personal fulfillment, but in the recognition that everything comes from the hand of God.

Questions for Further Study and Discussion

1. Should the Christian seek fulfillment in life? Explain "fulfillment" in your answer.
2. What are the practical results of viewing adversity with attention to purpose rather than cause?
3. What advice would Qoheleth offer Job?
4. Compare Qoheleth's approach to experience with the similar approach offered by C. S. Lewis in *Mere Christianity* (New York: Macmillan, 1986).

For Further Reading

Brown, W. *Ecclesiastes*. Interpretation. Louisville: Westminster John Knox, 2000.

Crenshaw, James L. *Ecclesiastes*. OTL. Philadelphia: Westminster, 1987.

Eaton, Michael. *Ecclesiastes*. Downers Grove, Ill.: InterVarsity Press, 1983. The most helpful of the evangelical commentaries.

Fox, Michael. *A Time to Tear Down and a Time to Build Up*. Grand Rapids: Eerdmans, 1999.

Gordis, Robert. *Koheleth: The Man and His World*. New York: Schocken, 1968.

Krüger, Thomas. *Qoheleth*. Minneapolis: Fortress Press, 2004.

Loader, J. A. *Ecclesiastes: A Practical Commentary*. Grand Rapids: Eerdmans, 1986. Not evangelical, but very stimulating insight into the book.

Lohfink, Norbert. *Qoheleth*. Minneapolis: Fortress Press, 2003.

Longman, Tremper, III. *Book of Ecclesiastes*. Grand Rapids: Eerdmans, 1998.

Moore, T. M. *Ecclesiastes: Ancient Wisdom When All Else Fails*. Downers Grove, Ill.: InterVarsity Press, 2001.

Ogden, Graham. *Qoheleth*. Sheffield, England: JSOT Press, 1987.

Provan, Iain W. *Ecclesiastes/Song of Songs*. NIVAC. Grand Rapids: Zondervan, 2001.

Seow, Chung-Leong. *Ecclesiastes*. Garden City, N.Y.: Doubleday, 1997.

Whybray, R. N. *Ecclesiastes*. NCBC. Grand Rapids: Eerdmans, 1989.

Zuck, Roy B., ed. *Reflecting with Solomon*. Grand Rapids: Baker, 1995.

CHAPTER
25

"Come away, my lover, and be like a gazelle or like a young stag on the spice-laden mountains" (Song 8:14). The Song writer was comparing the lover to a gazelle such as this one at En Gedi.

SONG OF SONGS

Key Ideas

- The goodness of humanity created male and female in God's image
- The dignity of human affections
- The sanctity of human sexual expression in the context of marriage
- The virtue of chastity before marriage and the virtue of faithfulness once married

Purpose Statement

The love poetry of the Songs celebrates the male-female relationship established by God at creation and the goodness of human sexual love expressed within the confines of God-ordained marriage.

Major Theme

- Positive dimensions of human love

God's Presence

The reflections in the Songs on the Genesis ideal of the male-female relationship recalls the intimate relationship humanity had with God before the Fall (Gen. 1–2). The associations of the power of love with death and jealousy may also hint at the divine presence since God loves his creation and his people Israel with a love as strong as death and his jealousy for his covenant(s) is like a burning fire (8:6–7).

467

Outline

One of the problems associated with the interpretation of the Song of Songs is identifying clearly who is speaking in the love poetry. Attempts to outline the Song are as numerous and varied as the interpretive approaches to the content of the book. The following outline assumes that the love poem relates the story of three primary characters (the Shulammite maiden, the shepherd lover, and King Solomon) in a series of sequential events.[1] The major headings or sections of the outline are essentially adaptations of the book divisions as found in the works of Calvin Seerveld and C. Hassell Bullock.[2]

I. Superscription (1:1)

II. The Shulammite Maiden in Solomon's Harem (1:2–3:5)
    A. The King and the Maiden Banter (1:2–2:2)
    B. The Maiden Seeks Her Absent Lover (2:3–3:5)

III. Solomon Woos the Shulammite Maiden (3:6–7:9)
    A. Solomon's First Proposal (3:6–5:8)
    B. Solomon's Second Proposal (5:9–7:9)

IV. The Shulammite Maiden Rejects King Solomon (7:10–8:4)

V. The Shulammite Maiden and the Shepherd-Lover Are Reunited (8:5–14)
    A. Maiden's Brothers See the Lovers Approaching (8:5a)
    B. Maiden Addresses Her Shepherd-Lover (8:5b–7)
    C. Maiden's Brothers Reminisce about Their Sister (8:8–9)
    D. Maiden Boasts of Her Chastity (8:10–12)
    E. Shepherd Beckons the Maiden for a Song (8:13)
    F. Maiden Responds in Song (8:14)

1. Note that although the authors of this survey appeal to the New International Version in Scripture quotations, they take an approach different from the NIV's presentation of the Song as a two-character love story.

2. Calvin Seerveld, *The Greatest Song* (Amsterdam: Trinity Pennyasheet Press, 1967); C. Hassell Bullock, *An Introduction to the Old Testament Poetic Books*, 2nd ed. (Chicago: Moody Press, 1988), 242–55.

The book takes its title from a phrase in the opening verse (1:1) and is variously understood as "The Song (of Songs)," "Songs," "Song of Solomon," or even "Best Song." The alternative name "Canticles" is derived from the Latin Vulgate version, which entitles the book *Canticum Canticorum* (Song of Songs).

The Song is placed among the books of wisdom and poetry in the Septuagint and most English versions. While not classified as wisdom literature in the strict sense, the Song shares some affinities with biblical wisdom in that the book is associated with wise King Solomon (1 Kings 4:29–34), concerns itself with the mystery of humanity created male and female, and offers instruction (at least implicitly) on behavior related to sexuality and marriage. The Song is grouped first among the five festival scrolls (**Megilloth**) in the Hebrew canon, and in later Judaism it was designated to be read as part of the Passover Feast, since it was understood to represent God's love for Israel.

The Writing of the Book

Traditional biblical scholarship has attributed the Song of Songs to King Solomon and dated the poetry to the late tenth century BC, largely on the strength of the book's title verse (1:1). Some ancient Jewish writers credit the work to King Hezekiah, the king of Judah who is accorded a prominent place in the preservation of Israelite wisdom literature (Prov. 25:1; cf. 2 Chron. 32:27–29).

The Amarna period art (14th century BC) is characterized by loving scenes between husband, wife, and children. This painting shows a couple in a garden scene reminiscent of some of the descriptions in the Song of Songs.

Allan Hise, courtesy of the Ägyptisches Museum, Berlin

The problems of authorship and the date of the Song are closely entwined. The inconclusive nature of the book's title further complicates the matter. The phraseology of the title verse or superscription may be understood variously as "of/to/for/about Solomon" (cf. the notations in Psalms 3:1; 4:1; 5:1; et al.). Thus, the title may imply that Solomon was the author of the poetry, that it was dedicated to him, or that it represents songs composed about him as a primary character in the action. Although Solomon's name occurs six times elsewhere in the book (1:5; 3:7, 9, 11; 8:11–12) and other Scripture attests his literary skill (1 Kings 4:29–34), these references assert nothing concerning his authorship of the book. Instead, they merely confirm Solomon's role as a key figure in the love story.

Another factor influencing informed opinion on the authorship and date of the book deserves mention. The interpretive stance adopted by the individual translator-commentator determines in large measure how one (1) outlines the text, (2) understands the poetry in respect to plot development, and (3) identifies the number of characters active in the story. This in turn colors the way one arranges and evaluates the various strands of evidence bearing on the questions of authorship and date.

For example, those who contend that the love story is a drama with two characters are likely to focus attention on the exotic vocabulary, the abundance of references to flora and fauna, and the apparent unity

Love poems were well known in the ancient world. In Egypt they are most prominent in the 18th and 19th dynasties (15th–12th centuries BC). In Mesopotamia they are often connected to sacred marriage festivals. Although this Old Babylonian scene is not part of the sacred marriage ritual, one part reads, "My beloved is sweet as honey, she is as fragrant to the nose as wine."
The Schoyen Collection MS 2866, Oslo and London

of geography within the poems and therefore decide on a date in the Solomonic age, if not Solomonic authorship (cf. 1 Kings 4:32–34). By contrast, those who understand the poetry as a love triangle with King Solomon cast as "the villain" would suggest a setting in the northern kingdom of Israel during the early period of the divided monarchies. A scholar using the typological or cultic approach would emphasize the linguistic features (e.g., Aramaic, Persian, and Greek influence) and the device of "literary fiction" in the poetry, in which Solomon represents "the great lover," and conclude that the book should be dated to the Persian period.

Given the uncertainties associated with understanding the title verse (1:1) and the unusual nature of the book's vocabulary and style, the Song of Songs is best regarded as an anonymous composition. The weight of literary, historical, and linguistic evidence seems to indicate a northern kingdom **provenance** and an early preexilic date for the writing of the book. Attempts to be more precise than this are tenuous and return relatively little benefit for the overall comprehension of the message and meaning of the love songs.

Historical Background

Aside from the ambiguous references to King Solomon (1:1, 5; 3:7, 9, 11; 8:11–12), clear historical parallels or allusions are lacking in the Song. Other than citing the reign of Solomon in general (ca. 970–930 BC), little else can be said about the historical background of the book. It is very likely that the love poetry reflects actual events associated with the reign of Solomon, possibly those summarized by the Old Testament historians in 1 Kings 3–11 and 2 Chronicles 1–9.

Solomon was dominated by sensuality, a trait he shared with his father David. This character flaw was evidenced in the extravagance of his kingship and the size of his royal harem, and eventually proved to be his undoing (cf. 1 Kings 4:20–28; 10:14–29; 11:1–3). Ironically, the sage who counseled young men against the wiles of the "foreign" woman was trapped in her snares (Prov. 5:1–23; 7:1–7; cf. 1 Kings 11:4–13).

Interpretation of the Book

No single book of the Old Testament has proved more perplexing for biblical interpreters than the Song of Songs. Centuries of careful study by scholars of various religious traditions and theological persuasions have produced little interpretive consensus. There are three primary reasons for the impasse.

First, the theme, the topic, and the frank language of the Song have confused, shocked, and embarrassed both Jewish and Christian readers—so much so that for generations the rabbis and early church fathers debated the value of the book and its place in the Old Testament.

Second, the nature and structure of love poetry does not lend itself to easy analysis. Much of the language of the book is unusual, if not unique and obscure, making translation and interpretation difficult. By definition, lyrical poetry is brief in length, concentrated in meaning, and often lacking smooth transitions. This poses a dilemma for commentators seeking to divide the book into smaller logical units. It also means uncertainty for identifying the number of characters in the love story and assigning these smaller units of speech to specific persons.

Third, the book is unfocused sociologically in that its setting is ambiguous, historical backgrounds and characterizations are vague, and the text seems to assume the moral teaching of earlier Old Testament books.

The several major interpretive approaches to the Song that have emerged over the years of scholarly study and analysis are summarized below.

1. *Dramatic.* The dramatic approach understands the Song as an ancient Hebrew play. This view, visible in church tradition since the third century AD, is based largely on analogy to Greek tragic drama, which developed in the sixth century BC. The poetry is considered a dramatic script intended for royal entertainment. The play, whether acted or sung, is usually outlined in six acts, each with two scenes. Speeches are assigned to the principal characters (two or three, depending on whether the shepherd is one and the same with the king), with the "daughters of Jerusalem" (or harem) represented by a female chorus.

Fig. 25.1. Interpreting Lyric Love Poetry

Leland Ryken's description of "lyric" poetry is a helpful guide to understanding the literary nature and the message of the lyric love poetry of the Song of Songs.* Several features characteristic of lyric poetry are present in the Songs, including

- A unifying theme that controls the entire poem ("Love is as strong as death," 8:6)
- Personal and subjective expressions of thought and feeling (e.g., "Arise, my darling, my beautiful one, and come with me," 2:10)
- Emphasis on emotion (e.g., "If you find my lover … tell him I am faint with love," 5:8)
- Concentrated intensity and compressed action (e.g., "I slept but my heart was awake," 5:2)
- Abrupt shifts in scene and between characters (see the outline above)

*Leland Ryken, *How to Read the Bible as Literature* (Grand Rapids: Zondervan, 1984), 109 – 14.

Terracota models such as this scene of a couple embracing seem to have been connected to fertility rituals.
Caryn Reeder, courtesy of the British Museum

2. *Typological.* The typological model recognizes the historicity of the book (whether it commemorates Solomon's marriage to the pharaoh's daughter or recounts the king's wooing of a Shulammite maiden) but subordinates the literal presentation of Old Testament history to a correspondent New Testament pattern of parallel. The traditional "type-antitype" fulfillment is read as God's covenant relationship to Israel by the Jewish interpreter or Christ's relationship to the church as his bride by the Christian interpreter.

3. *Cultic.* The cultic, or mythological, approach views the Song as a Hebrew adaptation of Mesopotamian fertility cult liturgy. Proponents argue that the word *beloved* is in fact a reference to the god Dod (at least in 5:9). Dod was the Syro-Palestinian equivalent of Tammuz in the Sumero-Akkadian Tammuz-Ishtar cult. The annual ritual was a reenactment of the ancient myth recounting the goddess Ishtar's search for her dead lover (Tammuz) in the netherworld, finally restoring him to life through sexual union and thus ensuring the continued fertility of the creation. It is assumed that the cultic associations of the Song were forgotten or consciously changed to make the book acceptable to Israelite faith.

4. *Wedding cycle.* Understanding the book as a wedding cycle assumes the Song is a collection of nuptial poems similar to the *wasf* of Arabic wedding ceremonies. The series of songs honoring the bride and groom was eventually formalized into a cycle of recitations that were finally incorporated into the wedding celebration.

5. *Didactic.* The didactic view does not deny the historical aspects of the Song. It does, however, discount the circumstances surrounding the occasion of book in favor of the moral and instructional purposes of the literature. The book is seen to present the purity and wonder of sexual love; promote ideals of simplicity, faithfulness, and chastity; and instruct on the virtues of human affection and the beauty and holiness of marriage.

6. *Allegorical.* The allegorical method is the oldest and remains the most popular approach to the Song in Jewish and Christian traditions—though the book nowhere claims to be an allegory. Allegory is defined as obvious symbolic representation in literature, or simply extended metaphor. Allegory says one thing but conveys a deeper or hidden meaning. The "allegorizing" of a text occurs when an interpreter understands a given passage as allegory even though it was not intended as such by the author. The allegorizing method as applied to the Song has yielded much the same interpretations as the typological

The Yorck Project/Wikimedia Commons, GNU

"Who is this coming up from the desert like a column of smoke, perfumed with myrrh and incense made from all the spices of the merchant?" (Song 3:6). Perfume was very appealing in a culture without deodorant or frequent baths. These Egyptians would wear cones of perfume on their heads, and the cones would gradually melt, with the perfume giving a continual aroma to the hair.

approach. The chief distinction is that the typological view accepts a historical basis for the setting, while the allegorical does not.

7. *Literal*. The literal, or natural, view takes the Song at face value and interprets the love poetry for what it appears to be—a sensual, even erotic, expression of emotions and passion as two young lovers voice their desire for each other. The literal-historical variation on this seeks to balance the natural sense of the literary qualities of the poem with an appreciation for the historical setting or situation prompting its writing. One of us assumes a love story with three main characters (King Solomon, the shepherd-lover, and the Shulammite maiden) and combines the literal-historical approach with elements of the didactic. In this interpretation the book would be considered a northern kingdom satire on the reign of Solomon and his exploitation of women (ironically to his demise) and a memorializing of the exemplary character of the Shulammite maiden who rejected the wooing of the king out of faithfulness to her commoner-lover. The other one adopts the literal view without the historical connections. In this interpretation the book is a collection of love poetry with no intended plot behind it. The poems are a unified composition that celebrates, illustrates, and warns of the power of sensuality.[3]

Structure and Organization

Like Psalms, Proverbs, and Lamentations, the Song of Songs is entirely poetic in literary form, with the exception of the superscription, or title verse. As lyrical love poetry, the Song has an idyllic flavor and

3. On this approach see further, Tremper Longman III, *Song of Songs*, NICOT (Grand Rapids: Eerdmans, 2001), 42–43, 70.

Questions for Further Study and Discussion

1. Why have both Jews and Christians preferred the allegorical interpretations of the Song of Songs?
2. How does the teaching of the book compare with the instruction in the rest of the Bible regarding human sexuality and marriage?
3. What role should the teachings of the Song of Songs play in the instruction of young people in the contemporary church?

For Further Reading

Alter, Robert. *The Art of Biblical Poetry*. New York: Basic Books, 1985.

Bullock, C. Hassell. *An Introduction to the Old Testament Poetic Books*. 2nd ed. Chicago: Moody Press, 1988. 223–55.

Carr, G. Lloyd. *The Song of Solomon*. TOTC. Downers Grove, Ill.: InterVarsity Press, 1984.

_____. "The Song of Songs." *A Complete Literary Guide to the Bible*. Ed. by Leland Ryken and Tremper Longman III. Grand Rapids: Zondervan, 1993. 281–95. Includes a helpful discussion addressing the problem of literary structure in the Songs.

Dorsey, David A. "Literary Structuring in the Song of Songs." *JSOT* 46 (1990): 81–96.

Fox, M. V. *The Song of Songs and the Ancient Egyptian Love Songs*. Madison: University of Wisconsin Press, 1985. A detailed comparison and literary analysis of the love song in the Old Testament and the ancient Near East.

Fuerst, W. J. *The Song of Songs*. CBC. Cambridge: Cambridge University Press, 1975.

Garrett, Duane A. *Proverbs, Ecclesiastes, Song of Songs*. NAC. Vol. 14. Nashville: Broadman, 1993. 347–432. Includes a useful summary of the various interpretive approaches to the book.

Garrett, Duane A. *Song of Songs*. WBC 23b. Nashville: Thomas Nelson, 2004.

Gledhill, Tom. *The Message of the Song of Songs*. Downers Grove, Ill.: InterVarsity Press, 1994.

Hess, Richard. *Song of Songs*. Grand Rapids: Baker, 2005.

Hill, Andrew E. "The Song of Solomon." *The Evangelical Commentary on the Bible*. Ed. by Walter A. Elwell. Grand Rapids: Baker, 1989. 452–66.

House, Paul R. *Lamentations*. WBC 23b. Nashville: Thomas Nelson, 2004.

Hubbard, D. A. *Ecclesiastes, Song of Solomon*. Preacher's Commentary 16. Nashville: Thomas Nelson, 2002.

Keel, Othmar. *The Song of Songs*. Continental Commentaries. Trans. by F. J. Gaiser. Minneapolis: Fortress Press, 1997.

Landy, Francis. "The Song of Songs." *The Literary Guide to the Bible.*
    Ed. by Robert Alter and Frank Kermode. London: Grafton, 1987.
    305–19.

Longman, Tremper, III. *Song of Songs.* NICOT. Grand Rapids:
    Eerdmans, 2001. Helpful introductory section treating issues of
    genre and interpretation. Views the book as an anthology of love
    poems, an erotic psalter of sorts.

Murphy, R. E. *The Song of Songs.* HER. Philadelphia: Fortress Press,
    1990.

Olhsen, W., ed. *Perspectives on Old Testament Literature.* New York:
    Harcourt, Brace, 1978. 283–88. A concise essay presenting a
    three-character interpretation, with emphasis on the message and
    teaching of the book.

Pope, M. *Song of Songs.* AB. Vol. 7. New York: Doubleday, 1977.
    Ponderous and technical analysis from the mythological or cultic
    perspective, including a comprehensive survey of the history of
    interpretation of the book and a thorough bibliography.

Provan, Iain. *Ecclesiastes/Song of Songs.* NIVAC. Grand Rapids:
    Zondervan, 2001.

Seerveld, Calvin. *The Greatest Song.* Amsterdam: Trinity Pennyasheet
    Press, 1967. A three-character adaptation of the book in critique of
    King Solomon and arranged for oratorio performance.

Webb, Barry. "The Song of Songs: A Love Poem and as Holy
    Scripture." *RefTR* 49 (1990): 91–99.

Cave 1 at Qumran was the first cave discovered. It included such finds as a scroll of Isaiah and a commentary on Habakkuk.

Todd Bolen/www.BiblePlaces.com

FORMATION OF THE OLD TESTAMENT SCRIPTURES

The Old Testament was composed over a thousand-year period roughly spanning the mid-second to the mid-first millennium BC. While the New Testament understands God to be the author of the Old Testament by inspiration of the Holy Spirit (2 Tim. 3:16), at least forty different writers have been identified as human authors. The text of the Old Testament was originally recorded in two languages, classical or biblical Hebrew and imperial Aramaic (Gen. 31:47; Jer. 10:11; Ezra 4:8–6:18; 7:12–26 only). Among the ancient scribes are such well-known biblical personalities as Moses, David, and Solomon. Lesser-known authors include Hebrew women such as Deborah (cf. Judg. 5:1) and Miriam (cf. Exod. 15:20–21), and non-Hebrews such as Agur and Lemuel (cf. Prov. 30:1; 31:1). The Old Testament contains five basic literary genres or types—law, historical narrative, poetry, wisdom, and prophetic utterance.

Text and Transmission

Writing in the Ancient Near East

The earliest systems of human writing predate 3000 BC and are found both in ancient Egypt and Mesopotamia. The initial stage in the development of writing was the pictogram in which pictures represented the equivalent material objects. Eventually pictograms evolved into ideograms, in which the picture symbols now represented ideas also. Over time, the pictograms and ideograms became more abstract (a type of shorthand) and signified both words (logograms) and syllables. The final stage of writing was the shift from the syllabic writing systems to the alphabetic script, in which the characters represent a single letter of the alphabetic writing system.

The Hebrew language of the Old Testament is an alphabetic writing system. It is classified as a Northwest Semitic language, in contrast to the syllabic writing systems of Assyria and Babylonia in Mesopotamia. Hebrew, along with Phoenician, Moabite, Ammonite, Edomite, and Ugaritic were alphabetic dialects derived from a common proto-Semitic alphabetic language system (cf. Isa. 19:18 where the prophet identifies the language of Hebrew as a Canaanite dialect).

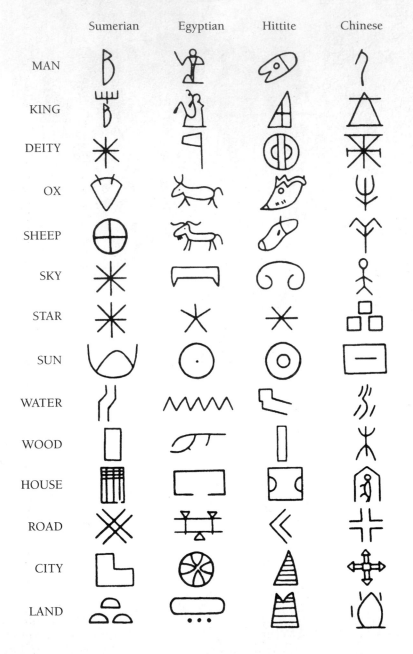

Figure 26.1. Pictograms in Early Civilizations
PICTORIAL SIGNS

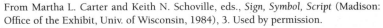

From Martha L. Carter and Keith N. Schoville, eds., *Sign, Symbol, Script* (Madison: Office of the Exhibit, Univ. of Wisconsin, 1984), 3. Used by permission.

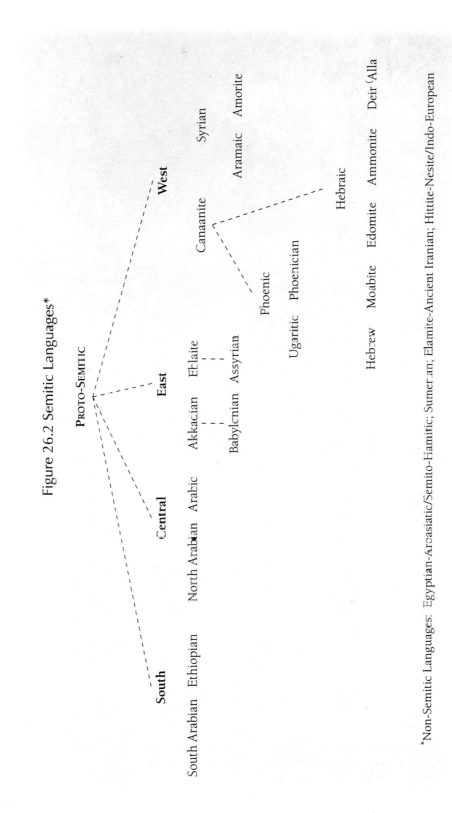

Figure 26.2 Semitic Languages*

*Non-Semitic Languages: Egyptian-Arcasiatic/Semito-Hamitic; Sumerian; Elamite-Ancient Iranian; Hittite-Nesite/Indo-European

This Hebrew inscription from the 8th century BC recounts the last stages of the digging of the water tunnel in the days of Hezekiah. It shows the form of Hebrew script during the monarchial period.

Z. Radovan/
www.BibleLandPictures.com

Writing Materials

A variety of materials were used as writing surfaces by the peoples of the ancient Near East. Monumental inscriptions were preserved on rock walls and stone slabs (see pictograms, Fig. 26.1). For example, the famous trilingual Behistun inscription of King Darius of Persia was etched in the rock face of a cliff. The Rosetta Stone and the Moabite Stone are other well-known examples of documents carved in solid rock. The Old Testament indicates that the Decalogue was carved in "tables of stone" (Exod. 32:15–16) and that later Joshua wrote a copy of the Law of Moses in stone (Josh. 8:32).

Other ancient writing materials included clay and wooden tablets (predominant in Mesopotamia but also known in Syro-Palestine at Ebla and Ugarit, cf. Isa. 30:8; Hab. 2:2), papyrus manuscripts and scrolls (used from the third to the first millennium BC, cf. Job 8:11; Isa. 18:2), and parchment (tanned animal skins). (The scroll of Jeremiah burned by King Jehoiakim may have been papyrus or parchment, cf. Jer. 36:2.) Ostraca (broken pieces of pottery) were commonly used as an abundant and inexpensive writing material throughout the ancient Near East, although they are not mentioned in the Old Testament. Beaten metal scrolls were occasionally used for special purposes. (A copper scroll was found among the writings left in caves along the Dead Sea by the Qumran community; see the section "Archaeology and the Old Testament" [p. 357] for a discussion of the Dead Sea Scrolls.)

The Old Testament makes no mention of the ink used for writing on scrolls, but it does list the iron stylus (Job 19:24; Jer. 17:1), reed pen (Jer. 8:8), a penknife for sharpening the pens (Jer. 36:23), and a writing case (Jer. 36:18) as instruments utilized in the writing process. The nature of the hand-copying process in the ancient world placed a premium on hearing, memorization, and public reading of documents—hence the emphasis on "hearing" the word of the Lord in the Old Testament. Spreading the written word also prompted the need for servants like message runners, heralds, and scribes (cf. 2 Sam. 18:19–23; Dan. 3:4).

Old Testament Text and Versions

The earliest manuscripts of the Old Testament were composed in the twenty-two consonantal characters of the Hebrew alphabet. Scribal schools continued the transmission of the consonantal texts until the time of the **Masoretes** (ca. AD 500–900). The Masoretes were Jewish scholars and scribes who improved word divisions and added vowel points or signs, punctuation marks, and verse divisions to the Hebrew Old Testament. Today the Hebrew text of the Old Testament is called the Masoretic Text (MT), signifying the important contribution of the Masoretes to the preservation of the Hebrew Bible.

In addition to the margin notes left by the Masoretes suggesting improved or corrected readings of individual words or verses, later developments in the Hebrew Bible included the subdivision of Old Testament books into chapters. First introduced in the Latin Bible by Stephen Langdon (1150–1228), chapter divisions were applied to the Hebrew Bible in 1518 (the Bomberg Edition). Numbers were assigned to the chapters in the Hebrew Bible by Arius Montanus (ca. 1571), having already appeared in the Latin Old Testament (ca. 1555).

The changing historical and political fortunes of the Israelite nation necessitated the translation of the Hebrew Bible into other languages. Several of these ancient versions are available in manuscript form and represent important witnesses to the text of the Hebrew Old Testament. The more important include the Samaritan Pentateuch (the Bible of the Samaritans dating to the fourth or fifth century BC), the Aramaic Targums (pre-Christian paraphrases of the Old Testament in Aramaic, the lingua franca of the Babylonian and early Persian periods, cf. Neh. 8:8), the Greek Septuagint (a by-product of the impact of Hellenism on the Jewish people, ca. 250 BC), Jerome's Latin Vulgate (AD 382–405), and the Syriac Peshitta (ca. AD 400?).[1]

Textual Criticism

The copying and translating of the Hebrew Old Testament over the centuries has proliferated the number of manuscripts available so that there are literally thousands of copies available in different languages from various time periods. Naturally the extended hand-copying process yielded errors of transmission. These human errors of sight, hearing, writing, memory, and judgment are called variants or variant readings of the text.

1. On the text and transmission of the Old Testament Scriptures, see further David Ewert, *A General Introduction to the Bible* (Grand Rapids: Zondervan, 1990), esp. 19–112; and Paul D. Wegner, *The Journey from Texts to Translations* (Grand Rapids: Baker, 1999), esp. 162–201.

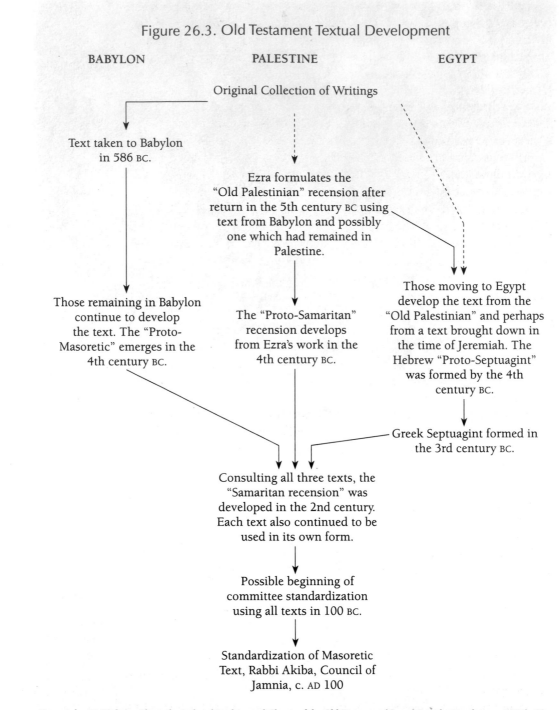

Figure 26.3. Old Testament Textual Development

BABYLON   **PALESTINE**   **EGYPT**

Original Collection of Writings

Text taken to Babylon
in 586 BC.

Ezra formulates the
"Old Palestinian" recension after
return in the 5th century BC using
text from Babylon and possibly
one which had remained in
Palestine.

Those moving to Egypt
develop the text from the
"Old Palestinian" and perhaps
from a text brought down in
the time of Jeremiah. The
Hebrew "Proto-Septuagint"
was formed by the 4th
century BC.

Those remaining in Babylon
continue to develop
the text. The "Proto-
Masoretic" emerges in the
4th century BC.

The "Proto-Samaritan"
recension develops
from Ezra's work in the
4th century BC.

Greek Septuagint formed in
the 3rd century BC.

Consulting all three texts, the
"Samaritan recension" was
developed in the 2nd century.
Each text also continued to be
used in its own form.

Possible beginning of
committee standardization
using all texts in 100 BC.

Standardization of Masoretic
Text, Rabbi Akiba, Council of
Jamnia, c. AD 100

From John H. Walton, *Chronological and Background Charts of the Old Testament* (Grand Rapids: Zondervan, 1994), 93.

Textual criticism, or lower biblical criticism, is the science of manuscript comparison. The goal of textual criticism is to establish or restore the written text of the Old Testament as close to its original reading as humanly possible. The practice or methodology of textual criticism includes gathering, sorting, and evaluating the variant readings of a given verse or passage of Scripture. The available manuscript data is then rated to select the most appropriate reading of the text in question based on the available data (cf. the margin notes in modern English Bibles in 1 Sam. 13:1, where textual criticism has been applied to restore the number indicating the length of King Saul's reign).

A word of caution is in order here, lest we be misled by those who emphasize the textual variants in the Old Testament manuscripts as evidence against the integrity and veracity of the Bible. Given its antiquity, the Old Testament exhibits a remarkable state of preservation. This is due in part to the meticulous copying procedures of the Hebrew and Christian scribes, the early and wide distribution of biblical manuscripts, and the reverence for and commitment to the Bible as "inspired Word of God" by Hebrews and Christians alike. Equally important was the work of the Holy Spirit, who inspired the human writers, illumined the readers, and superintended the canonization process.[2]

This Sumerian contract (ca. 2600 BC) from Shuruppak for the selling of a field and a house shows an example of Sumerian cuneiform, the oldest form of writing known.
Marie-Lan Nguyen/Wikimedia Commons, courtesy of the Louvre

Canon Definition and Formation

Definition

The word *canon* is not found in the Bible, although the root from which it derives occurs in 1 Kings 14:15 and Job 40:21. Originally *qāneh* meant a "reed" or "stalk" of papyrus, oil-grass, or sweet cane. Since reeds were used as measuring rods or ruling sticks for making straight lines, "canon" came to mean "measure" or "measuring reed." The term *canon* was first used as a theological expression in reference to the Holy Scriptures by Athanasius, bishop of Alexandria, in his Easter letter to the churches in which he outlined the contents of the New Testament canon (ca. AD 367).

As applied to the Hebrew Scriptures, the idea of canon has both intrinsic and extrinsic connotations. First, canon implies the individual books of the Old Testament demonstrated the inherent quality of

2. For example, prior to the discovery and subsequent publication of the Dead Sea (or Qumran) Scrolls, the oldest Hebrew manuscripts dated to around AD 900 (i.e., the Cairo Codex of the Former and Latter Prophets, AD 815; the Petersburg Codex of the Former and Latter Prophets, AD 916; the Aleppo Codex of the entire Old Testament, AD 900–950; and the Leningrad Codex of the entire Old Testament, AD 1008).

divine inspiration. This self-witness in conjunction with the illumination of the Holy Spirit permitted the recognition of these books as "word of God." Second, canon referred to the list or collection of books comprising the Hebrew Scriptures. This canon of Scripture was deemed supremely authoritative for faith and religious practice by the Hebrew community, and became the measure or standard by which later books of Hebrew history, tradition, and religious teaching were evaluated.

Canon Formation

Our knowledge of the formation process resulting in a fixed Hebrew canon remains sketchy. Unfortunately we have no ancient documents from the scribes detailing the various steps of the procedure that culminated in a Hebrew Bible. Two things do seem certain. The process was lengthy and involved, and it probably took place in stages over several centuries of Hebrew history. The generic outline of canon formation that follows does accommodate the available data on the topic:

Alphabetic scripts developed in the early second millennium BC. This one is the earliest known and is referred to as proto-Canaanite script.

The Schoyen Collection MS 5180, Oslo and London

Stage 1: "Authoritative utterances." Initially God's revelation to the Hebrew people (and others) was conveyed orally in most cases. (Note the **messenger formulas** along the line of "this is what the Sovereign LORD says," and "hear the word of the LORD" in the Old Testament, e.g., Isa. 1:10; Ezek. 5:5.) These authoritative utterances were then passed to succeeding generations as the "word of the Lord" in the form of received oral tradition (cf. Gen. 48:1–7).

Stage 2: Formal written documents. At some point these divinely inspired words, sayings, and speeches were recorded and preserved for the Hebrew community in written form. On occasion the authoritative utterance and the writing or inscripturating of the pronouncement occurred almost simultaneously (e.g., the Book of the Law in Exod. 24:3 [cf. Josh 1:8]; and Jeremiah's oracle to King Jehoiakim, Jer. 36). In other instances, the documentation of divine revelation took place some time after the historical event or circumstance prompting the word of the Lord. Often times that event or circumstance is recited as part of the context for God's communication to Israel (e.g., Exod. 15:1; Josh. 8:32; Judg. 5:1).

Stage 3: Collecting written documents. The collecting process was probably both lengthy and comprehensive—that is, long, given the millennium of Hebrew history recorded in the Old Testament (e.g., it is apparent that the Psalms came together over a period of five hundred years!), and comprehensive, given the number of ancient sources cited in the Old Testament that remain unknown to modern scholarship (e.g., the Book of the Wars of the Lord, Num. 21:14; the Book of Jashar, Josh. 10:13). Assembling the written records of the Hebrew experience with Yahweh into anthologies and books was partially a matter of convenience for the Israelite community, since it permitted easy access to and ensured continued preservation of the documents. More important, it signified the value, prominence, and authority of the writings collected for the religious life of the community. These books demanded the special attention of the Hebrew people (e.g., Deut. 31:24).

Stage 4: Sorting written documents and fixing a canon. The procedural details of sorting through documents are obscure, but we can discern the basic criteria applied to the documents for the purpose of "sorting" and delineating canon. It suffices to say that consensus choices among Hebrew religious leaders guided by the Holy Spirit of God during the course of Israelite history eventually resulted in a Hebrew canon of Scripture.

The Hebrews apparently had a "fixed," or established, canon of Scripture well before the time of Jesus Christ. The prologue to the Apocryphal Wisdom of Jesus Ben Sirach, or Ecclesiasticus, makes reference to a threefold collection of "great teaching" including the Law, the Prophets, and the Other Books of Our Fathers (ca. 200 BC). Jesus himself appealed to a threefold Hebrew canon consisting of the Law of Moses, the Prophets, and the Psalms (Luke 24:44).

It would seem there were at least four key periods during Old Testament history when the sorting of documents and the fixing of canon

Marie-Lan Nguyen/Wikimedia Commons

One of the most important in a long line of translations, the translation of Jerome—eventually referred to as the Vulgate—rendered the Bible into Latin about AD 400 and became the Bible of the Roman Catholic Church.

would have been crucial for the Hebrew religious community: (1) during the Sinai experience after the exodus, (2) during the shift from theocracy to monarchy in Israel, (3) at the time of the fall of Jerusalem and subsequent exile in Babylon, and (4) as part of the reforms of Ezra the scribe and Nehemiah the governor in postexilic Jerusalem.

Canon Selection Criteria

Unlike the New Testament, with its primary emphasis on apostolic authorship as the basis for canonicity, there seems to have been several factors or criteria important to the selection process for determining the Old Testament canon.

Foremost was the quality of inherent divine inspiration and authority recognizable to the leaders of the Hebrew religious community through illumination by the Holy Spirit (e.g., the direct manifestation of the Spirit of God in the case of Moses and the seventy prophets in Num. 11:16–30, and the fulfillment of the divine word, as in Jer. 28:9; 44:28).

Next, authorship was a key factor in evaluating books for canonicity. By and large the human writers of the books incorporated into the Hebrew canon held divinely appointed offices of leadership such as lawgiver, judge, prophet, priest, and king.

Third, the content of the individual books was examined for internal consistency of teaching and overall unity of theme and message with the covenant experience recorded in the other books recognized as "word of the Lord."

Last, the use of particular documents and books by the Hebrew religious community no doubt influenced canon selection. Those books read, studied, copied, and obeyed by the Israelites came to be recognized as canon.

In the final analysis, we have to assume the same Holy Spirit who inspired the human authors to write the books also superintended the Hebrew leaders during the canon selection process.[3]

Old Testament Canon History and Order

Canon History

The understanding of the Hebrew Scriptures as the "Old Testament" or "old covenant" is distinctly a Christian concept stemming from Jeremiah's reference to the "new covenant" (31:31–36; cf. Matt. 26:17–35) and the comparison made between the "former" and "better" covenant described in the New Testament book of Hebrews (cf. Heb. 9:15–28). In Judaism today, the Hebrew Scriptures are known as the "Tanak," an acronym reflecting the threefold division of the Old Testament: T for Torah or Law, N for Nebiim or Prophets, and K for Ketubim or Writings.

3. On Old Testament canon formation, see further David. N. Freedman, "Canon of the Old Testament," in *IDB: Supplementary Volume*, ed. K. Crim (Nashville: Abingdon, 1976), 130–36.

Egyptian hieroglyphics were one of the earliest forms of writing. As artistic as it is, it was extremely difficult to learn and kept literacy limited.

This tripartite division of the Hebrew Scriptures is attested, as we have already noted, as early as the second century BC in the prologue of Ben Sirach and later on by Jesus in Luke 24:44. But it is also affirmed in the Babylonian Talmud (*Baba Bathra* 14b–15a) and by a series of Jewish and Christian figures writing during the first four centuries after Christ (e.g., Philo, Josephus, Melito, Tertullian, Origen, Eusebius, Jerome, and Augustine).

The Hebrews enumerated twenty-four books in their Holy Scriptures. Samuel, Kings, Chronicles, and Ezra–Nehemiah were considered single books, while the twelve Minor Prophets were treated as a unified Book of the Twelve. Hence, the Hebrew canon contains fifteen fewer books than our English Old Testament of thirty-nine, although both contain the exact same material. The names or titles for the books of the Hebrew Scriptures were usually taken from the first line or verse of the text, whereas the English titles are derivations from the book headings in the later Greek and Latin versions of the Old Testament.

Canon Order

Apparently the Masoretic scribes established no guidelines for standardizing the order of the Hebrew canon, as early Old Testament manuscripts evidence no uniformity in the arrangement of the books of the Latter Prophets and the Writings. The same holds true for the Septuagint and early Greek texts of the Old Testament. Today's English versions repeat the Old Testament canon order of Jerome's Latin Vulgate, excluding the books of the Apocrypha.

"Disputed Books"

Later on, discussion did arise over the inclusion of certain books deemed "canon" by the Hebrew religious community. These disputed books, or *antilegomena* (i.e., "spoken against"), included:

Esther, because the book nowhere includes the name of God; Proverbs, because the practical nature of the wisdom made the book seem more like "earthly" than divine wisdom—and one need not necessarily "fear the Lord" to gain benefit from the wisdom teachings; Ecclesiastes, due to the pessimistic and hedonistic overtones of the book; Song of Songs, given the erotic nature of the love poetry; and Ezekiel, both for the prophet's bizarre antics and visions and for his teaching on sacrifice that seemingly contradicted the Torah of Moses.

It should be noted that the canonical status of these books was never in doubt. Rather, the questions were related more to the interpretation of the individual books and the scope of their use within the religious community. For example, it was once thought that the rabbinic council held at Jamnia or Jabne in or about AD 90 fixed the number and order of the Hebrew canon. However, it has since been recognized that the Jabne council did not discuss or settle the canon issue; instead, it discussed the interpretation of two particular books, Song of Songs and Ecclesiastes.[4] The completion of the Jewish Talmud in the fifth or sixth century AD essentially ended the discussions over the status of the "disputed books" in the Old Testament canon.

Canon Confirmation

Finally, it is important to understand that the Hebrew canon was established or fixed by the religious leadership of the Hebrew community. Later rabbinic and church councils did not determine canon, but merely affirmed or stamped their approval on the collection of divinely inspired and authoritative books already acknowledged as "word of the Lord" in the religious community.

Old Testament Apocrypha

The word *apocrypha* means "hidden." As applied to the collection of Jewish writings dating from the intertestamental period, the word has two connotations: (1) books that are "hidden away" because of their esoteric nature, or (2) books that are "hidden away" because they deserve to be—in that they were never recognized as canon by the Hebrews.

The Apocrypha is a collection of fourteen (or fifteen, depending on enumeration) books composed by pious Jewish writers between 200 BC and AD 100. These books were originally penned in Hebrew, Greek, and Aramaic and have been preserved in Greek, Latin, Ethiopic, Coptic,

4. Cf. Walter. C. Kaiser, *Toward Rediscovering the Old Testament* (Grand Rapids: Zondervan, 1987), 38–39.

Figure 26.4. Jewish and Christian Canons of the Old Testament

TANAK	ROMAN CATHOLIC AND ORTHODOX	PROTESTANT

Torah

1. Bereshith (Genesis)
2. Shemoth (Exodus)
3. Wayiqra (Leviticus)
4. Bemidbar (Numbers)
5. Debarim (Deuteronomy)

Nevi'im (Former)

6. Joshua
7. Shofetim (Judges)
8. Samuel
9. Melakim (Kings)
10. Isaiah
11. Jeremiah
12. Ezekiel
13. TereAsar (The Twelve)
   Hosea
   Joel
   Amos
   Obadiah
   Jonah
   Micah
   Nahum
   Habakkuk
   Zephaniah
   Haggai
   Zechariah
   Malachi

Kethu'bim

14. Tehilim (Psalms)
15. Job
16. Mishle (Proverbs)
17. Ruth
18. Shir Hashirim (Song of Songs)
19. Qoheleth (Ecclesiastes)
20. Ekah (Lamentations)
21. Esther
22. Daniel
23. Ezra – Nehemiah
24. Dibre Hayamin (Chronicles)

Pentateuch

1. Genesis
2. Exodus
3. Leviticus
4. Numbers
5. Deuteronomy

History

6. Joshua
7. Judges
8. Ruth
9 – 10. 1 and 2 Samuel
11 – 12. 1 and 2 Kings
13 – 14. 1 and 2 Chronicles
15 – 16. Ezra and Nehemiah
17. Esther
18. Judith*
19. Esther, including The Rest of Esther*

Poetry and Wisdom

20. Job
21. Psalms
22. Proverbs
23. Ecclesiastes
24. Song of Solomon
25. Wisdom of Solomon*
26. Ecclesiasticus (Wisdom of ben Sirach)*

Prophets

27. Isaiah
28. Jeremiah
29. Lamentations
30. Baruch, including The Letter of Jeremiah†
31. Ezekiel
32. Daniel, including The Rest of Daniel,* Susanna,* Song of the Three Holy Children,* Bel and the Dragon*
33. Hosea
34. Joel
35. Amos
36. Obadiah
37. Jonah
38. Micah
39. Nahum
40. Habakkuk
41. Zephaniah
42. Haggai
43. Zechariah
44. Malachi
45. 1 Maccabees*
46. 2 Maccabees†

Pentateuch

1. Genesis
2. Exodus
3. Leviticus
4. Numbers
5. Deuteronomy

History

6. Joshua
7. Judges
8. Ruth
9 – 10. 1 and 2 Samuel
11 – 12. 1 and 2 Kings
13 – 14. 1 and 2 Chronicles
15 – 16. Ezra and Nehemiah
17. Esther

Poetry and Wisdom

18. Job
19. Psalms
20. Proverbs
21. Ecclesiastes
22. Song of Songs

Prophets

23. Isaiah
24. Jeremiah
25. Lamentations
26. Ezekiel
27. Daniel
28. Hosea
29. Joel
30. Amos
31. Obadiah
32. Jonah
33. Micah
34. Nahum
35. Habakkuk
36. Zephaniah
37. Haggai
38. Zechariah
39. Malachi

*Apocryphal in Protestant canon
† Roman Catholic only

From Walter A. Elwell, ed., *Baker Encyclopedia of the Bible* (Grand Rapids: Baker, 1988), 1:301 – 2.

Arabic, Syriac, and Armenian. The Apocrypha contains six different genres or literary types, including didactic, religious, historical, prophetic (epistolary and apocalyptic), and legendary literature.

Initially, the books of the Apocrypha were added one by one to later editions of the Septuagint. This Greek translation of the Hebrew Old Testament was completed about 250 BC and made necessary by the impact of Hellenism on Judaism. These books were distinctly separated from the Hebrew Scriptures and not regarded by the Hebrews as part of the Old Testament. However, the Jewish scribes made no notations to this fact, which led to some confusion among the Greek-speaking Christians who adopted the Septuagint as their Bible. This was especially true after about AD 100, since subsequent copies of the Septuagint were transmitted by Christian scribes.

During the early centuries of Christianity there were conflicting opinions as to the canonicity of the Apocryphal books. For example, Greek and Latin church fathers like Irenaeus, Tertullian, and Clement of Alexandria quoted the Apocrypha in their writings as "Scripture," and the Synod of Hippo (AD 393) authorized the use of the Apocrypha

Figure 26.5. The Books of Apocrypha

Type of Book	Revised Standard Version	Catholic Versions
Didactic	1. The Wisdom of Solomon (c. 30 BC)	Book of Wisdom
	2. Ecclesiasticus (Sirach) (132 BC)	Ecclesiasticus
Religious	3. Tobit (c. 200 BC)	Tobias
Romance	4. Judith (c. 150 BC)	Judith
Historic	5. 1 Esdras (c. 150 – 100 BC)	3 Esdras* or 1 Esdras‡
	6. 1 Maccabees (c. 110 BC)	1 Machabees
	7. 2 Maccabees (c. 110 – 70 BC)	2 Machabees
Prophetic	8. Baruch (c. 150 – 50 BC)	Baruch chaps. 1 – 5
	9. The Letter of Jeremiah (c. 300 – 100 BC)	Baruch chap. 6
	10. 2 Esdras (c. AD 100)	4 Esdras* or 2 Esdras‡
Legendary	11. Additions to Esther (140 – 130 BC)	Esther 10:4 – 16:24†
	12. The Prayer of Azariah (second or first century BC) (Song of Three Young Men)	Daniel 3:24 – 90†
	13. Susanna (second or first century BC)	Daniel 13†
	14. Bel and the Dragon (c. 100 BC)	Daniel 14†
	15. The Prayer of Manasseh (second or first century BC)	Prayer of Manasseh*

*Books not accepted as canonical at the Council of Trent, AD 1546.
†Books not listed in Douay table of contents because they are appended to other books.
‡Numbering depends on whether Ezra and Nehemiah are titled 1 and 2 Esdras or Ezra and Nehemiah.

From David Ewert, *A General Introduction to the Bible* (Grand Rapids: Zondervan, 1990), 75.

Aleppo Codex is one of the earliest major copies of the Hebrew Bible. It dates to around AD 900 and is the product of the Masoretes.

Z. Radovan/www.BibleLandPictures.com

as canon. Yet others like Eusebius and Athanasius distinguished Apocrypha from the Old Testament.

The issue of Apocrypha as Old Testament canon was heightened with the publication of Jerome's Latin Vulgate (AD 405). Commissioned by Pope Damasus, this Latin translation of the Old Testament was intended to be the "popular" edition of the Bible for the Holy Roman Church. Jerome opposed the recognition of the Apocrypha as Old Testament canon and made careful notations in his Vulgate to that effect. But later recensions of Jerome's Vulgate failed to retain these clear distinctions, and soon most Latin readers understood no difference between the Old Testament and the Apocrypha.

The Reformation again brought the issue of Apocrypha as canon to the forefront of church discussion. As the reformers translated the Old Testament into the language of their constituencies, they discovered the Hebrew Bible contained no books of the Apocrypha. Thus, in their view these "lesser books" were either excluded from the Old Testament canon or appended as a separate and inferior collection. This discrimination between Old Testament canon and Apocrypha was anticipated by Wycliffe in his English translation of 1382. The Puritans are credited with the removal of the Apocrypha altogether from the covers of the English Bible. This tradition of excluding the Apocrypha still characterizes the majority of the English versions produced by Protestants.

The Holy Roman Church responded to the Reformers at the Council of Trent (1545–64). There the fathers reaffirmed the Vulgate as the Bible of the true church and pronounced the Apocrypha equivalent to canonical material (specifically, Tobit, Sirach, Wisdom, Judith, 1–2 Maccabees, Baruch, and the Additions to Esther and Daniel). Today this collection is usually called the Deutero-Canon, and it was substantiated as such by the Vatican Council of 1870. The Roman Catholic Church makes some appeal to the Deutero-Canon for religious doctrine, including the concepts of Purgatory, merit for good works, and the practice of prayers for the dead (cf. Tob. 12:9; 2 Macc. 12:43–45; 2 Esd. 8:33; 13:46; Sir. 3:30).

Figure 26.6. The Standard Selection of the Pseudepigrapha*

Legendary	1.	The Book of Jubilee
	2.	The Letter of Aristeas
	3.	The Book of Adam and Eve
	4.	The Martyrdom of Isaiah
Apocalyptic	5.	1 Enoch
	6.	The Testament of the Twelve Patriarchs
	7.	The Sibylline Oracle
	8.	The Assumption of Moses
	9.	2 Enoch, or the Books of the Secrets of Enoch
	10.	2 Baruch, or The Syriac Apocalypse of Baruch†
	11.	3 Baruch, or The Greek Apocalypse of Baruch
Didactical	12.	3 Maccabees
	13.	4 Maccabees
	14.	Pirke Aboth
	15.	The Story of Ahikar
Poetical	16.	The Psalms of Solomon
	17.	Psalm 151
Historical	18.	The Fragment of a Zadokite Work

*Since the discovery of the Dead Sea Scrolls, other books have come to light.
†1 Baruch is listed in the Apocrypha.

From David Ewert, *A General Introduction to the Bible* (Grand Rapids: Zondervan, 1990), 81.

The Westminster Confession of 1647 rejected the inspiration and authority of the Apocrypha and refused to accept the collection as part of the canon of Scripture. The Protestant churches have generally adopted this position regarding the Apocrypha. Although not widely appreciated nor observed today, Martin Luther's assessment of the Apocrypha still has merit. He held that the books of the Apocrypha were not equal to the Holy Scriptures, but are profitable to read and valuable for personal edification.

Old Testament Pseudepigrapha

Intertestamental Judaism produced a second body of extracanonical literature distinct from the Apocrypha known as the Old Testament **Pseudepigrapha** (or "books written under a pen name"). These eighteen books were composed by pious Jewish writers between 200 BC and AD 200. They were originally written in Hebrew, Aramaic, and Greek and have been preserved in Greek, Syrian, Ethiopic, Coptic, and Armenian.[5]

Although the collection remained outside the canon recognized in both Judaism and Christianity, the books were circulated and widely read in the early Christian church. In fact, the New Testament letter of Jude (vv. 14–15) quotes 1 Enoch and alludes to the Assumption of Moses (v. 9).

5. A full discussion of the character and significance of the Old Testament Pseudepigrapha is outside the scope of this survey. See further L. Rost's excellent introduction to the individual books of the Pseudepigrapha, *Judaism Outside the Hebrew Canon*, trans. D. E. Green (Nashville: Abingdon, 1976), 100–190. English translations of the Old Testament Pseudepigrapha include: R. H. Charles, ed. *The Apocrypha and Pseudepigrapha in English with Introductions and Critical Notes*, 2 vols. (Oxford: Clarendon, 1913); J. H. Charlesworth, ed., *The Old Testament Pseudepigrapha*, 2 vols. (Garden City, N.Y.: Doubleday, 1983, 1985); and H. F. D. Sparks, *The Apocryphal Old Testament* (Oxford: Clarendon, 1984).

Questions for Further Study and Discussion

1. What does it mean to say that the Hebrew Bible or the Old Testament is "inspired" by God?
2. How did the Hebrew religious community recognize divine inspiration in the books of the Old Testament?
3. Discuss the nature and purpose of textual criticism and its implications for biblical exposition.
4. What is the value of the Apocrypha and Pseudepigrapha for Old Testament study? Why are they largely ignored in Protestant scholarship and preaching?
5. On what basis is the Hebrew Bible or Old Testament considered a "closed" canon?

For Further Reading

Beckwith, R. *The Old Testament Canon of the New Testament Church*. London: SPCK, 1985.

Brotzman, Ellis R. *Old Testament Textual Criticism: A Practical Introduction*. Grand Rapids: Baker, 1994.

Bruce, F. F. *The Books and the Parchments*. 3rd ed. Old Tappan, N.J.: Revell, 1963.

_____. *History of the Bible in English*. 3rd ed. Oxford: Oxford University Press, 1978.

Carson, Donald A. *The King James Version Debate*. Grand Rapids: Baker, 1979.

Charlesworth, J. H., ed. *The Old Testament Pseudepigrapha*. New York: Doubleday, 1983, 1985. 2 vols.

Comfort, Philip W. *The Complete Guide to Bible Versions*. Wheaton, Ill.: Tyndale House, 1991.

deSilva, D. A. *Introducing the Apocrypha*. Grand Rapids: Baker, 2002.

Dewey, D. *A User's Guide to Bible Translations*. Downers Grove, Ill.: InterVarsity Press, 2004.

Ewert, David A. *A General Introduction to the Bible*. Grand Rapids: Zondervan, 1990. A current and readable presentation of general Bible introduction. Comprehensive, systematic, well illustrated. First published in 1983 under the title *From Ancient Tablets to Modern Translations*.

Fisher, M. C. "The Canon of the Old Testament." *EBC*. Vol. 1. Grand Rapids: Zondervan, 1979. 385–94.

Harrington, D. J. *Invitation to the Apocrypha*. Grand Rapids: Eerdmans, 1999.

Harris, R. Laird. *Inspiration and Canonicity of the Bible*. Grand Rapids: Zondervan, 1957.

Harrison, R. K. "The Old Testament Text and Canon." In *Introduction to the Old Testament*. Grand Rapids: Eerdmans, 1969. 260–88. Standard evangelical Old Testament introduction, though now somewhat dated.

Kline, Meredith G. *The Structure of Biblical Authority*. Grand Rapids: Eerdmans, 1972. The Old Testament canon characterized as "treaty-canon" originating out of the Old Testament parallels to ancient Near Eastern treaty or covenant literary forms.

Lewis, J. P. *The English Bible: From KJV to NIV*. Grand Rapids: Baker, 1981.

McDonald, Lee M. *The Formation of the Christian Biblical Canon*. Peabody, Mass.: Hendrickson, 1995.

Metzger, Bruce M. *The Bible in Translation: Ancient and English Versions*. Grand Rapids: Baker, 2001.

_____. *An Introduction to the Apocrypha*. Oxford: Oxford University Press, 1957.

Metzger, Bruce M., ed. *The Oxford Annotated Apocrypha*. New York: Oxford University Press, 1977.

Sparks, H. F. D., ed. *The Apocryphal Old Testament*. Oxford: Clarendon, 1984. English translation of the Old Testament Pseudepigrapha.

Trebolle Barrera, Julio. *The Jewish Bible and the Christian Bible*. Grand Rapids: Eerdmans, 1998.

Vermes, Geza. *The Dead Sea Scrolls in English*. 4th ed. New York: Penguin Books, 1995.

Wegner, Paul D. *The Journey from Texts to Translations*. 2nd ed. Grand Rapids: Baker, 2000. An expert guide on Bible origins and development.

_____. *A Student's Guide to Textual Criticism of the Bible*. Downers Grove, Ill.: InterVarsity Press, 2006.

Wurthwein, E. *The Text of the Old Testament*. Trans. by E. F. Rhodes. Grand Rapids: Eerdmans, 1979. Helpful treatment of the composition, transmission, primary versions, and textual criticism of the Old Testament.

PART V
THE PROPHETS

Aftermath oracles often offered hope to the people, and one aspect they addressed was hope for a future ideal king. This hope of a king who would bring victory over enemies and justice for his people was embedded in the message of the prophets. Assyrian kings were often portrayed in idealistic terms, as in this detail from the Balawat gates.

Werner Forman Archive/The British Museum

INTRODUCTION TO PROPHETIC LITERATURE

What Is a Prophet?

A prophet is someone who speaks on behalf of someone else. Most often in Scripture a prophet is a spokesperson or mouthpiece for God, though Exodus 7:1 speaks of Aaron as being a prophet for Moses (cf. Exod. 4:16). In modern politics this concept is well represented in the United States in the president's press secretary. He or she is the one who conveys the president's opinions, reactions, intentions, and the president's very words when necessary. The press secretary holding a news conference is never seen to be speaking for himself or herself, but is believed to be expressing only the words that the president desires the press secretary to speak. Another example would be the function of ambassadors to foreign countries who convey the official reactions and opinions of the government. Similarly, prophets are the mouthpiece of God, conveying God's opinions, reactions, intentions, and very words. In short, God's agenda, or program, is announced through the words of the prophets

The prophets are designated in the Old Testament by several different titles. The most frequent is *nabî*, which, though still somewhat controversial, appears to indicate that the prophet was "one who is called." A second title is "seer," which refers to the prophet's inclination to receive revelatory visions. Of course, the prophets did not always receive their messages through trances or visions; this was but one mode. Usually the text of Scripture does not specify how a message came.

The ministry of the biblical prophets tended to be clustered around times of crisis. Whether it was the religious crisis posed by the official sponsorship of Baal worship during the time of Elijah, the political crises caused by the Assyrian and Babylonian threats, or the identity crisis with which the postexilic community struggled, God used the prophets to offer guidance to his people in troubled times.

Prophecy in the Ancient Near East

Evidence of the existence of a prophetic institution has been found throughout the ancient Near East. Among the Mari tablets from

Figure 27.3. Categories of Prophetic Oracle

Oracular Categories	Description	Preexilic Emphasis	Postexilic Emphasis
Indictment	Statement of the offense	Focus primarily on idolatry, ritualism, and social justice	Focus on not giving proper honor to the Lord
Judgment	Punishment to be carried out	Primarily political and projected for near future	Interprets recent or current crises as punishment
Instruction	Expected response	Very little offered; generally return to God by ending wicked conduct	Slightly more offered; more specifically addressed to particular situation
Aftermath	Affirmation of future hope or deliverance	Presented and understood as coming after an intervening period of judgment	Presented and understood as spanning a protracted time period
			Religious: Now Socioeconomic: Potential Political: Eventual

The diversity of oracles demonstrates some key differences between the messages of the preexilic classical prophets and the postexilic ones. The indictment found in the preexilic prophets focused primarily on idolatry, ritualism, and social injustice (e.g., Isa. 1:10–15; Jer. 2:2–3:5; Mic. 3:1–3 respectively). In contrast, the indictment of the postexilic prophets often confronted the people's failure to give proper honor to the Lord (e.g., Zech. 7:5–6; Mal. 1:7–14).

Judgment (which constituted about half the oracles) in the preexilic prophets was usually political in nature and projected for the near future. The judgment oracles of postexilic prophets were more inclined to be interpretations of current crises than projections of future judgment (e.g., Hag. 1:6–11; Joel 1).

There were strikingly few instruction oracles among the prophets, probably because the law included all the instruction the people should have needed. In preexilic prophecy, the emphasis of the instruction was on returning to the Lord by ceasing wicked conduct (Jer. 3:12–13; Amos 5:14–15; Mic. 6:8). Postexilic prophecy had slightly more instruction, often more specifically addressed to a particular situation (e.g., Hag. 1:8; Mal. 3:10).

Finally, the aftermath oracles of the preexilic period generally offered hope, not for the deliverance of the generation that the prophet addressed, but for a future generation of Israel. This deliverance and restoration was usually projected after the judgment had come (with some exceptions—e.g., Mic. 5:5–6). The hope offered by the postexilic prophets did not have a set period of judgment intervening, but was presented as gradual restoration over a protracted period of time. Religious restoration was available for them immediately, with socioeconomic restoration coming gradually and political deliverance being an eventual outcome (e.g., Dan. 9).

Each of these messages has relevance to the prophet's audience and to us not so much for the information they offer of the present or the future, but for what they reveal about God. It must be remembered that prophecy is part of God's self-revelation. That self-revelation is to be found in the prophet's message, the proclamation of God's agenda. We come to know God by what he has done in the past (history) and by what his plans are for the future (prophecy). The fact that history and prophecy flow together in a single sovereignly devised and executed plan ought to produce a distinctive awe for the creator of that plan.

Prediction and Fulfillment

"Prediction" and "fulfillment" are two of the terms most often connected to prophetic literature, but both can lead to harmful misperceptions about the nature of prophecy.

The instruction offered by the prophets encouraged the Israelites to repent. This scene shows people in prostrate position humbly submitting to a higher authority—which is what God wanted from his people.

Todd Bolen/
www.BiblePlaces.com

Prediction

If someone today were to predict that the stock market would take a plunge and then took some action that actually caused it to happen, he or she would not be praised for the ability to predict. The aspect of predictiveness is diminished by the direct link to causation.

In the same way, the predictive element in biblical prophecy must usually be kept distinct from causation, else it ceases to be prediction. On these terms it is obvious that "prediction" would not be the best word to describe biblical prophecy. Prophets themselves were not predicting anything, but merely giving the word of the Lord. The prophecy was God's message, not the prophet's. If predicting is understood to preclude causation, then God cannot predict, for he is the final cause of all. So in the end, it must be recognized that prophecy is more interested in causation than in prediction. It is true that biblical prophecy spoke of events before they happened, but the purpose was that God would be properly recognized as having caused those events as a part of his ongoing plan.

Rather than regarding prophecy as prediction, we find it more helpful to consider prophecy "God's syllabus." The syllabus for a course does not "predict" what will happen in each class period of the term, but presents the instructor's plans and intentions for each period. The significance of the document is that the instructor is in a position to carry it out. Likewise, when a judge passes a sentence on a criminal, he is not "predicting" what will happen to that person. Rather, he is decreeing what ought to be done and is in a position to see that it is done.

This is like the relationship between God and prophetic literature. God was declaring his intentions and decreeing his judgments. Though these were still future when spoken, they could be considered prediction only in the broadest terms. It would not be accurate to speak of the prophets as predicting, for they were just the spokesmen. When a student assistant gives out a professor's syllabus, he or she is not predicting what the professor will talk about each day. It is the professor's syllabus; the student is but a delivery person. So it was with the prophets.

Fulfillment

"Fulfillment" can also be a misleading term. We have already noted that some people are inclined to neglect the message of the prophets in an often elusive search for fulfillments that inevitably leads to speculation that departs further and further from the text. It is often assumed that the prophets had specific events in mind, but that was not necessarily the case. It is not essential to be able to discern a prophet's intention in terms of fulfillment as long as the intended message is understood. The prophet was aware what the message was, yet he did not necessarily

Todd Bolen/www.BiblePlaces.com

Prophetic oracles spoke often of the coming domination of empires over Israel and Judah. The Assyrians reveled in portraying in their art their domination of others. This is a reconstruction of the gates of Balawat. The bronze bands are decorated with scenes of warfare, siege, and mutilation and humiliation of enemies. They portray what Israel had to look forward to when the prophetic judgments came to pass.

know what shape the fulfillment of the prophecy might take. It was the message that was inspired, and it was the message that was the medium of God's revelation. The fulfillment was almost incidental, though it was certainly important that it take place.

Whether or not the interpreter is able to identify the fulfillment with confidence is open to question. There are numerous passages in the Old Testament that, if read in the context of the time, would clearly suggest that certain things were going to happen in certain ways. As history unfolded, however, those things did not come to pass in the expected ways.

For example, if someone in the time of Isaiah had been able to read the text that we identify today as Isaiah 11:16, he or she would have supposed that the verse clearly and unambiguously suggested that the inhabitants of the northern kingdom would return from their exile in Assyria in a massive emigration comparable to the exodus. That did not happen. That it did not happen is not a blot on God's reputation, for who knows how the word could yet be fulfilled? But it suggests that assurance about fulfillment cannot always be achieved. Consequently, one must not become so absorbed in figuring out when and how fulfillment will take place that the message is neglected.

What is fulfillment? The Greek term translated "fulfill" in the New Testament is quite broad. When the New Testament authors spoke of something from the Old Testament as being fulfilled, they were certainly drawing a correlation between that Old Testament passage and something that was being said or done in their own time. At times the correlation is close and implies that the Old Testament was speaking directly to the New Testament event (e.g., Isa. 61:1 and Luke 4:18–19; Zech. 9:9 and Matt. 21:5). On other occasions the correlation is much looser and suggests only the vaguest relationship (e.g., Hos. 11:1 and Matt. 2:15).

To account for this wide range of possible connotations, fulfillment should be seen as indicating an *appropriate correlation* between the prophetic word and the event to which it is related. So when a New Testament author suggests that some event "fulfilled" an Old Testament passage, he is not suggesting that the Old Testament author was speaking or thinking of this event, but rather that an appropriate correlation can be drawn between the Old Testament and the event.

The Old Testament authors intended to communicate a message. Their writings show little interest in identifying the specific fulfillment of the message. In contrast, the New Testament authors specifically addressed fulfillment rather than trying to disclose the message of an Old Testament prophet (which would have been self-evident). Since Old Testament and New Testament authors focus on different aspects of the prophetic pronouncement, we are not under obligation to try to bring them into conformity with one another.

The New Testament authors were not using the Old Testament inductively to prove that Jesus was the Messiah. They had already accepted the fact of his messiahship. Instead, the Old Testament was used deductively to give further evidence of and to support that belief. Inductive proof was found in Jesus' miracles and in his words and deeds.

If the cited fulfillments did not necessarily represent the intentions of the Old Testament authors, one might wonder how the doctrine of

Tips for Reading Prophetic Literature

1. Think of prophecy as a syllabus explaining the outworking of God's plan rather than as simple prediction.
2. Be careful to distinguish between the message of the prophecy and the fulfillment of the prophecy.
3. The first step in interpreting a prophetic oracle is to identify to which category it belongs.
4. A vision is not the message but the occasion for the message.
5. The prophet's message is not hidden in uninterpreted symbols.

inspiration is maintained. Inspiration can be strongly affirmed as long as the perspective of the Old Testament about prophecy is understood. Prophecy as the word of God was expected to be appropriate to numerous situations as history unfolded. In other words, only time would tell how appropriate a prophetic statement might be. It had an obvious appropriateness to the contemporary audience, but there was no thought that its fitness was exhausted on the contemporary situation. Hindsight would come into play in order to identify other emerging appropriatenesses. Neither the prophet nor the audience had any confidence in being able to anticipate what form a future appropriateness might take. Such an insight could only come by revelation.

Therefore, the various appropriate situations that would emerge from a prophetic statement could not be considered part of the prophet's intention, yet by the same token he would not have objected to his prophecy being used in this expanded way. Consequently, the prophets would not have considered any apparently subjective correlations drawn by the New Testament writers as bad method. Endowed with inspiration, the New Testament writers were able to make reliable, acceptable, and appropriate correlations that the prophets did not anticipate even though further developments were expected.[3]

3. This understanding is built on a model using the significance of names in the Old Testament. For a fuller treatment, see John H. Walton, "Isaiah 7:14: What's in a Name?" *JETS* 30 (1987): 298–303.

Questions for Further Study and Discussion

1. From where did false prophets and prophets of other gods get their messages?
2. What distinctive evidences are there in the Old Testament that God has a predetermined plan for history?
3. Of what significance for eschatology is the principle that the vision is not the message, but the occasion for the message?
4. How are the "message" and the "fulfillment" different? What are the implications of this difference?
5. How much did a prophet understand his message? Or, was the object of the revelation of prophecy ever not actually the prophet and his audience? If so, why was the revelation given?
6. What are the implications of the statement, "Prophecy is more interested in causation than in prediction"?
7. What are the implications of the statement, "Prophecy is more interested in revealing God than in revealing the future"?
8. In what ways would the prophets be considered "champions of the covenant"?
9. Are fulfillments inspired? Explain your answer.

For Further Reading

Barton, John. *Oracles of God.* New York: Oxford, 1986.

Beale, G. K. *The Right Doctrine from the Wrong Text?* Grand Rapids: Baker, 1994.

Blenkinsopp, Joseph. *A History of Prophecy in Israel.* Philadelphia: Westminster, 1983.

Bright, John. *Covenant and Promise.* Philadelphia: Westminster, 1976.

Bullock, C. Hassell. *An Introduction to the Old Testament Prophetic Books.* Chicago: Moody Press, 1986.

Chisholm, Robert B. *Handbook on the Prophets.* Grand Rapids: Baker, 2002.

Gordon, Robert P. *The Place Is Too Small for Us.* Winona Lake, Ill.: Eisenbrauns, 1995. A collection of some of the best articles on the prophets.

Green, Joel B. *How to Read Prophecy.* Downers Grove, Ill.: InterVarsity Press, 1984. A good introduction to some of the key issues regarding prophecy.

Heschel, Abraham J. *The Prophets.* New York: Harper & Row, 1962. Classic study of the Hebrew prophets by a renowned Jewish scholar.

Holladay, John. "Assyrian Statecraft and the Prophets of Israel." *HTR* 63 (1970). 29–51. A good presentation of the categories of Israelite prophecy.

Koch, Klaus. *The Prophets.* 2 vols. Philadelphia: Fortress Press, 1982.

Lindblom, J. *Prophecy in Ancient Israel.* Philadelphia: Fortress Press, 1973. The classic study of the prophetic institution.

McConville, J. G. *Exploring the Old Testament: A Guide to the Prophets.* Downers Grove, Ill.: InterVarsity Press, 2002.

Nissinen, Martti. *Prophecy in Its Near Eastern Context.* Atlanta: SBL, 2000.

_____. *Prophets and Prophecy in the Ancient Near East.* Atlanta: SBL, 2003.

Russell, D. S. *The Method and Message of Jewish Apocalyptic.* Philadelphia: Westminster, 1964.

Sandy, D. Brent, and R. Giese. *Cracking Old Testament Codes: A Guide to Interpreting the Literary Genres of the Old Testament.* Nashville: Broadman & Holman, 1995.

Sandy, D. Brent. *Plowshares and Pruning Hooks.* Downers Grove, Ill.: InterVarsity Press, 2002.

Smith, Gary V. "Prophet," *ISBE.* Rev. ed. Grand Rapids: Eerdmans, 1986. 3:986–1004. An excellent introduction to the whole area of prophecy from a conservative perspective.

Uffenheimer, Benjamin. *Early Prophecy in Israel.* Jerusalem: Magnes, 1999.

Walton, John H. *Ancient Near Eastern Thought and the Old Testament.* Grand Rapids: Baker, 2006.

_____. "Isaiah 7:14: What's in a Name?" *JETS* 30 (1987): 289–306.

Westermann, Claus. *Basic Forms of Prophetic Speech.* Trans. by H. C. White. London: SCM Press, 1967.

Wilson, Robert R. *Prophecy and Society in Ancient Israel.* Philadelphia: Fortress Press, 1980. An exploration of the sociological aspects of prophecy.

"Isn't he the one whose high places and altars Hezekiah removed saying to Judah and Jerusalem, 'You must worship before this altar'?" (Isa. 36:7). High places like this one in Hazor were where unsanctioned worship took place. Hezekiah had destroyed them in his fervor for centralization of worship at the temple in Jerusalem.

Peter White

ISAIAH

Key Ideas

- The trustworthiness of the Lord
- The incomparability of Israel's God
- Divine sovereignty in judgment and deliverance

Purpose Statement

The purpose of the book of Isaiah is to demonstrate the trustworthiness of the Lord with regard to two kings that Isaiah advised. Ahaz did not trust the Lord. He ignored Isaiah's advice and followed his own schemes, and suffered the consequences. Hezekiah, in contrast, trusted the Lord and Jerusalem was delivered from the Assyrians. In the second half of the book the exiles are also encouraged to trust the Lord to bring deliverance.

Major Themes

- Sons' Names as Signs
- Servant
- Holy One of Israel
- Redeemer
- Eschatology

God's Presence

Because of the vision that launched Isaiah's ministry, the premise of trust in the book is based on the fact of the presence of a holy God dwelling in the midst of Israel. The book emphasizes that the Israelites are thereby in relationship with the sovereign God of the cosmos who holds history and the nations in his hands. The emphasis on the presence of God is especially explicit in the naming of Immanuel,

"God with us" in Isaiah 7:14, an idea that is fulfilled in the incarnation of Christ as God's presence came to earth in a remarkably innovative way.

Outline

I. Introduction
  A. Overture (1–5)
  B. Commissioning (6)

II. Assyrian Context: Scenario One
  A. Oracles at the Time of Syro-Ephraimite Coalition (7–12)
  B. Oracles Against Nations (13–23)
  C. Apocalyptic Conclusion to Oracles Against the Nations (24–27)

III. Assyrian Context: Scenario Two
  A. "Woe" Oracles at the Time of the Siege of Jerusalem (28–33)
  B. Apocalyptic Conclusion of "Woe" Oracles (34–35)
  C. Resolution of the Assyrian Crisis (36–37)
  D. Transition to Babylonian Crisis (38–39)

IV. Scenario Three: Projected Oracles Addressing Exiles (40–55)

V. Scenario Four: Projected Oracles Addressing Postexilic Situation (56–66)

The book of Isaiah is a collection of the prophetic sayings and oracles of the prophet Isaiah, who was the dominant prophetic voice in the tumultuous latter half of the eighth century BC (ca. 740–700). Some of the richest Hebrew literature known is found here as well as a bold and forthright presentation of the trustworthiness and sovereign power of the God of Israel.

The Writing of the Book

The unity of the book of Isaiah is a subject of no small controversy. The fact that the prophet lived in the eighth century BC makes it very diffi-cult for some scholars to accept that he could have identified Cyrus the Persian by name (44:28; 45:1), since Cyrus did not arrive on the scene of history until nearly two hundred years later. Even for those who are willing to accept the supernatural phenomenon of prophecy that looks into the future, this has sometimes seemed irregular when compared with other prophetic oracles. The only other instance in the Old Testa-ment of naming a person before his arrival is the naming of Josiah in

1 Kings 13:2, and that passage is further complicated by the probability that it was written in the time of Josiah. Technically, then, predictive identification such as this is unparalleled.

Even in a casual reading of the book of Isaiah in English we can detect a major shift occurring at chapter 40. The style becomes more poetic and theoretical. The tone becomes conciliatory rather than condemning. Indictment and judgment oracles that make up a large part of the first thirty-nine chapters become much rarer. The historical situation seems to have changed dramatically. The people being addressed are in exile rather than in eighth-century Judah. In light of these observations, one can easily understand why some are uncomfortable attributing the entire book to a single author writing in the eighth century.

It is commonplace for scholars to insist that there are at least two different authors of the book, separated from one another by at least 150 years. Typically, reference is made to a hypothetical "second Isaiah" and often an additional "third Isaiah" as the unidentified individuals credited with writing chapters 40–66 in the sixth and fifth centuries BC. More recently, computer analysis of writing style has been used to substantiate multiple authors.

Nevertheless, some scholars have felt that their view of biblical authority demands that the book be viewed as a unity. Consequently they have responded by fashioning a defense of the unity of the book and corresponding rebuttal of the objections to its unity. While this defense depends heavily on New Testament passages that associate the prophet Isaiah with the second part of the book (e.g., Matt. 3:3; 12:17; Luke 3:4; John 12:38–41; Acts 8:28; Rom. 10:16), evidence from the Old Testament is also used.

The testimony of the book itself certainly insists on the reality of supernatural prophecy that focuses on the future. The whole case for the sovereignty of God in Isaiah 40–48 is built around the Lord's ability to say beforehand what he is going to do and the challenge to the

out this section cannot be easily neutralized. The naming of Cyrus comes at a crucial climax of a highly structured poetic composition (44:24–28) and cannot easily be eliminated as if it were incidental or superfluous. Furthermore, the evidence that the book of Kings, completed by the middle of the exile, used the complete book of Isaiah as a source favors a preexilic date for the writing of the entire book.[1]

For those who do not view the statements of Christ as literary references, but as affirmations of authorship, the New Testament would require that Isaiah be considered the prophet who delivered these oracles to Israel, for he is identified at the least as their source. That does not necessarily mean that he wrote them down, but it does register that what was written represents faithfully what Isaiah said. We would therefore consider the eighth-century prophet Isaiah as the dominant, principle and determinative voice in the book. Furthermore, if 2 Kings used the book of Isaiah as a source, the book must have been written down fairly soon after Isaiah died. There is no reason to deny that it was put into written form during his lifetime, though such cannot be proved. On the whole, we remain unconvinced that the book of Isaiah must be divided among several authors. We consider it more productive to recognize four different scenarios in the book (the periods of Ahaz, Hezekiah, exile and post-exile—see below in the section on the organization of the book).

"At that time Medocach-Baladan son of Baladan king of Babylon sent Hezekiah letters and a gift" (Isa. 39:1). This Babylonian king, pictured on this boundary marker, was involved in revolts against the Assyrian rulers and perhaps wanted Isaiah to join a rebellious coalition.
Bildarchiv Preussicher Kulturbesitz/Art Resource, NY

The Background

The book of Isaiah is set against the background of the second half of the eighth century BC. It will be remembered that this is when the Neo-Assyrian Empire was taking its place as a greater world power than any previously known in history.

Two major events serve as the focus of chapters 1–39:

1. The invasion of Israel by the Assyrian king Tiglath-Pileser III serves as the backdrop to chapters 7–12. This came in response to the military action of Damascus (the capital of Aram) and the northern kingdom, Israel, against the southern kingdom, Judah. The reason for the aggression of Damascus and Israel against Judah (the Syro-Ephraimite War, 735–732 BC) is not given in the text. It is clear, however, that their action was considered a real threat against the survival

---

1. For proof of this, see John H. Walton, "New Observations on the Date of Isaiah," *JETS* 28 (1985): 129–32.

of the Davidic monarchy. The response of Ahaz, king of Judah, was to summon Assyria to police the region, an invitation that Tiglath-Pileser gladly accepted. The result was that Damascus was conquered, its people were deported, and all of Aram was incorporated into the Assyrian Empire (732 BC). Sections of the northern kingdom were annexed, and a new king was put on the throne. Several years later, Israel rebelled again and was totally assimilated into the Assyrian Empire, with the capital city of Samaria destroyed in 721; but this event is given very little coverage in the book of Isaiah.

2. The invasion of Judah by the Assyrian king Sennacherib in 701 resulted from Hezekiah's involvement in an anti-Assyrian coalition. It brought the destruction of many of the fortified cities of Judah, leading finally to the siege of Jerusalem. In contrast to his father, Ahaz, Hezekiah trusted the Lord for deliverance, and the Assyrian army was destroyed.

This was a time of fear and political uncertainty. The Assyrians terrorized the populace of the ancient Near East with an aggressive program of subjugation. A country could choose to be a submissive vassal paying annual tribute and supplying auxiliary troops to the Assyrians. Any sign of disloyalty, however, would bring territorial reductions and increased Assyrian control of the government—not to mention increased tribute demands. Behind all this lay the threat of ultimate deportation, with all political independence revoked.

The deportation program was designed to destroy any sense of nationalism or political identity. The goal was assimilation of foreign peoples into a massive ethnically and politically generic empire. For the Israelites this was a theological issue. They were a people chosen and set apart by God and living in a land promised and delivered to them by God. The Assyrian policy was a threat to the covenant distinctiveness of Israel.

Purpose and Message

The material of the book of Isaiah is arranged to highlight the trustworthiness of Yahweh, the covenant God. This is clearly seen in the

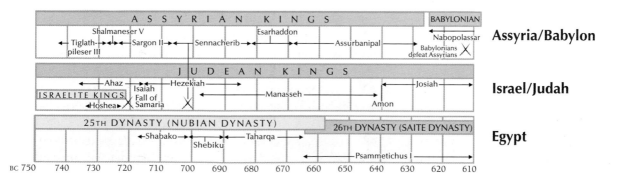

contrast between the actions of the two kings Ahaz and Hezekiah. Ahaz did not trust Yahweh, but sent for the Assyrians to aid him in time of political crisis (against the advice of Isaiah). This only resulted in replacing one crisis with another. Hezekiah, though he initially counted on Egyptian help, depended on Yahweh and was delivered in a mighty way. Hezekiah thus became a convincing example of how God in his sovereignty can bring deliverance. This was an important lesson for the Israelites in exile, who were thereby encouraged to respond to their crisis with trust.

Although some oracles explicitly give this emphasis (e.g., chaps. 30–31), it is more discernible in the arrangement of the oracles. The purpose of a prophet was to deliver the words that God gave him to say. The oracles of the first part of Isaiah (1–39) are largely oracles of indictment and judgment. Chapters 40–66 are more concerned with God's forgiveness, deliverance, and restoration of Israel.

Organization and Structure

There has been considerable dispute over the nature of chapters 1–5, since the formal commissioning of Isaiah is related in chapter 6. Some have contended that 1–5 contain oracles from before the time of the vision that Isaiah had in the year Uzziah died. Others believe that those five chapters serve as an introduction to the book by gathering selected oracles from many different periods of Isaiah's ministry. Whether or not this material was editorially gathered or preserves early material, it does serve as a suitable introduction to the book and its themes. Many of the indictment oracles come in this section.

Chapter 6 could be seen as a conclusion to this introduction, for it suggests that the people were not going to pay any attention to Isaiah's message. Isaiah's unheeded preaching would stand as a confirmation of the guilt of Israel established by the indictments in 1–5 and would lead to their eventual destruction.

The first historical scenario of the book attaches to the reign of Ahaz beginning about 735 and extending over the next several years. The purpose of chapters 7–12 is to highlight the failure of Ahaz to trust Yahweh and the results of that failure. These are mostly oracles of judgment but are interspersed with glimpses of future hope. The point of this is to show that, while Ahaz's failure was serious, it would not annul the covenant. God still intended to bring the promised kingdom after the period of judgment was over (e.g., chaps. 9 and 11).

The oracles against the nations (13–23) are properly placed here as demonstration of God's sovereign control over all the nations. The fact that Damascus and Israel were going to be unsuccessful in their attempted overthrow of the Davidic line, and the fact that Assyria suc-

King Sennacherib of Assyria invaded Judah during Isaiah's ministry and took some of the fortified cities (Isa. 36:1). But when he came against Jerusalem, God delivered King Hezekiah and the people (Isa. 37). Sennacherib is pictured here in a stone relief from his father's palace at Dur-Sharrukin.

Kim Walton, courtesy of the Oriental Institue Museum

cessfully invaded the west are neither incidental nor isolated. Israel was to trust Yahweh because he was in control over all that transpired politically or in any other realm. These oracles were not given for the sake of the nations whom they concern. Rather, through these oracles Israel was given a sense of the transcendent power of God. Chapters 24–27 conclude this segment by speaking generally of the deliverance of Israel and the destruction of her enemies.

The "Woe" oracles of chapters 28–33 shift the focus to the second scenario in the time of Hezekiah. In the last decade and a half of the eighth century BC Jerusalem was in potential distress (29), and Hezekiah was making alliances with Egypt (30–31). These oracles are filled with indictment for the nation's failure to trust Yahweh. Chapter 33 speaks of deliverance for the righteous ones in Zion, while chapters 34 and 35 speak of the wrath and judgment of Yahweh to fall on all his enemies.

The end of the Assyrian crisis (36–37) came when Hezekiah called on Yahweh to overthrow the armies of Sennacherib. It is interesting that the writer used the Assyrian officer to summarize the significant theological points. In his speech to Hezekiah's envoys, Rabshakeh insisted that the Egyptians would not be of any help to Israel. This parallels the idea that the Israelites were not to put their trust in Egypt. Rabshakeh made reference to Hezekiah's reforms (which he portrayed as making God angry, though the reader knows that they brought God's favor) and then presented the challenge that no other gods had been able to withstand the Assyrian armies. This heightened the irony of the situation, because the subsequent act of God's deliverance stands as testimony to the unique power of the God of Israel.

Chapters 38–39 function as a transition from the Assyrian crisis to the Babylonian crisis (scenario two to scenario three). Hezekiah's miraculous recovery from mortal illness came in response to his prayer and confirmed his standing as a godly king. But word of that recovery prompted Merodach-Baladan, the king of Babylon, to send envoys to Hezekiah with personal congratulations. Hezekiah took the liberty to show them the royal treasury. All this provided the backdrop for the oracle of Isaiah 39:6–7, which indicated that the Babylonians would be the ones to carry Judah into exile. This oracle sets the scene for the major literary and thematic shift that occurs with chapter 40.

The crisis related in scenario three (chapters 40–55) was the Babylonian exile spoken of in 39:6–7. If we accept this as the prophecy of Isaiah son of Amoz in the eighth century, we should note that he was not prophesying about the exile; rather, he was assuming it and addressing his message to those who were part of it. Was this intended to have meaning for Isaiah's eighth-century audience? Yes, for two reasons: (1) its emphasis was to establish trust in the sovereignty of God.

"To whom, then, will you compare God? What image will you compare him to? As for an idol, a craftsman casts it, and a goldsmith overlays it with gold and fashions silver chains for it" (Isa. 40:18–19). The image making that Isaiah describes is depicted in this relief from the tomb of the Egyptian high priest Ankhmahor (about 2300 BC).
Werner Furman Archive

Exile did not come because of any divine inability to deliver; whether God delivered (as in the destruction of Sennacherib's army) or not (as in the fall of Jerusalem), his sovereign plan was being carried out and everything was under his control; and (2) in keeping with the purpose of most "aftermath" oracles (see previous chapter), the people of Isaiah's time needed to be reassured that God would not fail to carry out his promises. After the period of judgment, God would bring restoration. This confidence and hope put the threat of punishment in a larger perspective.

The themes of chapters 40–55 include the coming deliverance of the exiles, the worthlessness of idols, the coming judgment on the nations, and God's use of a particular "Servant" as an instrument to carry out his plan. All this was directed toward the political and spiritual restoration of Israel. Throughout this section of the book the recurrent challenge is issued for the idols and pagan gods to reveal a plan for history, to show how it was followed in the past, and how it would be carried forward in the future. The extension of Yahweh's plan from the past into the future is presented as prima facie evidence of his sovereignty and uniqueness (41:21–29; 45:20–21; 46:7–11; 48:1–7).

Finally, in scenario four, chapters 56–66 project even further into the future to address those who have returned from exile. Upright living, the future glory of Jerusalem, and God's vengeance on his enemies are common topics. In all this, Yahweh laid out before Israel his agenda so that the people might understand and affirm his holiness, sovereignty, and faithfulness.

Major Themes

Isaiah was among the first of the classical prophets to the southern kingdom of Judah. In a sense he could be considered both classical and preclassical, for he served the king as adviser just as the preclassical prophets had done. Much of his message, however, was comparable to the message of the classical prophets, including the indictment of the people, the promise of exile and destruction as God's punishment, and the hope of future fulfillment of covenant promises. The most prominent traits and themes of Isaiah's prophecy are the following:

Sons' Names as Signs

Chapters 7–9 feature four sons whose names were given prophetic significance. Isaiah's own children—Shear-Jashub ("a remnant will return," 7:3) and Maher-Shalal-Hash-Baz ("quick to the plunder, swift to the spoil," 8:1–3)—had such names, and so did Immanuel ("God with us," 7:14; 8:8, 10) and the child identified in 9:6. These highlighted God's short-term and long-range agendas for Israel.

The Nations of
Isaiah 13–23

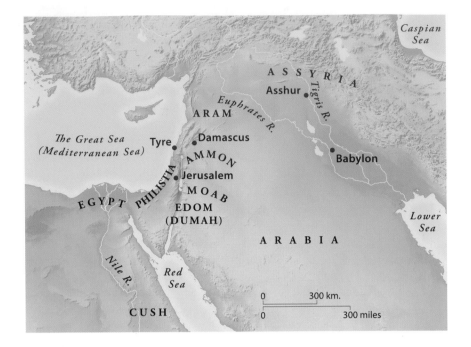

The Servant

Four sections in the book of Isaiah have been designated "Servant Songs," for they speak of a Servant who would be instrumental in fulfilling God's plans for Israel. These passages are 42:1–7; 49:1–9; 50:4–11; and 52:13–53:12; in addition, 61:1–3 shows some similarity to the Servant Songs, although the designation "servant" is not used. Israel is at times referred to as God's servant in the book (e.g., 41:8; 44:1) and Cyrus plays an instrumental role in God's program of deliverance; nevertheless, the description of the Servant in the songs goes far beyond what could be said of either of them. The function described for the Servant is strikingly parallel to the function ascribed to the future, ideal Davidic king elsewhere in the book (cf. chap. 11 and 55:3–5). The New Testament further confirms this as the preferred and common interpretation of these passages. Though the Servant is not called "Messiah" by Isaiah, the function and accomplishments attached to him lead many to that conclusion.

The Holy One of Israel

A title for God used almost exclusively by Isaiah in the Old Testament is "The Holy One of Israel." This title not only shows Isaiah's emphasis on the holiness of God, but also reflects the book's concern over the seriousness of Israel's offenses against that God. Reconciliation is God's ultimate goal. Punishment is used to effect reconciliation, and the Servant had a primary role in making it accessible to the people.

Yet, in the end God brought the people back to himself for his name's sake (43:22–28).

Redeemer

Another attribute emphasized in Isaiah is that Yahweh is the Redeemer of Israel. This title for Yahweh is used only four times elsewhere, but more than a dozen times in the book of Isaiah. All the references lie within chapters 40–66 (namely, 41:14; 43:14; 44:6, 24; 47:4; 48:17; 49:7, 26; 54:5, 8; 59:20; 60:16; 63:16). The verb is used another nine times as an action carried out by Yahweh (likewise all in 40–66: 43:1; 44:22–23; 48:20; 51:10; 52:3, 9; 62:12; 63:9). Again the focus is on the sovereign grace of God.

Eschatology

The eschatology (the study of the conclusion of God's agenda) found in the book of Isaiah is a kingdom eschatology. By that we mean that the emphasis is on the future kingdom of Israel. It is depicted as a kingdom centered in Jerusalem. Peace and prosperity will abound, and all the world will come to Jerusalem and marvel and be taught. Proper worship and the centrality of the law are significant characteristics of this kingdom. A descendant of Jesse will be on the throne, but this aspect of the kingdom is not prominent in Isaiah. The emphasis is on the fact that Yahweh will reign (24:23; 33:22; 43:15; 44:6) and will be the pride of the remnant of Judah and the glory of Jerusalem.

Questions for Further Study and Discussion

1. How important is the unity of Isaiah as a current theological issue?
2. Of what significance is it that prophetic activity becomes more prominent in times of crisis?
3. In what ways is the theology of Isaiah distinctive in the Old Testament?
4. How is the kingdom eschatology in Isaiah different in emphasis from eschatological approaches that are common today?

For Further Reading

Broyles, Craig C., and Craig Evans, eds. *Writing and Reading the Scroll of Isaiah*, 2 vols. Leiden: Brill, 1997.

Childs, Brevard. *Isaiah*. Louisville: WJK, 2001.

Goldingay, John. *Isaiah*. Peabody, Mass.: Hendrickson, 2001.

Hayes, John, and Stuart Irvine. *Isaiah*. Nashville: Abingdon Press, 1987. One of the more recent liberal treatments that argues for the unity of chapters 1–33 (where some scholars divide the book rather than after chap. 39) in the eighth century BC.

Holladay, William. *Isaiah: Scroll of a Prophetic Heritage*. New York: Pilgrim, 1988.

Lindsey, F. Duane. *The Servant Songs*. Chicago: Moody Press, 1985. A thorough analysis of the Servant material from a conservative perspective.

MacRae, Allan A. *The Gospel of Isaiah*. Chicago: Moody Press, 1977. A conservative treatment of chapters 40–56.

Motyer, Alec. *The Prophecy of Isaiah*. Downers Grove, Ill.: InterVarsity Press, 1993.

Oswalt, John. *Isaiah 1–39*. Grand Rapids: Eerdmans, 1986.

_____. *Isaiah 40–66*. Grand Rapids: Eerdmans, 1997. The best of the conservative commentaries.

Oswalt, John N. *Isaiah*. NIVAC. Grand Rapids: Zondervan, 2003.

Walton, John H. "Isaiah 7:14: What's in a Name?" *JETS* 30 (1987): 289–306. A treatment of the interpretation of Isaiah 7:14 and a discussion of the hermeneutical issues involved.

_____. "New Observations on the Date of Isaiah." *JETS* 28 (1985): 129–32.

Webb, Barry G. *The Message of Isaiah*. Downers Grove, Ill.: InterVarsity Press, 1996.

Wildberger, Hans. *Isaiah 1–12*. Minneapolis: Fortress Press, 1997.

_____. *Isaiah 13–27*. Minneapolis: Fortress Press, 1997.

Wolf, Herbert M. *Interpreting Isaiah*. Grand Rapids: Zondervan, 1985.
A conservative work with a textbook approach that provides a
very useful summary of Isaiah.

_____. "A Solution to the Immanuel Problem in Isaiah 7:14–8:22." *JBL*
91 (1972): 449–56. Support for the identification of Immanuel as
Maher-Shalal-Hash-Baz, Isaiah's son.

Young, E. J. *The Book of Isaiah*. Grand Rapids: Eerdmans, 1972. A
conservative classic in three volumes.

CHAPTER

29

Jeremiah rebukes the people for building a high place to Baal (Caananite storm God) at the "Valley of the Son of Hinnom" and sacrificing their children there (Jer. 7:31–32; 32:35). Because of this, it will be called "Valley of Slaughter" (Jer. 7:32; 19:6). This location is just outside of Jerusalem on the west side.

Jack Hazut

JEREMIAH

Key Ideas
- The law in the heart
- God's bringing an enemy against Israel
- God as the potter who destroys and builds up

Purpose Statement

The purpose of the book of Jeremiah is to call the people of Judah back to faithful dependence on the Lord. He warns them of the punishment of exile that is coming quickly upon them as the Babylonians expand their empire.

Major Themes
- God's Policy with Nations
- New Covenant
- False Prophets

God's Presence

Jeremiah makes it clear in his temple sermon that the presence of God is not to be considered a talisman of good luck or protection, independent of covenant adherence. God delights to live among his people, but he does not need a place of residence. The New Covenant anticipates a future advance in the covenant as it envisions the presence of God in his people. All of this is in preparation for the loss of God's presence in the destruction of the temple at the end of the book.

CHAPTER
30

"This is what the LORD Almighty says: 'Consider now! Call for the wailing women to come; send for the most skillful of them'" (Jer. 9:17). Women were often professional mourners in the ancient world, like this woman with dust on her head.

The Yorck Projet/Wikimedia Commons

LAMENTATIONS

Key Ideas

- God punishes sin.
- God's judgment is just.
- God instructs the faithful through suffering.
- God is faithful, instilling hope in the righteous.

Purpose Statement

The book of Lamentations commemorates the destruction of Jerusalem by the Babylonian armies of Nebuchadrezzar. The poems are both a testimony to divine justice and a call to repentance for the people of God.

Major Themes

- Human Suffering
- Divine Abandonment

God's Presence

God's presence in the book of Lamentations is expressed in a negative way through the motif of divine abandonment. The poet relates that God has spurned, rejected, and abandoned Judah—king, priest, and sanctuary (2:6–7). Previously, the prophet Ezekiel witnessed the departure of God's glory from the Jerusalem temple due to their covenant violations, including blatant idolatry (Ezek. 9:9; 10:18–19).

Outline

I. Lamentations for Jerusalem's Misery and Desertion (1)

II. Lamentation for the Daughter of Zion Cut Down in Yahweh's Wrath (2)

III. The Poet's Grief and Hope (3)

IV. The Horror of the Siege (4)

V. Zion's Disgrace Remembered; a Petition for Restoration (5)

Lamentations takes its title from the Latin Vulgate. The book's placement after Jeremiah in the English canon reflects the influence of the Greek Old Testament, the Septuagint, which in the title verse ascribes the poetry to the prophet Jeremiah. The Hebrew title, *'ēkāh*, is derived from the first word of chapters 1, 2, and 4. The interjection is usually translated "how" or "alas" and was commonly used in the opening line of Israelite funeral dirges. For example, there was David's lament over Jonathan's death, "How the mighty have fallen!" (2 Sam. 1:19), and Isaiah's taunt song against the king of Babylon, "How you have fallen from heaven!" (Isa. 14:12).

Lamentations is included in the third division of the Hebrew canon, "the Writings." The book is ordered third among the five books comprising the Megilloth, or "Festival Scrolls" (i.e., the Song of Solomon, Ruth, Lamentations, Ecclesiastes, and Esther), which are used on specified Jewish feast days. Lamentations is assigned to be read annually on the ninth day of Ab, the day of mourning for the destruction of the temple in Jerusalem (by the Babylonians in 587 BC and by the Romans in AD 70).

The book of Lamentations is entirely poetic in form. The five poems are coextensive with the five chapters of the book.

The Writing of the Book

The Septuagint and Jewish tradition both ascribe the writing of Lamentations to the prophet Jeremiah. This association was probably based on a misunderstanding of the statement in 2 Chronicles 35:25 that "Jeremiah composed laments for Josiah." The arguments for and against Jeremiah's authorship of the poetry approaches a stalemate. Evidence supporting the prophet, such as the similarities in tone and vocabulary between the books of Jeremiah and Lamentations, is countered by their differences in poetic style and theological perspective. It seems best to assign the composition to an unknown eyewitness of the fall of Jerusalem, since the text itself records nothing of authorship.

This collection of funeral songs for Jerusalem was probably composed sometime between the fall of the city in 587/586 BC and exiled King Jehoiachin's release from prison in Babylon (ca. 562 BC — cf. 2 Kings 25:27–30). The despairing tone of the petition for national renewal in the closing lines of the final poem (5:19–22) indicates that the writer apparently knew nothing of Jehoiachin's discharge from prison and its implications for the fulfillment of Jeremiah's prophecies for covenant restoration in Israel (Jer. 30–33).

The Background

The book is a response to the destruction of Jerusalem, and its aftermath, by the Babylonian armies of King Nebuchadrezzar in 587 BC. The biblical accounts of the invasion of Judah and the fall of Jerusalem are recorded in 2 Kings 24–25 and 2 Chronicles 36.

The prophets had forewarned Judah of the impending catastrophe for two centuries (cf. 2 Kings 21:12; 24:3). Sadly, the repetition of the threat of divine judgment only dulled the ears of the people and insulated them against the idea of repentance. Moreover, the delay of Yahweh's visitation had lulled the nation into a false sense of security (e.g., Jer. 6:13–14; Jer. 7:1–4). Lamentations bewails the day, warned of by the prophets, in which Yahweh would become "like an enemy," destroying Israel "without pity" (Lam. 2:2, 5).

Purpose and Message

In contrast with 2 Kings 24–25, which documents the historical data about the fall of Jerusalem, Lamentations captures the pathos of that tragic turn in Israel's covenant experience with Yahweh. The poems preserve the Hebrew response to the unthinkable and inexpressible — the utter destruction of David's Zion, the ruin of Yahweh's temple, and the divine abandonment of "the elect" of God. ("Zion" is a favorite expression for Jerusalem in Psalms, Isaiah, and Lamentations. The origin of the term is uncertain, but the Hebrew *Ṣîyôn* may be understood as "fortified tower.") While the tragedy did confirm the prophetic message and vindicate prophetic interpretation of the relationship between covenant stipulations and curses, this was of little comfort to the stunned survivors of the Babylonian onslaught.

Lamentations records "the day of the LORD" for Judah enacted in all its terrible fury. The threat of covenant curse became a grim reality and an unforgettable nightmare. Moses' admonition that covenant violations

These Roman coins graphically depict the captive status of Judah, a state first entered at the hands of the Babylonians and lamented in this book.

Todd Bolen/
www.BiblePlaces.com,
courtesy of the British Museum

"The LORD determined to tear down the wall around the Daughter of Zion. He stretched out a measuring line and did not withhold his hand from destroying" (Lam. 2:8). Jeremiah was not the only ancient voice to mourn in writing over the fall of his city. This "Lament over the Fall of Ur" tells how Enlil devastated the city with a great storm (early 2nd millennium BC).

Eric Lessing/Art Resource, NY, courtesy of the Louvre

jeopardized Israel's presence in the land of Canaan was revealed to be more than hollow theologizing. Yahweh had finally exacted punishment for Judah's covenant transgressions. The people of God had been "vomited" out of the land of Yahweh's covenant promise (Lev. 18:24–30). The only consolation for "the Daughter of Zion" was the knowledge that one day the nations would also drink from the cup of God's wrath (Lam. 4:21–22; cf. 3:55–66).

As funeral dirges, the poems of Lamentations were designed to offer a type of **catharsis** or purification to the survivors of Judah's calamity. This expression of sorrow and venting of emotions could never fully answer the questions related to the "how" and "why" of God's sovereign rule over human history. But it did allow the suffering Hebrews to deal honestly with their grief and to mitigate the trauma of Yahweh's abandonment.

The poet bared the soul of the penitent nation, bowed in shame and admitting her many transgressions and great rebellion (e.g., 1:14, 22). The purging of sin and guilt permitted the "widow of Zion" to acknowledge that Yahweh was indeed just in his judgment of Jerusalem's covenant unfaithfulness (1:18).

Only this response of confession and repentance could give meaning and substance to the words of future hope prayed in chapter 3. The very wrath of God signaled his covenant love for Israel. The loving father must punish his wayward child. The call to wait upon the Lord and his unfailing mercy instilled hope for Israel's future restoration, because the nation's history had demonstrated Yahweh will not cast off forever (3:21–29).

Structure and Organization

Lamentations as we have noted, comprises five poems. Three of the poems are funeral dirges, opening with the customary wail "how?" (chaps. 1, 2, and 4). The other two poems are cast in the form of the "lamentation" or "complaint," with chapter 3 being an individual lamentation and chapter 5 a community lamentation. The "lamentation" or

Figure 30.1. The Acrostic Structure of Lamentations

Poem 1 (22 three-line verses)	Poem 2 (22 three-line verses)	Poem 3 (66 three-line verses)	Poem 4 22 two-line verses)
a	a	a	a ....
......	......	a	......
......	......	a	b ....
b	b	b	......
......	......	b	c ....
......	......	b	......

"complaint" is distinguished from a "lament" in form and content. The former is an expression of grief over a catastrophe that is irreversible, while the latter is an appeal to a merciful God for divine intervention in a desperate situation.

Four of the five poems are alphabetic acrostics, each line in succession introducing one of the twenty-two letters of the Hebrew alphabet. The structure of the acrostic poem in chapters 1 through 4 may be outlined as in figure 30.1.

The purpose of the alphabetic acrostics in Lamentations is three-fold: (1) the acrostic form has mnemonic value—the poet preserves the memory of Jerusalem's tragedy through the recitation of the alphabet; (2) the acrostic poems convey the full expression of lamentation over Zion's destruction—effectual catharsis "from A to Z"; and (3) in constricting the range of artistic expression, the rigid use of the acrostic form enables the poet to devote full attention to the topic or theme at hand.

The concluding poem is not an acrostic, but it nevertheless follows the twenty-two verse pattern of poems 1, 2, and 4. The deviation from the formula may have been simply a stylistic choice or an emphatic ploy by the poet.

Poem 1 is a funeral dirge personifying the city of Jerusalem as a once proud and dignified woman, now brutally raped and abandoned by treacherous friends. This image is intensified by the use of words and phrases like "widow" and "queen" (1:1), and "Daughter of Zion" (1:6). The poem emphasizes the desolation, loneliness, and sense of abandonment felt by the survivors of the calamity (vv. 2, 9, 16, 17).

Poem 2 describes the vehemence of Yahweh's anger against Zion, and poem 4 records the grim aftermath of Yahweh's judgment. The Daughter of Zion's only comfort was the knowledge that the punishment for her sins had been accomplished (4:22). Some scholars suggest that the deliberate inversion of the sixteenth and seventeenth letters of the alphabet in chapters 2 and 4 serves to emphasize Judah's shame

CHAPTER
31

"Then they will know that I am the LORD their God, for though I sent them into exile among the nations, I will gather them to their own land, not leaving any behind" (Ezek. 39:28).

Eric Lessing/Art Resource, NY

EZEKIEL

Key Ideas

- Yahweh's sovereignty over Israel and the nations
- Dynamic relationship of the individual to the group
- Mysterious interplay of individual responsibility and divine judgment
- Babylonian exile as punishment for Judah's sin of idolatry
- Yahweh's faithfulness to his covenant promises
- Restoration of a New Israel under Davidic leadership

Purpose Statement

The purpose of the book of Ezekiel is to warn the people of Judah of the impending destruction of Jerusalem and call the people of God to repentance. The prophet also offers hope of future restoration for Israel in the promise of a new covenant and the return of God's presence to the Jerusalem temple.

Major Themes

- "Son of Man"
- Ezekiel's Chariot Vision
- Individual Responsibility
- Old Testament Apocalyptic Literature

God's Presence

Ezekiel witnesses the departure of God's glory from the Jerusalem temple prior to the final phase of the Babylonian conquest and exile of Judah due to their idolatry (9:9; 10:18–19). The prophet also promises the return of God's glory to a new temple (43:1–5).

vassal king. Jehoiakim subsequently died during the latter stages of the Babylonian siege of Jerusalem (598–597 BC). His son, Jehoiachin, ruled only three months in his place before the Babylonians overran and plundered the city (2 Kings 24:1–17).

King Jehoiachin and the royal family were deported to Babylon, along with another ten thousand people from the elite of Hebrew society (2 Kings 24:12–14). The prophet Ezekiel was among that number, and Jehoiachin's exile became the watershed by which Ezekiel dated his divine commission to prophesy and also many of his messages to the Hebrew captives in Babylon (Ezek. 1:1–3, 8:1; et al.).

Purpose and Message

The prophetic message and literary structure of Ezekiel are closely related. The book's three-part message is really a theodicy (i.e., a defense or interpretation of God's judgment of Judah and the resultant destruction), and it corresponds to the three dimensions or phases of Ezekiel's ministry to the Hebrew exiles. Chapters 1–24 predate the fall of Jerusalem and are directed to the rebellious house of Judah. The purpose of Ezekiel's divine commission as God's "watchman" was to warn a generation of obstinate and hardened Israelites of impending

The Nations of Ezekiel
25–32

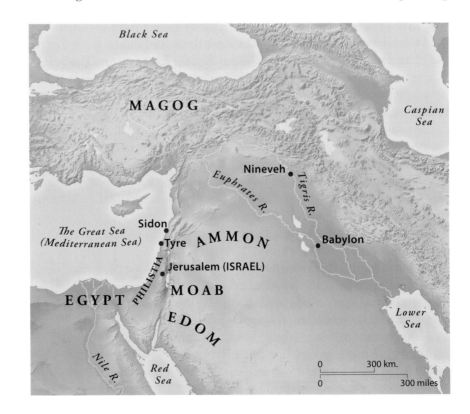

judgment (2:3–8), to underscore each generation's accountability for sin (18:20), and to call those willing to heed the counsel "Repent and live" (18:21–23, 32).

After the destruction of Jerusalem in 587/586 BC, Ezekiel turned his attention to the nations surrounding Israel that had been active participants in or gleeful onlookers to the "day of Jacob's trouble" (chaps. 25–32). Lest in their arrogance they assume an exemption from divine judgment, they too were warned that God had determined to visit them in wrath and vengeance for their misdeeds (e.g., 25:1–11). Implicit in this phase of Ezekiel's ministry was a reminder to Israel that Yahweh is indeed righteous and just in his sovereign rule of the nations (cf. 28:24–26).

Finally, in chapters 33–48 Ezekiel instills hope among the captive Hebrew remnant by encouraging them with the promise of a new "covenant of peace" superintended by the "Davidic shepherd" (34:20–31). Yahweh, the covenant-keeping God of Abraham, would once again restore the fortunes of Israel and Judah by joining them into a single nation under one messianic king—the Davidic prince who will rule forever. The Lord would cleanse his people, establish faithfulness in the land, relocate his sanctuary in their midst, and bless Israel through his "servant David" (37:15–28).

Structure and Organization

Thirteen of Ezekiel's messages are introduced by a date formula. The table below illustrates the general chronological arrangement of the prophecy, with three exceptions (29:1, 17; and 32:1). All three are oracles against Egypt and have been placed together with the other Egyptian prophecies rather than in chronological sequence.

The prophet's revelations from God were delivered to the Hebrew people orally and presumably recorded at a later date, as evidenced in expressions like "speak ... say" (14:4), "set forth an allegory" (17:2), "preach" (20:46), "confront" (22:2–3), and so on. The lack of strict chronological ordering of the literature may argue in favor of Ezekiel as the compiler of the oracles, since it is likely another later editor would have been more concerned with the deliberate sequencing of the dated materials.[1]

Chariot vision	1:1–3	June 593 BC
Call to be a watchman	3:16	June 593
Temple vision	8:1	Aug/Sept 592
Discourse with elders	20:1	Aug 591
Second siege of Jerusalem	24:1	Jan 588
Judgment on Tyre	26:1	Mar/Apr 587/586

1. The first year of Jehoiachin's captivity is dated to June 597 BC (2 Kings 24:12). The second siege of Jerusalem began in December/January 589/588 BC (2 Kings 25:1), and the destruction of Jerusalem came in September 586 BC (2 Kings 25:8). See K. S. Freedy and D. B. Redford, "The Dates of Ezekiel in Relation to Biblical, Babylonian and Egyptian Sources," *Journal of the American Oriental Society* 90, no. 3 (1970): 460–85.

Judgment on Egypt	29:1	Jan 587
Judgment on Egypt	29:17	Apr 571
Judgment on Egypt	30:20	Apr 587
Judgment on Egypt	31:1	June 587
Lament over Pharaoh	32:1	Mar 585
Lament over Egypt	32:17	Apr 586
Fall of Jerusalem	33:21	Dec/Jan 586/585
New temple vision	40:1	Apr 573

This book is one of the richest anthologies or collections of Hebrew literary forms in the Old Testament. Several types of prophetic and poetic speech are incorporated within the prophet's message, as shown in figure 31.1.

As drama, Ezekiel's words and actions gave "shock treatment" to a nation made callous by sin against the Lord. His bold and provocative language (especially the imagery of harlotry in chapters 16 and 23) was designed to scandalize and convict a people desensitized to the truth by a life of spiritual adultery. Meanwhile, his symbolic pantomimes served to underscore the urgency of the hour as Yahweh's wrath was about to be unleashed on Judah (e.g., chaps. 4–5; 12:1–7; 24:1–14; 37:15–23). Few heard the call of God. In fact, Ezekiel was likened to a "bard" skill-

Figure 31.1. Speech Types in Ezekiel's Message

Judgment oracle	Usually introduced by formula, "I am against you"	21:1 – 5
Aftermath or restoration oracle	Reversing judgment formula, "I am for you"	6:2 – 3; 20:46 – 47
"Woe" oracle of indictment		13:3 – 7; 34:2 – 6
Demonstration oracle	Usually containing "because … therefore" clauses	13:8 – 9; 16:36 – 42
Disputation oracle	In which popular proverb is recited and then refuted by prophetic discourse (e.g., the "sour grapes" proverb)	18:1 – 20; cf. 12:22 – 25
Lament Over Tyre Over Pharaoh		26:15 – 18 32:1 – 16
Wailing lament	Introduced by "wall"	30:1 – 4; 32:17 – 21
Riddles, parables, allegories	E.g., parable of the vine Allegories of eagle and cedars, lion, boiling pot, etc.	Chap. 15 Chaps. 17, 19, 23, 24, 27

fully playing and singing beautiful love songs to people who loved to listen — but refused to heed the warning of his message (30:30–33).

Finally, the overall structure of Ezekiel's oracles contributes to the basic purpose of the prophet's message — namely, the sovereignty of God. The oracles against Jerusalem (chaps. 1–24) reinforced Ezekiel's teaching on the sovereignty of Yahweh over Israel by calling attention to the curse of judgment for covenant trespass. Yahweh's sovereignty was then extended to Israel's neighbors as well in the oracles against the nations (chaps. 25–32). If Yahweh is sovereign over the nations, how much more is he the king over his elect people, Israel?

The concluding section of the book promises covenant renewal and the restoration of Davidic kingship in Israel (chaps. 33–48). The new temple vision confirmed Yahweh's sovereignty over Israel in vindicating his holiness for the sake of his covenant name (36:22–32). The repetition of the phrase, "and you will know that I am the LORD" (some ninety times in the book) stands as a not-so-subtle reminder of the certainty of God's judgment and the efficacy of the Sovereign Yahweh in "doing what he had spoken" (36:36).

Major Themes

"Son of Man"

The Lord addressed Ezekiel by the title "Son of man" some ninety times in the book. The phrase appears elsewhere in the Old Testament only in Daniel 8:17, and it is used to emphasize the humanity of the messenger in contrast to the divine origin and authority of the message. The expression also revealed the symbolic nature of Ezekiel's life and ministry for both the Hebrew captives in Babylon and those who remained in Jerusalem. Ezekiel played the "fool for God" in that his life was a living object lesson to the rebellious house of Israel (e.g., the pantomimes prefiguring the Babylonian siege and sack of Jerusalem and the exile of the Hebrews — chaps. 4–5). His unorthodox ministry and unconventional lifestyle were sanctioned by Yahweh and energized by the Holy Spirit as the "antidote" for a patient in the last stages of a "terminal disease." Ultimately these conditions ensured that Israel would know that a prophet of God had been among them (2:5; 33:33).

Ezekiel's Chariot Vision

The ecstatic visions of Ezekiel were essential to the overall message of the book for two reasons. First, they reinforce the correctness of the prophet's understanding of God's role in the fall of Judah and the destruction of his holy city Jerusalem. The predominant eschatological

"For the king of Babylon will stop at the fork in the road, at the junction of the two roads, to seek an omen: He will cast lots with arrows, he will consult his idols, he will examine the liver" (Ezek. 21:21). The ancients would often use a form of divination called extispicy, which involved reading omens from the organs of animals, such as the liver. These are clay models of a liver used for divination.
Marie-Lan Nguyen/Wikimedia Commons, courtesy of the Louvre

CHAPTER

32

"Then a mighty king will arise and do as he pleases. After he has appeared, his empire will be broken up and parceled out to the four winds of heaven" (Dan. 11:3). This is a widely recognized reference to Alexander the Great, who is in battle with the Persian king Darius III in this mosaic.

Eric Lessing/Art Resource, NY

DANIEL

Key Ideas

- Living a life of faith in an increasingly hostile world
- Sovereignty of God to deliver and prosper people of faith
- Sovereignty of God in international political affairs

Purpose Statement

The purpose of the book of Daniel concerns the sovereignty of God. As Daniel and his friends trust the Lord, God shows himself able to protect and deliver. Daniel's visions proclaim God's sovereignty over kings, nations, and empires. At the same time, his prophecies tell the people of Israel that the kingdom they were waiting for would be longer in coming than expected. In the meantime, they were to live out their faith in the midst of an unbelieving world, trusting in God for deliverance and protection.

Major Themes

- Kingdom of God
- Pride and Rebellion

God's Presence

In Daniel it is clear that God intends to continue to be present with his people even though the temple is destroyed and they are in exile. His presence protects them from oppression as they honor him in their decisions and behavior.

Outline

D aniel is one of the best-known yet most complex books of the Old Testament. It contains the story of a young Israelite taken forcibly from his homeland to be trained for diplomatic service in the great city of Babylon. He rose quickly through the ranks, becoming one of the most respected officials in the Babylonian government. His reputation remained even as the Babylonian Empire collapsed around him; though he was aged, his career reached its apex as he was appointed one of a triumvirate of officials second only to the king in the sprawling Medo-Persian Empire.

The Writing of the Book

The events of the book of Daniel are clearly set against the background of the sixth century BC. Nevertheless, many present-day scholars attribute the writing of the book to an author from the second century BC, specifically between 168 and 164 BC.

The reason for targeting this date and the precision of it are both derived from chapter 11 of the book. There Daniel discusses a number of kings whom he does not name but refers to as "king of the North" and "king of the South." As it turns out, however, the details presented in this chapter coincide quite closely with the history of the Middle East from the time of Alexander the Great in the fourth century BC (see vv. 3–4) through the time of Antiochus IV (Epiphanes) in the second century BC (vv. 21ff.).

1. Outline adapted from D. W. Gooding, "Literary Structure of the Book of Daniel.and Its Implications," *TB* 32 (1981).

Scholars who support the second-century dating of the book contend that Daniel fits into the category of apocalyptic literature, which they view as having certain traits in common. Among them are **pseudonymity** (attributing a piece of writing to a well-known person of the past to give it credibility) and *vaticinium ex eventu* (Latin, meaning writing about events that have already happened as if the author were living before they took place). These traits are observable in some Akkadian literature dating back to the twelfth century BC and are quite common in extrabiblical Jewish apocalyptic literature from the second century BC to the second century AD.

By including Daniel in this group, scholars imply that the book is thereby also pseudonymous (thus not written by Daniel or in the time of Daniel) and that the book contains *vaticinium ex eventu*. Since the book accurately reflects events that we know took place in the year 168 BC (vv. 31–39), it is supposed that the book was written soon after that date. If that is the case, it could not have been written long after that time, for these interpreters consider verses 40ff. to be an inaccurate prediction of how Antiochus IV (Epiphanes) would die. Since he died in 164 BC, the book would had to have been written before that time.

An additional feature that causes some to question the historicity of the book is the series of sensational events recorded in the narrative, such as the deliverance of Daniel's friends from the fire (chap. 3), the handwriting on the wall at Belshazzar's feast (chap. 5), and Daniel's ordeal in the lion pit (chap. 6). Such sensationalism was characteristic of much noncanonical literature of the intertestamental period.

A final objection concerns people and occurrences in the book that remain unconfirmed from extrabiblical sources. Darius the Mede (chaps. 6, 9, 11) has yet to be identified, and the seven-year insanity of Nebuchadrezzar has been thought to be more easily attributable to the last Neo-Babylonian king, Nabonidus.

While acknowledging the similarities that exist between Daniel and some of the intertestamental literature, some scholars are still wary of thereby attributing to the book of Daniel all the same characteristics. The book is different in many aspects from both the so-called Akkadian

This omen collection, called "shumma izbu," deals with the symbolic and ominological import of various deformities in newborn animals. Some of the descriptions are reminiscent of the characteristics of the beast in Daniel's vision in Daniel 7.

The Schøyen Collection MS 3000, Oslo and London

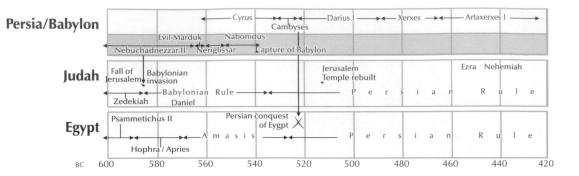

Persia/Babylon		

BC   600   580   560   540   520   500   480   460   440   420

apocalypses and the later Jewish apocalypses. Though it would not be denied that Daniel shares some features of apocalyptic literature, it is not easy to give a clear definition of apocalyptic, nor to differentiate it entirely from prophetic literature. More and more scholars choose to speak of a prophetic-apocalyptic continuum to accommodate all of the variables of the literature (see chap. 27). The further toward the apocalyptic side of the continuum a book leans, the more likely it is to have features such as pseudonymity or *vaticinium ex eventu*. But one could not infer that books toward the middle of the continuum such as Daniel would of necessity be so characterized.

In fact, the scenario that would be required for Daniel to be considered *vaticinium ex eventu* appears to face considerable problems. The four-year time span (168–164 BC) is far too short for a book of that time to be written, copied, circulated, and adopted as truth and then preserved as canon despite the apparent failure of its predictions.[2] On this count, it seems that the presuppositional rejection of supernaturalism is often partly responsible for the rejection of a sixth-century date for the book.

The identity of Darius the Mede is still in question. Attempts have been made to identify him with Gobryas, the governor of Babylon during the early years of Cyrus the Great, or with Cyrus himself. Both of these views remain speculative, and neither is without problems. As more information becomes available, more positive identity may become possible.

Finally, while it is true that the insane king of chapter 4 would be more easily identifiable with Nabonidus, it is not impossible to fit seven years of insanity into the reign of Nebuchadrezzar. To date, there is no attested activity by Nebuchadrezzar between 581 and 573 BC except the ongoing, drawn-out siege of Tyre.

The result of all of this is that we see no evidence to preclude dating the book to the sixth century BC. Furthermore, the linguistic evidence (in regard to both the Hebrew and the Aramaic of Daniel) points toward a time earlier than the second century, as does the appearance

2. For this argument in detail, see Gooding, "The Literary Structure of the Book of Daniel and Its Implications," 73–74.

of Daniel in the Septuagint (usually dated as early as the third century BC) and the Dead Sea Scrolls (from the first and second centuries BC). The fact that Daniel speaks in first-person narrative from chapter 7 to the end naturally suggests that he is the author, though the use of third person in the first part of the book may indicate that someone else laid out the framework and organized it.

The Background

In 626 BC Nabopolassar was enthroned as king of Babylon as the Babylonians declared their independence from the waning Assyrian Empire. Allying themselves with the Medes to the east, they began testing the strength of the Assyrians. By 612 the capital city of Nineveh fell, and with the collapse of the government after the fall of Carchemish in 605 the once mighty Assyrians became nothing more than a memory for the people of the Near East whom they had terrorized for almost a century and a half.

At the death of Nabopolassar, the throne was ably occupied by his son and field general, Nebuchadrezzar, in 605. At that time he assumed control of all the territories forfeited by the Assyrian capitulation, including Judah. The sons of Josiah occupying the throne of Judah proved themselves unable to accept a vassal role, as over the next two decades they became constantly embroiled in conspiracies against the Babylonians. This led not only to several deportations, but eventually to the destruction

When Nebuchadrezzar "was walking on the roof of the royal palace of Babylon, he said, 'Is not this the great Babylon I have built as the royal residence, by my mighty power and for the glory of my majesty?'" (Dan. 4:29–30). This sort of boast was common for kings of the ancient Near East and elsewhere, such as in this royal inscription found in east India.
Michael French, courtesy of the British Museum

of Jerusalem and the temple in 586 BC by the armies of Nebuchadrezzar. During all this time, Daniel was serving in the Babylonian court, for he had been among the first group taken to Babylon in 605.

Nebuchadrezzar's long and prosperous reign came to an end in 562, and not long after, the Persians began to build their empire under the leadership of Cyrus the Great. Over the next two decades the successors of Nebuchadrezzar performed so poorly that, by 539, Cyrus was welcomed into the city of Babylon as deliverer rather than as conqueror.

Within a year after gaining control of the Babylonian Empire, Cyrus established his policy of rule through benevolence by allowing many of the deported peoples to return and rebuild their homes and their sanctuaries (cf. Ezra 1:1–4). The people of Judah rightly viewed this as a fulfillment of the prophecies and a reestablishment of the covenant, and they looked forward to the formation of a worldwide theocracy with Jerusalem at its center.

Purpose and Message

The sovereignty of God is the core of this book and can be seen operating in both the spiritual and the political arenas. In the narratives of events in the lives of Daniel and his friends, the emphasis is on living a life of faith in an increasingly hostile world. God's sovereignty is seen in his ability to prosper or deliver those who are true to their faith convictions.

Babylonian, Median, Persian Empires

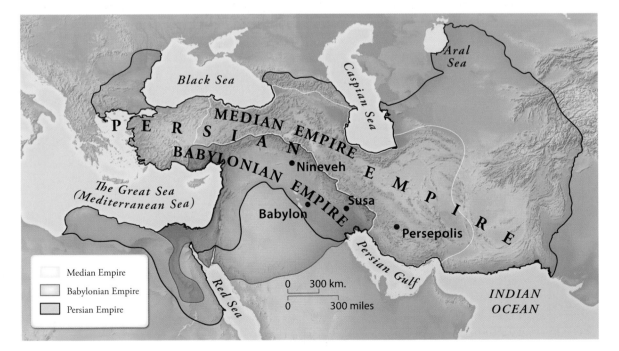

Median Empire
Babylonian Empire
Persian Empire

God's sovereignty in political affairs is addressed more directly in the visions of the book. The purpose was to deal with expectations of the exilic and postexilic communities. Based on their reading of the earlier prophets, the people of Israel were looking for the kingdom of God to be established upon their return from seventy years of exile. Daniel's visions informed them that four kingdoms were yet to come before the establishment of God's kingdom, and that while the return from exile would come within seventy years of Jeremiah's prophecy, this should not be confused with the full restoration. Rather than seventy years, the required span would be seventy weeks of years.

In the meantime the Israelites were to live out their faith in a Gentile world under circumstances that would make it more and more difficult to do so. They had to count on the sovereignty of God to sustain them generation by generation, crisis by crisis. They also had to trust the power of God to control the flow of world empires as they rose and fell. God's agenda is never in jeopardy; nevertheless, they were to be prepared for the long term.

"To these four young men God gave knowledge and understanding of all kinds of literature and learning. And Daniel could understand visions and dreams of all kinds" (Dan. 1:17). As captives in the Babylonian Royal Court, Daniel and his friends would have been trained in dream-reading techniques and used the literature that offered interpretations of dreams such as this omen tablet.
Todd Bolen/
www.BiblePlaces.com

Structure and Organization

The book can be seen to divide evenly between chapters 6 and 7, as shown in the outline, if the material is organized into events and visions. In this case, each half follows a chronological sequence, proceeding in chapters 1–6 from the first year of Nebuchadrezzar (chap. 1) through the last day of Belshazzar (chap. 5) and on into the reign of Darius (chap. 6). In chapters 7–12, the narrative begins in the first year of Belshazzar (chap. 7) and moves eventually to the third year of Cyrus (chap. 10).

When we consider some of the parallel structure of the book, however, another possible organization can be identified that places the major break between chapters 5 and 6. In this scheme, chapters 1–5 witness a steady deterioration in the attitude toward the Jewish religion. Highlights are the command to worship the statue (chap. 3) and the desecration of the sacred temple vessels (chap. 5). Chapters 6–12 show an increasing persecution of Jewish worship. Daniel is thrown to the lions when he refuses to alter his prayer habits (chap. 6). Pagan kings attempt to stop Israelite worship, and they desecrate the temple and altar (chaps. 8–12).

Besides this progression of hostile attitudes toward the Israelite religion, there are parallels between the sections. Chapters 1 and 6 both see Daniel refuse to adjust his practices to conform to expectations. Chapters 2 and 7 both deal with four empires. Chapters 3 and 8 both deal with kings who set themselves up as God and so interfere with proper worship. Chapters 4 and 9 have in common a sevenfold scheme of punishment (4:23, 25; 9:24–25). Chapters 5 and 10–12 both deal with the coming of the end.[3]

The court stories of chapters 1–5, then, show that during the initial reign of Gentile kingdoms over Jerusalem, only the first small indications of hostility toward Jewish religion were observable, and those were in isolated cases dealing with individuals. This small beginning was to escalate as time went by. In that sense, as of the Babylon of old, it may be said "If . . . they have begun to do this, then nothing they plan to do will be impossible for them" (Gen. 11:6).

Chapter 1 shows God honoring the act of faith of Daniel and his friends. In chapter 2 the sovereignty of God is evident in his providing Daniel with the interpretation of the dream and thereby sparing their lives. It is also evident in the contents of the dream, where we see a succession of kingdoms that conveyed to the Israelites that it was not yet time for the kingdom for which they had been waiting. Certainly this would have been a disappointing message for the exiles to hear. The main significance, however, is the fact that in God's agenda, the mighty empires of the world come and go, and they will all be superseded by the kingdom of God that will never be destroyed (2:44). This would give reason for continued hope.

The placement of chapter 3 implies that it may have been the dream of chapter 2 that had a role in inspiring the presumption of Nebuchadrezzar in building the statue for everyone to worship. Again, as in chapter 1 we see God honoring an act of faith with deliverance. A key statement is in 3:17–18: God may choose to provide deliverance or he may not, but his sovereignty is in no way threatened if he should not choose to deliver in any single instance.

Chapters 4–5 both demonstrate God's power and control over the Gentile kings and kingdoms. This goes beyond the assertion of chapter 2 that God has an overall agenda. Here we see the ability of God to intervene at any given point along the way to make his control evident.

In chapter 6 the insidious new development is that, unlike anything in chapters 1–5, we see a malicious conspiracy against Daniel specifically focused on his religious practice. Here it is the Gentile king who affirms the sovereignty of Daniel's God (v. 16).

3. Much more detail of this structure can be found in Gooding, "Literary Structure of the Book of Daniel."

Marie-Lan Nguyen/Wikimedia Commons, courtesy of the Louvre

The lion was symbolic of royal power. This roaring lion brings to mind the lion den into which Daniel was cast by decree of Darius the Mede.

A significant difference from the discussion of the four kingdoms in Daniel 2 is that chapter 7 shows clearly the perversity, especially of the fourth kingdom, and the hostility toward the godly (vv. 7, 25). Again, however, the emphasis is on the fact that after these pagan kingdoms, the kingdom of God is coming and will endure forever (vv. 16–18, 27).

The orchestrated persecution of chapter 8 moves well beyond the isolated incident that was reported in chapter 6. Both the pride of the king and his program of persecution make the Babylonians pale in comparison. Chapter 9 addresses the way in which Israel and her prophesied restoration fit into the four-kingdom framework. The information is given that Israel's persistence in rebellion meant that full restoration would be slow in coming, but this in no way implied any lack of control on the part of God. This also shows that, contrary to the expectations of those returning from exile, things would get worse before they got better.

Finally, chapters 10–12 speak of the eventual end of Gentile rule. Implicit in this, however, was the warning that there might be several periods of history that look like the end. It was not the task of the godly to know when the end was coming, but to persevere until the end that certainly would come in God's time. The assertion of Shadrach, Meshach, and Abednego in a very real sense stands as the central message of the book, namely, trust in the sovereignty of God sustains through crisis and persecution (3:16–18).

Major Themes

The Kingdom of God

That the kingdom of God is the climax of God's agenda for Israel and the world is communicated very clearly in the book of Daniel. The concept is introduced in chapter 2 as a kingdom that will never be destroyed (2:44), though in some senses God already rules an everlasting kingdom (cf. 4:3, 34–35). In 7:9–14 little additional information is given except in the introduction of one referred to as the "son of man" to whom the kingdom of God was given. From our vantage point we can surely identify this individual with Jesus, though that would not have been clear to the ancient readers. Yet there is no doubt that the "son of man" was recognized as a messianic figure, and this title became one of the most common to be connected to Jesus during his earthly ministry. Chapters 9 and 11 are concerned primarily with the time of the end that is to precede the setting up of the kingdom of God, but there is no discussion about that kingdom.

In contrast, the kingdoms of the nations are seen as temporary and exercising limited dominion. The Babylonian kingdom is the object of discussion in chapters 4–5; the Medo-Persian and Greek kingdoms are explicitly discussed in chapter 8; and the Greek kingdom, especially the Seleucid branch, is clearly the object of discussion in chapter 11.

The four-kingdom scheme presented in chapters 2 and 7 is a common motif in the literature of the time and afterward. The identification of the four kingdoms is not made in the book, though Nebuchadrezzar is identified with the first kingdom (2:38) and we would expect that the other two kingdoms mentioned explicitly in other sections — Medo-Persia and Greece — are two of the remaining three. Such identification, however, has relatively little significance. The pertinent facts for the context of the book are (1) the contrast between human empires and the kingdom of God, and (2) the latter is coming and will be everlasting.

Pride and Rebellion

A highly visible theme is the pride of kings that leads to their eventual downfall. Nebuchadrezzar's golden image and his pride over his accomplishments in building the city of Babylon (chap. 3); Belshazzar's pride demonstrated in the desecration of the utensils from the temple and his rebuke by Daniel (5:18–23); even Darius the Mede's vulnerability to the decree suggested by his administrators — all provide specific examples of this characteristic. Pride is seen further in the actions of the fourth beast of chapter 7, the little horn of chapter 8, the prince who was to come in chapter 9, and the king of the South in chapter 11.

While pride led to the downfall of the kings of the nations, it was Israel's rebellion against God that led to her punishment. Daniel's confession on behalf of the people of Israel acknowledged transgressing the law of Moses and ignoring the warnings of the prophets. So the pride and presumption of the nations was paralleled by the rebellion and disobedience of Israel, bringing the wrath of God.

The book of Daniel served to remind the people that their troubles would not be over when they returned from exile. Though judgment for the sins of the preexilic generations had been carried out in full, the people of Israel had still not reached the spiritual plateau that God wanted them to achieve. Expectations would therefore have to be put on hold and times of distress endured. But God gave them the hope of resurrection (12:2) and encouraged them to persevere through this important time of purging (12:10–13).

The Jezreel Valley was the site of many battles in ancient times. At its eastern end was the town of Jezreel, an administrative center for King Ahab. Hosea is commanded to name his first child "Jezreel" in memory of the blood that Jehu shed there in overthrowing the house of Ahab (2 Kings 9–10), which Yahweh would repay (Hos. 1:4–5). Jack Hazut

HOSEA

Key Ideas

- Yahweh's unchanging love for Israel
- Yahweh's jealousy for his covenant
- Yahweh's just judgment
- Yahweh's healing and restoration of the remnant

Purpose Statement:

The purpose of the book of Hosea is to warn the people in the northern kingdom of Israel of the impending Assyrian exile, demonstrate God's steadfast love for his people through his own marriage to Gomer, and call the people to repentance and covenant renewal with Yahweh.

Major Themes

- Hosea's Marriage
- Baalism

God's Presence

God's presence in the book of Hosea is embodied in his covenant relationship with Israel and illustrated in the metaphor of marriage, dramatized by Hosea's marriage to the prostitute Gomer.

Questions for Further Study and Discussion

1. Discuss how the various interpretive options for Hosea's marriage to Gomer illustrate or fail to illustrate Israel's covenantal relationship with Yahweh.
2. Discuss the ethical implications of God's charge to Hosea to marry a prostitute — specifically, the prophet's integrity and the risk of God's message being misunderstood and rejected.
3. What does Hosea mean by "acknowledging the Lord" (e.g., 4:1; 6:3)?
4. How were the religious, political, and social conditions of Israel similar as encountered by the prophets Amos and Hosea? How were they different?
5. What does Hosea have to say about "religious syncretism"? How do we avoid this mixing of pagan and orthodox religious traditions today?
6. Discuss Hosea's attitudes toward religious institutions, ritual, and liturgy. Can he correctly be called an "iconoclast"?

For Further Reading

Albright, William F. *Yahweh and the Gods of Canaan*. Reprint. Winona Lake, Ind.: Eisenbrauns, 1990. A standard work on Canaanite religion and its impact on Israelite religion.

Andersen, F. I., and David N. Freedman. *Hosea*. AB. Vol. 24. Garden City, N.Y.: Doubleday, 1980. Exhaustive and technical introduction and commentary. Fresh translation combines appreciation for the poetic nature of prophecy and careful linguistic study of the Hebrew text. The best book in English on the topic.

Beeby, H. D. *Grace Abounding: A Commentary on Hosea*. ITC. Grand Rapids: Eerdmans, 1989.

Brueggemann, Walter. *Tradition for Crisis: A Study of Hosea*. Atlanta: John Knox, 1968. Penetrating "tradition-history" analysis of Hosea as an interpretation of Mosaic law, with constructive suggestions for prophetic ministry in the contemporary situation.

Bullock, C. Hassell. *An Introduction to the Old Testament Prophetic Books*. Chicago: Moody Press, 1986.

Chisholm, Robert B. *Handbook on the Prophets*. Grand Rapids: Baker, 2002.

Craigie, Peter C. *Twelve Prophets*. 2 vols. DSBOT. Philadelphia: Westminster, 1985.

Emmerson, G. I. *Hosea: An Israelite Prophet in Judean Perspective*. JSOTSS 28. Sheffield, England: JSOT Press, 1984.

Garrett, Duane A. *Hosea, Joel*. NAC 19A. Nashville: Broadman, 1997.

Hubbard, D. A. *Hosea: An Introduction and Commentary*. TOTC. Downers Grove, Ill.: InterVarsity Press, 1989.

Kidner, Derek. *Love to the Loveless: The Message of Hosea*. Downers Grove, Ill.: InterVarsity Press, 1981. Readable and solid exposition of Hosea's message with insightful contemporary application.

Landy, F. *Hosea*. Sheffield, England: Sheffield Academic Press, 1995.

Limburg, J. *Hosea–Micah*. Interp. Louisville: John Knox, 1988.

Mays, J. L. *Hosea*. OTL. Philadelphia: Westminster, 1969. Valuable theological treatment of the book's message.

McComiskey, T. E. "Hosea." In *The Minor Prophets: An Exegetical and Expository Commentary*. Ed. by T. E. McComiskey. Grand Rapids: Baker, 1992. 1:1–237.

McConville, Gordon, J., and Ernest C. Lucas. *Exploring the Old Testament: A Guide to the Prophets*. Downers Grove, Ill.: InterVarsity Press, 2003.

Ostborn, G. *Yahweh and Baal: Studies in the Book of Hosea and Related Documents*. Lund, Sweden: Gleerup, 1956.

Smith, Gary. V. *Hosea/Amos/Micah*. NIVAC. Grand Rapids: Zondervan, 2001.

Stuart, D. *Hosea–Jonah*. WBC. Vol. 31. Waco, Tex·Word, 1987. Concise introductory sections on the historical background, message, literary structure, and themes of Hosea's book.

Wolff, Hans Walter. *A Commentary on the Book of the Prophet Hosea*. HER. Trans. by G. Stansell. Philadelphia: Fortress Press, 1974.

" 'Even now,' declares the Lord, 'return to me with all your heart, with fasting and weeping and mourning' " (Joel 2:12).

JOEL

Key Ideas

- Analogy of the locust plague to describe the coming day of the Lord
- The pouring out of the Spirit on all people as a prelude to judgment

Purpose Statement

Joel's concern throughout the book was to address "the day of the LORD." The locust plague was the beginning and the judgment would get worse. He called on the people to repent and when they responded positively, favor and prosperity were proclaimed.

Major Theme

- Locust Plague

God's Presence

The description of the day of the Lord is adopted in Acts as referring to the coming of the Holy Spirit, one of the major stages of God's presence where his people are indwelt and become the corporate temple of God.

Amos addresses in chapters 3–4 the sins of Samaria, the capital city of the northern kingdom of Israel. These are the ruins of Samaria's acropolis. Todd Bolen/www.BiblePlaces.com

AMOS

Key Ideas

- God holds the nations accountable for their social policy.
- Israel will not escape the judgment of the day of the Lord.
- True worship spawns social justice.
- God will restore a remnant of Israel.

Purpose Statement

The book of Amos forecasts disaster for the northern kingdom of Israel in the form of Assyrian invasion and exile as a result of entrenched religious hypocrisy and social injustice. The prophet also calls the people to repentance and promises hope for the future in the form of messianic restoration and blessing.

Major Theme

- Social Justice

God's Presence

The presence of God is inextricably linked to the practice of social justice in the book of Amos (e.g., 5:14).

Figure 35.1. Uzziah and Jeroboam II

Higher Old Testament Chronology		Lower Old Testament Chronology
791 – 740 BC	Uzziah (or Azariah)	783 – 742 BC
793 – 753 BC	Jeroboam II	786 – 746 BC

decades. The exact dates for Uzziah and Jeroboam II vary some two to seven years depending on the source consulted.[1] The alternative dating schemes for the reigns of the two kings are compared in figure 35.1.

The reference to "the earthquake" in the superscription provides little help in fixing the precise date of Amos's prophecy. Archaeological discoveries at sites like Samaria and Hazor attest such destruction by earthquake, and Zechariah's mention of the natural disaster indicates that the tremor was long remembered in Israel (14:5). Yet attempts to pinpoint the year in which the quake occurred are highly speculative. Consequently the time of Amos's prophetic activity is best assigned to the general time period ranging from 760–750 BC.

The biblical accounts of the reigns of Uzziah (or Azariah) and Jeroboam II are found in 2 Kings 14:17–15:7 and 2 Chronicles 26. Politically and economically, both kings brought stability and prosperity to their respective kingdoms. Territorial borders were expanded through successful military conquest against foreign foes, Israel and Judah even managed a peaceful coexistence, and commercial enterprise and agricultural production burgeoned.

The prophets of God, however, looked past the facade of the so-called golden age to the dry rot of social and moral decay in both Israel and Judah. Amos and Isaiah paint similar pictures of "real life" in the divided kingdoms. Contrary to all external appearances, these seers charged that the Hebrew nations were "loaded with guilt" (Isa. 1:4) and "ripe" for the judgment of God (Amos 8:1–2; cf. 3:9–15; Isa 3:13–15; 5:8–30).

Purpose and Message

Religious apostasy, moral and social collapse, and political corruption of the northern kingdom prompted God to send the Judahite Amos across the border to prophesy in Bethel of Israel. The shepherd-preacher's basic message to Jeroboam II and Israel was that "the end has come for my people" (8:2). Amos's pronouncement against the false priest Amaziah represented a condensed version of the prophet's word of judgment to the whole nation (cf. 7:10–17):

1. The higher chronology is based on Edwin R. Thiele, *The Mysterious Numbers of the Hebrew Kings*, rev. ed. (Grand Rapids: Zondervan, 1983); the lower chronology is based on John Bright, *A History of Israel*, 4th ed. (Louisville: Westminster John Knox, 2000).

"This is what the LORD says:
'Your wife will become a prostitute in the city,
    and your sons and daughters will fall by the sword.
Your land will be measured and divided up,
    and you yourself will die in a pagan country.'" (v. 17)

Both message and purpose spring logically from the book's general outline and are closely connected with the prophet's prediction of judgment and exile for Israel:

First message (2:6–16): Amos denounces Israel's sin and forecasts national disaster for the purpose of reminding the people of the consequences of covenant disobedience.

Second message (3:1–6:14): Amos condemns specific acts of social injustice and religious hypocrisy. The several purposes of this message include calling some to repentance of personal sin, encouraging a return to the standards of behavior consistent with Yahweh's covenant stipulations, and repudiating the popular notion that the "day of the LORD" was a day of national blessing only.

Third message (7:1–9:4): Amos relates five visions he experienced, all dealing with God's wrath and judgment on Israel. The visions served to reinforce the prophet's oracles against the nation, emphasize the certainty of Israel's destruction and exile, and introduce the remnant theme.

Fourth message (9:5–15): The prophet concludes his ministry to Israel with the promise of messianic restoration and blessing. Here

This is one of the possible sites of ancient Tekoa, the prophet Amos's hometown.
Bible Scene Multimedia/
Maurice Thompson

Bozrah was one of the major cities of the Edomites, on whom Obadiah pronounced judgment.

Todd Bolen/www.BiblePlaces.com

OBADIAH

Key Ideas

- The sovereignty of God
- The principle of retribution
- The restoration of Israel

Purpose Statement

The purpose of the book of Obadiah is to pronounce divine judgment against the nation of Edom for their role in assisting the Babylonians in the conquest of Judah, and to announce the future divine restoration of the people of Israel.

Major Themes

- Pride
- Lex Talionis
- Universal Judgment
- Restoration

God's Presence

The theme of divine presence in the book of Obadiah is implicit in the deliverance and holiness associated with Mount Zion (v. 17).

CHAPTER
37

Aerial view of modern Jaffa (Joppa).

JONAH

Key Ideas

- God's right to perform gracious acts of compassion
- God's delight in small steps in the right direction
- God's propensity for offering second chances

Purpose Statement

God reserves the sovereign right to be compassionate, even when those acts work against an already issued prophetic warning. God delights in gracious acts of compassion in response to small steps in the right direction. Certainly if God responded that way to Nineveh, the epitome of pagan wickedness, he would respond compassionately to his chosen people, Israel.

Major Themes

- Compassion
- Anger
- Theodicy

Moresheth-Gath, the likely hometown of the prophet Micah.   Todd Bolen/www.BiblePlaces.com

MICAH

Key Ideas

- An indictment of injustice
- The throne of David to be filled by a deliverer born in Bethlehem
- Right behavior, not manipulating rituals, as the proper response to God's anger
- The coming deliverance from the Assyrian threat

Purpose Statement

Micah is one of the few prophets who explicitly stated his purpose: "But as for me, I am filled with power, with the Spirit of the LORD, and with justice and might, to declare to Jacob his transgression, to Israel his sin" (3:8). This purpose is reflected in the large proportion of indictment and judgment oracles in the book.

Major Themes

- Deliverer
- What Does the Lord Require?

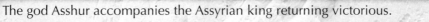

CHAPTER 39

The god Asshur accompanies the Assyrian king returning victorious.

Caryn Reeder, courtesy of the British Museum

NAHUM

Key Ideas

- The impending judgment of Nineveh
- Judah's coming release from the power of the Assyrian Empire

Purpose Statement

The purpose of the book of Nahum is to pronounce the doom of Nineveh. This was not just a case of the ebb and flow of history, but the action of the Lord's punishment against Nineveh. He announced Nineveh's doom, and he would accomplish it.

Major Themes

- Assyria and the Old Testament

Watchtowers such as this one in Samaria were part of both the urban and rural landscape. They were built in fields for overseers to watch the farmland and at a gate or a corner of a city wall for the defense of the city. They are sometimes used in metaphors of watchfulness: "I will stand at my watch and station myself on the ramparts" (Hab. 2:1).

HABAKKUK

Key Ideas

- God is just in dealing with nations.
- Judah was to receive punishment from the Babylonians, who would in turn be punished by God.
- Even when world events are confusing, we need to trust God and act with integrity.

Purpose Statement

The purpose of the book of Habakkuk is to examine the issue of God's justice on a national plane. The question at hand in the theodicy (the justification of God's ways with humanity) was, How can a just God use a wicked nation like Babylon as his instrument for punishment?

Major Theme

- God's Policy for Handling Nations

God's Presence

In the same way that God appears at the end of the book of Job in the storm, Habakkuk 3 portrays the arrival of the glory of God's presence to carry out judgment. The psalm is introduced in the last verse of chapter 2: "The LORD is in his holy temple; let all the earth be silent before him."

Outline

I. Discourse 1
 A. Prayer: Habakkuk's Complaint Concerning Judah (1:1–4)
 B. Answer: Oracle of Judgment—Babylon to Invade Judah
  (1:5–11)

II. Discourse 2
 A. Prayer: Habakkuk's Questions Concerning God's Justice
  (1:12–17)
 B. Instruction from God (2:1–3)
 C. Answer 1: Responsibility of the Righteous (2:4–5)
 D. Answer 2: Oracle of Judgment Against Babylon (2:6–20)

III. Discourse 3
 A. Prayer: Habakkuk's Request for Mercy (3:1–2)
 B. Reflection: The Sovereign Power of God to Deliver (3:3–15)
 C. Acceptance: Habakkuk's Trust in God's Sovereignty
  (3:16–19)

L ittle is known of the prophet Habakkuk, for no genealogical or historical information about him is given in the book. Unlike most of the other prophetic books, this one places a higher priority on addressing a particular topic rather than simply serving as a literary vehicle to preserve the oracles of the prophet (see chap. 27, esp. pp. 509–11). In this sense, for example, it is more like Jonah than like Jeremiah. Furthermore, the "wisdom" tone of the prophecy and its organization around the inquiries of the prophet distinguish it from the rest of the prophetic literature (see chap. 20, esp. p. 376). The wisdom tone is evident in its focus on the justice of God.

The Writing of the Book

There is little dispute concerning the unity or integrity of the book. There is more room for discussion, however, about the date of the prophecy. Parameters may be established from information within the book. In 1:5–6 the raising up of the Chaldeans (so KJV; "Babylonians," NIV) is presented as something astonishing and unexpected. The Chaldeans took control of the throne of Babylon, declaring independence from Assyria in 626 BC. By 612 Nineveh, the Assyrian capital, had fallen, but as early as 614, the alliance between the Medes and the Babylonians laid the foundation for their eventual success against Assyria. The statements of 1:5–6 would be most understandable if they were made prior to 626. Though they could possibly come as late as 615, any time beyond that would seem to trivialize the claim of these verses.

It should also be noted that this judgment on Judah at the hands of the Chaldeans was coming "in your days" (1:5). The judgment referred to could hardly apply to anything earlier than 597 BC, when Judah had its first major confrontation with Babylon. Calculating a generation prior to this suggests about 640 BC as the earliest likely date for the prophecy.

Josiah came to the throne of Judah in 640 BC, and some interpreters have felt that the negative conditions in Judah described in Habakkuk 1:2–4 would not be likely during the reign of a good king such as he. Yet it seems to stretch the chronological limits too far to extend the prophecy back into the reign of Josiah's wicked grandfather, Manasseh. It should also be remembered that Josiah was a child when he came to the throne, and he did not begin his reforms until twelve years into his reign. Even then, the reform focused more on matters of cultic practice than on a social agenda. As a result, the complaints of injustice by Habakkuk were not necessarily contradictory to the nature of the early years of Josiah's reign. The injustice fostered by the fifty-year rule of Manasseh would not have dissipated quickly.

The boundaries thus established for the prophecies of Habakkuk suggest that they should be dated somewhere between 640 and 626 BC, with 630 perhaps being the best estimate. This would make Habakkuk a contemporary of Jeremiah.

The Background

Ashurbanipal had come to the Assyrian throne in 668 BC and had inherited an empire that was at its height of glory. By the end of his reign, however, deterioration was evident and the momentous fall was to come within a score of years. Trouble arose as early as the mid-650s, when Psammetichus I, the Egyptian pharaoh, began to clear the Assyrians out of Egypt. Ashurbanipal was unable to prevent this, for he was largely preoccupied with the civil war taking place in the southeastern part of the empire. There his brother, Shamash-shum-ukin, backed by

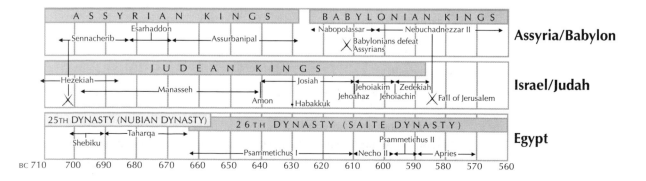

CHAPTER
41

Zephaniah warned that "Gaza will be abandoned and Ashkelon left in ruins" (2:4). These are some of the ruins at Ashkelon.

Todd Bolen/www.BiblePlaces.com

ZEPHANIAH

Key Ideas

- The coming day of the Lord
- The call to the humble to seek the Lord
- The universal impact of the coming judgment

Purpose Statement

The purpose of the prophecies of Zephaniah was to initiate change in Judah by pronouncing God's judgment on wickedness. Coupled with God's intention to punish came the proclamation of his intention to restore Judah. The message of Zephaniah was focused on the day of the Lord which, he contended, was fast approaching.

Major Theme

- The Day of the Lord

God's Presence

The prophet contrasts the injustice in Jerusalem to the righteousness of God's presence within her (Zeph. 2:1–5). He looks forward to a time when they will again experience the Lord's protection and deliverance: "The LORD your God is with you, he is mighty to save" (3:17).

CHAPTER 42

Haggai encouraged the people to continue rebuilding the temple during the reign of King Darius of Persia (Hag. 1:1). Darius also helped by issuing a decree that the Jews were allowed to do so (Ezra 6:1–12). This is Darius's palace at Persepolis.

HAGGAI

Key Ideas

- The importance of establishing proper priorities
- The value of the temple as a covenant symbol for Israel
- The faithfulness of God in renewing his covenant promises to David's descendants

Purpose Statement

The purpose of the book of Haggai is to initiate the reconstruction of the temple of Yahweh in Jerusalem upon the return of the Hebrews from Babylonian captivity.

Major Theme

- The Temple

God's Presence

The prophet affirms the presence of God's Spirit among the people as they commit to rebuild the Jerusalem temple (Hag. 2:4–5), and Haggai promises the glory of God will once again inhabit the completed temple in an even greater measure than before (2:9).

CHAPTER
43

Two olive trees mentioned in Zechariah 4 represent the leadership of Jerusalem—Zerubbabel and Joshua, the "two who are anointed to serve the Lord" (v. 14). Olives produced olive oil used for anointing, so the olive tree was an apt symbol for leadership.

Gabriella Bottka

ZECHARIAH

Key Ideas
- Repentance and covenant renewal
- Hope rooted in God's sovereignty
- Social justice
- Messiah

Purpose Statement

Zechariah is a tract for troubled times. First, the prophet rebuked the people for perpetuating the evil ways and deeds of their ancestors (Zech. 1:2–6). He exhorted them to repent and return to God in a renewed covenant relationship that demonstrated social justice (7:4–10). Finally, the prophet offered the people of Judah encouragement and hope for the future with promises of God's blessing and restoration (10:6–12).

Major Themes
- Messiah
- Old Testament Eschatology

God's Presence

The book of Zechariah opens with God, symbolized by the rider on the red horse (1:8), poised to reenter his temple once the sanctuary is rebuilt (1:16). Later, God declares he will be a wall of fire around Jerusalem and the glory within it (2:5). Finally, God promises he will return to Jerusalem and live there (8:3; cf. 14:5).

Outline

I. Prelude: Call to National Repentance (1:1–6)

II. Zechariah's Visions (1:7–6:15)
  A. Vision 1: Patrol Report of World at Rest (1:7–17)
  B. Vision 2: Horns and Craftsmen (1:18–21)
  C. Vision 3: Measuring Jerusalem (2:1–5)
  D. Postscript 1: Investiture of Joshua (2:6–3:10)
  E. Vision 4: Lampstand and Olive Trees (4:1–14)
  F. Vision 5: Flying Scroll (5:1–4)
  G. Vision 6: Woman in Ephah Basket (5:5–11)
  H. Vision 7: Four Chariots of Judgment (6:1–8)
  I. Second Postscript, Crowning of Joshua (6:9–15)

III. Zechariah's Messages (7–8)
  A. Justice and Mercy vs. Fasting (7)
  B. Jerusalem's Restoration (8)

IV. The Oracles (9–14)
  A. Oracle 1 (9–11)
    1. Messiah-King and his rule (9)
    2. Redemption of Israel (10)
    3. Messiah-King rejected (11)
  B. Oracle 2 (12–14)
    1. Israel's enemies destroyed (12:1–9)
    2. Israel cleansed (12:10–13:6)
    3. The shepherd and the sheep (13:7–9)
    4. The day of the Lord (14)

Haggai and Zechariah were complementary postexilic prophets. Zechariah was the younger and began prophesying about two months after Haggai's brief ministry. While Haggai called on the people to erect the temple of God, Zechariah summoned the community to repentance and spiritual renewal. His task was to prepare the people for proper worship and temple service once the building project was completed.

Zechariah means "Yah(weh) has remembered," which is the essence of his message to Jerusalem after the exile. The book's superscription identifies him as the son of Berekiah and the grandson of Iddo (1:1). Ezra records Zechariah as the son of Iddo (5:1; 6:14); here the word "son" was used simply to designate "any descendant." The frequency with which the name "Zechariah" appears in the Old Testament—some thirty-two people are called by it—invites misidentification. For example, Zechariah, son of Berekiah is not to be confused with Zechariah, son of Jeberekiah (Isa. 8:2).

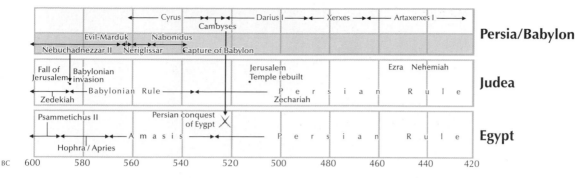

According to Nehemiah, Zechariah's grandfather, Iddo, returned to Jerusalem from the Babylonian captivity with Zerubbabel and Joshua (12:4). Elsewhere, Nehemiah lists Zechariah as the head of the priestly family of Iddo (12:16). This means Zechariah was a member of the tribe of Levi and served in Jerusalem as both a priest and a prophet.

The Writing of the Book

The date and history of the book of Zechariah are directly linked to one's view of the literary unity of the composition. Conservative biblical scholars have traditionally upheld the literary integrity of Zechariah, while scholars inclined toward more critical viewpoints have divided the book into two or three distinct literary segments. Those holding to a "Second" or even a "Third" Zechariah do so on the basis of perceived differences in style, vocabulary, theme, and genre (i.e., apocalyptic) between the sections.

Both scholarly camps readily assign the materials of chapters 1–8 to Zechariah the prophet of 520–518 BC. The chronology of Zechariah's ministry is keyed to the reign of the Persian king Darius (ca. 521–486 BC). Based on the three date formulas in the book, the specific dates for Zechariah's pronouncements may be converted as follows:

1:1–6	Year 2, month 8	=	Oct/Nov 520 BC
1:7–6:8	Year 2, month 11, day 24	=	15 Feb 519 BC
7:1–8:23	Year 4, month 9, day 4	=	7 Dec 518 BC

The time lag between these utterances of Zechariah and the actual composition of the prophecies is difficult to determine. Because chapters 1–8 fail to mention a rebuilt temple in Jerusalem, it seems likely that this portion of the book was compiled before the temple's reconstruction and dedication (ca. 520–515 BC; cf. Ezra 6:13–22).

Scholarly opinion is sharply divided over the remaining chapters of Zechariah. Conservative scholars ascribe them to Zechariah, son of Berekiah, and it is usually suggested that he wrote these oracles later in his life. They often cite the failure of the Persian expedition against

Foundation stones like this one often held important documents about the building of the temple. Zechariah 3–4 mentions a special stone inscribed and decorated with jewels. That could have been the foundation stone of the temple.

Todd Bolen/www.BiblePlaces.com, courtesy of the British Museum

Greece under King Xerxes as the event prompting the prophecies of chapters 9–14. They also emphasize the similarities in style, theme, vocabulary, and theology of the two parts of the book while attributing the differences to Zechariah's age, the peculiar nature of apocalyptic literature, and the changing historical and political circumstances of the later Persian Empire. The final draft of the book of Zechariah was probably completed sometime between 500 and 470 BC.[1]

Other biblical scholars assign chapters 9–11 to a Second Zechariah and chapters 12–14 to a Third. These alleged and unknown writers are supposed to have lived in Jerusalem sometime during the fourth to the second centuries BC. It is argued these anonymous oracles, along with Malachi, were appended to Zechariah 1–8 to complete the sacred number of the Twelve Prophets. According to this view, Zechariah may not have taken its final written form until the Maccabean period (ca. 160 BC). Evidence offered in support of the multiple author hypothesis includes the differences of style, tone, theology, and historical situation between the two parts of the book—most notably the reference to Greece in 9:13 (which is viewed as an allusion to the Hellenistic period)—and the distinctively apocalyptic flavor of chapters 12–14.

Like Haggai's prophecy, Zechariah's messages originated in Jerusalem and were intended for the people of postexilic Jerusalem and its environs. The spiritual apathy, despair, and sense of hopelessness pervading the early postexilic period of Hebrew history were the motivation behind Zechariah's exhortations and predictions.

1. Recent computer-assisted linguistic and grammatical analysis of Zechariah corroborates an early fifth-century BC date for Zechariah 9–14 and indicates that the literary break between chapters 1–8 and 9–14 is not nearly so pronounced as some scholars contend. Cf. Andrew E. Hill, "Dating 'Second Zechariah': A Linguistic Reexamination," *Hebrew Annual Review* 6 (1982): 105–34; and Y. T. Radday and D. Wickmann, "The Unity of Zechariah Examined in the Light of Statistical Linguistics," *Zeitschrift für die alttestamentliche Wissenschaft* 87 (1975): 30–55.

The Background

The setting for Zechariah's prophecy, like Haggai's, was the reign of Darius I, King of Persia (521–486 BC). Despite the Hebrews' return from Babylonian exile, there was little evidence of the program of covenant restoration Yahweh had promised Jerusalem (e.g., Jer. 30–33 and Ezek. 36–39). Selfishness crippled community spirit, and the general mood of the period was gloomy and dismal. In fact, only a small percentage of Hebrew captives had actually returned to Judah, and the city walls still lay in ruins, the temple of God remained a rubble heap, and drought and blight ravaged the land. Judah remained a Persian vassal state, and the surrounding nations continued to harass the leaders in Jerusalem and thwart their timid efforts to improve the bleak situation.

In response to this distress, God raised up two prophetic voices to initiate programs for the physical rebuilding and spiritual renewal of Jerusalem. Haggai was called to exhort and challenge the Hebrew community to rebuild the temple. He prophesied for only four months in the year 520 BC. Yet the people of God responded to his message and began the reconstruction of the temple (cf. Hag. 2:12–15).

The prophet Zechariah complemented Haggai's message in calling for a spiritual revival among the people (1:3–6; 7:8–14). His ministry began just two months after Haggai's, and his last dated message was delivered in 518 BC. So Zechariah's ministry in Jerusalem probably lasted more than two years. The reference to Haggai and Zechariah in Ezra 5:2 suggests that they continued to support and encourage the people until the temple was completed and rededicated to the worship of Yahweh with the celebration of the Passover Feast in 515 BC (Ezra 6:13–22; see further in chap. 42).

Purpose and Message

Zechariah's message was one of rebuke, exhortation, and encouragement—a tract for troubled times. First, the prophet upbraided the postexilic community because they had perpetuated the evil ways and deeds of their ancestors (1:3–5). The people were guilty of the very same covenant violations that sent a previous generation into exile (7:8–14).

The solution Zechariah offered to the problems of sin and rebellion among the people included genuine repentance and a return to God (1:3–5). Only spiritual renewal could foster true worship and meaningful service in the temple, which was now under construction at the prompting of the prophet Haggai. Only obedience to the voice of the

Kim Walton, courtesy of the Oriental Institute Museum

"The cover of lead was raised, and there in the basket sat a woman" (Zech. 5:7). Figurines were often included in foundation deposits. This Sumerian bronze foundation figurine is from the time of Rim-Sin, about 2000 BC.

This is a relief of Ashurbanipal, king of Assyria from 668 to 627 BC, carrying a basket with the ceremonial first brick for the rebuilding of a temple in Babylon. In Zechariah 3 the high priest Joshua is provided with a special turban as he is commissioned to build the temple and entrusted with the cornerstone. His turban may have served this same ceremonial function.

Z. Radovan/
www.BibleLandPictures.com

Lord would usher in the long-awaited blessing, prosperity, and righteousness of the messianic age (6:9–15; 8:13).

Yahweh's intention to "do good" to Jerusalem was contingent on the community's adherence to the stipulations of the covenant code, especially those governing behavior patterns (7:8–12; 8:14–17). Unlike later Jewish apocalyptic literature, with its heavy emphasis on the futuristic aspects of the restoration of Israel in the day of the Lord, Zechariah's message was laced with concern for social justice in the present. Before the nations of the world came to seek the Lord in Jerusalem, Israel had to seek the favor of Yahweh, render justice, and show kindness and mercy to Hebrew widows and orphans and to foreigners (7:9–10; cf. 14:16–21).

Zechariah explicitly stated that part of his duty as God's spokesman was to "comfort" and "strengthen" the people of Judah and Jerusalem (1:13; 8:9). His word of encouragement took several forms. For example, Zechariah's series of visions (1:7–6:8) reminded Israel that God still cared for his people and continued to rule the destinies of the nations for the ultimate benefit of his elect Zion (cf. esp. 2:6–13). The ordination of Joshua as the priest and Zerubbabel as the governor marked the resumption of divinely appointed leadership in Israel. This in turn rekindled messianic hopes and confirmed the divine blessing of the efforts to rebuild the temple and restore proper worship of God (cf. 4:6).

Finally, Zechariah's repeated reference to the words of the "former prophets" authenticated his own ministry and assured the Hebrew community that they had not misinterpreted Yahweh's earlier revelations (1:4; 7:7, 12). Despite their current distress, the people were not to despair. Zechariah's message confirmed God's intention to continue his covenant program with Israel. Their hope was not misplaced!

Structure and Organization

The book of Zechariah conveniently divides into two major parts. The first includes the introductory verse (or superscription) and the call to repentance (1:1–6), the seven night visions (1:7–6:15), and the two oracles addressing the topic of fasting (7–8). The second part consists of eschatological oracles, subdivided into two sections: the word of the Lord concerning Hadrach (9–11), and the word of the Lord concerning Israel (12–14).

Building on the literary analysis of P. Lamarche, Joyce G. Baldwin has identified chiasmic structure underlying both parts of Zechariah's prophecy. This pattern of inversion gives evidence of deliberate structuring of themes and argues for the unity of the entire work. It also supports the idea that Zechariah not only composed, but also arranged and edited his own visions and oracles.[2]

The chiastic arrangement of parts 1 and 2 is illustrated in figure 43.1.

The prelude of Zechariah calls the nation to repentance and thus complements Haggai's charge to rebuild the temple (1:1–6). The

2. Joyce G. Baldwin, *Haggai, Zechariah, Malachi,* TOTC (Downers Grove, Ill.: InterVarsity Press, 1972), 75–81, 85–86. Cf. P. Lamarche, *Zacharie IX-XIV : Structure littéraire et messianisme* (Paris: Gabalda, 1961).

Figure 43.1. The Structure of the Book of Zechariah

Part 1:

I. Prelude: Call to national repentance			1:1 – 6

II. Visions and postscripts

a		Vision 1. Patrol report of world at rest	1:7 – 17
	b	Vision 2: Horns and craftsmen (retribution for the nations)	1:18 – 21
	b¹	Vision 3: Measuring Jerusalem (the city protected by God)	2:1 – 5
	c	Postscript 1. Investiture of Joshua	2:6 – 3:10
		d Vision 4: Lampstand and olive trees	4
	b²	Vision 5: Flying scroll (retribution for evil)	5:1 – 4
	b³	Vision 6: Woman in ephah basket (Jerusalem purified by God)	5:5–11
a¹		Vision 7: God's chariots patrol the earth	6:1 – 8
	c¹	Postscript 2: The crowning of Joshua	6:9 – 15

III. Messages on fasting

a		The inquiry	7:1 – 3
	b	First sermon	7:4 – 14
	c	Covenant sayings	8:1 – 8
	b¹	Second sermon	8:9 – 17
a¹		The response	8:18 – 19

IV. Postlude: Entreat and seek the Lord

Part 2:

I. Triumphant intervention of the Lord: His shepherd rejected

a		The Lord triumphs from the north	9:1 – 8
	b	Arrival of the king	9:9 – 10
	c	Jubilation and prosperity	9:11 – 10:1
		d Rebuke for sham leaders	10:2 – 3
	c¹	Jubilation and restoration	10:4 – 11:3
	b¹	The fate of the good shepherd	11:4 – 17

II. Final intervention of the Lord: The suffering involved

c²		Jubilation in Jerusalem	12:1 – 9
	b²	Mourning for the pierced one	12:10 – 13:1
		d¹ Rejection of sham leaders	13:2 – 6
	b³	The shepherd slaughtered, the people scattered	13:7 – 9
c³		Cataclysm in Jerusalem	14:1 – 15
a¹		The Lord worshiped as King over all	14:16 – 21

Adapted from Joyce G. Baldwin, *Haggai, Zechariah, Malachi,* TOTC (Downers Grove, Ill.: InterVarsity Press, 1972).

physical rebuilding of Jerusalem and the temple were to be accompanied by a corresponding spiritual renewal. The night visions of the prophet substantiated his claim that "God will return to Israel" (cf. 1:3, 16; 2:10). The visions graphically outlined God's plan to bring peace to Israel, retribution to the nations who scattered Israel, restoration to the city of Jerusalem, divinely appointed leadership, a purging of evil from among the people of God, and the establishment of covenant righteousness in Zion.

The two sermons related to fasting connected the pursuit of social justice in the current age with the eventual reversal of Judah's fortunes among the nations in the age to come (e.g., 8:9–13). As Judah sought the favor of the Lord, so too the nations would one day seek the Lord in Jerusalem (cf. 7:2; 8:22).

Finally, the two eschatological oracles bolstered hope and encouraged the community by depicting the promised future kingdom of God.

This seven-spouted oil lamp found at Tell Dan (ninth century BC), sitting on a pedestal, is reminiscent of the oil lamp in Zechariah 4:2: "a solid gold lampstand with a bowl at the top and seven lights on it, with seven channels to the lights."

Z. Radovan/ www.BibleLandPictures.com

The book is cast in the "oracular prose," or combination of prose and poetry, which is typical of prophetic literature (except for the poetic materials in chaps. 9–10). The composition contains a variety of literary forms, among them:

- Exhortation with repentance oracle (1:1–6)
- Narrative in the form of a vision (1:7–6:8)
- Prediction with revelation and interpretation formulas (e.g., 5:1–4)
- Inquiry with instructional response (e.g., 6:1–8)
- Symbolic actions (6:9–15)
- Admonition with messenger and date formulas (7:1–7)
- Divine oracles of judgment and salvation (e.g., chap. 10)

Zechariah is often classified as proto-apocalyptic in contrast to the apocalyptic literature that appears in later Jewish writings of the intertestamental period (e.g., 1 Esdras and 1 Enoch). True, the book does exhibit features of apocalyptic writing: revelation in the form of visions, the presence of a divine messenger who also interprets the visions, the use of symbolism, and the themes of judgment for the nations and the ultimate triumph of God in human history. But many other features are absent, such as rigid determinism and pervasive pessimism, a rewriting of earlier history, and pseudonymity (writing under a false name).

Figure 43.2. Understanding Visionary Literature

- Be ready for the reversal of ordinary reality.
- Be prepared to use your imagination to picture a world that transcends earthly reality.
- Since visionary literature is a form of fantasy literature, you must exercise your imagination in picturing unfamiliar scenes and agents.
- Instead of looking for the smooth flow of narrative, be prepared for a disjointed series of diverse, self-contained units.
- Seek to identify the historical event or theological reality in salvation history represented by the symbolism in the passage.
- Read widely in visionary literature (both biblical visionary literature and extrabiblical fantasy literature).

Major Themes

Messiah

Zechariah has more to say about the messianic shepherd-king than any other Old Testament book except Isaiah. This foreshadowing of the Son of Man as Messiah is explained to the disciples by Jesus himself as a method of Old Testament interpretation (cf. Luke 24:44). Our approach (see fig. 43.3) identifies as "messianic" only those Old Testament passages that New Testament writers explicitly cited in reference or application to the life and ministry of Jesus of Nazareth as the Christ (while recognizing that some of these citations are at best only implicitly messianic in the context of Zechariah).

Figure 43.3. Zechariah's Messianic Prophecies

Come in a low and humble station of life	9:9; 13:7 (cf. Matt. 21:5; 26:31, 56)
Restore Israel by the blood of his covenant	9:11 (cf. Mark 14:24)
Serve as shepherd to a people scattered and wandering like sheep	10:2 (cf. Matt. 9:36; 26:15; 27:9 – 10)
Be pierced and struck down	12:10; 13:7 (cf. Matt. 24:30; 26:31, 56; John 19:37)
Return in glory and deliver Israel from her enemies	14:1 – 6 (cf. Matt. 25:31)
Rule as king in peace and righteousness in Jerusalem	9:9 – 10; 14:9, 16 (cf. Rev. 11:15; 19:6)
Establish a new world order	14:6 – 19 (cf. Rev. 21:25; 22:1, 5)

Old Testament Eschatology

Eschatology is the doctrine of end-time events, or the study of last things. Although Zechariah did not use the phrases "the day of the Lord" and "the kingdom of God," the book contributes greatly to our knowledge of Hebrew understanding of these end-time concepts.

Central to Old Testament teaching about the last days is the salvation of Israel, for "the LORD will save them on that day" (9:16). Zechariah predicted that this deliverance will be accomplished by a shepherd-king who will first be rejected and struck down (11:4–17). Yet his ministry will be one of peace and reconciliation and cleansing by the Holy Spirit (9:9–10).

A second concept associated with the day of the Lord in Zechariah is the regathering and restoration of Israel (10:9–12). Through the agency of his servant Messiah, God will again unify Judah and Israel and restore the fortunes of his elect. All this will come to pass after the nations have waged war against Jerusalem, only to be vanquished by the Lord (12:1–9; 14:1–5). Then Israel will mourn over "the one they have pierced," their repentance leading to cleansing and covenant renewal with Yahweh (12:10–13:9).

Yahweh's restoration of Israel is to culminate in the establishment of a new created order; the LORD himself will rule over all the earth. There will be a new Jerusalem, and the wealth of the nations will flow into Zion (14:6–15). Prominent in this restored city of David is the temple of Yahweh—the very temple Haggai and Zechariah had encouraged the postexilic community to build. The temple will stand as a symbol of the peace, righteousness, and holiness that will characterize the

Zechariah states that on the day of the Lord, "his feet will stand on the Mount of Olives, east of Jerusalem, and the Mount of Olives will be split in two from east to west" (14:4).

kingdom of God (14:16–21). Even the peoples of the nations will make regular pilgrimages to worship the God of Israel there (14:16).

This sequence of events comprising the day of the Lord was so compressed and condensed, historically speaking, that the distinctions made by later interpreters between the first and second advents of the Messiah became blurred in the prophets' minds into one coming. In fact, whole interpretive and theological systems have now been constructed in an attempt to understand Old Testament prophecies (i.e., **dispensationalism** and covenant theology).

However, Zechariah's perspectives on "that day" are consistent with the rest of Old Testament teaching in that they conform to the general pattern. Roughly this falls out as apostasy in Israel followed by oppression and scattering as judgment for sin. Israel's subsequent repentance then prompts God to regather the elect and restore the covenant blessings and judge the sin of the oppressive nations so that Israel might enjoy the presence of God in a kingdom experience (e.g., Ezek. 36–39; cf. Matt. 24).

CHAPTER
44

Edom is the nation which came from Esau, the brother whom the Lord "hated" because he "loved" Jacob (Mal. 1:2–5).

Todd Bolen/www.BiblePlaces.com

MALACHI

Key Ideas

- God desires wholehearted worship.
- God expects faithfulness in marriage.
- God hates divorce.
- The day of the Lord affects both the righteous and the wicked.
- An Elijah-like figure will announce the day of the Lord.

Purpose Statement

The prophet calls postexilic Israel to repentance for the purpose of covenant renewal with Yahweh (1:2–5; 3:7). This will enable the priests and people of God to restore proper temple worship (1:10–14; 3:9–10) and practice social justice within the community (3:5).

Major Themes

- Marriage and Divorce
- Elijah the Prophet

God's Presence

God's presence is implicit in the book of Malachi in the prophet's rebuke of the people for insincere worship and improper animal sacrifice (1:6–11). The eschaton will see the Lord suddenly enter his temple in Jerusalem to judge the wicked and purify the righteous (3:1).

oppression of the poor (1:6–13; 2:1–16; 3:5–10; cf. Ezra 9–10; Neh. 5:1–5; 10:32–39; 13:1–30).

Careful study of the Hebrew language of Malachi, however, reveals that the book has considerable linguistic similarities with Old Testament writings dated to the sixth rather than the fifth century BC. Based on the detailed information gleaned from this kind of technical linguistic analysis of the postexilic prophets, we conclude that Malachi was most likely composed in Jerusalem during the very early years of religious and social decline prior to the time of Ezra the scribe (roughly 500 to 475 BC).[1]

Persian influence on the thought and language of Malachi can be seen in the prophet's references to "a scroll of remembrance" (3:16; cf. Esth. 6:1; Dan. 7:10; 12:1) and "the sun of righteousness" (4:2). The book of remembrance, in which are recorded the names of the righteous, points to the continued theological development of the Hebrew belief in afterlife in the Old Testament. The unique expression "sun of righteousness" is reminiscent of the winged solar disk that represents the sun god in Mesopotamian and Egyptian **iconography**. The winged solar disk was often associated with the king and symbolized protection and assured his victory in battle. The imagery suggests that, in the same way, Yahweh would grant protection and restoration to those who feared his name when the fiery consummation of the day of the Lord should come.

The Background

The message of Malachi reflected conditions associated with the period of pre-Ezra decline (ca. 515–458 BC, or from the completion of the second temple to the ministry of Ezra in Jerusalem, assuming the traditional date for Ezra's journey to Jerusalem is correct). The second temple had been completed at the urging of Haggai and Zechariah (Hag. 1:1–6; Ezra 3:10–13; 5:1–2; 6:13–15), but the achievement ushered in no hoped-for messianic age (Mal. 3:6–12; cf. Zech. 8:9–23). Instead, the apathy and disillusionment that delayed the temple's reconstruction for nearly twenty years persisted within the restoration community. The expectations of a renewed Davidic state under Zerubbabel went unfulfilled (cf. Hag. 2:20–23). The material prosperity predicted by Haggai was only partially realized (2:6–9), and the streaming migrations of former Hebrew captives foreseen by Zechariah (8:1–8) proved to be as yet a mere trickle. Zechariah's call to a deeper spiritual life went unheeded and was even mocked by God's apparent failure to restore covenant blessings to Jerusalem (8:4–13; cf. 10:1–2; Mal. 3:13–15).

If the records of Ezra and Nehemiah are any indication, the messianic oracles of Zechariah and Malachi had little impact on postexilic morale (cf. Ezra 9:1–4; Neh. 5:1–8; 11:1–3). Given the testimony of scanty written documents to the contrary, even the prophetic voice

1. Cf. Andrew E. Hill, "Dating the Book of Malachi: A Linguistic Reexamination," in *The Word of the Lord Shall Go Forth: Essays in Honor of D. N. Freedman*, ed. C. Meyers and M. O'Connor (Winona Lake, Ind.: Eisenbrauns, 1983), 84–86.

soon ceased to be a factor in the Hebrew restoration community (Mal. 4:5; cf. 1 Macc. 4:46; 9:27; 14:41).

Jerusalem, which was likely a **satrapy** (or province) under the rule of a Persian governor, remained small, struggling, and insignificant in the vast Persian Empire—a social and political backwater. The ongoing petty hostilities with the Samaritans and the burdensome vassal status to Persia contributed to the skepticism and doubt that characterized popular response to Yahweh as God (Mal. 1:2). The Persians themselves were engaged in a titanic contest for control of the West against the Greeks. It was against this dismal setting that Malachi prophesied in Jerusalem as God's "divine messenger."

Purpose and Message

The predominant theme of Malachi's prophecy is Israel's covenant relationship with Yahweh and its ramifications. The prophet specifically cited the covenant of Levi (1:6–2:9), the covenant of the fathers and the covenant of marriage (2:10–16), and the messenger of the covenant (3:1).

The teaching of the six disputations in Malachi may be conveniently summarized.

Part of the situation Malachi addresses is a corrupt priesthood. To remedy the situation, the Lord promises that as a refiner and purifier of silver, "he will purify the Levites and refine them like gold and silver" (Mal. 3:3). This relief in the tomb of Mereruka (vizier under Pharaoh Teti, 24th century BC) depicts metalworkers at their task of refining metal.

Werner Forman Archive

CHAPTER

45

The photograph of all of the scenes included in the Dura Europas synagogue reminds us that all of the individual stories of the Bible offer a montage to communicate God's revelation of himself—the big picture of the Bible. Z. Radovan/www.BibleLandPictures.com

WHAT WE HAVE LEARNED

The God Who Does Not Change

Outlines fade away and kings' names often take their place only in the darkest recesses of the memory, but if nothing else is retained, the person studying the Old Testament should come away with an expanded view of God. In Exodus 3:14, as God is speaking to Moses from the burning bush, he offers "I AM" as his name, and it is from this that the name "Yahweh" is derived. The verbal form stresses the nature of Yahweh as "One who causes to be." While this has implications concerning creation and sovereignty, it can possibly be applied also to his election of Israel and his nature as the covenant-making God. His name is the introduction to his attributes. The key attributes of God emphasized in the Old Testament are summarized here by means of some of the clearest passages addressing them. These are among the greatest theological affirmations of the Old Testament, and they carry over into the New Testament and into today, for God does not change.

Creator

From the hymnic verses of Amos comes one of the many characterizations of Yahweh as the almighty creator:

> He who forms the mountains,
>   creates the wind,
>   and reveals his thoughts to man,
> he who turns dawn to darkness,
>   and treads the high places of the earth—
>   the LORD God Almighty is his name.
>
> (Amos 4:13)

There is nothing that God did not create. As discussed in the chapter on Genesis, the point of establishing God as creator is to establish him as the sovereign over the functioning world. There is a straight line of logic from Creation to Covenant to History to Eschatology.

Since God created everything, he is sovereign over everything. Nothing is beyond his power or knowledge; he is accountable or subordinate to no one; he shares his position with no other being. The universe works only as a result of his constant attention, and his is the only guiding hand. This is affirmed in the testimony

"But they were disobedient and rebelled against you; they put your law behind their backs. They killed your prophets, who had admonished them in order to turn them back to you; they committed awful blasphemies. So you handed them over to their enemies, who oppressed them. But when they were oppressed they cried out to you. From heaven you heard them, and in your great compassion you gave them deliverers, who rescued them from the hand of their enemies.

"But as soon as they were at rest, they again did what was evil in your sight. Then you abandoned them to the hand of their enemies so that they ruled over them. And when they cried out to you again, you heard from heaven, and in your compassion you delivered them time after time.

"You warned them to return to your law, but they became arrogant and disobeyed your commands. They sinned against your ordinances, by which a man will live if he obeys them. Stubbornly they turned their backs on you, became stiff-necked and refused to listen. For many years you were patient with them. By your Spirit you admonished them through your prophets. Yet they paid no attention, so you handed them over to neighboring peoples. But in your great mercy you did not put an end to them, or abandon them, for you are a gracious and merciful God." (Neh. 9:26–31)

God does not have to decide to be merciful. One should not think that justice is God's default attribute and mercy comes into play only as an intentional anomaly to the norm. It is just as natural for God to be merciful as it is for him to be just. God's attributes operate in perfect equilibrium.

Covenant-Making God

The election of Israel as God's chosen people was an act of grace, not of justice. God was under no obligation to choose anyone, and there was nothing Abraham or Israel did to deserve being chosen. Once they accepted their elect status (signified by circumcision), however, they also accepted God's expectations for them.

And now, O Israel, what does the LORD your God ask of you but to fear the LORD your God, to walk in all his ways, to love him, to serve the LORD your God with all your heart and with all your soul, and to observe the LORD's commands and decrees that I am giving you today for your own good?

To the LORD your God belong the heavens, even the highest heavens, the earth and everything in it. Yet the LORD set his affection on your forefathers and loved them, and he chose you, their descendants, above all the nations, as it is today. (Deut. 10:12–15)

As we have noted since the opening chapters, it was God's desire to be in relationship with his creatures. The covenant is his initiative to reestablish relationship and, as in any relationship, it involves loving response from his people.

Loyal

Once Yahweh entered into the covenant with Israel, he was characterized by steadfast loyalty to that covenant. His loyalty in reference to both the created order and the covenant with Israel is praised in Psalm 136. The term was translated "mercy" in the King James Version and rendered "lovingkindness" by the New American Standard Bible. The New International Version renders the word "love." While it is true that love, kindness, and mercy all result from Yahweh's covenant with Israel (among other things; see Deut. 7), it should be recognized that the driving force behind all these qualities was his loyalty to his elect people and the agreement that he made with them.

Redeemer

Finally, one of the most significant attributes to surface as a result of Yahweh's election of Israel is his deliverance of them. As his revelatory people, they witnessed his salvation.

> "You are my witnesses," declares the LORD,
>   "and my servant whom I have chosen,
> so that you may know and believe me
>   and understand that I am he.
> Before me no god was formed,
>   nor will there be one after me.
> I, even I, am the LORD,
>   and apart from me there is no savior.
> I have revealed and saved and proclaimed—
>   I, and not some foreign god among you.
> "You are my witnesses," declares the LORD, "that I am God."
>   (Isa. 43:10–12)

Key themes of the Old Testament: Covenant. This wall painting from an early synagogue at Dura Europas depicts Abraham as serenely receiving God's promise, "I will make you into a great nation and I will bless you; I will make your name great, and you will be a blessing. I will bless those who bless you, and whoever curses you I will curse; and all peoples on earth will be blessed through you" (Gen. 12:2–3).

Z. Radovan/
www.BibleLandPictures.com

Worship in the ancient world consisted most significantly of caring for the gods. In this Egyptian tomb painting, the food offering is stacked high before the god Osiris, and the worshiper holds a flagon to offer a libation.

RESPONDING TO GOD

The Old Testament as the Law of Love

The people of Israel were commanded to love the LORD their God as an essential part of their response of obedience to the covenant he enacted with the Hebrew nation after their exodus from Egypt (Deut. 6:5). The foundation for this law of love is laid down in the book of Deuteronomy, the account of God's covenant renewal with the second generation of Hebrews delivered from Egypt. Numerous times Moses implores Israel to love the LORD their God.[1] This command to love God reminds us that this covenant relationship with God involved more than an emotive response on the part of the people. Rather, it was primarily an act of the will.

The law of love is rooted in God's character, one of mercy, grace, patience, and abundant goodness and truth (Exod. 34:6–7). This brief "autobiography" of God is repeated several times in the Old Testament.[2] This covenant love is reciprocal, as the book of Deuteronomy also makes note of God's love for his people Israel (Deut. 4:37; 10:15; 23:5).

The law of love is dramatically demonstrated in his gracious revelation of himself and in the progressive unfolding of God's redemptive plan to reclaim, restore, and fully reinhabit his creation marred by human sin and subject to divine judgment (Gen. 3:14–19). The indication of God's intention to work within a fallen world is indicated as early as Genesis 3:15. Though neither Old Testament prophets nor New Testament apostles showed awareness of it, the early church saw this as a reference to the beginning of God's redemptive plan. They called it the *protevangelium* or "first gospel" as they recognized in it the announcment that both judgment of the Serpent and hope for humanity would come from human offspring. God's program is global but rooted in the family. God's vision to bless all nations through a family culminates in the unique offspring born into the family of Joseph and Mary of Nazareth. Remarkably, God designed a plan to restore his creation from the inside so to speak, working through humanity in the person of the last Adam to overcome the sin and rebellion of humanity (1 Cor. 15:45).

---

1. Deut. 6:5; 10:12; 11:1, 13, 22; 13:3; 19:9; 30:6, 16, 20.

2. E.g., Num. 14:18; Pss. 86:15; 103:8; Jonah 4:2; Mic. 7:18–19; cf. Jas. 5:11.

The OT condenses the law of love in two instances as a basic set of requirements enabling a proper relationship with God. The Sinai covenant called Israel to fear the LORD, to live in obedience to him by observing his commandments, and to love him with heart and soul (Deut. 10:12–13). The prophetic tradition summarized the LORD's requirements for Israel with the well-known triad of exhortations, namely: to practice justice, to love mercy, and to live in humble relationship with God (Micah 6:8). Clearly there is some overlap in the two charges and two essential ideas emerge from the passages: first, to fear or reverence the LORD, to completely love the LORD, and live in humble relationship with him speaks to our worship response to God; and second, to obey God's commands embodies social concern leading to social service. Jesus distills the OT law as a double love command, an all-consuming love for God and neighbor (Matt. 22:34–40).

One theological trajectory of the OT is the eventual worship of God by the nations, implicit in the covenant promise that Abraham and his descendants would be a blessing to all the peoples of the earth (Gen. 12:3). In one sense, the destination of human history as outlined in the Bible is the worship of the nations before God's throne.[3] Also from the very beginning of Scripture, God's plan for his people was an ethic, a lifestyle of doing what is just and right—the very pillars of his throne.[4] The NT confirms that God's intent for humanity across the covenants is the compassionate practice of social justice.[5] We will now explore these two responses to God, worship and social justice, individually.

Worship in Light of the Old Testament

Worship in the Ancient World

Among the peoples of the ancient Near East, worship involved a ritual response to deity. The gods were believed to have needs and the people were obliged to meet those needs, believing that by doing so they would earn the favor of their god. The needs of the gods included housing (the temple), clothing, a luxurious lifestyle befitting their rank, and, above all, food (the sacrifices) and drink (libations). In this way of thinking worship was part of a reciprocal relationship of mutual dependence. The gods were praised for their abilities to act on behalf of their people. The focus was on what they could do (or hopefully would not do) as opposed to recognition of who they were. No call to imitate the gods would have made any sense in this system, and the expected behavior of the people only served to contribute to a smoothly running society, which any ruler would desire.

These gods had not revealed themselves, so ritual responses were the result of logic—gods are greater than kings, so they must be treated even better than kings were treated. Their power was greater

3. Ps. 86:9; Isa. 66:23; Zech. 14:16; John 4:21–24; Phil. 2:9–11; Rev. 7:9.

4. Gen. 18:19; Ps. 89:14.

5. cf. Matt. 25:34–40; Jas. 1:27.

so they must be feared and pampered. The ritual system was designed in order to try to maintain this fragile symbiosis that framed their lives.

It was into this sort of world that Yahweh, the God of Israel, introduced the light of his character. Israel was given straightforward information of God's very nature and was led to understand that he had no needs. Their worship could then be directed toward recognition of his character rather than the meeting of his needs. He was worthy of worship not because of what he might do to them if they failed to meet his needs, but because of what he had done for them and for the continuing outworking of his plan. They were to imitate his character (a goal beyond the realm of possibility or desire in the rest of the ancient world) as he made his character known to them. The way in which they lived their lives reflected this call to holiness and righteousness, not simply as a nicety for a stable society, but as a response to who he was. Recognizing these important distinctives, we may now look more carefully at worship in the Old Testament.

In the New Testament parable of the Good Samaritan, Jesus drew attention to the law of love established in the Old Testament to explain how one should define the "neighbor" who is to be loved. This wood carving from the Church of St. Aegid in Germany (19th century AD) depicts the Samaritan's story.
Erich Lessing/Art Resource, NY, courtesy of the church St. Aegid, Gmund, Germany

What Is Worship?

Worship is a verb in the Old Testament. The Hebrew people were called to an active and whole person response to the God who initiated covenant relationship with their ancestors, Abraham, Isaac, and Jacob. Definitions of biblical worship abound. For the purpose of our study, worship in the OT may be defined as the expression of a relationship with God — always simple and complex at once, both an event and a lifestyle. The means by which God establishes relationship with humanity is through a series of covenant enactments. These covenants begin with Noah and his family, continue with Abraham, are renewed with his descendants, extended to the Israelite nation through Moses at Mt. Sinai, expanded to include kingship through the line of David, consolidated and universalized in the new covenant proclaimed by Jeremiah, and culminate with the fulfillment of the New Covenant in the Christ-event.[6] Covenants are initiated by God and regulated or maintained by stipulations or laws attached to the covenant agreements. The requisite response to God's covenant initiatives is absolute loyalty motivated by loving obedience (Deut. 30:15–16).

Knowledge of God Essential to Worship

Knowledge of God was central to Israel's worship response because covenant obedience was dependent upon Israelite understanding of Yahweh's words and deeds. The prophets attribute Israel's covenant failures to their lack of knowledge of God, indicting both the political leaders and the Levitical priesthood for failing to lead and instruct the people in the knowledge of the Lord. The pervasive knowledge of the Lord is one of the features of God's work of restoration in the eschaton. Not surprisingly, this knowledge of God will spread to the nations and they too will worship the LORD God of Israel. The incarnation of Jesus the Messiah became the ultimate expression of the knowledge of God, making known the Father to Israel and the world.[7] Knowledge of God is the foundation of worship. True worship is a response to a God who is known and flows out of our relationship with him.

Worship as a Response to God's Deeds

The exodus from Egypt was the defining event in ancient Israel's redemptive history and it was the basis for their worship of Yahweh. The Sinai covenant mediated by Moses is founded upon Yahweh's deliverance of Israel from slavery in Egypt. The mighty acts of God in humbling Pharaoh and overpowering the Egyptian gods marked the God of the Hebrews as the one truly omnipotent God among all gods. As a result, the expression "the God who brought you out of Egypt" becomes an identifying divine epithet in the OT.[8] Israel's worship response to God is contained in the psalmist's lyric, "I will meditate on all your works and consider all your mighty deeds. Your ways, O God, are holy. What god is so great as our God?" (Ps. 77:12–13). When viewed from the lens of the NT, the exodus event foreshadows the life and ministry of Jesus the Messiah, the Lamb of God and the ultimate Passover sacrifice.[9]

Language Describing Worship

The multidimensional nature of Hebrew worship is demonstrated in the various terms used to express worship in the OT. This rich worship vocabulary reveals important aspects of Hebrew religious belief and practice. For example, the word meaning "seek" (Heb. *dâraš*) is sometimes translated as "worship." This suggests worship is a quest for God not out of obligation or duty but freely and earnestly in gratitude for his

6. The sequence of references tracking these developments would include Gen. 9; Gen. 12, 15, 17; Gen. 26:2–5; 28:10–15; Exod. 19–24; 2 Sam. 7; Jer. 30–33; Luke 22.

7. For the biblical support for each of these concepts see Deut. 4:35; Ps. 100:3; Hos. 4:6; Mic. 4:12; Jer. 5:4–5; Mal. 2:7; Isa. 11:9; Hab. 2:14; Isa. 49:26; Zech. 2:9–11; John 1:18; cf. Heb. 1:1–2.

8. Expression of these ideas can be found in Deut. 4:32–40; Exod. 20:2; Deut. 3:23–24; Isa. 36:11–20; cf. Exod. 12:12; 18:10–11; Deut. 7:19; 8:14; 13:5; Ps. 81:10.

9. John 1:29; 1 Cor. 5:7.

goodness. The word meaning "fear" (Heb. *yârâ*) in the sense of awe and reverence is often used in the context of worship. The righteous fear or revere YHWH because of who he is as a unique, holy, just, loving, and merciful God, and for what he does as Creator, Covenant Maker, and Israel's Redeemer. Other key terms of worship in the OT include: "work" or "service" (Heb. *cabad*) in the sense of loyal service to God in the form of obedience to his commands; "bowing low" (Heb. *šâhâ*) is the most widely used expression for worship in the OT and connotes genuine humility on the part of an inferior being in the presence of a superior being; finally, a cluster of verbs of motion are sometimes found paired with words for worship in the OT (e.g., "draw near," Heb. *qârab*) suggesting that God is indeed approachable and that worship signifies nearness to God in terms of relationship with him.

Worship and Godliness

Several spiritual characteristics are foundational to the expression of worship as a lifestyle in the OT. Primary among them is the concept of the "fear of the LORD." The fear of YHWH in the OT wisdom literature is a response of reverent attitude that molds human behavior in conformity with the commandments of God. It is the fear of the LORD that provides the basis for the worship of God in the OT because only the fear of YHWH preserves the inscrutable nature of God and maintains the profound mysteries of life.[10] True worship of God springs from our inability to answer two simple questions posed by a biblical understanding of the fear of the LORD: O God, who is like you in power, righteousness, mighty deeds, and in pardoning sin (Ps. 71:18–19; Mic. 7:18–20)? And what are woman and man that God should look down from heaven and care for them and lift them up to sit with princes (Pss. 8:4; 113:5–8)? Other spiritual characteristics of the worshiper of God in the OT include: faith in God, separation from the world, and consecration to God in personal holiness.[11]

The spiritual character of God's people that is considered a prerequisite for worship is demonstrated in the OT by repentance and obedience:

1. *Repentance.* God's covenant blessings, and particularly deliverance of the Israelites, were contingent upon repentance and the washing clean of sin and evil. By repentance the OT means a turning away from sin and a forsaking of all evil and wickedness. It is an about-face from previous sinful behavior by an act of the will as well as emotional sorrow for wrongdoing. True repentance prompts the forgiveness of God and creates a new heart and spirit within the penitent. This new heart is the spirit of holiness which hates every false way and takes pains to avoid evil.

2. *Obedience.* Moses summarized the covenant demands incumbent upon Israel in one great requirement, "to observe the LORD's commands

10. Important verses emphasizing the fear of the Lord may be found in Exod. 20:20; Prov. 2:7, 10, 20: 3:4; Eccl. 3:11; Eccl. 3:12–15.

11. For these important concepts see Gen. 15:16; Hab. 2:4; Exod. 19:5–6; Lev. 20:24, 26; Lev. 11:44–45; 20:7.

Worship in ancient times was often portrayed and carried out with the accompaniment of musical instruments. This Sumerian tablet provides the earliest known list of musical instruments, dating to the 26th century BC.

The Schoyen Collection MS 2340, Oslo and London

and decrees" (Deut. 10:13). A lifestyle of covenant obedience was a sign or demonstration of genuine love for God on the part of the righteous. The charge of Jesus to his disciples is similar, "If you love me, you will obey what I command" (John 14:15). In fact, Jesus summarizes the response of worship to God in the OT by that first great commandment, to love God with our whole person (Matt. 22:37). This idea probably stands behind his teaching to the woman at the well in Samaria that true worshipers of God worship him in spirit and truth (John 4:23–24).

The spiritual character of God's people in the OT is expressed in devotion and in acts of worship such as thanksgiving, prayer and glorification of God.

1. *Devotion.* Perhaps the most prominent expression of personal spirituality in the OT is devotion to God as expressed in attention to praise. First and foremost, praise is a person— "He is your praise; he is your God" (Deut. 10:21). Yahweh's flawless character and mighty acts of grace in fulfilling his covenant promises to the Hebrews instilled the righteous with an overwhelming sense of trust and confidence in the God of Israel. The psalmists bid Israel to praise God, and those possessing the spiritual qualities of devotion and piety will naturally respond by making praise a priority in their lives.

2. *Thanksgiving.* Thanksgiving is the exaltation of God for his goodness as Israel's creator, redeemer, and king. Thanksgiving served to underscore the mercy of God in mediating his absolute holiness and human sinfulness, prompting the psalmist to sing: "Happy are those whose transgressions are forgiven, whose sins are covered" (Ps. 32:1). For the faithful Hebrew, life was praising God, particularly by recognizing him as the source of all life, blessing, and provision.

3. *Prayer.* Prayer is communion or fellowship with God that includes both listening to God's voice as well as speaking to him. Prayer expresses a broad range of responses to God, including some that have already been mentioned above: praise, thanksgiving, loving adoration, devotion resulting in a prayer or vow, communion, confession, petition or supplication, and intercession for others.

4. *Glorification.* The OT connects glorifying God with the divine deliverance and salvation of the righteous. God's glory is the revela-

tion of both his holiness and uniqueness, thus making Almighty God a glorious being. The heavens proclaim God's glory, and humanity as the pinnacle of God's creation, reflects the glory and honor of the Creator. Israel as God's special possession was created for his glory. Their worship of God was intended to glorify his name, serve as a beacon of saving light to the nations, and point to the eschaton when the glory of God fills the earth.[12]

Worship and Ritual

Numerous informal and formal rituals comprised the practice of Hebrew religion. The most prominent and elaborate of these were the sacrificial rites prescribed in the book of Leviticus and officiated by the Levitical priesthood. While the parallels between Israelite and ancient Near Eastern sacrificial practices attest the universal need to placate the gods, the Hebrew sacrificial system was distinctive in that it was directed toward the goal of personal and community holiness. Nothing in the teaching of the OT suggests that animal sacrifices were salvific or efficacious for individual or corporate Hebrew redemption. Instead, the sacrificial system was designed to maintain a relationship between God and his people that would allow him to continue to dwell in their midst, but it was never intended to determine their eternal destiny (cf. Paul's reflections on Gen. 15:6 and Hab. 2:4). In part, the purpose of Hebrew ritual sacrifice was didactic in that the enactment of symbolic atonement was designed to instruct the Israelites in the principles of God's holiness, human sinfulness, substitutionary death for the covering of human sin, and the need for repentance leading to cleansing and renewed fellowship within the community of faith and with God. This is why the apostle Paul could say that the OT law was put in charge to lead the people of God to the threshold of understanding Jesus as the Messiah (Gal. 3:24). It was an important OT precursor in the biblical teaching of justification of the righteous by faith mapped out in the Scriptures, culminating in Paul's doctrinal treatise on the subject in Romans 3–4.

The NT understands the sacrifices of the OT as theological types or illustrations pointing to the work of Jesus the Messiah. John the Baptist recognized and proclaimed Jesus as the Lamb of God who takes away the sin of the world, thus accomplishing what the blood of bulls and goats offered in ritual sacrifice could never achieve. Interestingly, Jesus fulfilled the roles of both the great high priest and the once for all sacrifice atoning for human sin. Finally, the NT writers found the new covenant equivalent of OT ritual sacrifice in the "spiritual sacrifices" offered by Christians to God through Christ Jesus. These sacrifices include generous and cheerful giving, worship—especially praise and thanksgiving and acts of kindness to others, prayer, and selfless service

12. These ideas can be found expressed in Ps. 50:15; Isa. 44:23; Ps. 19:1; Ps. 8:5; Isa. 43:7; Lev. 10:3; Isa. 49:6; Isa. 4:5; Hab. 2:14.

to Christ. All these and more are part of the spiritual worship Christians now offer God.[13]

Social Action in Biblical Context

God's plan for his people from the very beginning of Scripture was an ethic or lifestyle of doing what is right and just (Gen. 18:19). According to the psalmist, these two characteristics are the very pillars of God's throne (Ps. 89:14). The word "right" or "righteousness" (Heb. ṣdq) denotes conduct in accordance with the requirements of a particular relationship. Later, the Sinai covenant brokered by Moses will link this standard of behavior for the Israelites to the holiness of God and his continued dwelling among them (Exod. 19:6; Lev. 11:44–45). The term "just" or "justice" (Heb. mšpt) addresses the social implications of God's will and character, especially with respect to fairness and equity. This too was a part of Israel's obligation inherent in covenant relationship with God, another aspect of walking or living in what became known as "the way of the LORD".

The call to social justice contained within the stipulations of the Sinai covenant is far-reaching. Israel is charged to practice righteousness and justice with each other as members of the covenant community (Lev. 19:16–18). In addition, certain categories of disadvantaged and marginalized people groups are singled out as those in special need of righteousness and justice because they were susceptible to neglect and even oppression by others. The Law of Moses cites with particular concern the widows, orphans, the poor, and aliens within Hebrew society. These socially disadvantaged groups were not to be favored in the administration of covenant law, but neither were they to be neglected, exploited, and oppressed by those in positions of authority responsible for administering justice within the Hebrew social structure.[14] The Israelite practice of social justice was intended to have a global impact as well, as the nations will be drawn to the light of Israel's righteousness (Isa. 42:6; 60:2–3; Mic. 4:2).

In the call to social justice, the Bible does not idealize or romanticize poverty. Poverty is human need, social distress, and suffering and it is contrary to God's will. The Bible acknowledges poverty as a social reality and encourages a response of willing generosity. The Bible makes distinctions between several categories of poverty. Most common are those who are classified as materially poor. Closely related are those within social strata implying poverty, misery, exploitation, and need (e.g., the socially disadvantaged and marginalized groups like widows, orphans, foreigners, physically disabled, slaves, etc.). A third category are those who are identified as "spiritually poor," a necessity for receiving the kingdom of God and having an appropriate relation-

13. Biblical references supporting these ideas may be found in John 1:29–34; Heb. 10:1–10; Heb. 7–8; Rom. 5:6–11; Heb. 10:10, 12; 1 Peter 2:5; Phil. 4:18; Heb. 13:15–16; Rev. 5:8; 8:3–4; Phil. 2:17; 2 Tim. 4:6; Rom. 12:1–2.

14. Biblical passages demonstrating these concerns include Exod. 22:22; 23:6, 9; Exod. 23:3; Lev. 19:15; Exod. 23:2; Deut. 24:17.

ship with him. The Bible portrays God as an advocate for the poor. He is their refuge, he hears their needy cries, he provides for them, and he secures justice for them.[15]

All people, rich or poor, male or female, young or old, Jew or Gentile have dignity and value as persons made in God's image and thus have one Father (Mal. 2:10; cf. Matt. 5:45). The OT contains a considerable body of legislation aimed at providing justice for those socially disadvantaged. For example:

- Gleaning laws provided for the poor (Lev. 19:9–10; Deut. 24:17–22)
- A special tithe was collected for the poor (Deut. 14:28–29; 26:12)
- The sabbatical year allowed the poor to eat off the fallow land (Lev. 25:1–7; Deut. 15:1–11)
- The poor deserve impartial judgment, neither favored nor oppressed due to their status (Exod. 23:3–11; 30:15; Lev. 19:15)
- The poor were not to be denied justice nor exploited (Exod. 23:6)
- The poor among Israel were not to be charged interest on loans (Exod. 22:25)
- Certain items of security offered by the poor in lending was to be returned each day (Exod. 22:26–27; Deut. 24:12–13)
- The poor were allowed to make less expensive offerings (Lev. 5:7, 11; 27:8)
- The Year of Jubilee made provisions for redemption of property and the poor and enslaved (Lev. 25:8–55)

Although we would not treat these as binding laws for us today, they show us the heart of God and communicate how important it is to treat the poor with dignity and respect and to accept personal responsibility for their welfare as advocates for their just treatment.

Elsewhere in the OT, the Hebrew wisdom tradition affirms divine blessing for those who attend to the poor, and warns against mistreating the poor, because God is their advocate. Likewise, the OT prophets condemn those who oppress the poor; they promote social justice, and equate true spirituality with caring for the poor.[16]

The Golden Rule teaching of Jesus, doing unto others what you would have them do to you, sums up the Law and the Prophets and is in one sense an implicit call to social justice (Matt. 7:12). The OT provides the seedbed for Jesus' teaching on loving our neighbors, and even our enemies, as we would love ourselves. The biblical command to love one's neighbor is found in Leviticus 19:18, although in context the

15. Biblical support for these concepts may be found in Deut 15:4–11; Matt. 26:11; Exod. 22:21–27; Lev. 19:10; Exod. 22:21–22; Lev. 19:14; Deut. 24:17–22; Luke 14:21; Ps. 51:16–17; Mic. 6:8; Matt. 5:3–12; 11:25; Ps. 14:6; Isa. 25:4; Exod. 22:22–23; Ps. 34:6; Pss. 68:10; 82:3; 102:17; Ps. 140:12.

16. Statements in this paragraph are supported in passages such as the following: Prov. 14:21, 31; 19:17; 22:9; 28:8; 31:20; Prov. 21:13; 28:27; Prov. 14:31; 17:5; Amos 8:4–6; Isa. 10:1–4; Mic. 3:1–4; Jer. 5:26–29; Mal. 3:5; Isa 1:16–17; Amos 5:24; Mic. 6:8; Isa. 58:5–10.

injunction refers to fellow Hebrews. This neighborly love, however, is extended to the foreigner (i.e., resident non-Hebrew) later in that same passage (Lev. 19:33; cf. Deut. 10:19). Beyond this, the Hebrew wisdom tradition encourages compassion and generosity in caring for the needs of our enemies. So we see there is already an OT precedent for Jesus' teaching that extends the love of neighbor principle to anyone, and even to our enemies.

The NT continues the OT mandate for an ethic or lifestyle that practices social justice. Jesus preaches the Good News to the poor, a message of freedom, deliverance, and healing. The poor are identified as recipients of charity or alms, and the followers of Jesus have a duty to care for the poor. Jesus sent his disciples out in poverty, and he encouraged his followers to forego storing up earthly treasures. Deacons were appointed in the early church specifically to administer a food program for widows. Elsewhere, the NT encourages cheerful generosity, promotes attention to the socially disadvantaged, and warns against favoring the rich and discriminating against the poor.[17]

Continuity in the message emphasizing social concern across the Testaments is rooted in the character of God, especially: his compassion, generosity, hospitality, and acceptance.[18] At one level, the practice of social justice is the basis for separating the wicked from the righteous in the divine judgment at the end of the age (Matt. 25:31–46). More important, the litmus test of true religion in this age remains looking after widows and orphans in distress and keeping oneself from being polluted by the world (Jas. 1:27).

What are the practical implications of the biblical teaching on social justice? This question is all the more difficult when the human needs at the local, national, and global levels are so overwhelming as to induce despair leading to a paralysis of action. Yet we are reminded of the Starfish Story:

A traveler was walking along a beach when he saw a woman scooping up starfish off the sand and tossing them into the waves. Curious, he asked her what she was doing. The woman replied, "When the tide goes out, it leaves these starfish stranded on the beach. They will dry up and die before the tide comes back in, so I am throwing them back into the sea where they can live."

The traveler then asked her, "But this beach is miles long, and there are hundreds of stranded starfish. Many will die before you reach them—do you really think throwing back a few starfish is going to make a difference?"

The woman picked up a starfish and looked at it, then she threw it into the waves. "It makes a difference to this one," she said.[19]

<hr>

17. Statements in this paragraph are supported in passages such as the following: Luke 4:18–19; Mark 10:21; 14:3–7; 16:19–31; Matt. 6:1–4; Luke 11:41; 12:33; John 12:5; 13:29; Matt. 10:9–10; Luke 22:35–38; Matt. 6:19–21; Acts 6:1–4; 2 Cor. 8:1–15; 1 Tim. 6:18; Jas. 1:27; Jas. 2:1–13; 5:1–6.

18. For these attributes of God see Exod. 34:6–7; Ps. 112:4; Matt. 9:36; Col. 3:12; Jas. 5:11; Mal. 3:10; John 3:16; Eph. 3:20; Isa. 55:1–7; Matt. 11:28–30; Deut. 10:17; 2 Chron. 19:7; Acts 10:34; Rom. 2:11.

The starfish story reflects the biblical pattern of social concern. God's program of social intervention typically consists of empowering his people, sometimes corporately but most often individually, to help others one family, one person at a time. Whether the story of the kindness of Boaz to Naomi and Ruth or the ministry of Jesus to families and individuals in need, the biblical paradigm of social action emphasizes the rescuing of one "starfish" at a time. The practice of such social concern begins by slowing down, listening, and waiting so that we actually see the person in need (cf. Jas. 1:19). Next, we must learn to stop mistreating others by our stereotyping and judgmental attitudes (cf. Jas. 2:1–11). Finally, we must choose to get involved in tangible works of mercy that demonstrate our love for our neighbors. This response of obedience to God in loving our neighbor is motivated by loving God with our whole person—keeping the first great commandment first (Matt. 22:34–40).

Beyond this, what can one person do? Certainly as Christians we can hold people and situations in prayer; become an intercessor on behalf of the poor and those who work with the poor. We can become informed on the issues related to social justice and even lead study or discussion groups to share this knowledge with others. We can raise awareness by organizing local church or public events that draw attention to social justice concerns. Naturally, we can give generously of our financial resources to Christian faith-based agencies and organizations committed to the mission of social justice in the world. Finally, and most important, we can connect with those in need by volunteering in local church programs or Christian faith-based agencies and organizations engaged in ministries devoted to a biblical response to social concerns.

> No, the kind of fasting I want calls you to free those who are wrongly imprisoned and to stop oppressing those who work for you. Treat them fairly and give them what they earn. I want you to share your food with the hungry and welcome the poor wanderers into your homes. Give clothes to those who need them, and do not hide from relatives who need your help. If you do these things, your salvation will come like the dawn (Isa. 58:6–8 NLT).

---

19. *The Starfish Story*, based on Loren C. Eiseley, *The Star Thrower* (San Diego: Harvest Books, 1979).

Questions for Further Study and Discussion

1. What forms the essential content of worship as prescribed in the Bible?
2. How is the exodus-event a theological prototype of the Christ-event?
3. How does the biblical message of humanity created in God's image interface with the biblical message of social justice?
4. What are the implications of biblical teaching for our stewardship of creation and the practice of environmental justice?
5. How is our understanding of worship and social justice improved and enriched by the perspectives the global church brings to these topics?

For Further Reading

Barth, Christoph. *God with Us: An Introduction to Old Testament Theology*. Grand Rapids: Eerdmans, 1991.

Birch, Bruce C. *Let Justice Roll Down: The Old Testament, Ethics, and the Christian Life*. Louisville: Westminster John Knox, 1991.

Brueggemann, Walter. *Living Toward a Vision: Biblical Reflections on Shalom*. New ed. St. Louis: Chalice Press, 2001. Synthetic analysis of the Old Testament *shalom* and its implications for the church in light of New Testament teaching.

Dyrness, William. *Themes in Old Testament Theology*. Downers Grove, Ill.: InterVarsity Press, 1979. See especially chaps. 8, 9, and 10.

Dumbrell, William J. *The Faith of Israel*. 2nd ed. Grand Rapids: Baker, 2002. See especially pp. 57–68.

Haugen, Gary A. *Good News about Injustice: A Witness of Courage in a Hurting World*. Downers Grove, Ill.: InterVarsity Press, 1999.

Hill, Andrew E. *Enter His Courts with Praise!* Reprint. Grand Rapids: Baker, 1996.

House, Paul R. *Old Testament Theology*. Downers Grove, Ill.: InterVarsity Press, 1998. See especially pp. 169–96.

Levenson, Jon D. *Sinai & Zion: An Entry into the Jewish Bible*. New York: Harper & Row, 1985. A Jewish perspective on the theology of the Hebrew Bible based upon the two foci of ancient Israel's religion, Torah and Temple.

Millar, J. Gary. *Now Choose Life: Theology and Ethics in Deuteronomy*. Grand Rapids: Eerdmans, 1998.

Nardoni, Enrique. *Rise Up O Judge: A Study of Social Justice in the Biblical World*. Trans. by Sean Charles Martin. Peabody, Mass.: Hendrickson, 2004. Traces the roots of biblical teaching on social justice to Mesopotamian culture.

Ross, Allen P. *Recalling the Hope of Glory: Biblical Worship from the Garden to the New Creation*. Grand Rapids: Kregel, 2006. An inductive study of worship throughout the Bible.

Peterson, David. *Engaging with God: A Biblical Theology of Worship*. Downers Grove, Ill.: InterVarsity Press, 2000.

Rognlien, Bob. *Experiential Worship*. Colorado Springs: NavPress, 2005.

Stassen, Glen H., *Kingdom Ethics: Following Jesus in Contemporary Context*. Downers Grove, Ill.: InterVarsity Press, 2003.

Webber, Robert E. *Worship Old and New*. 2nd ed. Grand Rapids: Zondervan, 1994. A concise and readable biblical theology of worship that includes treatment of the history and practice of Christian worship.

Weinfeld, Moshe. *Social Justice in Ancient Israel and in the Ancient Near East*. Minneapolis: Fortress Press, 1995. A comparative study of the concepts of justice and righteousness in the literature of the OT and the literature of the ancient Near East.

Wright, Christopher J. H. *Old Testament Ethics for the People of God*. Downers Grove, Ill.. InterVarsity Press, 2004. An examination of the theological, social, and economic framework for OT ethics with application to contemporary issues of social justice.

CHAPTER 4

Among the sites that closely connect the Old Testament to the New Testament is Bethlehem, the hometown of David and the birthplace of Jesus. (See Micah 5:2.)

THE JOURNEY TO JESUS

Jesus as the Goal of the Old Testament

The Holy Scriptures of the Christian church contain two Testaments, but they comprise one Bible. The Old Testament, or Old Covenant, remains an essential part of the Christian Bible because the two covenants form one record of God's progressive and redemptive revelation to humankind. The promise of the "former" covenant finds its fulfillment in what the writer to the Hebrews called the "superior" covenant (Heb. 8:6).

The study of either covenant in isolation not only leads to an imbalanced and inadequate picture of God's self-disclosure and his purposes for creation, but also robs the Word of God of its full force as God-breathed truth and distorts its unified and unique redemptive message. This biblical scheme of redemptive history may be broadly outlined in the following fashion:

Triune God of the Bible

↓

Creation ↓ Fall ← Judgment → ← Redemption → Re-Creation

The apostle Paul said that the Christ child was born at exactly the proper moment in human history (Gal. 4:4). God the History Maker arranged the optimum historical, cultural, political, and theological environment for the birth of Jesus Christ and his church (cf. Isa. 14:24–27; Dan. 2:20–23). This made the Old Testament an integral part of God's "preparation history" for the coming Messiah. The New Testament writers clearly understood the importance of this continuity between the covenants, because the Hebrew Old Testament was the Bible for the early church. The Old Testament served as the source book for preaching (cf. Acts 2:14–36 and 3:12–26) and public reading in those apostolic days (cf. 1 Tim. 4:13). The apologetic of the early church was essentially to defend Jesus as the Christ by appealing to his fulfillment of Old Testament prophecy (e.g., Acts 4:5–12; 7:2–53; cf. Matt. 11:2–6, a method used by Jesus himself).

Related to this NT approach to understanding the OT is the methodology of biblical typology. Biblical typology is literary foreshadowing and one aspect of formal biblical interpretation or hermeneutics. Typology is a method of biblical exegesis that

Capernaum is the town where the ministry of Jesus began (Matt. 4:13–17).

Todd Bolen/www.BiblePlaces.com

establishes historical correspondence between OT events, persons, objects, or ideas and similar NT events, persons, objects, or ideas by way of prototype. The OT correspondent is identified as the "type"; the NT correspondent fulfilling or expressing the OT truth in a greater way is considered the "antetype." The NT offer numerous examples of biblical typology; prominent among them are the identification of Jesus Christ as the Passover lamb (1 Cor. 5:7), the great High Priest (Heb. 4:14–8:13), and the cross of Jesus Christ as the culmination of Mosaic sacrificial worship (Heb. 9–10). Jesus himself taught his followers to understand the typology of the OT Scriptures (cf. Luke 24:44–48; John 5:39, 46–47). Naturally, this approach does not override the need to read the OT in its own literary and historical context.

Bridging the Testaments: The New Testament Use of the Old Testament

The New Testament makes extensive use of the Old Testament in the form of direct quotation and indirect allusion. In fact, according to careful calculation, approximately 32 percent—nearly one-third—of the New Testament is composed of Old Testament quotations and allusions.[1] An analysis of these Old Testament quotations and allusions yields several major themes or emphases and shows us how the disciples of Christ broadly understood his statement about his "presence" in the Law, the Prophets, and the Psalms (cf. Luke 24:44).[2]

Figure 47.1 offers a representative sampling of the Old Testament verses most frequently cited in the New Testament.

The themes and emphases of these New Testament references to the Old Testament may be grouped under three major headings: those

1. For the details on this remarkable statistic, see Andrew E. Hill, *Baker's Handbook of Bible Lists* (New edition. Grand Rapids: Baker, 2006), 90–91.

2. Based on the Index of Quotations in *The Greek New Testament*, ed. K. Aland et al. 2nd ed. (New York: United Bible Societies, 1969), 897–920.

Figure 47.1. Use of the Old Testament in the New

OT Verse		Number of NT Occurrences
Psalm 110:1	The Lord says to my Lord: "Sit at my right hand until I make your enemies a footstool for your feet."	18
Daniel 12:1	At that time Michael, the great prince who protects your people, will arise. There will be a time of distress such as has not happened from the beginning of nations until then. But at that time your people — everyone whose name is found written in the book — will be delivered.	13
Isaiah 6:1	In the year that King Uzziah died, I saw the Lord seated on a throne, high and exalted, and the train of his robe filled the temple. (Cf. 2 Chron. 18:18; Ps. 47:8; Ezek. 1:26 – 28)	12
Psalm 2:7	I will proclaim the decree of the Lord: He said to me, "You are my Son; today I have become your Father."	10
Isaiah 53:7	He was oppressed and afflicted, yet he did not open his mouth; he was led like a lamb to the slaughter, and as a sheep before her shearers is silent, so he did not open his mouth. (Cf. Ps. 44:22)	10*
Leviticus 19:18	"Do not seek revenge or bear a grudge against one of your people, but love your neighbor as yourself. I am the Lord."	10
Deuteronomy 10:17	For the Lord your God is God of gods and Lord of lords, the great God, mighty and awesome, who shows no partiality and accepts no bribes.	8
Malachi 3:1	"See, I will send my messenger, who will prepare the way before me. Then suddenly the Lord you are seeking will come to his temple; the messenger of the covenant, whom you desire, will come," says the Lord Almighty.	8
Exodus 24:8	Moses then took the blood, sprinkled it on the people and said, "This is the blood of the covenant that the Lord has made with you in accordance with all these words."	7
Psalm 62:12	… you, O Lord, are loving. Surely you will reward each person according to what he has done.	7
Psalm 110:4	The Lord has sworn and will not change his mind: "You are a priest forever in the order of Melchizedek."	7
Deuteronomy 18:15	The Lord your God will raise up for you a prophet like me among your own brothers. You must listen to him	6
Genesis 15:6	Abram believed the Lord, and he credited it to him as righteousness.	5
Exodus 19:6	" 'You will be for me a kingdom of priests and a holy nation.' These are the words you are to speak to the Israelites."	5
Leviticus 18:5	"Keep my decrees and laws, for the man who obeys them will live by them. I am the Lord."	5

*The New Testament contains thirty-eight references to Isaiah 53 and twenty-four references to Psalm 22.

Much of Jesus' ministry took place around the Sea of Galilee, viewed here from the southeast.

Bible Scene Multimedia/Maurice Thompson

related to God Almighty, those related to Jesus as the Christ, and those related to humankind.

1. The New Testament writers highlighted several important aspects of God's nature and character as portrayed in the Old Testament, including the enthroned Sovereign of creation and the nations (e.g., Rev. 4:2ff.), the God of awesome deeds and power (e.g., Acts 26:8), and a God who is generous in extending his steadfast love without partiality (e.g., Acts 10:34). These themes were no doubt especially significant for the early Christian church, given the iron rule of the Romans within the vast empire.

2. Jesus Christ was foreshadowed in the Old Testament and recognized in the New Testament as Lord and King (Col. 1:15–20), as son of David (e.g., Matt. 9:27), as suffering servant and savior (e.g., Matt. 16:21), announced by the messenger of God (e.g., Luke 3:1–17), as the Lamb of God whose blood of the covenant purchased redemption for humanity (e.g., Matt. 26:28), and as the prophet greater than Moses and the eternal priest greater than Melchizedek (e.g., Heb. 3:1–6; 7:15–28). These christological themes constituted the basic message of salvation in Christ Jesus as the Son of God preached to the Gentiles, and they formed the chief apologetic of the early church demonstrating Jesus of Nazareth as Messiah to the Jews.

3. The New Testament identifies several areas of continuity with the Old Testament in regard to the need and destiny of humanity, including an impending day of distress and trouble as judgment for sin (e.g., Matt. 24:15–28), the need for deliverance and redemption by a blood covenant better than that of bulls and goats (e.g., Heb. 9:23–10:18), the priority of faith for relationship to God (Heb. 11:6), the need for holi-

ness (e.g., 1 Peter 1:16), and the demands of obedience to the decrees of God, issuing in "life" to the believer (e.g., Heb. 5:9). These emphases prove foundational for basic aspects of New Testament theology like eschatology (the doctrine of last things), soteriology (the doctrine of salvation), and sanctification (the pursuit of holiness by the believer).

Themes across the Testaments

Another useful model for bridging the Old and the New Testaments is tracing the theme of the covenant, the Old Testament conception of faith. Elmer A. Martens identifies four basic purposes or designs of Yahweh for Israel, including salvation or deliverance, the covenant community, the knowledge of God, and the land of covenant promise.[3] These designs not only capture the central message of Old Testament revelation, but also anticipate the person and work of the Messiah in the New. Thus, they serve as a grid by which key Old Covenant theological themes may be transposed and developed in the New Covenant.

1 God's design for salvation in the Old Testament demanded a faith commitment to God Almighty by acts of obedience to his word (e.g., Abraham's trek to Canaan and his offering of Isaac, cf. Heb. 11:8–22). Deliverance was accomplished by mighty deeds performed by Yahweh on behalf of his people Israel (e.g., the exodus from Egypt, Exod. 12–13), while worship of Yahweh was established on the principle

3. Elmer A. Martens, *God's Design: A Focus on Old Testament Theology* (3rd. ed. Richland Hills, Tex.: Scott Publishing, 1997), 18–30.

A model of the temple in Jerusalem at the time of Jesus.
Deror Avi

of substitutionary sacrifice for sin (cf. Lev. 1 – 7). Likewise, Jesus demanded a faith commitment shown in acts of obedience (e.g., the radical call to discipleship in Luke 14:25 – 33), and through his substitutionary and atoning sacrifice he defeated the final enemy — death itself (cf. 1 Cor. 15:20 – 28, 51 – 58).

2. God's design for a new relationship with humankind was enacted by treaty formula (e.g., Exod. 20 – 24), emphasized legislative holiness (e.g., Exod. 20:20), and was conditioned by the promise of blessing and the threat of curse (e.g., Lev. 26). The exodus-event was commemorated with a memorial meal and annual festival, the Passover (e.g., Exod. 12; 23:15). In the same way, the New Testament constituted a new covenant relationship with God (i.e., "friends" of God, John 15:14 – 15, and "heirs" with Christ, Eph. 3:6) and spawned a new community in which "all the believers were together and had everything in common" (Acts 2:44; cf. vv. 42 – 47). This new covenant was also legitimized by treaty formula (cf. Luke 22:7 – 30) and conditioned by the promise of blessing and the threat of curse (cf. 1 Cor. 11:29 – 31; 1 Peter 2:4 – 10), and commemorated with a memorial meal, the Lord's Supper (Luke 22:7 – 38; 1 Cor. 11:17 – 34). But this new covenant implemented an operative holiness through the dynamic power of the Holy Spirit (cf. Rom. 7:7 – 8:17).

3. Yahweh's design for a new relationship with humanity was based on the knowledge of God (Hos. 6:3). For the Hebrews this knowledge was disclosed in the revealed word spoken by Yahweh's servants (e.g., Isa. 6:8 – 13), divine acts of "salvation history" (e.g., Exod. 14:30 – 31), the divinely ordained offices of prophet, priest, king, judge, and sage

These are the steps leading to the Gates of Chuldah, one of the main entrances to Herod's temple in Jerusalem that would have been used by Jesus to enter the temple complex.

Z. Radovan/www.BibleLandPictures.com

(cf. Jer. 18:18), and the sacrificial system of the Hebrew religion (cf. Lev. 1–7).

This knowledge of God is a primary concern of the New Testament as well (cf. John 17:3; Phil. 3:10). Jesus Christ came to reveal or make known the Father (John 1:18), and he commissioned the church to make the word of God fully known to all people (not just the Hebrews, Col. 1:25). Elsewhere Paul described Christ Jesus as the believer's wisdom, righteousness, sanctification, and redemption (1 Cor. 1:30) and affirmed the "office" gifts of apostle, prophet, evangelist, and pastor-teacher so that all may attain the unity of faith and the knowledge of the Son of God (Eph. 4:11–13).

4. God's design for Israel included a land of covenant promise for the Hebrews (Gen. 12:1–3). The "covenant land" was a gift from a loving and gracious God and a reward for obedience to the stipulations of Yahweh's covenant (Deut. 30:11–31:8). The presence of the Hebrews in the land of Canaan symbolized rest and peace for the people of Israel (cf. Ps. 95:11), and served as a reminder of God's faithfulness to his covenant promises to the patriarchs (cf Pss. 106:45–46; 111:4–6).

More important, the land was symbolic of a way of life that included God's dwelling in the midst of his people and the restoration of order and balance in nature, human relationships (both within the community of Israel and extending to the "foreigner" and the socially disadvantaged), work and worship, space and time, and material possessions (cf. Exod. 25:8; Lev. 18–27).

The new covenant also focuses on God dwelling with his people, first by means of his indwelling Holy Spirit (cf. 1 Cor. 3:16–17; 6:19–20) and eventually with the very throne of God established among humanity (Rev. 21:1–4). The destination of the land of covenant promise as the symbol of peace and rest for God's people gives way to rest in Jesus the Messiah (Matt. 11:28–29; cf. Heb. 3:11, 18; 4:1–11). Likewise, the redemptive ministry of Jesus Christ initiated a new order of righteous behavior in the world (cf. Matt. 5–7) that ultimately gives way to complete and perfect re-creation of heaven and earth where "the old order of things has passed away" and "I am making everything new!" (Rev. 21:4–5).

The New Testament opens with the joyful response to God's fulfillment of long-awaited prophetic expectations. God's Messiah and Israel's salvation had arrived in the person of Jesus, the son of Mary (Luke 2). The timetable for the Lord's new covenant with Israel as predicted by Jeremiah was finally realized (cf. Jer. 31:30–33). Yes, the "promise" of the old covenant had given way to "fulfillment" in this new covenant, ushered in by Christ Jesus, but like Israel, the church of Christ was charged to wait—even prayerfully long—for his triumphant return (cf. 1 Thess. 1:9–10; Titus 2:11–14; Rev. 22:20).

During this interim period of tension between "the now and the not yet," the church of Jesus Christ anticipates the culmination of their salvation (cf. Matt. 24:13; 1 Thess. 3:12–13; 5:23), a completely restored and perfect relationship with God through Christ (cf. Phil. 3:17–21; Rev. 19:1–10; 21:1–8), full of knowledge of God in Christ (cf. 1 Cor. 13:8–13), and the blessing and rest of the new creation and the heavenly city (cf. Rev. 21:9–22:5).

Questions for Further Study and Discussion

1. What made the Roman occupation of Palestine during the first century AD the "fullness of time" according to historians?
2. What is the relationship of Israel in the Old Testament to the Christian church in the New Testament?
3. According to William Dyrness, the Old Testament is often useful in evangelistic situations because there is a natural bridge between it and the common people, especially in non-Western cultures. Discuss this concept. (Cf. William Dyrness, *Themes in Old Testament Theology* [Downers Grove, Ill.: InterVarsity Press, 1979], 15–19.)
4. How are the Old Testament and New Testament "continuous" and "discontinuous"?
5. The two Testaments correspond to each other "typologically." What is typology? What are the strengths and weaknesses of using typology to unify the Old and New Testaments? (Cf. Walter C. Kaiser, *The Uses of the Old Testament in the New* [Chicago: Moody Press, 1985], 103–44.)
6. How do we account for those occasions when the New Testament writers take liberties in quoting the Old Testament text? What does this mean for the biblical doctrine of the inspiration of Scripture?

For Further Reading

Baker, D. L. *Two Testaments: One Bible.* 2nd ed. Downers Grove, Ill.: InterVarsity Press, 1991. Standard work on the theological problem of the relationship between the Old and New Testaments.

Baylis, A. H. *On the Way to Jesus.* Portland, Ore.: Multnomah, 1986. Fresh, personal, and practical survey of the Old Testament, with great appreciation for the concept of two covenants—one Bible.

Bruce, F. F. *New Testament Development of Old Testament Themes.* Grand Rapids: Eerdmans, 1968.

Brueggemann, Walter. *Living Toward a Vision: Biblical Reflections on Shalom.* New ed. St. Louis: Chalice Press, 2001. Synthetic analysis of the Old Testament *shalom* and its implications for the church in light of New Testament teaching.

Dyrness, William. *Themes in Old Testament Theology.* Downers Grove, Ill.: InterVarsity Press, 1979.

France, R. T. *Jesus and the Old Testament.* Reprint. Grand Rapids: Baker, 1982. Detailed examination of Jesus' use of the Old Testament, with emphasis on how his interpretation shaped his understanding of his central role in salvation history.

Fuller, D. P. *Gospel and Law: Contrast or Continuum?* Grand Rapids: Eerdmans, 1980.

_____. *The Unity of the Bible.* Grand Rapids: Zondervan, 1992.

Kaiser, Walter C. *The Uses of the Old Testament in the New.* Chicago: Moody Press, 1985. Discussion of the hermeneutical uses of the earlier Testament in the later.

_____. *The Messiah in the Old Testament.* Grand Rapids: Zondervan, 1995.

Kuske, M. *The Old Testament as the Book of Christ.* Trans. by S. T. Kimbrough. Philadelphia: Westminster, 1976.

Longenecker, Richard N. *Biblical Exegesis in the Apostolic Period.* 2nd ed. Grand Rapids: Eerdmans, 1999.

Martens, E. A. *God's Design: A Focus on Old Testament Theology.* 3rd ed. Richland Hills, Tex.: Scott Publishing, 1997. A lucid, comprehensive, and readable description of Old Testament faith and its implications for New Testament faith.

Matthews, Victor H. *Old Testament Themes.* St. Louis: Chalice Press, 2000.

Scott, J. B. *God's Plan Unfolded.* Rev. ed. Wheaton, Ill.: Tyndale House, 1978.

Vang, P., and T. Carter, *Telling God's Story: The Biblical Narrative from Beginning to End.* Nashville: Broadman & Holman, 2006.

Walton, John H. *Covenant: God's Purpose, God's Plan.* Grand Rapids: Zondervan, 1994.

_____. "Isaiah—What's in a Name?" *JETS* 30 (1987): 289–306.

Wright, Christopher J. H. *Knowing Jesus through the Old Testament.* Downers Grove, Ill.: InterVarsity Press, 1992.

Youngblood, Ronald. *The Heart of the Old Testament.* Grand Rapids: Baker, 1971.

APPENDIX A:
CRITICAL METHODOLOGIES

Most critical methodologies have been developed to try to address the question, How should we approach the various literary genres that we find in the Bible? Was each book written at one sitting, or was there a longer process of composition? Could there have been previous editions of some of the books that have gone through stages of editing to reach the form in which we now have them? Were there later hands that reshaped material to give it a particular focus? Do some of the books incorporate texts of one genre into the context of another genre? All these questions are part of an attempt to understand the literary mechanisms as much as possible so that interpretation may proceed.

For much of the twentieth century, biblical scholarship was divided into camps labeled "liberal" and "conservative." While these terms broadly distinguish those who acknowledge less authority in the Bible (liberals) from those who held a more traditional view of biblical authority (conservatives), the absence of a generally recognized benchmark resulted in the use of "liberal" to designate anyone more open-minded than the person applying the label, while "conservative" might be applied to those considered anti-intellectual fanatics. These labels were therefore often used pejoratively to ridicule, caricature, or in other ways depreciate the perspective of the other's position. Recent years have witnessed some relaxation of the tensions and some cross-fertilization of ideas and methods without reducing the ideological chasm that separates the camps.

In this survey, reference has occasionally been made to "critical scholarship." This is neither a derogatory term nor a value judgment. It is a descriptive label that is generally brandished proudly by those to whom it is applied. "Criticism" here refers to the exercise of an expert sense of judgment about the text and should not be confused with "criticism" in the sense of making negative statements. Relative to the old terminology, it must be pointed out that "conservatives" and "liberals" alike use critical methodologies. Their respective presuppositions about the text, however, dictate to what extent and in what ways the various critical methodologies can be used. Contemporary evangelical scholars make extensive use of critical methodologies, but that use can be somewhat restricted by presuppositions about the nature and authority of Scripture.[1] The presuppositions of nonevangelical scholars leave them unfettered by such concerns and often promote, if not

1. *Evangelical* is a term in vogue to describe those who acknowledge the authority of the Bible. While it is a bit more precise than *conservative*, it can represent a range of beliefs.

demand, dismissal of supernaturalistic claims and reconstruction of biblical history and the text of the Old Testament. When we contrast "critical scholarship" and "evangelical scholarship" therefore, it is not to suggest that evangelical scholarship is uncritical or "precritical" in its approach to the Old Testament. Rather, it is a recognition that some scholars use critical methodologies more than others, depending on the nature of their presuppositions.

Some critical methodologies attempt to reconstruct the ways and means by which the text came to be in its present form. These are referred to as "diachronic," for they explore the history of the text and look for meaning in previous forms and settings of portions of the text. Other methodologies recognize that there may well be a history of the text but seek meaning in the form the text currently possesses. These approaches view the text as self-sufficient, requiring no outside information for interpretation and are referred to as "synchronic." Other terminology labels diachronic approaches as "historical-critical" and synchronic approaches as "literary."

Diachronic Methodologies

Textual Criticism

The aim of textual criticism is to identify errors that may have occurred in the process of copying and recopying the text by hand through the centuries. On one level, textual criticism is necessary when a given manuscript preserves one reading while another manuscript is slightly different. Frequently in Old Testament study, however, suspected transmission (copying) errors are identified and corrections suggested even when none of the manuscripts contains variant readings. This can be justifiable if the text makes little sense as it stands and a defensible alternative is available. The plethora of Old Testament manuscripts makes this situation much more common than in New Testament textual criticism.

Another feature adding to the complexity is that in the Old Testament, textual criticism often takes place on the basis of Septuagint readings. Because the Septuagint is a Greek translation of the Old Testament that originated no earlier than the third century BC, it is often difficult to judge whether the variant readings it offers represent an actual alternative in the Hebrew text or just an error on the part of the Greek translators or copyists. The goal of the text critic is to restore the text to its original canonical form.

Source Criticism

No one doubts that sources were used in the compilation of some books of the Old Testament. Chronicles and Kings both name sources that were available to them and from which they drew information (e.g., the Book of the Annals of Solomon, 1 Kings 11:41; the Records of Gad the Seer, 1 Chron. 29:29). For some two hundred years now, a growing consensus among scholars assumes that many more of the books of the Old Testament were compiled from written or at times oral sources.

Source criticism seeks to identify which sections of a given book belong to which hypothetical sources and then to analyze each source. Generally sections are assigned to different sources on the basis of perceived differences in style among parts of the book. Another criterion sometimes is a presupposed theory of theological development. For instance, many source critics would assume that the idea of a centralized place of worship was a relatively late development (perhaps not until the time of Josiah). Other "late" developments would include several of the festivals, the Aaronic priesthood, monotheism, and the future restoration of Israel.

As a result, any passage from an earlier book that shows concern or understanding about these matters would be assigned to a later source that may have made additions to the earlier work. These hypothetical sources are then analyzed for their style, interests, and theological parameters. This approach tends to fragment the text and has been criticized for being too vulnerable to circular reasoning. The speculative nature of its results has made it less popular in recent years to attach any certainty to its findings, but many persist in believing that most of the books of the Old Testament have resulted from the editing together of various sources, or at least show evidence of additions at the hands of sources other than the writer.

Form Criticism

Form criticism is not so concerned with working with the literary sources that may be behind a certain book as it is with identifying the oral history of the various parts of the text. The assumption is that many sections of any book had functions in society in their oral form that differ from how they are used in their present context. So, for instance, a number of psalms are sometimes identified as having been used for an annual "enthronement festival" in Israel. In labeling patriarchal narratives "sagas" or the narratives of Joshua "etiologies," form critics exercise great influence on interpretation, for with these identifications comes the implication that these narratives are of less historical value. As with source criticism, the difficulties lie in the speculative nature of the results and the neglect of the final form of the text.

Redaction Criticism

The redaction approach attempts to identify the logic and motivations of the author or, more often, the redactor (editor) who brought the sources together to produce the final form of the text. To a large extent the redaction critic works with the sources identified by the source critic, so this remains a diachronic approach, though it can be seen as providing a transition between diachronic and synchronic approaches. To put this another way, redaction criticism does treat the final form of the text, but it does so by examining how the redactor has reworked, reinterpreted, or in any way reshaped the sources to achieve his or her purposes.

The success of this method depends on the soundness of the source work and the strength of the evidence for the redactor's role and purpose.

Historical Criticism

The goal of historical criticism is to reconstruct the events that lie behind the biblical narratives. Since the narratives are usually produced with a theological motive or agenda, they may not clearly or completely present the details of the actual event. At other times scholars suspect the narrative of skewing the material, so they offer more substantial reconstructions. Historical critics may therefore offer reconstructions of what "really" happened in the plagues on Egypt or in the crossing of the Reed Sea. Anywhere God's supernatural intervention is portrayed can be subjected to an attempt to offer natural explanations. Likewise, there are sections of the historical literature that some would consider propagandistic or legendary (e.g., David fighting Goliath, the exploits of Samson). The historical critic would seek to identify a "historical kernel" in the account around which the "actual" event might be reconstructed.

There is very little objection to using historical criticism to fill in the gaps of what the Bible leaves unsaid about certain events. There is considerably more skepticism about using historical criticism to discard or discount some of the details given in the text in favor of the critic's reconstructions.

Synchronic Methodologies

Rhetorical Criticism

In an effort to be more holistic in its approach, rhetorical criticism assumes the unity of form and content. It is interested in discovering how the form of the literature aids the content in communicating the intended message. Literary structures such as chiasmus (a parallel pattern of words, lines, ideas, paragraphs, or rhyming scheme) and inclusio (beginning and ending a section with similar or identical lines) are identified, and even basic distinctions between poetry and prose become significant. Any feature that contributes to the literary art of the author is noted and analyzed. So, for instance, the inclusio in Ecclesiastes (1:2 and 12:8) can be used to identify the major premise of the author and to conclude that 12:9–14 are in some way extraneous to the major part of the book.

Structural Analysis

From a technical standpoint, structural analysis should be defined in relation to a philosophy of linguistics that has been expanded into the field of literary interpretation. In Old Testament studies, however, it has taken on a broader meaning and has come to refer to almost any method that is synchronic in its approach. This type of analysis focuses solely on the literary character and features of the text to derive their meaning. Thus, plot, character development, use of motifs, vocabulary, syntax, and other literary elements are explored in depth to the exclusion of historical or archaeological background or the history of the literature.

The Canonical Approach

In the canonical method, prehistory (sources, traditions, previous forms, redactions, etc.) of the text is ignored in favor of understanding the meaning of the final form (canonical form) of the text to the community of faith under whose aegis it took shape. This is a synchronic approach in that it takes final canonical form as the starting point for its analysis, though it is aware of layers in the text and at times seeks harmonization of those layers, thus having a diachronic element. It is interested in the interpretation of the text as a composite whole, a piece of Scripture. Furthermore, in this approach the canon as a whole can be viewed as a context rather than portions of books or the books themselves being the context.

Narrative Criticism

In narrative criticism the attention of the interpreter is focused on a close literary reading of the text that views the work solely as literature, in contrast to thinking of it as something that has a larger meaning. In this view literature is a work of art, not a work of philosophy or history. No moralization or spiritualization should be imposed on the text. Meaning is found in the plot, characterization, and formal structures of the text. These are the reason the narrative exists rather than providing only supporting structures for a larger meaning. Because of this, narrative criticism becomes very problematic for those who wish to attribute authority to a text. Furthermore, it is not at all clear that the ancient writers were doing literary art rather than simply using literary art.

	Diachronic (Reading in light of historical development)	Intermediary	Synchronic (Reading in light of context)
Author Intended Meaning: Words/Ideas/Message	Historical Criticism Literary Criticism	Form Criticism Redaction Criticism	
	Tradition Criticism	Rhetorical Criticism	Structuralism
Text Represented Meaning: Symbols/Structure	Textual Criticism Source Criticism		New Criticism Canonical Criticism
			Narrative Criticism
Reader Interpreted Meaning: Decoding Symbols/ Structure			Ideological Criticism Post-Structural Criticism Reader-Response

Writing and Reading Strategies

A close reading of a biblical book requires one to observe the use of certain strategies within the book. Three of the most important strategies, each occurring in a number of the aforementioned methodologies, are literary strategies, rhetorical strategies, and cross-textual strategies. Observing these strategies helps us to identify some of what the author is consciously bringing to the communication process.

Literary Strategies

Here we focus on the literary art of the writer (without resolving whether literary art is all there is). Authors such as R. Alter, M. Sternberg, J. Fokkelman, and L. Ryken have provided guides to understanding the literary strategies used by authors. These could include narrative strategies such as plot, setting and character development, or structural strategies such as chiasm, inclusio, ring structure, or palistrophe. Recognition of the use of such strategies by authors help the reader more effectively to take his or her place in the audience of the author.

Rhetorical Strategies

A writer makes many choices as he/she writes. Observing what an author chooses to include or to omit is an important part of interpretation. For example, the author of Esther chooses not to mention the name of God even once (and sometimes appears to have made an effort to avoid doing so). The interpreter will want to understand why. On the other side, the author of Genesis could easily have omitted the detail of Joseph failing to find his brothers but then encountering someone who told him where they were. The inclusion of this detail must be considered important.

A second choice concerns the arrangement of the material. Sometimes it is chronological, but at times there are other reasons. For example, why does the story of Judah and Tamar (Gen. 38) intrude into the middle of the Joseph story?

Finally, the author makes choices about what to emphasize and in so doing communicates what he/she considers important. In Old Testament narrative, for example, dialogue is often more important than character development. Being alert to these elements can help the reader to understand the rhetorical strategy of a book and thereby gain important information about what the author is trying to communicate.

Cross-Textual Strategies

All texts are cross dependent on other texts. Cross-textual strategies seek to identify the role and impact of other texts on the text under study. Sometimes a text will be intentionally alluding to other texts or even interpreting them. This could be reflected in a haphazard quotation, a vague allusion, or an outright analysis. This is called *intertextuality* and is what is taking place when the New Testament uses the Old Testament, or when Jeremiah is elaborating on the Davidic covenant. Intertextuality does not change the book that is being referenced, but it might offer a new or expanded understanding of that book.

In contrast, *innertextuality* refers to a process in which a book is subject to a series of additions, expansions or redactions that actually impose new ideas into the text. In this way the text can be seen as having competing voices within it. The focus of the initial author may be altered either subtly or radically to reflect the concerns of the later hands. In this way the text is not only reinterpreted, it is changed in the process to become something new.

Role of the Reader

In postmodern culture, the role of the reader has taken a more prominent position in interpretation. It has been recognized that we cannot get inside the mind of the author, reconstruct what he/she was thinking, or eliminate our own biases, cultural impulses, and personal needs from the interpretation process. In reader-response approaches, this recognition leads to the abandonment of any pretense of understanding what the author intended, being satisfied instead to allow interpretation to be personal and ever-changing to meet the needs of each new generation of readers or each cultural approach to the text. The problem with submitting to this approach is that it becomes impossible to retain the idea of authoritative text. Anyone's reading is legitimate and the text "means" whatever the reader might think it means or want it to mean.

For Further Reading

Alter, Robert. *The Art of Biblical Narrative*. New York: Basic, 1981.

Barton, John. *The Nature of Biblical Criticism*. Louisville: Westminster John Knox, 2007

_____. *Reading the Old Testament*. Louisville: Westminster John Knox, 1996.

Fokkelman, J. P. *Reading Biblical Narrative: An Introductory Guide*. Louisville: Westminster John Knox, 2000.

McKenzie, S., and S. Haynes. *To Each Its Own Meaning*. Louisville: Westminster John Knox, 1999.

Ryken, Leland. *How to Read the Bible as Literature*. Grand Rapids: Zondervan, 1984.

Sailhamer, John *The Pentateuch as Narrative*. Grand Rapids: Zondervan, 1992.

Sternberg, Meir. *The Poetics of Biblical Narrative*. Indianapolis: Indiana University, 1985.

Wegner, Paul. *A Student's Guide to Textual Criticism of the Bible*. Downers Grove, Ill.: InterVarsity Press, 2006.

APPENDIX B:
THE COMPOSITION
OF THE PENTATEUCH

Both the Old Testament and the New Testament make reference to Mosaic writing activity in connection with the Pentateuch (Exod. 24:4; John 5:46–47), and both covenants assert that Moses was the primary human author of the Pentateuch (Deut. 31:9; Mark 12:19). Until the age of the Enlightenment the large majority of Jews and Christians accepted the divine origin and the Mosaic authorship of the Pentateuch. Although a few dissenting Jewish and Christian scholars challenged the antiquity and integrity of a Mosaic Pentateuch, the scholarship of this period from the early church fathers to the Protestant reformation was essentially "precritical" in respect to the issues of Pentateuchal authorship and date.

However, traditional understanding of the Old Testament (and the New, for that matter) was questioned and overturned during the Age of Reason. This "enlightened" period of Western civilization spawned an era of critical study of the Bible rooted in a humanistic and scientific worldview that continues to shape the landscape of biblical studies. It was presumed that human beings were capable of a reasonable and natural understanding of themselves, the physical world, law, religion, and philosophy. Likewise, external authorities and nonrational assessments of nature, history, religious experience, and science were rejected. This concurrent rise of the scientific method (i.e., empiricism and scientific positivism), deistic theology in religion, and evolutionary theory in respect to origins has thoroughly influenced customary views on Pentateuchal authorship. As a result, several hypotheses or literary approaches to Pentateuchal composition have emerged from the past three centuries of scholarly discussion.

One Author Hypothesis

Hebrew, Samaritan, and early Christian tradition all regarded Moses as the author or compiler of the Pentateuch. The one-author view acknowledges that Moses wrote the entire Pentateuch apart from the account of his own death recorded in Deuteronomy 34. Some holding this view allow for the use of preexisting written sources by Moses, making him the compiler of portions of the Pentateuch.

Evidence adduced for the one-author view include the witness of the Pentateuch (e.g., Num. 33:2); the witness of the rest of the Old Testament and the New Testament to the "Law of Moses" (e.g., Judg. 3:4; John 10:5); the weight of Hebrew, Samaritan, and early Christian tradition; and the burden of material evidence given the eyewitness detail and familiarity with Egyptian language and culture demonstrated by the author.

This approach assumes the divine inspiration and supernatural origin of the (original) written documents through Moses. It also affirms the accuracy and reliability of the history as literally reported in the five books of the Pentateuch. All numbers are taken at face value (so some two million–plus Hebrews left Egypt at the exodus), and miracles happened as narrated, whether God used natural means or superseded natural law by intervening directly in time and space for the benefit of his people Israel (e.g., the miraculous path through the Sea of Reeds, or Yam Suph, is determined to be more than a mile wide to accommodate the millions of Hebrews passing through the waters).[1]

One Author—Later Editor(s) Hypothesis

The rise of rationalistic biblical criticism during the period of the Enlightenment brought serious challenges against the traditional view of Mosaic authorship of the Pentateuch. The so-called liberal repudiation of the Mosaic authorship view was grounded in phenomena within the literature of the Pentateuch itself. This approach constitutes a viable conservative alternative to the multiple-authorship theories characteristic of most modern critical biblical scholarship without rejecting the divine inspiration of the Old Testament Scriptures.[2]

The one author–later editor(s) hypothesis attempts to honestly address the objections to Mosaic authorship raised by the multiple-author hypothesis. These questions were primarily of a literary nature, like the differing style and vocabulary of the Pentateuchal narratives; the so-called literary doublets (i.e., two accounts of the same event, as in the creation versions of Gen. 1:1–2:4a and 2:4b–25); the historical anachronisms (i.e., references to people and places in the Pentateuch from later time periods, such as the mentioning of the Israelite kings in Gen. 36:31 or of the Philistines in Gen. 21:34); editorial insertions clearly designed to update a later audience (e.g., the reference to Egypt as "the district of Rameses," Gen. 47:11); and even disagreement between narrative accounts (such as the number and kinds of animals on the ark of Noah, Gen. 6:19–20; 7:2; 8–9).

Proponents of this approach respond to these literary difficulties in several ways. They assert that Moses used a variety of literary sources (e.g., Book of the Wars of the Lord, Num. 21:14) and appeal to the ancient Near Eastern literary conventions of repetition and duplication. They may cite the use of multiple names for deities (e.g., the Canaanite literature of Ras Shamra or Ugarit) or recognize the extrabiblical parallels in ancient Near Eastern literature illuminating biblical texts

---

1. This approach is represented by such scholars as Merrill F. Unger, *Introductory Guide to the Old Testament* (Grand Rapids: Zondervan, 1951); Norman. L. Geisler, *A Popular Survey of the Old Testament* (Grand Rapids: Baker, 1978); and I. L. Jensen, *Jensen's Survey of the Old Testament* (Chicago: Moody Press, 1978).

2. Representative evangelical perspectives of the one author–later editor(s) hypothesis include John W. Wenham, "Moses and the Pentateuch," in *The New Bible Commentary: Revised*, ed. D. Guthrie et al. (Grand Rapids: Eerdmans, 1970), 41–43; and William Sanford LaSor, David A. Hubbard, and Frederick W. Bush, *Old Testament Survey* (Grand Rapids: Eerdmans, 1982), 54–67.

(e.g., Egyptian and Mesopotamian creation and flood stories). Often archaeological evidence is cited supporting the reliability of the Pentateuchal narrative (e.g., the Nuzi Tablet parallels to patriarchal customs described in Genesis). Typically, apparent discrepancies are harmonized (e.g., understanding Paran in Num. 13:3 as a general place-name reference and Kadesh-Barnea in Num. 20:1 as the particular place-name equivalent). Finally, they emphasize the important role of later scribes in updating the ancient record, supplementing biblical narratives from parallel accounts, and correcting and clarifying puzzling data (e.g., the clarification of the Hebrew dry measure in Exod. 16:36).

Generally speaking, this approach acknowledges Moses as (1) the compiler of previously existing written sources into what we now know as Genesis, and (2) the author of the bulk of the other four books of the Pentateuch. In fact, while Moses did not write all the Pentateuch, these sections of the work are directly or indirectly attributed to the writing activity of Moses: Exodus 12, 20–24, 25–32, 34; Leviticus 1–7, 8, 13, 16, 17–26, 27; Numbers 1, 2, 4, 6, 8, 15, 19, 27–30, 33, 35; and Deuteronomy 1–33. Although editorial insertions in the Pentateuch are obvious, the greater questions involve the extent of that activity and the time frame in which it was completed. According to this view, the amount of editorial activity was minimal and the Pentateuch may have been completed in its present form as early as the time of the elders of Joshua's day (Josh. 24:26, 31) or as late as the era of Samuel the judge (cf. 1 Sam. 3:20–21).

Multiple Authors and Later Editor(s) Hypothesis

The multiple-authors approach to the composition of the Pentateuch was a response of rationalistic scholarship of the Enlightenment to the difficulties observed in the literature of the Pentateuch itself. For instance, why are there two versions of the creation story (Gen. 1:1–2:4a and 2:4b–25) or two accounts of the naming of Beersheba (Gen. 12:31; 26:33), or why is there apparent disagreement as to when the worship of Yahweh began (cf. Gen. 4:26; Exod. 6:2–3)? Or how does one deal with references to the Israelite kings (Gen. 36:31) and to the Philistines in Genesis (Gen. 21:34)? And what is meant by phrases like "to this day" (Gen. 32:32) and "at that time the Canaanites were in the land" (Gen. 12:6)?

These kinds of questions along with obvious differences in literary style and vocabulary in the Pentateuch gave rise to "source analysis" of the Pentateuch. While biblical scholars had raised questions about Pentateuchal authorship previously, it was the French physician Jean Astruc who initiated modern literary or source analysis of the Old Testament. His commentary on Genesis published in 1753 made the assertion, based on the use of divine names, that Moses used two parallel sources in compiling Genesis. One source identified God as Elohim (E), and the other referred to God as Yahweh (J). Later two other foundational sources were detected in the Pentateuch: D (the Deuteronomic source, largely the book of Deuteronomy), and P (the Priestly source, largely the legal and ceremonial texts of Exodus, Leviticus, and Numbers). Today this source criticism of the Pentateuch is most commonly associated with the Documentary Theory or Hypothesis. It assumes a four-source Pentateuch spliced together in the postexilic period, perhaps by Ezra the scribe.

The classical formulation of the multiple-authorship or Documentary Hypothesis was made by the German scholar Julius Wellhausen in 1876–77. Building on the work of earlier scholars such as K. H. Graf, Abraham Kuenen, and Hermann Hupfeld, Wellhausen postulated the view that the Pentateuch is a compilation of at least four major literary documents and that the composition process took some four centuries. The standard Graf-Wellhausen Documentary Hypothesis may be outlined as follows:

1. The J or Yahwist document, written by a Judean author during the ninth century BC. The name Yahweh predominates in this source, which is characterized by "epic style and colorful folklore," highlights patriarchal faith, and is given to anthropomorphism (i.e., representing Yahweh in human terms).

2. The E or Elohist document, written by a northern kingdom Israelite in the eighth century BC. The divine name Elohim predominates in this second document, which tends to be moralistic and prophetic. This source praises Jacob and Joseph and emphasizes the northern tribes like Ephraim, Manasseh, and Reuben, as well as the northern sanctuaries of Bethel and Shechem.

3. The combination of J and E. The clever interweaving of the two primary sources into a single document sometime after the fall of Samaria to the Assyrians in 722 BC was accomplished by a Judean editor (or editors).

4. The D or Deuteronomic source, ascribed to a "school" that produced the book of Deuteronomy and the final edition of the Former Prophets during the reign of King Josiah (ca. 630–600 BC). This D source is usually identified with the book of Deuteronomy and is equated with the finding of the "Book of the Law" that prompted Josiah's reform of Judean temple worship (622 BC; cf. 2 Kings 22–23). The D source is characterized by distinctive sermonic or **hortatory** style and covenant-legal vocabulary. Theologically the D source confines the worship of Yahweh to one central shrine (the temple in Jerusalem) and is marked by its strict adherence to a "blessing and curse" interpretation of Israelite history (i.e., "obedience to God brings reward, while disobedience brings punishment").

5. The P or Priestly source, distinguished by its uniform style, orderly arrangement of materials, and repetition of stereotyped phrases (e.g., "these are the generations"). This fourth major document contains liturgical and ritualistic texts, genealogical tables and statistics, laws and prescriptions—all unmistakable interests of the Israelite priesthood. The P source is assumed to be the product of postexilic priests about 500–450 BC.

6. These four literary sources compiled into a five-volume Pentateuch by a priestly editor (or editors) sometime around 450 BC, perhaps by Ezra the scribe (cf. Neh. 8:1–12).

Although refinements of the Graf-Wellhausen hypothesis have continued through the century since its introduction (including the further "atomizing" of the Pentateuch into sources like J1 and J2, E1 and E2, P1 and P2, K, L, N, and S), the four-source theory has remained solidified in this basic form (figs. A, B, C).

Figure A- The Development of the Pentateuch According to Source Analysis

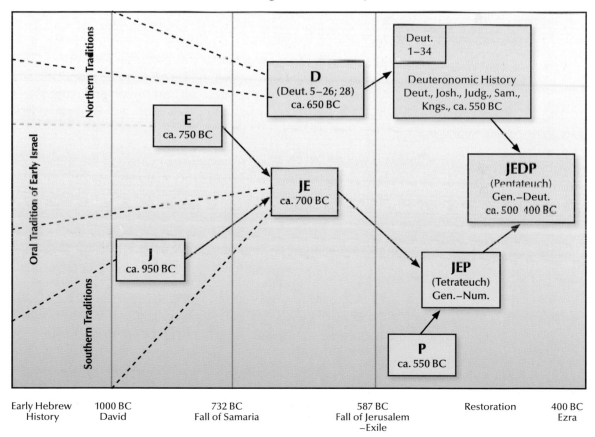

| Early Hebrew History | 1000 BC David | 732 BC Fall of Samaria | 587 BC Fall of Jerusalem –Exile | Restoration | 400 BC Ezra |

Figure B- Distribution of the JEDP Sources in the Pentateuch

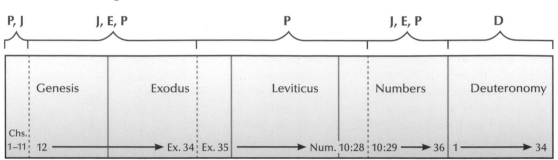

Figure C- Characteristics of Usage in the JEDP Sources

Features	Yahwist (J)	Elohist (E)	Priestly (P)	Deuteronomist
Divine Name	Yahweh	Elohim	Elohim	Yahweh
Divine Attributes	Walks and talks with us	Speaks in dreams, etc.	Cultic approach	Moralistic approach
Themes Emphasized	Blessing	Fear of the Lord	Law Obeyed	Obedience to the Law of Moses
Geography	Stress on Judah	Stress on northern Israel	Stress on Judah	Stress on whole land of Israel
	Uses "Sinai"	Uses "Horeb"		
	Calls natives "Canaanites"	Calls natives "Amorites"		
Literary Emphases	Narrative and stories	Narrative and warnings	Dry lists (genealogy) and schemata	Long homiletic speeches
	Earthly speech	Refined speech	Majestic speech	Speech recalling God's work
				Uses military imagery and has many fixed phrases

As a product of Enlightenment scholarship, the Documentary Hypothesis or Source Theory of Pentateuchal authorship was (and remains) rooted in the rationalism and skepticism of the age. The idea of deism ruled theology, so God was not conceived of as free to intervene in his creation. Thus, miracles, predictive prophecy, and even divine inspiration were impossible in a universe created by God but closed to his providential participation in human history. Evolutionary theory was applied to the development of Israel's history and religion so that the Hebrews were ever moving from the "primitive toward the complex" (or from polytheism to monotheism). Scientific positivism and the empirical method were also taken over by biblical scholars of the period and applied to the study of Scripture.

In the end, the Old Testament (even the entire Bible) was reduced to a merely human literary product, a sort of Hebrew "religious anthology." Human reason was now elevated above the Scriptures as final authority.[3]

Oral Tradition, Multiple Authors, and Later Editor(s) Hypothesis

The fourth hypothesis assumes that the oral transmission of Israelite historical traditions and folklore was foundational to the composition of the Pentateuch. By analogy to other ancient cultures and some contemporary societies, proponents of this approach conjecture that oral traditions were eventually written down or "crystallized" in document form. These small literary units were then collected and finally compiled into the five books of the Pentateuch. Many authors and editors were involved in shaping the contents of the literature in the movement from oral tradition to written text. While adherents of this position admit to the antiquity of many of the Old Testament traditions, the written form of the Pentateuch is usually assigned to the postexilic period of Israelite history.

This authorship hypothesis is often associated with the higher-critical methodology of **form criticism**. Form criticism attempts to identify the smaller literary units of the Pentateuch, explain their origin and life-setting (*Sitz im Leben*), and delineate the oral traditions that lay behind them. Important to this approach is determining the structure, genre, setting, and intent of each of the smaller literary units identified. The Old Testament narrative genre classifications include myth and folklore, legend and novelette, saga and history.

The efforts to identify the various literary types and forms of the Pentateuchal narratives have proven beneficial in understanding the Pentateuch as a literary composition. However, the approach has eroded the notion of historicity in the Old Testament in general and the Pentateuch in particular. The form critic declares that the Old Testament

3. See further Duane Garrett, *Rethinking Genesis* (Grand Rapids: Baker, 1991), especially pp. 13–87 on "The Documentary Hypothesis" and "Mosaic Authorship."

contains "no history writing" in the modern sense of the term. Biblical history is usually labeled "popular history" because it is believed the ancient writers indiscriminately drew from reliable historical documents as well as legend, folklore, and saga. The stance of the form critic to Pentateuchal historicity is one of skepticism at best.[4]

Later Editors of Hebrew Traditions Hypothesis

Still another theory contends that a group of editors collected and arranged Hebrew stories, folktales, and other literary materials and traditions (oral and written) into the five books of the Pentateuch during the Babylonian exile and postexilic periods of Hebrew history. The traditions collected are considered largely nonhistorical and shaped by later editors for specific religious and nationalistic purposes. For this reason the modern student of the Bible must approach the Pentateuch with a "certain skepticism," since neither the sources nor the motivations of the editors may be trusted.

As such, the Pentateuch is a thoroughly late composition in respect to both the time of its writing and in the traditions that it preserves. The early history of the Hebrews must be reconstructed largely on the basis of extrabiblical evidence, because the Pentateuchal traditions themselves have been "refashioned" by later editors to serve the purposes of a later generation facing persecution (i.e., those of the Babylonian exile). Especially important to this kind of Pentateuchal analysis is the nature of the community or group shaping the traditions, the geographical location of that community or group, the social and political and religious dynamics affecting the traditions, and the major themes, emphases, or motifs of the traditions.[5]

Pentateuchal Scholarship Today

The extremely hypothetical and subjective nature of Old Testament source analysis (e.g., the use of divine names as criteria for source division and "stylistic" differences), the faulty nature of many of the source analysis assumptions (e.g., the doublets or parallel accounts indicate diverse literary sources), and the inability of source critics to reach any consensus on the problems of Pentateuchal authorship have spawned numerous other approaches attempting to explain the composition of the Pentateuch (e.g., the wide disagreement among the subdividers of the text on the contents of the various sources). Form criticism and tradition history, the historical-archaeological approach, the social-sciences approach, the canonical approach, and the new literary criticism (e.g., narrative criticism and rhetorical criticism) have emerged as competing alternative theories to traditional source analysis for the modern biblical researcher.[6]

4. On form criticism, see further G. M. Tucker, *Form Criticism and the Old Testament* (Philadelphia: Fortress Press, 1971).

5. This hypothesis is usually considered part of the "tradition history" approach to Old Testament literature. See further W. E. Rast, *Tradition History and the Old Testament* (Philadelphia: Fortress Press, 1972); and Walter Brueggemann and H. W. Wolff, *The Vitality of Old Testament Traditions*, 2nd ed. (Atlanta: John Knox, 1982).

6. John Hayes and J. M. Miller, *Israelite and Judean History* (Philadelphia: Westminster, 1977), 64–69.

In fact, some biblical scholars have remarked that traditional source analysis is an exercise in "reductionism toward absurdity" and have observed that the multiple approaches to the complexities of Pentateuchal authorship have in effect canceled each other out. One commentator has gone so far as to say that the chaos in liberal scholarship today has put Pentateuchal studies in a most unfavorable position.[7]

So there is a growing movement away from the "microscopic" analysis of source criticism toward the "telescopic" analysis characteristic of literary analysis. This approach focuses attention on the whole picture of the Pentateuch as a literary composition, not on the individual pieces of the jigsaw puzzle. There is an increasing appreciation for the deliberate structuring of the Pentateuchal narratives into a unified composition. This has been due largely to the application of the techniques of literary criticism, especially structural analysis, to the five books of the Pentateuch.

For example, a series of books and articles have argued for the integrity of the Pentateuch as a unified composition and without exception have assigned a preexilic date to the work in its completed form. The common denominator of literary analysis characterizing each of these presentations emphasizes repeated words, phrases, and motifs in the narratives, artful **chiasmus**, parallel narrative structure, thematic coherence of larger literary units with smaller sections of the narrative, and the deliberate theological arrangement of literary units for didactic and mnemonic purposes in understanding the Pentateuch as a literary unity.[8]

Perhaps the current reactions to this new literary criticism and the view of the Pentateuch as a unified literary composition are indicators of future trends in Pentateuchal studies. On the one hand, the results of literary analysis may be presented as a viable alternative on equal standing with source analysis. On the other, it may be rejected (or more likely ignored) by scholars who will continue to look for creative ways to bolster the crumbling source analysis theory.[9] Apart from the literary considerations of Pentateuchal composition, the question of historical reliability remains.

7. Cf. E. P. Blair, *The Illustrated Bible Handbook*, rev. ed. (Nashville: Abingdon, 1987), 101.

8. Cf. Robert Alter, *The Art of Biblical Narrative* (New York: Basic Books, 1981); I. M. Kikawada and A. Quinn, *Before Abraham Was* (Nashville: Abingdon, 1985); Robert Polzin, *The Typology of Biblical Hebrew Prose*, HSM 12 (Missoula, Mont.: Scholars Press, 1976); G. A. Rendsburg, *The Redaction of Genesis* (Winona Lake, Ind.: Eisenbrauns, 1986); Gordon J. Wenham, "The Coherence of the Flood Narrative," *VT* 28 (1977): 36–348; Gordon J. Wenham, "The Date of Deuteronomy: Linch-Pin of Old Testament Criticism," *Themelios* 10, no. 3 (1985): 15–20, and 11, no. 1 (1986): 15–18; R. N. Whybray, *The Making of the Pentateuch: A Methodological Study* (Sheffield, England: JSOT Press, 1987).

9. As an example of the former, see J. L. Crenshaw, *Story and Faith* (New York: Macmillan, 1986), 60–62; for the latter, see J. H. Tigay, ed., *Empirical Models for Biblical Criticism* (Philadelphia: University of Pennsylvania, 1987). One major criticism of source analysis has been its exclusive application to biblical studies. Now source theory methodology has been applied to ancient Near Eastern documents.

GLOSSARY

acrostic. A poetic composition in which sets of sequential letters (e.g., initial or final letters of the lines) form a word or phrase or an alphabet.

Ahura Mazda. The supreme being of Persian Zoroastrianism represented as a deity of goodness and light, and whose symbol was fire.

alluvial. Clay, silt, sand, soil deposited by running water.

anthropomorphism. Describing a deity by terms and concepts that relate to human beings.

Apis. The Egyptian bull god, deity of agricultural and reproductive fertility.

Apocrypha. A collection of intertestamental Jewish literature, recognized as deutero-canon in some Christian traditions.

atonement. To "pay" for sin by means of sacrifice and offering, as a symbol of repentance and confession before God (cf. Ps. 51:16–17).

Baal. The Canaanite storm god, deity of agricultural and reproductive fertility.

canon. As applied to the Bible, a collection of religious books measured against the standard of divine inspiration.

catharsis. A purification, especially a purging of the emotions that brings release from anxiety and guilt and yields spiritual renewal.

charismatic leadership. Royal authority empowered randomly and spontaneously by God and established on the basis of inherent physical and spiritual characteristics.

chiasm(us). An literary device in which words or phrases parallel one another in reverse order (A-B-C-C-B-A).

chronicler. Commonly used designation for the author of the books of Ezra–Nehemiah and Chronicles, thought to be Ezra the scribe.

colophon. An addendum or postscript attached to a manuscript, sometimes containing facts relative to its writing.

concateny. A literary device in which a series of items are connected or strung together into a chain by the repetition of a word or phrase shared only by those literary units in sequence.

consort. A partner or associate, often used of a "spouse" of a deity in ancient Near Eastern religious contexts.

corpus. A collection of related writings.

covenant. A contract or treaty that establishes a relationship between two parties.

covenant theology. A theological system that understands God's relationship to humanity as a divinely established compact or covenant based on the analogy of the interrelationship of the three persons of the Trinity.

date formula. A stylized expression that records chronological information for the purpose of assigning a piece of literature to a specific historical period (often connected with the regnal years of a king [e.g., Hag 1:1, "the second year of Darius"], or even natural calamities [e.g. Amos 1:2, "two years before the earthquake"]).

Decalogue. The Ten Commandments.

Deuteronomistic school. (Hypothetical) Hebrew scribal guild of the seventh century BC responsible for shaping the historical literature of the Old Testament (Deuteronomy–Kings).

dirge. A funeral poem or song; a slow and mournful song or hymn of grief.

dispensationalism. A theological system that understands God's revelation and redemptive program as a sequential series of distinct stages of development.

divine oracle formula. Introductory statement indicating direct speech from God to a human agent (e.g., "the LORD said to Moses," Lev. 1:1; 4:1; 6:1; et al.).

Documentary Hypothesis. An approach to the authorship of the Pentateuch associated with source criticism that understands the five books as a patchwork composition of four (or more) literary documents.

dynastic succession. Royal authority legitimized by heredity; rulers of the same line of descent.

elect(ion). Theologically that predisposition of God resulting in the arbitrary selection or choice of the people Israel (through Abraham) to be his covenant people.

Enlightenment. A philosophical movement of the eighteenth century marked by a rejection of traditional social, religious, and political ideas and emphasizing rationalism and scientific methods (equated with Modernism).

eschatology. That branch of theology concerned with end-time events (i.e., the doctrine of last things).

foil. In literature, that which sets off or heightens (often a contrast between themes, characters, symbols, etc.).

foreshadow(ing). The literary device of prefiguring or indicating a significant person or event beforehand (see also *typology*).

form criticism. An interpretive method especially concerned with the analysis of the genre and structure of biblical texts and the historical impulse(s) prompting the shift from oral to written tradition.

Great Synagogue. A council of scribes and other Hebrew leaders reputedly founded after the Babylonian exile to reorganize Jewish religious life and culture.

Hellenism. The influence of Greek thought, language, and culture spread throughout the Near East after the conquests of Alexander the Great.

historiography. The writing of history or the product of historical writing; a collection of historical literature.

hortatory. Sermonic speech form that exhorts and warns.

iconography. Pictorial materials (especially conventional images and symbols) associated with a subject (often connected with kingship and religion in the ancient Near East).

idyll. A simple descriptive work (in prose or poetry) idealizing or romanticizing pastoral scenes and/or a rustic life.

illumination. The internal witness of the Holy Spirit confirming the quality of divine inspiration of the books of Scripture during the canonization process.

immanence. God's active presence and providential involvement in his creation (cf. Isa. 57:15).

intracultural. Divine revelation accommodating (with modification) or affirming the cultural norms of the Old Testament world.

lament. An appeal to a merciful God for divine intervention in a desperate situation.

lamentation. Expression of grief over a catastrophe that is irreversible.

Levant. Lands located along the 400 mile stretch of the Eastern Mediterranean between Turkey and Egypt (including modern day Syria, Lebanon, and Israel).

Levitical. Pertaining to the Levites, the priestly tribe.

lex talionis. The law of punishment identical to the offense.

libation. The act of pouring a liquid as a sacrifice to a deity (e.g., upon a stone, Gen. 35:14).

literary criticism. An interpretive method emphasizing the author's style, literary features, themes, and structure as keys to understanding a biblical text.

Masoretes. Jewish scholars and scribes who preserved the Hebrew Bible, improved word divisions, and added vowels, punctuation marks, and verse divisions (roughly between AD 500 and 900).

Megilloth. The Hebrew word for "scrolls" or "rolls." The term is used to describe the five books in the Hebrew Bible read publicly during the annual festivals of the Jewish religious calendar (Song of Solomon—Passover; Ruth—Pentecost; Lamentations—Fast of Ab commemorating the destruction of the temple; Ecclesiastes—Tabernacles; Esther—Purim).

Mesopotamia. The land between the Tigris and Euphrates rivers, known as the Fertile Crescent.

messenger formula. The clause "[*koh*] *'amar YHWH* ..." ("so Yahweh [has] said"), introducing a messenger speech (or prophetic oracle) and signifying the oral transmission of a message by means of a third party.

messiah (Heb. "anointed one"). Generally one set apart for a divinely appointed office, such as a priest or a king. Specifically, the title identifies a figure prominent in Old Testament prophetic writings who serves as Israel's deliverer-king (realized in Jesus of Nazareth according to the New Testament writers).

miracle. Divine intervention in human affairs, either in the superseding of natural law or in the intensification and timing of natural events.

oracle. An authoritative prophetic speech.

oracular prose. A hybrid literary form characteristic of Old Testament prophetic books and combining elements of prose and poetry.

Osiris. The Egyptian god of the underworld.

palistrophe. A chiastic literary device that inverts or counterbalances key themes hinging upon one fundamental teaching or idea.

pantheon. A divine assembly of gods and goddesses formally recognized by a society as participants in the experiences of community life.

Pentateuch. A Greek word meaning "five scrolls," applied to the first five books of the Bible.

proto-apocalyptic. An Old Testament prototype of apocalyptic literature that contains some of the elements and features of later intertestamental apocalyptic literature.

provenance. The original source, setting, or locale for a literary work.

pseudepigrapha. Extracanonical Jewish literature of the intertestamental period.

pseudonymity. The literary device of writing under a false or assumed name, commonly recognized as a feature of apocalyptic literature.

satrapy. A large administrative district or territory of the Persian Empire ruled by a governor called a "satrap."

seer. A technical term applied to certain of the Old Testament prophets, especially signifying divine revelation received in the form of a dream or vision.

Septuagint. The Greek version of the Old Testament, translated from the Hebrews by Hellenized Jews living in North Africa in the third century BC.

signet. A stamp or symbol of authority imprinted by means of a seal (as on a ring).

source criticism. A form of literary criticism especially concerned with the written documents' biblical author(s) used in composing extended biblical narratives.

steppe. Level and treeless land, usually arid.

superscription. A statement of classification and/or identification prefixed to a literary work.

supracultural. Divine revelation prohibiting or superseding the cultural norms of the Old Testament world.

suzerain. A superior feudal ruler; an overlord.

syncretism. The combining of different forms of religious belief and practice.

textual criticism. The science of comparing the variant readings of biblical manuscripts for the purpose of establishing the contents of the original text.

theocracy. A state or nation ruled directly by God.

theodicy. The philosophical and/or theological defense of God's goodness and omnipotence in view of the existence of evil.

theophany. An audible or visible manifestation of God.

topography. Natural or physical features of a region or land mass.

Torah. The Hebrew designation for the first five books of the Bible. The basic idea of Torah is "instruction in holiness" after the pattern of God's holiness.

tradition history (or tradition criticism). An interpretive approach that focuses on the history of the transmission of the biblical traditions by studying the oral traditions during the period of their transmission and by tracing the development of the written biblical documents, giving special attention to the theological emphases of the community editing and shaping those materials.

transcendence. Theologically, the notion of God's "otherness," his distinctness and uniqueness from the created order, his mysterious and unknowable nature (cf. Isa. 57:15a).

Twelve Prophets. Hebrew designation for the twelve books of the Minor Prophets in the Old Testament.

typology. One aspect of biblical interpretation that establishes a correspondence between Old Testament events, persons, objects, and/or ideas ("type") and their New Testament counterparts ("antetypes") by way of foreshadowing or prototype.

variant. Alternative readings of words and phrases in the Bible existing in manuscript traditions as a result of errors (and/or changes) associated with the copying (and/or translation) process.

vassal. A subordinate nation or people group (usually as a result of a treaty following conquest).

wadi. River bed or valley that is dry except during the rainy season.

INDEX

structure of, 606, 610–11

teachings of,

themes, 612–14, 715

Amurru, 190, 225

Anachronisms, 762

Anagogical method, 69–70

Analysis, "microscopic vs. telescopic," 769

Anatolia, 35–36, 182p, 189–90, 199

Ancient Near East, 37m,

Andersen, F. I., 375, 397, 417, 586, 592, 615, 648, 667

Anger of God, 114, 299, 506, 547, 637, 646

Animal sacrifice, 72, 88p, 118p, 128–36, 173p, 209, 263–64, 273, 322, 678, 701, 706, 732, 735

Antetype, 324, 744

Anthropomorphic language, 764, 770

Anti-Edomite theme, 622–23

Antilegomena, 492

Antiochus IV (Epiphanes), 568–69

Antitype, 472

Apis calf cult, 41, 115, 118p, 298, 770

Apocalypses, Jewish, 569–70

Apocalyptic literature, 496, 563, 569–70

Apocrypha, 331, 491–99, 770

Apodictic law, 151

Apologetics, 463

Apostasy, 206, 209, 240, 241, 245, 251, 260, 262, 314, 584, 591, 608, 671, 697

Appeasement, 412, 425, 601

Application of Old Testament, 27, 30, 729–30

Arabian desert, 37, 49, 333m, 528m

Arabian peninsula, 35, 41–42

Arad, 50m, 108, 143p, 144, 286p, 308p, 366

Aram, 38, 192–94, 271, 268m, 287m, 522–23

Arameans, 38, 48, 192–94, 238, 273p, 285f, 367, 461p, 584–85

Aramaic, 159, 271, 332–33, 339, 443, 458, 470, 481, 485, 492, 497, 570

Aramaic Targums, 485

Archaeological archives, 360–63

Archaeological record, 221–22, 285, 357–69

Archaeology, 357–69

Ark narrative, 258, 260–61, 269, 726

Ark of Noah, 76p, 80, 762

Ark of the covenant, 152f, 158p, 227, 231, 242, 260–61, 260f, 267, 269, 319, 323

Artaxerxes I, 330, 331f, 333, 335–36, 350f, 570f

Artaxerxes II, 336

Asa, 194, 212, 280, 282f, 289f, 300f, 301f, 302f, 310f

Asaph psalms, 421, 427f, 430

Asherah, 587p, 589, 590f, 612p

Ashkelon, 43m, 191, 281p, 367, 668p

Ashurbanipal, 196–97, 237p, 302f, 363, 504, 535, 653–54, 661–62, 670, 692p

Ashurnasirpal II, 193

Asia Minor, 35–37, 189, 198

Assonance, 383, 386

Assur, 184, 197, 320m

Assyria, 36–40, 48–51, 181–82, 190–92, 204p, 207p, 209p, 210p, 283, 286, 300–303f, 311f, 360, 364–65, 368, 428, 481, 502p, 513p, 525p, 583, 597, 643, 656, 692p

Assyrian campaign, 280–81f, 431, 503

Assyrian deportation, 51, 195, 285, 294m, 365, 513, 584, 764

Assyrian Empire, 181, 193–98, 195p, 282f, 294m, 349, 523, 535, 571, 631–32, 632p, 654, 661–62, 673,

Assyrians, 36–37, 48–49, 223, 237p, 238, 319p, 367p, 506p, 521p, 524–26, 557, 557p, 585, 632,

Astruc, Jean, 763

Aten, 114, 115f, 188, 447

Aten Hymn, 377, 378f

Atonement, Day of, 126, 134, 136

Atra-Hasis, 79, 85

Atra-Hasis Epic, 79, 83, 360p

Attributes of God, 21–22, 381, 415, 425, 435, 655, 715, 718–24, 766f

Authority from God, 26–27, 245, 296, 446, 506, 561

Authorship, 79, 103–4, 220, 282, 420, 469–70, 490, 522, 544, 678, 761–69. *See also* Editors

Baal, 238p, 281p, 293, 584p, 590f
Baal cult, 51, 295
Baal Epic, 362, 378
Baalism, 39, 194, 293, 299, 589–91, 671
Baal Melqart, 38, 194
Baal vs. Elijah and Elisha, 28p, 292f
Baal–Zephon, 108
Baasha, 194, 280f, 282f, 288f, 291f, 300–302f
Babylon, 49, 62, 139, 184, 185, 190, 196, 197,
    199, 284, 285, 294m, 302, 303, 311, 320,
    332, 333m, 338, 349, 361, 365, 366, 367,
    522, 526, 528m, 536, 544, 556, 561, 568,
    570
Babylonia, 36, 40, 51, 286, 312, 320, 337, 360,
    362
Babylonian Chronicles, the, 365–66, 663p
Babylonian deportation, 284, 320m, 365,
    535–36, 571
Babylonian Empire, 320m
Babylonians, 36, 42, 49, 197, 198, 285, 330,
    365, 526, 535, 544, 545, 557, 558, 571,
    575, 620, 654, 656, 660, 662, 663, 664,
    670, 679, 683
Babylonian Talmud, 282, 491
Baker, David W., 32, 222, 233, 602, 626, 657,
    667, 674, 711, 751
Balaam, 144f, 151, 154p, 366
Balaam Oracles, 60, 159
Baldwin, Joyce G., 97, 275, 355, 578, 684, 692,
    693, 698
Ban, the, 228, 230, 232
Bathsheba, 267, 429
Beersheba, 43m, 44, 50m, 89p, 127p, 374p,
    763
Belshazzar, 198, 366, 568–69, 573, 576
Ben-Hadad, 271p, 285f, 300f, 302f
Ben-Hadad II, 285f, 300f
Bethlehem, 50m, 249, 250, 642, 645, 646, 742p
Beth Shean, 45p, 321p
Biblical covenants, 166f
Biblical interpretation, 28–30
Biblical perspective, 96
Biblical scholarship, 753
Bimson, John, 121, 222

Black Obelisk, 286, 364
Black Sea, 37m
Blessing of Moses, 60, 164f
Blessing of Rebekah, 61
Blessings, 61, 166f, 176–77, 395, 448, 540
Block, Daniel, 165, 247, 254, 548, 564
Blood covenant, 695f, 746
Boghazköy tablets, 64
Book of Consolation, 534f, 537
Book of the Law, 57, 59, 167, 764
Book of the Wars of the Lord, 151, 762
Bright, John, 70, 73, 288f, 289f, 304, 325, 344,
    516, 608
Bullock, C. Hassell, 397, 437, 468, 474, 475,
    478, 516, 564, 592, 626
Byblos, 38, 185, 189, 223, 268m

Cain, 80, 85, 94
Calf cult, 41, 298–99
Cambyses, 199, 331f, 350f, 570f
Canaan, 36, 37m, 38–39, 44, 50m, 51–52,
    65, 67p, 80f, 81f, 86–90, 103f, 144–45,
    148–49, 170, 190, 222, 232, 239, 260f,
    368, 545–46, 625, 749. See also Palestine
Canaanite Pantheon, 167p, 237p, 241, 281p,
    293, 557, 584p, 590f
Canaanite religions, 129–30, 170, 245–46,
    281p, 298–99, 362, 589, 591
Canaanites, 38–39, 51, 224, 264, 295, 563
Canon, 487–97
    Christian, 493f
    confirmation of, 487–89
    definition of, 487–88
    formation of, 70, 444, 488489
    history of, 488–91
    Jewish, 489–91, 493f
    order of, 331, 491–92
    selection, 490–92
Canonical approach, 757, 758f
Canonical status, 70, 458
Cantata of David, 427f
Carchemish, 37m, 197–98, 605
Catharsis, 547
Cause and effect, 176, 208–10, 384, 447